VENEZUELA: THE CHALLENGE OF COMPETITIVENESS

Michael J. Enright
Antonio Francés
Edith Scott Saavedra

St. Martins Press
New York

VENEZUELA: THE CHALLENGE OF COMPETITIVENESS
Copyright © 1996 by Michael J. Enright
All rights reserved. Printed in the United States of America. No part of this book may be used or reproduced in any manner whatsoever without written permission except in the case of brief quotations embodied in critical articles or reviews. For information, address St. Martin's Press, Scholarly and Reference Division, 175 Fifth Avenue, New York, N.Y. 10010

ISBN 0-312-15851-3

Library of Congress Cataloging-in-Publication Data

Enright, Michael J.
 Venezuela, the challenge of competitiveness / by Michael J. Enright, Antonio Francés, Edith Scott Saavedra.
  p. cm.
 Includes bibliographical references and index.
 ISBN 0-312-15851-3
  1. Industries—Venezuela—Case Studies. 2. Industrial policy—Venezuela—Case studies. 3. Competition—Venezuela—Case studies. 4. Competition, international. 5. Business enterprises—Venezuela. 6. Venezuela—Economic conditions—1958- 7. Venezuela—Economic policy. I. Frances, Antonio. II. Scott Saavedra, Edith. III. Title.
HC237.E67 1996
338.60480987—dc20   95-46139
                                                   CIP

Book design by Acme Art, Inc.
First Edition: July 1996
10 9 8 7 6 5 4 3 2 1

Contents

List of Tables iv
List of Figures vi
List of Abbreviations vii

1. Introduction 1
2. The Structure and Performance of the Venezuelan Economy . . . 13
3. The Challenge of Competitiveness in the
   Modern World Economy 45
4. Venezuelan Industry Profiles 69
5. Venezuelan Industry Summaries 147
6. Venezuelan Factor Conditions 179
7. Demand Conditions, Related Industries,
   and Supporting Industries in Venezuela 243
8. Firm Strategy, Structure, and Rivalry in Venezuela 279
9. Government Policy and Competitiveness in Venezuela 307
10. Prospects for Venezuelan Firms and Industries 357
11. The Challenge of Competitiveness for the
    Venezuelan Government 373
12. The Challenge of Competitiveness for Venezuelan Firms 411
13. Final Thoughts 435

Appendix 443
Notes 449
Bibliography 475
Index 491

List of Tables

Table 2.1	GDP by Kind of Activity, Selected Latin American Nations, 1991
Table 2.2	Per-Capita GDP, Selected Nations, 1970 and 1988
Table 2.3	Real Growth in Components of Venezuelan GDP, 1987–1993
Table 2.4	Unemployment Rates, Selected Latin American Nations, 1986–1993
Table 2.5	Output, Factor Inputs, and Productivity Growth in Venezuela
Table 2.6	Inflation Rates, Selected Latin American Nations, 1970–1993
Table 2.7	Population Growth Rates, Major Latin American Nations, 1970–1992
Table 2.8	Export Composition, Selected Latin American Nations
Table 2.9	Venezuela's Leading Trading Partners, 1990 and 1992
Table 2.10	Principal Markets for Venezuela's Non-Traditional Exports, 1988–1993
Table 2.11	Net Foreign Direct Investment, Major Latin American Countries, 1979–1992
Table 4.1	Venezuelan Telenovela Exports, 1983–1993
Table 4.2	Latin American Forest Plantations, 1990
Table 4.3	Pulp and Paper Industry in Latin America, 1991
Table 4.4	International Tourism Receipts, Selected Countries, 1991
Table 4.5	Tourism Revenues as a Percentage of GDP, 1991
Table 4.6	1990 Petrochemical Exports, Selected Countries and Products
Table 4.7	Number of Producers of Petrochemical Products in Selected Countries, 1990
Table 4.8	World Production of Direct Reduced Iron
Table 4.9	Latin American Automobile Market, Selected Countries, 1992
Table 5.1	Sources of Advantage in Venezuelan Industry
Table 5.2	Sources of Advantage in Selected New Zealand Industries
Table 5.3	Sources of Advantage in Selected Canadian Industries
Table 5.4	Sources of Advantage in Selected Internationally Successful Swiss Industries
Table 6.1	Venezuelan Natural Resource Reserves
Table 6.2	The Electricity Sector, Selected Latin American Nations, 1992
Table 6.3	Occupation in Venezuela by Sector and Employment Category
Table 6.4	Worker Salaries in Manufacturing Industries, Selected Nations, 1991
Table 6.5	Ordinary Spending on Education, Selected Nations

List of Tables

Table 6.6	Total Public Spending on Education and Participation Rates, Selected Nations
Table 6.7	General Wage Increases in Venezuela
Table 6.8	Latin American Stock Markets
Table 7.1	Mexican and Venezuelan Petrochemical Clusters
Table 7.2	Brazilian and Venezuelan Iron and Steel Clusters
Table 8.1	Levels of Concentration and Rivalry in Venezuela, Selected Sectors, 1991–1992
Table 10.1	Projections for Selected Venezuelan Industries
Table 10.2	Exports of Selected Commodities, Selected Latin American Nations, 1992

List of Figures

Figure 2.1	Real Per-Capita GDP, Venezuela
Figure 2.2	Real Oil Income, Venezuela
Figure 2.3	Gross Fixed Capital Formation, Latin America
Figure 2.4	Venezuelan Trade
Figure 3.1	Competitiveness in Context
Figure 3.2	Miss Venezuela
Figure 3.3	The National or Regional Diamond
Figure 3.4	The National or Regional System
Figure 4.1	The Venezuelan Telenovela Industry
Figure 4.2	The Venezuelan Pulp and Paper Industry
Figure 4.3	The Venezuelan Tourism Sector
Figure 4.4	The Venezuelan Petrochemical Industry
Figure 4.5	The Venezuelan Steel Industry
Figure 4.6	The Venezuelan Auto and Auto Parts Industry
Figure 5.1	The Venezuelan Petroleum Industry
Figure 5.2	The Venezuelan Aluminum Industry
Figure 5.3	The Venezuelan Cocoa Industry
Figure 5.4	The Venezuelan Rice Industry
Figure 5.5	The Venezuelan Textile Industry
Figure 5.6	The Venezuelan Software Industry
Figure 5.7	The Venezuelan Engineering Industry
Figure 6.1	Evolution of Prices of Oil, Iron Ore, and Aluminum, 1960–1993
Figure 6.2	Educational Profile of the Venezuelan Workforce
Figure 6.3	Comparative Cost of Venezuelan Labor, 1991
Figure 6.4	Evolution of Compensation and Inflation in Venezuela
Figure 7.1	Venezuelan Entertainment Cluster
Figure 7.2	Forest Products Clusters, Chile and Venezuela
Figure 7.3	The Swedish Forest Products Cluster

List of Abbreviations

AD	Democratic Action
	Acción Democrática
ADR	American depository receipt
ALADI	Latin American Integration Association
	Asociación Latinoamericana de Integración
ALCASA	Aluminio del Caroní, S.A.
ALIM	Latin American Association of the Milling Industry
	Asociación Latinoamericana de Industria Molinera
ANDE	National Public Employees Association
	Asociación Nacional de Empleados Públicos
APEP	Association for the Promotion of Popular Education
	Asociación Promoción para la Educación Popular
APROCAO	Cocoa Processors' Association
	Agropecuaria Aprocao
APROSCELLO	Association of Certified Seed Producers of the Central Western Plains
	Asociación de Productores de Semilla Certificada de los Llanos Centro Occidentales
AREX	Auto-Reforming Reduction Technology
ASOQUIM	Association of Chemical Products Producers
	Asociación de Fabricantes de Productos Químicos
ASOTRIGO	Venezuelan Association of Industrial Millers
	Asociación de Industriales Molineros de Venezuela
AVE	Venezuelan Association of Executives
	Asociación Venezolana de Ejecutivos
BAP	Agrarian Popular Bank
	Banco Agrario Popular
BAUXIVEN	Bauxita de Venezuela C.A.
BCV	Central Bank of Venezuela
	Banco Central de Venezuela
BIV	Industrial Bank of Venezuela
	Banco Industrial de Venezuela

CACAOVECA	Cacao Venezolano, C.A.
CACM	Central American Common Market
CAD-CAE	Computer-Aided Design–Computer-Aided Engineering
CADAFE	Electrical Administration and Development Company
	C.A. de Administración y Fomento Eléctrico
CANTV	Venezuelan National Telephone Company
	C.A. Nacional Teléfonos de Venezuela
CARBONORCA	Carbones del Orinoco, C.A.
CARICOM	Caribbean Community
CAVECON	Venezuelan Chamber of Consulting Firms
	Cámara Venezolana de Empresas Consultoras
CAVN	Venezuelan Navigation Company
	Compañía Anónima Venezolana de Navegación
CCNA	National Rice Consulting Council
	Consejo Consultivo Nacional del Arroz
CCV	Comercializadora Cacao de Venezuela
CECONAVE	Cooperatives Central of Venezuela
	Central de Cooperativas de Venezuela
CEN	National Executive Committee
	Comité Ejecutivo Nacional
CENAC	National Center for Competitiveness
	Centro Nacional para la Competitividad
CEPAL	See ECLAC
CEPET	Center of Oil and Petrochemical Formation and Training
	Centro de Formación y Adiestramiento Petrolero y Petroquímico
CESAP	Center for Service to Popular Action
	Centro al Servicio de la Acción Popular
CIAT	International Center for Tropical Agriculture
	Centro Internacional de Agricultura Tropical
CMA	Agricultural Marketing Association
	Corporación de Mercadeo Agrícola
CONAHOTU	National Corporation of Hotels and Tourism
	Corporación Nacional de Hoteles y Turismo
CONAPRI	National Council for Investment Promotion
	Consejo Nacional de Promoción de Inversiones
CONATEL	National Telecommunications Commission
	Comisión Nacional de Telecomunicaciones
CONICIT	The National Council of Scientific and Technological Research
	Consejo Nacional de Investigaciones Científicas y Tecnológicas
CONINDUSTRIA	National Council of Industries

List of Abbreviations

	Consejo Nacional de la Industria
COPEI	Committee for Political Organization and Independent Election
	Comité de Organización Política Electoral Independiente
COPRE	Presidential Commission for the Reform of the State
	Comisión Presidencial para la Reforma del Estado
CORDIPLAN	Central Office of Planning and Coordination
	Coordinador de Planificación
CORPOINDUSTRIA	Corporation for Development of Small and Medium Firms
	Corporación para el Desarrollo de la Pequeña y Mediana Industria
CORPOTURISMO	Tourism Corporation
	Corporación de Turismo
CTV	Confederation of Venezuelan Workers
	Confederación de Trabajadores de Venezuela
CVG	Venezuelan Guayana Corporation
	Corporación Venezolana de Guayana
CVTV	Cadena Venezolana de Televisión
DRI	Direct Reduced Iron
EC	European Community
ECLAC	Economic Commission for Latin America and the Caribbean
	Comisión Económica para América Latina y el Caribe
EDELCA	Electricidad de Caracas
FAO	Food and Agriculture Organization (United Nations)
FAVENPA	Venezuelan Auto Parts Producers Association
	Fabricantes Venezolanos de Partes Automotrices
FDI	Foreign Direct Investment
FEDEAGRO	National Confederation of Farmer Associations
	Confederación Nacional de Asociaciones de Productores Agropecuarios
FEDEARROZ	National Federation of Rice Growers of Colombia
	Federación Nacional de Arroceros de Colombia
FEDECAMARAS	Venezuelan Federation of Chambers of Commerce and Production
	Federación Venezolana de Cámaras y Asociaciones de Comercio y Producción
FEDEINDUSTRIA	Federation of Small and Medium Enterprises
	Federación de la Pequeña y Mediana Empresa
FETRASALUD	Federation of Health Workers
	Federación de Trabajadores de la Salud
FII	Foundation Institute of Engineering

	Fundación Instituto de Ingeniería
FINTEC	Fund for the Promotion of Technological Innovation
	Fondo para el Desarrollo de la Innovación Tecnológica
FIOR	Fluidized Iron Ore Reduction
FIV	Venezuelan Investment Fund
	Fondo de Inversiones Venezolanas
FONAIAP	National Fund for Agricultural Research
	Fondo Nacional de Investigación Agropecuario
FONCACAO	National Cocoa Fund
	Fondo Nacional del Cacao
FONCINE	National Cinema Fund
	Fondo Nacional del Cine
FONCREI	Industrial Credit Fund
	Fondo de Crédito Industrial
FONTUR	National Urban Transportation Fund
	Fondo Nacional de Transporte Urbano
FUNDAMETAL	Foundation for Industrial Training in Metalworking
	Fundación Metalmecánica para la Capacitación Industrial
FUNINDES	Foundation for Research and Development (Simón Bolívar University)
	Fundación de Investigación y Desarrollo
GATT	General Agreement on Tariffs and Trade
GDP	Gross domestic product
GDR	General depository receipt
GNP	Gross national product
IAAIM	Autonomous Institute of Maiquetía International Airport
	Instituto Autónomo del Aeropuerto Internacional de Maiquetía
IAN	National Agrarian Institute
	Instituto Agrario Nacional
ICEI	Foreign Trade Institute of Venezuela
	Instituto de Comercio Exterior de Venezuela
IDB	Inter-American Development Bank
	Banco Interamericano de Desarrollo
IDEC	Institute for the Defense and Education of the Consumer
	Instituto de Defensa y Educación del Consumidor
IESA	Institute for Advanced Administrative Studies
	Instituto de Estudios Superiores de Administración
IMAU	Metropolitan Institute of Urban Cleanliness
	Instituto Metropolitano de Aseo Urbano
IMF	International Monetary Fund

List of Abbreviations

INAVI	National Housing Institute
	Instituto Nacional de Vivienda
INCE	National Institute for Educational Cooperation
	Instituto Nacional de Cooperación Educativa
INTERALUMINA	Interamericana de Alúmina, C.A.
INTEVEP	Venezuelan Institute for Petroleum Research
	Instituto Venezolano de Investigaciones Petroleras
IPOSTEL	Postal and Telegraphic Institute
	Instituto Postal Telegráfico
IVES	Venezuelan Steelmaking Institute
	Instituto Venezolano de Siderúrgia
IVIC	Venezuelan Institute of Scientific Investigation
	Instituto Venezolano de Investigación Científica
IVP	Venezuelan Petroleum Institute
	Instituto Venezolano de Petroleo
IVSS	Venezuelan Social Security Institute
	Instituto Venezolano de Seguro Social
JUNAC	Cartagena Agreement Commission
	Junta del Acuerdo de Cartagena
MAC	Ministry of Agriculture and Livestock
	Ministerio de Agricultura y Cría
MCCA	See CACM
MERCOSUR	Southern Cone Common Market
MIGA	Multilateral Investment Guarantee Agency
MTBE	Methyl tertiary butyl ether
NAFTA	North American Free Trade Agreement
NIC	Newly industrialized country
OCEI	Central Office for Statistics and Informatics
	Oficina Central de Estadística e Informática
OECD	Organization for Economic Cooperation and Development
OPEC	Organization of Petroleum Exporting Countries
OPIC	Overseas Private Investment Corporation
PAMI	Program for Attention to Mother and Child
	Programa de Atención a la Madre y la Infancia
PDVSA	The Venezuelan Oil Company, Inc.
	Petróleos de Venezuela, S.A.
PROFORCA	Productos Forestales C.A.
PROMEXPORT	Export Promotion Office
	Oficina de Promoción de Exportaciones

PROSERVIFACICA	Projects and Services of the Faculty of Sciences (Central University)
	Proyectos y Servicios de la Facultad de Ciencias
R&D	Research and development
RCTV	Radio Caracas Televisión
RECADI	Office of the Differential Exchange Rate Regime
	Oficina del Régimen de Cambios Diferenciales
SIDOR	Orinoco Steel Works, Inc.
	Siderúrgica del Orinoco, S.A.
SOE	State-owned enterprise
SUTISS	Single Union of Steel and Related Industry Workers
	Sindicato Unico de Trabajadores de la Industria Siderúrgica y Similares
TQM	Total quality management
UEC	USX Engineers and Consultants
UHF	Ultra-high frequency
UNIDO	United Nations Industrial Development Organization
VAT	Value-added tax
VENALUM	Venezuelan Aluminum Industry, Inc.
	Industria Venezolana de Aluminio, C.A.
VIASA	Venezuelan International Airlines, Inc.
	Venezolana Internacional de Aviación, S.A.
VTV	Venezolana de Televisión

1

Introduction

In September of 1994, Venezuela was in the midst of an economic crisis precipitated by a collapse of the nation's banking sector, a burgeoning public sector deficit, and uncertainty surrounding government policy. After strong economic growth in the years 1990 to 1992, the Venezuelan economy had contracted by 1 percent in 1993 and it was expected to contract another 5 to 6 percent in 1994. This situation contrasted sharply with that of other major Latin American nations, such as Chile, Argentina, Colombia, and Peru, which were experiencing solid economic growth. IMD, a leading Swiss business school, ranked Venezuela fortieth on overall economic competitiveness out of 41 nations covered in its *1994 World Competitiveness Report*.[1] To ride out the recession, Venezuelan firms, buffeted by high interest rates and uncertainty over government economic policies, had reduced investment and cut back on expansion plans. The economic system that had been put in place in the 1960s and 1970s had proven unable to generate sustained growth and prosperity. As the nation began to emerge from the crisis of 1994, firms and government were trying to find their way in the uncertain world of international economic competition.

In the 1960s and 1970s, Venezuela had embarked upon an ambitious program of state-led industrialization and import substitution. This program was similar to those adopted in other Latin American nations and was consistent with policies advocated at the time by the United Nations Economic Commission for Latin America and the Caribbean (ECLAC). The Venezuelan oil industry, especially after it was nationalized in 1976, was to be the source of funds for rapid industrialization, infrastructure investment, and generalized subsidies designed to achieve a variety of social and political objectives. Massive investments were made in state-owned enterprises designed to exploit the nation's natural resources by building up heavy industry in order to diversify the economy, create jobs, and earn foreign exchange. The Venezuelan government also intervened with a series of regulations, controls, and subsidies to correct what were seen as the deficiencies of immature markets. A paternalistic and interventionist ethos developed as the state became the dominant player in the economy.

Import substitution contributed to the development of numerous Venezuelan private-sector firms that emerged to serve the protected home market. Some became effective competitors, but many others depended on continued protection for their survival. Given extensive government regulation of business, many Venezuelan private-sector firms adopted strategies that were based more on political connections than on investments in new products or improved processes. Several local industries became dominated by oligopolies that divided up markets. A general lack of competition from domestic or foreign firms meant that most Venezuelan firms had little incentive to improve efficiency, develop new products, or invest in their workforces. Venezuela's family-controlled industrial groups engaged in vertical integration and diversification in order to grow within a small, protected domestic market. Labor relations within Venezuela were often confrontational, as labor and management fought over the division of oligopoly or politically derived rents.

The Venezuelan economic system appeared to make progress as oil revenues increased dramatically in the mid-1970s. In addition to the growth of the public sector, private companies made handsome profits and wages steadily increased in real terms. By the 1980s, however, the system began to collapse under pressures from falling commodity prices, a bloated public administration, and the inefficiency and corruption brought about by bureaucratic controls and distortionary policies. A financial crisis and substantial devaluation in 1983 were the first harbingers of decline. Venezuela was one of the worst performers in what became known as "the lost decade" of the 1980s, a decade in which nearly all of Latin America suffered from economic decline. By the end of 1988, the Venezuelan state, and the economic system that it had largely created, was rapidly approaching bankruptcy. Foreign reserves were depleted and a massive foreign debt had been accumulated. Hyperinflation, such as that which had beset other Latin American countries in the 1980s, appeared imminent. A number of state-owned enterprises increasingly drained the economy and required ongoing injections of capital. Many private-sector firms had become inefficient, uncompetitive, and overly reliant on governmental favors and protection.

It was under these conditions that Carlos Andrés Pérez was inaugurated for his second term as president of Venezuela in February 1989.[2] During the presidential campaign, Pérez had claimed that dramatic changes were necessary in order to save an economy that was teetering on the brink of disaster. The new administration embarked on a stabilization program similar to those being implemented in Argentina, Chile, and Mexico. Chile had been the first Latin American nation to undertake an economic liberalization program, in the early 1980s. Chile's program was followed by similar, though not identical, liberalization programs in Mexico (started in 1982-1983), Bolivia (mid-1980s), Venezuela and Argentina (1989), Colombia (1990), and Peru (1993-1994). The goals of these programs were the restoration of fiscal balance and the improvement of productivity through internal and international competition.

In Venezuela, reforms were introduced to reduce the role of the state in the economy, to eliminate subsidies, to decontrol prices and interest rates, to float the currency, to reduce trade barriers, and to change competition policy. Venezuela unilaterally reduced tariffs, joined the General Agreement on Tariffs and Trade (GATT), and negotiated a free trade agreement with Colombia. It restructured its debt through negotiations with the International Monetary Fund (IMF), the World Bank, and foreign banks. Subsidies to agriculture, to industries, and to consumers were reduced. The phone company, CANTV, and the national airline, Viasa, were privatized, and other privatizations were planned.

Economic performance began to improve after an initial period of painful adjustment unprecedented in the nation's recent memory. In the years 1990 to 1992, the Venezuelan economy was among the fastest growing economies in the world. Increased competition resulted in expanded consumer choice in many industries. Investment increased substantially in some sectors, such as forest products, mining, and tourism, that had been uneconomic under government controls. Some private Venezuelan firms made dramatic changes, cutting some product lines and focusing on improving efficiency in order to become more competitive in both the domestic and international markets. Some began to invest in overseas markets and some tapped foreign capital markets. The economic reform program also triggered an influx of foreign direct investment into the Venezuelan economy. Total net foreign direct investment in the years 1989 to 1992 was nearly ten times the total registered from 1979 to 1988. Most of the new investment came from the privatization of Compañía Anónima Nacional Teléfonos de Venezuela (CANTV) and Viasa. CANTV invested more in its first three years under the control of a consortium led by the American firm GTE than it had in decades under state ownership.

The reform program ran into substantial opposition, however, despite its similarity to the plans that were achieving a measure of success in other Latin

American nations. In Chile, the reform program was carried out initially under a dictatorial regime. In Mexico, reform took place under the leadership of the PRI, which had been in power for 60 years. In Argentina and Venezuela, the adjustment was carried out within a framework of open political confrontation. However, the Peronist Party in Argentina had been out of power and felt itself capable of pushing ahead with reforms. In Venezuela, the party of the government, Acción Democrática (AD), had been the principal architect of the statist system. This party resisted supporting the reforms of President Pérez, fearing the loss of popularity and the endangerment of its vested interests. In only a few instances, such as the privatization of CANTV, did AD support the reforms above and beyond its short-term interests.

Moreover, the perceived support by the Pérez government of certain domestic business groups earned the government the bitter enmity of powerful rival groups. As the commercial reform went forward, certain sectors of the economy felt affected by competition from imported goods and began a more active opposition to the reforms. Public discontent mounted, a reflection of economic decline, deteriorating public services, and a general disillusionment with the nation's economic and political institutions. Some well-known political figures and communications media fueled opposition to the Pérez government and its program of market-oriented reforms. Ironically, much of the general public came to view these reforms as the cause of the nation's economic difficulties rather than a potential solution. Improved macroeconomic performance did not satisfy the expectations of most Venezuelans. Many perceived the benefits of the new program to accrue mainly to large firms and financial institutions, particularly those linked to inner government circles. High inflation, falling real wages for many, an increase in the number of families in poverty, and poor public services fueled this perception. By 1992, employment had begun to grow substantially and real salaries began to recover. Nevertheless, most of the population perceived a growing deterioration in their living conditions.

Certain segments of the Venezuelan private sector, the supposed star of the new economic picture, had a difficult time adjusting. Venezuelan firms had been forced out of the safety of protection and subsidies into the uncertain world of international competition. At the same time, they had to deal with unreformed labor and capital markets and the absence of a state that was able to set and enforce clear rules in the new economic game. Some industries, such as autos, agriculture, chemicals, and some segments of the textile industry, were hurt by foreign competition. Oligopolies in distribution prevented the benefits of increased competition from accruing to consumers in other industries. Many Venezuelan firms seemed to have been unable or unwilling to make the changes necessary to become more efficient and competitive in a difficult and uncertain economic environment.

Important components of the economic reform program, including reform of the tax system and financial sector legislation, were systematically blocked in the Congress. Ambitious privatization plans slowed to a crawl after the sale of CANTV and Viasa. The "Social Megaproject," an effort to replace indirect subsidies with direct subsidies targeted to the poor, was only partially implemented. The weakness of the president's political position, his personal unpopularity, and charges of corruption within his private circle fostered coup attempts by elements of the armed forces in February and November of 1992. Free market policies lost support, and resistance against future attempts at reform arose.

President Pérez left office under the cloud of corruption charges in May 1993. Although the interim government of President Ramón J. Velásquez was able to push through several economic measures, including a tax package and a new banking law, 1993 was a year of political uncertainty and economic stagnation. Government spending was cut drastically in an attempt to close a widening budget deficit. Private-sector investment, from both domestic and foreign sources, fell sharply, and the nation went into recession after three years of impressive growth. Many businesspeople indicated that they were awaiting first the results of the December 1993 elections and then the economic policies of the new government before making investment plans.

On February 2, 1994, Rafael Caldera was inaugurated as Venezuela's president. Caldera, who was elected with 31 percent of the popular vote, had run as an independent candidate. The election represented a severe setback to Venezuela's leading political parties, Acción Democrática and COPEI, which had dominated the nation's political scene for more than 30 years, as well as a repudiation of the Pérez economic reform program. As a candidate, President Caldera had promised to clean up a corrupt political system, to raise a minimum wage that had become extremely low, to keep gasoline prices stable, and to repeal an unpopular value added tax. In his inaugural address the president called for a social program similar to the Mexican Solidarity movement, an economic policy based on fighting inflation and balancing the national budget, and fiscal reform to institute progressive taxes and increase tax collections. The president also called for the development of a more competitive economy based on a combination of private initiative and social responsibility.

The new government inherited an economy in recession and a crisis in the Venezuelan financial sector precipitated by the collapse of the nation's second largest bank, the Banco Latino, in January 1994 and the subsequent insolvency of several other leading banks. In an effort to deal with the financial crisis, the administration suspended economic freedoms guaranteed by the Venezuelan Constitution and began to exercise de facto control of a major portion of the banking sector. The resignation of a respected Central Bank president and concerns over government finances raised inflationary expectations and caused the value of the Venezuelan currency, the bolivar, to fall. In response, the administration established exchange controls, instituted price controls on a limited number of basic goods, and drafted laws that called for stiff prison sentences for "economic" crimes. In September 1994, the Venezuelan government announced a new program that sought to reduce the budget deficit, refinance the government's internal debt, reform the public administration, introduce selective elements of protectionism, and institute an industrial policy based on targeting a limited number of industries.

Substantial changes were under way in many Venezuelan industries. There were calls for the injection of private capital into state-owned oil, steel, and aluminum companies. The aluminum and steel industries, two of the nation's largest export earners, were in the midst of restructuring. Private-sector firms were attempting to cope with the banking crisis, exchange controls, and recession. Foreign investors cut back on planned investments or sought opportunities in other nations. Many firms looked forward to the implementation of the program announced in September 1994 and hoped for an improved economic climate.

A Nation Facing Choices

As 1994 came to a close, the Venezuelan economy faced a difficult future. The role of government in the economy had been reduced due to its lack of funds and resulting policy shifts. The traditional tension between statism and economic liberalism in Venezuela, which had swung toward liberalism in the early 1990s, had swung back, at least in part, toward statism. Historically, the AD governments had been more statist than those of COPEI, the Social Christian Party, including the first presidential term of Rafael Caldera (1969-1974) and the government of Luis Herrera (1979-1984), which tried to liberalize the economy. In contrast, in his second government (1989-1993), Pérez shifted away from the traditional position of AD, while Caldera, at the start of his second term (1994-), seemed inclined more toward statism. Caldera had separated from COPEI and presented an independent candidacy in the 1993 elections, and Pérez was expelled from AD in 1994. Although most observers agreed that it would be difficult to go back completely to the statist system of the past, it seemed equally difficult to move forward toward a modern market economy. The economy had not proven able to overcome the decline in real oil income experienced in late 1980s and early 1990s. It was also unclear what role the nation's leading institutions would play in the future. The government, the political parties, the major labor unions, and big business were all searching for a role in an uncertain future. What was certain was the need to improve the overall competitiveness of the Venezuelan economy and the ability of Venezuelan firms to compete in international markets.

The economic crisis of mid-1994 has showed the need for meaningful economic debate within the nation. The debate that emerged during 1992 and the 1993 presidential campaign left much to be desired. Denunciation of individuals often dominated the discussion of ideas or issues. A major reason for the lack of informed debate was the absence of a clear understanding of the nature of the economic problems that Venezuela faces. The illusion that oil income would be sufficient to ensure prosperity in Venezuela should have been shattered by the financial crisis of 1983 or the painful adjustment of 1989, but remarkably, neither event did so.

Perhaps the crisis of 1994 will finally bring about a clear understanding that the fundamental problem faced by the Venezuelan economy is that oil revenues will not be enough to ensure a high standard of living and that development of a more productive, competitive economy will be necessary to ensure prosperity. Only when such an understanding is widespread will the nation be able to develop effective solutions for the future. Unfortunately, popular perceptions of the causes of Venezuela's economic difficulties are often inaccurate. In such an environment, few seem willing to say that the task of change and reform has only begun and that a complete transformation of the Venezuelan economy is necessary to put the nation on the long and difficult road to prosperity. As a result, few have offered alternatives for the future that are both positive and realistic.

A clear economic vision will be necessary if Venezuela is to develop the competitive economy President Caldera called for in his inaugural address. Such a vision must come to grips with both the practices and ideologies of the past and the realities of the present. The reform program begun in 1989 was based on practicality and necessity rather than ideology. The absence of an underlying ideological base to the program, however, made it difficult to create an overall vision that could be readily explained to generate public support. The old statist system had failed, but no vision of what should replace it emerged. Without such a vision, it was easy for some to believe that a return to failed past policies might actually prove beneficial. While it had proven possible to tear down parts of the old system, building a new, more effective system had proven difficult.

What is needed in Venezuela today is a new vision, a new strategy for the main actors in the Venezuelan economy, including the state, management, labor, and the general public. Such a strategy should reflect the realities of the international economic environment. It also should reflect the fact that Venezuela is a land of potential. Its substantial natural resources remain largely underdeveloped. Many of its people are young, energetic, hardworking, and creative. The nation has been through a difficult period but has learned from its experiences. The Venezuelan public has learned that it has a voice in its rejection of corruption and the traditional political elites. In order to prosper, Venezuela will have to organize and mobilize its resources and its population to build a more productive economy that generates a higher standard of living for all its people.

Positive change will be difficult and will not be immediate. Many vested interests, with substantial influence over public opinion, have shown how far they are willing to go to defend their perquisites. These difficulties, however, do not mean that Venezuela should turn inward. They mean that the challenges, and rewards, of building a more competitive economy and a more prosperous future will be so much the greater. The purpose of this book is to contribute to the debate within Venezuela over the challenges to be faced in creating such a competitive economy.

Although these challenges reflect particularly Venezuelan circumstances, they are not so different from those faced in many other nations. All countries face the challenge of competitiveness in the modern world economy. Hundreds of millions of people live in poverty in the developing world. Throughout Latin America, nations have tried to adapt to the realities of international economic competition. Major reform programs are under way in Argentina, Chile, Colombia, Mexico, and Peru. Eastern European nations are trying to adopt more market-oriented economies after decades of stagnation under state socialism. Several East Asian nations are trying to follow the example of neighbors that have developed their economies by competing successfully in international markets. Competitiveness also has become a major concern in the industrialized nations, which have seen their economies stagnate in recent years. Democracies all over the world are struggling with the need to make difficult long-term economic choices while trying to address the short- and medium-term aspirations of their citizens.

Venezuela Competitiva

This book is the product of a research project titled Venezuela Competitiva carried out by researchers from Venezuela and the United States. The project had its genesis in July 1991, when Professor Michael Enright of Harvard Business School, who had served as research manager for the ten-nation study of industrial competitiveness that resulted in Michael Porter's book *The Competitive Advantage of Nations* (Porter 1990), addressed the Second Congress of the Venezuelan Chemical and Petrochemical Industries on the topic of competitiveness and conducted a seminar on the same topic at the Institute for Advanced Administrative Studies (IESA). Following his visit, members of the executive board of the Association of Venezuelan Executives (AVE) initiated discussions on the feasibility of conducting a large-scale analysis of the competitiveness of the Venezuelan economy. Researchers from IESA were soon brought into the discussions. The National Council for Investment Promotion (CONAPRI), the Fund for the Development of Technological Innovation (FINTEC), and subsequently the National Center for Competitiveness (CENAC) pledged their support. Work got under way in November of 1992 and proceeded throughout 1993 and the first half of 1994.

Since the start, this project has been a collaborative effort. The methodology and overall conceptual framework came out of work on international competitiveness at the Harvard Business School. Most of the research for this project was conducted in Venezuela by a Venezuelan research team headquartered at IESA in Caracas. Professor Julián Villalba helped to plan the project and got it under way. Professor Antonio Francés, IESA's director of research, took over the direction of the Venezuelan/IESA team in early 1993. The Venezuelan/IESA team, which included more than 35 professors, researchers, and experts, worked in close collaboration with Professor Enright and Edith Scott Saavedra, both located in Boston, Massachusetts. Professor Enright brought extensive experience in designing and carrying out such studies, as well as knowledge of other economies developed through his participation in studies of competitiveness in 15 other nations. Professor Francés, whose previous work includes numerous publications on international trade, corporate structure, and firm strategy, brought an extensive knowledge of Venezuelan firms and the Venezuelan economy and contributed substantial managerial, organizational, and conceptual elements to the study. Ms. Scott, whose prior international legal work involved clients from around the world, provided much of the conceptual and substantive guidance for the field research, undertook substantial additional research in support of the project, and managed the liaison between Boston and Caracas.

Research Design

The project was designed to be a comprehensive and exhaustive study of the Venezuelan economy, consisting of four major components. The first was an analysis of Venezuela's overall economic performance, including its macroeconomic performance, its performance on social indicators, and its trade and foreign investment performance. The second component was a series of papers on the themes and issues that have an important impact on Venezuelan industry in general. The third was a series of studies of specific Venezuelan industries chosen to provide a representative set that included some of the nation's most important sectors. The fourth component was an extensive set of interviews of government officials, businesspeople, community organizers, industry experts, and labor representatives carried out by the three authors of this book.

In the economy of every nation, there are vital leverage points that contribute to or detract from the competitive strength of local firms. The 14 "key issues" examined by this project included: education, training, foreign investment, technological development, new business formation, the informal economy, domestic rivalry, state-owned enterprises, international trade agreements, energy, environmental regulation, transportation, communications, and productivity growth. The goal was to understand the impact that each of these areas has had on the competitiveness of Venezuelan firms in both a general and a specific sense. In addition, a series of background papers were prepared that provided additional context for the project.

The 13 industries subject to study were chosen to provide a representative cross-section of the Venezuelan economy. This cross-section included several resource-based industries (oil, petrochemicals, steel, and aluminum), agricultural sectors (rice, cocoa, and pulp and paper), a service industry (tourism), two import substitution industries (automotive vehicles and parts, and textiles), and several that we chose to call "talent based" because talent plays an important role in competitive success in these industries (engineering, software, and telenovelas—a form of soap opera). We included some large export earners and some small ones, some industries that are successful in international markets and others that are less so, some industries that compete in global markets and others that compete in regional markets. The goal was not to provide strategic plans for individual sectors nor to pick future "winners and losers." Rather, as nations and their firms compete in individual industries, the goal was to study a representative set of industries to determine the sources of advantage and disadvantage, as well as the key leverage points, in the Venezuelan environment.

In all, Venezuelan researchers prepared 36 studies for this project. In addition to providing much of the basis of this book, many are outstanding pieces that can stand on their own. Many of the authors are among the foremost Venezuelan experts in their field. Several provided additional insights to the overall project. The authors of the key issue papers were Ignacio Avalos, Antonio Balaguer, Keila Betancourt, María A. Cervilla, Imelda Cisneros, María Elena Corrales, Lorenzo Dávalos Tamayo, Antonio Francés, Samuel Freije, Henry Gómez, Laura González, Elena Granell de Aldaz, Ana Julia Jatar, Janet Kelly, Juan Carlos Navarro, Carlos E. Paredes, Matilde Parra, Alberto Silva A., Carlos Suárez, Adolfo Taylhardat, and Horacio Viana. The authors of background papers were Francisco J. Briceño, Magín Briceño, Victor M. Calzadilla, Elba Julieta García, Luis García Montoya, Francisco González, Miriam Kornblith, Juan Carlos Larrañaga, José Malavé, Ramón Piñango, and Roberto Rigobón. The industry studies were authored by Luis Alvaray, Antonio Balaguer, María Eugenia Boza, Magín Briceño, María A. Cervilla, Carlos Enrique Dallmeier, Antonio Francés, Rosa Amelia González de Pacheco, Abdel Güerere, Luis Manuel Rivas Acosta, Ramón Rosales Linares, Rómulo Sánchez, Ana M. Segnini, and Nelson Vásquez. These papers are cited extensively in the text and appear in the bibliography.

Acknowledgments

Reliable industry data and business-related statistics are scarce in Venezuela. For this reason, the project placed particular emphasis on original field research. Interviews with industry participants, government officials, and industry experts, in Caracas and the interior, contributed to the industry studies and "key issue" papers as well as to the final report. We would like to thank the many executives, managers, public officials, community and labor organizers, industry experts, and others who generously donated their time to interviews.

We also thank the presidents and vice presidents of the Association of Venezuelan Executives, past and present, the boards of directors of the National Council for Investment Promotion, the Fund for the Development of Technological Innovation, and, more recently, the National Center for Competitiveness, who have given the project their support since its inception in 1992. Special thanks go to James Austin, Rodger Farrell, Janet Kelly, Ramón Piñango, Michael Porter, and the Project's Steering Committee, who reviewed and commented on the first draft of this book, to Rodger Farrell and Laura González, of IESA, whose hard work kept the research moving forward, and to Francisco Vázquez, who provided able research assistance. We extend our heartfelt thanks to the Project's Steering Committee, consisting of Adolfo Taylhardat, Hernán Oyarzabal, Luis Eduardo Paúl, Moisés Ramírez, José Rafael Rivas, Aquiles Viso, and Leonardo Vivas, for their tireless dedication and effort in steering this project towards fruition.

The principal sponsors of the project have been the National Council for Investment Promotion, the Fund for the Development of Technological Innovation, the Association of Venezuelan Executives, and the National Center for Competitiveness, in Caracas, Venezuela. Professor Enright's participation has been sponsored by the Division of Research at the Harvard Business School. The views expressed in this publication are those of the authors and do not necessarily reflect the views of any of the sponsoring organizations.

Structure of the Book

The remainder of this book is structured as follows. Chapter 2 provides an overview of Venezuela's recent economic and trade performance and the major macroeconomic challenges facing the nation in 1994. Chapter 3 sets forth the theoretical framework in which we will examine the competitive strengths and weaknesses of Venezuelan industry. Chapter 4 provides summary abstracts of six of the industry studies generated for the project: telenovelas, pulp and paper, tourism, petrochemicals, steel, and automotive vehicles and parts. Chapter 5 presents brief discussions of seven of the studies and the principal findings of the 13 industry studies. Chapters 6 through 9 discuss the determinants of national advantage within Venezuela at the national level. Chapter 10 highlights potential growth areas for the Venezuelan economy. Chapters 11 and 12 set forth the implications of the project for government and for firms. Chapter 13 provides some final thoughts and conclusions. A table of recommendations can be found in the appendix.

Our aim is to provide a comprehensive analysis of the present position of the Venezuelan economy and to set forth guidelines for government policy and firm strategy that the study has shown would contribute to the economic well-being of the nation. Our goal is not to provide a detailed legislative program nor a detailed consulting study of any particular industry. Rather, we hope to provide a new way of thinking that can be brought to bear by Venezuelan policy makers, managers, and citizens in their own endeavors and that will help Venezuela to move ahead, to build a more competitive economy, and to achieve a higher standard of living for its people. We have tried to identify where Venezuela does and does not measure up to other nations in the region and elsewhere. We have tried to be sympathetic, but honest and direct critics of the status quo. Anything less would be a disservice to our readers.

2

The Structure and Performance of the Venezuelan Economy

Before beginning a detailed discussion of the forces that have driven the Venezuelan economy, it is useful to provide a basic description of the structure of the economy and its performance over the last several years.

The Structure of the Venezuelan Economy

The basic structure of the Venezuelan economy in 1991 is compared with that of other major Latin American nations in Table 2.1. Manufacturing, mining and quarrying, and wholesale and retail trade were the largest single categories of economic activity. The importance of Venezuela's extractive industries, which were relatively larger than those of other Latin American nations, shows the greatest difference. This is due to the importance to the Venezuelan economy of oil, which accounted for a little over 22 percent of gross domestic product (GDP) in that year.[1] On the other hand, Venezuela's manufacturing; finance and business services; community and personal services; and agriculture, hunting, forestry, and fishing sectors were relatively smaller than those in several other Latin American nations.

Bimodal Size Distribution of Firms

The Venezuelan economy is characterized by a number of large state-owned and private companies and a substantial number of very small firms. In 1991, large firms, with more than 150 employees, accounted for only 9.3 percent of all manufacturing establishments, yet they generated 63 percent of manufacturing employment and 86.1 percent of manufacturing value added. At

TABLE 2.1
GDP by Kind of Activity, Selected Latin American Nations, 1991

Percent of Total GDP

Kind of Activity	Argentina	Brazil	Chile	Colombia	Mexico	Peru	Venezuela
Agriculture, hunting, forestry, fishing	8.3	10.8	8.7	22.5	8.9	6.6	5.5
Mining, quarrying	2.3	1.7	7.3	4.5	2.3	2.4	18.5
Manufacturing	25.4	25.0	20.5	20.8	22.2	25.0	19.9
Electricity, gas, water	1.9	3.6	2.5	1.1	1.4	0.6	2.1
Construction	5.5	7.1	5.8	3.0	3.9	8.6	5.5
Wholesale and retail trade, restaurants, hotels	15.4	7.1	18.5	11.4	26.7	18.7	18.3
Transport, storage, communications	4.7	5.5	7.4	8.8	8.4	5.9	5.7
Finance, insurance, real estate, business services	15.4	23.8	a	14.4	11.6	17.6	11.8
Government, community, social, personal services	18.5	23.4	29.3	13.7	15.7	14.3	12.5
Subtotal	97.3	108.0	-	100.3	101.2	99.7	99.8
Less: Imputed bank service charges	b	8.0	a	2.9	1.2	0.6	1.8
Plus: Import duties	2.7	-	a	2.5	-	0.9	2.0
Total GDP	100.0	100.0	100.0	100.0	100.0	100.0	100.0

[a] Included under Government etc. services.

[b] Included under each separate activity.

Source: Compiled from United Nations, ECLAC (1992b).

the other extreme, small firms, with between 10 and 50 employees, represented 65.8 percent of all manufacturing firms but only 15 percent of manufacturing employment, and a mere 3.8 percent of manufacturing value added. Medium-size firms (with between 50 and 150 employees), which often serve as motors of growth in developed economies, play a relatively minor role in Venezuela.[2]

State-Owned Companies[3]

State-owned companies are a prominent feature of the Venezuelan economy. Historically, the Venezuelan state took a very active role in developing the economy. State-owned companies were founded to foster economic development and to remedy market imperfections. The importance of oil and the view that foreign-owned oil companies were not operating in the best interests of the nation led to the nationalization of the industry in 1976. For many years, Venezuela's state-owned companies were viewed by politicians and many in the general public as superior for the long-term development of the nation's resources, as protection against monopolization in the private sector, and as a substitute for immature financial markets, which could not fund the large-scale investments necessary to develop the nation's potential. Over the years, state-owned companies extended their position within the economy.

As of 1993, there were some 202 state-owned companies in Venezuela. The largest, Petróleos de Venezuela (PDVSA, the national oil company) with 55,000 employees, and Siderúrgica del Orinoco, C.A. (Sidor, the nation's leading steel company) with 18,000, ranked first and third in employment among Venezuelan companies. Compañía Anónima Nacional Teléfonos de Venezuela (CANTV), the telecommunications company privatized in 1991, was second with approximately 22,000 employees. By one count, more than 327,000 people were employed by Venezuelan state-owned companies in 1989.[4] By law, the oil, gas, and iron ore industries are reserved to the state. In practice, state-owned companies have dominated the iron ore, steel, aluminum, electric power, communications, ports, airlines, mining, petrochemical, fertilizer, and milk industries. In addition, state-owned enterprises have had prominent positions in financial services, sugar mills, hotels, shipping, and cultural activities.

Venezuela's state-owned oil industry accounted for 22.2 percent of GDP in 1991. Nonfinancial, non-oil state-owned companies accounted for another 5.4 percent of GDP, down from 7.3 percent nine years earlier. Total public investment accounted for 59 percent of total investment in that year. State-owned companies have become a drain on the Venezuelan treasury in recent years. In 1991, for example, the state injected more than 51 billion bolivars (approximately $90 million) into the non-oil, nonfinancial state-owned enterprises.

The privatization of several state-owned companies, including that of CANTV (the national telecommunications company), Venezolana Internacional de Aviación, S.A. (Viasa) (the national airline), several hotels, and several banks, in the early 1990s signaled a change in policy toward state ownership. Many other companies were soon slated for privatization, but the process was virtually halted by the coup attempts of 1992. The privatization of CANTV left PDVSA and the

Corporación Venezolana de Guayana (CVG), a combination of corporation and regional development agency, as the largest state-owned companies in the economy. The CVG companies included Sidor; Aluminio del Caroní, S.A. (Alcasa) and Venezolana de Aluminio, C.A. (Venalum), the nation's largest aluminum producers; Electrificación del Caroní, C.A. (Edelca), the nation's largest electric company; Bauxita de Venezuela, C.A. (Bauxiven) and Interamericana de Alúmina, C.A. (Interalúmina), producers of bauxite and alumina, respectively; and Carbones del Orinoco, C.A. (Carbonorca), a producer of carbon anodes.

Industrial Groups

The Venezuelan private sector features a number of diversified and vertically integrated industrial groups that are large by Venezuelan standards, but medium-size by international standards. Venezuela's leading indigenous industrial groups include Polar (beer, agriculture, foods, packaging, and industrial equipment), Mendoza (agroindustry, building and construction materials, chemicals, banking, and financial services), Cisneros (ODC Group) (retailing, beverages, food and consumer products, broadcasting, entertainment, information and communications, aluminum, and mining), Boulton (airlines, travel agencies, shipping, insurance and financial services, ceramics and cement, and distribution), Phelps (broadcasting, entertainment, and food), Corimon (chemicals, building materials, juices, and packaging), Vollmer (sugar, rum, and financial services), and Machado/Zuloaga (iron, steel, auto parts, metal products, and electric power). These groups are generally controlled by one or a small number of families, with either the founders or direct descendants or relatives by marriage in charge.

Although some of the leading groups trace their history back to the mid-nineteenth century, several others were founded in the post–World War II era. Several of the local industrial groups grew up under the protection of import substitution policies instituted in the 1960s and restrictions placed on foreign ownership in the late 1960s and early 1970s. Some diversified to take advantage of the closed but small marketplace and focused substantial efforts on shaping government policies to their advantage.[5] Certain groups, including Polar, the Cisneros Group, and Corimon, have begun to make foreign investments of their own, growing into multinationals themselves from a Venezuelan home base.

Informal Firms[6]

At the other extreme in Venezuela is a substantial informal economy made up of sole proprietorships and microenterprises. It is estimated that the informal economy accounted for approximately 40 percent of total Venezuelan employment in the early 1990s. The informal sector in Venezuela covers a wide range of activities, from retailing to light manufactures. Most informal workers are in the tertiary sector. Commerce, services (such as electrical and automotive repairs), and transportation accounted for 62.8 percent of Venezuela's informal employment in 1991.[7] Informal firms and workers are also active in the garment, footwear, metalworking, and wood furniture industries. Several factors hinder the absorption of informal workers into the formal economy in Venezuela. The benefits and protections of the nation's labor legislation increase the marginal cost of labor and discourage the creation of jobs by the formal sector. In addition, most informal workers lack the education, skills, and capital resources to function productively in the formal sector. Informal workers on average earn less than workers in the formal sector, and this gap in incomes has widened over the past decade.

Importance of Multinational Firms

Foreign-owned multinational companies also figure prominently in Venezuela. Foreign multinationals dominated large portions of the Venezuelan economy until the 1970s, when Venezuela joined the Andean Pact restrictions on foreign investment. The oil industry was nationalized and the foreign presence was reduced in the banking, entertainment, and other sectors. From the mid-1970s until 1989, foreign direct investment was generally discouraged. Foreign capital entered Venezuela in the form of debt rather than equity during that period. In this way, Venezuelan firms could have access to foreign capital without giving up control. Privatization, the lifting of barriers to foreign direct investment, and market integration in the Andean Pact resulted in a sharp increase in foreign direct investment from 1990 to 1992.

Multinationals, sometimes affiliated with local companies or investors, figure prominently in the Venezuelan appliance, chemical, electronics, food, candy, glass, household goods, machinery, packaged goods, paper, pharmaceutical, soft drink, tobacco, and advertising industries. The privatization of CANTV made it the largest company in the Venezuelan private sector. Venezuela's auto assemblers are all foreign-owned companies. Legal restrictions have prevented foreign firms from playing a major role in the banking sector. In 1993, the new Banking Law opened several banking services to foreign firms.

Venezuela's Economic Performance

It is necessary to place Venezuela's economic performance in the appropriate context. There have been a number of different economic regimes in Venezuela over the last two decades. The impact of these regimes will be described in detail in Chapter 9. For now, a basic outline will suffice. As indicated in Chapter 1, Venezuela engaged in state-led, import substitution industrialization through the 1970s and most of the 1980s. In 1989, the nation embarked on a market-oriented economic reform program that freed prices, exchange rates, and interest rates. Some state-owned companies were privatized. The program also opened the nation to foreign competition and placed a much greater emphasis on exports as an engine of growth. Venezuela lowered tariffs, abolished many nontariff barriers, joined the GATT, opened most sectors to foreign capital, and negotiated a free trade agreement with Colombia. The reform process was largely stopped by opposition in 1992 and 1993. In early 1994, it was unclear what policies the new government that took office in February would follow.

Incomes

Venezuela experienced high economic growth from the end of World War II into the 1970s. In 1970, Venezuela's per-capita GDP was higher than that of Greece, Spain, Singapore, and Hong Kong, and only slightly below that of Ireland. (See Table 2.2.) The 1970s were boom years for the Venezuelan economy, with growth buoyed by high oil prices and massive public expenditures on consumption, social programs, and investments in industry and infrastructure. The boom, however, eventually came to an end. Real per capita income in Venezuela peaked in 1977 and began to decline. (See Figure 2.1.) Cuts in government spending, a major devaluation, and other restrictive policies in 1983 coincided with an 8 percent drop in per-capita GDP. By 1985, per-capita income had fallen to levels not seen since the mid-1960s. In 1988, even after three years of growth fueled by deficit spending, Venezuela's per-capita GDP was less than half that of Ireland, Spain, Singapore, and Hong Kong and only two-thirds that of Greece.

On the surface, the Venezuelan economy seemed to have outperformed those of the other major Latin American nations. Venezuela's per-capita income was still higher than that in most of Latin America. The nation had avoided the traumatic adjustments that had taken place in the early 1980s in Mexico, Argentina, and Chile. When purchasing power parity was taken into account, however, the story was somewhat different. By 1988, despite a higher per-capita GDP, Venezuelans actually had less purchasing power on average than Chileans, Argentines, Mexicans, and Brazilians. Of the major Latin American nations, only Colombia ranked lower in the average purchasing power of its citizens.[8]

TABLE 2.2
Per-Capita GDP, Selected Nations, 1970 and 1988

Venezuela 1970 = 100

Country	1970	1988	Growth Rate 1970-1988 (%)
Ireland	106.05	251.08	4.9
Venezuela	**100.00**	**92.98**	**-0.4**
Greece	94.35	143.41	2.4
Spain	90.08	237.05	5.5
Singapore	76.61	246.65	6.7
Hong Kong	72.58	262.89	7.4
Argentina	73.39	75.45	0.2
Brazil	36.29	67.03	3.5
Chile	68.55	47.37	-2.0
Colombia	27.42	35.99	1.5
Mexico	57.26	57.49	0.0

Sources: The Economist (1990), IMF Financial Statistics.

Falling oil revenue was a major contributor to the decline in output and income that Venezuela experienced in the late 1970s and the 1980s. Venezuelan oil revenues grew rapidly in the 1970s, tripling in real terms from 1970 to 1974 (see Figure 2.2) and then exceeding the 1974 peak in 1980. This increase in revenue was due primarily to increases in the price of oil. The real price of a barrel of Venezuelan oil in 1974 was roughly three and one-half times that in 1970. In 1980, prices were five times 1970 prices.[9] Venezuelan oil output actually declined through the 1970s due to the exhaustion of some wells, quotas from the Organization of Petroleum

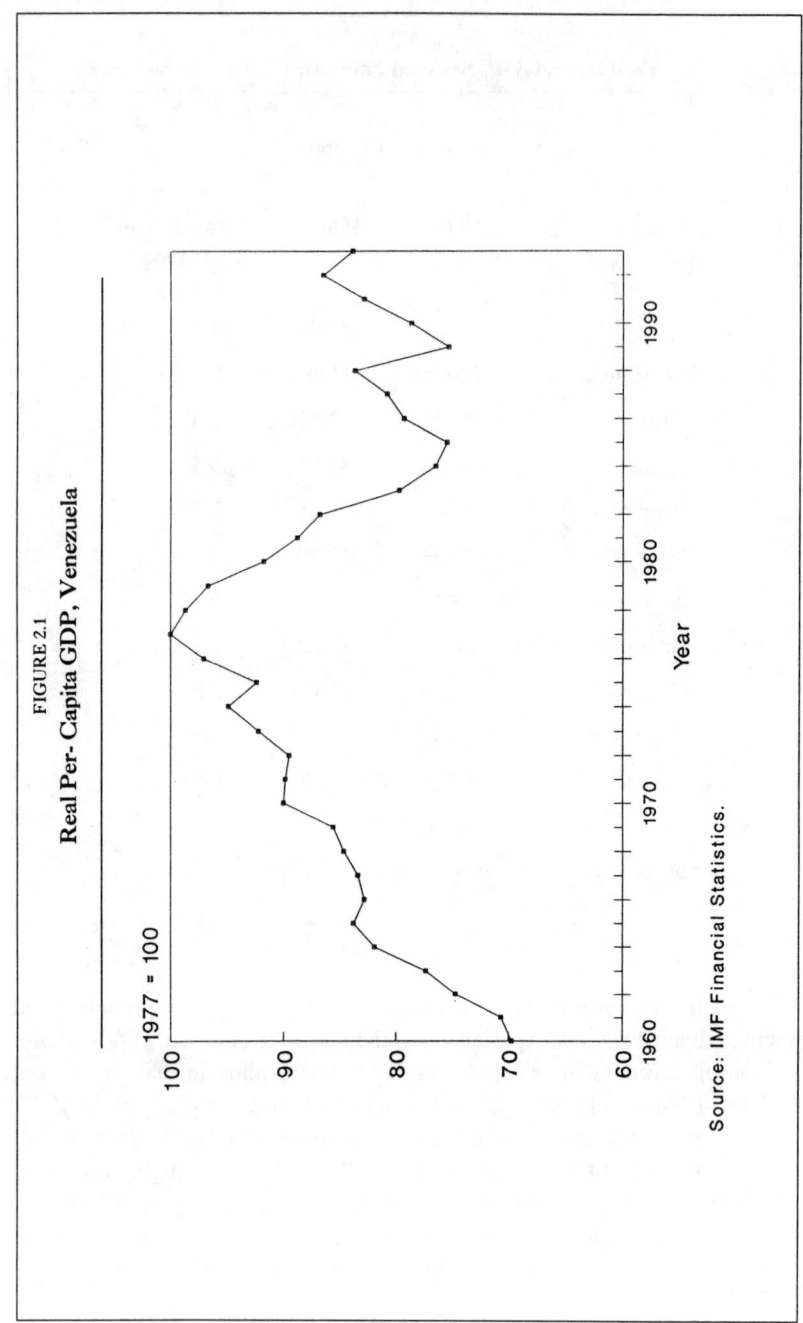

FIGURE 2.1
Real Per-Capita GDP, Venezuela

Source: IMF Financial Statistics.

Exporting Countries (OPEC) designed to reduce production and increase prices, and conscious efforts to conserve the oil resource. Venezuelan oil output fell from its high of 3.71 million barrels per day in 1970 to 2.30 million barrels per day in 1976, the year of nationalization, and to 2.16 million barrels per day in 1981.[10]

Venezuelan oil revenue fell dramatically in real terms after 1981. By 1988, Venezuelan oil sold for less than half the price it had just seven years earlier. Volume had continued to decline, reaching 1.77 million barrels per day in 1988. By 1988, real oil revenues had fallen 65 percent from their 1980 peak. This translated into a decline of roughly 70 percent in real oil income on a per-capita basis. Reduced oil revenues created two problems. The first was a reduction in revenues in the major industry in the economy. The second was that taxes on oil revenues accounted for approximately 75 percent of government revenues. The dramatic fall in oil revenues placed government finances in jeopardy and threatened an economic system in which oil revenues supported public services and political patronage as well as massive subsidies and investments in industrialization and infrastructure.

In 1989, the collapse of Venezuela's old economic system and the shock of adjustment resulted in an 8.3 percent decline in GDP. Per-capita GDP fell 10 percent (see Figure 2.1), the sharpest decline the nation had experienced in decades. Manufacturing output declined by 14.6 percent in real terms, while construction declined by 27.1 percent. After 1989, the Venezuelan economy began to perform admirably in macroeconomic terms. Real GDP growth was 5.3 percent in 1990, 10.4 percent in 1991, and 7.3 percent in 1992. (See Table 2.3.) Per-capita GDP increased by more than 14 percent in this period. Though much of the gain in 1990 came from higher oil revenues (which grew by 13.6 percent) brought on by the Persian Gulf War, the non-oil portion of the economy also grew strongly. Broader-based growth was recorded in 1991 as real oil revenues increased 10.3 percent, manufactures 10.8 percent, and construction 30.8 percent.

The economy grew again in 1992 despite a decrease in the oil sector. Construction (16.8 percent growth), manufacturing (12.1 percent), and services (8.7 percent) led the way. Venezuela's non-oil GDP rose by approximately 9.5 percent, the largest increase since 1976. There were indications that increased output was having an effect on the general welfare. By the end of 1992, real wages in Venezuela had regained their 1987 and 1988 levels.

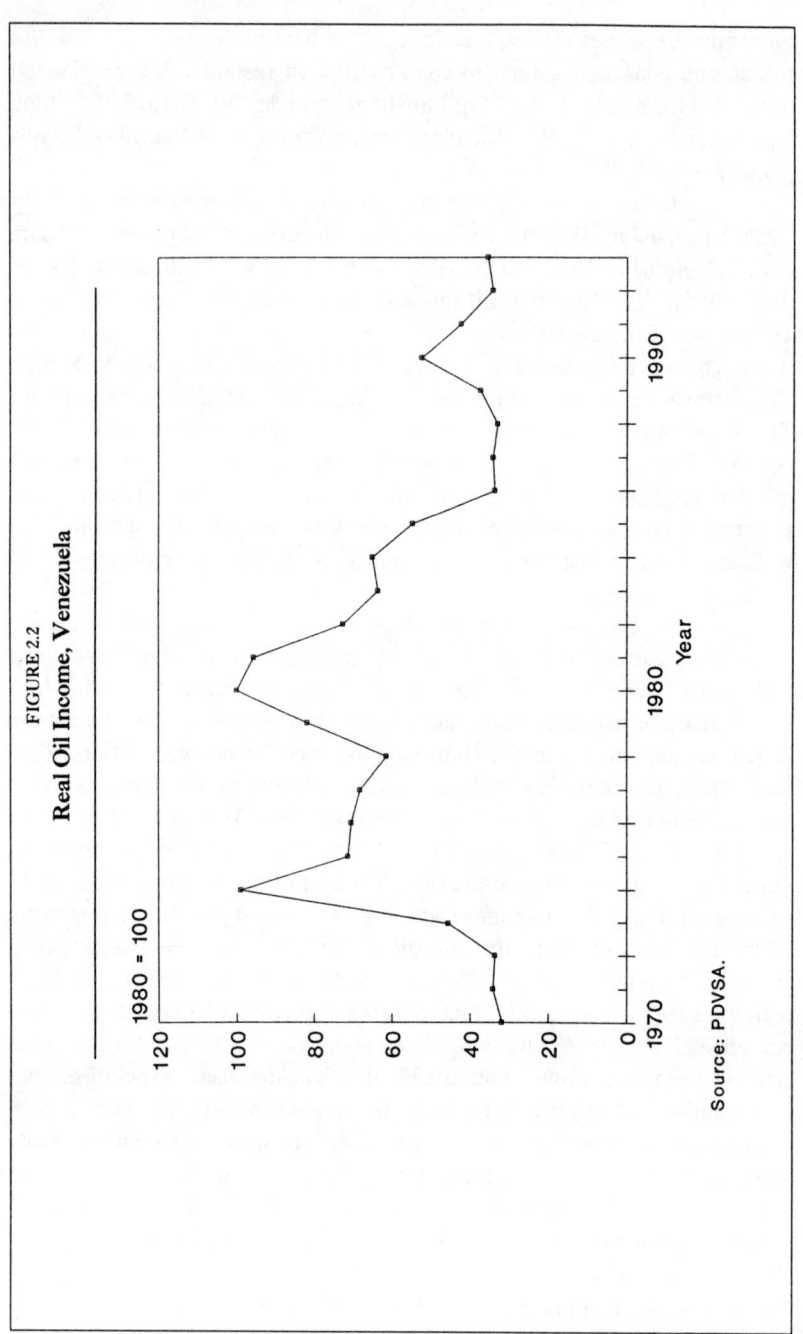

FIGURE 2.2
Real Oil Income, Venezuela

Source: PDVSA.

TABLE 2.3
Real Growth in Components of Venezuelan GDP, 1987–1993

Annual Growth Rate, Percent

	1987	1988	1989	1990	1991	1992	1993
Real GDP	3.5	5.8	-8.3	5.3	10.4	7.3	-1.0
Petroleum	-1.4	8.0	-0.4	13.6	10.3	-1.9	3.4
Nonpetroleum	4.4	5.7	-9.4	3.7	8.9	9.5	-1.7
Tradable	2.0	4.5	-12.1	3.6	8.5	9.5	-1.9
Agriculture	4.4	5.2	-5.1	-0.3	3.2	2.4	-3.9
Manufacturing	5.2	4.6	-14.6	4.9	10.8	12.1	-1.4
Nontradable	5.9	6.3	8.3	3.8	9.1	9.5	-1.6
Construction	6.4	7.9	-27.1	6.7	30.8	16.8	-1.6
Services	5.8	7.9	-6.9	3.4	6.9	8.7	-1.7

Source: Central Bank of Venezuela.

After three years of rapid growth, however, the Venezuelan economy entered a recession in 1993. GDP fell by 1.0 percent, despite a 3.4 percent increase in oil revenue. In contrast, other Latin American nations registered impressive growth, including Chile (approximately 6 percent), Argentina (6 percent), Peru (5.5 percent), Brazil (5 percent), Colombia (3.7 percent), Bolivia (3.7 percent), and Paraguay (3.5 percent).[11] The Venezuelan recession was felt throughout its non-oil economy, which contracted 1.7 percent, with declines in agriculture (3.9 percent), services (1.7 percent), construction (1.6 percent), and manufacturing (1.4 percent). A public spending reduction of 14 percent in real terms, in an effort to reduce the budget deficit, was in part responsible for the recession. According to the Economist Intelligence Unit, in 1993, Venezuela's per-capita GDP was just under $3,000. This was comparable to Chile, less than Argentina (approximately $6,800), Mexico (slightly under $4,000), and Uruguay ($3,600), but higher than Brazil ($2,700), Peru ($2,000), and Colombia ($1,300).[12]

Social Indicators

In terms of social indicators, Venezuela generally kept pace with other middle-income nations through the 1980s. Kelly (1992) examined a number of indicators of social performance, including those related to health, nutrition, education, and income distribution. Though Venezuela lagged behind the best performers among middle-income nations in individual indicators, in the late 1980s, Venezuelans were not on average worse off than the citizens of other such nations, several of which were experiencing economic problems of their own.

The deterioration of the Venezuelan economy can be seen in the levels of poverty experienced in the nation. The percentage of Venezuelans living below the poverty line increased from approximately 25 percent in 1981 to approximately 40 percent in 1989.[13] In addition, the portion of the Venezuelan population suffering from critical poverty increased from 5.1 percent in 1981, to 23.1 percent in 1987, and to 27.3 percent in 1989.[14] Though the percentage of the population in critical poverty stayed roughly the same from 1989 to 1992, growth in the economy allowed per-capita purchases of consumer goods and food to nearly regain their 1988 levels.

Employment

Unemployment was low in Venezuela throughout the 1970s and early 1980s. In 1978, for example, unemployment stood at just 4 percent. Jobless rates rose dramatically in the economic crisis of 1983 and 1984, reaching 15 percent in late 1984.[15] Unemployment declined in the mid-1980s, as borrowing fueled growth. Unemployment increased in 1989 and rose to more than 10 percent in the middle of 1990. (See Table 2.4.) Employment prospects gradually improved thereafter. By the end of 1992, unemployment stood at 7.7 percent. Net employment had increased by 884,000 since 1989. Nearly three-quarters of this new employment was in the private sector. Unemployment apparently fell in 1993 but was expected to rise to 8.5 percent by the end of 1994.[16]

Productivity

Venezuela experienced a productivity crisis in the 1970s and 1980s. The average annual output per worker in Venezuelan industry fell at a rate of 1.9 percent per year from 1965 to 1988. Over the same period, the output per worker in industry increased 2.7 percent per year in member nations of the Organization for Economic Cooperation and Development (OECD), 6.2 percent in the Asia/Pacific region, 2.7 percent in South Asia, and 2.5 percent in the Latin American/Caribbean region.[17] Productivity in industrial sectors dominated by state-owned enterprises was even worse, falling 9.2 percent per year in the late 1970s and 1.4 percent per year from 1983 to 1988.[18]

TABLE 2.4
Unemployment Rates, Selected Latin American Nations, 1986–1993

Percent of the Workforce

Country	1986	1987	1988	1989	1990	1991	1992	1993
Argentina	4.4	5.3	5.9	7.3	7.4	5.8	6.6	7.0
Brazil	2.4	3.7	3.9	3.3	4.3	4.8	5.9	
Colombia	13.0	11.1	10.1	9.0	10.2	9.8	9.2	7.9
Chile	8.8	7.9	6.3	5.3	5.6	5.3	4.4	4.5
Venezuela	11.0	9.1	7.7	9.2	10.4	9.5	7.8	

Source: United Nations, ILO (various years).

Paredes (1993) has calculated the growth rates of factor inputs, output, and productivity in Venezuela from 1921 to 1992. Total factor productivity (increased output through technological innovation and improved efficiency) growth was negative from 1974 to 1982 (minus 2.11 percent per year) and then again from 1983 to 1989 (minus 1.57 percent per year). Growth in labor productivity (output per worker) was negative for both periods (minus 0.07 percent per year and minus 3.25 percent per year), whereas capital productivity (output per unit of capital) registered a decline of 4.16 percent per year from 1974 to 1982 and a gain of only 0.11 percent per year from 1983 to 1989. (See Table 2.5.) If anything, Paredes concludes that these estimates may be high. The contribution of total factor productivity growth to output in Venezuela had been negligible for decades.

Productivity fell for a number of reasons, including the overall lack of incentives for firms to improve performance in a politically dominated import substitution economy, massive state intervention and controls, unreasonable expansion of inefficient state-owned enterprises in the late 1970s and early 1980s, initial productivity declines due to nationalization, and a sharp decline in investment activity in the mid- to late 1980s. In a politically dominated system, productivity improvements were neither as easy nor as sure a road to profit as obtaining

TABLE 2.5
Output, Factor Inputs, and Productivity Growth in Venezuela

Compound Annual Growth Rate, Percent

	1974-1982	1983-1989	1990-1992
Growth in:			
Output	3.14	-0.50	7.86
Factor Input	5.25	1.07	1.73
Labor	3.21	2.75	2.54
Capital	7.30	-0.62	0.93
Total Factor Productivity	-2.11	-1.57	6.13
Labor Productivity	-0.07	-3.25	5.33
Capital Productivity	-4.16	0.11	6.93

Source: Adapted from Paredes (1993).

government favors. Productivity improvement was not a primary, or even a secondary, goal of Venezuela's non-oil state-owned enterprises. In the mid-1980s, for example, some state-owned enterprises were ordered to increase their workforce by 10 percent in an effort to combat unemployment, with little regard for the impact on productivity. Other policies also affected productivity. Under the price control scheme then in place, Venezuelan firms in the private sector were able to obtain higher prices simply by showing that their costs had increased, regardless of the source of the cost increase.

The economic opening and reform program precipitated a spectacular increase in productivity in the Venezuelan economy. Total factor productivity increased at a rate of 6.13 percent per year from 1990 to 1992. Labor productivity increased at a rate of 5.33 percent, while capital productivity increased at a rate of 6.93 percent per year. All productivity measures showed improvements that had not been experienced in decades.[19] Increased competition and fewer distortions in the economy had resulted in substantial reductions in inefficiency throughout the economy.

Public Finances

In the early 1970s, the Venezuelan public sector ran small deficits and accumulated minimal external debt. The growth in oil revenues from 1974 to 1978 allowed the public sector to expand dramatically while maintaining an overall surplus. In the late 1970s and early 1980s, however, misguided interest and exchange rate policies encouraged the flight of capital from Venezuela. Interest rates were held below world levels in an environment with a fixed exchange rate and no capital controls. Investors naturally sought higher returns abroad. Capital flight was exacerbated by macroeconomic imbalances and the fear of a substantial devaluation (which came in 1983). Private holdings of dollar-denominated assets held abroad by Venezuelans increased by $29.2 billion from 1979 to 1983. The total value of foreign assets held by private Venezuelan parties was estimated at $45 billion by the end of 1983.[20] By 1988, this figure was estimated at $60 billion or higher.[21]

Capital flight resulted in the Venezuelan public sector financing the gains of the small number of private parties with dollar assets. It also limited the amount of private capital available for investment in the local economy. The government borrowed abroad to maintain an overvalued exchange rate as it supported capital flight by subsidizing foreign exchange. State-owned enterprises borrowed heavily from foreign sources in order to cover operational losses. This scenario, combined with attempts to maintain investment and consumption levels through international borrowing, increased the nation's foreign debt dramatically. In 1978, Venezuela's net public foreign debt was $0.5 billion. By 1983, this figure was $15.6 billion. By the end of 1988, the figure had reached $19.5 billion.[22]

Increased public sector debt was part of a larger crisis of public finance caused mainly by a rapid decrease in government revenues from the oil industry, which typically accounted for more than 75 percent of total government revenues. From 1981 to 1983, the government's real per-capita revenue fell by some 40 percent. In the latter year, the fiscal deficit exceeded 9 percent of GDP. A major devaluation and deep spending cuts were required to restore fiscal balance. The situation, however, worsened. By 1988, real per-capita government revenue from the oil industry was 75 percent below 1981 levels. Total government revenue per capita also had fallen by some 75 percent. Despite falling revenues, real per-capita government spending was virtually flat from 1984 to 1988. The result was a mounting public sector deficit, which reached 9.4 percent of GDP in 1988 and was projected to reach 12 percent of GDP in 1989. The Venezuelan state was rapidly going bankrupt.

Upon taking office in 1989, the new administration took quick action to try to reduce the budget deficit. It succeeded in reducing the public sector deficit, which was expected to reach 12 percent of GDP in 1989 in the absence of adjustment, to 1.2 percent of GDP. This was achieved through a drastic reduction in government spending; real per-capita government spending was cut in half. Given prior reductions in government expenditures, real per-capita government expenditures in 1989 were only a quarter of what they had been just eight years earlier.

Government finances and inflation remained problematic into the 1990s. The public sector showed small surpluses in 1990 and 1991 due to increased oil revenue during the Persian Gulf War in 1990 and 1991 and the sale of 40 percent of CANTV in 1991. In the absence of these two events, the public deficit would have been 6.9 percent and 5.3 percent of GDP in these two years.[23] The public deficit was officially recorded at 3.1 percent of GDP in 1991, a year in which government spending rose 11 percent in real terms.[24] In 1992, however, oil revenues declined and the public sector registered a deficit of 6.1 percent. In that year, the government's real per-capita revenues from the oil industry were only one-quarter of those received in 1980. Total government revenue per capita had fallen 80 percent over the same period. The consolidated public deficit fell to approximately 3.7 percent of GDP in 1993, as the result of spending controls instituted by the Pérez and Velásquez governments. Payments amounting to another 3 percent of GDP were deferred to 1994, however.

Throughout the period, Venezuela's tax base had been shrinking. Total tax revenues as a percentage of GDP fell at a rate of 7.43 percent per year from 1987 to 1991.[25] It was estimated that the failure to introduce a proposed value-added tax accounted for 50 percent of the 1992 government deficit. A value-added tax and a tax on business assets were approved in the latter portion of 1993. The value-added tax, however, was soon suspended due to public opposition and difficulties in its administration. During the 1993 presidential campaign, Rafael Caldera promised that he would repeal the value-added tax (which was expected to bring in tax revenues of 3 to 4 percent of GDP) and would reverse a decision to double gasoline prices (which would have brought the government another 1 percent of GDP in revenues). As of April 1994, the new government had not been able to reduce the nation's budget deficit appreciably.

Inflation

Inflation in Venezuela had historically been low by Latin American and world standards. In the 1970s, Venezuela actually had registered lower levels of inflation than a composite of industrial nations. (See Table 2.6.) In the 1980s, however, controls on prices, interest rates, and exchange rates masked growing

TABLE 2.6
Inflation Rates, Selected Latin American Nations, 1970–1992

Compound Annual Growth Rate of Consumer Prices, Percent

Country	1970-1979	1980-1988	1989-1991	1992
Argentina	132.94	286.34	1855.15	24.90
Brazil	30.52	212.14	1555.21	1008.70
Chile	174.56	21.85	21.62	15.40
Colombia	19.31	23.20	28.46	27.00
Mexico	14.38	74.50	23.10	15.50
Venezuela	**6.61**	**16.26**	**53.09**	**31.40**
Industrialized Nations Composite	8.12	5.85	4.59	2.97
Developing Nations Composite	14.22	34.18	73.92	51.90

Source: IMF Financial Statistics.

inflationary pressures. By 1989, they could be contained no longer. Inflation reached 84 percent as price, interest, and exchange controls were lifted. Though higher than Venezuela had experienced in decades, the inflation rate was far lower than the triple- or quadruple-digit inflation rates suffered by Argentina and Brazil in the 1980s or early 1990s. Venezuelan inflation settled down somewhat in 1990 as the economy began to recover. By 1993, government deficits, however, were again fueling inflation. Inflation for 1993 reached 45.9 percent, up from 31.4 percent in 1992 and 31.0 percent in 1991. Inflation was widely viewed as the greatest economic threat to the average Venezuelan and a prime cause for popular discontent. Given unsolved deficit problems, it was expected that Venezuela's inflation rate in 1994 would greatly exceed that of 1993 in spite of price controls adopted at midyear.

Exchange Rates

During the 1970s, rising oil income and a fixed rate policy combined to keep the Venezuelan bolivar stable at around 4.3 bolivars per dollar. By 1983, however, recession and macroeconomic imbalances forced a 50 percent devaluation. A dual exchange rate system was set up in which certain "priority" purchasers could receive foreign currency at preferential rates well below a true market rate. The official exchange rate increased from 7 bolivars per dollar in 1984, to 8 bolivars per dollar in 1986, to 14.5 bolivars per dollar in 1987. At this rate, the bolivar was substantially overvalued, impeding exports and making some Venezuelans with access to foreign exchange rich.

The exchange rate was freed and unified as part of the economic reform program of 1989. Under the "dirty float" exchange rate policy adopted at the time, the exchange rate went from 39.3 bolivars per dollar in February 1989 to 79.6 bolivars per dollar by the end of 1992. By the end of 1993, the exchange rate was at 106.2 bolivars to the dollar. By early 1994, the bolivar had fallen to more than 130 per dollar. Economists believed that the bolivar was generally undervalued in 1990 and overvalued in 1991 and 1992. Despite the steady devaluation, the bolivar was substantially overvalued at the beginning of 1994. In 1993, for example, the value of the bolivar fell 33.4 percent against the U.S. dollar, while the inflation differential between the two nations was 41.7 percent. In 1992, the bolivar had lost 22.6 percent of its value against the dollar, while the inflation differential was nearly 29 percent. According to *Business Venezuela,* the bolivar was overvalued by 17 percent of parity at the beginning of 1994, up from 8 percent the year before.[26] By mid-1994, only a few months after taking office, the Caldera administration introduced exchange controls. By that time the bolivar had approached 200 per dollar. The exchange rate was set at 170 bolivars per dollar and efforts were made to suppress black-market activities.

Investment

Gross fixed capital formation, which had been on the order of 20 to 30 percent of GDP in the early 1970s and had reached an incredible 42.5 percent in 1978, fell to just over 22 percent in 1988 (on par with that of other Latin American nations; see Figure 2.3). Given the overall decline in per-capita income, per-capita investment actually fell sharply during the 1980s. Gross fixed capital formation in Venezuela fell a total of 39 percent between 1988 and 1990, reflecting the uncertainty surrounding the country's situation and reductions in government investments.

Investment levels in Venezuela recovered somewhat in 1991, but remained below 1988 levels. Some estimated that over $1 billion in private offshore capital had been returned to Venezuela to support firms that faced difficulties in the new competitive environment.[27] In 1990 and 1991, the privatization program and outsiders' renewed confidence in the Venezuelan economic system attracted substantial amounts of foreign investment. Over-

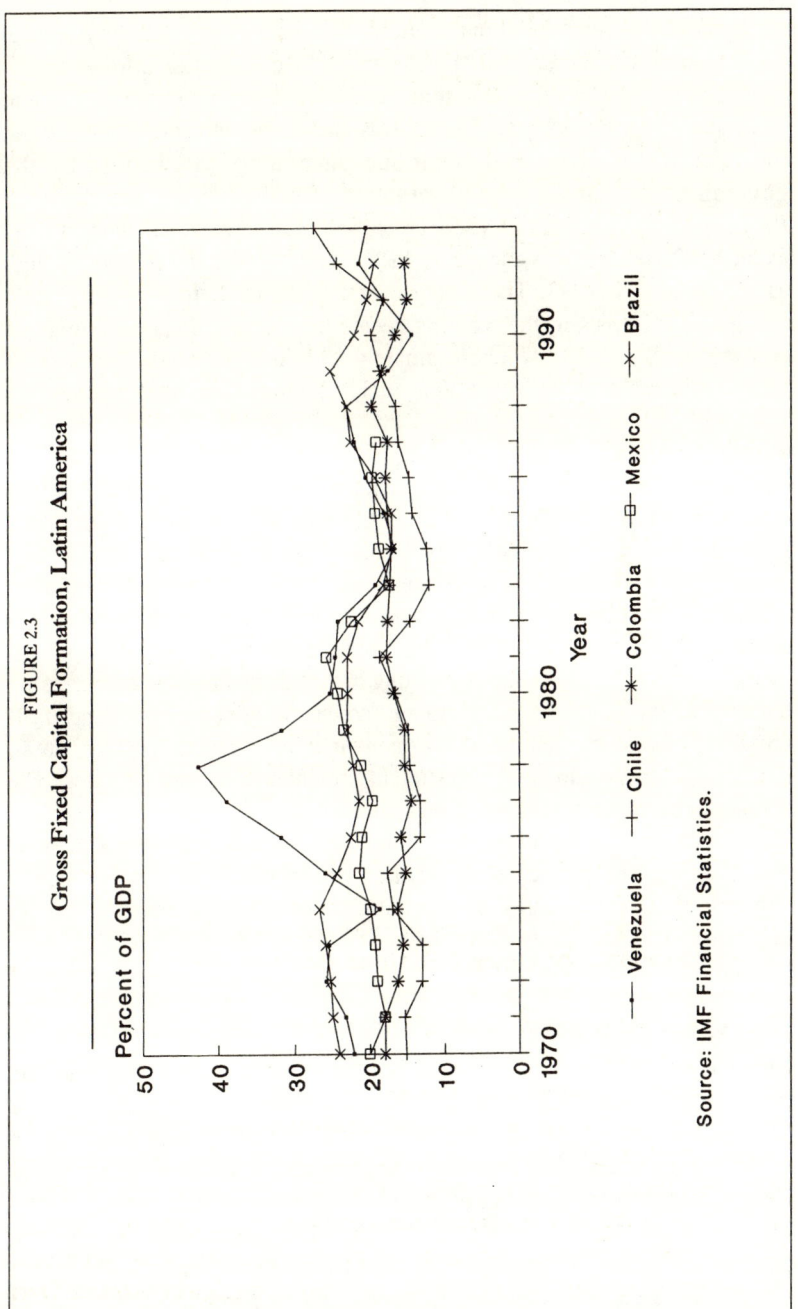

FIGURE 2.3
Gross Fixed Capital Formation, Latin America

Source: IMF Financial Statistics.

all, however, uncertainty about future government policy and the potential for further unrest caused many businesses to be cautious about investing.

The investment climate within Venezuela deteriorated substantially in 1992 and 1993. Investor confidence was shaken by two coup attempts and the resulting political and economic uncertainty, as well as by the government's shaky financial situation. In 1992, the Caracas Stock Exchange's main index fell 45.9 percent in dollar terms. Real interest rates exceeded 20 percent in Venezuela near the end of 1992 and climbed as high as 40 percent in 1993. The collapse of the Banco Latino in early 1994 precipitated a crisis in the banking sector that further dampened investor confidence. By mid-1994, approximately $5 billion, or nearly 7 percent of GDP, had been paid out by the Venezuelan Deposit Guarantee Agency.

Public Services

Reduced government income and inefficient administration led to a deterioration in public services in Venezuela. As indicated earlier, real per-capita government expenditures were cut in half from 1981 to 1984 and in half again in 1989. Government investment was the first to be cut, but soon the dramatic reductions in spending began to influence public services. In addition, many of the services had become bloated with political appointments and party functionaries, who hung onto their positions with increasing tenacity as the economy deteriorated. When the government found itself unwilling or unable to reduce employment or union perquisites in these areas, it cut back on funding for investments, maintenance, and supplies. The results were schools without books, hospitals without medical supplies, roads without repairs, and neighborhoods without water. By 1989, reduced real wages in the public sector resulted in the virtual collapse of public administration and a further deterioration of services. The situation did not improve much in the early 1990s, and in 1993 faltering public services were still a major issue in Venezuela.

Population Growth

Venezuela's population grew faster than that of other major Latin American nations from 1970 to 1988. (See Table 2.7.) The Venezuelan population grew at a rate of 3.86 percent per year from 1970 to 1980 and 2.58 percent from 1980 to 1988. This growth resulted in a very young population. By 1990, 37 percent of Venezuelans were under the age of 15 and 65 percent were under the age of 30.[28] The young population in turn created a high dependency ratio and placed a burden on people of working age who had to support the dependents. The upshot was that less income was spread over more and more people.

TABLE 2.7
Population Growth Rates,
Major Latin American Nations, 1970–1992

Compound Annual Growth Rate, Percent

Country	1970-1980	1980-1988	1988-1992
Argentina	1.75	1.39	1.22
Brazil	2.74	2.21	1.99
Chile	1.75	1.70	1.63
Colombia	2.35	1.96	3.12
Mexico	3.23	2.19	1.96
Venezuela	3.86	2.58	2.07

Source: IMF Financial Statistics.

Venezuela and the International Economy

The Venezuelan economy always has been closely linked to the international economy. Even in the days of import substitution, it was linked to the world economy through exports of oil; imports of capital goods, food, and industrial inputs; capital flows; and currency transfers. Venezuela traditionally relied on oil exports for a substantial portion of its GDP. Basic industries, such as aluminum and steel, were built up by state-owned entities that exported with the aid of export subsidies. One would expect that Venezuela's oil exports would cause an appreciation of the bolivar that would make exporting other goods difficult (a phenomenon known as the Dutch disease). The import substitution regime and policies that resulted in an overvalued currency, however, made exporting other goods even more difficult.

In most recent years, exports and imports both have exceeded 20 percent of GDP in Venezuela (see Figure 2.4), well above that in most other Latin American nations. The percentage has fluctuated with changes in oil prices and changes in GDP, which have influenced demand for imports. Exports reached more than 43 percent of GDP in 1974 as a consequence of the increase in oil prices during the oil shock of the early 1970s. Imports

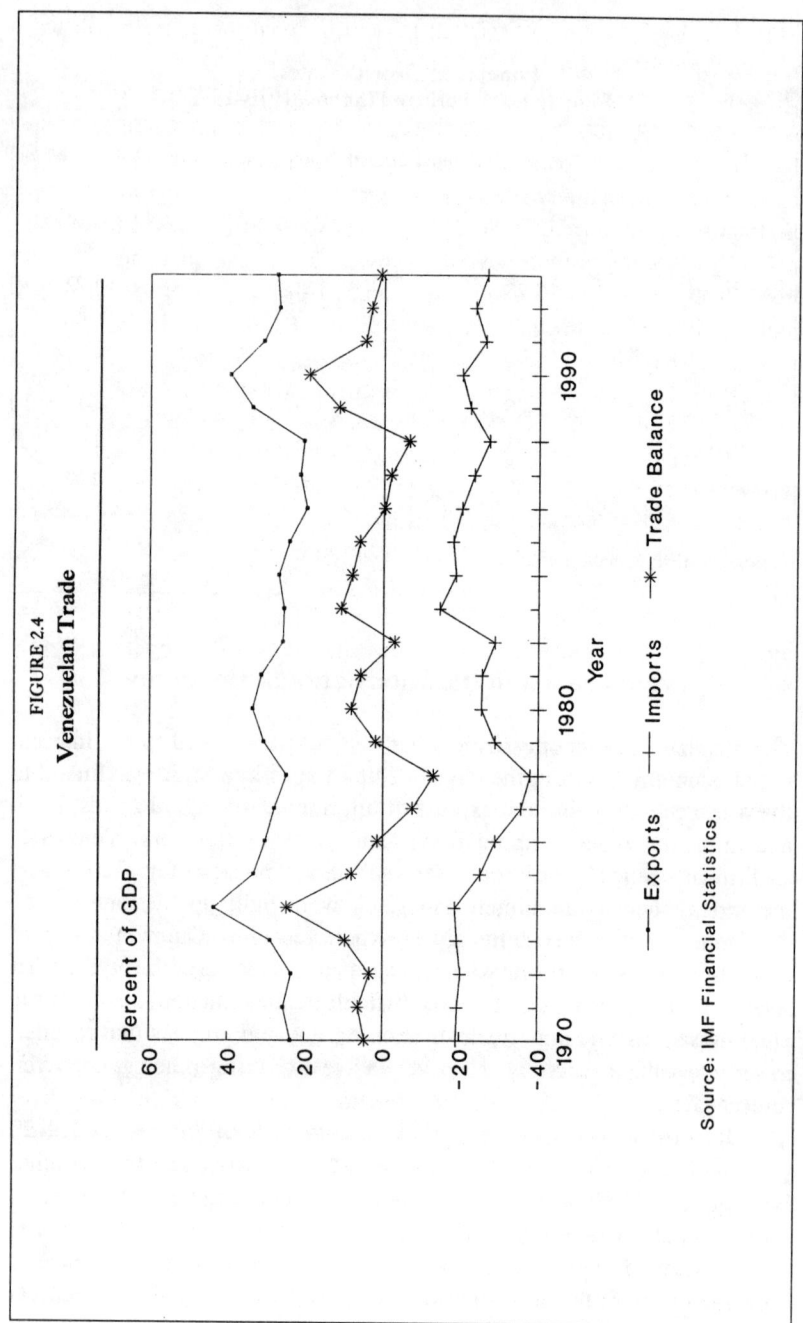

FIGURE 2.4
Venezuelan Trade

reached nearly 38 percent of GDP in 1978 as demand for capital goods and consumer goods peaked.

Though exports grew substantially as a percentage of Venezuelan GDP in 1989 and 1990, this growth was more the result of unique circumstances than the competitive success of Venezuelan firms. In 1989, those firms began to look outside the nation as domestic demand fell after the economic reform program was announced. In addition, Venezuelan firms rushed to export inputs and machinery that they had acquired before the announcement in order to obtain foreign exchange after the new government decided not to honor exchange guarantees made by the previous administration. The Iraqi invasion of Kuwait and the subsequent Gulf War resulted in a substantial increase in the price and volume of Venezuelan oil exports.

In 1991 and 1992, GDP increased, domestic demand picked up, firms adjusted inventories and production levels, and oil prices fell. Exports as a percentage of GDP fell in 1991 as did the nation's trade balance. In addition, imports increased from just over $7 billion in 1989, to more than $12 billion in 1992. In 1993, oil exports were $10.7 billion, or 75.4 percent of total exports of $14.2 billion. Total imports for the year were $10.84 billion, down 10 percent from 1992. In 1993, exports were 27.4 percent of GDP, whereas imports equaled 26.6 percent of GDP. Among major Latin American nations, only Chile had exports that were a higher percentage of GDP.

Venezuela's Export Industries

Venezuela's exports have been highly concentrated in a few product areas. (See Table 2.8.) In 1992, for example, oil and other fuels accounted for 81.3 percent of Venezuela's exports. Basic manufactures, mostly aluminum and steel, accounted for another 10.7 percent. This profile differed substantially from that of other Latin American nations. The export profiles of Brazil, Chile, and Mexico, for example, were much more diversified. Food and agricultural products accounted for more than half of Argentina's exports. Food and agriculture, crude materials (including minerals such as copper and silver as well as wood products), and basic manufactures (including processed copper and silver products as well as textiles) accounted for 86.2 percent of Chile's exports and 80.8 percent of Peru's exports. Food and agriculture (including coffee, other tropical crops, and cut flowers) and fuels accounted for 61.5 percent of Colombia's exports. Brazil and Mexico, the two largest Latin American economies, were the only nations with substantial exports of machinery and transportation equipment.

Venezuela exhibited substantial growth in nontraditional exports from 1989 to 1993. Nontraditional exports reached $3.28 billion, up 25.1

TABLE 2.8
Export Composition, Selected Latin American Nations

Percent of Total Exports

	Argentina (1992)	Brazil (1992)	Chile (1991)	Colombia (1992)	Mexico (1992)	Peru (1991)	Venezuela (1992)
Food and Agriculture[a]	54.6	25.0	25.9	33.0	11.1	21.2	2.5
Crude Materials[b]	9.0	13.9	23.1	6.5	3.9	24.1	0.8
Fuels	8.9	1.7	0.5	28.5	30.0	10.0	81.3
Chemicals	5.8	6.5	3.5	5.4	7.7	2.1	2.7
Basic Manufactures[c]	11.8	29.2	37.2	12.4	11.4	35.5	10.7
Machinery and Transport Equipment	7.5	22.4	1.2	2.3	31.7	1.0	1.5
Misc. Manufactures and Other[d]	2.4	1.4	8.6	12.0	4.5	6.1	0.7
Total	100.0	100.0	100.0	100.0	100.0	100.0	100.0

[a] Includes Food, Beverages, Animals, Animal and Vegetable Fats, and Tobacco
[b] Includes Hides, Oil Seeds, Wood and Wood Products, Textile Fibers, Minerals, and Metal Scrap
[c] Includes Rubber Products, Paper Products, Textiles, and Metal Products
[d] Includes Clothing, Photo Equipment, Electronics, Instruments, Toys, Etc.

Numbers might not add to 100 percent due to rounding.

Source: Calculated from United Nations Trade Statistics.

percent over 1992 and only slightly less than 1990. Between 1989 and 1993, there was an increase in virtually all major categories of nontraditional exports. Cisneros (1993) provides several examples of Venezuelan industries that became much more export oriented than they had been, including chemicals, transportation equipment, beverages, and tobacco. One of the goals of the 1989 economic reform program, an increase in private sector and nontraditional exports, appeared finally to be taking hold. In 1993, the private sector accounted for 68 percent of nontraditional exports, up from 35 percent in 1988.[29]

TABLE 2.9
Venezuela's Leading Trading Partners, 1990 and 1992

Percent of Total Exports and Imports

Country	Venezuelan Exports 1990	1992	Country	Venezuelan Imports 1990	1992
United States	51.6	54.6	United States	46.7	47.6
Dutch Antilles	0.3[a]	9.6	Japan	3.9	6.5
Netherlands	3.9	4.0	Germany	9.9	6.2
Colombia	2.1	3.6	Italy	4.8	4.5
Germany	3.7	2.4	Brazil	4.0	4.0
Japan	3.0	2.0	Colombia	2.0	4.0
Brazil	1.9	1.9	United Kingdom	3.0	2.2
Canada	2.6	1.1	Spain	2.2	2.2
Belgium-Luxembourg	1.4	0.7	Canada	2.9	2.0
United Kingdom	0.9	0.5	France	3.5	1.8
Ten-nation Total	71.2	80.7	Ten-nation Total	83.1	81.0

[a] This figure is suspect. Other sources give this figure as high as 7.2 percent. The same source as the rest of the table gives 6.5 percent in 1989 and 6.1 percent in 1991.

Source: United Nations (1992).

Venezuela's Trading Partners

In 1992, ten nations accounted for more than 80 percent of Venezuela's exports. (See Table 2.9.) The United States was the leading destination, accounting for more than half of Venezuela's exports. Other leading export destinations were the Dutch Antilles, the Netherlands, Colombia, Germany, Japan, and Brazil. Some of these can be explained by the export of oil. PDVSA owns several refineries and petroleum distribution outlets in the United States. Refineries in the Dutch Antilles have been major customers for Venezuelan oil, as has Germany, where PDVSA has a supply agreement

TABLE 2.10
Principal Markets for Venezuela's Non-Traditional Exports, 1988–1993

Millions of U.S. $

Market	1988	1989	1990	1991	1992	1993
ALADI[a]	45	110	220	192	249	281
Andean Pact[b]	197	286	403	372	571	862
Colombia	150	243	346	278	467	765
MCCA[c]	95	113	101	77	99	104
CARICOM[d]	50	60	64	58	72	55
Other Latin America	102	264	366	340	343	283
United States	413	753	907	580	585	746
Japan	385	454	397	324	285	220
European Community	234	546	641	461	369	499
Other	366	358	242	229	145	228
Total	1,887	2,944	3,341	2,633	2,718	3,278

[a] Non-Andean Pact ALADI (Latin American Integration Association) nations. Includes Argentina, Brazil, Chile, Mexico, Paraguay, and Uruguay.

[b] Bolivia, Colombia, Ecuador, Peru.

[c] Central American Common Market.

[d] Caribbean Common Market.

Source: OCEI data reported in Kline (1994).

with Veba Oil. The major export to Japan was aluminum from the Venalum joint venture between Mitsui and the CVG.

The United States (21.5 percent) was also the leading destination for Venezuela's nontraditional exports in 1992, followed by Colombia (17.2 percent), and Japan (10.5 percent). (See Table 2.10.) In 1993, Colombia was the leading destination for Venezuela's nontraditional exports, accounting for 23.3 percent of the total, ahead of the United States (22.8 percent) and Japan (6.7 percent). The percentage of Venezuela's nontraditional exports destined for Latin American and Caribbean nations increased from 25.9

percent in 1988 to 48.3 percent in 1993.[30] The increase in nontraditional exports and the increase in trade with Latin American nations was due to a more open trade regime than the one in place before 1989.

The dramatic increase in Venezuela's exports to Colombia (from 2.1 percent of total exports in 1990 to 3.6 percent in 1992 and from 8.0 percent of nontraditional exports in 1988 to 26.3 percent in 1993), for example, was due in large part to a free trade agreement between the nations reached in 1990. This agreement reduced tariffs to zero for most goods traded between the two nations and stimulated trade and economic activity between them. Total trade between the two nations increased from $372 million in 1989 to $924 million in 1992. This figure was expected to reach as much as $2 billion in 1993.[31] In some industries, including miscellaneous manufactures, Colombian firms have made substantial inroads into the Venezuelan market. In other industries, such as metal products, Venezuelan firms have carried the day. Complementarities between the two nations have been exploited in some industries, such as sugar, edible oils, cocoa, and vegetables. In sugar, for example, Colombia is among the world's most efficient producers, but lacks refining capacity.[32] Venezuelan firms have imported sugar for processing and reexport.

Foreign Direct Investment

Venezuela, which had discouraged foreign investment during much of the 1970s and 1980s, had received only $281 million in cumulative net foreign direct investment flows from 1979 to 1988. (See Table 2.11.) This represented only 0.67 percent of the net foreign investment flows registered by the seven largest Latin American economies. During the same period, Brazil had registered a net inflow of $16.9 billion; Mexico, $12.9 billion; Argentina, $5.3 billion; and Colombia, $3.9 billion.

From 1990 to 1992, foreign investment flows into Venezuela increased in the oil, petrochemical, pulp and paper, beverage, personal care, and glass sectors. Several multinational firms that were well established in Venezuela announced additional investments, including Procter & Gamble, Warner-Lambert, Mitsubishi, Chrysler, and Heinz. Procter & Gamble, whose operations headquarters for Latin America have been located in Caracas since 1987, chose the same city as the site of its Latin American Research and Development Center. Warner-Lambert, which maintains its Latin American administrative and management regional headquarters in Caracas, expanded its Schick razor operations. Venezuela also attracted new foreign investors, including GTE (United States), Iberia Airlines (Spain), United Distillers (United Kingdom), Makro (Netherlands), and Eastman Kodak (United

TABLE 2.11
Net Foreign Direct Investment,
Major Latin American Countries, 1979–1992

Millions of Current U.S. $

Country	1979-1988	1989	1990	1991	1992	Total 1979-1992
Argentina	5,326	1,028	2,008	2,439	4,693	15,494
Brazil	16,868	744	236	-42	1,308	19,114
Chile	2,044	184	249	576	739	3,792
Colombia	3,904	547	484	433	740	6,108
Mexico	12,911	2,648	2,548	4,742	5,366	28,215
Peru	301	59	41	-7	127	521
Venezuela	281	77	96	1,767	545	2,766
Seven-nation Total	41,635	5,287	5,662	9,908	13,518	76,010
Venezuela % of Total	0.67%	1.46%	1.70%	17.83%	4.03%	3.64%

Source: Calculated from IMF Financial Statistics.

States). In 1991, the sale of 40 percent of CANTV to a consortium led by GTE and of 60 percent of Viasa to Iberia Airlines pushed net foreign direct investment in Venezuela to nearly $1.8 billion. In that same year, U.S. firms accounted for more than 80 percent of all new foreign investment in Venezuela and an estimated 56 percent of accumulated foreign investment, followed by Spanish firms (7.4 percent of accumulated foreign investment), British firms (4.8 percent), Swiss firms (4.7 percent), and Japanese firms (3.6 percent).[33]

In 1992, a slowing in the privatization program caused foreign investment in Venezuela to fall to $545 million, well behind Mexico ($5.366 billion), Argentina ($4.693 billion), Brazil ($1.308 billion), and Colombia ($740 million). The nation experienced a sharp reduction in the amount of new foreign investment in 1993. Revenues from privatization, for example, were estimated at $350 million for 1993 versus $500 million the year before. Compared to the first 11 months of 1992, total capital flows from abroad fell 56.4 percent for the first 11 months of 1993.[34]

Venezuela's Economy and Economic Performance in Perspective

Although some aspects of the Venezuelan economy and its economic performance are unique or relatively unique, such as its oil income, many other aspects are not. Many developing nations have a similar mix of state-owned companies, relatively large local industrial groups, informal firms, and multinational companies. Most Latin American nations developed similar economic philosophies in the 1960s and 1970s, when it was hoped that state-led development would generate economic growth and social progress. Most Latin American nations fared poorly in the "lost decade" of the 1980s, when rising interest rates and falling commodity prices highlighted the inefficiencies of their economic systems. In the late 1980s, several Latin American nations began programs to open their markets, to reduce state involvement in the economy, and to reform their economies. As a result of these programs, most of these nations have seen a combination of economic growth and some public opposition.

Venezuela's economic performance declined in the 1980s as the effects of falling commodity prices, questionable economic policies, declining productivity, and the difficulties associated with state control became apparent. In some ways, Venezuela's adjustment appears to have been less severe than that experienced in other Latin American nations at the time. The decline in per-capita income in Venezuela in 1989 was not as sharp as those experienced in Mexico or Chile during their adjustment programs of the early 1980s. The mass bankruptcies and massive unemployment that many predicted would occur when markets were opened to foreign competition did not occur. After a traumatic 1989, the Venezuelan economy underwent a rapid turnaround. Productivity increased and national income grew. From 1990 through 1992, Venezuela had one of the fastest growing economies in the world.

The macroeconomic figures, however, do not tell the full story. Improvements in the nation's overall economic performance in the early 1990s were not translated into higher standards of living for a large portion of the population that had endured a substantial decline in real income. As a result, Venezuela's economic reform program met with a particularly strong backlash. Despite improvements, the perception of economic deterioration remained, even though most such deterioration had occurred before 1989. The conspicuous consumption of a privileged few reinforced the notion that the burden of adjustment had fallen on most other Venezuelans. The riots of February 1989, which reflected frustration that had been building for nearly a decade, shook the nation to its core. Two coup attempts in 1992 threatened Venezuela's democracy.

Difficulty in implementing a social safety net and the collapse of public services colored public perceptions. The failure of the Pérez government to dramatically improve social services proved devastating to its popularity.[35] Many farmers and manufacturers felt betrayed by open market policies and clamored for renewed protection. Workers were squeezed by a combination of wage stagnation and high inflation. The reform program became the lightning rod for the decade of decline that had preceded it. In fact, only a small part of the total economic reform program actually had been enacted by the end of 1992. Critical pieces, such as tax reform, on which the long-term success of the overall program rested, were not implemented. The two coup attempts in 1992 had a negative impact on the climate for investment and for business in general. The political uncertainty and paralysis of the latter portion of 1992 and all of 1993 stopped the positive momentum that had been building within the economy and contributed to the onset of recession. The stagnation of 1993 eventually gave way to an economic crisis in 1994. The public reacted favorably to the price and exchange controls instituted by the Caldera government in an attempt to stabilize the situation, although the long-term effects were not clear.

What is clear is that the Venezuelan economy has not allowed the nation's citizens to achieve a high and rising standard of living. Venezuelans, as people anywhere, naturally measure economic performance by the degree to which their lives are better or worse than before. The economic boom of the 1970s and early 1980s resulted in high expectations. For many people, the economic decline since the early 1980s resulted in a deep-seated pessimism. A 1989 poll indicated that 68 percent felt that they were worse off economically than the previous year. At the start of 1992, more than 57 percent of those polled claimed to be worse off. In addition, more than half of those polled thought that they would be worse off in six months. According to a survey taken in March 1992, a few weeks after the first of two coup attempts staged in that year, the major reasons why people sought a change in the government or were unwilling to defend it were personal economic difficulties due to inflation and the perception of government inefficiency and administrative corruption.[36]

Discontent and economic hardship also contributed to social unrest. By 1993, street crime had reached unprecedented levels, placing many Venezuelans at risk and causing others to retreat behind iron gates and security guards. Some observers warned of a widening social divide in which different classes of Venezuelan society have almost no interaction and in which the threat of the dissolution of civil society looms.[37] These realities have brought additional urgency to the search for economic progress.

This chapter has attempted to describe the overall performance of the Venezuelan economy. Such a description, however, does not provide nearly enough insight to improve performance. Instead, one must search for ways to improve the underlying features that influence economic performance. Ultimately, a nation's economic performance, both overall and in the international economy, depends on its resources and the productivity with which those resources are employed. A framework is needed that allows any firm or nation to assess these resources and the forces that influence productivity and competitiveness at the firm, industry, and national levels. In addition, a framework is needed to help explain the sources of advantage and disadvantage found in individual industries as well as the features that promote or hinder growth and development across the national economy. This framework can help organize positive efforts aimed at bringing about economic progress. Such a framework is the subject of the next chapter.

3

The Challenge of Competitiveness in the Modern World Economy

Competitiveness has become a vital issue for firms and governments throughout the world. While some nations, such as Japan and Asia's newly industrialized countries (NICs), have used the opportunities provided by international markets to develop and grow, other nations, including the United States and several in Europe, have seen wages and profits eroded under pressure from international competition. This chapter argues that there is no single magic source of competitiveness. At the national level, no single policy will support competitiveness. At the firm level, no single decision will create it. Competitiveness must be viewed as the result of interactions within a complex system. Nations and their firms will achieve greater success when competitiveness becomes the guiding principle of economic policy and firm strategy.

What Is Competitiveness?

Competitiveness can be defined for the company, for the industry, and for the nation. For the company, competitiveness is the ability to provide products and services as or more effectively and efficiently than competitors. In the traded sector, this means sustained success in international markets without protection or subsidies. Although transportation costs might allow firms from a nation to compete successfully in their home market or in adjacent markets, the concept of competitiveness usually refers to advantage obtained through superior productivity. Measures of competitiveness in the traded sector include firm profitability, the firm's export quotient (exports divided by output), and regional or global market share. In this sector, performance in the international marketplace provides a direct measure of the firm's competitiveness. In the nontraded sector, competitiveness is the ability to match or beat the world's best firms in cost and quality of goods or services. Measuring competitiveness in the nontraded sector is often difficult, since there is no direct market performance test. Measures of competitiveness in this part of the economy include firm profitability and measures of cost and quality. In industries characterized by foreign direct investment, the firm's percentage of foreign sales (foreign sales divided by total sales) and its share of regional or global markets provide measures of its competitiveness.

At the industry level, competitiveness is the ability of the nation's firms to achieve sustained success against (or compared to) foreign competitors, again without protection or subsidies. Measures of competitiveness at the industry level include overall profitability of the nation's firms in the industry, the nation's trade balance in the industry, the balance of outbound and inbound foreign direct investment, and direct measures of cost and quality at the industry level. Industry level competitiveness is often a better indicator of the economic health of the nation than competitiveness at the firm level. The success of a single firm from the nation might be due to company-specific factors that are difficult or impossible to reproduce. The success of several firms from the nation in an industry, on the other hand, is often evidence of nation-specific factors that might be extended and improved. To assess the competitiveness of an industry in which there is only one important firm, one must assess whether the success is due to monopoly rents, government support, or true efficiency. It is also important to note that a single firm's competitiveness does not necessarily imply an industry's competitiveness.[1]

For the nation, competitiveness means the ability of the nation's citizens to achieve a high and rising standard of living. In most nations, the standard of living is determined by the productivity with which the nation's resources are deployed, the output of the economy per unit of labor and/or capital employed. (See Figure 3.1.) A high and rising standard of living for all the nation's citizens can be sustained only by continual improvements in productivity, either through achieving higher productivity in existing businesses or through successful entry into higher-productivity businesses. Competitiveness at the national level is measured by the level and growth of the nation's standard of living and of aggregate productivity, and the ability of the nation's firms to increase their penetration of world markets through exports or foreign direct investment.[2] Although it is tempting to equate a nation's competitiveness in certain industries or sets of industries with competitiveness at the national level,

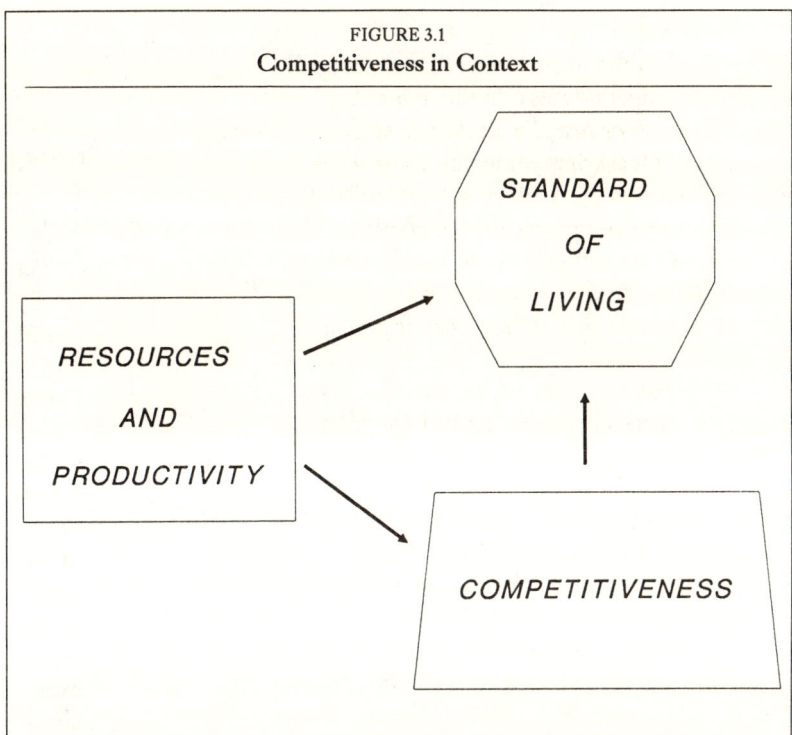

FIGURE 3.1
Competitiveness in Context

or with a positive balance of trade, this temptation should be avoided.[3] Comparative advantage dictates that any nation will be competitive in some industries and uncompetitive in others. A positive balance of trade has as much to do with the balance of domestic savings and investment as it does with the intrinsic capabilities of the nation's firms.

Why Is Competitiveness Important?

A nation's standard of living is increasingly dependent on the competitiveness of its firms. Competitiveness is vital if the nation's firms are to take advantage of the opportunities presented by the international economy. World trade and foreign investment have grown faster in the last several decades than world output. Competitiveness in industries subject to international trade and foreign direct investment can therefore provide substantial leverage for economic growth, especially in small nations, where competitiveness can allow firms to overcome the limitations of their small home markets in order to achieve their maximum potential. Competitiveness is also vital if a nation's firms are to guard against the threats posed by the international economy. International competition has become fiercer than ever before. Lower costs for transportation and communication, reduced trade barriers, and the spread of technology have combined to sharpen international competition. This competition has put unprecedented pressure on all a nation's economic actors, including management, labor, and government. In an environment in which the nation's firms must improve continually in order to meet the threat from an ever wider array of competitors, the failure of management, labor, or government to meet the challenge can spell disaster.

Competitiveness in the nontraded sector is also vital to the nation's economic health. The nontraded sector is a large portion of each economy. At a time when economic prosperity remains only a dream for most of the world's population, inefficiencies in the nontraded sector should be reduced to the greatest extent possible. In addition, the competitiveness of the nontraded sector has a substantial impact on the competitiveness of the traded sector, which relies on it for a wide range of goods and services. An inefficient, bloated nontraded sector can drag down the nation's productivity directly and indirectly through its impact on other nontraded and traded industries.

There is a growing realization that nations cannot avoid the rigors of international competition. No nation is totally self-sufficient. Nations are linked to the international economy through trade in goods and services, through international capital flows, and through commodity prices. The experience of developing nations in the 1980s has indicated that attempts to isolate an economy can have lasting detrimental effects. In the modern world, nations can try to run from the world economy, but they cannot hide. This is particularly true for small nations, where the costs generated by economic isolation in terms of rent seeking and losses in efficiency can be substantial, and for developing nations, where any loss of efficiency often means higher levels of poverty. The export-led growth of Japan and the Asian NICs and the relative stagnation of the import substitution economies of Latin America also have highlighted the link between international competitiveness and economic development.[4]

What Competitiveness Is *Not*

Just as it is important to understand what competitiveness is, it is important to understand what competitiveness is not. Consistently subsidized exports are not evidence that a firm or an industry is "competitive." Although infant industry arguments might support some level of subsidies in an industry's early stages, exports that depend on ongoing subsidies are more evidence of the nation's ability and willingness to subsidize than evidence of firm or industry competitiveness. Subsidized exports of agricultural goods from developed nations, for example, do not provide evidence of competitiveness. Unless the firm or industry is self-sustaining and can compete successfully on its own without subsidies, it is not truly competitive.

Competitiveness for the nation does not mean export success in every industry, or even most industries. Clearly, no nation can sustain a trade surplus in every sector of the economy. Indeed, the very specialization required to achieve international success in some industries implies that other industries will be less successful in terms of their export performance. Competitiveness in some industries allows a nation to improve productivity by allowing it to specialize in the industries and segments in which its firms are relatively more productive than firms in other nations and to import in industries where they are relatively less productive. All nations, even the most advanced and economically successful ones, have substantial portions of the economy in which they are not competitive. The Japanese economy, for example, is not competitive in aerospace, chemicals, most health care–related products, most services, and many other industries. The German economy is not competitive in most electronics, textile and apparel, and most international service industries. The United States is not competitive in many electronics, textile and apparel, and machinery industries.

Competitiveness for the nation does not mean preserving its existing industrial base. Nations progress when their firms improve productivity in industries or segments in which they already compete and when they gradually enter industries or segments that involve higher productivity. In this process, some industries are inevitably left behind. Exit from some industries is the natural consequence of the process of economic development. Governments that fight to save every industry can slow down economic advance by trapping resources that would be best deployed elsewhere. Instead of fighting to hold onto unproductive industries, nations and their firms should seek to find more productive outlets for their resources.

A nation is not "competitive" if it has low labor costs, a "favorable" exchange rate, or borrows its standard of living. Low wages can help a nation's firm to enter international markets. Ultimately, however, the nation's goal should be to achieve productivity that supports high wages. In Japan, Singapore, Taiwan, and Korea, for example, increased productivity has resulted in substantial increases in wages over the last two decades. Competitiveness based exclusively on low wages ultimately will be self-limiting unless productivity is increased through the development of higher skill levels, the incorporation of more advanced technology, or the institution of better management techniques. Similarly, the nation's goal should be productivity that supports a strong currency. Devaluations in order to gain export competitiveness provide advantages that are short-lived at best. Truly competitive nations are those whose firms compete successfully in international markets with strong national currencies. Finally, competitiveness refers to performance that is earned rather than borrowed. Performance that is fueled by deficit spending and borrowing, rather than by increases in productivity, cannot be sustained indefinitely. Debts eventually have to be repaid. Unless the debt is related to investments that result in higher returns than the interest rate, the debt will lower rather than raise the nation's standard of living.

The point is not that all nations have to be "competitive" by any single definition. Most nations are not "competitive" by any definition. This does not prevent them from competing in world markets, though it might limit their success in doing so. Rather, the point is that knowledge of what makes a firm, industry, or nation competitive provides a direction for improving firms and upgrading national economies. Every nation faces the challenge of improving productivity across industries. Some nations simply have farther to go than others.

The Sources of International Competitiveness[5]

Once we have established what competitiveness is and is not, it is vital to understand the sources of competitiveness. In his recent book *The Competitive Advantage of Nations,* Michael Porter (1990) set forth a framework for assessing the influence of the nation on the international competitiveness of its firms. In this framework, based on work by collaborators in ten nations, the determinants of competitiveness in a given industry are the *factor conditions*; *demand conditions*; *related and supporting industries*; and *firm strategy, structure, and rivalry* that are found in the nation. Nations succeed in industries in which these determinants provide the incentives, pressures, and capabilities to innovate and upgrade firm advantages.[6] The framework developed by Porter and his collaborators, often called "the diamond," provides a systematic alternative to explanations for competitiveness that focus on a single feature of an economy, such as natural resources, management practices, or government policy.

In this framework, *factor conditions* are construed broadly to encompass skill levels, technological capacity, and physical and business infrastructure in addition to more traditional factors, such as land, labor, natural resources, and capital. Factor conditions refer to the availability, creation, and selective disadvantages in these areas. The availability of resource endowments or a pool of low-skilled labor will help nations compete in resource-based and labor-intensive industries, respectively. Porter and his collaborators conclude that in more and more industries, however, competitive advantage comes from factors (such as knowledge and expertise) that are created rather than inherited. To Porter and his group, the most important factors in many industries are those that require significant public and private investment to create and those that are used in one or a few industries. Such factors foster advantage because they tend to be difficult to duplicate or source from a distance. Finally, they feel that in some cases, disadvantages in basic factors can be a stimulus to innovation that ultimately creates advantage. To foster innovation and advantage, such disadvantages must be selective, rather than systemic.

Demand conditions concern the size, sophistication, and segment structure of local demand. Porter and his collaborators conclude that the nature of local demand has a disproportionate effect on perceptions and responses to buyer needs. Their findings on the size of local demand are mixed. A large local demand can allow firms to achieve economies of scale in the local marketplace, an advantage in industries subject to long production runs or standardized products. A small local demand can force firms to make early moves into international markets, an advantage in industries that require local customization and a global presence. American firms have benefitted from a large domestic market in aerospace and fast foods, whereas Swiss firms have benefitted from a small domestic market in chemical and food products: in these sectors, Swiss firms were forced to enter international markets at a relatively early stage in their development. Sophisticated home demand, regardless of its size, places unique pressures on local firms to develop new products and processes, which often are sold subsequently on other markets. Swiss textile firms, for example, represent only 2 percent of the business of Swiss textile machinery firms, but their need for advanced equipment helps keep the Swiss machinery firms on the cutting edge. The structure of local demand often causes firms to develop expertise in serving segments which represent a disproportionate percentage of local demand. This expertise may then be used to serve the same segments in other nations. The high-performance segment of the German automobile industry provides one such example.

The *related and supporting industries* category refers to the presence of world-class suppliers and firms in industries related by common technologies, distribution channels, or target markets. World-class suppliers often provide local firms with superior machinery or inputs earlier than their foreign customers. Local firms that are world leaders in related industries are often the source of technology and expertise that can be spread across industries. A good example would be the robotics industry: here Japanese firms are the world leaders, not only in robotics, but in most of the major component technologies. Related and supporting industries play an important role in the formation of industry clusters (defined in the next section), which in turn play an important role in the process of economic development.

Firm strategy and structure includes the distinct national patterns that can be observed in company and individual goals, typical firm strategies, and typical organizational structures. Nations succeed in those industries in which the strategies and structures that work well in the industry work well in the nation. There are relatively few industries in which both Swedish and Italian firms are internationally successful. The industries in which Swedish firms succeed often are characterized by the need to manage far-flung multinationals and complex organizations. The industries in which Italian firms are internationally successful tend to be characterized by small firms, relationship sales, and family ownership. The strategies and structures that work well in the industries in which Swedish firms tend to succeed simply do not work as well in industries in which Italian firms tend to succeed and vice versa.

In his book, Porter groups *domestic rivalry* with firm strategy and structure even though one might wish to separate determinants that are inside the firm (firm strategy and structure) from those that are outside the firm (rivals). Rivalry among local firms provides an important stimulus to innovation and upgrading of firm capabilities. Tough local rivalry sharpens the skills that companies can then use in international markets. Competition from foreign companies also can provide stimulus to innovate and improve but does not create an advantage for the nation's firms. Domestic rivalry was found to be an important contributor to competitive success even for small nations, such as Sweden, Switzerland, and Denmark.

According to Porter and his collaborators, *government* policies and *chance* events are best understood by addressing their impact on local factors; the size, sophistication, and segment structure of local demand; the development of related and supporting industries; and the strategies and structures of local firms as well as the level of rivalry among them. Government influences the determinants through its impact on factor costs and availability, its role as a purchaser, its impact on the goals of firms and individuals, and its impact on the nature of competition within industries. Porter and his collaborators found that government's role in creating competitiveness is inherently partial. Governments rarely can create a truly competitive industry without some other favorable conditions. Chance events may unfreeze existing industry structures and shift advantage to new competitors by changing the relative importance of the various determinants. Chance events include wars, natural disasters, supply shocks, and events beyond the direct control of nations or firms in the industry.

Industry and Geographic Clusters[7]

The determinants identified by Porter and his collaborators are systemic in nature. They can reinforce each other in a positive or negative manner. Advanced factors in the form of technological capabilities can stimulate the development of industries that employ related technology. Local rivalry can foster more sophisticated demand (as firms compete through creating higher quality or more variety in their goods) and the development of specialized skills (as firms compete to develop new products and processes). The interdependence of the determinants is apparent in the formation of industry clusters. Nations tend to succeed and fail in clusters of industries that are related through vertical (buyer or supplier) and horizontal (such as common technology, channels, and customer base) linkages. As economies grow and develop, competitive advantage often spills over from one industry to others. An industry emerges from the local environment, often due to some specific local demand, factor, or related industry. Soon suppliers develop to serve it. Developed expertise spreads to other industries that have similar requirements. The cluster grows wider and deeper as new industries emerge from the local milieu.

Geographic concentration reinforces the development of clusters through close interaction among firms. Rivalry among geographically concentrated firms takes on personal as well as economic attributes, stimulating additional investments in products and processes. Spinoffs take advantage of new opportunities, fill gaps in the industry's product lines, and provide new sources of supply. Local demand becomes increasingly sophisticated as it distinguishes among the products and services supplied by local firms. Geographic concentration also allows public and private entities to make focused investments in industry-specific education, training, and infrastructure that would be difficult to make if the industry were more dispersed.

Miss Venezuela, An Illustration[8]

The "Miss Venezuela" phenomenon illustrates how the determinants can be used to understand success in international competition. Venezuela leads the world in international beauty pageant winners. In the past 14 years, it has produced more Miss Universes and Miss Worlds, counted together, than any other nation. Venezuelans have won Miss Universe three times and Miss World four times, for a total of seven crowns in these two contests. The United States is the first runner-up, with a total of five crowns, and Puerto Rico the second runner-up, with a total of four crowns. With only 0.4 percent of the total world population, Venezuela has captured more than 20 percent of all international pageant crowns (including Miss Universe, Miss World, Miss Suramérica, Miss America Latina, Miss Costa Internacional, Miss Globo, and many others). In this sector, each of the four determinants (factor conditions; demand conditions; related and supporting industries; and firm strategy, structure, and rivalry), alone and in combination, works to confer competitive advantage.

Importance of Advanced Factors

Basic factors are important to success in beauty pageants, but in reality they play less of a role than is often thought. Industry experts like to point out the advantages of Venezuela's warm climate, which promotes an active, beach-going, and beauty-conscious population. However, created factors are more important to Venezuela's international success. Year after year, Venezuela's pageant business keeps one step ahead of international beauty, fashion, and marketing trends, combining expertise with creative talent. This is the factor that confers the most powerful advantage in international competition.

Education and training are an important source of advantage in international pageants. Some Venezuelan girls start competing at a very young age in "little league" pageants. Caracas is home to a nucleus of coaches, personal trainers, beauty technicians, and designers who combine their talents to create Venezuela's image on international walkways. Each year, these professionals teach an aspiring class of Miss Venezuela contestants the skills they will need to compete for national and international crowns, and several have been hired as consultants to pageant organizations in other nations. Each contestant undergoes a ten-month course in beauty, presentation, etiquette, and physical fitness. Expert plastic surgeons and dentists also engage in more direct forms of "factor creation."

Sophisticated Demand

Venezuela has a national passion for beauty pageants, as reflected by the television ratings of "Miss Venezuela" and "Chica 2001." Even regional and junior pageants attract a viewing public. Many Venezuelans have opinions about which contestant should win the national title and also care about the fate of their contestants on the international stage. When Miss Venezuela

1992 placed first runner-up to Miss Puerto Rico for the Miss Universe title, the nation felt the loss. At the same time, the "political correctness" of beauty pageants is not an issue in Venezuela. There is no social stigma associated with being a "Miss." Each new Miss becomes an instant celebrity, wins access to high society, and is offered rich professional opportunities. Some have used their titles as an entrée into commerce and politics.

The per-capita consumption of personal care products in Venezuela is among the highest in Latin America. (See Chapter 7.) Venezuelan women are sophisticated consumers of cosmetics and fashion. This translates into a discerning and sophisticated audience for the national beauty pageants.

A Rich Mix of Related and Supporting Industries

Related and supporting industries also are a source of advantage for Venezuela in beauty contests. The television industry is the most closely related. Television ratings in Venezuela are among the highest in the world. Ninety-seven percent of Caracas households have a television set. (See Chapter 4.) This fact has generated strong domestic demand for television advertising, which in turn generates revenues for the national pageant business.

Local fashion designers contribute to the high quality of Venezuelan pageants. The bathing suits, footwear, and many of the evening gowns modeled by the Miss Venezuela contestants are designed by national talent. Venezuela also boasts world-class talent in makeup, hair styling, and modeling. The best Venezuelan television production expertise is comparable to that in the United States. In addition, a related cluster of internationally competitive entertainment sectors, including music recording, and other entertainment industries, contribute to the success of the Miss Venezuela productions. (See Chapter 7.) Contestant winners and runners-up supply a constant flow of new talent into the television, advertising, and modeling industries.

Integrated Firm Strategies and Structures

The structures and strategies of the Venezuelan firms involved in the beauty pageants confer competitive advantage. Each of the two leading national beauty pageants, Miss Venezuela and Chica 2001, is owned and produced by a national TV broadcaster. The Miss Venezuela operation is part of Venevisión, the self-styled "Channel of Beauty," which is a member of the Organización Diego Cisneros (ODC Group). Its younger rival, Chica 2001, is affiliated with Radio Caracas Televisión, which is part of the Phelps Group. This corporate ownership provides deeper funding and greater continuity in management than is the case in beauty pageants in most other countries of the world.

The stations have powerful incentives to produce a successful pageant. The winner of Miss Venezuela, aired by Venevisión, goes on to compete for Miss Universe, while the first runner-up goes on to compete for Miss World. Venevisión holds exclusive broadcasting rights for each of the two international contests. These two broadcasts, in turn, will fare better in the national ratings if the Venezuelan contestants have won the loyalty of home viewers and are likely contenders for an international crown.

Intense Rivalry

Rivalry takes place at many levels in the beauty pageant "industry." Given the rewards of winning, competition is good-natured but fierce among the contestants themselves. At the industry level, the pageants are a battleground in the ratings war between television broadcasters. Venezuela is one of the few nations that has a long history of intense rivalry among multiple private television broadcasters. (See Chapter 4.) This competition stimulates broadcasters to upgrade and to enhance their pageant productions each year.

An Absence of Government Involvement, Favored by Chance

The beauty pageant "industry" was allowed to grow without state intervention and has not been subject to government regulation. Chance has had a larger impact on international success than government. Two ODC Group executives who played a major role in transforming the Miss Venezuela pageant into a world-class competition, Ignacio Font and Osmel Sousa, emigrated to Venezuela from Cuba. Without the contribution of these two individuals, Venezuela might never have captured the leading share of international pageant titles.

The Venezuelan System

The Venezuelan beauty pageant system shows that even small countries can succeed in international competition as long as the system of determinants provides the incentives, pressures, and capabilities to innovate and to upgrade advantage. Beauty pageants are a national pastime and a business that attracts many of Venezuela's talented individuals. Training techniques developed over decades hone the talents of the competitors. Sophisticated demand from a discerning public pushes the companies involved in the business. Advanced related and supporting industries assist in developing competitive advantages. Firm strategies and structures make the beauty pageants integral parts of larger company strategies. Rivalry stimulates the contestants and companies to ever greater efforts to succeed. The specialized,

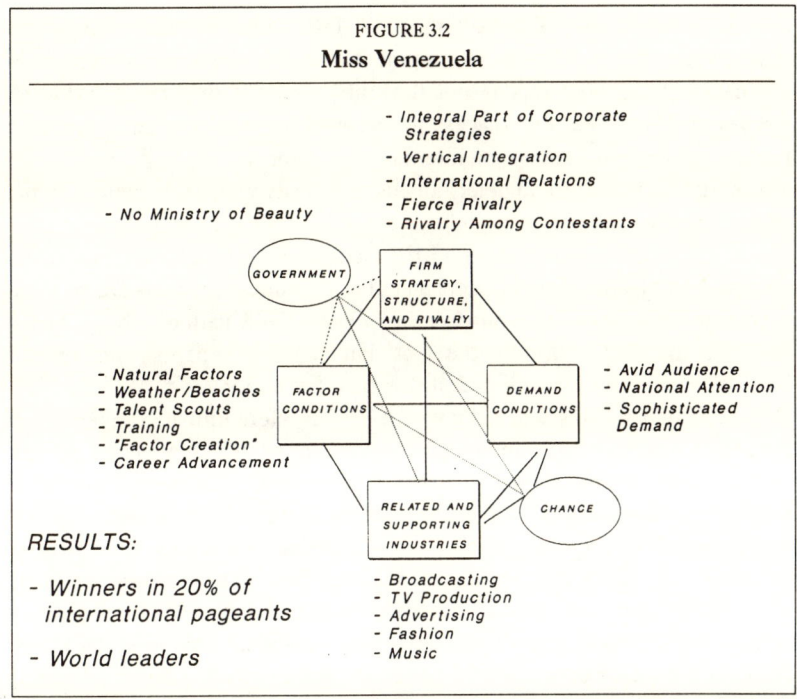

FIGURE 3.2
Miss Venezuela

interdependent system that has developed around beauty pageants has provided the advantages that propel Miss Venezuela into the international winner's circle year after year. (See Figure 3.2.)

Extensions to the Basic Framework

The Basic Framework and Export Success

A number of extensions to the basic framework found in Porter's book are required to relate it directly to success in international competition. The framework found in Porter's book identifies potential sources of advantage and disadvantage that a nation's firms might draw from the national environment. A nation need not, however, have advantages in all determinants for its firms to achieve export success. In order to achieve such success in a given industry, the nation needs a "critical mass" of favorable conditions in the determinants. What constitutes a "critical mass" of favorable conditions will differ by industry. The examples found in Porter's book—the Japanese robotics industry, the Italian ceramic tile industry, the German printing press industry, and the U.S. medical equipment industry—have advantages in all the determinants, but this is not the only way a nation can provide an environment that leads to success in international competition. A nation's firms can achieve success in international competition if the nation has advantages in one or more determinants and parity with other nations in the others. British chemical and pharmaceutical firms have succeeded in international competition even though British demand conditions and related and supporting industries for chemical and pharmaceutical products are no more favorable than those in a number of industrialized nations. Swiss banks continue to prosper despite the fact that banking expertise and related industries are as well developed in several other nations.

A nation's firms will achieve success in international competition if the nation has advantages in one or more determinants that are large enough to overcome disadvantages in other determinants. Japanese firms have become world leaders in Latin-letter typewriters due to their expertise in first mechanical and then electronics manufacturing, spillovers from related industries, and fierce competition among local firms. These advantages have allowed the Japanese firms to succeed despite disadvantages in local demand conditions. (Relatively few Latin letter typewriters are used in Japan.) New Zealand is a major exporter of dairy goods due to its unique natural conditions for growing grass and advanced farming techniques. These advantages have overcome the disadvantages of domestic demand that is relatively small and unsophisticated compared to that in other OECD nations and a monopoly export structure that has limited incentives to develop new products and markets.

The relative importance of a single determinant, or any subset thereof, will differ from industry to industry. In particular, the relative importance of the different determinants will be related to the key competitive variables in the industry. Marketing expertise is critical in consumer packaged goods, many services, and fashion-related industries. Competitiveness in these industries often depends on the presence of sophisticated demand in the home market. Low-cost labor is vital in labor-intensive commodity industries, such as the low-priced segments of the apparel and footwear industries. Competitiveness in these industries depends on the presence of low-cost labor and a certain level of infrastructure development. Product development skills are vital in industries that rely on technology development, such as aerospace, advanced electronics, and software. Competitiveness in these industries depends on highly educated and trained people, cutting-edge demand, the presence of related technologies, and research-based firm strategies. In general, the higher the technology, or the earlier in the product life cycle, the more important it is to have favorable conditions in all the determinants. In industries that are later in their product cycle, demand is often equally as sophisticated in a number of nations and technology is often widely available. Under these conditions, advantages in a subset of the determinants can result in success in international competition.[9] In other industries, such as mineral or natural resource industries, a single determinant, factor conditions, is decisive. Saudi Arabia, for example, exports oil because it has oil, not because it has favorable demand conditions; related and supporting industries; or firm strategy, structure, and rivalry.

The relative importance of the different determinants in an industry depends on the drivers of competitive success in that industry. It is a mistake to assume that the mix of determinants required for international success is the same across industries. The upshot is that the nation or nations with a critical mass of favorable conditions in the determinants that are most important for a particular industry will have an advantage versus other nations. Similarly, it is a mistake to conclude that having advantages in all the determinants is the most preferable and sustainable situation. The sustainability of national advantage in a given industry depends on the nature of competition in that industry, how these advantages map to the determinants, and how both change over time. An advantage in a single determinant (a unique natural resource, for example) might prove more sustainable than temporary advantages in several determinants.

Foreign Demand, Economic Integration, and Competitive Advantage

Some claim that industry is globalizing, the world is a single marketplace, and local demand conditions are irrelevant to the success of a nation's firms in international competition. The ten-nation study reported by Porter concluded that this was not the case. Companies still seem to respond more quickly and more completely to local demand than to demand in other nations. The signals sent by local demand appear to reach firms more quickly and clearly than signals sent by foreign markets. This is particularly true in industries that are fashion related or are early in their product life cycle. Serving large or sophisticated foreign demand might provide a nation's firms with rough parity in demand conditions with firms from other nations, but it will not give the first nation's firms an advantage. As long as there are differences in the character of demand among nations, foreign demand will be an imperfect substitute for advanced domestic demand. Proximity in distance, language, and culture allows a firm to obtain quantitatively and qualitatively superior information. While learning to serve foreign demand might be necessary to overcome disadvantages in domestic demand conditions, it will not give a nation's firms an advantage.

The trend toward regional trade pacts and free trade areas in the 1980s and 1990s has increased the size of the market that firms from a region can easily address. For goods in which demand is homogeneous across the nations in the free trade area, economic integration can be viewed as an effective extension of the domestic market. In such industries, competing within the free trade area can be an end in and of itself or might provide a stepping-stone to penetration of wider markets. Reduction in trade barriers, however, does not make the German consumer as sophisticated a consumer of cheeses as the French consumer. It does not make the French purchaser of printing presses as sophisticated as the German purchaser. It does not give the Canadian consumer or firm the same tastes and sophistication as the Mexican consumer or firm. Thus, in industries in which the particulars of local demand provide important signals to firms, economic integration is less effective in extending the local market. It is important not to confuse *access* to markets with *similarities* in tastes or *sophistication* of demand. Free trade agreements might accelerate the homogenization of demand conditions across nations, but they do not do so completely, or overnight.[10]

Domestic Rivalry and Competitive Advantage

One of the most striking findings of Porter and his collaborators was the importance of local rivalry in helping to create national advantage in industry. Competition has long been identified as a key stimulus to innovation and improvement on the part of firms. The study found that active domestic rivalry was a key stimulus to improvement and innovation, even in small nations such as Switzerland and Sweden. Switzerland is the home of two of the world's leading dye companies, three of the world's leading pharmaceutical companies, three of the world's leading banks (plus many medium-size banks), several of the world's leading freight forwarders, and numerous machine tool, textile machinery, trading, chocolate, and medical products firms. Sweden has many leading companies in paper and a number in specialty steel and packaging machinery. It is also the home of two leading truck and two leading rock drill companies. Small industrialized nations tend to succeed in industries in which domestic competitors gain scale through exporting rather than by dominating the domestic market. Local competition tends to force them into international markets at an early stage of their development.

Many economists and businesspeople believe that scale economies (usually of unspecified nature or magnitude) make domestic competition wasteful. This view tends to focus on the static advantages of scale rather than on the dynamic advantages of rivalry, and reflects a domestic market orientation rather than a global outlook. It fails to take into account the fact that in modern competition, the size of the world market might be a better benchmark than the size of the local market. When a nation's firms are global in outlook, they are limited not by the size of the domestic market but by how much of the regional or global market they can penetrate before the appropriate resources are exhausted. Nations, even small ones, tend to be better off with multiple competitors that compete with each other locally and globally, obtaining scale economies through exports rather than through limits on local rivalry. Though there are cases in which scale economies are so large that only a few companies can operate efficiently worldwide (large commercial airframes is one example), such cases are less common than many would have us believe.

Porter does not make a clear distinction between the number of competitors and the ferocity of competition in an industry. The number of competitors in an industry does not directly determine the level of rivalry in a nation (though clearly there has to be more than one competitor, and the presence of many competitors often tends to increase rivalry).[11] *The important determinant is not the number of rivals, but the nature and ferocity of competition among the firms in the industry.* Fierce domestic rivalry can be found in industries with as few as two competitors in a nation. In contrast, in some industries hundreds of cartelized local "competitors" do not compete with each other at all. Competition that forces firms to become more efficient and to develop new products and incorporate more advanced technology provides overall benefits to the economy. Competition that seeks to monopolize inputs or distribution channels does not. Competition to improve efficiency and reduce costs benefits the economy. Competition that results in mindless price wars without increased efficiency or lower costs does not.

Recent efforts at international economic integration (including the North American Free Trade Agreement [NAFTA] and the Europe 1992 Program) have attempted to foster efficiency gains by increasing competition through the reduction of trade barriers. Unilateral openings in New Zealand, Venezuela, and elsewhere have been predicated on the same reasoning, that competition from foreign firms will improve the efficiency of domestic firms. Several nations have found it politically easier to open to foreign competition than to stimulate domestic competition, even though it would seem more effective to stimulate domestic competition first (so that firms learn how to compete) and then open up to foreign competition. In many nations, firms wield enough political power to resist the enactment or enforcement of tough domestic pro-competition laws. In terms of stimulating firms to become more efficient foreign competition is clearly better than no competition at all.

The question that emerges is whether domestic competition, competition among local national firms, provides any additional benefits beyond those provided by competition from foreign firms. Foreign competition is not a perfect substitute for domestic competition. First of all, foreign competition cannot, by definition, provide an advantage to a nation's producers. Allowing competition from foreign firms might give the nation's firms parity in terms of rivalry, but not an advantage. Second, rivalry from foreign firms tends not to be as immediate or as personal as rivalry from domestic firms. Third, the asymmetry in sources of advantage across nations means that it is often possible to compete against foreign companies through the use of static advantages rather than dynamic advantages that result in constant improvement and innovation. Consider a Korean firm competing against Japanese and American firms on the basis of low labor costs. In the absence of local competition, the Korean firm does not have to improve; all it has to do is use its labor cost advantage. When we add another Korean competitor, however, the equation changes. The original firm has no labor cost advantage over its local rival. Instead, it must compete in a more sophisticated fashion and develop higher-order sources of advantage. Eventually, the Korean companies do not rely just on low-cost labor. Instead, they compete on a much wider basis, focusing on constant improvement to compete with each other as well as with foreign firms.

Foreign Direct Investment and Competitive Advantage[12]

International competition and competitiveness manifests itself not only through trade but also through foreign direct investment. In the 1980s and 1990s, foreign direct investment actually has been growing faster than world trade. Foreign investments can be divided into two basic categories, those designed to serve local markets and those designed to serve export markets. Investments to serve local markets can be further divided into those that gain market access (get around existing or potential trade barriers) and those that minimize transportation costs (where production costs plus transportation costs are higher for export sales than for foreign production). Investments to serve export markets can be further divided into those that source simple factors of production (low-cost labor or natural resources) and those that source higher-order advantages (specialized skills and expertise). The categories need not be exclusive. Several U.S. firms, for example, have set up facilities in Ireland in part to get access to the European Community (EC) market and in part to take advantage of relatively low labor costs and tax breaks that Ireland offers vis-à-vis other EC nations.

In cases of foreign direct investment, a question arises as to the location of competitive advantage. In particular, does foreign direct investment (FDI) reflect competitive advantages of the host country, the home country of the multinational firm, or both? The answer depends on the type of foreign investment. Investments designed to get around tariff barriers or to serve local markets in products with high transportation costs usually reflect advantages that the multinational company has developed in its home nation. In these cases, FDI represents the firm's attempts to spread its advantages over space when exporting is impractical or expensive.[13] Investments that source basic factors of production generally reflect advantages of both the host country (low-cost labor or natural resource deposits) and the home country of the multinational (which put the company in a position better to utilize the low-cost labor or resources). Investments that source higher-order advantages (Japanese investments in the U.S. motion picture industry, for example) generally reflect competitive advantages of the host country. In order to determine the location of competitive advantage in industries involving substantial amounts of foreign investment, one must determine the key competitive variables, success factors, and determinants in the industry and assess whether advantages in these elements come from the host nation, the home nation, or both.

A hierarchy of benefits to the host nation is associated with foreign investment. The modern multinational firm can spread its activities across the globe. In general, the more of these activities that take place in the host nation, the greater the benefit in terms of spillover into the local economy. Investments that involve a world or regional mandate for a particular product line or a regional headquarters often provide the greatest benefits to the host nation because they typically involve important activities such as strategy formulation, technology development, some advanced production, and marketing. On the other hand, investments that involve a single activity or part of an activity (screwdriver assembly plants or natural resource extraction, for example) usually provide less in the way of spillover into the local economy. One might argue that a host country should be more concerned with the activities that a foreign-owned firm engages in than the industry in which it competes.[14] This is not to say that these investments hurt the host nation. On the contrary, nations compete actively to obtain the benefits of just these investments. It is not surprising, however, that foreign investments in isolated activities tend to form few linkages with the host economy that can be sources of local advantage. One reason why manufacturing and assembly investments are made in countries other than the home nation is that these activities can be separated from those that provide the investing company with competitive advantages. In short, it is very difficult to attract foreign investment that is accompanied by the activities that provide the greatest spillovers to the host country. Doing so more or less requires that conditions in the host country be favorable for those activities. Subsidies or low-cost labor generally do not create such conditions.

The benefits of foreign direct investment for the host nation can include inflows of capital, technology, skilled personnel, and management expertise, most of which are usually in short supply in developing nations. Foreign direct investment is often complementary to the local economies of developing nations, where the industries dominated by multinational companies are often different from those dominated by indigenous firms.

Competitiveness Analysis for Industries and Nations

This discussion allows us to develop a new framework for assessing the competitiveness and prospects for competitiveness of a national industry. The first step is to identify the key success factors for the industry. This includes an assessment of the key competitive variables in the industry, the appropriate generic strategies (low-cost, differentiated, or focused), and the nature of consumer demand. The second step is to map the key competitive variables (or key success factors) for the industry to the determinants to understand which determinants are the most important and what constitutes a critical mass of favorable conditions for that industry. The third step is to assess the position of the nation and its firms versus competitor nations and firms in terms of the most important determinants. Doing so provides insights as to how a nation's firms compare to foreign competitors and to how a national environment compares to that of other nations. The last step is to identify mechanisms to exploit the advantages and minimize or overcome the disadvantages found in the local environment.

The process of assessing the competitiveness of a national industry can be extended into a competitiveness analysis for a nation as a whole. The first step is to identify the types of industries in which the nation's firms succeed and fail. The sources of advantage and disadvantage found in the nation are then isolated from an analysis of the competitiveness of a representative set of industries. The determinants are used to understand

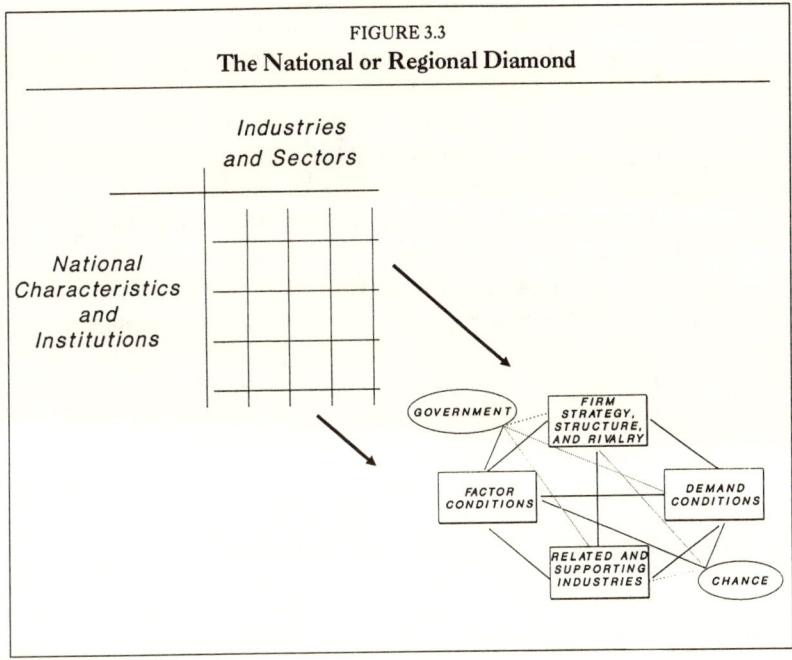

FIGURE 3.3
The National or Regional Diamond

the recurring patterns of advantage and disadvantage in both the traded and nontraded sectors of the economy. Finally, mechanisms are identified to exploit the advantages and to minimize or overcome the disadvantages in the national environment. The analysis of the nation should reflect both the traded and nontraded sectors of the economy, since the same determinants that provide the pressures, incentives, and capabilities to innovate and improve in industries in the traded sector (factor conditions; demand conditions; related and supporting industries; firm strategy, structure, and rivalry) will determine the competitiveness of the nontraded sector as well. Again, each nation must develop its own plan to enhance its advantages and overcome its disadvantages.

The components of a competitiveness analysis of a national economy are shown in Figures 3.3 and 3.4. In order to understand the forces that influence the competitiveness and productivity of a national environment, one must analyze the sources of advantage and disadvantage in individual industries as well as the national institutions and characteristics that cut across the economy. Such a crosscutting analysis allows one to construct a "national diamond," in which the sources of advantage and disadvantage for

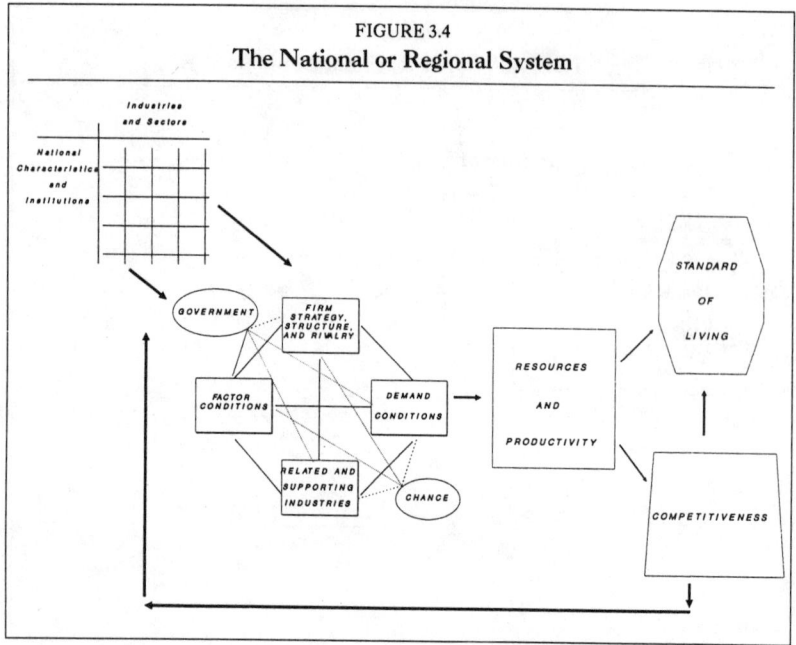

FIGURE 3.4
The National or Regional System

the nation are arrayed. Figure 3.4 closes the loop by showing the linkages between individual industries, national institutions and characteristics, the nation's resources and productivity, national competitiveness, and the nation's standard of living.

As indicated, the traded sector provides a unique window into the relative performance of national economies. It is in the traded sector that direct comparisons can be made between productivity levels of firms from different nations. Here too is where one can best see how the economic structures of different nations provide their firms with advantages or disadvantages. Exposure to international competition creates for each industry an absolute productivity standard necessary to compete with foreign rivals. Even if an industry is relatively more productive than others in the national economy, it will be unable to export unless it is also competitive with foreign rivals. Understanding why a nation can or cannot achieve high productivity becomes central to understanding economic development and prosperity. The nontraded sector is important in its own right and through its links with the traded sector. Efficiency or inefficiency in the nontraded sector can lead to advantages or disadvantages in international competition in the traded sector. Examination of the nontraded sector, however, does not provide the same opportunity for assessing the performance of a nation's firms and institutions in direct competition with those of other nations.

The Challenge of Competitiveness in Developing Countries

Porter's book reflected research on the determinants of international competitive success in industrialized and newly industrialized nations. If Porter and his collaborators had focused on the industries in which developing nations have achieved export success, the resulting determinants of international competitiveness would have been the traditional Ricardian notions of low-cost labor and natural resource endowments and the influence of governments and chance events. Much of the export success of developing nations has relatively little to do with factors creation; stimulating demand conditions; related and supporting industries; or the positive aspects of firm strategy, structure, and rivalry. In fact, developing nations usually have disadvantages in these areas with respect to industrialized nations.

Does this mean that the extended framework developed in this chapter is of no use to developing nations? To the contrary, the extended framework identifies potential sources of advantage in international competition. The fact that developing nations tend not to generate many of the potential sources of advantage identified above helps explain their limited penetration of world markets. In fact, the extended framework can be used to help explain why it is so hard for developing countries to develop. Development is a systemic and interdependent process. The extended framework helps to organize and to characterize the influence of features unique to developing countries that hold back development, *and in the process it helps to identify some of the key leverage points for these nations*. Thus such analysis becomes extremely important for developing nations. In addition, firms from developing nations often compete with firms from developed nations. It is therefore important to understand all the potential sources of advantage of competitor nations, be they developed or developing.

Developing nations have particular characteristics that can be viewed through the lens of the extended framework. They often have disadvantages in factor conditions in terms of infrastructure, science and technology, human capital, and financial markets. They often are characterized by limited purchasing power and a lack of advanced or sophisticated demand. In addition, they tend to lack the well-functioning markets necessary for the emergence of world-class related and supporting industries. Developing nations often are characterized by firm strategies and structures that try to minimize economic and political risk rather than maximize profits. Such nations often lack the domestic rivalry that stimulates innovation and improvement as well as competition from foreign firms that might serve as an imperfect substitute. Governments in developing nations often intervene in their economies for noneconomic reasons, which often are worthy in their own right, but sometimes hurt economic development. Even when attempting to intervene for economic reasons, governments in developing nations often intervene in a manner that distorts incentives for firms and individuals in ways that hinder the nation's ability to meet its long-term economic objectives. Understanding these dynamics allows one to identify the key leverage points that might be used to stimulate the competitiveness of a nation's firms and to promote its economic growth.

The extended framework developed in this chapter presents a set of questions rather than a set of answers. These questions must be answered in the specific context of each nation. While the answers might be different in developing nations from those in industrialized nations, the questions are still the same.[15] Each nation faces its own challenge of competitiveness. The next several chapters are devoted to addressing the challenge of competitiveness in the context of a single developing nation, Venezuela.

4

Venezuelan Industry Profiles

This chapter analyzes the dynamics of competitive advantage and disadvantage in Venezuela that have shaped six of the industries studied for this project: telenovelas, pulp and paper, tourism, petrochemicals, steel, and automotive vehicles and parts. Summary discussions of the remaining seven industries studied for this project are included in Chapter 5. The studies lead one to believe that Venezuela has substantial competitive potential. Most of the industries discussed in these chapters appear to be improving their competitiveness. The question is not so much the direction of this movement, but its speed and completeness.

The Venezuelan Telenovela Industry[1]

The case of the Venezuelan *telenovela* (soap opera) industry is instructive concerning the present and potential sources of advantage in the Venezuelan economy. At the start, however, it may be necessary to lay aside some preconceptions. Our discussions with Venezuelan businesspeople and policy makers suggested that many within these circles view the telenovela as trivial (mere popular entertainment) and that their view of the product colors their view of the telenovela industry. In fact, as we will discuss, the telenovela industry is one of a small number of industries in Venezuela with a dense pattern of competitive advantage, similar to the patterns of advantage found in many globally competitive industries in more advanced economies. In 1992, foreign licensing revenues from Venezuelan telenovelas were estimated to have reached between $40 million and $60 million,[2] which places Venezuelan telenovela "exports" on par with the export earnings of such domestic industries as automotive vehicles ($53 million), clothing and textiles combined ($49 million), and pulp and paper ($45 million). When it comes to a nation's economic growth, there are neither "good industries" nor "bad industries" (except if illegal); there are only industries in which the nation's firms can compete successfully and those in which they cannot.

According to local industry executives, in 1993 Venezuela led the world in the production and export of telenovelas, ahead of main rivals Mexico, Argentina, and Brazil.[3] Between 1983 and 1993, Venezuelan producers licensed more than 184,000 hours of telenovela programming abroad for broadcast in at least 38 countries. Venezuela is first in international markets, not in oil or aluminum, but in an industry where human talent and creativity are paramount. It has achieved this leadership position despite the fact that rivals Mexico and Brazil have the two largest television networks in Latin America and together account for 54 percent of Latin American television stations.[4]

The telenovela industry shows that it is possible in Venezuela to have a situation in which each of the four determinants is a source of competitive advantage. It shows that Venezuela can compete and win in talent-based industries against much larger rivals. This industry also highlights the importance of local rivalry and private sector initiatives in the development of competitive advantage.

The Telenovela: Chance Beginnings

The telenovela is a Latin American genre of TV fiction consisting of a series of sequential episodes, normally one hour in length, which generally are shown six days per week. A successful telenovela may run for about six to eight months from start to finish and often includes between 200 and 250 episodes, although there have been successful telenovelas outside that range.[5] The central plot is often, though not always, a romance between two protagonists with story lines often drawn from classic tales. Telenovelas evolved from the early radio soap operas produced before the onset of television by U.S. producers of personal care products.[6]

In the early 1950s, the U.S. companies Procter & Gamble and Colgate Palmolive introduced the telenovela in both Venezuela and Cuba. The first Venezuelan telenovela, *La criada de la granja* ("The Dairy Maid"), was aired in 1953. At the time, telenovelas broadcast by Radio Caracas Televisión were actually produced by Procter & Gamble and Colgate Palmolive, and the actors were on their payrolls. By chance, the next major stimulus came from Cuba, when the nucleus of talent on which the Cuban industry was based fled the Cuban revolution. Although some people went to the United States and Spain,[7] several very talented individuals from the CMQ Channel of Havana moved to Caracas. They brought know-how in acting, casting, and production and, perhaps most important, writing a successful libretto. Cuban entrepreneurial drive would also contribute to building the Venezuelan industry.

Television came early to Venezuela, first airing in 1952 as a public broadcast medium. The next year the government opened the field to private investors. Since then, there have always been at least two strong private competitors in the Venezuelan television sector. The Phelps Syndicate entered in 1953 with Radio Caracas Televisión (RCTV) and a competing group of investors with a station called Televisa. In 1961, the Cisneros Group and ABC acquired Televisa and changed its name to Venevisión. In 1964, the Vollmer Group, the Time/Life CBS consortium, and an investor formerly of the Cuban station CMQ founded a third private station, Cadena Venezolana de Televisión (CVTV). Over the succeeding decades, competition among private investors proved a powerful engine of growth, for Venezuelan television broadcasting in general and telenovelas in particular.

During the 1960s, the introduction of videotape technology to Venezuelan television opened new artistic and commercial possibilities. *El derecho de nacer* ("The Right to Be Born") aired in 1965, was the first Venezuelan-produced telenovela of 200 chapters in length and was a major success. The telenovela genre known as the *culebrón* (or "long snake," an allusion to its long and twisting plot) soon became a cultural phenomenon in Venezuela with a broad domestic audience. The 1960s were a golden decade in Venezuela for TV advertising of consumer goods, such as packaged goods, tobacco, and beverages. Television was reaching ever-larger numbers of Venezuelan viewers across different geographic regions and income levels. Although most TV programming was imported, the local television industry invested in its own production facilities and developed its own production expertise. At the time, each of the Venezuelan broadcasters had equity ties with one of the "Big Three" of U.S. television: Venevisión with ABC, Radio Caracas Televisión with NBC, and Cadena Venezolana de Televisión with CBS. This continued into the 1970s, when restrictions on foreign investment resulted in Venevisión and RCTV buying out their partners. CVTV was acquired by the Venezuelan state and transformed into Venezolana de Televisión (VTV).

The Rise of Export Strategies

In the 1970s, Venezuelan television producers began to license telenovelas for broadcast in several small Latin American nations, such as Panama and Costa Rica. In the 1980s, Radio Caracas Televisión and Venevisión established an international marketing arm in Miami, Florida, called Coral Pictures. Coral Pictures soon separated into two rival firms, Coral Pictures and Venevisión International. Two particularly attractive markets, Spain and the United States, proved difficult to penetrate. Spanish broadcasters doubted that a Venezuelan product could ever interest Spanish viewers. Televisa of Mexico, the largest Spanish-language television producer in the world, controlled most of the U.S. Hispanic broadcasting market.

After several years of trying to penetrate the Spanish television market, Radio Caracas Televisión hired a well-known sales representative from inside the Spanish television industry. In 1987, the first Venezuelan telenovela was broadcast on Spanish television. Soon thereafter, *Cristal,* produced in Caracas by RCTV, became the most popular telenovela ever shown in Spain, attracting nearly 7 million viewers. It was followed by a string of additional Venezuelan successes, including "Abigail" (RCTV), *La dama de rosa* ("The Lady of Rose") (RCTV), and *La revancha* ("The Revenge") (Venevisión). By the end of the decade, Venezuela had displaced Mexico and Brazil as the leader in the Spanish telenovela market.

After the breakthrough in Spain, Venezuelan telenovelas penetrated markets worldwide, reaching 38 countries by 1993.[8] They have been watched in Latin America, Spain, the Spanish-speaking United States, Italy, Germany, Turkey, Greece, Israel, the Philippines, and Pakistan. Broadcasters throughout the former Soviet Union, from Russia to the former Soviet Turkish republics, have bought Venezuelan telenovelas. In 1993, broadcasters in countries of the Far East, including China, Hong Kong, Japan, and Korea, were expressing interest in Venezuelan telenovela programming, and the Venezuelan producers hoped that they might become major customers. In the spring of 1993, the Venezuelan telenovela *Cara sucia* ("Dirty Face"), produced by Venevisión, ranked number one in the Nielsen ratings of U.S. Hispanic broadcasters for three months. See Table 4.1 for figures on Venezuelan telenovela exports.

Traditionally, telenovelas were marketed abroad only after they completed their first run in the home market. In the 1990s, however, the trend is for earlier transmission abroad. A series that has a proven record of success at home is more easily marketed abroad and will command a premium price. The price received per hour will vary substantially according to the foreign market in question. The value of telenovela licensing rights in a foreign market depends on the population coverage of the broadcasting station, the size of the advertising market, and per-capita disposable income. There is little price competition between rival exporters in an individual market. In 1993, prices ranged from $8,000 to $12,000 in Spain per hour (on national

TABLE 4.1
Venezuelan Telenovela Exports, 1983–1993

Title	Countries	Chapters	Hours Exported
Radio Caracas Televisión, 1983-1993			
1. *Señora*	18	229	7,557
2. *Cristal*	25	246	6,888
3. *La dama de rosa*	21	228	5,928
4. *Topacio*	20	187	5,797
5. *Abigail*	22	257	5,654
Top Five			31,824
Additional 68 telenovelas exported			58,985
Total exports		8,083	90,809
Venevisión, 1983-1993			
1. *La revancha*	18	247	4,446
2. *Pasionaria*	15	254	3,810
3. *Paraíso*	15	253	3,795
4. *Niña bonita*	16	199	3,184
5. *Inés Duarte, secretaria*	13	238	3,094
Top Five			18,329
Additional 46 telenovelas exported			66,779
Total exports		.	85,108
Marte Televisión, 1990-1993			
1. *María María*	14	198	2,772
2. *Emperatriz*	10	211	2,110
3. *La traidora*	8	180	1,440
4. *La loba herida*	6	214	1,284
5. *Las dos Dianas*	6	137	822
Total exports		940	8,428
INDUSTRY TOTAL, 1983-1993			184,345

Source: Güerere (1993b), RCTV, Venevision International, Marte TV.

networks), to as little as $140 per hour in Nicaragua for the same telenovela chapter.[9]

In 1993, the Venezuelan industry was making investments in production and broadcast companies throughout the Western Hemisphere. Venevisión had acquired equity interests in a broadcast station in Chile and had acquisitions in process in Argentina and Colombia. In October 1991, Venevisión entered into a joint venture agreement with Televisa of Mexico for the distribution of programming throughout Latin America. Venevisión's largest shareholder became a member of the board of directors of Televisa. In 1992, Venevisión and Televisa, as part of a joint venture with Hollywood producer Jerold Perecchio, each acquired a 25 percent interest in Univisión, the most-watched Spanish language network in the United States, as well as 12.5 percent equity interest in its affiliated broadcast stations. Radio Caracas Televisión, in partnership with International Television Inc. (INTV), has launched a satellite channel, GEMS, directed at Hispanic women in the United States and Latin America.

Advanced Factor Conditions

The Venezuelan telenovela industry relies for success on specialized expertise in writing, acting, and production. Writing is critically important to success in telenovelas. Venezuelan telenovela writers are first rate and include world masters of the craft.[10] In 1993, there were approximately ten top telenovela writers in Venezuela under contract to the producers, each of whom headed up a small team of script writers. In addition, there were approximately 40 well-respected free-lance writers nationwide. These numbers are very small both in absolute terms and in relation to total employment within the Venezuelan television industry, which in 1993 was estimated at 10,200 persons.

Although talent is a prerequisite to telenovela script writing, training and experience are also important. Few of the leading telenovela writers in Venezuela are graduates of universities, much less the national arts school. Some come from the intelligentsia, others from theater, and some talented people arrive at the studio doors with no special background and are trained in-house. The Venezuelan TV industry has managed to involve some of the nation's leading authors in writing telenovelas, including José Ignacio Cabrujas and Salvador Garmendia, whereas in other Latin American nations leading authors usually look on TV writing with disdain.

Industry executives interviewed for this study agree that there is in Venezuela a deep talent for acting. The pervasive interest in acting and media careers among today's youth ensures a steady flow of aspiring actors through the doors of the producers' talent scouts. Venezuela boasts excellent television producers and a strong innate aptitude for technical aspects of production. Workers are quick and adept at mastering new filming and lighting equipment. In addition, over the past decades, the major Venezuelan studios have taken the lead in training the skilled artists and workers whom they need in order to compete.

Advanced Demand Conditions

The size, sophistication, and segment structure of Venezuelan demand for telenovelas all have had a substantial impact on the industry and its export success. The Venezuelan population is not large, but a "hit" television program generally reaches a percentage of the total population that is extremely high in international terms. In 1993, television sets were present in at least 89 percent of all Venezuelan households.[11] TV ownership rates were even higher in Caracas, where there were televisions in 97 percent of all households and in 94 percent of the lowest-income households.[12] More than 90 percent were color television sets. In 1993, on any given night, roughly 8 million people, or 40 percent of the Venezuelan population, were watching the current leading telenovela. A strong telenovela might reach 28 percent of the population in a noontime slot or 50 percent in a prime-time evening slot. In contrast, the most popular TV program on United States network television in 1993, *Roseanne,* reached between 22 percent and 25 percent of the U.S. population. Social critics, in fact, voice concern over the hold of television on the Venezuelan public.

The nature of advertising in Venezuela has stimulated demand for telenovelas. TV's reach makes it a very powerful advertising force in the nation. This is reflected in the cost of reaching 1,000 persons (or "cost per thousand") in Venezuela, which in 1993 was $2.16 for prime-time television compared to $14.19 for magazines.[13] The low cost, in absolute and relative terms, of getting advertising messages to TV viewers makes television the medium of choice for Venezuelan advertisers. Total spending on television advertising in Venezuela by independent buyers was estimated at between $270 million and $300 million in 1993.[14] The advertising market has grown at a healthy rate since the 1960s, providing funds that have fueled the growth and maturation of the nation's television industry in advance of many other nations.

Venezuelan demand for telenovelas is sophisticated in international terms. Venezuelans have been watching television, and telenovelas in particular, for four decades, and the most successful telenovelas since the birth of the genre are a part of the collective memory. Venezuelan audiences also have been exposed to foreign programming, especially U.S. programming, since the early years of television, which in turn has made them more demanding TV viewers. Venezuela's tradition of affluence and cosmopolitan tastes in fashion and other consumer goods also contribute to an attractive telenovela product. In the 1980s, Venezuelan demand for telenovelas preceded, and was predictive of, foreign demand. For example, the telenovelas *Cristal* and *Topacio* reached the top of national rating charts before becoming hits in foreign markets. Venezuela is an important test market for telenovelas from other Latin American countries, which often are aired in Venezuela first in order to assess their export potential.

Venezuelan producers have a modest advantage over other Spanish-language producers and a larger advantage over producers from non–Spanish-speaking countries because of the segment structure of Venezuelan demand. Venezuelan demand for Spanish-language TV fiction developed early and was a precursor of similar demand in many other Spanish-speaking nations. Although Venezuelan producers have started to export to a wide range of non–Spanish-speaking nations, the core of their international market can still be found in Spanish language audiences. The Venezuelan accent appears to be better received in Spain and throughout Latin America than the Mexican or Argentine accent. This advantage may be waning as Venezuelan actors are lured to other countries. It was their success in Spain that gave the Venezuelan firms the impetus to enter the wider world marketplace. Venezuelan firms have an advantage over firms from non–Spanish-speaking nations in an international Spanish-speaking market with more than 400 million viewers.

Integrated Structures and Strategies

Telenovelas are an important part of the integrated corporate structures and strategies of their parent companies. As such, they receive enhanced corporate investment and support. Each of the two leading Venezuelan telenovela producers belongs to a major industrial group within the Venezuelan economy. The Organización Diego Cisneros is active in a wide range of business sectors, including supermarkets, department stores, entertainment, petrochemicals, computers, and telecommunications. Its communications division encompasses television and radio production and broadcasting, advertising and postproduction services, beauty pageants, and musical recording (records, tapes, and videos). Radio Caracas Televisión is part of the Phelps Group, which also owns radio stations, newspapers, magazines, a local airline, and hotels.

There are several direct links between the telenovelas and the leading firms' overall entertainment business strategies, which are discussed in the next section. In addition, there are several indirect connections. Although most of the major broadcasters' advertising revenues come from independent customers, each producer also airs advertisements of products from affiliated companies. In this way, telenovelas form part of the marketing strategies of firms that are within the corporate group or are related indirectly through common ownership ties. Related advertisers generally pay for advertising spots, but at a discount. As a rule, the Organización Diego Cisneros and its related companies do not advertise on RCTV, and the Phelps Syndicate and related firms do not advertise on Venevisión. Exceptions to this rule are generally short-lived, not for business reasons, but because of personal animosity between the two groups.

Fierce Rivalry for Revenues and Viewers

The Venezuelan television industry is propelled by fierce domestic rivalry for domestic advertising revenue. Despite the growing importance of foreign licensing revenues, domestic advertising income is still the lifeblood of the industry. However, there is more to this than mere business rivalry. Rather, it is a feud between people at the top who know each other well, do not like each other, and are not afraid to show it. This is a sharp contrast from the situation in Mexico and Brazil, where in the past there was little or no rivalry in television production.

The principal rivals in the Venezuelan television industry are the two private producer/broadcasting giants, Venevisión and Radio Caracas Televisión. Early attempts to divide up the market between them dissolved in the 1980s, with the strong growth of local and international markets. More recently, the granting of new open-circuit concessions by the state to regional operators and the entry of Marte TV into telenovela production have injected new dynamism into the sector. Independent producers, headed by Marte TV, have been producing telenovelas, miniseries, and feature films, which have been purchased by the national channels and, in certain cases, even sold to foreign markets. Marte Televisión has established itself rapidly as a successful producer of TV programs, including telenovelas. Between 1990 and 1993, it produced seven telenovelas, equivalent to more than 1,300 hours of programming.

The television ratings war is waged daily, and telenovelas are on the front lines. The war to be first starts at the drawing board and imbues the entire creative and production process. The producers groom their own writing, producing, and acting talent in-house, and in the past they have not been shy to "poach" rival talent. The search for new talent is constant and relentless. Otherwise, a competitor might come up with the next new star.

Both Venevisión and RCTV monitor ratings on an ongoing basis. This continuous monitoring has a direct and immediate impact on the shape and content of Venezuelan telenovelas that often goes beyond that found in programming in the United States. By the time an individual telenovela episode is aired, production often has advanced about 25 chapters into the future. If an individual chapter or group of chapters falters in the Venezuelan ratings, it is too late to reshoot the immediately succeeding episodes. Existing footage, however, is often edited to boost the plot's dramatic tension. In a real sense, a first-run telenovela that has run an entire season on Venezuelan television has survived a trial by fire. As mentioned, the first Venezuelan telenovelas to conquer foreign markets were broadcast overseas after they had been aired in their entirety at home. Their dramatic hold over foreign viewers was forged in the furnace of home competition.

Venezuela is a world leader in telenovelas largely because of strong domestic rivalry. Members of the industry are the first to point this out. A director of market research for one producer said it best:

> Some people see competition as an ugly word, but I don't. I see competition as a wonderful thing. Anywhere in the world where you see competition in the marketplace, it works to the benefit of the marketplace. Everyone has to push that much harder and do that much more.... Venezuela is the first in the world in telenovelas, ahead of Mexico, although we have a population of only 20 million people. Twenty million people is nothing in Mexico—we could fit in Mexico City alone. But with the monopoly, the Mexican producer could afford to slip up from time to time on sound, lighting, actors. The audience would watch anyway, because there was only one producer. In Venezuela, we can't afford to slip up. That's why Venezuela is number one.

A Vibrant Entertainment Cluster

The Venezuelan telenovela business is part of a cluster of industries related to popular entertainment. Caracas is the home of internationally successful recording, fashion, beauty pageant, and advertising industries. These sectors are linked by common ownership, expertise, talent flows, and marketing strategies. Together with Miami and Mexico City, Caracas is one of the most important recording centers for popular music in Spanish. The entertainment and recording sector in Caracas attracts talented singers from throughout Latin America and the Caribbean. Venezuela's largest recording firms, Sonográfica and Sonorodven, have the promotional clout and international licensing networks to launch talent to international stardom. (See Chapter 7.)

Music is an integral part of the telenovela. Every telenovela series has a theme song, which is heard on TV in millions of households. Both RCTV and Venevisión work in tandem with related recording firms to maximize the commercial synergies between telenovelas and popular music. The theme songs from telenovelas produced by Venevisión, for example, are performed exclusively by Sonorodven musicians. Aspiring singers sometimes take on roles in the telenovela as part of their recording contracts. If they are successful as actors, their mass TV exposure builds an advance demand for future recordings at home and abroad. The international singing career of the Venezuelan actor José Luis Rodríguez, popularly known as El Puma, for example, was preceded by the success of a series of locally produced telenovelas in which he starred.

Beauty pageants supply a continuous flow of talent to television. As mentioned, Venezuelans on the whole take beauty contests seriously, and Venezuelan contestants have won a disproportionate share of international beauty titles over the last few decades. (See Chapter 3.)[15] Venevisión, the self-proclaimed "Channel of Beauty," produces the Miss Venezuela contests. RCTV followed suit with the Chica 2001 contest. Both companies employ talent scouts that search for potential contestants and then groom and train them for the competitions. Pageant winners already have public name recognition, which boosts telenovela ratings and makes them a valuable asset to local television production. Pageant winners with less acting ability readily find spots in television commercials.

The wardrobes worn by telenovela actors and actresses also tie into the domestic design and clothing industry. Clothes shown on the programs often start fashion trends, and program credits sometimes give the names and addresses of stores selling the wardrobes and accessories. With the devaluation of the bolivar, there has been growing demand for local designers, and new fashion houses are rising to the challenge. The telenovelas showcase their designs and at the same time benefit from the added allure of fashion.

Caracas is also home to one of the most competitive television advertising industries in Latin America. In commercial production, particularly the staging and shooting of commercials, the city is considered more advanced than its Latin American neighbors and nearly on par with Miami and Los Angeles. (See Chapter 7.) This first-rate production capability is not just an offshoot of the television studios. Many of the finest advertisement producers in Caracas learned their craft independently.

The State's Contribution to Competitiveness

The Venezuelan government opened the television sector to private competition in the early 1950s and has kept it open over time. This is its single greatest contribution to the industry, and it has had long lasting, positive consequences. Of the three national broadcasters active in 1970, only one, CVTV, was nationalized, and its publicly owned successor failed to develop into a major broadcasting force. The other two, RCTV and Venevisión, were allowed to remain in private hands, and they grew into industry leaders. In contrast to Brazil, and (until recently) Mexico, in Venezuela the state has allowed competition among private broadcasters.

Since 1980, the government has been very active in granting new concessions to regional broadcasters throughout Venezuela, thereby allowing new entry into the industry. In 1993 alone, new broadcasters in the provinces include TV Guayana (Puerto Ordaz), Telesol (Cumaná), TV Oriente (Anzoátegui) and Llanovisión (Barinas). Seven UHF channels have been assigned in Caracas, plus several others in the interior. Although the newcomers operate on a much smaller scale than RCTV and Venevisión, they represent an important infusion of new talent, opinions, and entrepreneurial dynamism into the sector.

Venezuela's democratically elected regimes have contributed to the industry's development by supporting the freedom and independence of the media even in times of national crisis. The state, however, also has adopted some restrictive policies. During the 1960s and 1970s, telenovela scripts had to be sent to the government for review by public censors. Censorship strictly prohibited certain themes, such as the kidnapping of children, illegitimate births, and extramarital relationships, forcing scriptwriters to resort to awkward plot twists, such as secret marriages, to permit the development of the story line. Not until the 1970s, when censorship ceased, did plots become less restricted. The Venezuelan product became more sophisticated, resulting in such famous series as *La Señora de Cárdenas* ("Mrs. Cardenas"), a breakthrough in dramatic quality. Since then, there have been efforts to regulate telenovelas in an effort to protect young viewers. As is the case in the United States and elsewhere, in Venezuela the influence of television on children is cause for concern in educational and political circles.

Opportunities and Challenges

The early 1990s have been a time of change for Spanish-language broadcasting in the Western Hemisphere. The industry is being reshaped by Mexican, U.S., and—increasingly—Venezuelan interests. As countries from Latin America, to Europe, to Asia privatize their television stations and open up the airways to new technologies such as cable television, demand for commercial programming is growing rapidly, both at home and abroad. Because Venezuelan producers were early entrants in the export of television fiction, they are well positioned to take a leading role in international markets. In 1993, the Venezuelan telenovela industry was expanding. Over several years, Venevisión and RCTV had invested considerable amounts in modernizing and expanding technical equipment and installations. Marte TV, which entered production in 1990, had its own installations with studios, equipment, and other facilities. Investment atrophied only in state-owned stations.

In 1993, the production capacity of the telenovela sector, including Venevisión, RCTV, and Marte TV, was estimated to be between eight and twelve telenovelas per year.[16] Expansion plans then under way were expected to increase this total to approximately 19 per year within ten years. By the year 2003, Venezuela probably will possess a fiber optic cable system, which will further fuel demand for television fiction. The question is whether the conditions are in place for the industry to take full advantage of growing demand and of the deep financial pockets of the major producers.

One challenge to the expansion of the industry is the growth potential of the Venezuelan talent pool. In any country, there will be limits to the pool of truly first-rate talent in writing, filming, acting, and directing. In the international marketplace of the 1990s, creative talent is increasingly mobile. Some of Venezuela's former telenovela stars, for example, have relocated to Miami, Argentina, and Spain, where they are earning much higher salaries than the Venezuelan producers can, or care to, pay. Venezuelan writers are also being lured to new markets. A shortage of writers may become a constraint on future growth, because writers are the most important specialized factor in telenovelas. Compared to its tradition in the other fine arts, such as music, graphic arts, and acting, Venezuela's literary tradition is relatively weak. Thus expanding the pool of first-class writing talent at the same rate as capital investment may prove difficult. Over the coming years, the leaders of Venezuelan industry will have to redouble their efforts to identify and train new talent, in writing and other areas.

Another challenge to the Venezuelan industry will come from foreign rivals. Mexico's Televisa is the largest producer of Spanish-language programming in the world, with holdings in television broadcast channels, cable television, radio stations, music recording and distribution, and publishing businesses. Televisa has a strong international presence in telenovelas and for the past several years has pursued a strategy of boosting its presence in foreign markets. In 1991, Televisa established production studios in Chile and Argentina, as part of its plan to "Latin Americanize."[17] In 1992, it set up a production studio in Brazil to produce telenovelas and miniseries in Portuguese, using Brazilian artists, for the Brazilian market and for sale

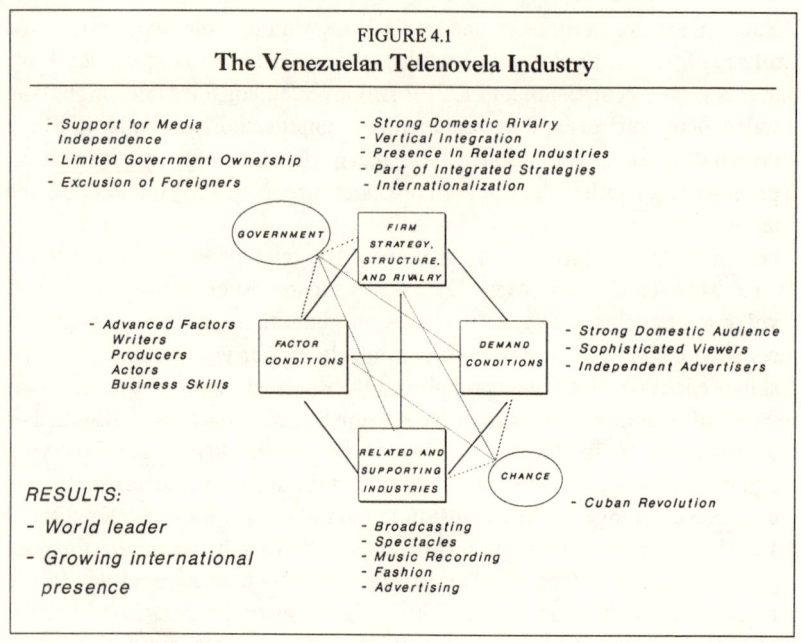

FIGURE 4.1
The Venezuelan Telenovela Industry

abroad.[18] Argentina and Brazil are also a major presence in foreign markets, including those throughout Latin America. Smaller producers, such as Chile and Colombia, are trying to expand their production and their share of foreign markets.

Lessons from the Venezuelan Telenovela Industry

Several lessons can be learned from the Venezuelan telenovela industry. The developed nations are not the only ones that can succeed on the basis of advanced factor conditions, sophisticated demand, advanced related and supporting industries, increasingly international strategies, and fierce domestic rivalry. The unique attributes of the Venezuelan telenovela diamond are what have allowed this country to develop competitive advantage. (See Figure 4.1) Venezuela need not rely exclusively on natural resources to succeed in international competition. It can provide an environment that develops the skills of its people to compete in the international marketplace.

This industry highlights the importance of domestic rivalry in stimulating the constant improvement that leads to export success. Venezuela is one of the few nations in the world with strong, long-standing local rivalry in television. Even though the battle for dominance between Venevisión and

Radio Caracas Televisión has moved into foreign markets and foreign alliances, the strongest motivation for success abroad continues to be rivalry at home. The future success of Venezuelan interests on a hemispheric basis will depend in large part on the preservation and stimulation of rivalry in the domestic market. This is especially critical now that Mexico, Venezuela's principal foreign rival, has injected a powerful new dynamism into its television sector with the privatization of the state's former broadcasting holdings.

Finally, Venezuelan firms can succeed in international competition without the direct involvement of the state. The state has made positive contributions to competitiveness in this sector by promoting private ownership of the airwaves, allowing competition among producers, and promoting freedom of expression. Although its performance in some of these areas leaves room for improvement, its overall contribution to the growth of telenovelas and television in Venezuela has been positive and has been characterized more by self-restraint than active interventionism. This is in sharp contrast to other industries to be discussed in this chapter, such as pulp, petrochemicals, tourism, and steel, in which the state set out to be the primary motor of growth. In telenovelas, the private sector has identified its own opportunities and charted its own path to world success.

The Venezuelan Pulp and Paper Industry[19]

In 1991, the Venezuelan paper industry produced an estimated 652,000 tons of paper and cardboard, making it the fourth largest producer of paper and cardboard in Latin America after Brazil, Mexico, and Argentina.[20] This output was based mostly on recycled fiber and imported pulp. The industry produced only a small quantity of pulp (88,000 tons). Its total paper and cardboard exports totaled $44.6 million, or 2 percent of total non-oil exports.[21]

Venezuela has some of the most favorable conditions in the world for the production of pulp, the major raw material for paper and cardboard products. Its basic factor advantages are more favorable than those of the leading pulp producers in the world, Canada and the United States. Compared to these countries, Venezuela has better growing conditions, a shorter life cycle for trees, abundant water, highly competitive energy costs, and low-cost labor. Compared to Chile, Venezuela has better growing conditions, more lands suitable for forest plantations, competitive energy costs, and much easier transportation to the North American and European markets.

Venezuela even has advantages in terms of land and energy costs and location with respect to neighboring Brazil.

Despite these basic factor advantages, Venezuela does not produce pulp in significant quantities. Instead, it annually imports more than 160,000 tons of pulp and nearly 200,000 tons of recycled fiber to support its domestic paper and cardboard industry.[22] Comparisons with Chile and Brazil are informative. In 1991, for example, Chile produced 1.1 million metric tons of pulp, 435,000 for domestic use and 665,000 for export; in 1992 it increased pulp capacity to 2 million metric tons. Brazil produced 4.84 million metric tons of pulp in 1991, primarily from short-fiber trees, of which it exported 1.37 million metric tons.[23] As mentioned, Venezuela, with better natural conditions for forestry, produced only 88,000 tons of pulp and exported none.

Why have the Chilean and Venezuelan experiences been so different? Twenty years ago, the Chilean government decided to promote the development of a pulp and paper industry through the granting of land concessions to private plantation operators and the provision of incentives to private investment. At about the same time, the Venezuelan state also decided to promote the development of forest plantations and pulp production—by keeping ownership and management of the forest plantations primarily in its own hands.[24] By 1993, the Chilean private sector had planted more than 1.6 million hectares of forest plantations and had invested more than U.S. $2 billion in pulp plants. In contrast, the Venezuelan state had planted 436,389 hectares of forest, but it had not produced any pulp. The Venezuelan private sector managed 89,000 hectares and produced 88,000 tons of pulp per year. See Table 4.2 for a comparison of Latin American forest plantations.

The case of the Venezuelan forest plantations shows that basic factor endowments are not enough to confer competitive advantage. Across a broad range of natural resource industries, Venezuela has not been able to transform rich natural endowments into world-class industries. There are certain common themes throughout these experiences. Basic factor advantages are not advantages in the marketplace where the government controls and mismanages the resources to be developed, local competition is stymied, and domestic production is shielded from the rigors of international market forces. On the other hand, these examples also show that there is a substantial potential upside that might be realized through effective resource management and development strategies for the nation's natural resource-based industries.

Between 1990 and 1993, market distortions in the Venezuelan pulp and paper sector were largely corrected. Subsidized pulp imports and an overvalued currency no longer sent the wrong signals to local business. As of the

TABLE 4.2
Latin American Forest Plantations, 1990

Thousands of Hectares

Wood Type	Argentina	Brazil	Chile	Colombia	Venezuela
Eucalyptus	188	816	131	48	12
Pine	367	576	1,305	93	373
Other	82	46	119	86	-
Total 1990	637	1,437	1,555	227	385
Estimate 2000	987	2,300	2,020	597	825

Source: Briceño (1993).

early 1990s, members of the Venezuelan industry were starting to make substantial investments, anticipating the eventual recovery of international markets. However, because the reforms were recent and still tentative, Venezuela's advantages in pulp and paper were only in the early stages of development. It will take decades for the nation's potential to be realized fully, even under favorable circumstances.

The Evolution of the Pulp and Paper Industry

Starting in the 1960s, the Venezuelan paper industry was protected by high tariffs on paper and cardboard products. Tariffs on imported pulp were kept low, the bolivar was overvalued, and the state subsidized the purchase of inputs and capital equipment. The result was that Venezuelan paper companies were able to import pulp at subsidized prices that were well below their full market value. The Venezuelan paper producers located their plants along the central corridor of Caracas, Maracay, and Valencia, for proximity to the ports of entry of imported pulp and to domestic users. Some also engaged in the cultivation of short-fiber plants, such as cane, to produce pulp on a small scale. However, at that time, the technology to process short-fiber woods into high-resistance paper was not available. Long-fiber plants, such as pines, were preferred for the manufacture of high-quality and high-resistance paper and cardboard.

The states of Monagas and Anzoátegui, up to 900 kilometers away from the principal paper plants, contain vast tracts of land ideally suited to the growing of Caribbean pine and other trees. These are not tropical forests, which Venezuela also has in abundance. Rather, they are flat scrub lands with sandy soil that have no competing uses. Their potential for controlled forest plantations was first discovered by the Venezuelan Ministry of Agriculture and Livestock (MAC), which planted Caribbean pines on an experimental basis in the early 1960s. After several trials, the Corporación Venezolana de Guayana (CVG) established a 720 hectare plantation program in Uverito in 1969, as the base of a large-scale project. The Venezuelan state recognized the economic potential latent in these lands, deemed the plantations of strategic interest to the nation—and kept them under government control. Over the next 20 years, a series of state agencies would carry out the planting and management of the largest pine plantations in Venezuela.

In general, the highest value-added use of plantation pines is their conversion into pulp. Since 1969, the Venezuelan state has courted private investment to establish an efficient-scale pulp plant in the nation that would generate meaningful employment and export earnings.[25] More than two decades have come and gone, and the initial plantings are past their prime, but there is still no pulp plant to use the pines in Venezuela. A state-of-the-art, efficient-scale pulp plant costs an estimated $700 million to $850 million (in 1993 dollars). However, private investment of this magnitude requires basic guarantees regarding the terms of investment as well as adequate long-term supplies and reasonable prices of key raw materials and inputs. For one reason or another, the CVG has been unable to grant such guarantees. As a result, private investors have not come forward to invest in such a plant.

In 1980, plans were drawn up for a Kraft pulp mill with an annual capacity of 400,000 metric tons. Market conditions were good and a consortium of Venezuelan paper manufacturers were eager to participate. Alleged conflicts of interest within the government and the unwillingness of the CVG to define its terms of sale, however, killed the project after only six months of discussion.[26] In 1985, new plans were drawn up, this time for a combined pulp plant and newsprint mill. After three years, a joint venture was formed between the CVG and the Venezuelan Investment Fund as principal shareholders; two foreign partners that would supply technology, Abitibi Price and Bowater; and Grupensa, a Venezuelan firm associated with the leading national newspapers. By this point, however, the state was in financial difficulty, and international pulp prices were on the verge of collapse. In 1989, the Venezuelan Investment Fund withdrew from the project. Abitibi Price soon followed. Union Camp took its place. Then the CVG withdrew.

Negotiations were started with the Venezuelan paper manufacturer, Grupo Delfino, to acquire 20 percent of the project. In August 1992, with the world pulp market in a slump worsened by economic recession, Bowater withdrew and Union Camp put its investments on hold.

In the early 1990s, the CVG faced the pressing problem of what to do with trees that lose commercial value quickly after reaching maturity. Those planted in the early 1970s were already past their prime, and more came ready for harvest each year. In 1992, Forest Products, Inc. (PROFORCA), the CVG agency managing most of the forests, had 6.5 million stereo cubic meters of wood over 15 years old, which will be beyond use well before any pulp plant is constructed. If a 400,000 ton pulp mill had been in operation in 1993, as originally planned, it would have used an estimated 2.5 million stereo cubic meters of pine per year and would have earned more than $260 million per year in revenues, even at depressed prices.[27] However, as of 1993, there were no large-scale harvesting operations of state-owned pines.

In the absence of a pulp mill, PROFORCA settled for lower value-added alternatives. In 1993, various sawmills were converting pines into boards. Letters of intent had been signed to install two large-scale chipping plants, which would convert some of the state-owned pines into wood chips, and a plant to produce boards, primarily for export. However, in terms of value added, earnings, and employment, chipping plants are a distant second best to pulp production. Private-sector firms that invested in plantations with the understanding that the pulp mill would go forward also had to find an outlet for their trees.

Over the years, the private sector played a leading role in the domestic paper and cardboard industry but only a secondary role in forestry plantations. In 1972, the Delfino Group, one of the nation's largest paper producers, inaugurated a plantation project in the south of the Anzoátegui state. A mixed public-private company, Corporación Forestal Guayamure, was eventually formed to manage these plantations. The Delfino Group and others followed the initial investment with additional ones. However, a combination of factors hampered the growth of a private plantation sector. The CVG declined to grant private investors concessions to its largest plantations. Under the Agrarian Reform Law, would-be investors had little certainty of secure tenancy in plantation lands.[28] At the same time, subsidized pulp imports made reliance on imported pulp more attractive than long-term investments in pulp plantations. Price distortions due to protection and subsidies reduced the incentive to produce pulp in Venezuela despite the country's natural advantages.

TABLE 4.3
Pulp and Paper Industry in Latin America, 1991

Thousands of Metric Tons

	Argentina	Brazil	Chile	Colombia	Mexico	Venezuela
Pulp						
Production	667	4,839	987	266	707	88
Export	71	1,375	665	0	0	0
Import	37	96	0	60	320	168
Paper and Cardboard						
Production	963	4,888	482	559	2,896	652
Export	31	1,077	121	16	120	39
Import	185	371	115	107	464	176

Source: Briceño (1993).

The Venezuelan situation contrasts sharply with that of Brazil and Chile, where governments decided that the private sector would do a better job of forest development than the public sector. These nations passed forestry legislation, provided some subsidies to planting, and monitored the industry closely. Brazil and Chile came from nowhere to become major world players in less than 30 years. Chile enjoys a substantial trade surplus in a number of forest product industries, including rough logs, pulpwood chips, pulp, paper, lumber, and lumber products. (See Table 4.3 and Chapter 7.)

Economic Reforms and the Pulp and Paper Industry

During the decades of import substitution, the Venezuelan paper and cardboard producers expanded paper operations to take advantage of the captive domestic market. Although there was captive demand for many product types, demand for any particular good was small, usually less than minimum efficient scales of production. Protected from import competition, domestic producers divided up the market, with the result that generally only two producers were active in each major product category. It was a cartelized market with little head-to-head competition. Venezuela became largely self-sufficient in most categories of paper and cardboard, with the exception of newsprint and cigarette wrappers, which were imported.

The economic reform program initiated in 1989 had a dramatic impact on the Venezuelan pulp and paper industry. Venezuela opened its markets to imports of paper and cardboard products, eliminated input subsidies, and allowed the currency to float. One result was an increase in imports and a major improvement in quality and selection on the part of domestic producers. The inflow of competitive products from Colombia and elsewhere pressured local producers to restructure costs, to improve, and to innovate. This, in turn, stimulated growth in exports. In the early 1990s, Venezuelan paper producers were exporting a variety of paper products to the United Kingdom, the Caribbean islands, Colombia, Ecuador, Central America, the United States, and Mexico. Tissue paper was the leading export, with industrial cardboard and corrugated paper a distant second and third. (See Chapter 7.)[29]

A major issue facing Venezuelan paper manufacturers is whether to reduce their dependence on imported pulp. From 1989 to 1993, the world pulp and paper markets were depressed, burdened by recessions in the United States and Western Europe. The price of U.S. Southern Pine pulp went from $810 per ton in late 1989 to $450 a ton in the last quarter of 1991, before recovering slightly to $520 per ton in early 1992.[30] The low prices of imported pulp have allowed Venezuelan paper manufacturers to compete against imports of finished products in the home market. On the other hand, industry forecasters expected international pulp and paper prices to start to climb again later in the 1990s. If pulp prices rise significantly, Venezuelan paper producers will be hard-pressed to protect their market share from low-priced paper imports. Brazil, a close neighbor that produces large quantities of low-cost paper, mostly from short-fiber eucalyptus, has already invaded the Argentine market. By 1993, Venezuelan paper producers had reduced cost through the aggressive use of local recycling and the development of small and medium-scale plantations, but for most paper products, not to a level where they could compete internationally with the lowest-cost Latin American producers.

In the early 1990s, low international pulp prices due to a depressed world market favored importation of pulp and dampened enthusiasm for large-scale investments in Venezuelan pulp mills, at least in the short term. However, Venezuelan paper manufacturers were formulating creative responses to the problem of securing a long-term supply of pulp at a competitive price. They were investing in greater pulping and recycling capacity as well as small- and medium-scale plantations of both long- and short-fiber trees. In 1993, the Grupo Delfino owned or had ownership interests in more than 67,000 hectares of Caribbean pines, a thermo-chemical-mechanical pulp plant for Caribbean pine with an annual capacity of 24,000 metric tons, and plants for the recovery of recycled fiber. Smurfit owned more than 12,000 hectares of plantations, with a total of 60,000 hectares planned. It had a short-fiber wood pulp with 15,000 metric ton capacity and a cane pulp mill with 50,000 metric ton capacity. Papeles Venezolanos had over 12,000 hectares of pines and eucalyptus either under cultivation or in the planning stage, and a wood pulp plant with a 36,000 metric ton capacity. Venepal, a domestic company which does not own forestry plantations in Venezuela, had purchased 25 percent of Celgar, a Canadian pulp producer with a production capacity of 420,000 metric tons of long-fiber Kraft pulp, in order to reduce the risk and costs associated with pulp imports.[31]

The privately owned pulp plants installed to date in Venezuela are far from efficient scale, which, as mentioned earlier, is currently between 300,000 and 500,000 metric tons annually for a state-of-the-art Kraft pulp plant. In 1993, despite low prices, some Venezuelan paper producers were considering major investments in domestic forest plantations and pulp capacity. Some were reportedly weighing the viability of investing, together with foreign partners, in efficient-scale Kraft pulp mills to utilize state-owned and privately grown pines. The potential benefits are immense, but so are the risks, and the outcome will depend on future market developments, the strategies of foreign competitors, and, ultimately, the ability of the Venezuelan industry to compete on cost with the lowest-cost producers in the world. (See Figure 4.2.)

Unfulfilled Potential

Although the Venezuelan pulp and paper industry remains largely undeveloped, it has vast potential. Venezuelan forestry land is among the least expensive anywhere. Planting costs are low.[32] Low land and planting costs and fast-growing trees mean low-cost logs, the single largest element of variable cost in the production of pulp. With a growing cycle of 12 to 15 years, compared to 60 years or more in northern latitudes, Venezuelan plantations should be able to harvest three to four generations of pines in the time required for a Canadian grower to bring one crop to harvest. Hydroelectric power and abundant reserves of natural gas should keep energy costs equal to, or lower than, that of major competitors. The Orinoco River should provide ample water for the production process and easy transportation of products, with good access to potential port sites. Moreover, the sources of

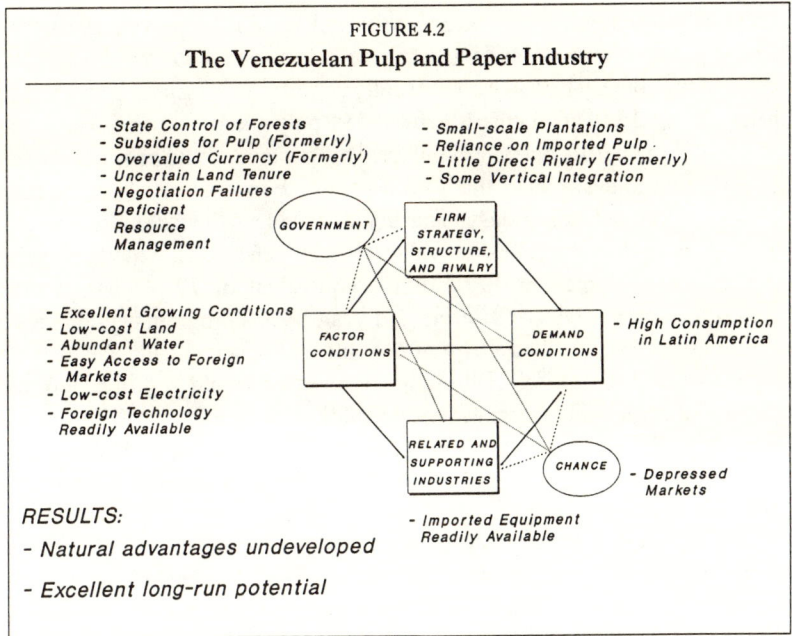

FIGURE 4.2
The Venezuelan Pulp and Paper Industry

RESULTS:
- Natural advantages undeveloped
- Excellent long-run potential

energy and water are located very close to the existing plantations of Caribbean pine and the future site of projected pulp and saw mills. Venezuelan labor costs are well below those in the United States and are unlikely to rise much above the level of Latin American competitors. Geographically, the nation is also well situated with respect to the major export markets of North and Central America and Europe, in comparison with such regional competitors as Brazil, Chile, and Argentina.

The Venezuelan government has designated about 9 million hectares for coniferous forest plantations; as of 1993, only 6 percent of these lands were being used.[33] Current forecasts project that a total of 825,000 hectares will be under cultivation within the next ten years. In 1993, the Venezuelan paper industry was reportedly considering long-term investments that could expand forest plantations to 1.6 million hectares by the year 2010.[34] When we consider that more than 19 million hectares of land are suitable for plantation forests in the nation, we begin to see the immensity of the long-term, untapped potential for forestry in Venezuela.

If Venezuela were to create the conditions to exploit its basic factor endowments in forestry, its pulp and paper industry could be a very important contributor to the economy. For example, if two pulp plants of approximately

400,000 metric ton capacity each were brought on line by the year 2010, they would generate, directly and indirectly, an estimated 6,800 well-paid jobs in areas of the country that are economically depressed.[35] Assuming an average price of U.S. $650 per metric ton, these two pulp plants also would generate $520 million in gross revenue annually. This revenue would be split between exports and domestic sales that would substitute for imports. Thus the total change in Venezuela's trade balance in pulp could reach $520 million a year. That is more than ten times the value of total Venezuelan exports of pulp, paper, and cardboard in 1991, or the equivalent of 20 percent of total Venezuelan non-oil exports during that year. Such a program would require a total investment of at least $1.4 billion, most of which would have to come from foreign sources.[36] Growth in the pulp sector would in turn benefit the paper and cardboard sector, generating additional benefits for the economy as a whole. While two pulp plants would make a major economic contribution, they would represent only a small fraction of Venezuela's long-term potential in this sector.

Venezuela's potential advantages in pulp and paper lie mainly in basic factor conditions. In many industries, the absence of several elements—advanced demand, world-class technology development, well-developed related and supporting industries, and internationally oriented strategies on the part of local firms—would limit the nation's ability to export. In the pulp and paper industry, however, the pace of technological change is rather slow. Leading edge technology and forest management expertise are generally available through major multinational companies. Most products are sold in standard grades on the basis of price. Increasingly, the name of the game is low-cost factors of production and the management capability to develop them. In this industry, the other determinants are less vital to international success.

Under favorable world market conditions, the Venezuelan pulp and paper industry has great promise. However, guaranteeing private investors either secure, long-term access to inputs through long-term leases or private ownership of the forest plantation lands is essential. Only through increased participation by the private sector will Venezuela harvest competitive advantage from its natural endowments in this industry.

Lessons from the Venezuelan Pulp and Paper Industry

A number of lessons can be learned from the story of the Venezuelan pulp and paper industry. Proper development of natural resources requires a long-term strategy and clear and binding long-term commitments. Issues surrounding land tenancy, power costs, and raw materials supplies must be resolved before the pulp and paper industry can develop to its full potential. Policies that change quickly will not support the development of any industry with a long time horizon. Such industries require stable policy environments and a business infrastructure that can finance development that has a long-term payback. Private sector companies will not wish to rely upon state entities that have a history of changing terms and conditions with political cycles.

It will take time to develop Venezuela's nontraditional export industries. The damage done by past policies must first be repaired and the new strategies that are now possible developed. It has been only five years since the market was opened, the bolivar was floated, and subsidies removed. In the forest products sector, the main forestry lands are still in the hands of the state, not the private sector. While some uses for Venezuela's forest resources can be developed quickly, others will take more time. It takes roughly five years to construct a new large-scale pulp and paper facility. It takes 12 to 15 years to grow a forest of Caribbean pines. It will take years or decades before Venezuela can make up for the time it has lost and truly develop its sources of competitive advantage in the industry.

Access to modern, effective capital markets will be required if the Venezuelan economy is to reach its full potential. To do so, large investments, on the order of hundreds of millions or even billions of dollars, will be necessary. The lack of long-term financing at reasonable rates within Venezuela is a critical shortcoming that hinders any investment that takes time to bear fruit. Deeper equity markets, pension funds managed by institutional investors, banking reform, and a financially sound government, which would result in lower local and foreign-based interest rates, will be necessary if the Venezuelan private sector is to make large, long-term investments. Otherwise, only foreign firms and a few large local groups will be able to participate. Private sector firms, reflecting the lack of long-term capital markets, have asked the Venezuelan government to subsidize private sector plantation development. A much better solution would be to implement policies that stabilize government finances, strengthen equity markets, and create pools of capital in the hands of institutional investors who could afford to take a long-term perspective. The Venezuelan government should think long and hard before agreeing to any subsidized financing. Private sector firms should consider raising equity capital if long-term loans are not available.

Venezuela has paid a huge price for "getting prices wrong" in terms of the distortions introduced by the subsidies and preferential exchange policies of the past. These distortions not only diminished the efficiency of Venezuelan public spending, they also sent the wrong signals for Venezuelan investment. Distortions large enough to make imports more cost effective than investing in what might be the world's most favorable location for forestry and pulp production might be difficult to imagine, but that is precisely what happened in this industry in the 1980s. Though the Venezuelan pulp and paper industry represents an extreme case, the distortions of the old system changed hundreds or thousands of investment decisions throughout the economy, each inflicting its cost on the Venezuelan economy in terms of inefficient spending and foregone opportunities.

Finally, this industry shows the consequences of extending state intervention beyond its optimal duration. The state did contribute to starting up the forestry sector in the 1960s and 1970s by identifying the economic potential of Venezuela's forestry lands and founding experimental plantations. However, it decided to develop the sector itself rather than open it fully to participation by private enterprise. The cost of this decision has been very high. In telenovelas, Venezuela has no natural resources yet the private sector has built an industry that is a world leader. In pulp, Venezuela has what might be the finest natural resources in the world, but the state has failed to produce pulp for export after 30 years of trying.

The Venezuelan Tourism Sector[37]

International tourism is a young sector of the Venezuelan economy that grew rapidly during the 1980s. In 1992, Venezuela's tourism sector earned $282 million in foreign exchange (down from $365 million in 1991), ranking fourth after petroleum, aluminum, and iron and steel. Venezuela's balance of trade in tourism was, and remains, negative. In 1991, Venezuela did not rank among the world's top 60 tourism earners (neighboring Colombia ranked sixtieth), but Venezuela ranked thirty-second in the world in tourism expenditures, with total expenditures in 1991 of more than $1 billion.[38] Tourism has substantial long-term potential in Venezuela as a source of revenue and employment, but there are obstacles to overcome. This sector highlights issues specific to the development of service-based industries in a developing economy. It also illustrates the foregone opportunities that ensue when government intervention lingers beyond its useful life.

Venezuela possesses spectacular natural conditions for tourism. It has 2,400 kilometers of Caribbean coastline (more than Caribbean islands so famous for beach tourism), Andean mountains, Amazonian rain forest, and unique regions such as the *Llanos* (extensive floodplains renowned for their semiaquatic birds and animals) and the *Tepuyes* (ancient mountain formations that rise from the forest in the southeastern corner of the country).

However, Venezuela has not yet found ways to manage its tourism resources effectively. Some seem to believe that Venezuela is so rich in natural attractions that there is room for error in developing the service and business side of the sector. In the words of one sector spokesman, "Venezuela is an extraordinary country, so extraordinary that even if we should do things badly, it will come out ahead in its touristic development and in its economic and social development."[39] In the words of another, "in tourism we have left the matter up to nature. In effect, to God, who provides for fine beaches, awesome natural beauty, a magnificent variety of climates and terrain, and we leave it at that."[40] In tourism, as in many other industries in Venezuela, there is a tendency to rely too heavily on natural resource endowments as a source of competitive advantage.

Venezuela does have natural advantages, but only creative development and marketing of these advantages will lead to success in the marketplace. Tourism is a sector in which created factors—infrastructure and human skills, including service, management, and marketing skills—are becoming more and more important in the quest for competitive advantage. Competition in international tourism is fierce and is focusing increasingly on the quality of service. For example, Venezuela's competitors in the Caribbean are now defining competitiveness in terms of "achieving the highest possible standards for the total tourism product."[41] It will be essential for Venezuela to offer first-rate services and infrastructure and also to master the fine art of differentiating its tourist products in international markets. See Table 4.4 for a comparison of tourism receipts in selected nations.

The Most International of Services

Tourism is the largest service activity in the traded sector worldwide. In 1989, tourism and travel accounted for more than $2.5 trillion in gross output, or 5.5 percent of world gross national product (GNP).[42] Over the past 30 years, international tourism has grown considerably faster than world trade in goods. The international tourist purchases a series of services from different businesses, including international and local transportation, lodging, meals, and entertainment. Tourists are defining the notion of vacation increasingly in terms of the consumption of services. Disney World, in Orlando, Florida, a wonderland whose attractions are entirely man-made, is perhaps the best example of this trend.

The two major tourist products offered by Venezuela are beach vacations and ecotourism vacations. In the beach resort segment, Venezuela competes primarily with the islands of the Caribbean and Mexico. In 1991, Venezuela ranked fifth among Caribbean destinations in total inter-

TABLE 4.4
International Tourism Receipts, Selected Countries, 1991

Millions of U.S. $

Country	Receipts	World Rank
United States	45,551	1
Spain	19,004	4
Switzerland	7,064	8
Mexico	4,355	12
Argentina	2,336	26
Brazil	1,559	31
Puerto Rico	1,445	34
Bahamas	1,222	38
Jamaica	764	49
Chile	700	51
Colombia	410	60
Venezuela	**365**	**n.a.**
Uruguay	333	n.a.
Costa Rica	310	n.a.
St. Maarten	310	n.a.
Peru	277	n.a.
Guatemala	211	n.a.
Ecuador	189	n.a.
Trinidad and Tobago	101	n.a.
Belize	95	n.a.

Source: United Nations, World Tourism Organization (1993).

national visitors, with an estimated 600,000 visitors, of whom only about one-half, or 300,000, were tourists.[43] In contrast, the Bahamas, a leading Caribbean destination, attracted 1.4 million international visitors.[44] Jamaica, the United States Virgin Islands, and Puerto Rico each attracted more international visitors than Venezuela despite their smaller size and much more limited endowment of natural attractions.[45] Mexico, which was not included in the Caribbean statistics, registered 16.5 million foreign

TABLE 4.5
Tourism Revenues as a Percentage of GDP, 1991

Foreign Tourist Spending

Country	Percentage of GDP
Portugal	6.0
Greece	3.6
Spain	3.6
Ireland	3.4
Switzerland	3.0
New Zealand	2.5
Chile	2.2
Mexico	1.9
Venezuela	**0.6**
Brazil	0.4

Source: World Economic Forum (1993).

visitors in 1991.[46] Table 4.5 shows that tourism accounts for a relatively small percentage of Venezuelan gross domestic product (GDP).

In the early 1990s, ecotourism, which attracted about 15 percent of Venezuela's foreign visitors, was growing faster than conventional resort tourism in the nation. It attracts high-income travelers willing to spend hundreds of dollars per day to experience nature with the assistance of expert guides. Compared to resort tourism, it is an inherently low-volume activity because its destinations are ecologically delicate and support relatively small numbers of visitors. However, ecotourists spend much more per capita than do beach tourists. In this segment, Venezuela competes with such countries as Belize, Costa Rica, Trinidad and Tobago, Peru, and Ecuador.

Building a Service Sector

Prior to 1982, the Venezuelan tourist sector catered primarily to domestic visitors.[47] Thereafter, the devaluations of the bolivar made Venezuela an affordable Caribbean destination for winter visitors from abroad. Foreign demand spurred rapid growth and, in such locales as Margarita, outstripped the existing supply of accommodations. The 1980s were the era of the "charter" or "all-inclusive" deal, in which the vacationer paid a flat fee in advance for transportation, meals, lodging, and entertainment. The arrangement brought many visitors, but their per-capita spending was low. Many of the new hotel operators had a background in construction, not services, and were not oriented toward serving tourists. The aim was short-term profit, perhaps at the expense of return visitors and long-term development.

By 1994, the Venezuelan tourism sector was larger and more sophisticated. Large investments had been made in tourist facilities, infrastructure, and training. Many hotels and travel agencies in Caracas and the interior, both large and small, had mastered the art of serving the customer. However, the level of service throughout the sector as a whole was uneven.[48] An issue of an English-language Venezuelan tourism newspaper reported on a hotel fire caused by careless workmen, allegedly corrupt activities in a tourist port, and the overnight abandonment of a group of tourists by their pilot after poor weather forced an unscheduled landing. In the words of two British tourists on the trip, "we would have expected an apology from the airline and tour company but they seemed at a loss to understand why we were complaining."[49] The tourist newspaper that reported these incidents soon was banned from some Venezuelan hotels and could not find a Venezuelan printer willing to print subsequent editions.[50]

These incidents are not recounted here to characterize the tourist sector overall. As Corpoturismo has documented, the great majority of tourists who visit Venezuela comment favorably on their trip upon departure.[51] However, the Venezuelan tourist sector must be able to compete for tourists in the international market. Even a small number of unhappy incidents can be a source of competitive disadvantage for a sector that attracts foreign tourists on the basis of reputation. In 1990, only 16 percent of foreign tourists decided to visit Venezuela on the basis of television or printed advertising, while 27 percent were influenced by the recommendation of their friends.[52] Under these circumstances, Venezuela's tourist sector must speak for itself by sending home satisfied customers.

Tourists and immigrants always have been welcome in Venezuela and many travelers enjoy the service, hospitality, and warm reception that they receive. These facts could be turned into a competitive advantage if service levels are brought up to par. Building a world-class tourist sector from the ground up is a large undertaking. High-quality service requires infrastructure and well organized management. It also requires a commitment throughout the sector to mastering the service ethic. Creating a commitment to service is a major challenge for Venezuela, where many still equate the term "service" with "servility." This is a reflection, in part, of the youth of the Venezuelan tourism sector, which began to focus on the international tourist segment only around ten years ago. In the words of one industry member, "we were a rich country, at least in our own minds up till 1983. And the thinking was that a rich people do not work in tourism."[53]

The State's Involvement

Until the late 1980s, the state maintained a policy of active intervention in tourism. Corpoturismo, the central regulating agency for the sector, was created to be all-powerful in its regulation of market transactions. Corpoturismo classified hotels into categories defined by number of stars, which in turn determined the daily rates that each hotel was permitted to charge. The goal was to protect consumers by ensuring that they receive fair value for their money. Corpoturismo also regulated the substance and price of tour packages and required that all applications to set up new tourism companies be accompanied by economic and financial feasibility studies.

The results were not conducive to growth or good service. The hotel rating system lost credibility when it became common practice to "buy" stars by making illicit payments to public employees. This resulted in "star inflation," whereby customers paid more for less. There was a saying in the industry that a five-star hotel in Caracas was worth only three stars in Paris.[54] Regulation of package content discouraged innovation in the sector. In one instance, a hotel put together a package to attract tourists traveling as families, which included day care in the fixed price; Corpoturismo disapproved it on the ground that day care was not an item to be included in packages but instead must be optional.[55]

Government regulations created barriers to entry across the tourist sector, from hotels to travel agents to bus drivers. This was exacerbated by the large number of public entities with jurisdiction of one sort or another over tourism. Not only were numerous permits required, but in some cases the requirements of different regulatory agencies conflicted, all of which added to the time and cost of setting up business. According to Boza (1993), more than 300 steps were required to acquire a hotel permit.

State ownership and operation of hotels in Venezuela got its start in the 1950s under the dictatorship of Marcos Pérez Jiménez. Before 1983, Venezuela was an expensive destination attracting relatively few foreign tourists, and the private sector had little interest in making major investments in tourism. A state agency, the National Corporation of Hotels and Tourism (CONAHOTU), was created to fill this vacuum, and it either constructed or financed construction for most of the modern hotel rooms in the country. CONAHOTU contracted the management of the largest hotels to international operators but retained management of several medium-size hotels for the next 20 years.[56] By the mid-1980s, the Venezuelan government owned more than 20 hotels and tourist facilities around the country. Of these, some of the largest were operated by multinational concessionaires, including Hilton, Intercontinental, Sheraton, and Meliá. The remaining hotels were managed directly by Corpoturismo. The quality of management in the latter, for the most part, was poor, and hotel installations were allowed to deteriorate.[57]

The state has not promoted infrastructure specifically related to tourism on a sustained basis. With few exceptions, it has invested in infrastructure in general, not in tourism-related projects. On the island of Margarita, for example, the state constructed highways and roads, projects of a general nature that were not fine-tuned to the needs of tourist development. Venezuela's track record in this area reflects political values that do not support building for affluent tourists infrastructure that is lacking in local communities. In some competitor nations, such as Mexico or Aruba, governments aggressively court foreign investment in tourism by guaranteeing to provide infrastructure. The government's willingness to make such commitments confers a competitive advantage over rival sites in other countries.

Corpoturismo did try to promote foreign awareness of Venezuela as a tourist destination. Successive boards approached the task with enthusiasm and commitment. However, it has been reported that they failed to master the "ABCs of publicity" and spent their resources on publicity ventures with minimal returns.[58] In 1989, Jamaica spent $42.8 million on marketing and $6.7 million on advertising to promote its tourism sector. The Bahamas spent $29.7 million on marketing and $4.6 million on advertising.[59] In 1990, the resort of Cancún, Mexico, spent $4.7 million on advertising in the United States alone.[60] In contrast, Venezuela's entire national marketing and advertising budget for the promotion of tourism was only about $2 million.[61]

Playing Catch-Up

In the late 1980s and early 1990s, Venezuela made positive policy changes in the tourism sector. By 1993, there was less regulation and red tape and more promotion of investment. Starting in 1986, Corpoturismo gradually phased out price regulation of hotels. The elimination of price controls had a salutary impact on the hotel sector, stimulating investment. In 1993, plans were under way to discontinue the review and approval of tourist packages, a move that would stimulate innovation and growth in both the hotel and tourist agency sectors. The Tourism Law of 1993 provided for a new Fund for Tourism Promotion and Training, although as of December 1993 the fund had not been financed because of legal technicalities in the tax laws.

The state also relinquished, at least in part, its role as owner and manager of hotels. As of 1993, several hotels formerly owned by the state had been sold to private owners, for a total sales price of $17.4 million, or on average $31,200 per hotel room.[62] However, approximately 20 hotels and tourist facilities (including tourist lodges and camps) had not been privatized, and Corpoturismo still operated eight hotels. The president of Corpoturismo, responsible for planning and promoting Venezuelan tourism at the national level, still signed paperwork when a state-owned hotel bought new supplies. The status of future privatizations was uncertain.

In the early 1990s, the state took steps to attract new private investment in tourism. These included the liberalization of restrictions on foreign investment, the creation of tax incentives for investments in hotels, a new financing program funded by the Inter-American Development Bank (IDB), and a debt equity conversion program. However, as of 1993, much remained to be done. The rules of the game and investment climate were still too uncertain for many potential investors. The two coup attempts in 1992 and the ensuing political instability led to a sharp decline in tourist arrivals and discouraged some potential investors. Corpoturismo, which was seriously understaffed and underfunded, had not undertaken the task of inventorying public lands and granting land concessions for new hotels. Even the most basic public statistics on the national tourism sector were deficient. The long-term use of the national parks was a difficult issue still to be resolved. Potential investors want proof of a strong promotion policy, but as of 1993, the Fund for Tourism Promotion and Training had not been financed, and Venezuela's total annual promotional and marketing expenditures were a mere $1.7 million.[63]

The government has an important role to play in tourism, in such areas as infrastructure, human resources, data collection and analysis, the promotion of the nation in foreign markets, the promotion of private investment, the management of state lands, and long-range planning. If Venezuela is going to compete successfully in coming years for inflows of tourists and foreign investment, Corpoturismo must be provided the human, financial, and technical resources to perform its tasks effectively.

Tourism is a labor-intensive sector. Foote and Hawkins (1991) estimate that the Venezuelan hotel sector alone employs between 15,000 and 30,000 workers. As a rule, each five-star hotel room generates one job directly and many more jobs indirectly.

The vast majority of these jobs require only basic skills combined with the right attitude, the so-called service mentality. Nevertheless, the Venezuelan tourist sector faces an across-the-board shortage of qualified employees.

The most serious shortage exists at the level of service workers who come into daily contact with tourists—such as receptionists and porters. These positions require basic literacy, numeracy, and foreign language training, abilities that should be imparted at the primary and secondary school level. Unfortunately, the public schools are failing at their task. As of 1992, 53 percent of Venezuelan students abandoned school before the end of the ninth grade, and 37 percent did not even finish primary school. (See Chapter 6.)[64] Those who stay on in secondary school do not, on average, develop the foundation required for entry-level jobs in hotels, except for menial employment. Workers with basic skills are a sought-after elite, who often aspire to immediate advancement and are dissatisfied in entry-level positions.

The state and the private sector both offer a number of training and educational programs at the secondary or postsecondary level. The National Institute of Educational Cooperation (INCE), through INCE TURISMO, has graduated an estimated 92,000 trainees in hotel and tourism-related areas since 1977.[65] Both public and private universities offer tourism-related courses of study at the postsecondary level. The Simón Bolívar University has run a campus devoted to tourism studies, with very good results. The Hotel Tamanaco Intercontinental has run a successful in-house training program for workers at all levels, serving as a regional training center for Latin America. The Prado Río Hotel School, sponsored by the government of Mérida, has shown promising initiative in the hands-on training of superior technicians.

Many children, however, never make it to the secondary school level. They leave school so early and so deficient in learning that they cannot apply to INCE, much less become a superior technician or university graduate. The state and the private sector must invest in them early and well if Venezuela is to be internationally successful in tourism or, indeed, any other service sector.

A New Role for the Private Sector

Since the late 1980s, the Venezuelan tourism sector has grown significantly in size and sophistication. The primary motor of growth, prior to the coup attempts of 1992, was strong foreign demand. Tourist arrivals increased at an average rate of 14.2 percent per year between 1986 and 1991.[66] Private investors, led by the local banking sector and foreign joint venture partners, invested aggressively in hotels, transportation, and travel agencies. Private investments between 1990 and 1993 in new hotel and resort facilities that were either in operation or under construction as of 1993 were estimated by the National Council for Investment Promotion to exceed $600 million.[67] The banking crisis of 1994 adversely affected many of these projects.

In the 1990s, international hotel chains, and international travel wholesalers and reservation system networks, are playing an increasingly important role in attracting and directing transnational tourist flows. Systems of this nature already are influencing tourist flows in Venezuela as well as other Latin American nations. Foreign investors also contribute private capital and expertise. For these reasons, the continued presence of foreign firms will be important to the competitiveness of the tourism sector. However, Venezuelan tourism also would benefit from a much deeper pool of national expertise in hotel management. In contrast to neighboring Colombia, Venezuela has very few nationally owned and operated hotel chains. If the Venezuelan private sector is to increase its participation in the hotel industry, it needs to adopt a new mentality. It needs to think long term, not short term. It needs to focus on the delivery of high-quality services and to target specific niches and market its services effectively. Real estate investment is only part of the hotel business.

Industry members often observe that Venezuela has lacked a true commitment to tourism.[68] As we have seen, tourism presents many long-term opportunities for the economy. It generates foreign exchange in large quantities and creates many thousands of skilled and semiskilled jobs. It also raises political issues regarding the use of natural resources (such as national parks) and funds needed for infrastructure. A national consensus to promote tourism will achieved only if the private sector unites and makes it happen. The private sector is fragmented and the costs of this fragmentation are high. The private industry federations must be united and vigorous. There is much to be done. Greater support can be generated for tourism in business and political circles. Industry associations need to identify the needs of the sector as a whole and to formulate a long-term agenda to meet those needs.

Concerted action by the private sector is needed to promote higher levels of service throughout the sector, to deepen local management and marketing skills, and to promote human factor creation in tourism. Quality control is essential not just for the future growth of the sector but also to make the best use of the hotels and other assets already in place. The industry as a whole can take steps to ensure that all providers meet minimum standards of service, by implementing quality control programs for hotels, tour operators, airlines, and ground transportation companies. Mechanisms, such as complaint books, can be made available to tourists. It is important that tourists have confidence that their comments will be reviewed and acted upon. In the area of promotion and marketing, participants in the Venezuelan tourism sector need to ask themselves what they have that interests specific foreign markets and to focus on those targets that they can really satisfy.

Human factor creation also needs greater emphasis. The private sector can provide tourism trainees with hands-on experience to a greater extent than it does now. Private-public partnerships can be set up to improve the teaching of basic skills at the primary and secondary school levels, to teach about service-oriented careers, and to provide scholarships earmarked for education in tourism. At the postsecondary level, the private sector can work with universities and institutes to bring course curricula into closer alignment with business needs. National data bases can be set up to provide statistical information on domestic and foreign markets. Libraries can be endowed with updated reference books on tourism. As of 1993, there was a serious shortage of data on tourism, national and international, in Venezuela, and students interested in tourism had difficulty finding up-to-date information. (See Figure 4.3.)

Lessons from the Venezuelan Tourism Sector

Several lessons can be drawn from the case of the Venezuelan tourism sector that are applicable across industries. The tendency in Venezuelan business and government sectors to overestimate natural resource endowments as a source of competitive advantage is not unique to tourism. We see it in forestry, aluminum, petrochemicals, and other sectors. Natural resources, even spectacular ones, do not create wealth by themselves. They must be developed in an intelligent fashion by people with the skills to produce, market, manage, innovate, and compete.

Tourism, like other service sectors, can serve as a motor for the creation of the types of human resources that the entire economy needs to become more competitive. Building this sector right will require public and private sector investments in primary and secondary education, business education, hands-on training, and knowledge resources. All of these investments are important leverage points for economic growth. For example, strengthening the Venezuelan tourism sector will require developing a stronger service ethic among students, workers, and management. This should have beneficial spillover effects in other areas of the Venezuelan economy, by promoting a clearer understanding of the importance of putting the customer first.

If any country is to realize its potential in today's international markets, the government must perform its core functions well. Tourism is a good example, because of the importance of public infrastructure, foreign promotion, data collection, stewardship of the public lands, and long-term planning.

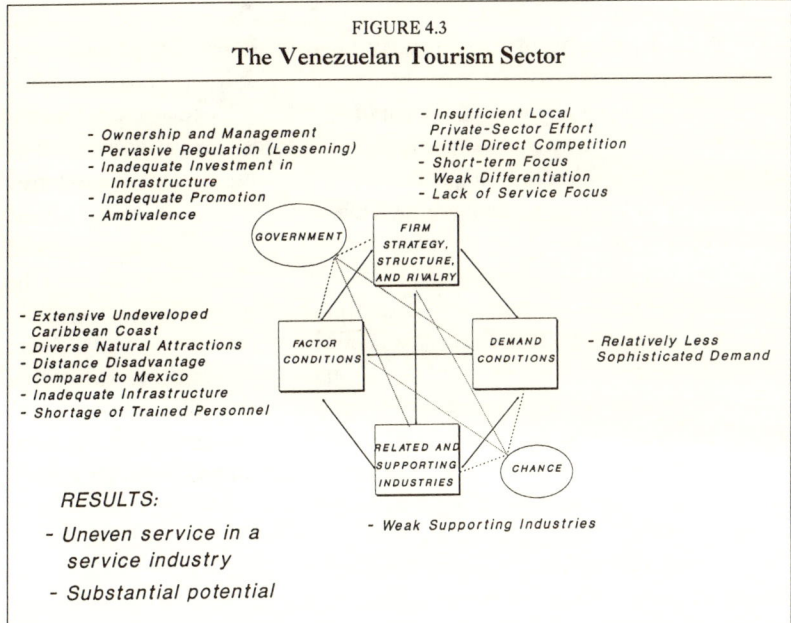

FIGURE 4.3
The Venezuelan Tourism Sector

These are difficult tasks. Changing from the role of active participant to the role of promoter and planner has presented the Venezuelan government with a new set of challenges. A good start has been made in this direction, but the country must make a clear commitment to a long-term strategy.

The tourism sector, like many other sectors in the Venezuelan economy, is new to international competition. Some growing pains as Venezuelan operators become familiar with international standards are to be expected. The Venezuelan tourism sector has substantial potential. Both the government and the private sector are learning what is involved in competing in this service sector in international markets. The speed and extent of this learning will in large part determine the future of the Venezuelan tourism sector.

The Venezuelan Petrochemical Industry[69]

The petrochemical sector is one of Venezuela's leading sectors in terms of its contribution to manufacturing GDP and exports. In 1992, petrochemicals were the nation's fifth largest export, earning $260 million in foreign exchange.[70] Venezuela produces petrochemicals primarily for domestic consumption, exporting about 32 percent of its production.[71] However, the nation is highly dependent on imports. In 1992, its imports of chemicals and petrochemicals exceeded its exports by almost $1.1 billion. The petrochemical industry highlights a number of issues that the Venezuelan economy faces, including the role of state-owned companies, capital costs, natural resource pricing, technology acquisition, and responses to market pressures. Questions also arise concerning Venezuela's ability to take advantage of natural resources in downstream industries.

Petrochemicals, a Challenging Business

The world petrochemical industry is a challenging business. Efficient scale production generally requires very large capital investments. Large investments, high fixed costs, and commodity products mean that petrochemical firms tend to compete on price in order to increase sales volume and keep capacity utilization high. Margins are also under constant pressure from substitute products, including other petrochemicals and nonpetrochemical products such as metal, wood, and glass.

Petrochemicals are generally classified as basic, intermediate, or advanced products. Most basic and intermediate petrochemical products are commodities produced with mature technologies. The key to success in basic petrochemicals is to offer low prices, large volumes, and a reliable supply. Success in intermediate products, such as polymers, often involves offering a variety of products and meeting the particular specifications of individual clients. At this level, research and development (R&D) focuses more on developing new product applications than on major product breakthroughs. Marketing efforts focus on meeting customers' specific needs in terms of quality, price, and delivery. More advanced products, such as engineering plastics and polymers, draw on new technologies and obtain the highest prices. Technological sophistication and in-depth knowledge of customers' needs are essential to success in these products. As a nation moves from basic to advanced petrochemical products, possessing low-cost raw materials becomes less of an advantage.

The petrochemical industry is generally cyclical, with growth correlated directly to periods of general economic growth and, in most countries, inversely to the price of petroleum. However, the Venezuelan petrochemical industry differs from most with respect to its relation to petroleum prices. The primary raw material of much of Venezuela's petrochemical production is based on natural gas, rather than oil, while its use of petroleum as a raw material is much less developed. Venezuela's abundance of natural gas is an important factor advantage in many product lines, such as olefins, in contrast to other countries that import naphtha (a petroleum derivative) as a raw material. The Venezuelan petrochemical sector is less dependent on petroleum than those of many other countries, and Venezuelan gas-based olefins become more price competitive as international oil prices rise.

The Venezuelan petrochemical industry produces mainly basic industrial inputs (including ammonia; methyl-tertiary-butyl-ether, or MTBE; and sulfuric acid), fertilizers (urea, nitrogen-phosphorous-potassium formulas, and ammonia sulfate), plastics (such as high-density polyethylene, low-density polyethylene, polypropylene, polystyrene, and polyvinylchloride), and olefins (ethylene and propylene). Venezuela also produces smaller quantities of aromatics (cyclic hydrocarbons and their derivatives, including benzene, toluene, and o-xylene). Engineering plastics and polymers, products at the high end of the value added chain, are not produced in Venezuela.[72] Pequiven, a wholly owned subsidiary of the state oil company, PDVSA, is the largest Venezuelan producer of primary petrochemicals, while mixed Pequiven–private sector companies supply a variety of products, from olefins, to intermediate products, to plastic resins used directly in the manufacture of consumer goods. In 1990, the total sales of Pequiven and the mixed enterprises amounted to about $800 million. (This was less than one-third of the sales of the Canadian firm Nova, which, in turn, ranked twentieth worldwide in sales.) A smaller segment of firms are totally owned by private capital; these account for about 30 percent of the industry's total production. The most important of these firms manufacture resins and tend to be integrated downstream into the production of paint products. Table 4.6 compares exports of selected nations for several petrochemical products.

The State Builds an Industry

For 40 years, the state has played the lead role in the Venezuelan petrochemical industry. In the 1950s, it formed the Venezuelan Petrochemical Institute (IVP), which set about to design and build an industry that would use the natural gas and petroleum by-products of the oil industry and in which the state would be the primary producer. It also encouraged the formation of a series of mixed enterprises, with capital from the state and from national and foreign investors. Química Venoco, Nitroven, and Monomeros Colombo-Venezolanos all got their start during the 1960s. The state-owned plants were the principal producers of fertilizers, chlorine and caustic soda, and explosives. The production of the mixed enterprises focused on polystyrene and polyethylene (for the production of plastics), alkylbenzenes and polyphosphates (for detergents), and basic industrial inputs such as aluminum sulfate, phthalic anhydride, and chlorofluorocarbons. Some privately owned

TABLE 4.6
1990 Petrochemical Exports, Selected Countries and Products

Millions of U.S. $

Country	Acyclic Hydrocarbons[a]	Polyethylene	Cyclic Hydrocarbons[b]	Urea	Polycarbonates
United States	442	1,130	1,093	139	88
Holland	1,073	1,242	1,353	149	66
Germany	167	1,488	546	44	46
Canada	160	668	535	208	n.a.
Saudi Arabia	64	535	247	55	-
Indonesia	-	792	0.6	191	-
South Korea	24	122	245	-	n.a.
Singapore	48	338	64	3	-
Brazil	54	156	191	24	2
Mexico	11	13	1	37	-
Argentina	-	68	-	-	-
Venezuela	**8**	**25**	**0.8**	**34**	**-**

[a] Mostly olefins.
[b] Includes aromatics.

Source: Balaguer and Segnini (1993), citing United Nations (1991) and Stanford Research Institute (1990).

companies, such as Resimon, also started up at this time, focusing on the production of intermediate products for use in paints and consumer and industrial chemicals. There never were legal restrictions on the participation of private capital, domestic or foreign, in this industry.

The size and sophistication of domestic demand have been important factors in the rise of competitive petrochemical industries worldwide. The nations that built the first petrochemical industries in the 1950s had large and sophisticated home markets. Later, countries such as South Korea and Taiwan started their petrochemical industries with the production of ethylene, an input used by their export-oriented textile sectors in polyester fibers. In those countries, export-oriented industries (textiles and, later, consumer electronics) provided a major stimulus to petrochemical production. Venezuelan domestic demand for petrochemicals always has been relatively small and unsophisticated. From the start, the Venezuelan industry was structured to serve this demand. Its earliest production concentrated in fertilizers, urea in particular, for local consumption. Although the industry eventually diversified its production, the limited size and sophistication of domestic demand translated into small production volumes and a focus on basic products that would have serious long-term consequences for the industry.

In international markets, the sudden rise in world oil prices in 1973-1974 shifted comparative advantages in petrochemicals to countries that produced petroleum and gas, which could set transfer prices for feedstocks at levels lower than world prices. This stimulated the rise of new export-oriented petrochemical industries in the Middle East and Africa. In contrast, Venezuelan policy and industry continued to focus on import substitution. Protection was provided by a high effective tariff rate and by import licensing requirements. Plants constructed to serve the Venezuelan market were far smaller than the minimum efficient scale for production. Except for the urea plants, many of the major plants built before 1989 are much smaller than the international average. Such plants would never be able to compete effectively on international markets. At the time, however, this was not a concern because the industry was protected from foreign competition.

The Venezuelan petrochemical sector grew in size in the 1970s. By 1977, it was producing approximately 600,000 metric tons per year, 60 percent for the domestic market and 40 percent for export, and employed over 2,200 workers. However, capacity utilization was only 25 percent and the industry's financial performance was dismal. In 1977, the IVP's losses were estimated at $140 million.[73] In 1978, the IVP was transformed into Pequiven, which in turn was made a subsidiary of PDVSA. PDVSA launched an effort to rehabilitate the petrochemical sector. It improved the management and operations of the state-owned firms and, over the course of five years, managed to turn a small profit. By 1986, Pequiven felt sufficiently confident to try to expand the industry within the protected market. Investments were made to diversify production for national consumption, rather than to expand exports.

Worldwide, the petrochemical industry is generally dominated by only a few producers per product line. However, the firms within each oligopoly tend to compete fiercely with each other. Successive generations of petrochemical products have distinct product life cycles that are driven by evolving industrial demand. Leading firms invest heavily in R&D to ensure leadership in future product generations. High investment and fixed costs make capacity utilization critical to profitability. This generates strong pressure for firms to expand their market shares, and they do so by competing on efficiency, price, quality, and innovation. Firms also face competition from substitute products, petrochemical and nonpetrochemical, which pressure them to maximize the efficient operation of their plants.

TABLE 4.7
Number of Producers of Petrochemical
Products in Selected Countries, 1990

Country	Ethylene/ Propylene	High-Density Polyethylene	Benzene	Polycarbonates
United States	22	16[a]	24	3
Germany	8	4	7	1
Japan	11	13	10	6
Canada	4	4	6	n.a.
Brazil	4	5	8	1
Mexico	1	1	2	0
Argentina	4	2	2	0
Venezuela	1	1	1	0

[a] Includes high- and low-density polyethylene.

Source: Balaguer and Segnini (1993), citing Stanford Reseach Institute (1990), Chapman (1991), UNIDO (1990/1991).

The industry structure built by the Venezuelan state was different from that found in most other nations. By promoting import substitution in a small domestic market, the state built scale inefficiencies into the industry. In many instances, product lines were concentrated in a single producer. (See Table 4.7.) Local rivalry was essentially precluded, as was rivalry from foreign products and substitutes. Within their protected market, local producers had little incentive or opportunity to develop the technological proficiency and business skills critical to survival in world markets. Overall, levels of technological proficiency were low, as were capacity utilization rates. Domestic firms as a whole did not seek out and identify customer needs. Because the domestic producers of end products were also protected from imports, user industries felt little competitive pressure, which limited their sophistication as buyers. They exerted little pressure on Venezuelan petrochemical firms to improve efficiency or quality, or to move downstream to products with specialized applications. Meanwhile, the state's program of fertilizer subsidies fed demand for urea and other petrochemicals used in fertilizers, instead of more advanced petrochemical products.

The Opening: New Pressures and New Growth

The economic opening that started in 1989 resulted in major changes for the Venezuelan petrochemical industry. Tariffs were lowered, prices were deregulated, and subsidies were reduced or eliminated. The political climate for private investment improved. The state sought to redefine its role from that of the major industry participant to a promoter of growth. It reoriented its growth policies for the sector, toward new businesses, toward exports, and toward global markets. The timing of these events was in some ways unfortunate. World prices for petrochemicals fell dramatically in the early 1990s, with prices for some products reaching record lows. Within Venezuela, real interest rates rose to high levels as economic uncertainty increased and banks were forced to adjust to the new environment. Imports, mainly from the United States, put severe pressure on Venezuelan petrochemical prices. Many Venezuelan chemical firms were not ready for the changes. Subscale petrochemical facilities designed to serve the domestic market, for example, were now forced to compete with world-scale plants in other nations. These reforms raised the level of competition in the industry, even among Pequiven's joint ventures. In polyethylene, for example, different Pequiven joint ventures were once directed at different markets. By 1993, they were competing with each other in the marketplace.

The risk profile of the industry changed dramatically. Under the old system, import levels for a petrochemical product not produced in Venezuela could be monitored in order to determine local demand. Then a plant could be built, often with subsidized financing, to meet this demand. Once the plant came on stream, imports would be reduced or forbidden and prices that ensured profitability could be negotiated with the government. In such an environment, private investors' investment in petrochemical facilities was often risk free and very profitable. In the years following the economic opening, investment became much more risky. Financing was no longer subsidized, local firms had to compete with imports, and prices were set on world markets. The result was that it was possible to invest in a plant, have it brought on line on time and on specification, and have it lose money due to falling world prices. Technological proficiency is a necessary, but not sufficient, condition for success in the petrochemical business.

Despite these difficulties, during the early 1990s state and private investors were seeking out and acting on promising investment opportunities. The commercial opening also made it possible to develop projects for the export market that would not have been viable otherwise. As of 1993, investments for petrochemical expansion planned from 1993 to 1998 totaled approximately $1.5 billion. These projects included new facilities for methanol in Jose ($670 million) (start-up anticipated in late 1994), linear-low-density-polyethylene at El Tablazo ($250 million), and aromatics in Cardón ($231 million). These plants were expected to produce primarily for export markets, a focus that would permit the exploitation of economies of scale. All of these plants would have installed capacities greater than the international average.

In addition, during the early 1990s many Venezuelan chemical firms were responding to changes in their environment by changing the way they did business. Prices, efficiency, and pleasing the customer were all taking on new meaning. Before the commercial opening, firms did not have to worry about marketing their petrochemical products in the home market. Afterward, they started developing new marketing skills. Competition and the high cost of capital forced some firms to become more efficient, to reduce inventories, and to improve management. Several firms made substantial efforts to improve quality and efficiency. Several were addressing export markets, some for the first time. Companies that had not marketed outside Venezuela began to set up commercial offices in other countries.

The economic opening did not change PDVSA's status as a monopoly supplier of feedstocks, Pequiven's status as a monopoly supplier of basic petrochemicals, or the status of various mixed companies as monopoly producers of intermediate products. According to industry sources, attitudes and operating procedures within PDVSA and Pequiven did not change all that much in the early 1990s. What did change was the pressure for short-term profitability in both PDVSA (due to heavy taxation and cash-flow problems) and Pequiven (which as of 1993 had to be self-sufficient). In 1993, some in the industry were worried that pressure for profitability would cause PDVSA and Pequiven to charge monopoly prices for feedstocks and inputs and to divert supplies to foreign buyers.

Despite the increase in sophistication of local demand after the commercial opening, domestic demand remains a source of competitive disadvantage. The Venezuelan market is small in world terms. In 1990, Latin America represented only 4 percent of total world consumption of petrochemicals, and Venezuela, in turn, accounted for only 4 percent of Latin American consumption, far behind Brazil (50 percent of Latin American consumption) and Mexico (39 percent of Latin American consumption). Domestic demand is weighted heavily toward traditional products, such as urea, and is relatively undeveloped in specialty petrochemical products. Balaguer and Segnini (1993) observe that compared to world demand, Venezuelan industrial customers tend to place less importance on quality and more importance on price. If the resins and transforming sectors, in particu-

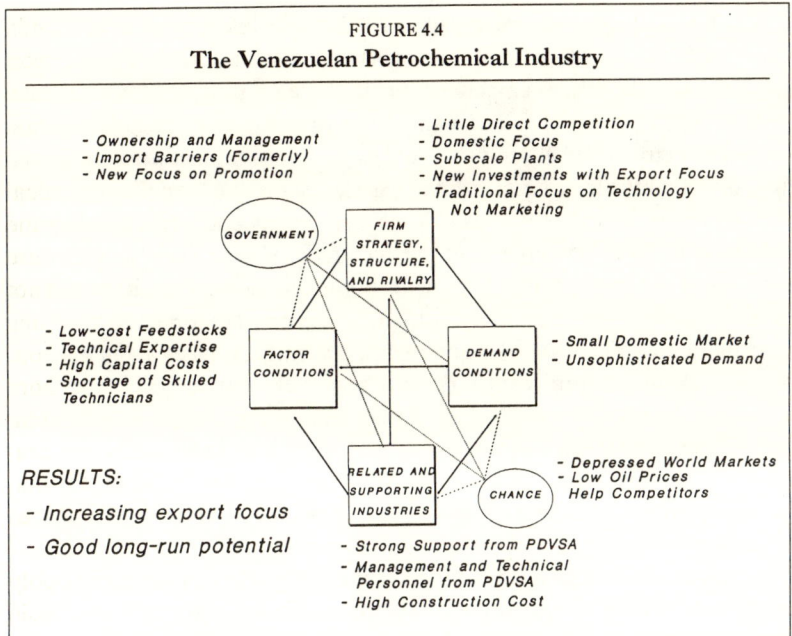

FIGURE 4.4
The Venezuelan Petrochemical Industry

lar, are to conquer export markets, they will need to learn how to compete on the basis of quality as well as price.

In 1993, the Venezuelan petrochemical industry was a mixed lot in terms of cost competitiveness. In some product lines, including those derived directly from natural gas and especially from methane, Venezuelan producers operated world-scale plants and compared favorably in cost with producers in other parts of the world. This was the case with respect to urea and also should be the case with respect to methanol when new capacity comes on line. In numerous other product lines, Venezuelan firms operated subscale plants that had much higher costs than competitors elsewhere, a legacy of the import substitution period. (See Figure 4.4.)

Challenges Going Forward

High Investment and Capital Costs. Contrary to popular belief, petrochemicals is an example of an industry in which natural resource advantages do not by themselves guarantee success. Venezuela's advantages in materials costs are indeed important. Across the petrochemical product spectrum, the nation needs low raw materials costs to be competitive in international markets. Yet while low materials costs are necessary, they are not sufficient.

Firms can have low raw materials costs and still lose out in international markets, because materials costs are only part of the total cost structure. Other cost items of the utmost importance include the cost of investment and the cost of capital, and in this area Venezuelan firms are at a disadvantage.

For petrochemical products such as ethylene and methanol, depreciation directly related to investment is the most significant item in the overall cost structure. Investment costs in Venezuela are generally reported to be on the order of 20 to 25 percent higher than in the United States and Europe, with some estimates reaching 80 percent higher. This is due in part to the need to import components, construction equipment, technology, design capabilities, and construction expertise. On average, it takes about one year longer to build a petrochemical plant in Venezuela than in the United States or Europe, in part due to a lack of infrastructure.[74]

High capital costs are coupled with high investment costs in Venezuela. Efficient production of petrochemicals demands large, capital-intensive plants, which can require investments of hundreds of millions of dollars. Very few Venezuelan firms can afford investments of this magnitude, especially in an environment with very high real interest rates and a world petrochemical environment with historically low prices. In the early 1990s, real interest rates in Venezuela have been on the order of 5 percent higher than in the United States or Europe. It is very difficult to make such investments unless one has access to dollar-denominated loans and expects to receive sales revenues in dollars. As a result, the Venezuelan industry must look to foreign capital. The risk premium for Venezuela due to doubts about the nation's intentions to honor its debt is a serious problem. During the early 1990s, this premium was as high as 13 percent. Pequiven has looked to foreign capital, even encouraging the construction of 100 percent foreign-owned facilities, such as a new Dow facility at El Tablazo.

Technology Acquisition and Assimilation. The world petrochemical industry is technology intensive, and technological capacity is an important component of competitiveness. This is true across the product spectrum, from basic to advanced petrochemicals. In the case of a developing nation such as Venezuela, which acquires most of its technological capabilities by licensing existing technologies, technological capacity encompasses far more than product and process development. It also includes the capacity to negotiate technology transfers and to acquire, to use, to assimilate, and to improve technologies.[75]

Some Venezuelan petrochemical firms have been successful in adapting and improving upon imported technology, including Química Venoco (see Chapter 6), and Polilago's low-density polyethylene plant, which reached 115 percent of its original capacity in 1992. The Venezuelan Institute for Petroleum Research, an affiliate of PDVSA, has developed patented technology in the field of catalytic distillation based on technology purchased from British Petroleum. There are other similar cases, but they are exceptions. Most technology transfers have taken the form of turnkey contracts, and the level of technology transfer has been insufficient. Traditionally, Venezuelan firms have had relatively little negotiating power vis-à-vis their licensors. The industry itself has tended to view technology as a commodity that can be purchased, rather than a dynamic, human asset.

Balaguer and Segnini (1993) have observed two common patterns of technology assimilation in the Venezuelan petrochemical industry: first, situations in which world-class or efficient-scale technology has been acquired but in which Venezuelan firms lack the technological expertise and experience to utilize their full installed capacity, and second, situations in which the firms have mastered thoroughly the technical operations of their plants but the plants themselves use second-tier technology as a result of low levels of competitive pressure in the industry. The first situation can lead rapidly to heavy losses in today's market, characterized by high capital costs and low profitability. The cost advantages derived from inexpensive natural gas and efficient-scale plants can easily be lost if firms are not able to take advantage of installed capacity in an efficient manner. In Venezuelan projects, there have been many cases of complications and work stoppages caused by technical and management errors.

The industry can do much to boost its technology capacity. Negotiation skills can be sharpened. Licensing agreements can be structured so that the future operators of the Venezuelan plants gain firsthand experience in the engineering and construction phases of each project and receive training in the licensor's plants and R&D centers. Cooperation agreements can give Venezuelan firms access to future technology improvements by the licensor. The R&D division of the Venezuelan firm can be given an active role in the negotiation and acquisition of technology, a strategy that has been successful in other developing countries, including Brazil. Many steps may be taken to build or strengthen the "technological memory" of the firm, to ensure that valuable knowledge of the licensor is transferred and systematized. Licensors often know about much more than the productive process, including information on clients, their needs, and potential product applications, and systems can be set up to transfer and store such knowledge.[76] The importance of improving the industry's technological capacity, broadly defined, bears emphasis and applies across the entire product spectrum, even to natural gas derivatives such as urea and methanol where Venezuela has its greatest cost advantages and where technologies are mature.

Feedstock and Input Costs and Availability. Possession of natural resources is not an advantage if one has to pay more for the resources than competitors, or if resource availability is uncertain. Under the import substitution regime, input prices were not an issue. Local petrochemical firms that bought inputs from Pequiven at regulated prices also sold their output at regulated prices. They had little reason to focus on input prices as long as negotiated output prices guaranteed a comfortable profit. In contrast, with the introduction of foreign competition and with prices to customers determined by market forces, input costs become critical to a firm's ability to compete. By 1993, input prices were major issues for the Venezuelan industry.

In situations where market forces determine the price of natural gas, the price tends to reach equilibrium at the marginal cost of production (including profit) plus a premium for natural resource exhaustion. This rule tends to operate in competitive markets such as the United States and Europe. However, it does not operate in Venezuela, where natural gas is produced as a by-product of oil exploration. There is no extraction cost for "associated gas" beyond the cost of extracting petroleum. The costs of separation, purification, and transportation are incurred independently of oil production, but in Venezuela these steps in the production chain take place in conditions of low competition. As a result, the pricing of natural gas in Venezuela has for years been a question of accounting conventions, and pricing methodology has lacked clarity. The absence of specific marginal costs has made it difficult for the state to justify any particular tariff structure. In contrast, aromatics, which are the other major raw material for the Venezuelan petrochemical industry, are a tradeable product produced by refining petroleum. Thus, the prices of Venezuelan aromatics are determined by market forces.

The basic petrochemicals produced by Pequiven are building blocks for the rest of the Venezuelan petrochemicals industry. The industry chamber, Association of Producers of Chemical Products (ASOQUIM), has argued that the price of these basic petrochemical inputs should be set equal to United States Gulf Coast Price minus transportation costs, because that is the best price that Pequiven could get otherwise. Pequiven, which enjoys a local monopoly in many petrochemicals and is under pressure to be profitable, has taken the position that downstream customers should pay United States Gulf Price plus transportation, because that is the best price that the customers could get otherwise. However, this raises raw material costs, which are critical to Venezuela's advantage in petrochemicals.

We have seen that capital costs are high and that Venezuelan investment costs for petrochemical facilities are higher than those of the main competitors, U.S. firms. We also know that labor costs are a small portion of total costs in the petrochemical industry. In view of this, if Venezuelan firms are to compete successfully with U.S. firms in export markets, they must have either more efficient facilities, operate their facilities more efficiently, or have access to lower-cost feedstock and inputs than their U.S. competitors. Venezuelan firms will be able to compete successfully in their own market, on the other hand, if the product is nontradeable for technical or safety reasons, or if raw materials costs, tariffs at 12 to 15 percent, and transportation costs faced by competitors offset Venezuela's higher capital and investment costs.

It will be difficult for Venezuelan firms dependent on Pequiven for basic petrochemical inputs to compete successfully in international markets unless prices are set in a way that promotes efficiency and provides a low-cost resource. The same can be said of the prices that PDVSA charges Pequiven for feedstocks. If PDVSA is to maximize its profits, then it should sell feedstocks at a monopoly price to capture as much value as it can. This situation has implications for the structure of the industry. It will be difficult for downstream companies to develop if they must pay higher prices for feedstocks than competitors. On the other hand, artificially low prices might not create the right incentives for efficiency and might be subject to action under United States or European Community trade laws if "subsidized" or "dumped" products are exported to the United States or EC.

In other nations, dilemmas such as this are often prevented or resolved by vertical integration (resource companies forward-integrating into chemicals and chemical companies backward-integrating into feedstocks), or through long-term contracts. For example, an integral part of Exxon's business strategy in petrochemicals is to optimize the "synergies" between the company's refining and petrochemical production operations so as to obtain economies of scale and cost reductions in petrochemical production.[77] In Venezuela, vertical integration does exist in several segments of the petrochemical industry, but its overall level is low, and rigidities prevent firms from taking full advantage of potential scale efficiencies and low-cost inputs. Several petrochemical companies have long-term contracts with Pequiven that guarantee supplies, but Pequiven is not guaranteed feedstock supplies by PDVSA and occasional interruptions force it to import feedstocks to meet contractual obligations. One obvious solution is for Pequiven and PDVSA to reach agreements that guarantee feedstocks to Pequiven either at predetermined prices or at prices pegged to a market index. Vertical rigidities are particularly harmful in products such as polyethylene and plastic resins, where raw material cost is a relatively large component of total cost when compared to the cost structure of other petrochemicals.[78]

How Far Downstream Can We Go? In many nations, there is a natural desire to try to expand resource-based advantages into downstream industries. The Venezuelan petrochemical industry, in some ways, represents the downstream expansion of the oil and hydrocarbon sector. It is questionable how far downstream the industry can go and still be competitive in world and regional markets. As mentioned earlier, the sources of competitive advantage vary among basic, intermediate, and advanced petrochemical products. In basic petrochemicals, nations and firms that can produce at low cost and sell into commodity markets can succeed. Low-cost feedstocks, access to world-class technology, capital costs, and efficient plant operation are the key determinants of success. Natural resources alone do not ensure competitiveness in even basic petrochemicals. In intermediate goods, marketing, service, and applications research also become vital. In advanced products, advanced and sometimes proprietary technology and close contact with leading edge customers are key to success.

Left on its own, the Venezuelan industry probably would not be able to compete on world markets in anything but basic petrochemicals. It would lack both the technological skills and the marketing expertise to compete in the other portions of the industry. The joint venture structure that the industry has developed, however, makes it possible for Venezuela to compete in more than just basic petrochemicals. Foreign joint venture partners supply the technological and marketing skills to design facilities and market the end products in foreign markets. Given the state of Venezuelan capital markets, they also must supply capital. In theory, doing so would allow Venezuela to participate in any portion of the industry in which it could attract the right foreign partner and develop the skills to actually operate the facilities.

At the regional level, as of 1993, the Andean Pact nations (Colombia, Peru, Ecuador, and Bolivia) offered a promising potential market for Venezuelan petrochemicals, including plastic resins. Venezuela has the best-developed petrochemical industry in the region, which already accounts for its largest export market. The proximity of the Andean Pact nations makes them a natural market for Venezuela because many petrochemicals have high transport costs. At the same time, Venezuelan firms face several challenges in penetrating this regional market. Overall, competition is stronger and demand is more sophisticated in the regional market than in Venezuela. As Balaguer and Segnini (1993) point out, in contrast to the domestic market, Venezuelan firms must "win" the regional market. The firms will have to seek out customers and market opportunities. Regional exports in the plastic resins segment will depend on the ability of Venezuelan firms to identify clients and client needs, to develop differentiated products for specialized applications, and to provide specialized technical support for their products. This will be a challenge because it represents a new orientation for many Venezuelan firms.

To a large extent, the future success of Venezuelan petrochemicals in the regional market will depend on the domestic industry's ability to improve its overall technological capacity, marketing abilities, and organizational structure at the firm level. Strategies to raise awareness across the industry of the importance of product quality to success in export markets are urgently needed. These changes must be rapid because of existing and potential foreign competitors, including the United States.

Lessons from the Petrochemical Industry

A number of lessons can be drawn from the Venezuelan petrochemical industry. The industry shows that when subject to market pressures, Venezuelan firms, industries, and industry associations start to focus on developing human resources, on infrastructure requirements, on efficiency, on quality, on marketing, and on customer service. They start to assess their resources carefully and to identify opportunities in foreign markets. The absence of market pressures in the past not only limited incentives to operate effectively, it also limited the understanding of what operating effectively means. According to one manager in the petrochemical industry, "Under the old system, we never even knew how inefficient we were." The petrochemical industry was in many ways ill-equipped to move from import substitution to competing on world markets, but significant changes were made during a short period of time. The petrochemical experience also shows that it takes some time for the benefits of change to be seen. As of 1993, some of the older, subscale plants were having difficulties, though many were fully depreciated. Newer plants were coming on stream at a time when world prices were depressed. It will be a few more years before some of the most recent investments are fully up to speed.

At the same time, the petrochemical industry shows the importance of putting Venezuela's macroeconomic house in order. In petrochemicals, as in other capital-intensive industries, high interest rates due to the inflationary pressures of the public deficit and uncertainty over economic policy have made Venezuela a very difficult place to invest. In many industries, substantial investments have been deferred until better macroeconomic conditions prevail. As of 1994, it is nearly impossible to overestimate the chilling effect that macroeconomic conditions are having on investment and on economic growth throughout the economy.

Another lesson involves the role of foreign direct investment and state-owned firms in the Venezuelan economy. Joint ventures with foreign-owned firms are probably the best training ground for Venezuelans to gain the technical and marketing skills necessary to expand the local petrochemical industry. Thus Venezuela's ability to attract foreign direct investment from world-class companies is absolutely critical to the industry's future. By combining resource advantages with technological and marketing expertise, these foreign investment joint ventures provide the best way for Venezuela to participate in the downstream portion of the petrochemical industry. State-owned firms have had both positive and negative effects on the industry. PDVSA and Pequiven have been the main sources of trained individuals and technology development in the Venezuelan industry. They also have been leaders in developing the skills of local suppliers and engineering consulting firms. These have been major contributions to the industry and to the country. On the other hand, the monopoly positions of the state-owned enterprises affects their performance.

The Venezuelan petrochemical industry does have the potential to be quite successful in certain product lines (particularly those based on compounds containing one or two carbon atoms, C1 and C2 derivatives). It offers some solid opportunities for growth well into the future. However, given the realities of international competition, world market prices, and the nonresource inputs to the industry, petrochemicals will not be a bonanza for Venezuela, as some may have hoped. Some people in Venezuela believe that, because oil was so profitable, miracles can be expected from other resource-based industries and that anything less than a miracle is not worth the effort. Petrochemicals looks like a close cousin to oil, and when people see the size of the resources and the scope of planned investments in petrochemicals, there is the danger that they will expect too much and either be complacent or disappointed with the results. It is important to think in terms of solid diversified growth rather than hope for a miracle in any given sector.

TABLE 4.8
World Production of Direct Reduced Iron

Millions of Metric Tons

Country	1990	1991	Percentage
Venezuela	**3.15**	**3.94**	**20.4**
Mexico	2.47	2.49	12.9
EEC	1.60	1.70	8.8
Indonesia	1.41	1.43	7.4
Saudi Arabia	1.09	1.12	5.8
Argentina	1.03	0.94	5.0
India	0.72	1.18	6.1
Others	6.35	6.47	33.6
Total	17.92	19.29	100.0

Source: De Sanctis (1993).

The Venezuelan Steel Industry[79]

In 1991, Venezuela exported $490 million worth of iron and steel products, which, after aluminum, comprised its second-largest non-oil export.[80] Venezuela was the twenty-eighth largest steel producer in the world[81] and the third largest steel producer in Latin America, ranking in size below Brazil and Mexico and just above Argentina. Its total annual production of 3.1 million metric tons of liquid steel represented 8 percent of Latin American production.[82] In contrast to most steelmaking capacity in Latin America and the rest of the world, the Venezuelan industry uses electric arc furnaces rather than conventional blast furnaces. Venezuela is the largest producer in the world of briquetted direct reduced iron (DRI) used in electric furnace steelmaking. Seven plants in the region of Guayana account for an estimated 20 percent of world production of direct reduced iron (DRI), of which 25 percent is exported. (See Table 4.8.)[83] Venezuela has the only complete flat-rolled steel installation in the Andean Pact, Central America, and the Caribbean.

For most of its history, the Venezuelan steel industry served a relatively small domestic market protected by high import barriers. The CVG carved up the sector by product lines and by preempting other players created a de facto monopoly for itself in most products—including flat-rolled steel, slabs, and seamless tubular products for use by the oil industry. In other product areas, such as prereduced ore, blooms and billets, and shapes and rebar, private industry had the opportunity to participate. In 1993, the industry consisted of Sidor (Siderúrgica del Orinoco C.A.), a state-owned firm with an installed production capacity of 3.6 million tons (78.8 percent of the national total); Sivensa, the largest steelmaker in the private sector, with an installed production capacity of 830,000 tons (18.2 percent); and five smaller private sector steelmakers with a combined installed capacity of 140,000 tons (3 percent).[84] Sivensa appeared to be responding to new opportunities in the domestic and export markets. Sidor had an important export presence and had implemented a restructuring program. However, Sidor seemed weighted down by problems with production and productivity as well as by the burden imposed on its management by the requirements and pressures intrinsic to state control.

The Evolution of the Venezuelan Steel Sector

Alvaray (1993) has identified four distinct phases in the history of the Venezuelan steel industry. From 1950 to 1962, the industry's primary focus was the sale of iron ore in international markets. There was relatively little domestic value added or impact on the national economy. The abundant iron ore in Guayana inspired the notion of building an integrated industry there. A private consortium, the Iron and Steel Syndicate, took preliminary steps in this direction, but the government decided to reserve the Guayana steel industry to the state because of its "strategic" importance to national development. In 1962, the CVG oversaw the entry into operation of the first steel plant in Guayana, and Sidor was founded two years later.

For the next 21 years, from 1962 to 1983, the Venezuelan steel industry was built on an import substitution model. By the early 1970s, Sidor had built up a production capacity of 1.2 million tons directed at the domestic market.[85] It was still, in international terms, a relatively small steel producer with moderate expansion plans.[86] In 1974, oil prices rose and the influx of petrodollars inspired the Venezuelan government to order Sidor to accelerate and expand its planned expansion program, known as Plan IV.[87] Sidor invested approximately $5 billion in an additional 3.6 million tons of production capacity, including direct reduction, milling, and casting facilities, for a total production capacity of 4.8 million tons. Its product line was broadened substantially beyond long products and seamless tubes to encompass flat products from hot-rolled steel to steel sheet. The primary policy objective in expanding product lines was to promote industrialization, through the growth of the steel sector and encouragement of user industries.[88] Most of this expansion was financed by debt. The government instructed Sidor to borrow "against a government pledge of future capitalization."[89] However, the bonanza oil income was quickly exhausted and the government did not fulfill its pledge.[90]

In 1983, the Venezuelan economy contracted and the industry began to target export markets as a matter of financial necessity. At first, exports tended to be a function of domestic demand, with lower export volumes in years of high domestic consumption. However, as more production capacity came on line in the 1980s and domestic consumption failed to keep pace, exports became an integral part of the industry's strategy. At the same time, the interest obligations generated by Plan IV began to weigh heavily on Sidor, absorbing much of "the cash flow it needed to remain competitive."[91]

The import substitution regime in steel products involved significant import tariffs (as high as 25 percent ad valorem). Tariffs combined with the high freight expenses intrinsic to the steel industry served as an effective barrier to most imports, and this was reinforced by a policy of import licenses. Import licenses were required even for those products not manufactured by the domestic producers, and for a time the discretionary power to grant or deny import license applications was in the hands of Sidor itself. On the other hand, the government subsidized certain user industries by setting domestic prices for some steel products below production costs (such as rebar sold to construction firms, barbed wire sold to cattle ranchers, or steel sheet sold to packaging firms). To encourage exports, the government provided export incentives of approximately 25 percent, depending on the value added of the product.[92]

By 1990, largely as a result of the Plan IV expansion, Sidor had incurred a total interest expense of $3.87 billion, of which it had paid $2.97 billion.[93] Sidor's interest-to-sales ratio of 15.4 percent was among the highest in the world steel industry, far above the Latin American average (9.2 percent) or the average for steelmakers in industrialized nations (between 0.3 percent and 5 percent).[94] Its older plants, especially those dating back to the 1960s, were burdened by a lack of modernization, and operative problems were widespread. Persistent political intervention in management also had taken a toll on Sidor's financial performance.

The commercial opening brought major changes in the rules of the game to the steel industry. Import tariffs were reduced and import licenses were eliminated. The state stopped setting domestic steel prices. Export subsidies were phased out. In 1989, Sidor was presented with a new corporate mission, "to produce for profit and for export, and concentrate only on the product lines that generate the highest returns."[95] In response, Sidor undertook a program of industrial restructuring. In the early 1990s, it modernized its production capacity, cut costs, and cut back on its products to eliminate unprofitable product lines. Sidor made significant reductions in its workforce. The oldest production facilities, those that predated the Plan IV expansion, were closed, reducing overall capacity to 3.6 million tons. In May 1993, the state capitalized $904 million (60 percent) of Sidor's debt and an additional $166 million in accumulated interest.

In contrast to Sidor, Sivensa followed a strategy of steady growth on a smaller scale. The company's original plant predates the firm itself, having been founded in 1950 as a small scrap-recycling installation. Over the succeeding decades, Sivensa built up installations in Antímano, Caracas, to a production capacity of 200,000 tons. Starting in 1980, Sivensa launched an expansion program that included the acquisition of two domestic steelmaking firms, acquisition of 60 percent ownership of the Fluidized Iron Ore Reduction (FIOR) briquette plant, and the construction of both a steel plant and briquette plant in Guayana. In 1993, Sivensa had a total steelmaking capacity of 830,000 tons.[96]

The segment structure of domestic demand has evolved with the Venezuelan economy. In the 1950s, a period of great expansion in the oil industry, demand was heavily weighted toward tubular products used in the oil industry. In the mid-1970s, construction materials predominated, and in recent years, the growth of the metalmechanics industries has shifted demand again, this time toward flat products.

Direct Reduction Iron: Lengthy Learning, Promising Results

Venezuela has immense endowments of iron ore, natural gas, and hydroelectric power but it lacks the metallurgical carbons used in conventional steelmaking. This scarcity served as an important incentive to innovation. In the 1970s, Sidor and foreign investors such as U.S. Steel and Exxon invested heavily in a new, experimental technology—direct reduction—whereby iron ore is converted into direct reduced iron, an intermediate product used as an input in electric arc furnaces. Direct reduction consumes natural gas in large quantities but dispenses with the need for metallurgical carbons in the steelmaking process.

On a conceptual level, building a steel industry based on DRI/electric arc technology had several attractions. It offered a potential solution to the scarcity of metallurgical carbons and, at the same time, a way to take advantage of Venezuela's low-cost hydroelectric power and natural gas. Nevertheless, it was a bold decision. At the time, DRI technology was still being developed and had not been applied commercially on a large scale. Sidor hoped to build 3.8 million tons of production capacity based on DRI technology at a time when the largest plant in the world had a maximum capacity of 450,000 tons per year.[97] In 1973, when Sidor made the decision to acquire the HYL and Midrex direct reduction technologies from foreign sources, "the processes of direct reduction constituted a radically new avenue in technological development in the world steel industry. By nature they were closer to the technology used in the petrochemicals sector."[98]

In 1973, U.S. Steel opened a plant in Venezuela using its own proprietary technology, but the plant had operational difficulties and was closed in 1982. In 1976, Exxon, a group of national and foreign investors, and the CVG started up a direct reduction plant based on FIOR technology. The plant encountered difficulties, causing its foreign investors to withdraw. Also in the 1970s, Sidor opened DRI plants using Midrex (a U.S. technology acquired by Kobe Steel) and HYL (a technology developed by the Mexican firm Hojalata y Lamina, S.A.). The HYL plants were never successful and were eventually closed.

Between 1977 and 1983, the technical performance of Sidor's direct reduction plants was poor and they operated at a loss. Production problems were widespread and persistent, and were reflected in low capacity utilization rates and financial losses. Although problems might be expected during start-up of an experimental technology of this kind, some DRI plants elsewhere did report levels of productivity during start-up that exceeded design parameters.[99] Viana (1984) has found that the underlying problems at Sidor were in a "lack of human resources capable of maintaining an efficient operation and a lack of technological and managerial capacity, which produced a process of fragmented learning."[100]

Mastery of large-scale DRI production occurred in the mid- to late 1980s. In the late 1980s, two successful plants using Midrex technology, the OPCO and Venprecar plants, commenced operation. In 1988, 12 years after it was founded, the FIOR plant (now owned by Sivensa and Sidor) attained its full production capacity of 400,000 metric tons of briquetted reduced iron per year.[101] FIOR has been developing its own, improved direct reduction process. Although the technology used in the FIOR plant was originally imported, over time Venezuelan engineers have developed it to such an extent that it has for practical purposes become a Venezuelan process.[102] Sivensa and Sidor have been granted three U.S. patents related to the FIOR process technology. As of 1993, FIOR was working with Voest Alpine of Austria to develop a technology for the new process, with the aim of building a new plant with an annual capacity of 1 million metric tons. Sidor also has developed its own direct reduction process, Auto-Reforming Reduction Technology (AREX), which it has patented in the United States. Test trials of AREX in existing plants have resulted in production increases of up to 25 percent, and as of 1993, the AREX process was being marketed in other countries.[103]

The recent achievements of Sidor and Sivensa in DRI process technology are exceptional when compared to Venezuela's overall performance in technology development. In the case of DRI, Venezuelan engineers have mastered and improved upon the original, imported technology. Their technological contributions have given rise to a domestic DRI sector that is the world's largest and that is in an excellent position to compete in the growing world market for synthetic scrap. At the same time, progress along the learning curve was relatively slow.[104]

Natural Resource Advantages, Uneven Human Resources

The basic inputs used in direct reduction and steelmaking are iron ore, natural gas, electricity, and scrap. Venezuela possesses immense endowments of these natural resources. (See Chapter 6.) Domestic prices of iron ore and natural gas are among the world's lowest. So are the electricity rates charged to the steel sector, which are based on long-term marginal cost. Venezuela's cost advantages in basic inputs have a strong impact on production costs of briquetted reduced iron, at the base of the steel product chain. In 1991, the total production cost in Venezuela of briquettes was the lowest in the world, at $70 per ton, followed by Trinidad, at $105 per ton.[105] In the case of Sivensa, a cost advantage also exists at the next step up the product chain in the semifinished segment. In 1991, Sivensa's production costs for billets compared favorably to those of most international competitors.[106] Metal feedstock, in the form of direct reduced iron or scrap, is the most important element of cost in the production of semifinished products, and in the case of the electric arc furnaces utilized in Venezuela, low-cost electricity is also an important cost advantage. In the case of finished products, Sidor's production costs do not compare favorably overall to those of the world leaders,[107] due to inefficiencies in the production process and technological problems in Sidor's installations.

Venezuela possesses a valuable pool of expertise in direct reduction, made up of managers and engineers with decades of experience. In other respects, however, the national steel industry is deficient in human resources, despite the efforts of Sidor, Sivensa, INCE, the universities, and technological institutes. In 1990, a study of workers leaving Sidor for other jobs found that more than half of them had six years or less of formal schooling.[108] Compared to workers in the world's leading steel industries, this is a very low level of education. Venezuelan firms also suffer from a high rate of employee turnover (the average time on the job in this industry is less than ten years), which inhibits the accumulation of knowledge and experience. Sidor's overall labor productivity has compared very unfavorably to that of leading steel producers in other nations.[109] In contrast, labor productivity in the direct reduced iron segment is up to international standards.

Growing Competitive Pressures in the Domestic Market

Traditionally, there was little rivalry in the Venezuelan steel industry. Prices were controlled by the state. Sidor held a monopoly in the areas of flat and tubular goods, which accounted for more than 60 percent of total industry sales. Although private firms, including Sivensa and some much smaller producers, were active in long products along with Sidor, Sidor and Sivensa acted as a duopoly, tacitly dividing markets by geographic region and product dimensions. For example, Sivensa was more active in small rebars, while Sidor concentrated on larger rebars.

In 1993, Sidor was still the sole domestic producer of flat products, which represented 52 percent of the Venezuelan steel industry's sales.[110] It was likely to retain its domestic monopoly in flat products for the foreseeable future. Nevertheless, the commercial opening introduced new competitive pressures for the Venezuelan steelmakers. By 1993, in many product lines, imports were only incipient, but the domestic producers were keenly aware of the potential for import competition. The extended CIF price of hypothetical imports, calculated to reflect the likely price of imported steel at the client's factory gate, became the price to beat. One product segment where imports made strong inroads, eroding 16 percent of Sidor's erstwhile monopoly, was wire rod.[111] Trinidad accounted for nearly half of these imports. The opening of the market and freeing of prices also introduced rivalry between domestic steelmakers in their area of greatest overlap, rebars, causing Sidor and Sivensa to compete actively against each other for the first time.

The domestic market consumes two-thirds of Venezuelan steel production. Annual apparent consumption of steel products fluctuated around the 2 million metric ton mark during 1983-1993.[112] Most domestic buyers have not been in a position to enforce quality standards on Sidor, especially in those areas where it holds a monopoly. Import barriers served to limit the potential of local demand to pressure for improvements in product quality and terms of delivery. In the early 1990s, however, with the opening of the markets, domestic buyers were becoming more demanding with respect to product quality and prompt delivery. Clients in the petroleum, packaging, and boiler industries were forging closer relations with the domestic steelmakers in an effort to boost product quality.

Room for Improvement in Related and Supporting Industries

Related and supporting industries have not realized their full potential as a source of competitive advantage to the Venezuelan steel industry. Venezuelan steel producers benefit from inexpensive electricity supplied by the CVG company, Edelca. Iron ore and natural gas also have been available at very attractive prices, which has stimulated the development of the industry. However, the steel sector has been dependent for most raw materials and basic inputs on state-owned monopolies that in the past were not always fully responsive to the needs of domestic clients. Iron ore is an illustrative example. The quality of Ferrominera Orinoco's supplies of iron ores to local firms has been uneven.[113] Local firms believe that Ferrominera Orinoco has given preferential treatment to foreign clients.[114]

In 1993, Ferrominera's management was placing new importance on serving local clients and was taking steps to stimulate local demand. At the same time, the requirements of foreign buyers were exerting pressure on Ferrominera Orinoco to improve the quality of its products, which in turn was benefitting local customers. The firm was implementing quality improvement programs that benefitted both foreign and domestic clients, and domestic purchasers were demanding higher-quality ore in order to increase their yields.[115]

Most of the steel consumed within Venezuela is transported from Guayana to its destination by truck.[116] The high cost of overland freight from Guayana is a problem for user industries, which purchase steel Free on Board (F.O.B.) Puerto Ordaz, and is a potential source of vulnerability vis-à-vis imported steel which could enter the country from maritime ports much closer to domestic clients' facilities. Two factors contributing to high freight costs are the poor condition of the highways, made worse by the practice of overloading trucks, and the low level of competition within the local trucking transportation sector.

The steel sector itself has played an important role in stimulating the growth of downstream industries, such as metalworking. It has served as a center for the development of technology and formation of skilled human resources, which have spread downstream. Sivensa has contributed to the development of technology and skills through Fundametal.[117] Sidor is the largest training center for personnel in steelmaking and metalworking in the country, many of whom have gone on to other industries and taken their skills with them.

Export Prospects and Challenges

The Venezuelan steel industry currently exports about one-third of its production. Fifty-five percent of the nation's steel exports are sold in the South American, Central American, and Caribbean markets.[118] Venezuela's export presence in Colombia, Central America, and the Caribbean has benefitted from regional market integration agreements, especially the free trade agreement with Colombia. Asia, which accounts for 22 percent of exports, is a promising market but high transport costs are a factor. Exports to the United States and Europe have encountered import restrictions in certain product segments and represent only 20 percent and 3 percent, respectively, of total steel exports.[119] Although the initial growth of Venezuelan steel exports benefitted from currency devaluations and export incentives, from 1983 to 1993 the Venezuelan steel producers made a concerted effort to penetrate foreign markets and to develop market intelligence, especially within Latin America.[120]

Venezuelan steelmakers need to expand their presence in export markets. The domestic market is the fourth largest in Latin America, after Brazil, Mexico, and Argentina, but it is too small to support economies of scale. The demand for steel in Venezuela, as in other nations, is closely tied to the performance of the economy, and short-term projections of domestic GDP growth underscore the need to boost exports. As of 1993, Sidor, which was burdened by excess capacity in certain product lines, still faced difficult challenges in expanding export sales. In the past, it has been plagued by inefficient production and at times has had to sell product below international prices to compensate for poor quality and slow delivery.

Future prospects for exports of Venezuelan steel vary by product segment. As discussed earlier, Venezuelan firms are low-cost producers of briquettes. As of 1993, the world market for DRI was strong and promised to grow in coming years. The U.S. steel industry has been shifting toward minimills, which rely heavily on scrap or direct reduced iron for their metal input. The minimill sector has moved into producing the best grades of steel, which in turn require high-quality scrap or reduced iron. The supplies of high-quality scrap in the United States are under severe pressure. Venezuelan firms should be well positioned to meet this demand for direct reduced iron, if they are aggressive in identifying and developing new buyers that need high-quality product.

As of 1993, Venezuelan export prospects for semifinished products, such as billets, were also promising. International trade in this segment was incipient but growing. Sivensa, which has mastered the production technology, has had success in exporting billets. In 1993, Sidor still suffered from operational difficulties and had not yet succeeded in raising its capacity utilization rate above 70 percent. Nevertheless, given that electricity represents 20 percent of total production costs, Sidor should have the potential to become cost competitive in this product segment. At prices of about $220 per ton, it should be possible for the Venezuelan producers to sell large quantities of billets in the markets of the Andean Pact, Central America, and the Caribbean.[121]

The future export prospects of flat products (hot rolled steel, cold rolled steel, and steel plate) is uncertain due to the inefficiencies of Sidor's plants and will depend to a large extent on whether the productivity and manufacturing quality of these installations are improved.[122] Sidor has the only production complex for flat products within the Andean Pact, Central America, and the Caribbean. Outside this geographic area, export markets are somewhat limited due to import barriers in the United States and Europe and the high cost of freight to Asia.

Nonflat products (rebars, steel wire, and shapes) are relatively unattractive for export. As Alvaray (1993) points out, although the Venezuelan producers have mastered the production technology in this product segment and this is the only segment where internal rivalry exists, these factors alone are not sufficient to confer a competitive advantage. Worldwide, the production of nonflat steel products tends to be local, dictated by the availability of inputs and the existence of local demand. Technological and capital barriers to entry are relatively low. As a result, many countries have at least some domestic production capacity in nonflat products. Prices are relatively low compared to other steel products, which makes the cost of transportation an important factor. The situation is not expected to change in the foreseeable future.

Although there is excess supply worldwide in tubular goods, Venezuela may have export potential in this segment as well. As of 1993, Venezuela was the only producer of tubular goods in the Andean Pact, Central America, and the Caribbean, areas that have growing petroleum sectors. Tubular goods production requires very large capital investments (an estimated $3,000 per metric ton for lamination and finishing alone); however, these goods command higher prices than other steel products. In the near future there will be at least two Venezuelan producers of tubular goods, Tuborca and BCPA, and other entrants are possible.[123]

Capital Requirements and the Need for Foreign Investment

Restructuring the Venezuelan steel industry will require large infusions of capital in the near future. As of 1993, Sidor had embarked on an ambitious modernization program that was projected to cost on the order of $750 million and would include modernization of its flat product installations. Ferrominera Orinoco was developing a $500 million investment program, which included a new pellet plant. Sidor's new seamless tubes plant would require $500 million, to be supplied by private investors. Two more direct reduction plants were under study, which would mean $550 million in new investments. Overall, between 1993 and 1997 the industry might absorb as much as $2.3 billion in new investments. With the state in fiscal crisis and the state-owned firms highly indebted, it is estimated that nearly half of this total will have to come from private investors. As this volume of investments exceeds the supply of private Venezuelan capital, foreign investment will be critical to the growth of the sector. Foreign partners also can supply markets for Venezuelan output and technology to modernize local plants and to improve productivity.

Whether the steel sector will be able to attract foreign investment in the amounts required will depend on several key factors. It will be important to establish a long-term pricing policy (of at least ten years) for iron ore, natural gas, and electricity in order to guarantee a return on investment. Also important will be a scheme of national and municipal taxes that provides either initial exemptions or a progressive application of tax rates. In addition, investors will need assurances as to the availability of infrastructure, especially adequate transportation systems for inputs and products.[124] (See Figure 4.5.)

Lessons from the Steel Industry

The history of the Venezuelan steel industry offers valuable insights for the economy as a whole. It shows that even in a nation such as Venezuela, with varied and vast endowments of natural resources, a selective factor disadvantage can serve as a stimulus to the creation of advanced factors that are a powerful source of competitive advantage. Twenty years after the industry made the decision to incorporate DRI/electric arc technology, Venezuela is the leading producer of direct reduced iron in the world and possesses electric arc steel plants that are well positioned in the incipient world market for semifinished steel of high metallic purity. The nation's rich endowments of

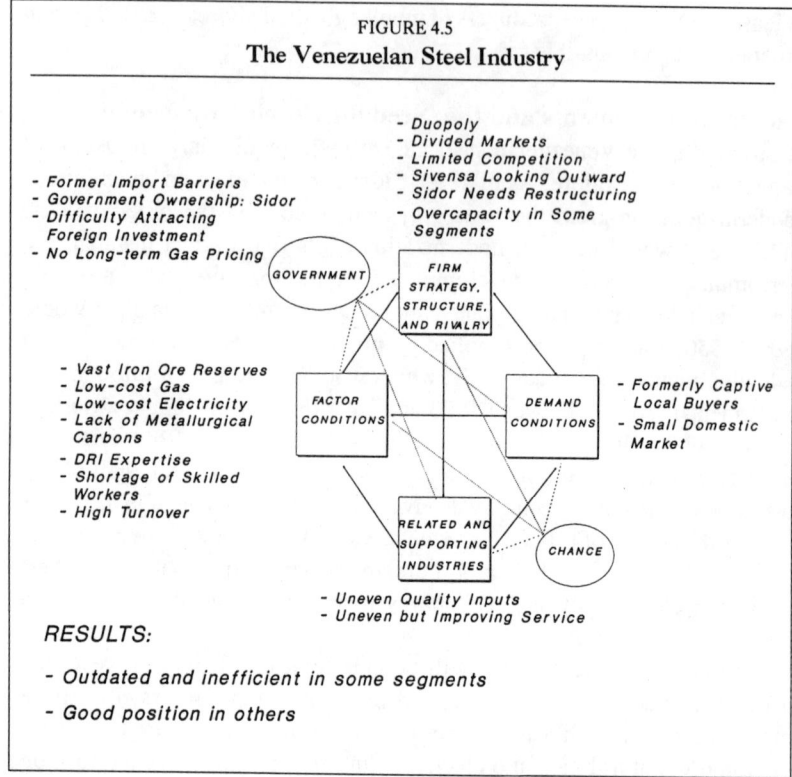

FIGURE 4.5
The Venezuelan Steel Industry

natural gas and hydroelectric power made this avenue of development possible, but it is unlikely that Venezuela would have pursued it had the country also possessed reserves of the high-quality metallurgical carbons used in conventional steelmaking. The selective disadvantage in metallurgical carbons pressured the local industry to upgrade by developing higher-level competitive advantages via technological innovation. In this respect, the Venezuelan experience in DRI/electric arc technology has counterparts in internationally successful industries around the world, including the Italian ceramic tile industry and the German chemical industry.[125]

The Venezuelan experience in direct reduced iron also sheds light on the nature of technological development and innovation during the import substitution regime. The success of Venezuelan engineers in developing world-class proprietary technology is unusual in the Venezuelan experience but not unique. In several industries, including petrochemicals (for example, Química Venoco) and aluminum (for example,

Venalum), there have been other isolated examples of firms that imported production technologies, mastered the technologies, and proceeded to achieve technological breakthroughs of their own.[126] In such cases, Venezuelan engineers committed to optimizing the productive performance of the plants have been the driving force behind technological learning. However, within an environment of protectionism and state subsidies, they operated largely independently of the sorts of competitive pressures that, in open markets, add financial urgency to the process of technological learning. According to Viana and associates (1993), Sidor's experience with DRI tends to support the argument that processes of technological learning within environments of protection and subsidies can, in certain cases, have a higher social cost than would otherwise be the case.[127] The challenge going forward will not be to recoup sunk costs but rather to ensure that in the future, Venezuelan industries will be subject to the sorts of competitive challenges and pressures that stimulate cost-effective technological learning and innovation.

The Venezuelan Automotive Industry[128]

In 1992, the automotive sector (automobile assembly and parts production) accounted for about 10 percent of Venezuelan manufacturing value added, 10 percent of manufacturing employment, and 25 percent of manufacturing earnings (largely attributable to auto parts).[129] In 1991, 73,000 automotive vehicles were assembled in Venezuela, or about 3 percent of Latin American production, while Mexico and Brazil, with 989,000 units and 880,000 units, respectively, together accounted for 87 percent of Latin American automotive production.[130] In 1992, Venezuela exported $75 million in auto parts and $53 million in assembled vehicles[131] and imported about $2 billion in vehicles and parts,[132] for a sharply negative balance of trade.

The story of the Venezuelan automotive sector illustrates the costs and limits of protecting "infant" industries. For 30 years, the Venezuelan government has cultivated a domestic industry within a complex system of protections and incentives. It has done so because the sector lacks sources of advantage. From the start, domestic demand was too small to support efficient full-scale production or assembly. Firm strategies were distorted by government policies that eliminated rivalry among producers. Within this context, the local assembly operations of multinational corporations developed on a small scale in Venezuela. A large number of parts producers sprang up within a protected market to serve the local assemblers, but by the late

1980s, only a select group had targeted the major foreign markets. Most remained inwardly focused.

Between 1990 and 1993, the Venezuelan automotive sector was opened to increased foreign competition. The opening was only partial, but it rapidly yielded benefits for consumers of autos, who had greater choices and more competitive prices; for auto assemblers, who boosted efficiency by restructuring sourcing patterns; and even for some parts manufacturers, who targeted international markets with greater urgency. The competitiveness of the sector as a whole improved. In September 1993, the Venezuelan government announced a change in course that will increase protection once again, though the market will remain far more open than it was before 1989.

The questions raised by the automotive policy are important issues for the economy as a whole. How much does the Venezuelan consumer pay for "protection" from imports and for the jobs that the auto sector generates? Does "protection" help or hurt the most promising of Venezuelan firms, those that might be able to develop competitive advantages? What are the future implications for other sectors? Autos and agriculture are only two of the sectors of the Venezuelan economy that have lobbied heavily, and succeeded, in obtaining special treatment. While producers in these industries have received much press, little attention has been paid to the plight of the Venezuelan consumer who must pay inflated prices to support inefficient producers, or to the signals that such protection sends to the rest of the economy.

A Small Market

The Venezuelan automotive industry assembles, rather than produces, cars and buses, jeeps, pick-up trucks, and commercial vehicles from a combination of imported and domestically produced components. The engine and transmission assemblies are imported, as are a variety of additional components, including most stamped steel pieces used for vehicle exteriors. In 1992, components represented on average 84 percent of the total value of vehicles assembled in Venezuela. Imported parts accounted for approximately 60 percent of total value, and domestic value added (domestic parts and labor) about 40 percent.[133] The auto parts industry manufactures a wide range of components that are used in vehicle assembly or are sold as replacement parts, including stamped pieces, seats, axles, shock absorbers, valves, pistons, brakes, tires, clutches, wheels, glass, electric parts, and batteries.

The small size of the Venezuelan auto market has shaped its development. In 1992, the two largest auto markets in Latin America were Mexico

TABLE 4.9
Latin American Automobile Market, Selected Countries, 1992

Country	Thousand Units[a]
Mexico	1,210
Brazil	1,115
Argentina	310
Venezuela	**146**
Colombia	84
Ecuador	49

[a] Includes local production and imports.

Source: The Venezuelan Automotive Chamber (CAVENEZ) and the Venezuelan Auto Parts Producers (FAVENPA).

and Brazil, with markets of 1.2 and 1.1 million units, respectively. In contrast, the Venezuelan market totaled only 146,000 units. In that year, Venezuela, Colombia, Peru, and Ecuador combined represented a small market of approximately 300,000 units. (See Table 4.9.)

Vehicle assembly is a scale-intensive industry. Worldwide, an efficient-scale plant requires an annual capacity of at least 250,000 units. The assembly plants in Venezuela, which were set up to serve the home market, operate on a fraction of the scale of the biggest assembly plants in Latin America. The installed capacity of the eight largest assemblers in Venezuela in 1990-1991 ranged from 10,000 to 34,200 units per year.[134] In 1991, Fiat, for example, had an installed capacity in Venezuela of about 16,000 units and a capacity utilization rate of 57 percent. In the same year, Fiat had an installed capacity in Brazil of 230,000 vehicles, 50,000 kits for assembly, and 300,000 motors annually.

Small scale means relatively high costs for auto assembly. In 1993, there was wide consensus that Venezuelan assemblers would not be able to compete with imported autos on the domestic market without tariff protection.[135] Natural trade barriers, such as transportation costs, cannot overcome the scale inefficiencies of the small, local plants. Venezuelan autos are cost competitive with imports today only because of substantial tariffs on imported cars, which are in effect a tax on the Venezuelan consumer.

The auto parts industry is also very scale intensive. For many parts, if a Venezuelan plant operates at minimum efficient scale, which it must if it is to compete on price with the leading world producers, its output would be greater than total national demand. The only way to operate at efficient scale in these parts products is to export. Some first-tier Venezuelan parts producers do so. As of 1993, parts producers such as Ejeven, Rualca, and OCI Metalmecánica placed more than 40 percent of their production in foreign markets.[136]

The Brainchild of Policy

The Venezuelan automotive industry is the product of an aggressive import substitution policy. The main aims of this policy were the creation of industrial employment and technological development, and the conservation of foreign exchange.[137] In the early 1960s, the government created incentives for the major multinational auto companies to invest in local assembly operations by erecting high tariff barriers and outright import prohibitions and by promoting the establishment of local plants. The main attractions for the foreign auto companies were a guaranteed, though small, local vehicle market and an expanding market for replacement parts. Prior to 1962, Chrysler, General Motors, and Renault were the only major firms with assembly operations in Venezuela. Ford, Jeep, American Motor Company, and others invested in assembly plants during the 1960s and 1970s, and Fiat, Nissho Iwai, and Toyota followed thereafter.

One of the goals of the automotive industrial policy was to promote the development of a Venezuelan-based and Venezuelan-owned auto parts sector. To this end, the government imposed high tariffs and import restrictions on auto parts and prohibited the auto assemblers from investing in auto parts production. It also required that locally produced parts constitute a significant percentage of the value added of the finished vehicle (through so-called integration requirements), creating a captive market for local parts production. The 1960s and 1970s saw the formation of numerous Venezuelan auto parts manufacturers to supply the assemblers and the after market, in such segments as stamped pieces, brakes, electric parts, laminated glass, and wheels.

In 1965, only 56,568 vehicles were assembled in Venezuela. This small market could not support efficient-scale assembly plants. At the same time, the Venezuelan consumer—arguably the most sophisticated in Latin America—placed a premium on a wide selection of up-to-date models. The proliferation of models assembled by local plants drove down scale efficiencies and profits. The Venezuelan state responded by gradually reducing the number of models that could be produced locally, from 116 in 1966 to 43 in 1986, while at the same time increasing integration requirements.[138]

Until 1990, competition and rivalry played a negligible role in this sector. The goals were employment and preserving foreign exchange rather than efficiency. Vehicle prices were set by mutual agreement between industry and government, an arrangement that ensured profitability. Although there were eight major assemblers in the market overall, only a few, at most, would be active within the same general product line. For example, Toyota and Chrysler sold jeeps, while Ford and GM sold light commercial vehicles. Models were allocated by government license among companies, and any innovation in this area, such as the introduction of a new model, was subject to government approval. In general, the assemblers competed for customers by invoking their international reputations, by establishing widespread dealer networks, and by offering reliable supplies of spare and replacement parts. These strategies helped to win sales but did little to promote the competitiveness of local assembly operations. The local assemblers also competed for government approvals, including permits to import components and to obtain subsidized foreign currency.

Like the assembly sector, the auto parts sector was structured to minimize competitive pressures. Prior to 1990, with a few exceptions, Venezuelan auto parts producers enjoyed a captive market. In 1993, in Venezuela there was only one producer for at least 55 types of auto parts and only two producers for 35 types of parts.[139] Where multiple producers existed per part, there was a tendency to specialize in distinct product subcategories, which obviated head-to-head competition. No doubt, this resulted in part from the need to maximize economies of scale in a small market. The result, however, was that there was little fear of a competitor trying to steal an existing account or of an existing customer finding an alternative supply. The assemblers tried to demand the same standards of local suppliers as they did internationally, but, in fact, they often were forced to accept low-quality items and late deliveries. There were even complaints that the local assembly operations were not making efforts to adapt their international standards to the skills and capacities of the local suppliers. While most parts producers turned their attention inward, a small number of firms, such as Danaven, Rudeveca, Ejeven, and Rualca, did look outward to foreign markets for technology, capital, and customers.

The government tried to promote sales to foreign markets by granting subsidies for exports on nontraditional products, including autos. However, despite isolated successes, the exports of the vehicle sector were negligible—about 1 percent of production.[140] Despite an average tariff of 100 percent on assembled vehicles and 45 percent on auto parts, the trade balance of the automotive industry was sharply negative, more than $450 million in 1988 for passenger vehicles and $220 million for auto parts.[141]

A Partial Opening: New Winners and Losers

The end of the 1980s ushered in a period of rapid change for the Venezuelan automotive industry. In 1989, a year of painful adjustment for the Venezuelan economy, the auto market temporarily collapsed. Domestic vehicle production fell from 123,000 units in 1988 to 26,000 units.[142] In 1990, Venezuela restructured its automotive policy. Under the new policy, tariffs on assembled vehicles, which had averaged about 100 percent, were reduced sharply. In 1991, tariffs on imported passenger vehicles with an invoiced value of $15,000 or less were reduced to 25 percent and to 40 percent for vehicles priced above that amount.[143] Tariffs on auto parts imported for use in assembly of passenger vehicles were reduced to 5 percent. Assemblers were no longer required to incorporate nationally produced parts in their vehicles. Although they were required to contribute to foreign currency earnings, they could meet this requirement in a variety of ways, including the use of local parts, the export of finished vehicles, and the export of parts produced in Venezuela. Import licenses, manufacturers' licenses, and export subsidies also were eliminated as part of the policy reforms.

After the opening, imports fueled fierce competition in the Venezuelan auto market. Imports of vehicles surged over the next three years, accounting for 40 percent of all units sold in Venezuela in 1992. Many of these imports entered through new channels—an estimated 27 percent of total sales in 1992 were made independent of the established assemblers.[144] Meanwhile, although the market was recovering from its depression in 1989, climbing to 146,000 units in 1992, it had not recovered to its all-time maximum of 189,000, reached in 1978. This fact exerted pressure on the local assemblers, who had to fight for their share of the market.

For the first time, assemblers were free to supplement or to replace lines of locally assembled vehicles with imports from their foreign operations. They scrutinized their locally assembled models to determine which, if any, were viable under the new import regime. Many factors played a role in determining viability, including the international objectives of the parent company, the capabilities and cost structures of plants existing in the region, the cost of potential imports (including freight, which might vary considerably by model), and the potential sourcing of components for local assembly.

The result of the new competition was increased variety and consumer choice. In 1990, there were 8 major assemblers producing fewer than 50 models. By 1993, more than 24 auto companies were present in Venezuela, through assembly or import operations, selling an estimated 250 or more models.[145] Even LADA, the Russian automaker, made inroads, especially in the low end of the market. The overall quality of Venezuelan produced vehicles and parts greatly improved.[146] Competition had created a greater selection of models than had been seen in decades. Venezuelan consumers quickly learned to engage in comparative shopping. Lower-priced imports, increased efficiency, and other factors helped to mitigate inflation, keeping price increases lower than they would have been otherwise.

Increased imports and specialized vehicle production, in turn, dramatically changed the nature of the auto parts market. With a 5 percent duty on parts, assemblers had the option of sourcing components abroad. The mix of parts purchased locally was changing. As assemblers rationalized their sourcing patterns, some chose to buy fewer parts from Venezuelan suppliers. Domestic demand for vehicles still had not recovered completely from the market contraction of 1989. Under these pressures, the Venezuelan auto parts producers had to compete fiercely on price and quality with the world leaders from the United States, Japan, and Europe, many for the first time.

Some Venezuelan parts manufacturers have had notable successes in supplying local assemblers in the face of competing imports. For example, by 1993, 20 percent of Ford's Venezuelan suppliers had qualified at Ford's Q-1 level. Changed conditions in the home market also spurred some leading parts producers to step up their efforts to penetrate foreign markets. Sidaven, a producer of chassis components, refocused its efforts from the home market to exports. In 1989, Sidaven sold 95 percent of its production in Venezuela,[147] but by 1993, it exported 85 percent of its production and aimed to become a world exporter.[148] For those parts suppliers that already had reached world-class quality standards, the next challenge was to become cost competitive in the major world markets. In 1993, several firms were making major efforts in this direction.

Most Venezuelan auto parts firms, however, lacked the resources of Sidaven or the other first-tier companies. For many of these firms, the new market was very difficult. To compete successfully, they had to be able to demonstrate their reliability to potential buyers through statistical process controls—something many of them lacked. Others lacked the experienced management required to restructure their costs. In addition, their captive market for replacement parts was being eroded by the proliferation of new imported models, many of which would not generate demand in the replacement market for parts produced by local industry. A small company could no longer meet its targets for the year by negotiating a single contract with a local assembler. The total number of Venezuelan auto parts firms fell, from 160 firms in 1988 to about 120 firms in 1992. Total employment in the Venezuelan auto parts sector fell by 7,000 between 1988 and 1992.

The Auto Pact: A Step Backwards?

In September 1993, the Venezuelan government signed an auto pact with Colombia and Ecuador that set common external tariffs and a regional content requirement. Under the agreement, Venezuela's tariff rate on imports of cars, small buses, and most trucks was 35 percent in 1994. At the assembly level, the pact required Venezuelan assemblers to use significant quantities of regionally produced parts in their local operations. The agreement set a floor on regional value added of 40 percent for most vehicles in 1994 and 45 percent in 1995. This froze local content at 1992 market levels in 1994 and thereafter will increase it well beyond the regional content levels that had been reached under open competition.

The stated purpose of the 1993 auto pact was to increase competition and efficiency.[149] In fact, the agreement will do just the opposite. There will be no efficiencies from increased competition, because there will be less competition. Nor will the pact stimulate efficiencies of scale to any great extent. In its entirety, the Andean Pact auto market is only 300,000 units—too small to support efficient-scale production. There will be some short-term jockeying for position as assemblers realign production and parts manufacturers work out their pattern of specialization in a small regional market. This will halt and partially roll back the trend toward improvement over the past few years, with potential ramifications for quality, price, and reliability of delivery. There will be renewed calls for the assemblers to lower standards to accommodate suppliers that refuse to meet them. The assemblers, with increased costs and less competitive pressure, are likely to raise prices.

The increased tariffs and lower productivity will hit the pockets of middle-income consumers hardest. These same consumers were just becoming accustomed to comparing prices, enjoying a wider selection of vehicles, and receiving better service. Meanwhile, costs will be lowered on imported luxury cars for the wealthy.

There might even be costs in that part of the sector that appears to gain the most from the 1993 auto pact. By 1993, a number of Venezuelan auto parts firms already had penetrated international markets and, as part of the struggle to win market share in these markets, had achieved the quality and

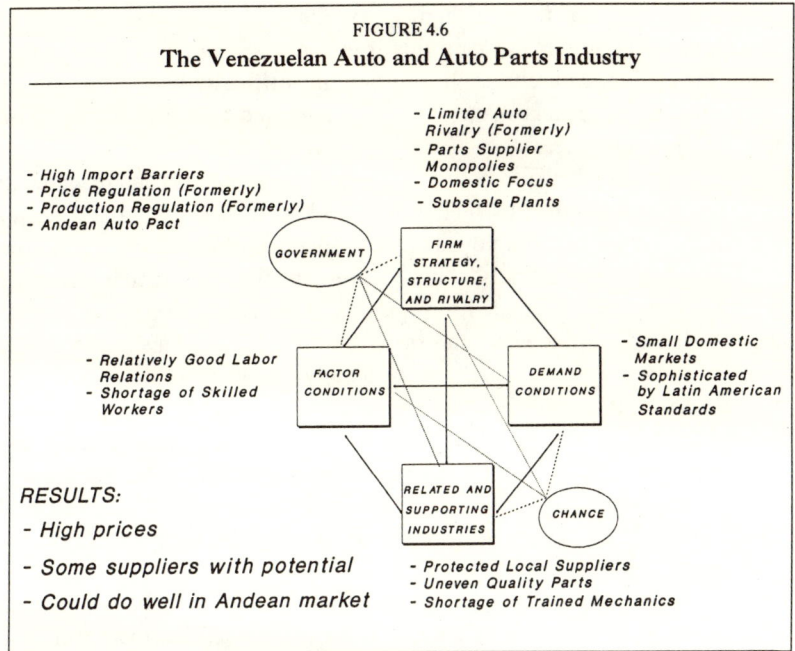

FIGURE 4.6
The Venezuelan Auto and Auto Parts Industry

efficiencies needed to compete both at home and abroad. While some of these companies will continue to pursue export markets under the 1993 auto pact, others might not. After all, why should they struggle to meet higher standards and tougher competition in international markets when the local market provides a safe haven free from such concerns? Even those that do will have to make different trade-offs in their decisions to serve a protected market against limited competition or to serve export markets against tougher competition. It is not clear that these companies will be able to achieve their true export potential, especially outside the Andean Pact, in this environment. (See Figure 4.6.)

The Costs of Protection

Does the Venezuelan auto policy make economic sense? Some argue that the purpose of the auto policy is to create and to protect jobs that would not exist under a free market regime. Auto sector jobs, the argument goes, provide the steady income and manufacturing skills that Venezuela's workforce needs. This argument has been an important rationale for Venezuela's protection of the automotive sector over the past 30 years. Others argue that it makes sense as a form of luxury tax. Only the relatively well off in Venezuela can afford to buy cars, this argument goes, and therefore it makes sense to "tax" auto purchases. In addition, the difficulty in collecting taxes in general in Venezuela makes an easily collected tax, such as tariffs on automobiles, attractive.

The Venezuelan automotive sector does generate jobs and revenue. In 1992, it employed approximately 6,000 workers in assembly. Estimates of the number of workers employed in the production of auto parts range from 19,000 to 45,000 workers.[150] Auto parts production and vehicle assembly together have been estimated to represent as much as 10 percent of total manufacturing employment, and these are well paying jobs.[151] Domestic sales revenues were $1.53 billion for locally produced vehicles and $540 million for locally produced components. The industry also provides a market for some raw materials produced in Venezuela, such as steel and aluminum. In 1992, assuming a weighted average tariff of 30 percent and $1.114 billion in after-tariff sales of imported automobiles, the tariff would have yielded $257 million in revenues. These were the main benefits of the automobile policy in effect in 1992.

Who pays the costs of protection? Consumers pay higher prices than they would in the absence of a tariff. If we assume a 30 percent weighted average tariff, this would imply a pretariff import value of $857 million in 1992. In that case, an average tariff of 30 percent would represent $257 million in tariff payments and another $353 million (out of domestic vehicle sales of $1.53 billion) in higher prices paid to domestic assemblers, for a total of $610 million in artificially high prices. If we assume 50,000 employees in the Venezuelan industry, which is at the upper range of employment estimates made by industry experts, this means that the consumer pays $12,200 in tariff subsidies for every auto sector job. At 25,000 employees, the low end of industry estimates, this means that the consumer pays $24,400 in tariff subsidies per job. Although this simple calculation oversimplifies the tariff structure, correction does not materially affect the result. If we accept the luxury tax argument and only take the $353 million into account, the range of consumer subsidy per auto sector job is between $14,120 and $7,060. This is still very high for an industry in which compensation and benefits averaged approximately $8,500 per worker.[152]

The auto pact of 1993 will raise these subsidies further. For a 35 percent tariff, assuming no fall-off in demand, the total of tariffs ($300 million) and higher prices paid to domestic assemblers ($413 million) would be $713 million. This would give a range of consumer subsidies of $28,520 to $14,260 per auto sector job. If we exclude the tariff figure, the range of subsidy would be from $16,520 to $8,260 per job. If, on the other hand, we assume that the auto pact of 1993 results in an effective incremental increase in the tariff of 5 percent (from 30 percent to 35 percent), this would mean an increment of $113 million (assuming away impact on demand). If this were to preserve 10,000 jobs (a generous assumption, since approximately 2,500 assembly jobs and 7,000 auto parts jobs were lost from 1988 to 1992), it would mean a transfer from consumers of $11,300 per job. If it preserves 7,500 jobs, it would mean a tariff subsidy of $15,066 per job. Even if we accept the luxury tax argument and reduce the calculated subsidies accordingly, the incremental subsidies per incremental job would be on the order of $6,000 (saving 10,000 jobs) to $8,000 (saving 7,500 jobs).

Although higher prices are a cost to the consumer, with respect to the Venezuelan economy as a whole, they represent transfers to the treasury, to auto assemblers and parts manufacturers, and to auto sector employees. High prices for new automobiles will tend to increase prices for used cars as well. The costs to the economy as a whole come about through the deadweight loss associated with reduced demand at artificially high prices for both new and used cars. This loss cannot be estimated from available data. Presumably consumers would spend at least some of the money that they saved on auto purchases on other items, which would increase employment in other industries. While a much more detailed analysis would be necessary to reach precise estimates, the simple calculation gives us an idea of the magnitude of the transfers paid by consumers. Questions of this nature rarely received much attention in the past, but in today's Venezuela, transfers and costs should become a major part of the discussion of protection.

Venezuelans need to ask themselves some very hard questions about their automotive policy. Is this a jobs program? If so, it is a very expensive one. Can Venezuela afford it, given its costs to the consumer? If the answer is that the policy is in fact a luxury tax on the rich, then the question is: Is there a more effective and efficient way to collect taxes? Moreover, if the aim is to impose a luxury tax, why not tax vehicles assembled in Venezuela as well as imports? In addition, if the tax is to be on the rich, why does the 1993 auto pact lower the tariff rate for cars with a CIF value higher than $15,000, while raising it for less expensive cars? If the purpose of protectionism was to give the Venezuelan auto parts producers a chance to get established, does it make any sense to continue it now, when competition against the world's best in foreign markets might in fact be their best medicine? Ultimately, the auto pact, and auto protection in general, is a policy choice to be made by Venezuelans. Many nations protect their auto industries. The problem is that protection of such a scale-sensitive industry involves particularly high transfers in nations with small markets. It is to be hoped that in Venezuela such choices will be fully informed ones.

Warning Signs

There are a number of warning signs in the auto pact of 1993. The first is the seeming disregard for consumers. Although Venezuelan consumers might wind up with more choice and lower prices than they would under a system in which the Venezuelan market was protected from all outside competition, they probably will wind up with less choice and higher prices than under the policy that was in effect in 1992. The second is that political influence and protection rather than efficiency and competitiveness seem to be guiding this policy. The road to profits in the auto sector might once again involve government intervention rather than investment and productivity. The third is that some Venezuelan managers, who lobbied for local content requirements of up to 80 percent, seem to be more intent on seeking out preferential treatment than in getting on with the business of creating a more competitive nation. Finally, the policy sets a questionable precedent in using the Andean Pact as an excuse for protection. Once free trade arguments are used to disguise protection in one industry, it becomes easier to do so in other industries. This is a cause for concern in the context of a nation that is in many ways new to open competition in the world trade environment.

Conclusion

This chapter has identified sources of advantage and disadvantage faced by particular industries in Venezuela. The six industries profiled illustrate important issues that cut across the nation's economy. A number of positives emerge from the profiles. In certain industries and segments of industries, Venezuela holds its own with the world's best competitors. It has substantial potential in some others. The economic opening has forced firms to focus on improving productivity and efficiency and has encouraged investment in nontraditional industries. Although some firms have had difficulties in adjusting, others have moved to take advantage of new opportunities. The profiles show that local and foreign firms can and will invest to build their companies and industries in Venezuela when given the opportunity. The profiles also indicate that there could be a substantial payoff to the nation for getting prices right, for investing in human resources, for improving local capital markets, and for better management of the nation's resources.

The industry profiles also point out a number of obstacles to development and progress in the Venezuelan context. The availability of oil rents in the 1970s and early 1980s helped to fund industrialization based on import substitution rather than intrinsic efficiency. Import substitution policies distorted incentives and made it uneconomical to develop certain resources and industries within the nation. They also limited the incentives for firms to improve their efficiency and learn how to serve customers. Government intervention has helped to create industries in Venezuela, but it also has left them hampered by bureaucracy and politicization. The profiles show that even well-intentioned government policy can have counterproductive results. They highlight the importance of developing deep, long-term capital markets. Venezuela has far to go before its capital markets can support long-term strategies, particularly in capital-intensive industries. Finally, the cost of protection has been, and continues to be, paid by Venezuelan consumers.

These positives, negatives, and issues found in the Venezuelan economy will be addressed further in subsequent chapters.

5

Venezuelan Industry Summaries

The six industries profiled in Chapter 4 illustrate important issues for the Venezuelan economy. Although space considerations preclude us from providing detailed abstracts of the other seven industries we studied in this project, here we discuss them briefly. These discussions highlight the salient features of the industries and identify the issues that they face going forward.

Petroleum[1]

The oil industry has accounted for roughly 25 percent of Venezuelan GDP since the 1970s. Venezuelan exports of petroleum and its derivatives reached about $12 billion in 1991 and $11.2 billion in 1992.[2] In 1991, petroleum and its derivatives accounted for 81 percent of Venezuela's total exports, while all of Venezuela's non-oil exports combined amounted to $2.85 billion.[3] Given its importance to the economy, the petroleum industry features prominently in remaining chapters in this book. In this chapter we highlight some of the key attributes and challenges of the industry.

Profitability in the oil business depends largely on two factors: oil reserves and low production costs. Venezuela has both. Its proven oil reserves are the sixth largest in the world. Its cost of production is higher than in the Persian Gulf States but is relatively low compared to most other oil-producing countries. The Venezuelan petroleum industry also possesses highly professional and competent managerial and technical staffs. PDVSA has been a center of technology development, management training, and supplier development, not just for the petroleum industry but for the nation as well. (See Chapters 6 and 7.)

Because of its high profile, PDVSA attracts some of the best business and engineering talent in Venezuela. It sometimes has difficulty keeping this talent, especially with the recent increases in professional salaries in the private sector. PDVSA has acted as a training ground for Venezuelan engineers and management. Former PDVSA employees populate most of the leading Venezuelan engineering and consulting firms. Many of the managers in the chemical industry, and other industries for that matter, were once employed at PDVSA.

Since 1976, when the oil industry was nationalized, PDVSA has proven its ability to succeed in international oil markets. It has developed downstream capabilities and marketing channels through acquisition in the United States and alliance in Europe. The most pressing question for the Venezuelan oil industry is whether the state and the political parties will give PDVSA the financial and operational independence that it needs for future growth. PDVSA predicts that if the fiscal drain on the oil sector continues unabated, oil production and revenues will peak in the year 1997 and decline steadily thereafter.

Issues Facing the Industry

Product Mix and Yields. In recent years, the bulk of the nation's oil reserves has shifted toward heavy and extra-heavy crudes just as world demand has moved in the opposite direction, toward light crudes. This puts a premium on making the most of Venezuela's remaining light crudes, which in turn requires capital investment. It also places a premium on exploring for as-yet undiscovered light crude reserves. Regions where there is a likelihood of finding light crudes include northeastern Monagas, Amacuro, northeastern Barinas, offshore the Orinoco Delta, west and east of the Maracaibo basin, and northeastern Guárico. Exploring these areas and developing new fields will require substantial investments—an estimated $4 billion.[4]

PDVSA also needs to maximize yields from existing wells. Doing so will entail stepping up application of techniques to increase output of the older wells that are still producing and also reactivating wells that have been allowed to cease operation because of high operating costs (the so-called marginal wells). Many other areas also will require significant capital investments, such as projects to turn extra-heavy crudes into higher-quality synthetic crudes and projects for the commercial production of Orimulsion, a fuel derived from bitumen. PDVSA has devised comprehensive plans to maximize production and earnings. The total capital costs required to do this are estimated at $37.8 billion through the year 2003.

Price Volatility and Decline. Volatility in oil prices is one of the major sources of uncertainty in the Venezuelan economy. Over the last several years, the economy has been subject to fluctuations in oil revenues that have averaged 6 percent of GDP. Fluctuations of this magnitude would be difficult for any nation. Former Cordiplan minister Ricardo Hausmann has proposed the creation of an oil stabilization fund that would be used to even out the fluctuations in oil revenues. It is not clear whether Venezuela has the funds or the political will to do so at this time.

Perhaps more important than price fluctuations has been the overall price decline since the early 1980s. Much of the increase in Venezuela's standard of living in the 1970s and subsequent decline in the 1980s can be attributed to changes in oil prices. In late 1993, real oil prices reached their lowest level since the mid-1970s. Prices could fall even lower once Iraq reenters world markets. Venezuela can do little to affect world oil prices other than to do its best to look out for its interests in the Organization of Oil Exporting Countries (OPEC).

Heavy Tax Burden. The dilemma faced by PDVSA, and the country as a whole, is that the state is siphoning off too much oil revenue. As of 1993, the state taxed the oil industry at 67.7 percent on net taxable income and inflated the export revenue tax base by adding a markup of 20 percent to export earnings. At the same time, PDVSA was required to supply the domestic gasoline and oil market at subsidized prices that barely covered production costs. Every year, the requirements of the domestic market grow, and, as a result, the availability of products for export shrinks. All of this reduces PDVSA's cash flow and the capital available for productive investment.

According to PDVSA projections, if its fiscal burden is not mitigated, national production would rise slightly from 1993 levels and peak at about 2.7 million barrels per day in 1997. Thereafter, production would fall into a steady decline, sinking to about 1.7 million barrels per day by 2012. National oil income (PDVSA's before-tax earnings) would fall by about one-third. In contrast, PDVSA projects that if its fiscal burden is relieved and it pursues its plans for growth, national oil production would rise to nearly 5 million barrels per day by 2012, boosting national oil income by 100 percent.

Future Challenges.[5] Any analysis regarding PDVSA's future must start with the recognition of the basic limitations that are constraining its development: a lack of financial resources for investment and of the political support that it needs in order to adopt strategic options that will ensure its long-term growth. Although these two limiting factors also affect other oil companies, in Venezuela they assume added seriousness because the firm's shareholder is a sovereign state.

State ownership of PDVSA seriously constrains its financial resources and financing options. In order to finance additional investments in the petroleum sector, PDVSA must compete for public funds that normally would be used by the government for its recurrent expenditures and investment. Moreover, state ownership is an obstacle to financing the expansion of PDVSA through conventional means such as bank loans or bond issues, because such debts would be considered additional sovereign debt, of a country that already has the fourth largest external debt in Latin America.[6]

The simplest way to finance an aggressive expansion of the Venezuelan oil industry would be through the participation of foreign capital. While this foreign capital could be invested only in downstream segments or in the petrochemical sector, as has been done to date, such a course of action might create a problem of imbalance between the volume of crude oil and of oil-based products. Moreover, in an international market characterized by a combination of a world recession and competitive pressures from other OPEC members, it is particularly important to ensure overseas markets for Venezuelan petroleum production. Alliance with foreign firms is an effective way to secure foreign market access for Venezuelan petroleum and its derivatives.

For these reasons, the best options for developing the Venezuelan oil industry would involve foreign investments in the traditional areas of the industry. However, this avenue of expansion would require substantive changes in the petroleum legislation now in effect and, in turn, very considerable political support. If these changes are accomplished, PDVSA then would be free to adopt a development strategy similar to that of the major transnational oil companies, which would involve greater production at home and abroad, greater processing capacity at home and abroad, and the widening of distribution channels in foreign markets. These actions would permit risk diversification and the exploitation of fiscal advantages in the countries that would receive Venezuelan investment.[7] (See Figure 5.1.)

Aluminum[8]

In 1992, Venezuela exported aluminum and related manufactures worth $710 million, which placed aluminum first among non-oil exports.[9] Venezuela ranks ninth in terms of primary aluminum production capacity, ac-

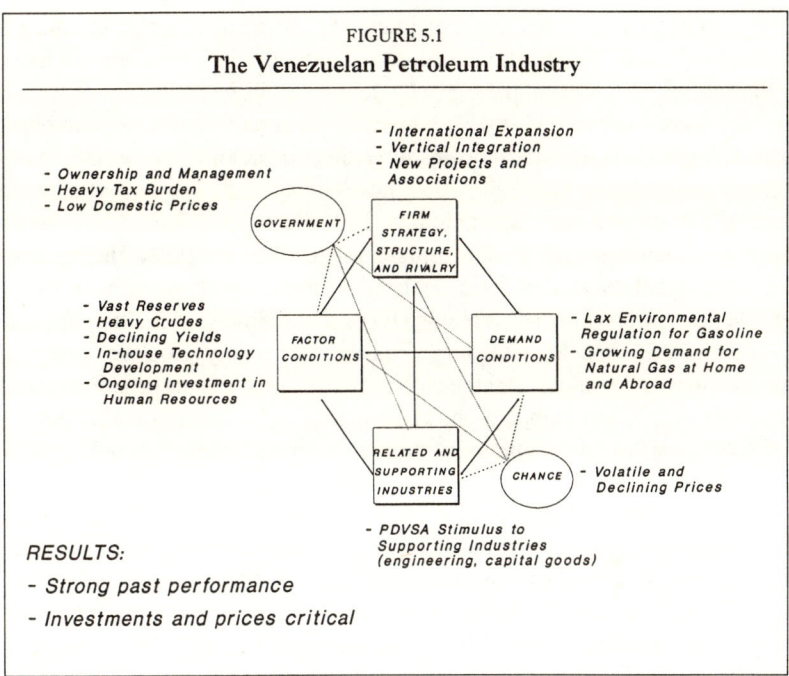

FIGURE 5.1
The Venezuelan Petroleum Industry

RESULTS:
- Strong past performance
- Investments and prices critical

counting for an estimated 3.3 percent of the world total.[10] With its vast supplies of low-cost hydroelectric power and deposits of high-grade bauxite, Venezuela should be the lowest-cost producer of primary aluminum in the world. However, the Venezuelan industry has had difficulty translating its natural factor advantages into cost leadership, despite subsidies, capitalization of debts, and other preferential treatment by the state.

Over the past three decades, the Venezuelan state has built the aluminum sector from the ground up.[11] It has invested heavily to provide low-cost energy, raw material inputs, capital, infrastructure, and production technology. At the same time, state ownership has constrained the ability of the Venezuelan aluminum producers to evolve into cost-efficient competitors in the world market. The two major producers of primary aluminum in Venezuela, Venezolana de Aluminio (Venalum) and Aluminio del Caroní, S.A. (Alcasa), are both majority owned by the Corporación Venezolana de Guayana (CVG). The CVG has divided products, as well as foreign and domestic markets and clients, between the two firms so as to avoid rivalry. Domestic purchasers of primary aluminum have lacked the bargaining power to pressure the two firms to innovate or improve.[12] The state for many years shielded Alcasa and Venalum from financial pressures and market discipline. (See Chapter 7.) At the same time, the Venezuelan firms suffered from political pressures incompatible with long-term efficiency. Venalum and Alcasa were subject to frequent changes in management and political pressures to generate positive short-term results, which tended to inflate long-term costs.

Primary aluminum accounted for 100 percent and 83 percent, respectively, of Venalum and Alcasa's sales in metric tons in 1991. The international commodity market for primary aluminum is very volatile. In 1993, world prices were severely depressed by excess supplies in both the Western world and the former Soviet Union. Producers of primary aluminum compete on cost in world markets, and the cost of electric power is the most important element in this cost competition. The existence of a local, low-cost supply of bauxite also can confer a significant cost advantage, though this is secondary.

The Venezuelan industry should be able to convert low-cost energy into an important cost advantage in aluminum production, but this effort is still under way. The cost to Venalum and Alcasa of hydroelectric energy produced by Edelca is very low in world terms and compares favorably to prices charged to Canadian aluminum smelters by Hydro Quebec and Manitoba Hydro. (See Chapter 6.) Bauxita de Venezuela (Bauxiven) produces bauxite from deposits located 600 kilometers distant from Puerto Ordaz, where the rest of the industry is located. Bauxiven has encountered a series of difficulties and not until 1993 was it able to provide Interalúmina, the alumina producer, with an adequate supply of bauxite. Carbonorca, a public company in which Venalum and Alcasa are the primary shareholders, produces carbon anodes for primary aluminum reduction. It generated losses in its first few years and required capital contributions from the aluminum firms. Carbonorca was established on the premise that the Venezuelan industry was going to expand in the near future; because expansion has not occurred as anticipated, the firm is encountering difficulties. As of early 1994, Carbonorca was supplying Venalum with anodes to redress a temporary deficit caused by the reconstruction of Venalum's furnaces. It will be difficult for Carbonorca to become profitable unless it exports its future production, which at present does not appear to be feasible.[13]

The total costs of Venalum and Alcasa over the last several years probably never will be fully understood, due to less-than-transparent state capitalizations and other practices.[14] Both Venalum and Alcasa have reported losses since 1991. González de Pacheco (1993) has estimated that based on the costs reported in the firms' own annual reports, in 1991 Venalum's total costs (including return on investment) were below the international average for aluminum producers in Western nations. However, Venalum did not fall within the 25 percent of this international production capacity with the lowest costs. Venalum unofficially reports that it has made substantial reductions in its cost of production in 1993. According to González de Pacheco (1993), in 1991 Alcasa's costs of production (including its reduction, lamination, and foil operations) placed it within the quartile with the highest costs. According to Alcasa, its cost of production for laminating operations in 1991 ranked, in international terms, in the same quartile as Venalum. In 1993, Alcasa's debts, which had been exacerbated by costly expansion, reached $678 million, equal to 281.7 percent of sales.[15] Its interest expense per metric ton rendered even its most efficient lines unprofitable at 1993 world prices.[16]

Issues Facing the Industry

Lack of Skilled Human Resources. Venalum and Alcasa are suffering from shortages in skilled human resources. Skilled blue-collar workers have left in large numbers, as a result of the severance payment system, opportunities for speculative investment, and uncertainty over the industry's future. The effects of labor flight have been exacerbated by a hiring freeze, which has made it impossible to fill the posts left empty by the departed workers. The high rate of turnover among skilled workers and technicians makes it difficult for the Venezuelan firms to progress along the learning curve and to optimize production. The early 1990s also have witnessed the flight of white-collar employees from the aluminum companies. Venalum and Alcasa would benefit from more professional expertise in finance and international marketing, including sales contract negotiation and foreign market intelligence.[17]

Mastering the Basics. Aluminum is traded in three basic forms: primary, semifinished, and finished. Primary aluminum is a commodity whose price is subject to volatile fluctuations in world supply and demand. The leading producers of aluminum in the industrialized nations are shifting their focus from basic aluminum and its inputs to semifinished and finished aluminum products, with higher value added.[18] However, it is necessary to master the efficient production of primary aluminum before advancing downstream to semifinished and finished aluminum, markets that demand greater technological, management, and marketing expertise. The immediate challenge that the Venezuelan industry faces in this regard is to overcome the operational and management difficulties in the primary aluminum sector that have kept it from fully realizing its potential cost advantages.

Restructuring and Privatization. In July 1993, the recently appointed president of CVG, Francisco Layrisse, announced a major restructuring of the industry. Bauxiven, Interalúmina, and Venalum were soon in the process of being merged into a single company, Bauxilum. As of May 1994, the legal merger between Bauxiven and Interalúmina was complete. Venalum's merger into the new firm was awaiting the approval of its minority Japanese shareholders and was expected to proceed without difficulty. The three companies already were functioning as an integrated firm. This eliminated several layers of management and permitted better coordination of firm policies and activities. The merger also was expected to reduce personnel costs and to bring the organization of the Venezuelan aluminum industry more into line with the structure adopted by the most successful firms worldwide. It was expected that Venalum's Japanese minority shareholders would be invited to participate in the unified firm.

Alcasa's financial crisis was too severe to permit its inclusion in the new company.[19] As of 1994, Alcasa was doing everything possible to find a partner and thereby continue to operate. Alcasa transferred part of its holdings in other companies to its creditors, principally Interalúmina. Its holdings in its foil plant at Guacara were partially divested in order to pay debts to local banks, forming a new firm, Aluminios de Carabobo, in which the banks held a majority interest. Nevertheless, Alcasa continued to face serious difficulties, especially because of its inability to pay its debts to Edelca and Interalúmina, its major suppliers.

It is hoped that further privatization will allow a fresh start for the Venezuelan aluminum industry. Under effective management, the industry should be able to parlay its natural advantages into long-term profitability.

Attraction of Foreign Investment. It is unlikely that the capital and expertise necessary to put the Venezuelan aluminum industry on a firm footing will be available from Venezuelan sources alone. No doubt foreign capital and expertise will be required. It will be very important that negotiations with foreign companies be transparent so that the Venezuelan people and Congress will know what to expect going forward. It is important, for example, that the Venezuelan people understand that Alcasa is more a liability of the state than an asset, and its future sale or closure must reflect this fact. (See Figure 5.2.)

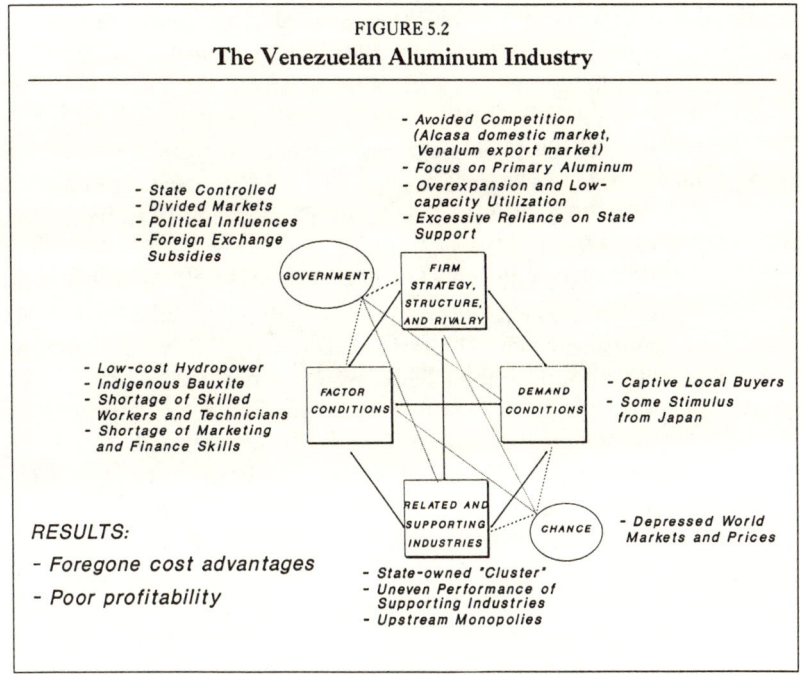

FIGURE 5.2
The Venezuelan Aluminum Industry

Cocoa[20]

Venezuela possesses excellent growing conditions for the cultivation of fine cocoa as well as unique, local varieties of specialty cocoa beans. In the eighteenth century, Venezuela was a major producer of cocoa, and its cocoa was considered to be the world's finest. Sixteen million cocoa trees, stretching from Cumaná to Maracaibo, were the mainstay of Venezuela's colonial economy.[21] Venezuela's shift to coffee in the nineteenth century and oil in the twentieth century sent the cocoa industry into decline. In the meantime, new producers around the world entered mass cocoa production. Today, the world's largest producers include the Ivory Coast, Brazil, Ghana, Malaysia, and Indonesia. Venezuela is only a marginal producer in international terms. In 1992, for example, Venezuela exported approximately 7,000 metric tons of cocoa beans and derivative products worth about $9.7 million, which accounted for less than 0.2 percent of world exports of cocoa beans.[22]

The cocoa exported by Venezuela is categorized as "fine or flavor cocoa." "Fine or flavor" cocoa is used primarily in dark chocolate of high quality, including plain, vanilla, and semisweet chocolates and chocolate coatings. It is a specialty product that is not used in mass-produced chocolate.[23] The highest-quality "fine or flavor" cocoa normally commands a premium over ordinary cocoa in international markets. Purchasers value the quality of the cocoa bean (aroma, color, and size), reputation, consistency, and reliability of delivery. Traditionally, seven or eight types of Venezuelan cocoa beans were sold on international markets under recognized names such as Carúpano, Río Caribe, Carenero Superior, Chuao, and Maracaibo, which had built up brand loyalties among international buyers.

From 1975 to 1991, the National Cocoa Fund (FONCACAO), a state marketing board, held a monopoly over the purchase, distribution, and export of Venezuelan cocoa beans. The marketing board was created to support particular political constituencies. FONCACAO eliminated the brand-based marketing system for cocoa exports, thus destroying the brand recognition that had helped Venezuelan sales in foreign markets. Instead, it set three generic product designations for Venezuelan cocoa beans: "extra fine," fine first class *(fino de primera)*, and fine second class *(fino de segunda)*.

FONCACAO was not a demanding purchaser. As a result, producers had little incentive to produce cocoa beans up to international standards. Large traditional growers stopped production. The quality of their beans and the quality of Venezuelan product suffered—in a market where quality and reliability are of paramount importance.[24] In 1991, FONCACAO lost its monopoly over the collection, marketing, and export of cocoa beans. The three principal purchasers of the 1991-1992 harvest were FONCACAO, APROCAO (the Cocoa Processors Association), and CACAOVECA (Venezuelan Cocoa, Inc., the leading association of cocoa farmers). FONCACAO was still exporting, but it was debilitated by funding cuts. CACAOVECA encountered the sorts of logistical problems to be expected in collecting and storing large quantities of cocoa beans for the first time. Between 2,000 and 3,000 metric tons of low-quality beans made it to the international market, further eroding the reputation of the Venezuelan product.

As of 1993, Venezuelan cocoa growers could sell their product directly in the domestic and international markets. CACAOVECA was planning to expand and to rationalize its system for receiving and storing cocoa beans, and to improve its cash and product flow. Steps were being taken to improve the quality of Venezuelan cocoa beans for export. The Comercializadora Cacao de Venezuela (CCV), which was formed in 1992 as a joint venture with the growers to sell high-quality Venezuelan cocoa beans overseas, was taking steps to reintroduce Venezuelan brand names to the market and to provide financing to selected producers to improve the productivity of their plantations. Cacaotera Santa María was working with selected local producers to improve the quality and uniformity of their product. Palmaven and Chocolates El Rey were jointly investing, through Agropecuaria Palmacao S.A., in a new cocoa plantation for future export of first-quality cocoa to specialty users. Palmaven and French investors were cultivating Porcelana cocoa (once world famous), south of Lake Maracaibo, for export.[25] In the domestic market, increased competition in the chocolate candy segment, brought about by imports of chocolate, was boosting the sophistication of local demand for cocoa beans.[26] Venezuelan agroindustry was becoming more selective in purchasing cocoa beans, and purchase price was now more closely linked to quality.

Issues Facing the Industry

International Market Trends. The Venezuelan cocoa industry faces several challenges in the coming years. An oversupply of basic cocoa beans in world markets is predicted through the year 2000, and prices are depressed. "Fine or flavor" cocoa also faces increased competition from ordinary cocoa and other confectionery ingredients. Many of the world's largest manufacturers of chocolates have discontinued the use of "fine or flavor" cocoa in favor of ordinary cocoa beans in order to maximize economies of scale in purchasing and processing.[27] Small chocolate makers, who used to buy specialty cocoa beans and grind them in-house, are increasingly purchasing ground cocoa from the larger cocoa processing firms.[28] To succeed under these conditions, it will be essential for Venezuelan cocoa exporters to target the specialty niche market and to establish Venezuelan cocoa as a product that is of consistent quality and availability.

Low Productivity. Venezuela possesses "criollo" cocoa varieties that produce beans renowned for their aroma as well as growing conditions that are uniquely suited for the production of high-quality cocoa. However, the average cocoa plantation in Venezuela reflects decades of neglect. Most cocoa producers are peasant farmers (the average holding is less than five hectares) who are undercapitalized and do not invest in the basic maintenance needed to keep their cocoa plants productive.[29] Many trees are old and infected. In some cocoa-producing areas, cultivation, fermentation, and drying techniques have hardly advanced since the eighteenth century. The traditional Venezuelan cocoa plantation has an average yield of only 300 kilograms per hectare.[30] It is estimated that these yields would double if local farmers applied fertilizers, herbicides, and some mechanization. Modern, plantation-style cultivation easily can produce yields of 1,000 kilograms per hectare, with some yields as high as 2,400 kilograms per hectare. However, weaknesses in the "criollo" cultivars from which much fine or flavor cocoa is produced (such as susceptibility to disease) is a constraint on yields, and additional agricultural research to develop improved strains of "criollo" cocoa is urgently needed.

Shortage of Technical Expertise. There is a shortage of Venezuelan technical expertise in cocoa growing. Efforts by state-sponsored researchers to breed more disease-resistant strains of cocoa have backfired. Hybridization did strengthen the resistance of the trees, but it had a negative impact on aroma, flavor, and fermentation. As the hybrid trees have been planted in local plantations, it is common to find as much as 20 percent unfermented cocoa mixed in with properly fermented cocoa.

Building a New Reputation. The key to getting a good price for cocoa on world markets is to offer a differentiated product and to establish direct relationships with the final customers. One option for Venezuelan growers would be to specialize in certain specific varieties of cocoa and to develop direct relationships with end users in the United States, Japan, and elsewhere. It will be crucial to convince foreign buyers that Venezuela will indeed provide a continuous and reliable supply of differentiated cocoa. Building a solid reputation in the international cocoa market is a long-term proposition that will require long-term commitment from the industry. The industry needs to improve local cocoa yields, to attract additional private investment in modern plantations, and to promote the development of improved cocoa hybrids. One urgent task is to work to eliminate or to reverse the damage done by the introduction of poor-fermenting or non-flavor trees. (See Figure 5.3.)

Rice[31]

In 1992, the Venezuelan rice sector harvested about 600,000 metric tons of paddy rice, which accounted for approximately 0.1 percent of world rice production.[32] Venezuela grows rice primarily for domestic consumption and over the past decade has engaged in export only sporadically, in years of domestic surplus. In 1992, a year of unusually high rice exports, Venezuela exported approximately 50,000 metric tons of rice worth around $14 million.[33] Nevertheless, rice is Venezuela's leading grain export. Venezuela possesses favorable natural conditions for the cultivation of rice, including extensive tracts of arable land, good topography, and good climate. This

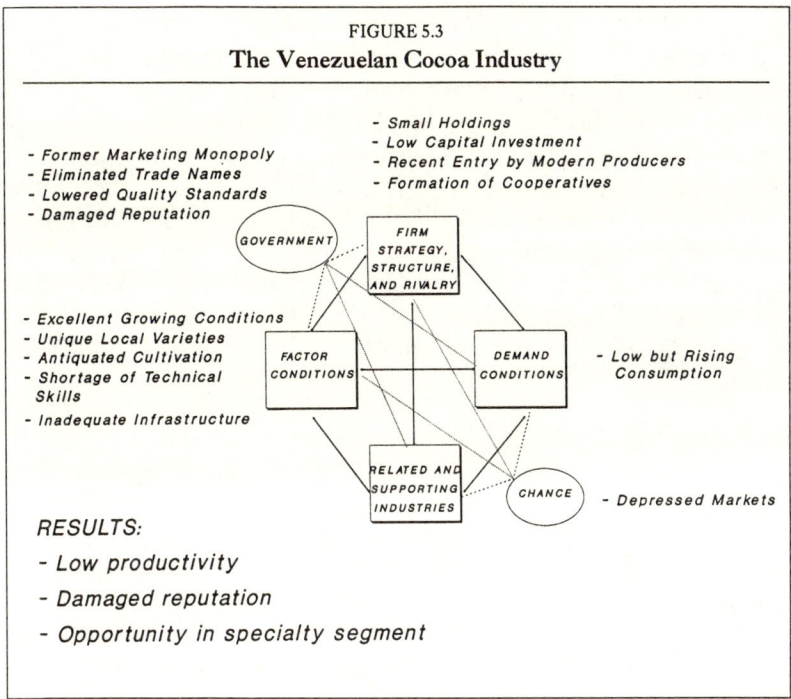

FIGURE 5.3
The Venezuelan Cocoa Industry

RESULTS:
- Low productivity
- Damaged reputation
- Opportunity in specialty segment

natural potential has been expanded by substantial investments in modern agricultural equipment (such as tractors and combines), irrigation and other infrastructure, and cultivation technology. The rice milling sector has the most modern plants and the largest installed capacity within the Andean Pact.

The economic rules of the game in the Venezuelan rice sector are still in a state of flux. For several decades, the state intervened heavily in this sector. Until 1984, the state, through the Corporation for Agricultural Marketing (CMA), bought and stored all domestically grown rice, and brokered it to domestic millers. During the 1980s, the state set a minimum price per ton at the producer level. It also heavily subsidized fertilizers, up to 80 percent of sales price, and made subsidized financing available to growers through state agencies and the private banking sector. Subsidized foreign exchange was available for the purchase of imported inputs such as pesticides.

Following the commercial opening, protectionist barriers to rice and other grains were lowered and the state largely eliminated producer subsidies. Interest rates and producer prices were freed. Costs, including the cost of financing, rose faster than prices, and profits fell sharply. This is a sector that has given high priority to investing in modern agricultural infrastructure and cultivation technologies. The national average yield per hectare increased 30 percent between 1980 and 1993. However, many farmers are weighted down by inefficiencies that are in large part the legacy of the marketing board system. Many lack the ability to dry and to store their crops. This raises the risk of spoilage because rice must be dried promptly upon harvesting, and it forces farmers to sell their crop immediately after harvest, regardless of market conditions. Under the old system, they had little incentive to invest in drying and storing capabilities, because these functions were performed by the state and they had no need for the marketing flexibility that these capabilities would confer.[34]

Issues Facing the Industry

Finding New Markets. Demand for rice in Venezuela is relatively low, a reflection of the nation's highly urban population and cosmopolitan tastes. Per-capita annual consumption is 16 kilos, compared to about 30 kilos per person in Colombia and 60 kilos in Brazil.[35] The domestic market will continue to expand at or slightly above the rate of population growth. However, the rice milling sector was operating at only 50 percent capacity in 1993. If this sector is to raise its capacity utilization rates significantly in the short term, it will be necessary to boost domestic demand through advertising and to penetrate export markets. In the past, Venezuela exported rice in small quantities to Colombia, the United States, the Caribbean islands of Aruba, Grenada, and Saint Martin, and Spain, but the nation is not yet an established participant in the international rice trade. The major obstacles faced by Venezuelan rice producers in developing export markets are the presence of strong, subsidized foreign competitors, protectionist barriers against rice imports, and the weak price competitiveness of their product in most markets.

International Market Conditions. The international rice market is highly volatile and is dominated by major low-cost producers such as Thailand and the United States, which subsidize their rice production. Import barriers also distort international markets. Venezuela's export of 50,000 kilos to Colombia in 1992 resulted in a countervailing duty suit against Venezuela before the JUNAC (Cartagena Agreement Commission), and a settlement is being negotiated. Venezuela must protect its interests effectively in negotiations with Colombia if it is to develop a regional market for its rice. In northern Colombia alone, an estimated 10 million inhabitants have a high per-capita consumption of rice. According to some estimates, costs of production per metric ton in Venezuela are lower than those in Colombia.[36]

Boosting Productivity. To succeed in world markets, Venezuelan rice would have to compete on the basis of price with the world leaders, including the United States, Thailand, and Vietnam. However, Venezuelan rice cannot compete on price with rice from the United States in most export markets. Venezuelan rice exports also face competition from rice imports from Thailand and Vietnam, even within the Andean Pact. In 1992, negotiations to sell Venezuelan rice to Peru failed because the Venezuelan rice could not compete on price with rice from Thailand and Vietnam, due in part to the high cost of freight overland from Venezuela to Peru.

The cost per hectare of growing rice in the United States and Venezuela is comparable, but yields per hectare are much higher in the United States (on average, 6,600 kilos per hectare) than in Venezuela (on average, 4,000 kilos per hectare).[37] The principal challenge faced by the Venezuelan rice sector is to boost yields substantially while containing costs. Many areas urgently need an adequate supply of certified seed and the development of improved varieties suited to local conditions. (It is estimated that in Portuguesa State, fully 48 percent of cultivated area is sown with uncertified seeds,[38] resulting in lower yields and higher cultivation costs than otherwise would be the case.) It also will be important for growers and agroindustry to reduce inefficiencies across the entire process of drying, storing, and processing rice. For example, it is not unusual for different varieties of rice to be dried together in a single lot, which causes higher spoilage rates than would otherwise be the case. Cost efficiency also could be improved by adapting the varieties of rice seed sown by the growers to the specific processing requirements of agroindustry.

Private Sector Initiatives. Venezuelan rice producers have taken steps to improve productivity and efficiency. As of 1993, most technicians who advised rice growers had been trained thanks to the initiative and participation of the agricultural associations. This is a very significant contribution given that no technical school in Venezuela graduates technicians skilled in rice cultivation. APROSCELLO (Association of Certified Seed Producers of the Central Western Plains) has directed a series of workshops for training specialists in rice cultivation and for identifying problems in plantation management, with the support of the International Center for Tropical Agriculture (CIAT). APROSCELLO, among others, also has been active in programs that provide financing and technical assistance to growers as well as research programs to promote the production and sale of high-quality seeds. As of 1993, rice growers and processors were considering new initiatives to promote research in rice cultivation that would utilize the resources of the agricultural research agency, FONAIAP. For such efforts to succeed, it will be essential to devise and to implement effective mechanisms for technology transfer to the growers.

Government Policies. After provisional President Ramón Velásquez took office in 1993, government policies toward agriculture, including rice, took a turn toward increased protection of local producers and government market intervention. In the fall of 1993, the ministry of agriculture took steps to increase protection by modifying the "price band" scheme to raise the levels of duties on imported foodstuffs. Since then, the government has exempted agricultural producers from the Pro-Competition Law, an open invitation to return to past price-setting practices. This permitted producers and agroindustry, under the auspices of the ministry of agriculture, to agree to raise prices at the producer level. In January 1994, the government set a ceiling on retail prices for rice (and other products of "primary necessity"). Since then, the government and certain sectors, including agroindustry, have begun discussions aimed at setting "concerted" prices in an effort to control inflation. If past experience is any indication, new producer subsidies or "minimum" producer prices, which would hit the poor particularly hard, are not far behind. In 1994, the executive issued a decree requiring commercial banks to refinance the debts of agricultural producers at preferential terms.

As discussed, the Venezuelan rice producers have made progress in improving yields and costs, but still have to improve cost efficiencies before they can compete on price with the lowest-cost producers in the world. The shifts in policy during the 1993-1994 period suggest that the government is willing to support a rice-producing sector in Venezuela in return for political support from certain interest groups. It is not at all clear that this is an effective use of Venezuela's scarce resources. (See Figure 5.4.)

Textiles[39]

In 1992, Venezuelan exports of textiles and related manufactures (including clothing) totaled $49 million.[40] The nation's balance of trade in textile and related manufactures was sharply negative, with imports valued at $379.1 million in 1991.[41] The Venezuelan textile sector developed as an import substitution industry, and, with the exception of synthetic fibers, its tradi-

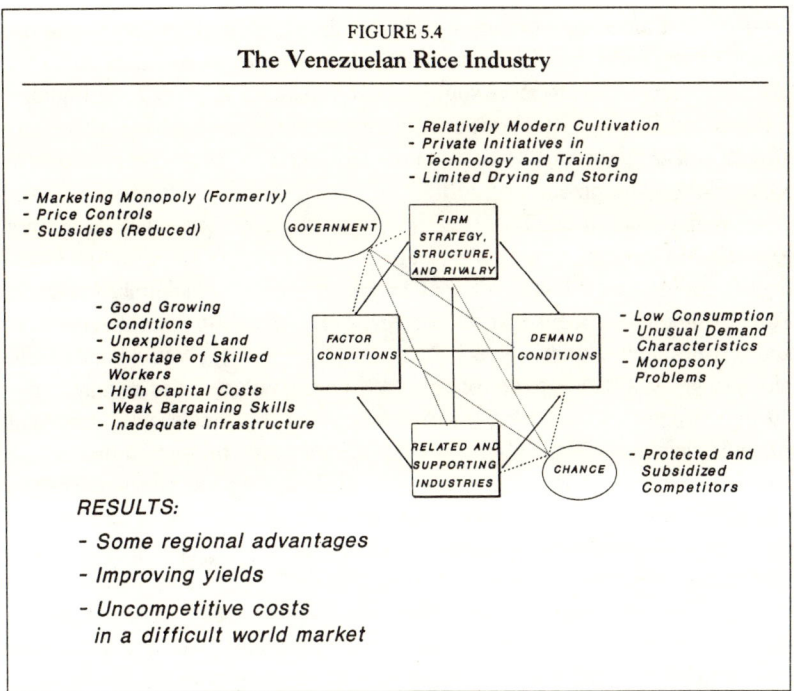

FIGURE 5.4
The Venezuelan Rice Industry

tional focus has been on the domestic market, not exports. By the 1980s, levels of import duties exceeded 100 percent for certain textile categories.

Within this closed market, the principal textile producers focused on distinct market segments. In linens, for example, the major textile companies produced and marketed products directed at consumers with different levels of purchasing power. The textile producers colluded for import restrictions and competed for subsidized financing and other favors. They also competed by vertically integrating into distribution and sale of textiles. Competition for customers was directed more at customer financing than at price or product quality. The smaller clothing manufacturers, essentially garment workshops, had difficulty obtaining financing from banks. The textile companies met this need and in effect added financing to their other lines of business.[42]

The domestic textile firms, on the whole, were unable to realize economies of scale because of the small size of the domestic market. Production inefficiencies translated into higher prices. Many products (though not all) were deficient in quality. Venezuelan clothing manufacturers, who wanted smaller lots, greater variety, higher quality, and faster turnaround in order to satisfy their customers, had no choice but to accept the terms of the local textile industry. While consumer demand pressed for greater variety in styles, more sophisticated finishing, and smaller individual lots, the textile producers continued to produce a limited variety of fabrics, slowly and in large lots. Many Venezuelans shopped in duty-free zones in Margarita or Miami, and smuggling was widespread.

With the commercial opening, import duties on textiles and clothing were lowered to 20 percent. Venezuelan clothing manufacturers responded by importing textiles in unprecedented volumes. Low prices were not their only attraction. Foreign suppliers offered smaller lot sizes; a greater variety of colors, designs, and finishes; and shorter delivery times. As of 1993, local textile plants often required up to 180 days to deliver an order. Foreign plants often required only 30 days to complete the order. When time is added for shipment (90 days) and customs clearance (30 days), the average delivery time on foreign orders was 150 days—still less than local plants. Nevertheless, long lead times compelled clothing manufacturers to maintain very high inventory levels—more than 60 days of raw materials—which in turn inflated their working capital and made it difficult to compete on price with clothing imports.[43]

The market opening sharply increased competitive pressures on Venezuelan textile producers. Domestic producers lost 30 percent of the domestic market between 1989 and 1993, and some were having difficulty competing in the new environment. However, several leading textile firms were responding vigorously and were beginning to compete on the basis of price, delivery times, and, above all, variety, on which the Venezuelan consumer of fashion places a premium. There was also an increased focus on exports. The synthetic fiber producers, Sudamtex and Mantex, began to export before the commercial opening and continued to do so thereafter. In 1991, exports accounted for more than half of Sudamtex's sales. Some Venezuelan firms, such as Jeantex of Grupo Telares Maracay, a denim manufacturer, were able to penetrate the highly competitive Colombian market. In 1992, Grupo Telares Maracay exported about 15 percent of its production and planned to raise that percentage to 40 percent in 1994.[44] It had marketing offices in Colombia, Italy, and the United States and planned to open more distribution channels in foreign countries.[45]

Issues Facing the Industry

Weakness in Basic Factors. Retroactive obligations under the labor laws impose a heavy burden on textile producers. Legal restrictions on the dismissal of employees in times of economic downturn are especially difficult for small textile firms and firms in the garment sector. The textile sector as a whole neglects investment in training. Only a handful of firms, such as Sudamtex, engage in the continuous training of personnel. Although the government provides some training through INCE-Textil, it will be incumbent upon the textile firms themselves to satisfy most of the training needs of the sector. Doing so will require a strong commitment from management. Two areas where the need for training is especially urgent are finishing and equipment maintenance.[46]

The quality of the Venezuelan textile industry's industrial plant is uneven. Many firms purchased new equipment during the preferential dollar regime of 1984 to 1988. However, as of the early 1990s, much of the nation's spinning and finishing plant was outdated. Most spinning equipment was more than 20 years old, and there was a serious shortage of skilled labor and modern equipment in finishing. Overall, the sector's spinning and finishing operations are not up to the standards of sophisticated local demand.

Debt and the Quality of Management. For years, Venezuelan textile firms had access to capital at preferential terms provided by the state. As of 1993, many were having difficulty obtaining financing, and those that could were paying very high interest rates. With certain exceptions, such as Sudamtex and Mantex, the sector tends to have a high debt/equity ratio, exacerbated by management practices that have inflated financing costs. It is common for 10 percent of all production to be waste or reprocessing, and in some cases this percentage is as high as 20 percent.[47] Often plants are not well maintained, inventories are poorly managed, product spends too long in process, and sales are inadequately forecast. All of this results in a greater need for working capital, higher production costs, and higher prices than would otherwise be the case.

Responding to Demand. Following the commercial opening, the domestic textile companies began to compete on the basis of price, delivery times, and variety. Product quality improved greatly in the years after the market opening. However, progress has been hampered by poor relations between the textile and clothing sectors. For decades, the two sectors competed for government favors, and antagonism still exists between the textile and clothing producers' associations. The larger Venezuelan clothing manufacturers have begun importing textiles directly.

Diverging Interests. In the early 1990s, the interests of the textile and clothing sectors diverged sharply. Textiles and clothing received the same level of duty protection from imports. Many textile firms were in favor of raising import duties on imported fabrics, which in turn would raise the costs of the clothing sector. Some clothing manufacturers were in favor of reducing import duties

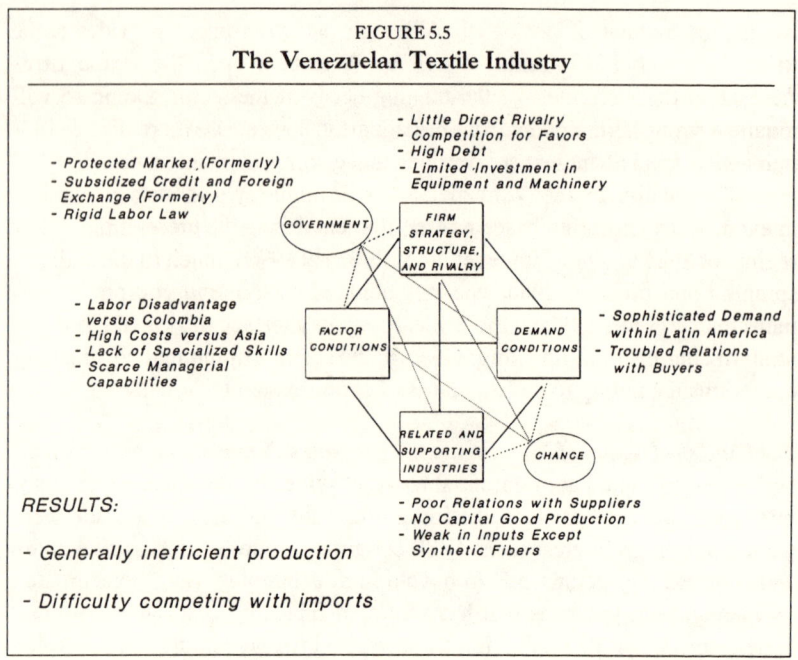

FIGURE 5.5
The Venezuelan Textile Industry

on textiles, in order to help the domestic clothing sector compete with imported garments, especially from Asia. Some clothing manufacturers supported an increase in import duties on imported clothing, which would erode even further the purchasing power of Venezuelan consumers.

Because most textile producers oppose lowering duties on textile imports, it is unlikely that the government will do so in the immediate future. This is likely to occur only if consumers bring strong social and political pressure to bear on the government. A combination of lower import duties on textiles, combined with strong controls at customs on unfairly traded imports, would benefit consumers, place local clothing manufacturers in a better position to compete on costs, and help to preserve garment worker jobs. The Venezuelan clothing sector is by far the larger employer. The textile sector employs approximately 25,000 workers.[48] While OCEI estimated 28,509 jobs in the clothing sector in 1990, other sources estimate that when workers in the informal sector are taken into account, the Venezuelan clothing sector employs as many as 120,000 workers.[49] (See Figure 5.5.)

Software[50]

The Venezuelan software industry is a relatively young sector, for which industry-wide sales data are not available. This industry has its origins in the importation of computer hardware. Venezuelan hardware users needed Spanish-language software tailored to their new equipment. Venezuela had a good supply of software talent, due to the relatively high level of software instruction in leading universities, and local firms were formed to satisfy this demand. Some worked in tandem with the hardware importers. Over time, the sector diversified into additional areas, including software for a wide variety of specific applications and industrial and commercial users. The local software developers encountered a ready domestic market for their products. Many market niches were open for exploitation and relatively few domestic firms existed. As a result, firms tended to specialize in specific areas, and there was little direct competition.

After their initial success at home, several Venezuelan software producers decided to venture into foreign markets. In some instances, the computer hardware firms provided the incentive by importing Venezuelan software applications into other Latin American markets where local programs were not available. In other instances, local entrepreneurs acted from their own initiative. In the early 1990s, Venezuelan software was being sold on a small scale to other Latin American countries, to Spain, and to Spanish-speaking communities in the United States.

Venezuelan software exporters have learned several important lessons in export markets. The more developed the market, the higher is the degree of competition in the software industry. Users in more sophisticated markets demanded a software product that met international industry standards; in the Venezuelan market, it had been possible to win client acceptance on the basis of intrinsic quality, without reference to international standards. Pricing turned out to be a very important factor in foreign markets, which had not been the case in Venezuela. Moreover, contractual requirements were very specific, and Venezuelan firms learned that they would lose sales if they did not control their production processes carefully and meet specifications for delivery dates and quantity.[51]

Another lesson from foreign markets is that foreign firms respond quickly to competitive challenges from imports, often assimilating and improving upon the imported innovation. One Venezuelan firm launched its software in Spain with initial success. For two years, the Venezuelan software gained market share as a result of its high quality. However, the Spanish firms responded by upgrading the quality and quantity of their competing solutions, and regained market share. The Venezuelan firm closed its offices in Madrid and now sells in Spain through a distributor. It had matured in a domestic market where there was no direct competition and, therefore, no need to master the essential skill of responding to innovative challenges.

Issues Facing the Industry

The Need for Strong Copyright Protection. For many years, software received little if any intellectual property protection in Venezuela. In 1989, Microsoft started a "consciousness-raising" campaign to crack down on local software pirates. Microsoft later was joined in this effort by Lotus and Ashton Tate. This campaign focused primarily on large firms and corporate users, such as banks, insurance firms, engineering and consulting firms, manufacturing firms, and distributors of computer equipment. By mid-1994, 36 legal actions had been brought, almost all of them before the enactment of the new Copyright Law of 1993. Most of these cases have reached an amicable settlement, whereby the infringing firm acquires rights to use the software. The copyright law, approved in August 1993 after eight years in Congress, expressly extends copyright protection to software and is starting to be enforced against software pirates. The law also is starting to change attitudes toward software piracy.

Fierce Foreign Competition. The Latin American market for software is growing rapidly. In the early 1990s, the race was on to become the industry standard in the Spanish-language segment for many applications. Despite Venezuela's endowment of well-trained and talented software designers, Venezuelan firms are generally behind the leading Chilean firms. Chile lowered import barriers to software in the late 1970s, and its software designers have had to respond to strong competitive pressures in the domestic market. Since 1985, Chilean software producers have joined together to promote their products in foreign markets, mitigating the heavy costs of overseas promotion. Chile's largest software manufacturer, Sonda, which is owned 50 percent by Digital Equipment Corporation (DEC), joined forces with DEC in late 1991 to adapt Sonda software to Digital hardware. As of 1993, they were marketing these products in 14 Latin American countries.[52] IBM and Chile's largest power company have formed a firm to design software for power companies. Chilean software firms are taking advantage of the nation's regional lead in areas such as privatization, securities exchanges, pension funds, and statistics record keeping to sell software and related services in these areas to purchasers in other Latin America countries.

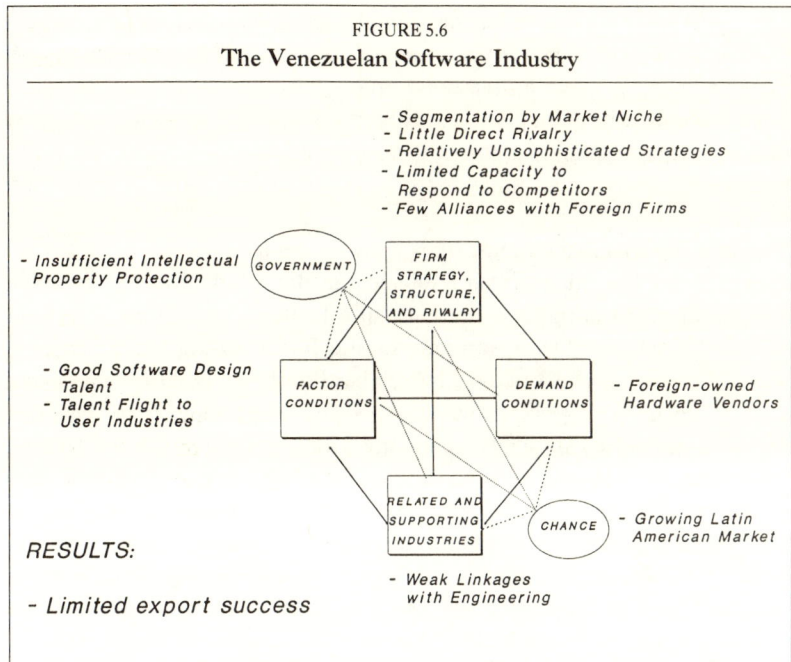

FIGURE 5.6
The Venezuelan Software Industry

Some analysts predicted that Chilean software exports would grow from between $5 million and $14 million in 1992 to $100 million or more in a few years.[53]

Design Talent Is Not Enough. Venezuela has a good pool of software design talent. The leading public and private universities graduate well-trained students. However, technical talent is not enough to compete and win in this industry. In this sector, weak domestic competition and the lack of marketing expertise have hampered the country's export potential. The nation's pool of talent, however, provides a solid base upon which to build. (See Figure 5.6)

Engineering Consulting Services[54]

Engineering consulting is a sector in which the Venezuelan government, through its state-owned companies, has been a source of sophisticated demand. After the Venezuelan petroleum industry was nationalized, a "Buy Venezuelan" policy was introduced to stimulate the growth of local engineering firms. This policy has been implemented in a fair and transparent fashion and has promoted development of the local industry. However, with the state facing fiscal crisis, the Buy Venezuela policy has reached its limits. If the national engineering consulting services sector is to grow, firms must find new opportunities at home and in foreign markets. In 1992, the Venezuelan engineering consulting services sector earned about $8 million in export revenue.[55]

The Venezuelan oil industry is a highly demanding and sophisticated client. It has played a primary role in the development of Venezuelan engineering consulting firms through an effective strategy that combined preferential treatment with high, and continually increasing, quality requirements. One example is Maraven, which has developed an elaborate system to detect errors in projects and has prepared an Engineering Control Manual. The oil industry also promoted competition among Venezuelan engineering consulting firms by holding competitive bidding contests that took into account price estimates and credentials. Engineering firms have applied the learning gained from these projects to activities in other engineering segments. Outside the oil industry, the biggest recent projects have been the Caracas Metro and the heavy industry of Guayana, including the Sivensa steel plants and the Macagua hydroelectric dam and power plant.

Although demand in Venezuela has been highly sophisticated, it also has been less diversified than in Venezuela's principal regional rivals in engineering consulting services, Mexico and Brazil. The Venezuelan market is relatively small compared to the market in those countries, and it has been subject to strong fluctuations dictated by movements in world oil prices. These factors have made it difficult for Venezuelan engineering firms to develop specialized expertise in diverse areas.

Rivalry among Venezuelan engineering consulting firms is fierce. Firms compete for markets, contracts, and specialized personnel. Because domestic demand is relatively small, the growth of any individual firm is often at the expense of its rivals. Rivalry expresses itself in all aspects of the business, including pricing, quality, managerial capability, project deadlines, and financial capacity. At the same time, the firms respect professional and ethical standards—because of their own professionalism and the high standards for professional and ethical behavior set by PDVSA and its affiliates. The quality of Venezuelan engineering services is high. Although the firms in general do not have the technological resources or capabilities of the world's leading engineering firms, many have successfully joined forces with foreign firms to obtain access to leading edge capabilities.

Issues Facing the Industry

The Cost of Keeping Up. Since the mid-1980s, leading international engineering firms have adopted computerized design methods, known as Computer Aided Design–Computer Aided Engineering (CAD-CAE), which have greatly enhanced automated calculation and design. In 1993, international firms developed more than 60 percent of their projects on CAD-CAE systems, and leading firms were approaching 100 percent automation, with substantial use of three-dimensional systems. By 1991, Venezuelan firms were using two-dimensional CAD-CAE, but the world's leading firms were increasingly using three-dimensional CAD-CAE.[56] The increasing cost of such technological systems, which must be imported, is a burden to most Venezuelan firms. Keeping up-to-date in technology will be an important and ongoing challenge. Venezuela is heavily dependent on foreign technology, and few new products are developed in the country. There is a danger that Venezuelan engineering services firms might lose competitiveness in the area of project design. In 1993, many were diversifying their activities and placing new emphasis on procurement and construction services as well as works inspection and maintenance, in which familiarity with the locality is an important advantage.

A Volatile Home Market. In the early 1990s, the Venezuelan market for engineering consulting services was volatile. The oil industry represented about 60 percent of the national market in person-hours in 1991. However, the oil sector experienced a significant reduction in its volume of investments in 1992. As a result, the Venezuelan market shrank by 50 percent between 1991 and 1993, and the engineering industry had to cut its capacity by 40 percent.[57] Whether the domestic market for engineering consulting services recovers depends on two factors: whether PDVSA is able to go ahead with its expansion plans, and whether the government pushes forward with the privatization of the basic industries and utilities and opens up new areas of activity to foreign investment.

Venezuelan engineering consulting firms are responding to changing market conditions by diversifying into new areas (such as telecommunications and transportation), forming associations with foreign firms, and targeting foreign markets. In 1992, the leading Venezuelan engineering consulting firms exported an estimated 5 percent of their services. They hoped to reach export levels of between 20 percent and 30 percent of services over several years.[58]

International Market Conditions. In foreign markets, Venezuelan firms face stiff competition from local firms and the major international firms. Protectionist barriers to entry are also widespread. Mexico, for example, restricts

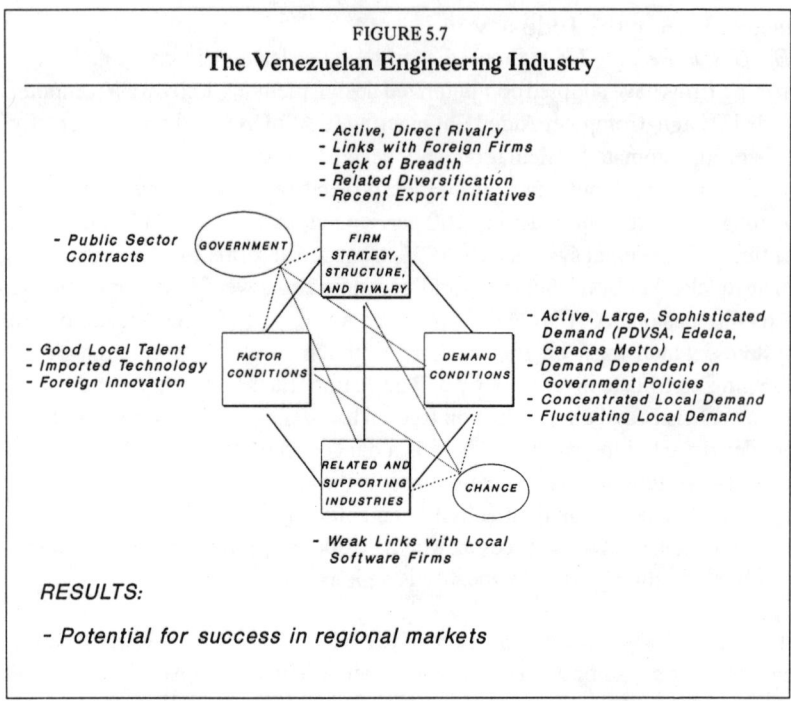

FIGURE 5.7
The Venezuelan Engineering Industry

foreign investment in engineering services and also restricts imports of foreign engineering. Brazil requires that foreign firms associate themselves with local partners. The most promising foreign markets for Venezuelan engineering services appear to be in the Andean, Central American, and Caribbean regions. Taken together, these foreign markets could represent a market at least equal to the Venezuelan market at its height—and might grow to be much larger in the long run. The oil industry is growing in Colombia, Ecuador, and Trinidad. Venezuelan engineering consulting firms are well positioned to exploit opportunities in the Andean Pact. Some firms already are present in other Andean Pact countries and have formed "multinational Andean companies" that enjoy preferential treatment. Venezuelan engineering consulting firms also enjoy preferential treatment in Central America and the Caribbean through various cooperation agreements. However, competing with local and regional competitors in foreign markets will not be easy. It will demand new skills and abilities on the part of Venezuelan firms, which traditionally have been turned inward toward the Venezuelan market. (See Figure 5.7.)

TABLE 5.1
Sources of Advantage in Venezuelan Industry

Industry	Inherited Factors	Created Factors	Demand Conditions	Related & Supporting Industries	Firm Strategy & Structure	Rivalry
Resource-based						
Oil	+++	+			+	
Petrochemicals	+++			+		
Steel	+++	+				
Aluminum	+++					
Agriculture						
Rice	+					
Cocoa	++					
Pulp, Paper	+++					
Import Substitution						
Textiles						
Autos and Auto Parts						
Services						
Tourism	++					
Talent-based						
Engineering		+	++		+	+
Software		+				
Telenovelas		++	++	++	++	++

Venezuela's Pattern of Competitive Advantage

In the last two chapters, we have seen the sources of competitive advantage and disadvantage in the 13 industries studied as part of this project. When we aggregate the results of our analysis for these sectors, overall patterns of competitive advantage that are reflective of the Venezuelan economy as a whole emerge. Table 5.1 summarizes the sources of advantage in the industries studied. While it is difficult to capture the essence of hundreds of pages of industry studies in a single table, the table does allow for an overall picture of the sources of advantage in the Venezuelan economy. A plus sign indicates advantage in regional or global terms. Two plus signs indicate strong advantage, and three plus signs indicate truly extraordinary advantage. The operative question is: Does this determinant provide a source of competitive advantage in today's international marketplace? For simplicity, we have not included indications of determinants in which Venezuela has distinct disadvantages. These can be identified from the profiles and abstracts of the last two chapters.

Venezuela has some strong factor advantages in resource-based industries and in some agricultural sectors. These are concentrated in inherited

TABLE 5.2
Sources of Advantage in Selected New Zealand Industries

Industry	Inherited Factors	Created Factors	Demand Conditions	Related & Supporting Industries	Firm Strategy & Structure	Rivalry
Resource-based						
Methanol	++					
Pulp, Paper	++					
Agriculture						
Wool	+++	++		+		
Dairy Products	+++	++		+		
Meat	++	++		+	+	
Kiwifruit	+++	++		+	+	
Service						
Tourism	++					
Consulting/ Engineering		++	++	+	+	+
Innovation-driven						
Software		+	++		+	+
Yachts		++	+++	+	++	++
Electric Fencing		++	+++	+	++	++

Source: Adaption of data from Crocombe, Enright, and Porter (1991).

factors. However, as we have seen, even extraordinary natural resource advantages do not necessarily guarantee success in the international marketplace or profitability in world markets, particularly in industries experiencing depressed prices. In Venezuela's resource-based industries and agriculture, there are fewer sources of created advantage. Industry participants interviewed across a variety of industries, including petrochemicals, steel, aluminum, pulp and paper, tourism, rice, and cocoa, identified the nation's shortage of skilled technicians as a serious constraint on their ability to compete. Indigenous technology, expertise, or management provide advantages in only a few of these industries.

No determinant is a source of competitive advantage in the two import-substitution industries studied, textiles and automotive vehicles and parts. This pattern is not unique to Venezuela. If these industries as a whole had strong advantages, they would not require protection from imports. In talent-based industries, in contrast, far more determinants are sources of advantage. These sectors did not inherit factor advantages but instead created them. Some of these sectors benefit from favorable national demand and

TABLE 5.3
Sources of Advantage in Selected Canadian Industries

Industry	Inherited Factors	Created Factors	Demand Conditions	Related & Supporting Industries	Firm Strategy & Structure	Rivalry
Resource-based						
Market Pulp	+++					
Aluminum	+++		+	+		
Styrene	++		+	+		
Nickel	+++	+		+	+	
Import Substitution						
Autos and Auto Parts						
Pulp, Paper Equipment			+			
Service						
Geophysical Consulting	++	++	++	+	++	
Innovation-driven						
Ice Skates		++	+++	++	++	++
Flight Simulators		+			+	
Industrial Explosives	+		++	+	+	+
Central Office Switches	++	++		++	+	

Source: Adapted from Porter and the Monitor Company (1991).

others from strategy, structure, and rivalry. The telenovelas sector shows strong sources of advantage across the entire set of determinants.

Three additional tables are included for purposes of comparison. In each case, data from the original sources listed has been adjusted to correspond to approximately the same standard of advantage as the Venezuelan chart. Table 5.2 summarizes the pattern of advantage for a selection of New Zealand industries. Most of New Zealand's exports are in agricultural and related industries that take advantage of the nation's excellent growing conditions (dairy products, meat, fruit, wine, etc.). Over time, New Zealand has broadened its advantages in these industries by developing world-class farming expertise and by developing some strength in related and supporting industries. It also exports in a number of industries in which local innovation is an important component. These industries can be further separated into those in which local demand and talent have played a significant role in the development of export success (engineering consulting, construction, and software, for example) and those in which New Zealand has advantages in all the points of the determinants (electric fencing and yachts). It should be noted that New Zealand has relatively few industries in this latter category.

Table 5.3 summarizes the pattern of competitive advantage for a selection of Canadian industries. The pattern of advantage in Canada's resource-based industries is not much different from that in Venezuela. Many of its strongest advantages are concentrated heavily in inherited factors. This is not surprising in industries in which inherited factors are key to a nation's competitive position. However, Canadian resource-based industries have been able to develop additional sources of advantage, particularly in related and supporting industries. Like Venezuela's import-substitution industries, Canadian import-substitution industries have scarcely any sources of advantage. Again, if there were sources of advantage, these would not be import-substitution industries. In contrast to Venezuela, however, Canada is successful in a series of other industries designated here as "innovation-driven industries." These are industries in which expertise and innovative capabilities are vital to success. In these industries, Canada has overall a far denser pattern of advantage. This is similar to Venezuela's pattern of advantage in telenovelas, but in the Canadian case it applies to a far larger number of industries.

Table 5.4 summarizes the sources of advantage in a sample of internationally successful Swiss industries. This chart is different from the ones set forth for Venezuela, New Zealand, and Canada in that only successful industries are shown. (Switzerland has unsuccessful as well as successful industries.) Successful Swiss industries exhibit a much denser pattern of advantage than even the successful Venezuelan, New Zealand, and Canadian industries profiled. Inherited factors are absent here, while far more determinants, including created factors of production, are present as advantages. The Swiss example is an extreme one, even among industrialized nations, in terms of the density of advantage present in its internationally successful industries. The Swiss pattern in these and many other industries is truly representative of an export base built upon human resources rather than natural resources. Worthy of note is the role that domestic rivalry has played in Switzerland's internationally successful industries. Switzerland is a small nation, with a small home market. In several of the industries in the table (as well as in many others), Swiss firms have achieved scale economies by exploiting international markets. In this way, these industries have reaped the benefits of domestic competition while escaping the constraints of a small domestic market.

These comparisons are not meant to cast the Venezuelan economy in an unfavorable light. There is nothing unusual about Venezuela's pattern of competitive advantage. It is more or less what one would expect to see in

TABLE 5.4
Sources of Advantage in Selected Internationally Successful Swiss Industries

Industry	Inherited Factors	Created Factors	Demand Conditions	Related & Supporting Industries	Firm Strategy & Structure	Rivalry
Dyes		++		+	++	+
Pharmaceuticals		+++	+	++	++	++
Watches		+++	++	+	++	+
Textile Machinery		++	+	+	+	+
Banking		++	++	+	++	++
Trading		++	++	++	++	++
Chocolate		++	+	+	++	+

Source: Adapted from Borner, Porter, Weder, and Enright (1991).

countries at its level of development. Most developing nations have limited advantages outside of their natural resource position or low-cost labor. One important feature of the Venezuelan pattern is evidence of the existence of pockets of world-class expertise, advanced demand, creative firm strategies, and local rivalry. Looking across the tables, it is clear that as countries develop, they gradually enter a broader range of industries and develop denser patterns of advantage. New Zealand has broadened its base of agricultural industries and has begun to branch out into industries related to its agricultural advantages as well as some other industries that serve its unique demand conditions. Over time, Canada has deepened its sources of advantage in certain resource-based industries. In addition, it has gradually developed advantages in other industries that are not dependent on natural resources. Switzerland shows a particularly dense pattern of sources of advantage in its internationally successful industries. These four nations are at different stages in their development. There is no reason to expect the patterns of advantage to be the same. The tables do, however, suggest the type of progression that allows a nation to develop its economy and the types of advantages that nations might develop and exploit.[59] The next several chapters will analyze Venezuela's sources of advantage and disadvantage systematically and in detail.

6

Venezuelan Factor Conditions

Venezuela's factor conditions provide several sources of advantage or potential advantage for the nation and its firms. These include a variety of natural resources that provide the basis for a substantial portion of its economy and the vast majority of its exports. Venezuela also has some pockets of world-class skills and expertise. These advantages, however, have not been sufficient to ensure the nation's prosperity. Many of Venezuela's natural resources remain largely undeveloped. World market conditions have reduced the returns on investment in some of Venezuela's resources. A lack of leading edge infrastructure, specialized and advanced human resources, and a modern financial system have combined to limit growth and development. Although progress has been made on many fronts in the last several years, Venezuela's factor conditions will require substantial improvement to support higher levels of productivity and competitiveness. The attitudes developed through years of reliance on natural resources have limited the nation's ability to develop the human, knowledge, and capital resources necessary to build a more productive economy.

An Economy Based on Natural Resources

The Venezuelan economy always has been dominated by industries that exploit the nation's natural resources. In the colonial era, Venezuela was an exporter of cocoa and tobacco. In the nineteenth century, the nation exported large quantities of coffee, rubber, and other tropical products. Agricultural exports gave way to exports of oil starting in the 1920s. While important progress has been made in the last few decades, the Venezuelan economy is

TABLE 6.1
Venezuelan Natural Resource Reserves

	Units	Reserves[a]	World Rank	Output[b]	Years Supply[c]
Petroleum	Million barrels	63,330	6	876	72
Light Crudes	Million barrels	6,557	n.a.	221	30
Gas	Million cubic feet	3,581,809	8	29,043	123
Iron Ore	Thousand metric tons	1,960,000	11	18,877	104
Coal	Thousand metric tons	540,000	n.a.	2,450	220
Bauxite	Thousand metric tons	320,000	14	1,052	304
Potable Water	Km^3	n.a.	44	4.1	n.a.

[a] Reserves as of the end of 1992.
[b] Annual figures are for 1991.
[c] Estimated at 1991 levels of production.

Venezuela's population of 20.7 million ranked thirty-eighth worldwide. Its land area of 911,000 Km^3 ranked twenty-eighth.

Source: PDVSA, Ministry of Energy and Mines, *The Oil and Gas Journal*, World Bank.

still extremely dependent on industries based on exhaustible resources, which still generate more than 90 percent of total exports.

Vast Energy Resources

The most prominent of Venezuela's resources is, of course, oil. In 1993, Venezuela's proven oil reserves of approximately 63.3 billion barrels placed it sixth in the world behind Saudi Arabia, Iraq, Kuwait, Iran, and Abu Dhabi. (See Table 6.1.)[1] In the Orinoco bituminous belt, Venezuela has the world's largest known deposits of extra heavy crudes. In 1992, Venezuela produced 2.3 million barrels of oil per day, which placed the nation seventh in the world, behind Russia, Saudi Arabia, the United States, Iran, China, and Mexico. Venezuela's oil production in that year equaled approximately 9.5 percent of OPEC output and 3.8 percent of world oil output. PDVSA, the Venezuelan state oil company, was the fifth largest oil company in the world in terms of output, behind the state oil companies of Saudi Arabia, Iran, China, and Mexico. The average Venezuelan well produced on the order of 189 barrels a day, whereas the average well in Saudi Arabia produced more than 5,800 barrels a day and the average well in Iran produced 4,900 barrels a day.[2] Venezuela has a cost disadvantage in oil production as compared with the Persian Gulf States and a cost advantage compared to oil producers outside the Persian Gulf. In the early 1990s, the total cost of producing a barrel of oil in Venezuela was roughly $3 per barrel, compared to $1 per barrel in the Persian Gulf.[3] The Venezuelan cost disadvantage will increase over time as Venezuela's light oil reserves are depleted.

Some 72 percent of Venezuela's proven reserves are heavy and extra-heavy crudes, which require more expensive and technically challenging refining processes and receive lower prices than light crudes. In 1992, for example, PDVSA's direct production costs averaged $1.04 per barrel of light crude versus $1.39 per barrel of heavy crudes.[4] Heavy oil also brings lower prices in the marketplace. The price of Tía Juana light crude, for example, was $16.97 per barrel in July 1993, while the price of Tía Juana heavy crude was $10.41 per barrel.[5] Venezuela has a 30-year reserve of light crudes and a more than 200-year reserve of extra-heavy oil. As PDVSA's product mix shifts toward heavier crudes, its profit margins get squeezed on both sides. PDVSA hopes to expand its production to 4 million barrels of oil per day by the year 2002, 3.2 million from traditional areas and 0.8 million from the Orinoco belt.[6] The latter is to be exploited by a joint undertaking consisting of PDVSA, Total (France), and a consortium lead by Itochu-Marubeni (Japan). PDVSA's expansion plan, including natural gas and chemical operations, is expected to require nearly $38 billion in new investment.

Venezuela also has 3.6 trillion cubic meters in proven reserves of natural gas. Substantial gas resources associated with oil deposits are located in the western part of the country around Lake Maracaibo. In addition, 4 billion cubic feet of gas reserves are found off the Paria Peninsula in the eastern part of the country. At $0.50 per million BTU in 1993, Venezuelan natural gas prices were among the lowest in the world, on par with Saudi Arabia. This compared favorably with prices in Trinidad ($1.32), Mexico ($2.40), and Canada and the United States ($3.00). Venezuela's natural gas can provide substantial competitive advantages for industries that use it for energy or processing. An extensive gas pipeline system supplies the main industrial areas in the country, allowing several large firms to use inexpensive natural gas to produce their own electricity. Natural gas is also the principal feedstock for the Venezuelan petrochemical industry. In addition, the demand for natural gas in export markets is likely to be strong in coming years due to the fact it is considered environmentally friendly as compared to oil or coal. In 1993, the Venezuelan Congress approved the Cristóbal Colón liquefied natural gas project (after a two-year delay due to political resistance

TABLE 6.2
The Electricity Sector, Selected Latin American Nations, 1992

	Installed Capacity MW[a]	Annual Consumption KWH/per capita	Energy Intensity BEP/10^3	Average Price (US Cts./KWh)		
				Residential	Commercial	Industrial
Argentina	17,197	1,293	2.9	9.49	10.69	6.35
Brazil	54,135	1,470	3.0	6.88	7.59	4.11
Colombia	8,925	817	3.2	2.01	5.88	4.45
Chile	5,100	1,318	2.3	11.12	10.09	6.02
Mexico	21,500	1,070	3.1	4.95	12.87	5.43
Peru	4,187	563	4.0	4.24	9.86	5.03
Venezuela	**18,822**	**2,335**	**3.5**	**2.05**	**5.94**	**4.17**

[a] Includes self-generation.

Source: CAVEINEL.

to foreign investment in the hydrocarbon sector). This $5.5 billion project will bring together Exxon, Shell, Mitsubishi, and Lagoven (a PDVSA subsidiary) to exploit the Paria Peninsula reserves and serve export markets.

Venezuela has tremendous electricity-generating capacity. A total of 11 private and public sector companies are engaged in electricity generation, transmission, and distribution. Venezuela produces and consumes far more electricity on a per-capita basis than other Latin American nations. (See Table 6.2.) The Caroní River is the site of one of the world's largest hydroelectricity-generating networks. Investments of more than $5 billion over the last two decades have added 10,000 megawatts to the system. Thermal power plants, using Venezuelan oil and natural gas (use of natural gas in Venezuelan thermal power plants increased from 42 percent in 1980 to 77 percent in 1990) provide a further 7,500 megawatts of capacity. An additional 7,500 megawatts of capacity on the Caroní and 6,000 megawatts in thermal capacity were originally planned for the late 1990s and early 2000s, though the state of public finances will force revision of such investment plans. At present, Venezuela exports electricity directly to Colombia. In addition, Venezuela's hydropower can be considered exportable in that electricity generated by hydroelectric facilities frees oil and natural gas for export.

In Venezuela, electricity rates have been set so that business users subsidize residential users, in contrast to the situation in Argentina, Chile, and Brazil, where industrial rates have been lower than residential rates. In 1992, most Venezuelan industrial and commercial customers paid rates twice and three times those of residential consumers, respectively. Nevertheless, Venezuelan electricity prices were relatively low in world and regional terms. (See Table 6.2.) The Venezuelan steel and aluminum industries, which are largely owned by the CVG, which also runs the nation's main hydroelectric facilities, enjoy transfer prices that are significantly lower than those charged to other Venezuelan industries. In the early 1990s, these Venezuelan industries paid between nine and 15 mills[7] per kilowatt hour for their electricity,[8] compared to a range of 15 to 20 mills for aluminum producers in Canada and a range of 21 to 30 mills for aluminum companies in the United States, New Zealand, and elsewhere.[9] CVG's transfer prices will have to be reconsidered, since the long-term marginal cost of generation in the late 1990s and early 2000s could be as high as 20 mills, depending on the cost of fuel. Venezuela will maintain a cost advantage in electric power for basic industries, but the extent of that advantage will depend on the mix and costs of hydro- and thermal generation (newer hydro facilities are becoming more expensive and the mix will tend more toward thermal generation over time), the efficiency of the generation and transmission facilities, the extent of cross subsidization, and the magnitude of theft of electricity. (Cadafe estimates that such losses can amount to 30 percent of delivered power in some areas.)

The price of electricity is, however, not the only consideration. The quality of electricity service in Venezuela ranges from excellent to poor, depending on the area of the country. Fluctuating voltages and outages plague many areas and make it difficult to use the public network for processes that are sensitive to line voltages or for which the interruption of service creates major problems. (One major chemical plant, for example, has had to shut down repeatedly due to fluctuating voltages.) Many large Venezuelan firms possess their own electrical plants for self-generation and cogeneration. These firms are able to take advantage of Venezuela's low costs for natural gas and oil and above all, enjoy better quality and continuous service.

Extensive Mineral Deposits

Venezuela has extensive mineral wealth. There are 1.96 billion metric tons (or a 100-year supply at current usage rates) of proven iron ore reserves. Total Venezuelan bauxite reserves are estimated at 320 million metric tons and the bauxite deposits at *Los Pijiguaos* in Bolívar state are among the richest in the world. More than 4.2 million hectares have been opened to gold and diamond exploration under state concessions in the Guayana region.[10] Venezuela was the seventh largest exporter of raw diamonds in the world in the early 1990s. Its proven coal reserves are estimated at 540 million metric tons. (See Table 6.1.) In addition, Venezuela mines and exports aragonite, asbestos, barite, bentonite, calcite, granite, gypsum, kaolin, lime, marble, pumice, quartz, salt, silicon sand, and sulfur.[11]

Despite its wealth of mineral deposits, Venezuela has been a large net importer of minerals. Uncertain jurisdiction over mining contracts and mineral rights continues to hamper the development of the nation's mineral resources. Before 1983, a greatly overvalued currency made it easy to fill requirements with imports. At prevailing exchange rates, it was impossible to produce many of these minerals competitively in Venezuela. Many of the nation's mineral resources have been developed only recently. For example, the local coal industry started large-scale production only in 1987. In 1992, Venezuelan coal production was expected to reach about 2 million metric tons, well behind that of Colombia (12 million metric tons).[12]

The Corporación Venezolana de Guayana (CVG) has exploited the nation's iron and bauxite deposits with mixed success. In the early 1990s, Ferrominera Orinoco produced about 19 million metric tons of iron ore annually, of which about 6 million tons were consumed in the domestic market and the remainder was exported.[13] Although Ferrominera Orinoco has had problems with the quality of its exports in the past, as of 1993 it was working to improve its position in world markets. It was upgrading and diversifying its products by using higher-quality ore deposits, focusing on calibrated products rather than run of mine, and introducing new production processes. Bauxita de Venezuela (Bauxiven) has encountered transportation, management, and other problems. When it was founded in 1979, its projected annual production was about 6 million metric tons. In 1991, Bauxiven supplied Interalúmina with only 1.05 million metric tons of bauxite, or 30 percent of its requirements.[14] Since then, progress has been made; as of 1994, Bauxiven was supplying Interalúmina with 100 percent of its requirements.

In the area of gold and diamond mining, the state has resorted to granting concessions to private firms as well as forming mixed companies with contributions of private capital. However, private enterprise has been stymied by a morass of conflicting regulations and a jurisdictional struggle between the CVG and the ministry of energy and mines.[15] Meanwhile, as of 1993, an estimated 40,000 illegal miners continued to prospect in the Guayana region using primitive and environmentally dangerous methods, to the detriment of the watershed of the Caroní and Orinoco rivers.

Physical Geography and Geology

Venezuela's location on the northeastern coast of South America gives it good trading access to major markets in the eastern and southeastern United States and in Europe. Its accessibility to the Panama Canal also gives it good trading access to Pacific markets. Venezuela has a wide variety of climates and landscapes, including 2,400 kilometers of Caribbean coastline, snow-covered mountains, vast savannas, tropical rain forests, and unique features such as the Tepuyes table mountains and the Angel Falls. These locations, in combination with a wide variety of flora and fauna, should make Venezuela a tourist's dream. In 1993, tourism was the nation's fifth largest earner of foreign currency and was widely regarded as underdeveloped. (See Chapter 4.)

Agricultural Potential

Venezuela's varied climates and topography hold potential for a wide variety of tropical and semitropical crops. Venezuela's Chuao and Porcelana brands of cocoa achieved fame in Europe in the 1700s, and their distinctive quality is still dependent on Venezuelan growing conditions. Venezuela produces fine coffee, which in the nineteenth century was a mainstay of the economy. In Zulia state and elsewhere, Venezuela has excellent conditions for tropical fruits such as mangoes, bananas, and plantains, and for innovative crops such as manioc, which is used in the production of starch. Venezuela has lands well suited for rice, which under irrigation can yield two harvests per year.[16] Cattle farms are found in western Venezuela, and the *llanos* (floodplains) in south-central Venezuela are suitable for the grazing of livestock, including water buffalo.

Despite its advantageous growing conditions, Venezuela lags behind other Latin American nations, including medium-size and small nations, in many agricultural exports. In 1992, Venezuela exported $24 million in bananas, approximately $10 million in cocoa and cocoa products, $14 million in rice and $12 million in coffee.[17] In contrast, the prior year, Ecuador exported $718 million in bananas and $105 million in cocoa and cocoa products; Uruguay exported $120 million in rice; and Costa Rica exported $265 million in coffee.[18] Venezuela's modest volume of agricultural exports can be explained in part by past government policies toward agriculture. In the 1970s and 1980s, subsidies, price controls, guaranteed state purchases, high tariff barriers, and an overvalued currency resulted in an inwardly focused agricultural sector that produced primarily for the domestic market. In certain sectors or products, producers and government officials agreed on prices and profits, financed by the state. Public money supported the large-scale production of temperate-zone crops for domestic consumption, while many export opportunities in tropical and semitropical crops went unexplored. Attempts to reform these policies in 1990 and 1991 met with at least partial success.

Changes in government policy in the years 1990 to 1992 resulted in agricultural investments based on Venezuela's comparative advantages. For the first time in decades, producers began to seek out areas where Venezuelan produce could compete successfully in international markets and began to build a new export base. The cocoa and coffee sectors began to invest to improve the quality of the Venezuelan product, for international consumption. Investments were made to bring Porcelana cocoa back from extinction. Banana cultivation was expanded in the area south of Lake Maracaibo and in Monagas, regions possessing excellent sunlight and climate for this crop. Installation began of irrigation systems in Zulia's plains for a variety of fruit and vegetable crops. Yucca began to be cultivated on a large scale for starch. New biotechnology firms began to work to improve the commercial potential of nontraditional crops. Mangoes, once not considered a marketable crop, began to be grown for export.

Excellent conditions exist in Venezuela for growing trees for pulp and paper production. Extensive tracts of open land in Monagas and Anzoátegui states are superb for pine cultivation and have no competing commercial uses. More than 400,000 hectares of tree plantations already exist in Venezuela, but this is a small amount compared to Chile and Brazil. Technical advances in pulping have allowed short-fiber trees that grow in Venezuela on 12-year cycles to be competitive with long-fiber trees that grow on 90-year cycles in Canada and Scandinavia. With abundant land, water, natural gas, river transportation, and electricity, Venezuela has the potential to become the lowest-cost producer of pulp and paper in the world. Nine million hectares have been set aside by the government for forest plantations, but in 1993 only 6 percent were under cultivation.[19] Uncertainty over property rights and over raw materials supplies and the ineffective use of forestry plantations by state enterprises have limited Venezuelan forestry and the associated pulp and paper industries to date.[20] (See Chapter 4.)

Untapped Fishing Resources

Venezuela's fishing and fisheries resources have been largely untapped. The nation has a modern commercial fishing fleet that in 1993 ranked second among Latin American nations in the Pacific and first in the Atlantic. Venezuela's long Caribbean coast and extensive river networks have substantial potential in aquaculture for high-yield species such as cachama, tilapia, trout, and shrimp. Until 1992, the government banned the production of tilapia (pink snapper) for environmental reasons, but this ban was lifted. In 1991, average costs of production for tilapia in Venezuela were less than half the international average.[21] The market for tilapia imports in the United States is expected to grow dramatically during the 1990s. Investors who ventured into fish and shrimp farming are finding that Venezuela's conditions are excellent. Venezuela produced 1,200 tons of shrimp in 1992 on farms located along the coast, far below its potential, and exported $36 million in shrimp and other shellfish. Ecuador, with similar natural conditions, exported $493 million in shrimp and other shellfish in 1991.[22]

Falling Rates of Return in Resource Industries

In the late 1980s and early 1990s, Venezuela's resource-based industries experienced falling rates of return. Commodity prices are depressed in many of Venezuela's existing and potential natural resource industries. In some industries, prices are cyclical and happen to be at their low point due to the current world recession. In other industries, however, there are signs of a secular decline in prices that might never be reversed. In some cases, such as steel and aluminum, demand is shifting away from traditional products to newer, higher-technology products, such as special alloys and engineering plastics. Demand for fossil fuels has been affected by environmental concerns, conservation efforts, and alternative energy sources. In other cases, new foreign competitors, such as Russia, have arrived on the scene starved for cash and ready to undersell the market. At the same time, costs in many of Venezuela's resource-based industries are rising as resources become depleted and environmental costs increase. Together, these factors reduce the rates of return of Venezuela's existing resource-based industries and make it more difficult for the nation to break into other resource-based industries. This trend will make it more difficult for Venezuela's resource-based industries to carry the economy into the future.

Commodity prices have fallen across a wide range of products. Figure 6.1 shows the movement of oil, iron, and aluminum prices in the early 1990s. Real oil prices fell from their highs of the early 1980s to their lowest levels since the early 1970s. Iron prices also fell. The average price per pound of

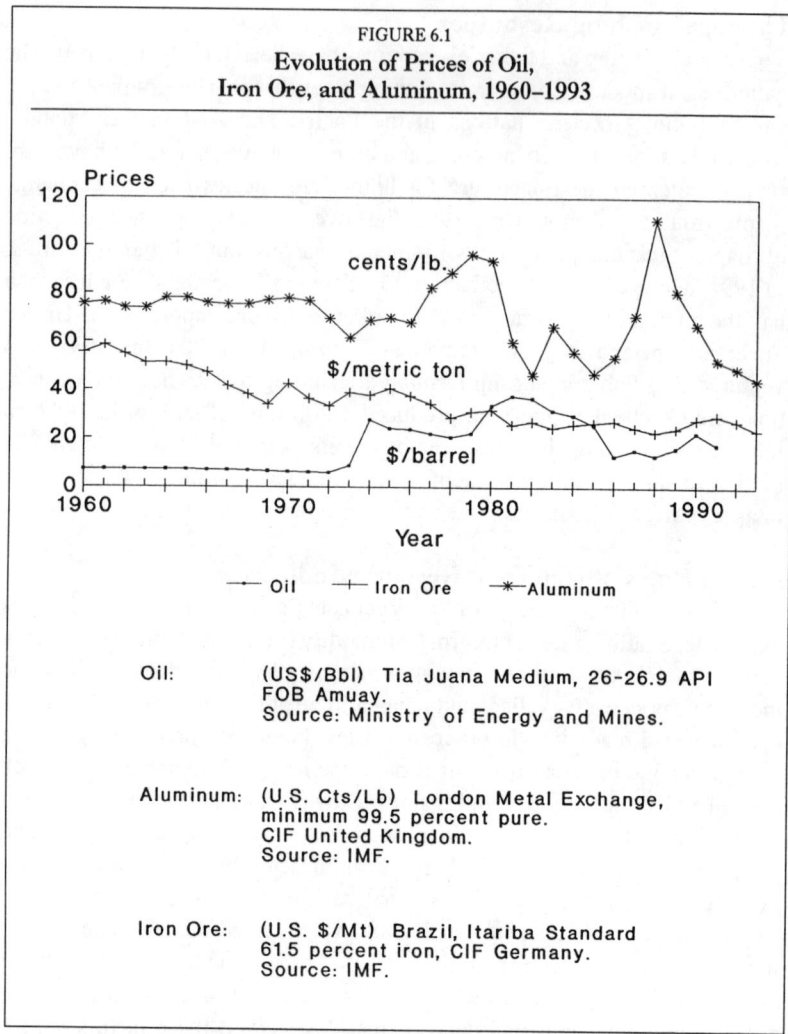

FIGURE 6.1
Evolution of Prices of Oil,
Iron Ore, and Aluminum, 1960–1993

Oil: (US$/Bbl) Tia Juana Medium, 26-26.9 API FOB Amuay.
Source: Ministry of Energy and Mines.

Aluminum: (U.S. Cts/Lb) London Metal Exchange, minimum 99.5 percent pure. CIF United Kingdom.
Source: IMF.

Iron Ore: (U.S. $/Mt) Brazil, Itariba Standard 61.5 percent iron, CIF Germany.
Source: IMF.

primary aluminum fell from $1.06 in 1988 to $0.60 in 1992[23] and even lower in 1993. These were not isolated cases. World prices were also depressed for pulp and paper, rice, cocoa, and petrochemicals. The price of pulp (Southern Pine) fell from $810 per metric ton in 1989 to a low of $450 per metric ton in the fourth quarter of 1991 and had recovered only partially by 1993.[24] The price of rice (Thai White 5 Percent Broken) fell from $433 per ton in 1980 to $287 per ton in 1990.[25] Cocoa bean prices on the New York Mercantile

Exchange (Ivory Coast beans) fell from $2,066 per metric ton in October 1987 to $1,294 in February 1992.[26] By May 1993, real cocoa prices on the New York spot market were the lowest in history. In 1992, petrochemical profitability worldwide was at an all-time low.[27]

Although some of these markets will recover, many will remain volatile or depressed due to the recent entry of new competitors. In the oil industry, the prospective reentry of Iraq will cap world prices in the short to medium term. In the longer run, the development of oil industries in the former Soviet Union could further limit prices. Russia has already flooded world markets with cheap primary aluminum produced in plants that, for all intents and purposes, are fully depreciated. In the 1980s and early 1990s, Chile and Brazil came from nowhere to become major exporters of wood pulp. Brazil exported 1.37 billion metric tons of pulp in 1991. Vietnam has burst upon the international rice market, increasing exports from roughly 0.10 million tons to 2 million tons between 1987 and 1991.[28] Indonesia, a new entrant in international cocoa markets, was expected to harvest a record crop of 200,000 metric tons of cocoa beans in 1992-1993. (The prior year, Venezuela harvested only 16,000 tons of beans.)[29] Asian nations, such as Korea and Taiwan, have engaged in massive expansions of their petrochemical facilities, which have influenced prices worldwide.

Meanwhile, several of Venezuela's resource-based industries face increasing costs. Costs in the oil industry are rising as the best and most productive fields become depleted and PDVSA exploits more marginal fields. Over the next decade, the profitability of the Venezuelan oil industry is expected to fall sharply. The costs of environmental compliance will result in rising production costs in many Venezuelan industries, including everything from oil and petrochemicals to textiles and consumer products. This trend will be accelerated by the Environmental Crime Law, which attaches heavy fines and penalties to offenses against the environment. Between 1987 and 1992, PDVSA and its subsidiaries spent approximately 3 billion bolivars on environmental cleanups and the incorporation of environmentally friendly technology. Faced with rising contaminant levels in Lake Maracaibo, Pequiven has had to construct a new plant at El Tablazo to avoid the use of mercury cells in the production of caustic soda and chlorine.[30]

Infrastructure in Need of Upgrading

Venezuela's infrastructure cannot be considered an advantage in international competition. Much of its infrastructure was built in the boom years of the 1950s, 1960s, and 1970s. A lack of investment in the 1980s, however, resulted in a marked deterioration. In the early 1990s, privatization has resulted in dramatic improvements in some areas of infrastructure, most notably in telecommunications and the ports. Although Venezuela's infrastructure compares relatively well to that of other nations in the region, there is still much to be done before it can provide distinct advantages to Venezuelan firms.

Transportation Good by Regional Standards, but Not Good Enough

Venezuela's transportation system is widely regarded as good by regional standards, but it is not adequate to support Venezuelan industry and exporters. Most domestic freight within Venezuela travels by truck. As of 1993, highways carried more than 80 percent of Venezuela's domestic shipping (not including oil products). The railroads, in contrast, are used to cover specific routes. As of 1993, the only commercial line in operation, between Puerto Cabello and Barquisimeto, was in poor repair. An additional 200 kilometers of track were planned, including a 44-kilometer line between Caracas and Cúa. Venezuela has the least railway coverage among the large Latin American countries.[31]

Venezuela's system of highways is the most extensive and best developed in the Andean Pact. It has more than 30,000 kilometers of paved roads, compared to Colombia and Peru, countries of similar size, with only 10,000 kilometers of paved roads each. Public spending on highways in Venezuela, however, has been ambitious but haphazard, with a definite preference to start new systems rather than to complete or improve existing ones. By the early 1990s, certain highways had been under construction for 15 years and thousands of kilometers of roads had fallen into disrepair. Only 26 percent of Venezuelan roads were considered to be in good condition, while 54 percent were in fair and 20 percent in poor condition.[32] In a 1993 survey of Venezuelan manufacturing firms by Horacio Viana (hereafter the Viana survey), 30 percent of the firms surveyed identified the condition of the nation's roads as an obstacle to their growth.[33]

Venezuela's heavily subsidized domestic gasoline prices have been among the lowest in the world. Nevertheless, freight costs have been high in Venezuela when compared with nations outside the Andean Pact. Despite lower fuel and labor costs, trucking costs in Venezuela have been comparable to United States costs as a result of lower productivity and the high costs of financing and equipment.[34] There has been little competition in the private trucking sector within Venezuela, and service has suffered as a result. High freight costs have placed a heavy burden on local producers who transport unprocessed goods over long distances within the nation. Logs for conversion into pulp, for example, often are hauled 900 kilometers from forest plantations to pulp plants at high expense. Tropical fruit producers have complained of the high cost of transporting their perishables to Caracas from Zulia state. The oil and steel industries have tried to minimize freight expenses by maintaining internal trucking fleets.

Many Venezuelan firms have found the high cost of overland freight in neighboring countries to be an obstacle to trade within the Andean Pact. Some of Venezuela's largest rolling stock must stop and unload at the Colombian border because the Colombian roads, with their narrow shoulders, cannot accommodate them. The high cost of shipping passenger vehicles overland has been a constant problem for the Venezuelan automotive industry. Although Venezuelan rice production is more cost efficient than Colombian production, land freight costs have been a major burden. As of 1993, the average freight cost to ship Venezuelan rice to the major Colombian markets, such as Bogotá, Cali, and Barranquilla, was more than 3,000 bolivars per ton on a product that sold for roughly 18,000 bolivars per ton.[35] In 1992, an initiative by Venezuelan millers to sell rice to Peru failed because of the prohibitive costs of shipping rice overland.

Most of Venezuelan international trade is shipped through the ports of Puerto Cabello, La Guaira, Maracaibo, and Guanta. Historically, Venezuela's maritime ports have been a drag on commerce and a major disadvantage for the nation's exporters and importers. Exporters were often obliged to make illicit payments or gifts to customs workers in order to "expedite" *("habilitar")* shipment. Failure to do so might require reshipment or might cause part of the shipment to disappear and require issuance of letters of credit to foreign customers. Importers, especially of finished goods, often suffered losses of merchandise. Incompetent ports management stymied efforts by Venezuelan producers to penetrate foreign markets. For example, a Venezuelan bathing suit manufacturer who won an order from a client in Italy took merchandise to the port of La Guaira for shipment. Part of the order ended up in England and the rest in Spain.[36]

Administration of the ports passed to regional authorities in late 1991 and early 1992. These authorities, in turn, turned to the private sector to manage cargo. Improvements in productivity and quality of service were almost immediate. In the port of Puerto Cabello, the average length of time spent at dock was cut from 163 hours in 1991 to 65 hours in 1992. Port personnel was reduced from 8,500 workers to 135 workers. Firms no longer had to pay two sets of ports workers, one to do the work and the other not to. Instead of losing $5 million per year, as it had, the port earned a profit of $9 million in 1992.[37] The reorganization also stimulated the growth of local service industries. In 1993, more than 583 private firms operated warehouses and other facilities at ports (not including La Guaira), compared to 213 in 1991.[38] Venezuelan managers report that though Puerto Cabello, in particular, has improved, further progress in port and customs administration is needed.[39] Many Venezuelan firms have complained of the widespread failure of customs officials to enforce tariffs on imports. The result is that firms that play by the rules have been forced to compete with those that have reduced their costs by avoiding the tariffs. The president of one textile firm went so far as to call for the elimination of tariffs to ensure that all firms compete on a level playing field.[40]

The Venezuelan oil, steel, cement, and aluminum industries use their own relatively efficient port facilities. As mentioned, the oil industry operates its own transportation fleet to export oil and oil products. Other industries are served by national and international carriers, including the government-owned Venezuelan Navigation Company (CAVN). Most industrial plants are located near seaports or fresh water ports. Navigation channels in the Orinoco River and Lake Maracaibo are cleared periodically, but ship size is limited to about 80,000 tons. On the other hand, agricultural production is usually carried out in areas distant from the main ports and suffers from higher transportation costs. Exporters have complained about the comparatively high freight costs they must pay, which carriers attribute to low volume.

Venezuela is served by about 50 airports. Three of these airports, Simón Bolívar International (Caracas Maiquetía), Porlamar (Margarita), and Maracaibo, receive regular international traffic. Domestic passenger traffic was approximately 6 million passengers in 1991, down from nearly 8 million in 1988. International traffic was around 1 million passengers in 1991. Total air freight traffic was around 100,000 tons in 1991. The cost of internal air freight was comparable to or higher than United States costs on a per-ton basis.[41] As of 1993, Venezuela's airport infrastructure was generally acknowledged as inadequate to meet existing demand. Regional airports used to be under the authority of the Autonomous Institute of Maiquetía Airport (IAAIM), an arrangement that did not promote their efficient regulation. Steps have been taken to transfer regulatory authority to regional governments, which should have stronger interest than the IAAIM in improving local airports.[42]

In 1993, approximately 40 international flights departed the Simón Bolívar International Airport at Maiquetía daily, and the number of flights continued to grow. However, Maiquetía has been having difficulties handling the existing passenger flows. Despite its favorable location, the airport is not a hub for connections throughout Latin America, and it will not become one without major structural expansion and service improvements. As of 1993, the lack of capacity at Maiquetía and other airports was making it difficult for local carriers to expand operations and made it less likely that new airlines would want to start up operations in Venezuela.[43] The ministry of transport and communications was considering major infrastructural improvements, and in the meantime had taken steps to improve passenger security and comfort at the airport.[44] In 1993, students from the Simón Bolívar University helped passengers arriving from overseas to exit the airport without harassment by hucksters, which made a big difference to arriving tourists and business travelers. Noticeable improvements included refurbished waiting rooms and the installation of public telephones. However, the long lines and the inefficient processing of passengers remained pressing problems and continued to give foreign visitors negative impressions of Venezuela.

Ground transportation in the major cities poses problems for most Venezuelans. In 1993, the average worker in the Caracas area spent two hours or more commuting each day. Traffic jams paralyze the city's main arteries during rush hour, and rush hour is growing longer. Those workers who do not own cars often must surmount imposing obstacles to get to work on time. Many walk from their homes outside Caracas to major roadways, placing their personal safety at risk, and then catch buses or hitch rides from passing commuters. The Caracas Metro has helped to alleviate congestion somewhat, but the two lines in operation in 1993 did not cover enough of the city. As of 1993, the Metro had plans to add four lines (including one under construction) and 50 stops by the year 2010, and construction had started on a commuter rail linking Caracas and Cúa in the neighboring Tuy Valley. The urban buses, many of which were run by small operators, suffered from a lack of capital and rising maintenance costs, and tended to be in poor repair. The National Urban Transportation Fund (FONTUR) was administering a $400 million program to improve bus service in the major cities and was providing financing to private bus operators.

The legacy of import substitution has left Venezuela without the infrastructure needed to export in substantial quantities. The nation, for example, lacks the specialized facilities required for the export of perishable goods,[45] such as the refrigerated storage needed to export tropical fruits. As of 1993, Maiquetía was the only airport in Venezuela with refrigerated storage, and demand exceeded supply. Maritime ports had containers for grain imports but not for grain exports. Agricultural producers in remote areas, such as the cocoa farmers near Carúpano, have been at a disadvantage because local ports are relatively undeveloped and receive infrequent maritime service. Venezuelan exporters who ship in small volumes often pay high rates.

Potential in Telecommunications

A nation's teledensity (number of phone lines per 100 inhabitants) correlates to its level of economic development. According to ECLAC (1992a), expansion of nonresidential telephone density is a cause of economic growth, while expansion of residential teledensity is an effect of that growth. In 1989, Venezuelan teledensity was only 8.2 lines per 100 inhabitants. Given Venezuelan's per-capita income levels at the time, this suggests substantial unmet demand for telephone lines. Venezuela ranked below Spain and Argentina, with teledensities of 28.1 and 10.2, respectively, but above Colombia (6.7) and Mexico (5.6).[46]

Historically, Venezuela's telecommunications services have been very weak. The poor quality of service hindered not only the competitiveness of Venezuelan firms, but also normal firm operations and the everyday life of subscribers. A history of rates that were too low to cover costs, disinvestment, politically appointed managers, poor labor relations, and low morale combined to create a system that reduced efficiency across the economy. Particularly hard hit were the service sectors, such as banking, tourism, and transportation.

In 1991, CANTV, the state-owned telephone monopoly, was privatized. Forty percent of its stock was sold to a consortium of private investors led by General Telephone and Electronics (GTE), and another 11 percent was sold to company employees. The new owners found a system in collapse. In the first two years after privatization, CANTV invested more than $1 billion in the Venezuelan phone system, or more than had been invested in its entire history under government control. In those first two years, CANTV exceeded its targets by adding more than 200,000 new subscribers per year as well as nearly 14,000 public telephones.[47] CANTV committed to increase teledensity to 18 lines per inhabitant by the year 2000, by which date it will serve 4.4 million subscribers. CANTV also committed to raising Venezuelan telephone service to international standards. As of 1993, the nation's firms felt the need for improvement urgently in their day-to-day operations. In the Viana survey, 40 percent of the firms surveyed identified telecommunications as an obstacle to their growth.[48]

Venezuela has an opportunity to become one of the leaders in Latin America in telecommunications by the year 2000. GTE has the technology, know-how, capital resources, and business skills to develop the Venezuelan market to its fullest potential. In 1991, the cellular communications sector was opened to competition, ushering in a new Venezuelan lifestyle for the 1990s. By 1993, more than 120,000 Venezuelan subscribers were served by Telcel (affiliated to Bell South) and Movilnet (affiliated to

CANTV) in ten urban areas. CANTV holds exclusive rights to switched telephone service only until the year 2000, when competition will open up in this area. In the meantime, Sprint and MCI are already competing with CANTV to provide private circuit service. By 1993, TDI, founded by AT&T, had become affiliated with CANTV. Competition among providers was stimulating rapid growth of international data transmission, private lines, trunking, and value-added services.[49]

Venezuela is not alone in its efforts to build a state-of-the-art telecommunications system. The telephone systems of Argentina, Chile, and Mexico also have been privatized, and ambitious telecommunications expansion is being undertaken in these countries. For example, as of 1993, Argentina planned to raise its teledensity to 17.3 lines per inhabitant by 1997.[50] Chile's short-term teledensity targets were comparable to those of Venezuela and Argentina.[51] Mexico raised its teledensity to eight lines per inhabitant in the early 1990s, had further increases in process, and was in the process of phasing out tariffs on telecommunications equipment from the United States under the North American Free Trade Agreement (NAFTA).[52] Large investments in cellular systems were being made in Argentina, Mexico, and elsewhere, and direct competition was heating up the Mexican cellular market.[53]

Should Venezuela become a regional leader in telecommunications, this would provide valuable support for its industries, particularly information-intensive industries, including banking, retailing, transportation, tourism, and professional services. It would also make Venezuela more attractive as a location for foreign investment and as a transportation hub. (In Asia, several nations are making telecommunications a source of competitive advantage. Singapore, for example, will boast the world's most advanced phone system by the year 2000. The nation is using this system to develop a sophisticated service economy.) The communications sector also could be one of the major sources of economic growth in Venezuela during the 1990s. In 1991, the telecommunications industry accounted for less than 1 percent of GDP. Juan Mijares, former managing director of CONATEL, the telecommunications regulatory agency, has estimated that the sector could account for as much as 6 percent of GDP by 1996.[54]

The future of the Venezuelan telecommunications sector will depend on the government keeping its commitment to allow the gradual but steady rate increases necessary to fund the investments required to build a modern communications infrastructure. In 1993, rates for local service were between one-third and one-half of rates in the United States, Argentina, Chile, and Mexico, where telecommunications were also privatized. It will take time for service to improve, and it also will take time for the public to learn how to value these improvements. In this respect, the Venezuelan public's traditional aversion to paying for telephone service could become, in the hands of a populist administration, a threat to growth, not only of the telecommunications sector but the economy as a whole.

Postal service in Venezuela is provided by a public agency, the Postal and Telegraphic Institute (Ipostel). Service is considered slow and unreliable.[55] In the early 1990s, it ranked beneath the best Latin American postal services as well as that of neighboring Colombia within the Andean Pact. The poor quality of Ipostel's service has stimulated demand for alternative forms of communication. Most large and medium-size firms in Caracas use in-house motorcycle messengers for urban deliveries. A number of specialized document delivery companies exist for those who prefer to contract for the service. Facsimile transmission is also very popular and is improving in reliability as the phone connections improve. Some of these substitutes, however, can be very expensive. In addition, poor and unreliable service limits the distribution channels that Venezuelan firms can use in the domestic market. The purchase and delivery of merchandise by mail (such as the mail order catalog business found in the United States), for example, is not common in Venezuela. It is difficult to foresee dramatic improvement in the public mail service in the near future. Further development of private services, and the growing use of facsimile machines and data transmission, will increasingly substitute for the public postal service, at the same time making its improvement less likely. Domestic retailers probably will continue to be disadvantaged by the absence of a cheap and reliable system for the delivery of goods.

Shortage of Information Resources

In advanced economies, the dissemination of reliable business information contributes to business growth and new business creation. Information flows are essential to gaining competitive advantage. The competitive success of any firm depends on its leaders' ability to respond to the right signals in its environment, whether they relate to rivals, markets, suppliers, or new technologies. Although information flows to the firm from many sources, including informal networks, there is no substitute for reliable business and economic data in firm decision making.

As of 1993, the information resources available in Venezuela were insufficient and were not a source of advantage to the nation's firms. The Central Bank of Venezuela generally was considered the best source of data on the economy as a whole. The Central Office of Statistics and Informatics

(OCEI) has provided a number of useful surveys, including its survey of households, but has lacked the resources to provide comprehensive, up-to-date industry statistics. There have not been reliable censuses of manufacturing or service industries, and agricultural statistics frequently have been estimated from a baseline that was developed in the 1960s. In 1993, a major debate in the tourism sector involved disagreements over estimates of the number of tourist arrivals due to alleged inaccuracies in record keeping. Official estimates of the number of people employed in tourism and tourism-related industries have been inaccurate by an order of magnitude. Industry-wide sales data for the Venezuelan software sector, as well as many others, have not been available, making it difficult to evaluate its domestic and export sales performance in relation to regional competitors. Venezuela's agricultural statistics have been in a state of disarray. In the course of this project, we were repeatedly confronted by the absence of reliable business data in Venezuela.

In Venezuela, as in many other countries, certain factors conspire against information disclosure and dissemination. Most firms are privately held and are not subject to disclosure regulations. Some leading Venezuelan firms do not even supply financial information to their banks. Many companies represent the principal source of wealth of their owners. In several state-owned companies, accounts apparently have been obscured to hide the extent of subsidies and cross-subsidies.[56] Venezuelan managers are extremely reluctant for information on their performance to spread to suppliers, competitors, buyers, and labor (which might use the information in contract negotiations or in pressing profit-sharing claims), in part for economic and competitive reasons and in part for cultural reasons. In a nation where information does not flow freely, knowledge is power. Nearly all information is considered private information, which can be traded for other useful information but is rarely "disclosed."[57]

Nevertheless, since the mid-1980s, there has been a significant increase in the amount, and quality, of general and specific business information available in Venezuela. This has reflected the growing sophistication of Venezuelan firms, as they have become more concerned with product quality, productivity, and global and regional business trends. There also has been a marked increase in the number of consultants offering economic studies and forecasts. By the early 1990s, market research, provided by the Venezuelan firm Datos and others, was used by a number of Venezuelan and foreign-owned companies. Venezuela's National Center for Competitiveness (Venezuela Competitiva) has been working to strengthen the nation's base of industrial statistics.

One source of economic and business information that has been growing in importance in Venezuela is the business press. The press in general is highly developed and influential in the nation. A tradition of democratic freedom and independence has allowed the press to carry substantial political weight. National daily newspapers include *El Universal, El Nacional, Ultimas Noticias, 2001, El Diario, El Globo,* and the English-language *Daily Journal.* The business press flourished in the early 1990s following the economic opening. *Economía Hoy* and *Reporte de Economía* appeared and business magazines proliferated. Leading publications on the economy and business have included *Gerente Venezuela, VenEconomía, The Monthly Report, Business Venezuela,* and *Número.* In addition, there are a large number of specialized publications. Through these publications, economic and business news have received a great deal of coverage.

Despite the business press, many Venezuelan firms have only limited knowledge about the business and economic information being generated in the outside world. Within Venezuela, it is sometimes difficult to gain access to the studies carried out in the nation by the United Nations, the World Bank, the International Monetary Fund (IMF), and other international organizations, particularly those carried out on particular industries and sectors. This is not reflective of the educational background of the nation's executives, many of whom have received all or part of their business training overseas. Rather, it points to the need for the systematized collection and dissemination of business-related materials within the country, by industry associations and other groups.

Infrastructure in Need of Investment

Venezuela's infrastructure clearly will require substantial investments, in management and people as well as in money, in order to bring it up to world standards. It is worthy of note that the greatest improvements in infrastructure in the early 1990s have come in telecommunications and the ports, where private firms have started to provide far better service than was achieved under state control. In 1994, the government announced a program to build roads and railways by private concession. It was hoped that this program would upgrade transportation infrastructure substantially in Venezuela.

Uneven Human Resources

A nation's competitiveness in the modern world economy, and its standard of living, is largely determined by the productivity of its people. This productivity, in turn, depends on the skills and capabilities obtained through education and training. Investments in education, training, and skill building are the most important investments that a nation can make. This fact has not been lost on the people of Japan and the newly industrializing nations of Asia, which have built, or are building, their economies through investments that increase the skills, capabilities, and productivity of workers and managers. In Latin America, Chile has set the creation of the best education system in the world as a major goal. These nations are overcoming their disadvantages in natural resources by developing advantages in human resources.

The Venezuelan economy has a severe shortage of skilled and semiskilled workers with technical know-how, the people who actually maintain the plants and keep the equipment running.[58] Granell and Parra (1993), in their study of human resource formation and competitiveness in Venezuela, found that most plant operators in industry have only a primary education.[59] In 1990, 50 percent of Sidor's employees were found to have six years or less of formal schooling, indicating an educational level in the steel industry below international standards.[60] Throughout Venezuelan industry there are technicians who cannot read equipment manuals and secretaries who have not mastered the basic rules of spelling.[61] In many sectors, such as tourism, workers with basic literacy and numeracy are an elite, which leads to high turnover rates and dissatisfaction in entry-level jobs. In the Viana survey, nearly 50 percent of the firms surveyed identified a shortage of qualified workers as an obstacle to their growth.[62]

During the early 1990s, approximately 40 percent of the nation's employed workers were in the so-called informal sector of the economy. Most of these workers earned less than their formal sector counterparts, and the gap between the income of formal and informal workers was widening. In their study of the informal economy and competitiveness in Venezuela, Betancourt and Freije (1993) found that the existence of such a large informal economy in Venezuela is a symptom of the country's weakness in human factor creation.[63] (Although immigration also has contributed to the low educational level of the informal sector overall, in 1991, only about 8 percent of informal workers in Venezuela were foreign immigrants.) Many of the workers in the informal sector have poor education and training, which makes it difficult for them to find jobs in the modern sector. Modern industry, from telecommunications to tourism, demands well-grounded basic skills such as reading, writing, mathematics, and general cultural knowledge. Betancourt and Freije estimate that if the productivity of the informal sector were raised to that of the formal economy, Venezuela's GDP would increase by nearly 30 percent.

TABLE 6.3
Occupation in Venezuela by Sector and Employment Category

Field	1977	1980	1985	1991	1992	1993[a]
			Thousands			
Total Employed Persons	4,332.7	4,753.6	5,201.2	6,830.5	7,003.9	7,001.3
Modern Sector	2,604.6	2,906.6	2,922.0	4,233.2	4,228.3	4,216.6
Private Sector	1,720.6	1,888.2	1,780.3	2,906.6	2,964.1	2,986.7
Owners	130.9	135.3	126.8	133.7	175.4	177.3
Employees/Workers	1,539.2	1,721.8	1,637.2	2,712.7	2,750.1	2,769.6
Professionals/Technicians	50.6	31.1	16.3	60.2	38.6	39.8
Public Sector	884.0	1,018.5	1,141.6	1,326.6	1,264.2	1,229.9
Informal Sector	1,728.1	1,847.0	2,279.2	2,597.3	2,775.6	2,784.7

[a] 1993 figures based on January through June.

Source: OCEI, Household Survey.

Labor Force Facts

The Venezuelan labor force is relatively small (7.5 million people in 1992) and relatively young. Between 1981 and 1990, it grew at an annual average compound rate of 4 percent, faster than the labor forces of Brazil (3.7 percent) or Mexico (3.5 percent).[64] The rapid growth rate will continue because of the youth of the nation's population. (In 1990, 37 percent of the nation's population was under the age of 15[65]). In 1993, private-sector employment accounted for 71 percent of the labor force employed in the modern sector of the economy, with the public sector accounting for the remaining 29 percent. (See Table 6.3.) The ratio of females (32 percent of the total workforce) to males (68 percent) was rising along with the rate of female participation in the workforce.[66] Informal workers accounted for roughly 40 percent of the workforce.

The educational profile of the Venezuelan workforce has changed substantially in the last three decades. The portion of the workforce consisting of illiterates and persons with no schooling decreased from 48

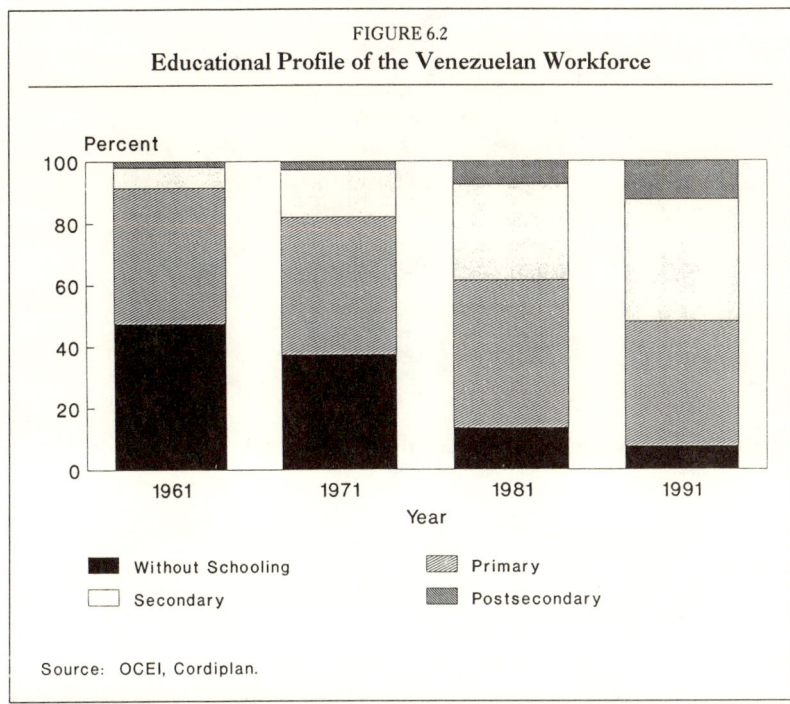

FIGURE 6.2
Educational Profile of the Venezuelan Workforce

Source: OCEI, Cordiplan.

percent in 1961 to 7.4 percent in 1991. The portion with only a primary school education fell from 45 percent to 40 percent, while the portion with secondary schooling increased from 7 percent to 44 percent and the portion with higher education increased from 1.8 percent to 12.9 percent of the workforce. (See Figure 6.2.)[67] Nevertheless, a major challenge going forward will be to develop the skills and educational base of present and future workers. In a 1992 study, the National Council for Investment Promotion found that "a key problem in Venezuela is that the growth of the industrial sector has been faster than the development of human skills."[68]

From 1940 to 1960, Venezuela experienced rapid urbanization. Large numbers of farmers entered the urban workforce. At the same time, almost 1 million European immigrants arrived in Venezuela, many establishing themselves as artisans, shopkeepers, and technicians. Many of them left afterward, lured by better opportunities in the burgeoning European Community, but the majority remained and entered the business and professional middle class. In the 1970s and 1980s, immigrants arrived from Colombia, including many special-

TABLE 6.4
Worker Salaries in Manufacturing Industries, Selected Nations, 1991

	Thousand U.S.$/Year	U.S.$/Hour
United States	30.2	11.8
Argentina	8.4	3.3
Brazil	5.7	2.2
Mexico	6.4	2.5
Venezuela	**4.6**	**1.8**

The hourly salary was estimated using an average income of 14.5 months per year, and 176 working hours per month for all countries.

Source: Towers Perrin.

ized workers, and from Chile and Argentina, including a large number of professionals fleeing dictatorial regimes. However, overall immigration fell substantially. The number of foreign-born residents officially peaked at 1.2 million in the late 1970s. Reduced immigration has limited what had been a major source of technical and business skills for the nation.[69]

Relatively Low-Cost Labor

The cost of labor in Venezuela (before adjustment for retroactive severance payments, and the inflation and interest rates that affect severance payments) became the lowest in Latin America after the 1989 devaluation. (See Table 6.4.) In 1991, Venezuelan labor costs were below those of other Latin American countries for construction workers, department managers, electrical engineers, bank tellers, secretaries, and female textile workers.[70] However, the labor costs of machinists, auto mechanics, and salespeople were higher than in other Latin American countries, reflecting the nation's shortage of skills in these areas. (See Figure 6.3.) The Union Bank of Switzerland estimates that in 1991, Venezuelan labor costs overall were 20.4 percent lower than the Latin American average. Salaries in Venezuela were 80 to 90 percent lower than in Europe or the United States.[71] Venezuelan salaries did not keep pace with inflation in the late 1980s and early 1990s. (See Figure 6.4.)

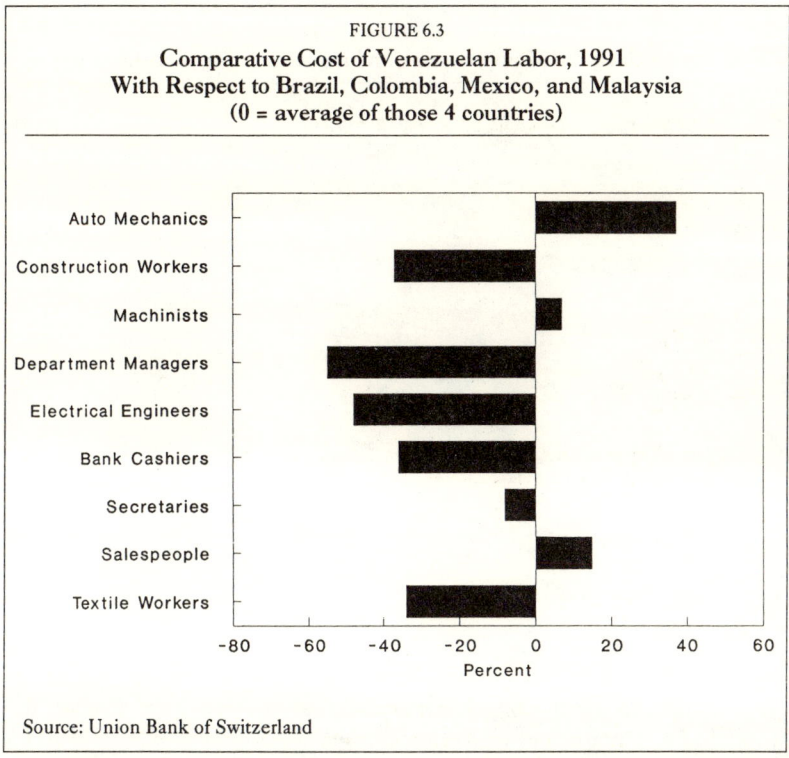

FIGURE 6.3
Comparative Cost of Venezuelan Labor, 1991
With Respect to Brazil, Colombia, Mexico, and Malaysia
(0 = average of those 4 countries)

Source: Union Bank of Switzerland

Although Venezuelan wages are relatively low in regional terms, competing exclusively on the basis of low labor costs is not an attractive route to economic growth. At the low end of the wage scale, labor cost advantages are precarious. There always will be countries somewhere in the world with larger and poorer populations than Venezuela, more than ready to steal away foreign markets and foreign investment based solely on cheap labor. Low-cost labor is a basic factor advantage, like raw natural resources, and it is not as effective a leverage of economic growth as skilled labor, which generates higher level competitive advantages. Improving Venezuela's standard of living will depend on raising the productivity of its workforce through improved education and training, not on keeping labor costs low.

Rigid Severance and Dismissal Rules

Venezuela has not instituted a viable social safety net for its people, via social security payments or a national pension fund. The Social Security Institute

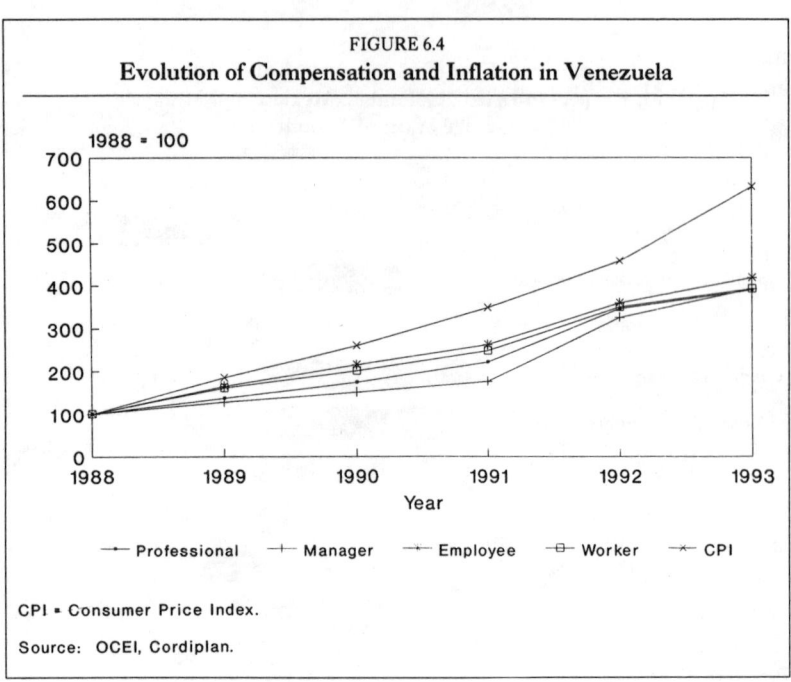

FIGURE 6.4
Evolution of Compensation and Inflation in Venezuela

CPI = Consumer Price Index.
Source: OCEI, Cordiplan.

is widely viewed as corrupt beyond redemption. Only a small percentage of Venezuelans qualify for and collect unemployment insurance. The only security that most Venezuelan workers accumulate is their severance payment, which is in effect a tax that is paid in by firms over the course of a worker's employment and is paid out when employment ends. However, Venezuela's system of severance payments is an inadequate substitute for virtually nonexistent unemployment insurance and retirement funds, and the rigidity that it generates hinders job creation in the formal economy.

Legal restrictions on worker dismissal in Venezuela are among the most rigid in Latin America. By law, Venezuelan workers have the right, upon dismissal from employment, to a severance payment equal to one month's salary, based on their average monthly wage during their final year of employment, multiplied by the number of years of employment. Workers dismissed for unjust cause are entitled to collect double indemnity. In effect, most employers pay double indemnity as a matter of course, because of numerous pro-labor biases in the law. Employers are required to contribute to each worker's severance fund in regular installments and to pay interest on these contributions.[72] The combination of retroactivity and interest payments means that, in effect, firms must pay twice for the effects of inflation and salary increases. These provisions have an inflationary impact on prices. As firms cannot go back and charge higher prices to customers who bought goods five years ago in order to cover the costs of retroactive severance schemes, they must charge higher prices to today's customers.

The severance provisions distort the hiring, training, and promotion of workers in the Venezuelan economy. They make it costlier to keep workers on payroll for extended periods than to dismiss them and to hire new workers. For most firms, it is cheaper to fire workers and to replace them than to promote them, since each increase in salary inflates the final payment to be made on their leaving the firm. This dynamic discourages firms from hiring people for the long-term, promoting them to higher levels of responsibility, or investing in their training or education. Managers of firms that place a high value on human resource training confided in interviews that they have to struggle against these very real disincentives. The same dynamic probably is also at work in the vast majority of firms that place less emphasis on worker training. The results are very costly in an economy that is constrained by a lack of trained and specialized workers. Many workers are caught in the revolving door of short-term employment, and others are shut out of the formal economy altogether.[73] (See Chapter 9.)

In the 1980s and early 1990s, Chile (and to a lesser extent, Argentina and Colombia) took steps to liberalize their legal provisions governing severance and dismissal.[74] Chile and Argentina do not grant severance payments to workers who terminate their employment without "just cause." Both countries recognize as "just cause" the fact that a firm is experiencing economic difficulties, and levy lower severance payments in such cases. Colombia recognizes economic difficulties as "just cause" for terminating workers in the case of small firms; Venezuela does not.

Creative and Flexible Workers

Although it is difficult to generalize about a nation's workers as a whole, the managers interviewed for this study emphasized many positive aspects of the Venezuelan workforce. According to managers in a broad range of industries, Venezuelan workers are favorably disposed to learning on the job, pick up new skills quickly, and are adaptable. Several foreign managers with experience in Venezuela and Colombia reported that Venezuelan workers are more willing to learn new things and more adaptable to changes on the job than their Colombian counterparts.[75]

Managers of multinational firms, with international experience, suggest that Venezuelan workers are talented at tasks involving creativity, flexibility, and challenge.[76] The manager of a multinational paper company claimed that Venezuelan workers welding production equipment created welds under difficult conditions in the field that were superior to those made in the factory in the United States. A factory manager for a multinational hardware factory (specializing in locks) was very favorably impressed by the attitudes and performance of Venezuelan workers, compared to those of U.S. and Italian workers in the same type of production. In his opinion, the Venezuelan workers exhibited a positive and flexible attitude, whereas the Italian and American workers followed guidelines literally and limited their efforts to reaching the target production quota.[77]

However, managers tended to rate Venezuelan workers less favorably in terms of overall discipline and attention to detail. According to one German manager, given the same assignment, a German worker will read the instructions from start to finish, devise a plan, and then start the task at hand. The Venezuelan will start work first and read instructions as needed, generally without a plan. Venezuelan workers, on average, need to learn to think strategically. Colombian workers won higher praise for their reliability in following orders and attention to detail. Several managers explained that they delegate at their own risk in Venezuela.[78] Unless they have a truly exceptional assistant or are particularly successful at motivating their employees, the chances are high that their orders simply will not be carried out in their absence.

Some managers also pointed out that their employees do their best to get to work regularly and on time despite long commutes, dangerous neighborhoods, personal insecurity, and inadequate health care. Malavé and Piñango (1993), in their study of social conditions and competitiveness in Venezuela, observe that, in the opinion of some managers with broad experience in managing workers, the Venezuelan worker "can and does achieve high levels of productivity when he is well directed and appropriately equipped. Instead, his limitations come from the social surroundings where he lives. For example, the cause of absenteeism and high labor turnover should be sought in such factors as deficient nutrition, the inefficiency of and frequent interruptions in health, water and transportation services, in addition to the severe personal insecurity typical of the poorest neighborhoods."[79]

Education and Competitiveness
The investments that a nation makes in its people, particularly in their education, are among the most important of all national investments. Given Venezuela's per-capita income, the amount spent per student is far less than that spent in the industrialized nations. (See Table 6.5.) Nevertheless,

TABLE 6.5
Ordinary Spending on Education, Selected Nations

U.S. $ per Student per Year

Country	Year	Primary	Secondary	Tertiary
Mexico	1990	133	261	744
United States	1986	3,281	6,638	4,812
Brazil	1990	225	256	1,421
Chile	1989	223	178	639
Colombia	1991	76	118	442
Venezuela	**1988**	**104**	**281**	**1,162**

Spending per student corresponds only to public spending plus support to private education.

Source: UNESCO.

Venezuela has devoted up to 20 percent of its government budget on education, a relatively high percentage in regional terms. (See Table 6.6.) On the other hand, other nations with similar and even lower income levels, such as Chile and Costa Rica, have achieved better results than Venezuela in their educational investments. As Juan Carlos Navarro finds in his study on education and competitiveness in Venezuela, the problem is not so much the amount of money spent on education (although it might be argued that a nation always should spend more on education, given its transcendental importance to competitiveness). Instead, the problem lies with the effectiveness of spending within the system and the allocation of resources between educational levels.[80]

Vastly Expanded Education. Since the 1960s, Venezuela has vastly expanded its system of public and private primary and secondary schools. It has created dozens of institutions of higher learning, including universities, technological institutes, university colleges, and institutes for the training of teachers. (The private education sector, though smaller than the public education sector, is significant, with total spending on private education

TABLE 6.6
Total Public Spending on Education and
Participation Rates, Selected Nations

	Year	Percent of GDP	Percent of Government Spending	Net Schooling Rate, Primary	Net Schooling Rate, Secondary
United States	1989	5.3	12.4	99	81
Mexico	1990	4.1	n.a.	98	44
Venezuela	**1989**	**4.1**	**18.8**	**61**	**20**
Brazil	1988	3.9	n.a.	88[a]	16[a]
Chile	1990	2.9	10.4	86	55
Colombia	1989	2.9	21.4	73[b]	36[b]

[a] 1990
[b] 1991

Source: UNESCO.

equal to about 37 percent of public spending.) In 1989, the nation's education system accommodated 5.2 million Venezuelan students from the primary through university levels, up from 1.5 million in 1961. Venezuela has reduced adult illiteracy from 37 percent in 1965 to 9 percent in 1990.[81] From 1965 to 1990, enrollment, as a percentage of age group, has increased from 95 to 105 percent for primary school, from 27 to 56 percent for secondary school, and from 2 to 28 for university and technical school.[82] Nevertheless, there is growing concern among many Venezuelans that students are not learning the skills and knowledge needed for success in a competitive world economy.

Inadequate Primary and Secondary Education. Most Venezuelan children are not receiving the education that they need in order to be competitive in the modern economy. As of 1992, 37 percent of Venezuelan students dropped out of school before completing primary school, and 53 percent of all students dropped out before completing the ninth grade.[83] By ninth grade, 95 percent of all public school students had repeated at least one school year.

According to Navarro (1993), on average, a student requires one year and four months to advance one grade within the public school system. Venezuelan public schools spend 18 years' worth of educational resources to take a child through nine grades, twice as much as an efficient system would require. Only 60 percent of children in the corresponding age group attend primary school and only 20 percent attend secondary school, figures well below other Latin American countries. This fact shows that Venezuelans attend school later than the normal age.[84] (See Table 6.6.)

The official Venezuelan school year is 900 hours (180 scheduled school days of five hours each). In the early 1990s, at least one-third of that total has been lost to teacher strikes and other problems, yielding a total school year of less than 600 hours.[85] During the 1992-1993 school year, teachers' strikes canceled approximately 35 days out of the annual total of 180 days, and an additional 15 days were lost to political disturbances; the teachers' unions would not make the lost days up by extending the school year.[86] Additional days were lost due to interruptions in basic services and other problems. In contrast, children in Japan attend school 1,650 hours per year.

More serious than the nation's short school year is the inefficiency and ineffectiveness of the educational system during the relatively few hours devoted to teaching.[87] According to Navarro (1993), on average, there is only one book for every 17 children in the Venezuelan public schools. Teachers often spend half of class time writing out the day's material on the chalkboard, due to the shortage of books. The teachers themselves are poorly paid and tend not to represent the highest-ranking graduates of the educational system.[88] According to the World Economic Forum (1993), in 1990, the average yearly wage of a Venezuelan primary school teacher was $2,500, a figure lower than the corresponding wages in Korea ($15,400), Singapore ($9,700), Malaysia ($4,300), and Brazil ($3,250), but above that in Mexico ($2,100) and India ($1,100).

In 1992, Venezuelan children 13 years of age ranked twenty-eighth in a sample of 31 nations in a test of reading comprehension skills, above only Nigeria, Zimbabwe, and Botswana. By this age, nearly half of all Venezuelan students have left school and entered the informal economy. The educational performance of those who have stayed on, presumably the top half of the class, bodes ill for the prospects of the many who have left to join the labor force prematurely. In a study of a representative sample of sixth grade students conducted by the ministry of education, students on average scored seven points out of a maximum of 20 points in basic academic skills appropriate to their age level; private school students scored only somewhat better than public school students.[89]

According to a conservative estimate, in 1991, 53 percent of Venezuelan children under 14 years of age lived below the poverty line.[90] As Malavé and Piñango observe in their study of social conditions and competitiveness in Venezuela, most of the population is young and poor. Poor children generally live "in urban communities characterized by a high degree of social disorganization: abandonment, child and juvenile delinquency, lack of public services, [and] school absenteeism."[91] However, these factors must not be accepted as an excuse for the failings of the public schools.[92] Other Latin American countries, with less money to spend and students with lower income levels, have had more success in public education than Venezuela. Within Venezuela itself, certain nonprofit schools, operating in low-income neighborhoods and working with children from the same social pool as the public schools, have achieved significantly better results at lower cost, as in the case of Fé y Alegría.

Another Way? Since 1955, Fé y Alegría schools have been educating children and youths from low-income families throughout Venezuela with the support of the Catholic Church. In 1993, there were 109 schools in the national Fé y Alegría network, including five schools that offer agricultural programs. They emphasize preparing the student for productive work, which is seen as an appropriate means of self-realization and community growth, and they tailor their programs to the needs of each community. Many also offer night workshops for adults. Fé y Alegría also has created two schools in Maracaibo and one in San Felix dedicated to training unemployed youths who have dropped out of school.[93]

The Fé y Alegría schools generally have achieved better educational results than the public school system even though they operate in the same neighborhoods, teach the same sorts of youngsters, and even, in some cases, use the same teachers as the public schools, at a cost savings of 22 percent per student.[94] It is not uncommon for a primary school teacher to teach in the public school in the morning and then in a Fé y Alegría school in the afternoon, where he or she is more effective. The Fé y Alegría system has been adopted in other Latin American countries, including Ecuador, Panama, Peru, Bolivia, El Salvador, Colombia, Nicaragua, Guatemala, and Brazil. The relative success, even on a small scale, of alternatives to public education show that there is nothing intrinsic in Venezuela that prevents the development of a successful primary education system. The Fé y Alegría example shows that, at its core, the problem with the Venezuelan public primary schools is not primarily financial. Rather, it is a question of whether public resources can be spent efficiently and well.

The Higher Education Sector. Venezuela's higher education sector is not generating specialized human resources in the varieties or quantities needed by local industries to compete in international markets. The most popular areas of study are social sciences (43 percent of graduates in 1988), engineering, architecture and technology (22 percent), and education (17 percent).[95] The social sciences, including legal studies, are by far the most popular course of study for university students in Venezuela. Internationally, a negative correlation has been found between the percentage of graduates majoring in law and accounting and a nation's rate of economic growth.[96] In many of the industries studied in this project, including petrochemicals, steel, aluminum, pulp and paper, rice, and cocoa, shortages of specialized professionals and technicians are a source of competitive disadvantage. For example, despite the relatively high popularity of engineering as a field of study, the chemical industry reported that in 1993, the number of qualified graduates was not satisfying industrial demand.[97]

The Venezuelan university system, which has grown greatly in recent decades, is uneven. Public universities range from the very prestigious, such as Simón Bolívar University, to the less prestigious. Private universities and colleges are also a mixed lot. Attrition rates are high and many university students take extra years to complete their courses of study. In the late 1980s the public universities graduated on average only one of every three students who entered the system. While the costs of instruction in the public universities were three times higher than those in the private universities, the private universities managed to graduate two out of every three students enrolled.[98]

The public universities control most research and development centers in the country, an arrangement that for years divorced Venezuelan R&D from the needs of industry. The private sector responded to the lack of connection between the public universities and business by creating private universities and supporting private educational institutions. The best of these schools are fine indeed, but they are insufficient to bridge the gap between the university sector and the needs of the economy. There have been some promising signs of improvement in the interaction of business and the public universities. As public budgets shrank in the 1980s, the private sector became a more important employer for graduates of public universities. The universities also needed to look for new funding. Several universities started to offer a range of extension courses to professionals, government, business, and communities. Research-oriented universities and departments created institutes to cater to the technological, training, and consulting needs of industry. The current trend is clearly toward closer ties between university and business, although progress is slow.

An outstanding university R&D center has been the Foundation for Research and Development (FUNINDES), a nonprofit institution that has operated at the Simón Bolívar University since 1986. Its aim has been to link the scientific, technological, and management capacity of the university with the Venezuelan productive sector. Since its founding, it has established ties with approximately 300 firms, mostly in the Caracas metropolitan area. In 1992, contracts between FUNINDES and firms totaled 600 million bolivars (around $8.3 million), an amount equal to about 10 percent of the university's budget. FUNINDES has had a good reputation in the productive sector, and its ties with Venezuelan firms have grown stronger from year to year.[99]

Misallocation of Educational Resources. Venezuela spends a disproportionately high percentage of its education funds at the top of the educational pyramid (and on students who, from an economic perspective, need it the least). Throughout the 1980s, more than 40 percent of government spending on education in Venezuela was devoted to higher education. This spending pattern is very atypical within the Latin American nations, which tend to spend one half of what the Venezuelan government spends on higher education (in percentage terms) and at least four times more on secondary education.[100] Neighboring Colombia, for example, has allocated about 26 percent of its education spending to higher education. Colombian public planners believe that even 26 percent is too high, because public spending on higher education is "not well targeted in terms of redistributive effect."[101]

The current pattern of public spending on education in Venezuela subsidizes the affluent. A Venezuelan student who attends public schools from preschool through the end of the Diversified Cycle (high school) will end up receiving from the state less than half the education subsidy received by a youth whose family has paid for private schools and whose only participation in the public school system is five years at public university. (These families tend to be more affluent.)[102] The result is a two-tiered education system, in which most poor children attend inadequate schools and drop out well before they might take advantage of the publicly funded universities, and in which more affluent children attending public universities receive a disproportionate amount of public support. The hope that state funding of higher education would lead to more equality in opportunity has foundered on the reality that most poor children drop out long before they reach university. One result is a highly skewed labor market, sharply stratified by education, training, and pay.

Technical Training Shortage. Education in Venezuela, as in much of Latin America, traditionally has been geared to preparation for university and a prestigious degree as a lawyer, physician, or engineer. Venezuelan culture does not value technical careers as highly as careers in law, medicine, or engineering. Venezuela lags behind not only developed countries in its formation of technical skills but its neighbors as well. In 1993, the World Competitiveness Report ranked Venezuela last among 15 developing countries in the availability of skilled personnel.[103] Granell and Parra (1993) found that only 2 percent of Venezuela's operators and artisans have any formal technical education. They also found that there were *fewer* workers with technical training in the manufacturing sector in 1993 than there were in 1981.

Various technical curricula have been implemented at the secondary school level, including several experimental initiatives. However, the technical courses of study continue to suffer from a lack of prestige that discourages enrollment. Only 17.7 percent of secondary school students were enrolled in the technical *bachillerato* (high school) course of study during the 1990-1991 school year, down from 26 percent in 1981.[104] Institutions of higher education offering three-year degrees in computer programming, tourism, marketing, and other white-collar occupations were opened in the 1980s. In 1988, these schools, together with teacher institutes, attracted 35 percent of higher-education enrollment, compared to 53 percent for public universities and 12 percent for private universities.[105]

The typical students at Venezuela's technical schools come from low-income families.[106] Upon graduation, they receive certification as "middle technicians." Many hope to pursue postsecondary technical training subsequent to graduation, in order to become "advanced technicians" and thereby enhance their earning power. However, the postsecondary educational system in Venezuela places obstacles in their way. Technical courses of study are offered primarily by private three-year institutions, not the public universities. These university colleges and technical institutes charge tuition fees. The graduates of the technical schools, who for the most part have limited financial resources, face the prospect of paying what are for them enormous sums in tuition (approximately 50,000 bolivars per semester in 1994), in order to study at night and work during the day, while students from middle- and upper-class families attend public universities nearly free of charge.

Leading companies in Venezuela, in services, natural resources, and manufacturing, tend increasingly to take care of their training needs themselves, whereas smaller companies must rely on the National Institute for

Educational Cooperation (INCE) and informal on-the-job training to fill the existing gap in technical education. INCE, a public institution that offers short training programs to young people, bears much of the burden of the nation's vocational training. INCE was restructured in the early 1990s and has experimented with new educational methods, including a program that has combined training and on-the-job practice based on the German dual training system. The reformed INCE drew good reviews from most managers interviewed as part of this project, but it is inadequate to meet the training needs of the entire economy. In 1992, INCE graduated a total of 12,184 apprentices from its National Apprentice Program and about 340,000 students total from courses that it sponsored directly or indirectly. In that same year, the head of INCE estimated Venezuela's national training deficit at 86 million course hours.[107] INCE alone hardly makes a dent in Venezuela's need for training.

Support of INCE by private and public firms has been lukewarm at best. Many firms do not participate in the INCE apprenticeship program, preferring to pay a fine instead. One exception is Nestlé Venezuela, S.A. As the general director of Nestlé Venezuela points out, the difference between vocational training schools in Switzerland and Venezuela is that in Switzerland, private industry structures training institutes, and private industry cares that these institutes work.[108] In Venezuela, private firms have offered only limited support for schools in general. As will be discussed, Siemens has cooperated with the Escuela Don Bosco. The Venezuelan-German Chamber of Commerce and Industry also has been active in supporting secondary schools. In 1993, IBM ran a program to promote the in-school use of computers, and the Banco Mercantil had implemented a program for the maintenance and repair of public schools.[109]

Training and the Private Firm. The scarcity of skilled workers in Venezuela is a serious obstacle to economic growth, as shown by the Viana survey.[110] According to the Viana survey results, 42 percent of the manufacturing firms that tried to hire technical workers in 1991 had difficulty doing so; 31 percent had difficulty hiring laborers. The firms tended to blame the shortage of trained workers on the government and its perceived failure to supply a sufficient pool of trained labor.

The studies by Granell and Parra (1993) and Viana and associates (1993) indicate that Venezuelan firms as a whole fail to understand the importance of a well-trained workforce. Most Venezuelan firms engage in training on a reactive, rather than proactive, basis, in order to respond to immediate problems and needs.[111] Many businesses still consider training an expense rather than an investment in improving capacity, in part due to high turnover rates and contractual conditions imposed under the present labor law.[112] Although there are notable exceptions, on average Venezuelan firms spend very little on training. Granell and Parra estimate that Venezuelan companies spend on average 0.2 percent of revenues on training, compared to 3 percent in Japan and 2 percent in Germany. According to international estimates, a professional should devote 80 hours per year to continuing education. In the most advanced Venezuelan firms, this number seldom exceeds 20 hours. As a result, the gap between technological advances and Venezuela's human resources is growing wider.

Venezuelan firms do not spend more on training for a number of reasons. The notion that training is primarily the responsibility of government is still widespread in the private sector. Training normally leads to payroll increases and higher personnel costs, which are magnified many times over as a result of the severance provisions in the labor law. These provisions create strong incentives not to train personnel and encourage high rates of employee turnover. Some firms are reluctant to engage in training because newly trained employees are often lured away by better-paying offers from other firms. Some firms complain that the INCE's deductions program does not sufficiently recognize amounts spent by firms with in-house training activities.[113]

Granell and Parra find that there also are deeper reasons underlying Venezuela's low rate of investment in human resources, reasons that highlight the shortcomings of Venezuelan management. It is difficult for Venezuelan firms to evaluate the return on this particular investment. Effective training requires good planning and understanding of a firm's needs. Some Venezuelan firms still are not subject to competitive pressures and therefore do not feel the need to increase productivity and product quality; under these circumstances, firms are unlikely to invest in their human resources. In addition, many Venezuelan firms are still operating with old technologies and equipment, which do not require specialized skills. Out of the 600 manufacturing firms included in the Viana survey, 337 firms reported to have *reduced* their training and human resources development efforts after the domestic market was opened up in 1989. Only 129 firms reported to have increased their efforts in this regard.[114]

Noteworthy Investments in Training. Despite this overall picture, important contributions to training have been made across the Venezuelan economy by private firms (both domestic and multinational), state-owned enterprises, and industry associations. Many of these efforts accelerated since the economic opening in 1989. While there are far too many worthy examples to discuss them all here, those that follow have been selected to give a sense of the high-quality results that are possible in Venezuela when industry assumes a leadership role in training

FUNDAMETAL. The Foundation for Industrial Training in Metalworking (Fundametal) was founded as a private nonprofit organization in 1976, in order to upgrade the technical skills of Sivensa's workforce. Its primary focus has been on training skilled workers, technicians, and other employees up to the middle-manager level. Fundametal has offered a variety of training programs aimed at improving on-the-job performance, an apprenticeship program in cooperation with INCE, and training programs that lead to degrees at the middle-technician and university levels. Since its founding, it has opened its doors to other firms in the central region of Venezuela, including suppliers and contractors to the Sivensa Group.[115]

CEFORME/METALGRÁFICA. CEFORME is a training center funded jointly by Industrias y Plásticos Metalgráfica, a member of the Polar group of companies, and INCE. CEFORME offers a four-year program to teach workers the technical skills required for specialized jobs. In 1991, it instituted an advanced four-semester course to provide graduates of its first program with additional training opportunities. This program has received support from INCE-Metalminero and the *Deutsche Gesellschaft für Technische Zusammenarbeit* (GTZ). The firm has invested approximately 100 million bolivars (around $1.4 million in 1992) to install a training center to provide services to other firms with similar training needs. Participants in CEFORME's programs study and simultaneously produce goods and services for sale, which help with financing. Participants receive a salary and other benefits, pegged to the level of training that they receive. The higher the level of difficulty, the higher the salary. In 1992, CEFORME had an enrollment of 160 students.[116]

SIEMENS. Siemens is a multinational corporation active in the areas of heavy industry, automation, communications, telecommunications, health, and the control of industrial processes. Until the mid-1980s, its technical and managerial personnel came primarily from Europe. In 1986, the firm decided to incorporate Venezuelan personnel at these levels, a difficult task due to the shortage of Venezuelans with technical training. To remedy this problem, Siemens set about to train its workers in-house. As of 1993, Siemens had training programs in technical areas such as communications and information, telecommunications networks, energy and automation, and electromedicine. It also offered programs in administration, finance, and foreign languages. In 1992-1993, Siemens planned to sponsor 341 courses in Venezuela and overseas, which would translate into 38,763 person-hours.[117] Siemens has participated in an apprenticeship program in coordination with the technical school Don Bosco. Students have received stipends from Siemens and trained to become technicians at its facilities while attending school. After graduation, students have gone on to work for Siemens. Siemens has had very good results with its Venezuelan technical trainees.[118]

CARACAS METRO. The Caracas Metro is one of the most efficient public services in Venezuela. Since its founding, the Caracas Metro has emphasized training at all levels. As of 1993, it had three separate training units, which gave courses, workshops, talks, and seminars. In 1992, the Metro's 4,500 employees devoted 347,606 hours to training courses. The Training Center (CEN), which was equipped with modern simulation labs, directed the training of train operators as well as station and maintenance workers. All candidates for operator positions underwent a rigorous process of selection (only one in ten were selected) and an additional two to three months of training. The Caracas Metro also offered a wide variety of incentives for continuing education, including a program for financing higher studies. An employee who completed three years of service with excellent evaluations could apply for financial aid to attend university courses in areas of interest to the employee and the firm. The Caracas Metro is not always able to reap the benefits of its training efforts. Because it is a public agency, its salaries cannot compete with those offered by private firms, and the Metro suffers from a high rate of talent flight.[119]

Rapidly Growing Management Training. Management training is relatively new in Venezuela, but it has developed fast. The Institute of Advanced Administrative Studies (IESA), several universities, and a number of private companies offer a wide range of courses, of variable length, cost, and quality, covering a wide range of subjects. Continuing education courses for professionals are increasingly common, often organized by professional associations for engineers, physicians, economists, lawyers, or executives. Leading private and public sector companies often send their top managers and professionals to training courses and seminars in Europe and the United States, and even Japan. Executives and professionals in small and medium-size firms and organizations have far fewer opportunities to participate in such courses.

In the early 1990s, the evolving nature of domestic demand for management training suggested that Venezuelan managers were increasingly concerned with professionalism and modernization.[120] Among Venezuelan firms, demand for management education rose sharply. Enrollments in

IESA's Center of Managerial Development grew from 1,528 participants in 1984 to more than 5,000 participants in 1994. Demand for managerial courses at IESA became more sophisticated and varied, with growing interest in the designing of "in company" and specialized programs. In 1993, the most popular subject areas included finance, marketing and sales, production, and total quality. IESA faculty noted a marked increase in demand for case studies, practical experience, and problem solving and for professors with close ties to business and consulting. A CEPET survey showed that Venezuelan firms were most concerned with such issues as quality, productivity, and competitiveness, followed by ethics and values, leadership, and teamwork.[121] In this respect, the concerns of Venezuelan management in 1993 were similar to those of managers in many other countries.

Strained Labor/Management Relations

Unions are strong in Venezuela and have enjoyed broad political and popular support. Venezuela's four confederations of labor unions, each of which is affiliated to international labor organizations, represent Social Democrat, Christian-Democrat, and Socialist political movements. The largest is the Venezuelan Workers Confederation (CTV), which is considered the umbrella labor confederation and is linked to the Democratic Action party (AD). Public sector labor unions, many of them affiliated to CTV, are larger and more powerful, as a rule, than private-sector unions.

Venezuelan labor laws provide for collective bargaining, and more than 1,000 collective contracts are signed every year. One-quarter of the labor force is covered by collective contracts, including one-half of all workers in the public sector and one-third of those in the private sector.[122] Some contracts cover a given trade, such as the construction industry, while others are specific to a given company. Sometimes the largest firms in an industry sign industry-wide contracts, which have to be honored by the smaller, less efficient firms, to their disadvantage.[123] The number of strikes has been relatively small, and concentrated in the public sector, where unions are highly politicized and salaries have lagged well behind both inflation and market levels of compensation. Strikes by school teachers and by judiciary personnel have been frequent in the early 1990s; both fields are highly underpaid and hard-hit by inflation.

Labor/management relations in Venezuela traditionally have been adversarial. In the days of large oil rents and import substitution, unions and managers lobbied, negotiated, and vied for shares of the oil rent and special

TABLE 6.7
General Wage Increases in Venezuela

Year	Minimum Wage (bolivars/month)
1936	None
1960	300
1970	450
1974	900
1985	1,500
1986	2,010
1988	2,610
1989	4,000
1991	6,000
1992	9,000
1994	15,000

Until 1992, increases in the minimum wage were accompanied by general increases in wages and salaries.

Source: *Legal Gazette.*

treatment. Over time, labor representatives used the clout of the major political parties to win favorable terms from management in contract negotiations. Since 1984, in fact, the union confederations have focused on achieving blanket salary raises by government decree (see Table 6.7), shifting their activity from negotiating with business to government lobbying.[124] This immersion in interest politics and perceived corruption eventually separated the traditional union leadership from the concerns of the rank and file. Meanwhile, managers lobbied for government favors and used their firms' market power to pass on the costs of labor contracts to consumers.

Overall, Venezuelan labor and management have not joined forces to increase productivity in the workplace, although there have been some noteworthy exceptions. There is a continued tendency in Venezuela to look upon labor/management negotiations as a zero-sum game. Gain by either side seems to come at the direct expense of the other. In this context, some labor leaders keenly mistrust all talk of competitiveness and improved productivity as just another "trick" by management to enrich itself at labor's expense. As one labor leader explained, "We are cynical about discussing productivity improvements with management. When a private employer arrives at the table with a proposal to improve productivity, he is already circulating it among his political friends to turn it into a law and bind us. This is ridiculous. Productivity cannot be imposed from above."[125] Many labor leaders reject the call for improved competitiveness altogether. As the union spokesperson explained, "What does competitiveness mean to the Venezuelan on the street? It means neoliberalism. It means everything bad that has happened to this country over the past four years."[126] Organized labor in Venezuela still has not come to terms with the notion that future improvements in standards of living for workers have to come from increased productivity within mostly private firms.

On the other hand, management itself is responsible for many of the problems in the workplace. Labor's suspicion of employers has been fed by a number of unscrupulous businessmen too ready to cheat workers, creditors, or customers, to make a quick profit and get their money out of the country. Some Venezuelan managers tend to take a negative view of their workers' potential and abilities, while holding a highly favorable view of themselves.[127] Many managers have failed to show genuine concern for their employees' working conditions. They have tended not to consider the opinions of workers, and in the past there was little effort to create the type of participatory work environments in which the Venezuelan worker seems to do best.[128] Improving these basic shortcomings can make a great improvement in worker productivity and satisfaction. An experience at CANTV in the early 1990s bears this out: "Before privatization, the firm had a workshop for telephone repair that repaired about five telephones per week. Today, the same workshop is repairing about three hundred telephones per day. The only change was to replace the manager. The person who runs the workshop today is someone who comes out of his office, speaks with the employees, asks their opinion, and fixed the rest rooms and eating area. These very significant changes were achieved with the very same personnel."[129]

In several cases Venezuelan labor and management have joined forces to increase workplace productivity. For example, some firms (both domestic and multinational) have implemented incentive programs that give workers the opportunity to acquire new skills and knowledge. Ejeven, a Sivensa company, has instituted an Incentives for Learning Program, designed by Fundametal, which provides workers the opportunity to advance to successive levels of work-related knowledge and simultaneously to increase their earnings. This program has stimulated learning and given workers the opportunity to raise their standard of living. Gates, also a Sivensa company, has instituted a similar program. Although in 1993 it was too early to measure the long-term impact of the Gates program, the general manager believed that the program, together with other programs for excellence in manufacturing, already was yielding improvements in production quality, increases in workers' suggestions and participation, a decline in employee turnover, and improvements in the climate of the workplace.[130]

When Ford Motor Company introduced a "pay-for-learning" program in its Valencia plant in 1991, initially it encountered some resistance from both the labor unions, with whom it had to negotiate, and some managers, who initially took a short-term view and were impatient to see results. Teaching materials had to be prepared specially to suit the workers' comprehension level. Ford also found it necessary to offer special facilities to its workers, such as after-hours transportation, and administering the program required changes in the plant's payroll and information systems. The biggest challenge, however, came from competitors, who tried to hire away the trained personnel. In response, Ford found new ways to boost worker participation and to increase the worker's sense of belonging to the company.[131]

Procter & Gamble's plant in Barquisimeto has implemented a system of work multiabilities, which encourages workers to participate in different areas of the production process, and which remunerates each worker in accordance with his or her acquired knowledge. The aim was to give workers the opportunity to become more flexible and to build a knowledge base that enables them to make a greater contribution and to take on more decision making. Since this system was adopted in 1980, productivity has increased, quality has improved, and operations have become more flexible. In addition, worker performance improved, teamwork was strengthened, and there was a greater "sense of belonging."[132]

In addition, there have been instances where, subsequent to the market opening, management and labor pulled together as a team in the face of new competitive pressure. Faced with competition from imports, a Venezuelan agribusiness firm decided to adopt new production methods to lower costs. Doing so would require its plant technicians to apply statistical process controls. None of the existing workers, who had been with the firm for many years, had more than a primary education. The head of the firm met with the workers, explained the situation, and offered them the opportunity to take an in-house mathematics course. All of the workers passed the course promptly and mastered the new production process.[133]

Reactions by unions of public sector employees to attempts to restructure state-owned enterprises have been mixed. Juan Carlos Larrañaga, in his study of Venezuelan labor and competitiveness, observes that traditional unions, such as the Federation of Health Workers (FETRASALUD) and the National Employees Association (ANDE), have refused to cooperate with efforts to streamline the labor force in the public health service and the public administration as "a point of honor."[134] In contrast, the Union of the Workers of the Steel and Related Industries (SUTISS) was participating actively in Sidor's efforts to restructure its labor force, including the Employment Protection Fund. The fund has been retraining specialized workers dismissed as a result of Sidor's restructuring in order to facilitate their reentry into the labor force by giving them new skills and abilities.

Limited Technological Resources

Competitiveness in the modern world economy depends on the ability of a nation's firms to develop or to incorporate modern technology. Though relatively few developing nations generate much in the way of new technology, technological skills are just as important to them as in industrialized nations. Such skills are required to assess, to utilize, and to adapt modern production equipment and processes, even if they are developed elsewhere.

Venezuela lacks a tradition of science and technology. Under the import substitution regime, Venezuelan industry paid relatively little attention to technology, viewing it as another input to be purchased on the international market. Horacio Viana (1993) found that the result has been relatively high imports of capital goods, combined with poor performance in productivity growth and manufactured exports.[135] Overall, Venezuelan firms have not fully understood the fact that expertise is required in technology's selection, negotiation, and use. Levels of technological learning have been low, and, as a consequence, the firms have tended to depend on suppliers permanently. Moreover, the low level of assimilation of technology has had repercussions in the way the imported technologies were used and, as a consequence, in the productive performance of Venezuelan firms.[136]

Few Resources Devoted to Research and Development

Venezuela and its firms have engaged in relatively low levels of research and development. In 1991, Venezuelan research and development expenditures were equal to 0.31 percent of GDP, roughly comparable to that of Brazil and Mexico, but lower than in Korea (1.83 percent) and Taiwan (1.41 percent). In 1970, Venezuela had approximately one-half as many researchers as Korea. By 1989, Venezuela (with just over 5,000) had only one-eleventh as many researchers as Korea, which had more than 56,000.[137] Between 1970 and 1989, the annual rate of growth in the number of researchers was 3.8 percent in Venezuela; the corresponding growth rate in Korea (1970-1988) was 13.7 percent. Future trends are less encouraging. It is estimated that by the year 2000, Korea will have a total pool of researchers numbering more than 150,000, while Venezuela will have fewer than 13,000.[138]

Another cause for concern, in addition to the limited resources devoted to research and development within Venezuela, is the distribution of researchers between the public and private sectors and by industry. In Venezuela during the 1980s, fewer than 10 percent of all researchers were employed by the manufacturing sector; in countries such as Korea and Singapore, this percentage was much higher, 49 percent and 40 percent, respectively, in 1987. Moreover, in Korea, 37 percent of researchers active in R&D worked in private manufacturing, while the corresponding percentage in Venezuela was a mere 2.8 percent, lower than the percentage of researchers in the nation's extractive industries.[139] Thus the manufacturing portion of Venezuela's private sector represents a very small percentage of a very small research and development pie.

The Public Sector Predominates

The Venezuelan government and state-owned enterprises have accounted for more than 90 percent of the nation's total R&D expenditures. The state has never had an official policy for technology assimilation, that is, a policy directed to the assimilation of technology by Venezuelan firms.[140] (See Chapter 9.) Most research in Venezuela is carried out by universities and the public sector. One of the most pressing problems for the nation is how to promote the development of technological capacity within its firms.

The National Council of Scientific and Technological Research (CONICIT) is the main funding agency for research and development. CONICIT projects have been devoted to basic science (30 percent), social sciences (18 percent), engineering (17 percent), agriculture (17 percent), and medicine (12 percent).[141] In the early 1990s, CONICIT has emphasized programs to promote excellence in research, technological parks, and new technologies.

One CONICIT initiative has been its Program of Firms with Technological Basis, designed to help researchers, university institutions, research centers, and private businesspeople to start up firms to develop and to market the results of innovative research.

The Foundation Institute of Engineering (FII), assigned to the ministry of development, is the leading multidisciplinary engineering center in Venezuela. The FII has been active in efforts to transfer and to generate technologies to support producers of goods and services, in order to strengthen their competitive capacity. It has carried out activities of technological research and development in such areas as industrial automation, microelectronics, electrical measurements, telecommunications studies, applied informatics, ceramics and refractive products, industrial design, industrial systems, and materials technology. The FII has worked closely with many leading Venezuelan companies (such as PDVSA, CANTV, CADAFE, Polar, and Sivensa) and has transferred more than 400 projects to industry since its inception in 1982. In 1992, its capitalization was 650 million bolivars (about $9 million), and it had 160 employees.[142]

The Fund for the Promotion of Technological Innovation (FINTEC) was created in 1981 to foster technological innovation in the private sector. Most of the projects that received FINTEC support involved companies in the informatics and electronics sectors founded by researchers affiliated with universities or national research centers. Only four of the 37 projects that benefitted from FINTEC support were ultimately considered successful. Their major problem was insufficient managerial capabilities, particularly in the area of marketing.[143] FINTEC was dissolved in 1992. A new national center for competitiveness, Venezuela Competitiva, has been formed to promote the competitiveness of Venezuelan firms.

The Venezuelan Technological Institute for Petroleum (INTEVEP), an affiliate of PDVSA, is the closest that Venezuela comes to a world-class research center. INTEVEP originally was founded to address the operational problems of the PDVSA subsidiaries. In the early 1990s, its mission was to serve as a center for research and technological support for the national oil and petrochemical industries as well as to promote operational continuity and international competitiveness in the oil business. With 989 scientific and engineering employees, 551 technical personnel, and 208 administrators, it was the only Venezuelan research institute to operate on a scale similar to research centers of industrialized countries. INTEVEP, which ranks just below the technological leaders in the world oil industry, has made important achievements in processes, equipment, and catalyzers. Its best-known process is Orimulsion. It has formed three associations with third parties to market the new processes known as ETHEROL, ORIMATITA, and PROMISOX. INTEVEP has attributed its success in large part to its dual-track career system for personnel, which has provided advancement opportunities in both management and technology, and to its continuing education courses at the professional level.[144]

Low Levels of Private Sector R&D

The Venezuelan private sector does relatively little research and development. Most Venezuelan firms still fail to see the connection between technological expertise and competitiveness. In Viana's survey of Venezuelan manufacturing firms, 70 percent of all companies, regardless of size, reported that in the wake of the commercial opening, they were making greater efforts to improve the quality of their products.[145] However, Viana found that Venezuelan firms were *cutting back* on R&D. In 1988, 20 percent of large firms surveyed (those with 150 or more employees) and 80 percent of small firms surveyed (between ten and 20 employees) did not invest in R&D. In 1992, 40 percent of large firms surveyed and 90 percent of small firms surveyed did not invest in R&D.

Under the import substitution regime, it was not to be expected that Venezuelan firms would possess strategies for technological development. Only a few firms carried out technological activities, and these were basically directed at modifying imported technology, almost always as short-term measures as part of "defensive reaction" to unexpected problems. These changes were not incorporated into firm memory in a systematic fashion, and as a result they did not result in an overall learning process that could strengthen the firm's capacity to innovate.[146] Even in the days of import substitution, however, there were exceptions. Some firms, motivated primarily by their own internal plant technology, made serious efforts to assimilate and to improve upon acquired technology. (See Chapter 4.)

One of these cases was Química Venoco. The firm started operations in 1969 with the start-up of a plant that manufactures dodecylbenzene (DDB) and linear alkylbenzene (LAB), chemicals used in the manufacture of synthetic detergents. The plant and associated technology were acquired turnkey from Phillips Petroleum and PONA Engineers. The installed capacity of the original design was 13,620 metric tons per year. By the early 1990s, the plant's capacity in DDB mode was 66,000 metric tons per year and its capacity in LAB mode was 100,000 metric tons per year. According to the firm's directors, this increase in plant capacity was the product of 24 years of technology management and of incremental improvements in the acquired technology. These improvements have involved investments that are relatively small compared to their contribution to the value of the plant and their impact on competitiveness. In 1993, the Química Venoco plant was one of the five largest in the world in terms of capacity, with a total investment equivalent to a plant one-third its size.[147]

In the years following the commercial opening, certain Venezuelan firms took the lead in developing forward-looking strategies for technological development. These strategies included the formation of in-house research and development centers, research contracts with domestic and foreign laboratories, and programs for technological learning. Remavenca (Polar Group), Protinal, and Alfonzo Rivas, for example, set up internal R&D centers and were systematically integrating their business and marketing strategies with R&D projects. Each introduced new products successfully in the Venezuelan market. Small firms also have been successful in this area. Venezuela possesses a small but noteworthy group of small electronics firms that have very able personnel, have generated their own technologies, and have exported products such as private telephone systems, voltage regulators, telephone blockers, and electronic taxi meters.[148] A number of foreign-owned firms also perform research and development in Venezuela. In 1993, Procter & Gamble was investing $20 million to establish a regional R&D facility in Caracas. In making its decision, P&G considered Venezuela's central location in Latin America, proximity to the United States, quality of workforce, infrastructure, and improving communication system.

These firms, however, were the exceptions. Most technological changes in Venezuelan firms occur through investment in physical equipment rather than through the development of personnel. The idea is still widespread that productivity gains are achieved by replacing existing equipment with more modern equipment. There is little thought of improving productivity by mastering technology.[149] Management emphasizes the acquisition of tangibles over intangibles such as knowledge and information.

Most Venezuelan firms are still unsophisticated in their purchase and use of technology. The Viana survey indicates that most firms buy machinery and equipment out of catalogs, on the basis of existing relations with suppliers, and that they have little experience in technology negotiations. It is uncommon for Venezuelan firms to negotiate technology acquisitions on a piece-by-piece basis, primarily because they lack a sophisticated understanding of what they are buying.[150] As a result, technology ends up being seen as a "black box." This precludes the continuous improvement of productivity through mastering technology. As Viana (1993) concludes, many Venezuelan managers seem not to understand that knowledge is critical to the ability to select, acquire, use, and adapt new technology.

Promising Capabilities in Design

Product innovation draws upon a variety of capabilities, including design capabilities. While Venezuela does not have an impressive track record in technological innovation, it has developed a promising set of capabilities in the field of design, including fashion, graphic design, architecture, and the fine arts.[151] What is missing is the link between design and industrial mass production of high-quality products for the international market. Unless this link is created, an important potential source of competitive advantage will remain untapped.

Venezuela is one of the few Latin American countries to boast a substantial pool of truly first-rate designers in haute couture. Some, like Carolina Herrera, Guy Meliet, and Angel Sánchez, have become established outside of Venezuela. Margarita Zingg, Oscar Carvalho, Cora Escobar, and Rafael Enrique Ramírez also are known outside Venezuela, although they primarily have served the domestic market. Jewelry and accessories designers, such as Eleazar Molina, also have enjoyed an international clientele. Some Venezuelan designers were originally trained as architects. Others move in international social circles or have worked for international designers abroad. Venezuela also has benefitted from the immigration of highly skilled European seamstresses and other artisans, to develop a high-quality fashion establishment.

At the firm level, Tropicana has manufactured women's fashion collections for export and Rori has sold its lines of men's and juvenile's clothes in the United States. Lony and Riviera have exported swimwear to the United States and Europe. Dorita Vera started by designing swimwear for friends in 1986 and later began exporting to Florida and the Caribbean, manufacturing in Caracas and Colombia. Despite these examples, it is still the norm for manufacturers of mass-consumption clothing in Venezuela to "tropicalize" European fashion rather than to tap the talents of Venezuelan designers. Because Venezuelan designers focus on an elite market, high-volume production has been a major stumbling block. For example, one Venezuelan designer won the contest for Coca Cola's women's uniform for Latin America, but local factories virtually collapsed trying to fill the first order.

Graphic design, which is well developed in Venezuela, is also a potential source of competitive advantage. Larry June and Gerd Laufert were the first to achieve prominence. Designers John Lange, Bárbara Brándli, and Alvaro Sotillo are well known for their designs of books and packaging, and Santiago Pol has received international prizes for his poster designs. Victor Húgo Irazabal and Karmle Leizaola are known for their ground-breaking graphic design for the *Economía Hoy* daily newspaper. Jorge Blanco and Soledad Mendoza have achieved a reputation for corporate image design. Graphic designers are employed by advertising companies such as Ars and CORPA and by high-quality printers such as Editorial Arte, Editorial Color, and Editorial Ex Libris. Production has been small and focused on the domestic market. Montana Gráfica, a firm of the Corimon Group, has produced high-quality packaging for export as well as for the domestic market.

Several private foundations promote graphic design, including the Fundación Neumann, Fundación Polar, and the Sofía Imber Museum of Contemporary Art. Also, a number of design schools are training new talent. Graphic design in Venezuela is creative, modern, and uninhibited. It has a substantial export potential if the good design can be wedded to mass production and marketing. However, technical support is in short supply and poses a serious bottleneck to mass production. Industrial design, in contrast, is less developed in Venezuela than fashion or graphic design. Most product designs have been adopted from abroad. Consumer and industrial products designed in Venezuela usually lack an artistic design of their own.

Architecture, landscaping, interior design, furniture design, and urban design are well developed in Venezuela. Among contemporary architects, the late Carlos Raúl Villanueva and Fruto Vivas, who has directed urban renewal plans in some Caracas barrios, have achieved international reputations. Max Pedemonte leads a group of architects well known for the integrated design of Metro de Caracas. Lander Quintana has designed low-cost "self-constructed minimal housing" that is exported to Belize, Nicaragua, and El Salvador. However, Lander Quintana is an exception. Typically, design is produced by a small group of highly sophisticated professionals, working for an elite market, with few connections to mass production. In fact, the links of Venezuelan design to pure art are more evident than are those to industry.

Limited and Antiquated Financial Markets

Venezuela's limited capital markets have hindered the economy's competitiveness. The nation's banking sector lacks the capital, experience, and expertise to provide the resources necessary for the economy to grow. Venezuelan equity markets remain thin and risky. International sources of capital are available to only a few Venezuelan companies. Small and medium-size firms have found it very difficult to obtain capital. Venture capital is almost nonexistent. High real interest rates have contributed to a tough investment climate. Despite these difficulties, there have been several signs of progress. The reform program instituted in 1989 freed interest rates and exchange rates, allowing rates to reflect market conditions. The Venezuelan Central Bank has been made autonomous. A banking law enacted in 1993 was expected to increase competition and supervision in the banking sector. Much remains to be done, however, before the Venezuelan financial markets are able to support the development of a modern economy. The banking crisis of early 1994, in which government agencies had to pump billions of dollars into a faltering banking system, and the economic dislocations caused by the crisis showed the costs of an inadequate financial system.

An Undercapitalized and Undersupervised Banking Sector

The Venezuelan banking sector has long been the major player in the Venezuelan financial market. In 1992, commercial banks controlled 73 percent of the financial resources in Venezuela; 66 percent was controlled by the seven largest banks.[152] This situation differed substantially from that in most developed countries, in which 15 to 35 percent of funds were controlled by commercial banks and the remainder were in the hands of institutional investors, insurance companies, and other financial institutions and investors. The large majority of the credit portfolios of Venezuelan banks had maturities of less than one year (typically 90 days). Long-term financing has become difficult or impossible to obtain from Venezuelan banks. The high real interest rates experienced in the early 1990s have made bank finance very expensive for most companies.

In general, Venezuelan banks have been undercapitalized and undersupervised. A number of important Venezuelan banks have been the "house banks" for local industrial groups. Some have engaged in questionable activities, such as making loans to affiliated companies or individuals without proper guarantees or credit analysis, accounting gimmicks, manipulating loans in order to gain control of client companies, and failing to acknowledge and to reserve for nonperforming loans. Some banks have taken over failed client firms, preferring to keep them operating or to search for a buyer than to close them down and write them off. The result has been an increase in interest rates and spreads to nonaffiliated companies and other customers in order to compensate for deteriorating loan portfolios. Balance sheets and income statements have been artificially bolstered by sales of assets to related companies. These questionable practices helped cause the collapse of the Banco Latino, the nation's second largest bank, in early 1994 and the ensuing crisis, which resulted in government intervention in the rest of the banking sector.

The Venezuelan banking sector is still feeling the effects of failed financial policies of the past. In the early 1980s, the Venezuelan government capped interest rates at levels lower than those available in the United States and elsewhere. The result was an unprecedented outflow of capital. In 1993, Venezuelans held offshore some $60 billion to $80 billion in capital. In contrast, the domestic financial sector has been estimated at $17 billion. With interest rates that were fixed by law, banks made only the lowest risk loans to the most solid clients, or to companies and individuals with special relationships with the banks. The state guaranteed the debts of many private firms, turning private debt into public debt in the process. Banks made up their losses on loans through informal commissions, gains obtained by channeling funds to less regulated financial activities, or manipulation of the differential exchange regime that was in place through most of the 1980s. This period left several legacies. Venezuelan firms have traditionally relied on short-term debt financing for much of their capital needs. Negative interest rates led Venezuelan firms to maximize their debt and minimize their equity. Banks focused on analyzing financial guarantees rather than credit, project, or risk analysis. In fact, many bank managers and employees lack the training necessary to provide such analysis.

The Venezuelan banking sector also has been a fairly tight oligopoly, in the absence of competition from foreign banks, which have been excluded from the market for the most part. (This has been changing with the 1993 Banking Law.) The reform program of 1989 did not open up the financial sector to outside competition. As a result, the banking sector had far less reason to improve efficiency and make needed changes than other sectors of the economy.

The Central Bank Law passed in 1992 conferred substantial autonomy on the Venezuelan Central Bank. Many believe that the clarity and stability of Central Bank policy was the single greatest contributor to economic stability in Venezuela during 1992 and 1993. To support the bolivar and avoid renewed capital flight, the Central Bank has relied on open market operations, principally the sale of zero-coupon bonds. Central Bank rates increased from 30 percent at the end of 1991, to 40 percent at the end of 1992, to 50 percent in March 1993. As a result, passive and active interest rates in the banking sector soared to over 50 percent and 70 percent in early 1993. Such rates reflected the inability of the Venezuelan government to balance its budget and a loss of confidence in the Venezuelan economy as a result of political turmoil. The bank also began to enforce capital adequacy regulations that prompted many banks to try to move quickly to clean up their balance sheets. Some banks have used creative accounting and sales of assets from one bank affiliate to another to prop up their balance sheets. Extraordinary income, often from such less than arm's length transactions, has been the major source of recorded profits for some banks in recent years.

The Banks in Crisis

In December 1993, the collapse of the Banco Latino revealed the delicate situation of the Venezuelan financial system, giving rise to a crisis without precedent. A generalized run on other banks and on the bolivar took place. During the first quarter of 1994, at least 12 institutions encountered serious difficulties, obliging the Central Bank to intervene massively in aid of the sector.

In terms of repercussions, the fall of the Banco Latino was very different from earlier bankruptcies. The collapse of the Banco Nacional de Descuento in 1978 and of the Banco de Comercio in 1985 occurred without consequences for the rest of the financial system. The same was the case with the nine financial institutions (the majority of which were *sociedades financieras,* or financial societies) that failed between 1982 and 1983. In contrast, the failure of the Banco Latino has had a great impact on firms not related to the financial system and on a wide segment of the population, and became a complex political problem for the Caldera government. In other aspects, many of the elements present in the Banco Latino crisis are common to the earlier situations: corruption, traffic in influence, and other sorts of irregular practices, including the self-issuance of loans and the financing of the activities of the political leadership. This fact in part explains why financial sector's restructuring was delayed during President Pérez's second term in office.

The General Banking Law, passed in the last quarter of 1993, has the potential to reshape the Venezuelan financial sector substantially. The law will allow the formation of universal banks that can combine the activities previously dispersed among commercial banks, investment banks, mortgage banks, and leasing companies. Foreigners will be able to invest in Venezuelan banks, to set up their own local banks, and to invest in other financial institutions.[153] Finally, the law sets more stringent capital adequacy rules and provides for an independent Superintendency of Banking, with greater regulatory powers and an independent source of financing. Though the details of the law's implementation remain to be seen, the new legislation represents a marked improvement that should lead to greater efficiency, competition, transparency, and confidence in the Venezuelan banking sector. All will be necessary to create a strong banking system.

TABLE 6.8
Latin American Stock Markets

	Argentina	Brazil	Chile	Colombia	Mexico	Peru	Venezuela
Number of listed companies							
1992	175	1,158	245	80	195	287	66
Market Capitalization (million U.S.$)							
1992	18,633	45,261	29,644	5,681	139,061	2,630	7,600
1988	2,025	32,149	6,849	1,145	13,784	n.a.	1,816
Market Capitalization / GDP							
1992	0.08	0.11	0.76	0.14	0.42	0.08	0.15
1988	0.02	0.10	0.31	0.03	0.08	n.a.	0.07
% of Latin American Market Capitalization							
1992	9	18	12	2	57	1	3
Trading Values (million U.S.$)							
1992	15,679	20,525	2,029	554	44,582	398	2,631

Source: IFC (1993), IMF Financial Statistics.

Undeveloped Equity Markets

Venezuela's equity markets are not sufficient to support the equity capital needs of the nation. Venezuelan stock and equity markets remain largely undeveloped when compared to those of other Latin American nations. There were 66 companies listed on the Caracas Stock Exchange at the end of 1992, compared to 245 in Chile and 287 in Peru. Only ten to 15 Venezuelan companies had shares that were liquid and actively traded. Total market capitalization was roughly $7.6 billion, or roughly 3 percent of total Latin American capitalization, at the end of 1992. This was far lower than the capitalization of the equity markets in Mexico, Brazil, Argentina, and Chile. Whereas the capitalization of the stock markets of Mexico, Brazil, and Argentina should be expected to exceed that of the Venezuelan market, it is noteworthy that Chile, a country with a population roughly two-thirds that of Venezuela, had a stock market capitalization four times that of Venezuela. (See Table 6.8.) (This is largely due to the system of pension funds and the favorable economic climate found in Chile.) Futures and options are not traded on the Caracas Exchange.

There are several reasons for the small size of the Caracas Stock Market, including the motives of Venezuelan managers, risk to investors, and an antiquated clearing and settlement system. Venezuelan firms are usually family-owned, and many prefer to retain control of their company rather than risk diluting control through the issue of equity. Many managers do not wish to comply with the disclosure requirements of the stock exchange, fearing that information on firm operations and profitability, information vital to the potential investor, would be used against the company by suppliers, customers, or workers. Venezuelan managers are used to funding their investments with retained earnings (profits for many leading Venezuelan firms were very high in the days of government subsidies and protection) or with loans from friendly banks. Those Venezuelan companies that do issue stock usually sell only a small portion of the company, leaving control in the hands of a few families or partners. While investors in these companies can share in the company's profits or losses, they do not exercise any real direction or control over management.

Both the absence of laws to make insider trading and market manipulation criminal offenses and insufficient supervision increase the risk to equity investors. Informal reports from experts have indicated that two people working together probably could manipulate a single stock on the Caracas Exchange and that three people working together could move the whole market. Concentration of the brokerage business (four brokerage firms accounted for 64 percent—by value— of the equity transactions made in 1992) has led to further allegations of insider trading and market manipulation. The resulting risk keeps investors out of the Venezuelan equity markets. Sophisticated Venezuelan investors often prefer to invest in countries with more stable currencies and better protected markets or to invest in real estate. Foreign fund managers, who control tens of billions of dollars, hesitate to invest in the Venezuelan market.

The Venezuelan exchanges are extremely inefficient from an operational standpoint, although computerized systems for trading are being installed in an effort to improve efficiency. Equity transfers in Venezuela are governed by the 1919 Commercial Code, which requires all stock transfers to be made manually in the books of the company concerned. This regulation makes the settlement and clearing process a nightmare. Finally, the relative absence of pension funds and institutional investors in Venezuela sharply limits the capitalization and stability that long-term investment of pension funds would bring to the market. As a result, the only major sources of equity capital available in Venezuela are foreign multinationals, large indigenous industrial groups, and the state, each of which gives rise to questions of concentration of economic power.

The Caracas Stock Exchange soared in 1990 and 1991. The stock index rose 549 percent in 1990 and 64 percent in 1991 as the same shares were sold and then resold at a higher level. According to one expert, people gambled at the racetrack on Saturday and Sunday and on the stock market from Monday through Friday. The market underwent a sharp decline in 1992 as two coup attempts and the resulting political uncertainty diminished investor confidence. As of 1993, the Caracas market remained thin and volatile. Few companies have used the equity market to raise capital. The advent of mutual funds and investments of insurance companies and employee savings funds have provided additional capital to the market, but significant reform will be necessary to attract substantial new funds into Venezuelan equities.

Lack of Strong Oversight

Supervision of the Venezuelan banking system and capital markets traditionally has been weak. Regulators have lacked the legal backing and resources to track down and to prosecute violators. The regulatory agencies have lacked the independence from governmental authorities and the financial resources to do their job properly. The limits imposed by the public administration salary structures have made it difficult to attract people with the requisite financial expertise to serve as regulators. The sanctions that regulatory agencies have been able to impose have lacked the teeth necessary to ensure compliance with regulations. As of 1993, sanctions for transgressions of capital market regulations, for example, were punished with nominal fines that had not changed in bolivar terms since 1973. The 1993 Banking Law provides the Banking Superintendency with greater powers to intervene in the banking sector and an independent funding mechanism, both of which are critical to its ability to monitor and to regulate the banking sector. The draft Capital Markets Law, which had not been passed by Congress by the end of 1993, could do the same for capital markets.

A Trend toward Disintermediation

Venezuelan firms have gone increasingly to the debt market on their own, rather than borrowing from commercial banks. Historically, fixed and negative real interest rates and subsequent credit rationing on the part of the major commercial banks resulted in informal mechanisms for obtaining funds at market rates. In the early 1990s, the large spreads charged by the commercial banks, their limited expertise, and the growing sophistication of investment banking, mostly through the activities of foreign investment banks in Venezuela have caused firms to issue commercial paper. In Venezuela, commercial paper is usually placed with the help of brokerage houses and other financial institutions that can compete favorably with commercial banks due to their focus on large transactions (which reduces costs) and the fact they are not subject to the same cash reserve requirements. The major limitation of this direct placement of commercial paper is the difficulty in actually placing it. Since the "nonbank" institutions have been forbidden to receive deposits on their own account, it has been necessary to complete both sides of the transaction at the same time.[154]

Historically, the volume of brokerage transactions that take place outside the stock exchange has been much higher than that of transactions on the exchange.[155] In general, off-the-exchange transactions of instruments in foreign currency have been more important than transactions of instruments in bolivars. The major instruments in foreign currency traded off the exchange are ministry of defense promissory notes, bonds issued by the Republic of Venezuela, and bonds issued by private firms on the Euromarket. In fact, the most active capital market in Venezuela is actually for debt instruments rather than equities.

Nonexistent Venture Capital

As mentioned earlier, venture capital is almost nonexistent in Venezuela. The nation has lacked the expertise and financial sophistication to support a real venture capital market. Venture capitalists tend to demand high returns in the medium term in order to justify their investments. In Venezuela, relatively few investors who are used to 30, 40, or 50 percent returns for relatively risk-free short-term investments, such as the Central Bank's zero-coupon bonds, are willing to risk investing for the medium or long term in any Venezuelan company, no less a start-up. Finally, venture capitalists in developed nations generally try to liquidate their positions through initial public offerings within a few years of their initial investment. Given the limited Venezuelan equity markets and even more limited market for initial public offerings, venture capitalists in Venezuela would be unable to cash out of their investments. As a result, even with a good, marketable idea, Venezuelan entrepreneurs often find it impossible to obtain the financing necessary to create more than a very small business. The lack of an active venture capital market places another limitation on the development of new firms in Venezuela. In industrialized countries, venture capitalists are often the major sources of advice to new companies on the difficult tasks of starting and building a company. Without an active venture market in Venezuela, this valuable source of experience and advice is generally not available to new firms.

State Financing in Flux

In industrialized nations, private savings provide the vast majority of funds used for productive investment. In Venezuela, oil rents, channeled through the government's budget, provided a steady source of investment capital from the 1940s into the 1980s. The oil, steel, aluminum, and petrochemical industries received the largest investments. In addition, the government gave loan guarantees to many private companies. Official investment and lending slowed dramatically in the 1980s. The importance of state-owned companies in Venezuela, however, has meant that the state has remained a substantial source of industrial finance. In the case of PDVSA, it is actually the state-owned company that has financed the state rather than the other way around. Many other state-owned firms have required constant injections of capital to keep them going. Several of these firms have focused on "operating earnings," excluding debt service, instead of profitability in reporting their results. The mentality seems to have been that debt had been imposed upon the firms because the government had not capitalized all their debts. The net effect has been to obscure performance and levels of government subsidies.

The government developed several mechanisms to provide financing for private-sector firms, mostly for small and medium-size ones. The Corporation for the Development of Small and Medium Firms (Corpoindustria) was created in 1974 to aid firms through technical and financial assistance. Corpoindustria aimed to fill a gap in the financial system by providing a source of long-term—up to 20 years—loans for small and medium-size businesses. The Industrial Credit Fund (FONCREI) was designed to provide loans to new companies at rates equal to 90 percent of market rates for up to five years. In 1993, FONCREI was involved in administering several lines of credit from multilateral organizations and was trying to access international capital markets through the issue of debt securities. The Industrial Bank of Venezuela (BIV) has operated as a commercial bank to provide loans of short and medium term at market rates. These organizations have been less than successful. Some have become politicized, while others have been plagued by charges of corruption and favoritism. For example, officials frequently forced the BIV to extend and to roll over bad loans to companies run by people with the right connections. The government's debt/equity conversion program focused on export industries with two exceptions; the program was used to restructure the debt of media companies and of small and medium-size business. According to some sources, companies with ties to the leaders of the organization that coordinated the debt/equity conversion program for small and medium-size companies got preferential treatment.

Corpoindustria, FONCREI, and BIV represented attempts to fill gaps in the financial markets that were often brought on by other governmental policies. Their activities were curtailed sharply in the early 1990s.

Limited Access to International Capital

Venezuela has had limited access to foreign capital to make up for the shortfalls in domestic capital markets. The three major sources of foreign capital have been loans from multilateral development agencies, stock offerings and private placements by Venezuelan firms on international capital markets, and foreign direct investment. Between 1989 and 1993, total financial backing from the World Bank and the IMF has totaled $7.5 billion. In the period from 1989 to mid-1993, the World Bank approved loans to the Venezuelan government totaling $2.4 billion. These loans were targeted for a number of specific projects involving economic policy, social investments, infrastructure projects, and management reforms. The International Finance Corporation has helped to finance 33 private-sector projects by approving loans worth $326 million.[156] Loans from multilateral development agencies should be viewed as extraordinary sources of capital, to be used for specific projects. Multilateral agencies should not be viewed as long-term sources of capital for the Venezuelan government or for Venezuelan firms. Venezuela's goal, in fact, should be to reach levels of income that will make it ineligible for multilateral loans. In addition, it must be remembered that the funds from multilateral agencies are loans that must be repaid with interest. They are not a substitute for sound fiscal and monetary policies that would allow Venezuela to better fund the adjustment process internally.

Some large Venezuelan firms, including Corimon, Sivensa, Venepal, and Mavesa, have obtained financing in the United States, selling ADRs (American Depository Receipts) and GDRs (Global Depository Receipts) worth a total of several hundred million dollars on the New York Stock Exchange. Other firms, including Cerámicas Carabobo, Grupo Zuliano, and Corporación Grupo Químico, have placed dollar-denominated bonds in foreign markets. PDVSA has used export credits and foreign debt to obtain financing, including six bond issues, totaling $1 billion, placed on the Euromarkets from 1991 to 1993. PDV America, a PDVSA subsidiary, has placed another $1 billion in bonds in the United States. Despite these examples, most Venezuelan firms do not have access to international financial markets. Such access has been limited to Venezuela's largest and most solid firms, or to those that can show a steady stream of dollar-denominated earnings. While international capital markets will not provide funding for the majority of Venezuelan firms, a select few can escape the limitations of the Venezuelan capital markets and obtain financing on terms roughly similar to their counterparts in developed nations. Even firms that can access international financial markets, however, pay a price for the relative backwardness of local financial markets in terms of country- and company-specific risk premiums.

The final potential source of foreign capital is foreign equity investment in Venezuela. Such investment, in theory, could take two forms, portfolio investments by foreign institutional investors and foreign direct investment. As indicated earlier, the absence of insider trading laws, insufficient supervision, and the antiquated settlements and clearance system generally have kept foreign fund managers from investing in Venezuelan equities. After 15 years of discouraging foreign direct investment, Venezuela reversed its policy and began to welcome it once again in 1989. Foreign direct investment increased dramatically after the economic opening, with the beginning of privatization of Venezuelan state enterprises. Foreign firms have invested in wholly owned enterprises, have formed joint ventures with Venezuelan firms, and have bought portions of existing firms. Given the limits on other sources of funds in Venezuela, foreign direct investment will have to play a major role in supplying the capital that the economy will need over the next decade. Despite changes in regulations regarding foreign investment, many people in Venezuela are suspicious of foreign firms. The government has not done nearly as much to attract foreign investment as have other nations, both in the region and around the world.

Financial Markets Need Modernization

The state of Venezuela's financial markets provides far more disadvantages than advantages to Venezuelan firms. In the early 1990s, firms have found it very difficult to obtain the funds to make needed investments at affordable rates. This has hurt the nation's ability to foster the founding, growth, and restructuring of firms. In many instances, the lack of modern capital markets has made the state or foreign multinationals the only organizations with the capital necessary to make large investments. Venezuela will need to develop a strong local banking sector and sources of domestic equity necessary to support a modern, growing economy. Some necessary steps, such as the Central Bank Law and new Banking Law, have been taken, but, as the financial crisis of early 1994 has shown, many more are needed before Venezuela's financial markets will be up to the task.

Venezuelan Factor Conditions in Context[157]

At this point, it is useful to place the discussion of Venezuelan factor conditions in a wider context. Although Venezuela has many unique features, the nation shares many similarities with other developing nations in terms of its factor conditions. Three aspects of factor conditions common in developing nations are scarcity of factors, competition based on natural resources, and reliance on low-cost labor.

Scarcity of Factors

Perhaps the biggest difference between developed and developing nations is the general scarcity of resources found in the latter. This scarcity makes resource allocation a critical task for the developing nation. Scarcity affects all aspects of economic and social life in most developing nations. Poverty, functional illiteracy, and poor nutrition hold back productivity. Developing nations often lack the education and training needed to foster the skills required to compete in advanced industries. They often lack the technology base and management skills needed to identify, adopt, and employ modern production practices. Poor physical and business infrastructure often hold back development. In addition, developing countries tend to lack information about markets and competitors, both domestic and foreign, necessary to formulate medium and long-term strategies.

Investment capital is often in scarce supply in developing nations. Savings rates tend to be low, due to low incomes and the fact that a high portion of income must be spent on subsistence. The nation's wealth is often in the hands of a relatively small number of people who prefer to seek investments that are less risky, politically and economically, in the industrialized nations. The lack of strong financial institutions in developing nations also hinders the accumulation and deployment of capital. The banking sectors are often not well developed. Thin and risky equity markets are often open to manipulation. Foreign debt has become difficult to obtain. Foreign banks have been less willing to extend credit to developing nations since the debt crisis of the early 1980s, and multilateral development agencies have only partially filled the gap. Foreign direct investment, one potential source of investment capital, has been a highly charged issue in many developing nations. Fears of loss of sovereignty and domination or exploitation by multinationals have resulted in limits on foreign investment in many nations. In the 1990s, as more countries open to foreign investment, many are finding that the competition for limited investment funds can be severe.

Competing on Natural Resources

Many developing nations compete on the basis of natural resource endowments. Some nations that compete on the basis of natural resources have become wealthy. Saudi Arabia has become rich due to its oil wealth. Canada is a very wealthy economy that competes in the international marketplace largely on the basis of natural resource endowments. These nations became wealthy because they possess natural resources that are abundant and unique enough, relative to the size of the population, to support high per capita incomes. Most nations that compete on the basis of natural resources, including many developing nations, are not that fortunate. Natural resources are subject to depletion, substitution by resource-reducing technological change, and reductions in demand due to conservation. Falling prices have plagued many commodities in the 1980s and 1990s, substantially reducing the terms of trade of many developing nations. In addition, exploiting natural resources often entails substantial environmental costs.

Heavy reliance on natural resources for competitive advantage poses another danger. Resource-rich nations often use their resources inefficiently and often fail to develop other sources of advantage. They tend to focus on administering resource wealth rather than creating new wealth through investments in education, training, and technology development. Attitudes and policies often develop that stunt the upgrading of individual skills and firm capabilities. Large, powerful resource companies emerge that have a tendency to resist competition and press for subsidies. Government policies are prone to focus on spreading the rents rather than on promoting dynamism and efficient resource utilization.

Some believe that the logical way to promote economic growth is to stimulate industries that employ the natural resources exported by the nation. Calls to "capture more value" or "add more value" at home are often heard in natural resource-exporting nations. The framework developed in Chapter 3 can be used to help determine the nation's ability to move downstream beyond natural resource–based commodities. To assess the nation's ability to move downstream, one must identify the key competitive variables and success factors in the downstream industry to understand which determinant or set of determinants are decisive. Then one must compare the nation's advantages and disadvantages and potential advantages and disadvantages in these determinants with those of competitor countries. In this way, it should be possible to determine if resource advantages are enough to compete successfully in downstream industries.[158] In general, developing countries will succeed in downstream industries only if they improve their situation in other determinants or find ways to overcome their disadvantages.

Reliance on Low-Cost Labor

Firms from developing nations often compete in international markets on the basis of low-cost labor. This is generally due to a scarcity of highly trained workers, limited science and technology infrastructure, and a lack of large or sophisticated demand, elements that are often essential to fostering more advanced sources of advantage. The wealth of an economy relying on cheap labor is inevitably constrained by the low wages it depends on to compete. Competing on low-cost labor places a fundamental cap on a nation's standard of living unless it can upgrade its skill levels to support higher wages over time. Otherwise it will be trapped with low wages and will be vulnerable to firms from other nations with even lower-cost labor. This is particularly true in footloose industries where multinational firms can shift production locations quickly. The price-sensitive segments of the footwear and apparel industries, for example, have moved from one low-wage nation to another as wages increase and as minimal levels of infrastructure become more widespread. Korean international construction firms, for example, have seen their position in basic projects involving unskilled labor threatened by firms employing labor from Malaysia or Thailand. The experience of certain Asian nations, which initially used low-cost labor to penetrate international markets and then developed more advanced advantages, however, shows that competing on low-labor costs can be a stepping-stone to other sources of advantage and an improved standard of living.[159]

The Challenge of Competitiveness

There are clearly similarities between factor conditions found in other developing nations and those described in the bulk of this chapter. Similarities point out common problems that a number of nations are attempting to overcome or common advantages that they are attempting to exploit. There are also differences between the factor conditions found in Venezuela and elsewhere. As we have tried to show, Venezuela ranks ahead of other nations in Latin America in some areas and behind them in others. These differences represent potential sources of advantage (or disadvantage) that might be exploited (or overcome) in order to promote the progress of a particular national economy.

Meeting the challenge of competitiveness in Venezuela will involve further developing and exploiting the nation's factor advantages in natural resources, topography, and location as well as pockets of advanced skills and expertise. It also will involve improvements in infrastructure as well as improvements in education, training, and technological expertise to better match the capabilities of the workforce with the needs of the economy. It also will involve a more flexible labor regime in which management and workers invest in improving their skills. Meeting the challenge of competitiveness will involve the creation of a financial system and an investment climate that attract capital from domestic and foreign private investors. These issues will be further addressed in subsequent chapters.

7

Demand Conditions, Related Industries, and Supporting Industries in Venezuela

Two of the determinants of national competitiveness identified in Chapter 3 (demand conditions and related and supporting industries) involve vertical and horizontal linkages in the economy. For ease of exposition, here we assess the position of Venezuela with respect to these determinants. This chapter also addresses the role of clustering, the development of groups of industries linked through vertical and horizontal relationships, in the Venezuelan economy.

Demand Conditions in Venezuela

As indicated in Chapter 3, the demand conditions found in a nation can be an important stimulus to the nation's firms. In particular, nations tend to succeed in international competition in industries in which the size, sophistication, and/or segment structure of local demand provides local firms with the impetus to develop new products or improve their capabilities. Sophisticated demand is particularly important in that it often provides local firms with a unique set of signals that anticipates demand elsewhere. Favorable demand conditions often operate in consort with other determinants in a virtuous circle in which the favorable demand conditions stimulate the development of skills and capabilities that in turn provide better products that contribute to the size and sophistication of local demand.

Venezuelan Consumer Demand

Venezuelan consumer demand is, on the whole, of moderate size and sophistication. Although in a general sense, Venezuelan consumer demand conditions confer few advantages on its firms, some Venezuelan industries have benefitted from the characteristics of this demand.

Moderate-Size Domestic Market. With a population of more than 20 million people, the Venezuelan consumer market is of moderate size. For many products, the Venezuelan consumer market was far too small for firms to reach efficient scale under the (export discouraging) import substitution regime that was in effect through the 1970s and 1980s. The typical Venezuelan auto assembly plant, for example, had a capacity of 10,000 units per year, in contrast to some Mexican and Brazilian plants with capacities of hundreds of thousands of units per year.[1] (See Chapter 4.) Even in industries with moderate scale economies, such as textiles, Mexican and Brazilian producers (with home markets of roughly 90 million people and 150 million people, respectively) have achieved substantial benefits over producers in small Latin American nations.[2] (See Chapter 5.) Other examples in which the moderate size of Venezuela's domestic demand is a potential source of disadvantage include pulp and paper products, certain domestic appliances, and candies.

The size of the Venezuelan consumer market also is influenced by the purchasing power of individual Venezuelans. Roughly 5.3 million Venezuelans have the type of purchasing power that marketers usually target.[3] In 1992, the A and B segments of the population, which include the very wealthy (A), and top executives, leading industrialists and politicians, and some highly successful professionals (B), represented roughly 2 percent of the population, or approximately 500,000 people.[4] The middle class, or C segment, represented 21 percent of the population, or approximately 4.8 million people. The D segment, which included mostly semiskilled workers, accounted for 34 percent of the population. The E segment, which included people who lived in marginal circumstances, represented 43 percent of the population. The 1992 figures showed a substantial shift from those of 1983 and 1984, when the A and B segments made up 3 percent; C segment, 25 percent; D segment, 40 percent; and E segment, 32 percent.[5]

Falling income levels since 1982 have limited the discretionary expenditures of many Venezuelans. According to the Central Bank of Venezuela, the average Venezuelan family spent 32 percent of its income on food and drink in 1984 and 43 percent in 1990. According to some private-sector sources, this figure reached 68 percent in 1993.[6] The result has been reduced demand for consumer durables and other discretionary items. The dramatic fall in demand for autos in the late 1980s was only one such example.[7] The egalitarian nature of Venezuelan culture and society, however, tends to lead all social classes to imitate, to the extent allowed by their purchasing and borrowing power, the consumption patterns of the rich. Thus, actual purchases of some consumer goods are higher in Venezuela than might be expected from purchasing power alone. This broadens a market otherwise restricted by the size of the population and purchasing power.

Free trade agreements have increased the size of the market to which Venezuelan firms have direct access. Venezuela's free trade agreement with Colombia gives Venezuelan firms access to a total market of 52 million people. As of 1992, there were about 92 million people in the wider Andean Pact with an estimated annual consumer purchasing power of $23 billion.[8] However, access to this wider market does not ensure competitive success. There are differences in tastes among the Andean Pact nations, and years of import substitution has stunted the ability of many Venezuelan companies to serve this potential market. In the early 1990s, many people found that their limited capacity and capabilities placed them in a less-than-optimal position to exploit the opportunities of the broader Andean market.[9]

Moderately Sophisticated Domestic Consumer. Venezuelans generally have adopted the consumption patterns of the advanced Western nations, but at a lower level of sophistication. The growth of income from the oil industry, starting in the 1920s, allowed Venezuela to become a sophisticated importer of consumer goods. In the 1950s and 1960s, Venezuela became a leading importer (at least on a per-capita basis) of French perfumes and champagne, Italian leather goods and furniture, German cars, and American domestic appliances. During the boom years in the late 1970s, Venezuelans of the upper and middle social classes drank premium Scotch whiskey, vacationed at Disney World, and shopped for Pierre Cardin outerwear. Shopping trips to Miami were common. In the 1980s, consumer demand suffered within the constraints of a closed domestic market and falling real incomes.

The import substitution regime hurt the sophistication of Venezuelan consumer demand by constraining consumer choice to the relatively narrow variety offered in most product areas. Across the spectrum of consumer goods, from processed foods to chocolate bars to stationery supplies, Venezuelans had to accept the few models or varieties manufactured or assembled locally. Lack of outside competition also allowed Venezuelan firms to sell products of quality below international standards. Faulty auto parts, short-lived light bulbs or hand tools, unreliable appliances, and ill-finished tableware, among others, plagued the consumer. Nevertheless, the desire for better-quality goods remained strong. Shopping trips to the free port of Margarita Island and wholesale bootlegging fed this demand during the 1980s.

Many Venezuelan exporters have had to adapt their products in order to obtain acceptance in upscale foreign markets. Yukery, for example, modified the fruit and sugar content of its fruit juices to sell them in the European Community. Alimentos Margarita had to meet strict kosher rules to offer its canned fish products in Israel. Rori changed the wool and polyester content in the cloth that it used in men's clothing to meet more demanding U.S. fiber content requirements. While Venezuelan firms should, and must, modify products to sell in international markets, the fact that these markets require modifications often means that the firms must undertake substantial efforts and investments to enter foreign markets.

Distribution and Retailing Limit Options for Consumers. Fixed prices, industry concentration, and collusion within Venezuela's distribution and retailing sectors have further limited consumer choice and, therefore, sophistication. Before 1992, government regulations required that the selling price of most goods (PVP, sales price to the public) be fixed by the manufacturer. Competition at the retail level entailed discounts and promotional bargains (three for the price of two, for example). From the middle of 1992 to early 1994, retailers were allowed to set most selling prices. The idea was to encourage consumers to pressure for competition among retailers. Many consumers clamored for renewed governmental regulation to curb what were perceived as excessive retail markups. In fact, retailer margins tend to be rather high in Venezuela, and as of 1994, price-fixing agreements remained the rule rather than the exception for small grocery shops, pharmacies, coffee shops, bakeries, hardware stores, and other well-organized small businesses.

Venezuelan demand suffers from a lack of standards and sophistication in distribution channels. Concentration and collusion in distribution has limited the variety of products available to the Venezuelan consumer. Distribution of agricultural produce, for example, has been concentrated in the hands of a limited number of intermediaries who do not classify their produce by origin, variety, or quality. The Venezuelan consumer does not have a choice between Porcelana, Chuao, and Carúpano cocoa, or between Zulia or Aragua mangoes, but instead must buy undifferentiated products. Fruit, produce, cut flowers, seafood, and dairy products sold in Venezuela routinely fail to meet international standards. Crops developed specifically for export, including mangoes, plantains, and cashew nuts, are geared to international standards, but the resulting improvement in quality has not yet had an impact on production for local consumption.

Unsophisticated Consumption of Public Goods and Services. Venezuelans traditionally have been relatively unsophisticated consumers who have placed too low a value on public goods and services. The widespread attitude that goods and services provided by public agencies or state-owned enterprises should be free has hurt the nation's ability to provide such goods and services. The administration of a number of state-owned enterprises, which are often guided by political rather than economic goals, has fostered this attitude, to detrimental effect.[10]

As Kelly and González (1993) found in their study of state-owned enterprises and competitiveness in Venezuela, Venezuelan consumers have tended to assume that they have a right to low prices for public goods and services and that price increases are always unjustified. Venezuelan consumers have tended not to demand improvements that might justify price increases. Instead, they have insisted on paying rates that are too low to cover needed investments and often have participated in corrupt practices to try to get the service that they want. CANTV, before privatization, provided a prime example. Telephone rates, which increased at a rate lower than inflation, did not generate revenues sufficient for the company to expand its network or to provide adequate service. Demand exceeded supply, creating a black market in which new phones were obtained through a variety of illegal means. Over time, customers developed very low expectations and rarely demanded improvements. Customers had received the service too cheaply for too long for customers to place a value on the service.[11] In 1994, Venezuelan prices for basic phone service were still low by world standards, and there was still substantial opposition to price increases.

Signs of Increasingly Astute Shopping Behavior. Venezuelans are learning gradually how to become more astute shoppers. During the early 1990s, the availability of imported products, such as processed foods, chocolate candies, stationery supplies, and clothing, made the Venezuelan consumer a more value conscious shopper.[12] In many industries, consumers were demanding that local firms meet the quality, packaging, and pricing standards of imports. For example, in processed foods, a sector where Venezuelan consumers traditionally were sophisticated in regional terms, imports made the market very competitive and price-sensitive, and by 1993 consumers were becoming even more demanding than before.[13]

Falling incomes have made many Venezuelan consumers more value conscious in their purchases than they once were, but not to the extent that might be expected. As of the early 1990s, many Venezuelans had not adjusted their spending to their new income levels. Instead, they were running down savings and taking on debt in order to maintain consumption. Less affluent consumers often let their families' basic needs go unmet in order to purchase appliances or attractive clothing. A 1991 IESA study documented the resistance of many Venezuelans to making changes in spending patterns in the face of economic difficulties.[14]

Venezuelan consumers are only beginning to realize that they can exert pressure on local manufacturers and retailers to improve products and service. There is no well-organized consumer movement in Venezuela. After the commercial opening, the Superintendency of Consumer Protection was transformed into the Institute for the Defense and Education of the Consumer (IDEC). However, this agency was not able to refocus its efforts toward consumer education and away from its original mandate, which prior to the opening was to protect consumers from unauthorized price increases.[15] In 1994, IDEC reverted to its old role of enforcing price controls. The consumer learning process will take time, and it will be possible only if the economy remains open.

Demand Advantages in World Markets. In a few sectors, local demand is giving rise to actual or potential advantages in world markets. These are the exceptions, not the rule, but they show that domestic demand can indeed be a source of competitive advantage for Venezuelan exports in global markets. These exceptions tend to be concentrated in products where Venezuela shows high levels of per capita consumption. In some cases, the source of advantage is the sophistication of local demand. In others, highly elastic demand (price-sensitive consumers) has stimulated local producers to maximize production efficiencies, resulting in cost advantages in international markets.

An outstanding example of sophisticated demand as a source of advantage is found in the Venezuelan telenovelas (soap operas) industry. Venezuelan audiences for this type of program are considered the most discriminating in Latin America, and perhaps in the world.[16] Soap operas from Mexico, Argentina, and Puerto Rico have been tried out on Venezuelan audiences before being widely marketed. Venezuelan television ratings (measured as the percentage of a nation's population that watches television) have been among the highest in the world.[17] One major reason is long exposure to highly competitive private television channels dating from the 1950s—something rare outside the United States. (See Chapter 4.)

There also are pockets of sophisticated Venezuelan demand in women's and juvenile fashion wear, sports footwear, and swimwear. Clothing has been an important status symbol in Venezuela for many years, and per-capita consumption of clothing is high compared to other Latin American countries.[18] The Venezuelan high-fashion market originally was served by imports. A combination of sophisticated demand, falling purchasing power due to the 1983 devaluation of the bolivar, and import restrictions stimulated the local fashion industry in Venezuela in the 1980s.[19] Several former retailers and local designers began to design clothes for the Venezuelan marketplace. The Venezuelan fashion market has become more discriminating after the economic opening. Although some local designers have fallen victim to competition from imports, others have continued to thrive in the more demanding environment.

Some Venezuelan clothing and apparel products that reflect sophisticated local demand are finding acceptance in world markets. Tropicana has been able to export affordable women's fashion clothing to the United States. Thom Sailor has introduced its sport shoes successfully to the United States. Local fashions reflective of Venezuela's beach culture also are finding acceptance in upscale export markets. Textilera Avila has exported its Riviera brand swimwear to Germany, where it enjoys an exotic image. Dorita Vera has exported swimwear with a Latin flavor to the United States, Europe, and throughout the Caribbean.

Although the demand for luxury goods in Venezuela is relatively large (generated by its highest income groups), it never has been large enough to foster export-oriented luxury goods industries. Venezuelan demand for luxury goods has been served largely by imports, as the wealthy have ample funds for both travel and purchasing. In contrast, Venezuelan demand for low-cost but good-quality consumer goods is a source of actual or potential advantage in some commodity products.

Tissue paper is a good example of a commodity product in which Venezuelan firms have started to compete on cost in global (as well as regional) markets. Venezuelans consume more paper products per capita than citizens of any other Latin American country except for Panama. Until 1989, the production of rolls of tissue paper in Venezuela was subsidized, and domestic consumption was concentrated heavily in the premium tier ("Class A" paper). Since 1989, Venezuelan demand for tissue paper has become very price sensitive and has refocused toward "Classes B and C" paper. Venezuelan demand for low-cost tissue paper of acceptable quality is similar to demand in many foreign markets. In 1991, Venezuela exported tissue paper to the United Kingdom ($7.7 million) and the United States ($2.2

million) as well as to the Caribbean (Trinidad and Tobago, $2.7 million), and Central America. Venezuela was the third largest exporter of tissue paper in the Americas (including the United States).[20]

Demand Advantages in Regional Markets. In certain products, Venezuelan demand is a source of actual or potential advantages in regional, rather than world, markets. High rates of domestic consumption can permit companies to reap economies of scale and thereby gain regional cost advantages. High rates of domestic consumption often are accompanied by a relatively high degree of demand sophistication in regional terms. Venezuela has demand advantages over other Latin American nations in a number of areas, including fashion, television and advertising, packaging, alcoholic beverages, and cosmetics.

In the early 1990s, per-capita consumption in Venezuela was among the highest in Latin America for beer, personal care products, pasta, canned goods, paper, and juvenile fashion. Venezuelans are discriminating purchasers of beer, and in 1993 Polar was successfully exporting beer developed for Venezuelan consumption to southern Florida. Cervecera Nacional was exporting beer to the Puerto Rican beer market. As mentioned, Venezuelan consumers are sophisticated purchasers of processed food products in regional terms.[21] Local food processors are continually improving existing products and developing new products to meet this demand, and Nestlé Venezuela and Alfonzo Rivas & Cia. have been exporting processed food products to other Latin American and Caribbean countries. Milpa, a supplier to the Venezuelan National Housing Institute (INAVI), has successfully exported low-cost modular housing units to Central America and the Caribbean countries, taking advantage of designs developed for the Venezuelan rural environment.

In 1993, Venezuela had the highest per-capita consumption of personal deodorants and dentifrices in Latin America. It used to have the highest per-capita consumption of cosmetics, and as of 1993 it tied with Mexico for first.[22] The sophistication of local demand for personal care products has been high, not just in regional but also in world terms. For example, according to Procter & Gamble, Pantene became Venezuela's top-selling shampoo within four months, an "incredible" market acceptance for a "premium" product, evidence of the highly sophisticated Venezuelan demand.[23] The sophistication of local demand led Valebrón, a Venezuelan soap manufacturer, to produce a wide variety of upscale soaps based on natural plant extracts.[24] In 1994, the firm still imported fragrances from Switzerland and France for use in its local soap production, because, in the words of

Valebrón's general manager, "[Venezuelan] consumers are appreciative and will select our brands over those of the multinationals" despite difficult economic times.[25] Valebrón started exporting soaps to Colombia and Panama and was targeting other markets in the Andean Pact and the Caribbean.[26]

In Latin American markets, consumer goods produced in Venezuela often are perceived as up-market, and many are accepted without adaptation. Such has been the case with processed foods, beer, and sports footwear. Thom Sailor sport shoes have been sold in Puerto Rico without any product modifications. In 1993, the beer sold by Polar in southern Florida was identical to that consumed in Venezuela; only the packaging was different. Venezuelan computer software programs have received positive reviews from buyers in smaller Spanish-speaking countries.[27]

Sophistication of demand on a regional basis is a potential source of competitive advantage, but it will not create competitiveness by itself. In many areas, Venezuelan consumer demand is considered more sophisticated than Colombian demand. However, trade flows since the signing of the Colombia-Venezuela free trade agreement indicate that relatively few Venezuelan firms have been able to turn this into an advantage. In the years following the agreement, exports from Venezuela to Colombia consisted mainly of metal and chemical products, whereas the reverse trade was more diversified. (See Chapter 2.)

Differences in demand between the two countries can pose unexpected challenges for would-be exporters. Some Colombian producers have found it difficult to meet the more sophisticated tastes of the Venezuelan market. In textiles, for example, some Venezuelan observers expected the free trade agreement to result in a massive influx of Colombian fabrics. However, the deluge did not occur, in part because much of the Colombian product did not satisfy Venezuelan tastes, which place a premium on variety and attractiveness in color and design.[28] In 1993, Venezuela exported more textiles to Colombia than it imported from that country.[29] Colombian consumer demand is not always predictive of consumer demand in Venezuela, even in products where national tastes are similar. The Venezuelan firm Alfonzo Rivas & Cia., for example, developed a ready-mix for *buñuelos* (fritters) for the Venezuelan market, based on the success of this type of product in Colombia. However, the higher retail prices in Venezuela of additional ingredients used in cooking the ready-mix made the product uneconomical for many Venezuelan households.[30] These cases highlight the need for firms on either side of the border to conduct country-specific market research in their specific product segments.

Advantage Due to Specific Aspects of Local Demand. Some Venezuelan companies have developed competitive advantages by meeting the challenges of serving specific aspects of local demand. Appliance manufacturer Madosa developed a strategy of identifying and solving consumer problems found in the Venezuelan environment.[31] The company has "tropicalized" its products to serve the Venezuelan market by reengineering its motors to tolerate widely fluctuating voltages, by developing a method for purifying the water and ice cubes dispensed by its refrigerators to counter poor water quality, and by resizing and simplifying some products to match the needs of Venezuelan households. These changes have helped the firm to cement its position as the leading appliance company in Venezuela and to begin exports to other nations in the region.

In the processed foods sector, Alfonzo Rivas & Cia. has developed new products formulated to satisfy Venezuelan tastes, including an instant mashed potato product, two ready-to-eat children's cereals, and an instant milkshake. The firm surveyed its target market and found that Venezuelan consumers expressed desire for an instant shake with a "really thick" consistency, a product that at the time did not exist in Venezuela.[32] It formulated a new product, conducted taste tests on a sample of 5,000 people, and finalized the product on the basis of this research. The product, *Tris Tras*, has been very successful.[33]

Other Venezuelan firms have taken advantage of the fact that Spanish is spoken so widely, especially in the Western Hemisphere. This can be a source of advantage compared with firms from non-Spanish speaking nations, which generally do not focus on the Spanish-speaking market. In some cases, it also can be an avenue to success in broader global markets. Venevisión has been building an empire of television networks throughout the Spanish-speaking Americas, including the United States.[34] When Venezuelan telenovelas were first exported by Radio Caracas Televisión and Venevisión in the late 1970s and early 1980s, their earliest foreign markets were Spanish-speaking.[35] Their stellar successes in Spain in the late 1980s opened doors into other European countries, and by 1993 they had penetrated an estimated 38 countries worldwide.

Focusing on the Spanish-speaking market also led to broader international success in children's books. In the 1960s and 1970s, Venezuelan demand for children's books was high in regional terms because the national public libraries had money for book purchases, financed by oil revenues.[36] At the time, the supply of children's books in Spanish worldwide was very limited, partly because the concept of "easy-to-read" books for children was not part of the cultural tradition. Ediciones Ekaré, a local publisher of children's books, began operation as part of a public agency whose mission was to supply children's books to the national library system. It later became an independent, nonprofit organization. When Ediciones Ekaré first set up a stall at the international children's book fair in Bologna, along with the best publishers in the world, it was viewed as a novelty.[37] In 1982, its first major success, *La calle es libre (The Street Is Free)* won international acclaim. Since then, the book has sold 200,000 copies in translation to countries that are among the world's most discriminating purchasers of children's books: Canada, Germany, England, Denmark, Norway, Sweden, France, Holland, and Switzerland. While Venezuelan public sector demand for children's books was an essential factor behind the rise of Ediciones Ekaré, the primary motor of success was a talented and visionary editing team. Ediciones Ekaré is an isolated case of international success in book publishing, which as a sector is not well developed in Venezuela.

Venezuelan Industrial Demand

Historically, much of Venezuelan industry was transplanted from the developed countries. Imported technology, machinery, equipment, inputs, and parts traditionally were combined with local labor, raw materials, and energy. Under the import substitution regime, local demand was too small and volatile to support a sizable capital goods industry in the way the larger Mexican and Brazilian markets supported capital goods industries in those nations. Oil shocks and government policies have combined to create an investment roller coaster, making it difficult for Venezuelan firms to plan long-term investments. PDVSA and government investments have risen and fallen with oil revenues. In the past, uncertainty over government policy made it difficult for firms to plan more than a few months ahead. In the early 1990s, political instability and economic uncertainty kept hundreds of millions of dollars of investments on hold. Uncertainty over industrial demand in Venezuela, in turn, has hampered the industries that supply capital goods and industrial inputs, especially to cyclical industries such as construction and textiles. As a result, it is often easier for foreign suppliers, who are less reliant on the uncertainty of the Venezuelan market, to supply the nation's industrial demand.

Large and Sophisticated Demand from the Energy Sector. Since Venezuela's oil industry is one of the world's largest, it is not surprising that Venezuelan demand for inputs and services for that industry is also among the world's largest. PDVSA is the largest Venezuelan customer for a wide range of products and services, including steel tubes, engineering services, valves, and electric transformers. PDVSA's demand can fluctuate substantially. In the late 1980s and early 1990s, PDVSA unveiled a multiyear $50 billion investment program. These plans were later cut back substantially, but not until after several suppliers of products such as drilling equipment began to gear up to serve the anticipated demand. Several had to downsize when the demand failed to reach expectations.

PDVSA also has been a sophisticated customer that has fostered the development of several related industries in Venezuela. It has given preference to local suppliers, while imposing increasingly stringent quality standards and fostering competition. The company also has commissioned consulting studies of Venezuelan suppliers in order to identify a select number of firms for highly intensive training and assistance in preparing for export. Venezuelan consulting engineering, capital goods, and industrial construction firms have been the main beneficiaries of this policy. PDVSA actively has sought out export opportunities for local suppliers, some of whom have successfully entered the international market. Venezuelan valves for the oil industry have been sold in Mexico, Colombia, and the United States. Química Venoco has sold oil lubricants in such export markets as Ecuador, Peru, and Honduras, where it has competed against large multinational firms. Its product was of international quality due in part to the stringent requirements of PDVSA.

The Caroní River watershed is the home of Edelca's hydroelectric complex, one of the world's largest. This complex, including dams at Guri and Macagua, has created an enormous demand for engineering services, cement, reinforcing bar, aluminum, and other inputs. The civil construction industry has grown substantially in the area of Puerto Ordaz as a consequence of the large projects carried out in the region. Local engineering firms have worked closely with foreign companies in the design and construction of the dams. By all accounts, Edelca has been a sophisticated and demanding consumer of engineering services, equipment, and materials.

Import Substitution and Industrial Demand. Under the import substitution regime, government-controlled prices generated a cost plus mentality on the part of many Venezuelan firms, which usually were able to pass on increases in costs to consumers. Many Venezuelan firms did not monitor the quality of their inputs or recognize the costs associated with low-quality inputs. Limited competition made product quality not much of a selling point and did not force Venezuelan companies to ensure that their inputs were of the highest quality. Until 1989, Venezuelan manufacturing firms were largely forbidden to import raw materials or intermediate goods that were manufactured in the country. In addition, Venezuelan producers of particular commodities often were given control over imports. Sidor, for example, had a de facto monopoly on the production and importation of most steel products. Alcasa and Venalum were duopolists in aluminum. Industrial companies had to accept what the local companies supplied. Sometimes Venezuelan firms were granted protection in exchange for their promise to manufacture certain goods. As a result, they were able to be exclusive suppliers of the products that they promised to manufacture.

The opening up of the Venezuelan market to foreign competition after 1989 greatly increased the level of competition many Venezuelan firms experienced. Under the new commercial policy, manufacturers were able to import inputs and local suppliers were forced to offer competitive terms in order to sell their products. Venezuelan industrial buyers became more demanding and sophisticated in response to the increased demands that they faced in their own markets and the choices that they were given. Some industrial linkages have been reduced as a consequence of market liberalization, but linkages that could not hold up in a free marketplace are unlikely to have been sources of advantage in any case.

A Lack of Stimulus from State-Owned Enterprises. With certain notable exceptions, such as PDVSA, Edelca, and the Caracas Metro, Venezuelan state-owned enterprises have not been demanding buyers of inputs and services, nor have they stimulated higher quality standards and competitiveness on the part of their suppliers.[38] Venezuelan suppliers have tended to view the state-owned enterprises as a guaranteed market. At the same time, the state-owned enterprises have tended to buy from any domestic supplier that appears in order to create new potential political "friends" and to maintain relationships with others. The attitude seems to be "He who buys from everyone does not make enemies."[39] Customers of the state-owned enterprises, which are powerful public monopolies, usually cannot or do not exert effective pressure to improve state-owned enterprise procurement.

State-owned enterprises have been in charge of purchasing technologies and choosing partners for heavy industrial projects. Often they have had to choose between competing offers by foreign multinationals. These choices, particularly in the case of the CVG, sometimes appear to have been made (or not made at all) on the basis of political or personal choices rather than the best bid or offer. Delays in the development of the aluminum, pulp, and mining industries, for example, can be attributed to the CVG's historical intransigence.

In the area of agriculture, the state marketing boards, in their role as purchasers, introduced disincentives to quality and innovation among producers. For example, the National Cocoa Fund (FONCACAO) implemented an oversimplified definition of cocoa bean categories. It did not sufficiently differentiate between different grades of quality of Venezuelan cocoa beans in setting prices to the producer. As a result of this and other practices, cocoa growers had no incentives "to maintain or improve the quality of their products. Consistency plummeted, and supply guarantees were frequently violated. In frustration, many long-time international buyers simply turned elsewhere."[40] This situation was particularly harmful because a reputation for consistency in quality and delivery is essential to success in the international market for fine cocoa beans, the type produced and exported by Venezuela.

Unsophisticated Private-Sector Demand for Capital Goods. The Venezuelan private sector has a history of relatively high imports of capital goods combined with poor performance in productivity growth and manufactured exports.[41] This history underscores the fact that in Venezuela, "technology has been understood as a merchandise, always available in the marketplace," acquired already incorporated into machines, equipment, and technical assistance.[42] Many Venezuelan firms imported capital goods during the 1980s, paying for them with subsidized foreign currency. However, most of these firms did not understand that the imported technology would require a high level of expertise in its selection, acquisition, and use. Because their levels of technological learning have been low, many Venezuelan firms have fallen into a permanent dependence on their suppliers. Because they never became sophisticated users of the technologies that they purchased, their productive performance has suffered.

Venezuelan firms are not leading edge customers for most capital goods. These goods tend to be imported after they have been developed and proven in other nations. In the Viana survey, nearly 400 manufacturing firms out of a sample of 600 reported that they bought standard machinery and equipment from catalogs, without any associated nontangible assets. One hundred firms acquired equipment designed by vendors. Fewer than 50 firms purchased machinery and equipment designed by themselves, and relatively few firms reported that they modified purchased equipment. Only a handful reported they had entered into patent or brand licenses.[43] Such evidence suggests that the type of leading edge firms that provide early and advanced demand for capital goods are not present.

Pockets of Sophisticated Private-Sector Demand. Despite the general tendencies, a number of pockets of sophisticated demand exist in the Venezuelan private sector. In the early 1990s, several companies began to work directly with suppliers to improve the quality of their inputs. Mavesa instituted a program to create a group of reliable suppliers for its palm oil business that involved training farmers in production technology and business skills. Many farmers rapidly made the jump from peasant to modern businessman. Sivensa was working with the CVG to try to improve the reliability of the latter as a supplier. After the economic opening, a number of private-sector firms began to threaten to change suppliers if state-owned enterprises did not improve. Others resorted to imports to obtain varieties or quality not available in Venezuela. For example, Ruedas de Aluminio C.A. (RUALCA), a manufacturer of aluminum rings used in cars, started to import aluminum alloys not supplied by the CVG.

The Venezuelan subsidiaries of multinational firms have provided a sophisticated source of demand for a number of Venezuelan industries. Several of the multinationals with operations in Venezuela are among the leaders in their industries worldwide. Many of these multinationals have worked closely with their suppliers to bring Venezuelan inputs up to acceptable, if not international, standards. Between 1989 and 1993, multinational auto companies raised the standards that they demanded from local suppliers. Foreign-owned auto assemblers, such as Ford, worked with leading Venezuelan auto parts makers in qualifying auto parts for use in international markets. CANTV was developing close contacts with a wide range of local suppliers. Companies such as Heinz and Procter & Gamble (P&G) have been sophisticated clients for local suppliers of inputs and advertising agencies.

Multinational producers of consumer goods, such as P&G, also have been very demanding of their local suppliers of raw inputs and packing materials. This demand has provided some local suppliers with the experience they needed in order to start supplying foreign markets. Montana Gráfica, a Venezuelan producer of flexible packaging, has exported to the Caribbean, Central America, Colombia, and Argentina. Its primary customers have been firms that produce mass consumer goods in Venezuela, many of which are multinational companies that have very high quality standards for their packaging. In contrast, the publishing sector is not well developed in Venezuela; this fact is reflected in the quality of paper produced locally for use in printing books, which has been of lesser quality than the paper and cardboard produced locally for use by the consumer goods sector.[44]

Related and Supporting Industries in Venezuela

Related and supporting industries can be a potent source of competitive advantage. Leading industries in developed countries often are enriched by the presence of a diverse set of local suppliers of inputs, services, machinery, and equipment, whose productive efforts "support" the competitiveness of the user industries. Related industries often cross-fertilize each other with ideas, talent, and expertise. Technology and expertise often spill over from one industry to related industries. Industries that use similar inputs deepen or widen the market for goods and services, stimulating the growth of common suppliers. In some industries, a common customer base can provide opportunities for shared activities.

Suppliers of Natural Resources

Venezuela's vast endowments of natural resources should result in supply advantages for a number of the nation's industries. Unfortunately, natural resource advantages often do not turn into advantages for downstream firms in Venezuela, due to import substitution policies that made it uneconomical to develop some resources (such as mining and forestry resources), differences in sources of competitive advantage between upstream and downstream industries, the prevalence of state-owned firms in natural resource and raw materials industries, and difficult general business conditions.

Venezuela's state-owned companies have not been the best suppliers in terms of their readiness to understand and to supply customer needs. To quote a manager from one Venezuelan state-owned enterprise, "We are a monopolist and we act like a monopolist. We charge high prices like a monopolist. We provide lousy service like a monopolist."[45] Such attitudes are hardly conducive to fostering the competitive advantage of downstream industries.

The CVG companies, at times, have been notorious as suppliers. In iron and steel, these companies have performed poorly in "supporting" domestic industrial users, although in 1993, improvements were under way. In 1993, Ferrominera Orinoco's management was placing new importance on serving domestic clients and was working to upgrade and to stimulate local demand.[46] For many years, domestic purchasers of aluminum had no choice but to accept inexact product specifications from Alcasa, which also imposed delivery terms on its domestic buyers and requested that domestic orders for laminated and foil products be received a full three months in advance of delivery.[47] Pulp and paper producers traditionally have found it very difficult to negotiate with the CVG for rights to CVG-managed forests. (See Chapter 4.)

PDVSA and its subsidiary Pequiven sometimes have been less than optimal suppliers. At times, PDVSA has sold raw materials and feedstocks on the export market and has left Pequiven scrambling for inputs and unable to meet its own obligations to customers. Schemes that require Venezuelan chemical companies to pay Pequiven prices that are higher than Gulf Coast (U.S.) prices are unlikely to result in a strong, export-oriented petrochemical industry. Some buyers have complained that Pequiven has been slow to enter into supply contracts for basic inputs.

Few Suppliers of Capital Goods

Some types of supplier industries, such as capital goods industries, are not well-developed in Venezuela. Capital goods industries fall into this category. In industrialized countries, technology and expertise often are transmitted from one industry to another through capital goods. The Italian ceramic tile industry, which borrowed production technology developed in the local glass industry, is one such example. In Germany, capital goods industries provide a backbone around which much of the economy is built. Some Latin American nations, such as Argentina, Brazil, and Mexico, experienced a "second phase" of import substitution that fostered domestic manufacturing of capital goods. In the mid-1980s, Brazil and Mexico produced 74 percent and 62 percent of their respective capital goods requirements, but Venezuela produced only 23 percent.[48] The Venezuelan economy appears to lack the diversity, dynamism, and entrepreneurial tradition that characterize nations that have managed to build strong capital goods sectors despite limited domestic market size, such as Sweden, Switzerland, Belgium, and the Netherlands.

Local producers of capital goods and industrial services face barriers to entry not only in international markets but in Venezuela as well. Many Venezuelan industrial buyers prefer to purchase capital goods and services from foreign companies. This attitude is especially prevalent with respect to machinery, equipment, and sophisticated services. In Venezuela, most sophisticated machinery and equipment for the generation of electricity, for example, has been sourced abroad. Capital goods of a less complex nature, such as steel towers and other structures, aluminum and copper electrical cables, electrical transformers, steel pipes, and boilers, have been sourced in Venezuela. Multinational enterprises tend to use their customary sources of capital goods, and national firms often acquire their new plants via turnkey contracts.

The tendency of local firms to rely on foreign suppliers of capital goods is not surprising. Firms in many developing nations are in roughly the same position. The tendency does make it absolutely critical, however, for Venezuelan firms that rely on foreign suppliers to keep up-to-date on technological developments made in the most advanced of the foreign supplier and user industries and that they develop long-term strategies to ensure access to the most modern equipment. Venezuela's negative trade balance in capital goods is not alarming as long as imported capital goods are used to increase productivity.

Poor Supplier-Buyer Relations

In order for supplier-buyer relationships to be a source of competitive advantage, suppliers and buyers must work together to solve common problems and to promote joint efficiency. In Venezuela, the import substitution system worked against the formation of effective working relationships between supporting industries and their clients. The system created incentives for firms to integrate vertically and discouraged the growth of independent, focused suppliers who specialized on particular inputs or equipment. Incentives to please one's customer, to innovate, and to improve were largely absent, because markets were guaranteed and there was little or no competition based on quality and cost. Because the key to profitability was market power within a protected environment, producers organized themselves into groups to increase their power. Supplier-buyer relationships were widely viewed as zero-sum transactions, in which the supplier or the buyer benefitted at the expense of the other.

The linkages between buyers and suppliers within Venezuela tend to be weak. The Viana survey found that 27 percent of the Venezuelan manufacturing firms surveyed did not maintain relations with their suppliers of raw materials, and 47 percent did not maintain relations with their clients.[49] Historically, vertical integration in Venezuela has resulted from the perceived need to control access to basic raw materials. In some industries, companies could get access to imported inputs only if they had a presence in the upstream industry. In others, integration has been fostered by the desire to ensure supplies of certain inputs, such as bottles or cans, or distribution channels. Venezuelan firms could not count on markets to supply their inputs at reasonable prices. When protection was reduced starting in 1989, many groups linked by supplier-buyer ties came into open conflict. Buyers, under pressure from imported end products, began to import inputs, which in turn put pressure on their local suppliers. Mutual distrust grew with diverging interests.

The zero-sum mentality has persisted to a large extent. One example has been the Venezuelan textile and clothing sector; here antagonism between clothing producers and textile manufacturers has prevented them from working together to innovate and improve.[50] (See Chapter 5.) Further upstream, the traditional estrangement between Venezuelan textile manufacturers and cotton growers has impeded the competitive improvement of both sectors. The physical characteristics of much of the cotton grown in Venezuela are not suitable for high-quality fabrics, and imports are meeting local demand for high-quality cotton. However, the two sectors have weak relations, and certain textile producers have entered the cotton farming business. The auto and auto parts sector provides another example. While some Venezuelan parts firms have worked hard to meet assemblers' quality standards, some others have called for lower standards, and many have lobbied for protection that would reduce the pressures to improve quality and lower costs. Following the commercial opening, negotiations between the local grain producers and agroindustry broke down, in part because the sectors lacked a tradition of dealing with each other directly without government involvement.

Some aspects of these supplier/buyer conflicts are actually positive signs. Reduced protection and increased competition were supposed to pressure Venezuelan firms to be more efficient. The number and extent of the conflicts among Venezuelan suppliers and buyers show that this has indeed been occurring. They also show how dramatically inefficient and uncompetitive Venezuelan firms had become. The nation may well have to go through a period in which market forces weed out the inefficient and reward the efficient before we can expect Venezuelan firms to realize the advantages of effective relationships between efficient suppliers and buyers. In this regard, calls for protection are causes for great concern. As long as the possibility (real or perceived) of protection exists, there will be powerful disincentives to form effective linkages between buyers and suppliers throughout the economy. Only when both buyers and suppliers are convinced that they must compete in an open environment will they find ways to work together in a mutually beneficial fashion.

Clusters in the Venezuelan Economy

"Competitive clusters" are groups of competitive industries (industries that have achieved success in international markets or have achieved world-class quality and cost position) linked through supplier-buyer linkages; through related technologies, expertise, or customer base; or through a combination thereof. Clusters consisting of buyer, supplier, and related industries are important because national economies tend to grow through their development.

Venezuela has relatively few clusters of competitive industries. The reason is a history of poor supplier/buyer relations, limited generation of new technology, limited pockets of world-class expertise, and the mixed impact of government policy. State investments in heavy industry in Venezuela followed what could be described as a "cluster creation" strategy. Indeed, most of what could be called "clusters" of export industries in Venezuela are under state ownership. Although state investment has made a positive contribution by founding industries, state-owned enterprises, outside of the oil sector, have been a mixed lot in terms of their contribution to competitive cluster formation. State-owned and managed clusters operate according to a set of dynamics that can serve to impede, rather than promote, competitiveness.

An outstanding example of a cluster of related and supporting industries that *is* competitive in regional (and, in some sectors, global) markets is Venezuela's entertainment cluster, which owes its creation to the private sector. In early 1994, there were signs that new clusters might be forming in the wake of the economic opening, although this was still in the very early stages. In addition, a greater emphasis on privatization and more transparent public policies, if forthcoming, could extend some existing clusters that have stagnated under state control.

Venezuela's Clusters

The following clusters of industries contain Venezuela's major export industries: petroleum and petrochemicals, aluminum and steel, mass media entertainment, and pulp and paper. These clusters generally include a main industry, some supplier industries, and some customer industries.

Petroleum and Petrochemicals. In Venezuela, the petroleum and petrochemical industries are under the umbrella of PDVSA, a government-owned corporation. They form an industrial cluster, sharing the same policies and, to a large extent, the same supporting industries. The Venezuelan petroleum industry consists of the Petróleos de Venezuela parent company and its operating subsidiaries. The main source of advantage for this cluster, of course, is the presence of large reserves of oil and natural gas. The cluster produces and exports crude oil and refined products, including a broad range of fuels and lubricants. The petrochemical industry consists of Pequiven (a PDVSA subsidiary) and a number of mixed capital firms created around

TABLE 7.1
Mexican and Venezuelan Petrochemical Clusters

MEXICO		VENEZUELA	
Industry	Trade Balance (Million U.S. $)	Industry	Trade Balance (Million U.S. $)
Basic Hydrocarbons			
crude oil	8,900	crude oil	5,100
liquefied propane, butane	16	refined petroleum	8,700
light petroleum oils	224		
petroleum lubricants	54		
Basic Chemicals			
ethylene glycol	52		
phenol	10		
phtalic anhydride	16		
terephtalic acid esters	96		
other polyacids	76		
Chemical Products			
polyamides	15	alkyds, polyesters	32
anti-knock preparations	28	polyethylene	33
		polystyrene	15

Includes all petroleum and petrochemical products in which the respective nations achieved a positive trade balance of U.S. $10 million or greater in 1990.

Source: Calculated from United Nations Trade Statistics.

Pequiven, with private capital and both national and foreign participation. In the early 1990s, suppliers to the petroleum and petrochemical industries, including engineering consulting firms, some capital goods firms, and suppliers of metal-mechanical inputs, such as tubes, valves, and pumps, started to export.

Table 7.1 compares the export performance of the Venezuelan and Mexican petroleum and petrochemical clusters. It shows the petroleum and petrochemical industries in which each nation had net exports in excess of $10 million in 1990, according to United Nations statistics for that year. As of 1994, a number of projects were under way within Venezuela that were expected to increase substantially the nation's ability to extend the cluster into liquefied natural gas and additional petrochemical products. In addition, in reading the chart, one must keep in mind the fact that Mexico's economy is much larger than Venezuela's.

Aluminum and Steel. The Venezuelan aluminum industry developed under the state-owned CVG in the southeast of Venezuela. The industry is vertically integrated and includes bauxite mining, alumina production, aluminum smelting, and the manufacture of aluminum foil—all under the control of the CVG.[51] The industry's most important input, electricity, is supplied by Edelca, another CVG company. Downstream manufacturing, which is carried out by private or mixed capital enterprises, includes aluminum wire, cables, and auto parts. Although the Venezuelan aluminum "cluster" has been a substantial source of exports, including alumina, aluminum, cables, and aluminum rings, it can hardly be called a cluster of competitive industries. Truly competitive industries are those that succeed in world markets without the need for subsidies or protection. Although some parts of the cluster might fit this description, others do not. In aluminum, for example, Alcasa has been heavily subsidized, and Venalum saw its profits virtually disappear when world prices fell and export subsidies were eliminated.

Historically, state ownership insulated the CVG companies active in bauxite, alumina, and aluminum from financial market pressures. Alcasa, for example, was able to start a plant modernization program by capitalizing its debts and issuing paper on the private market.[52] When it failed to generate sufficient earnings to finance its cash flow, it began to space out its payments. It could choose among various alternatives, such as not covering its employee obligations, or not keeping up to date with its payments to Social Security, the national training institute (INCE), or the housing policy fund. Alcasa was able to delay its payments to Edelca for electricity, to Interalúmina for alumina, and to the CVG for its contribution to corporate functions. Alcasa went so far as to sell its deliveries in advance, which hurt future earnings, in order to generate cash. In the case of aluminum, the state-owned "cluster" shielded some members from market discipline, with costly results. Privatization and transparent negotiations with foreign investors hold out the best hope for the development of a vibrant aluminum cluster.

The Venezuelan steel "cluster" includes the mining of iron ore and the production of iron pellets and briquettes, primary steel, flat products, extruded shapes, seamless pipes and tubes, and auto parts. Most of the industry is controlled by the CVG, which is integrated from iron ore to finished steel. Sivensa, the leading private steel manufacturer, is partially integrated, using both steel scrap and briquettes as inputs. The natural gas used in iron ore reduction is provided by a PDVSA subsidiary, CORPOVEN, while the electricity used for steel production is provided by Edelca, a CVG company.

Domestic steel production helped generate downstream activities in several sectors, including wire and wire mesh, pipes and tubes, steel roofing materials, boilers, some parts and equipment for the petroleum industry, packaging and containers, and auto parts. Of major importance to the growth of these areas was the existence of a reasonably reliable domestic supply of steel. The major private-sector steel producer, Sivensa, has contributed to the development of a number of downstream areas by investing in new plants and by finding foreign joint venture partners to provide additional capital, expertise, and access to foreign markets. In addition, trained personnel, expertise, and technology have radiated out of the steel sector into downstream activities.[53] For example, Sivensa's Foundation for Industrial Training in Metalworking (Fundametal) has played an important role in teaching job skills and the use of new technologies in metalworking to firms within the Sivensa Group, their suppliers and distributors. Sidor, the state-owned steel company, has had many of the same problems as the state-owned aluminum companies. Nevertheless, it also has made a very important contribution to professional and technical training in the steel and related industries.

The Venezuelan iron and steel "cluster" exports iron ore, iron pellets and briquettes, steel and steel products, and auto parts. On the surface, the basic structure of the Venezuelan iron and steel cluster compares reasonably well with that of Brazil. The main difference is that Brazil is much better developed in terms of transportation equipment, machinery, and other downstream users of steel. Venezuela, however, is competitive now in only a few products, particularly iron ore, direct reduced iron pellets and briquettes (DRI), semifinished products (billets), and some auto parts. Table 7.2 lists the iron and steel industries with trade balances in excess of $10 million in 1990 for the two countries. Brazil's sector appears much more developed, as one might expect given the relative size of the two economies.

Mass Media Entertainment. The Venezuelan mass media entertainment cluster is an outstanding example of a cluster that is competitive in regional, and in some instances global, markets. Venezuela is a world leader in the production and foreign licensing of telenovelas, as discussed in Chapter 4. Telenovelas are produced by both national television networks, Radio Caracas Televisión and Venevisión, as well as by an independent producer, Marte Televisión. The networks and independent producers also produce other television programs including drama series and comedy series.[54] Related industries include radio (with 192 AM radio stations and 107 FM

TABLE 7.2
Brazilian and Venezuelan Iron and Steel Clusters

BRAZIL		VENEZUELA	
Industry	Trade Balance (Million U.S. $)	Industry	Trade Balance (Million U.S. $)
iron ore concentrates	1,600		
iron ore agglomerates	755		
pig iron	418		
ferromanganese	34	ferrosilicon	26
ferrosilicon	117	iron, steel blocks, lumps	11
other ferroalloys	202		
iron, simple steel blooms	753	iron, simple steel blooms	44
other alloy blooms	46	iron, simple steel coils	25
iron, simple steel coils	502		
iron, simple steel wire, rod	185	iron, simple steel wire, rod	59
high carbon steel wire, rod	13	high carbon steel wire, rod	13
stainless steel bars	28	iron, steel bars, hotrolled	59
other alloy bars	44		
iron, steel bars, hotrolled	264		
iron, simple steel heavy plate, rolled	299	iron, simple steel thin plate, rolled	118
iron, simple steel medium plate, rolled	30	other iron, simple steel plate, sheet	33
other alloy steel medium plate	16		
iron, simple steel thin plate, rolled	63		
tinned plates, sheets	57		
other iron, simple steel plate, sheet	46		
iron, simple steel wire	12	other iron, steel pipes, tubes	42
iron, steel seamless tubes	17		
other iron, steel pipes, tubes	111		
iron, steel tube fittings	31		
rough iron castings	13		

Includes all basic iron and steel products in which the respective nations achieved a positive trade balance of U.S. $10 million or greater in 1990.

Source: Calculated from United Nations Trade Statistics.

radio stations nationwide in 1993), subscription television, fashion, video recording, music recording, movie production, and live shows. Advertising, modeling, and beauty contests provide marketing skills and talent. With the introduction of fiber optic cable links in Venezuela, telecommunications will grow in importance as a related and supporting industry to radio and television.

Demand Conditions, Related Industries 267

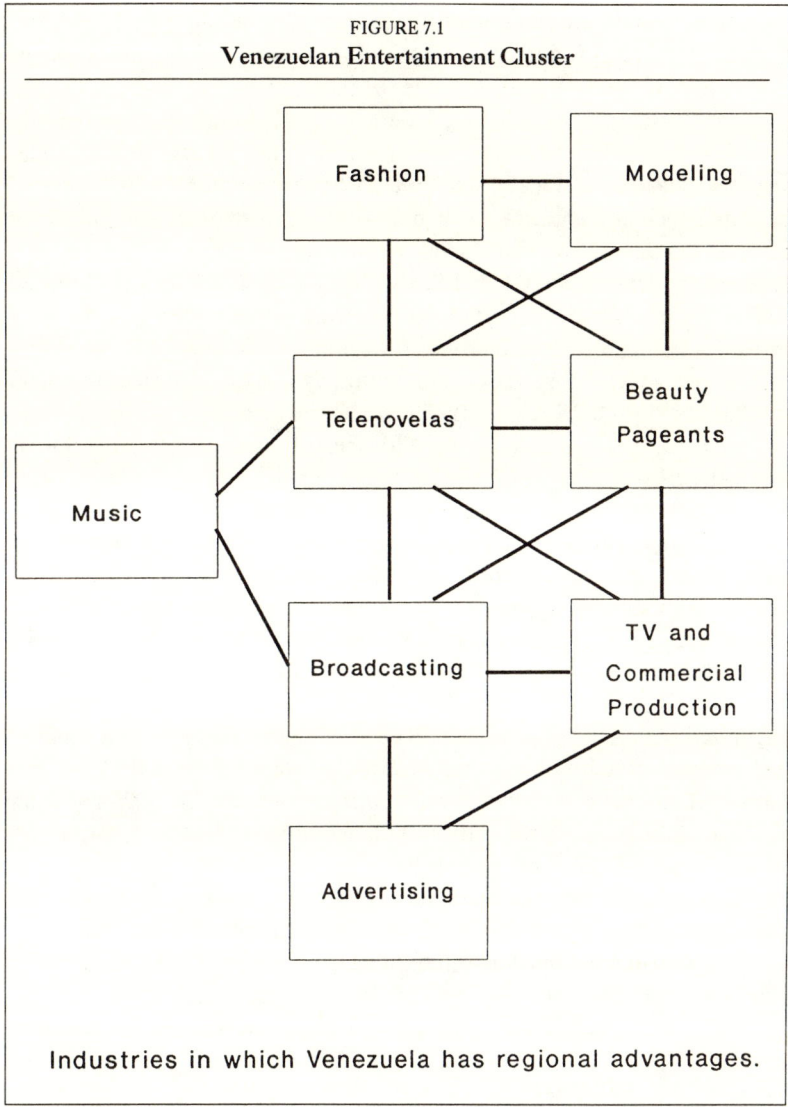

FIGURE 7.1
Venezuelan Entertainment Cluster

Industries in which Venezuela has regional advantages.

Figure 7.1 shows some of the entertainment industries in which Venezuela is considered to be on par with or superior to the best in the region. Because there are relatively few statistics on these industries, the chart was developed using information obtained from industry experts.

Venezuela's entertainment cluster includes, along with television, a music recording industry that has substantial export potential. As of 1993, approximately 9 million copies of music recordings were sold each year in Venezuela, of which 85 percent were Venezuelan and Latin American titles. (In the early 1980s, the government decreed the mandatory broadcasting of local music in an effort to counter the influence of imported rock and roll.) More than 2 million copies of titles recorded in Venezuela, mostly by Venezuelan artists, were sold abroad, mainly in Mexico, the United States, and Spain. Only a small amount of recorded material is physically exported, to nearby countries such as Colombia and Panama. The rest is licensed to foreign or multinational recording companies. The local market is dominated by Sony (a multinational firm that has acquired CBS Records) and two domestic firms, Sonográfica and Sonorodven, which are affiliated with the two main Venezuelan television networks.

According to industry sources, Venezuela and Mexico are the main sources of musical talent in Latin America in popular modern genres. (In tropical dancing music, Puerto Rico, the Dominican Republic, and U.S. Cubans dominate.) The popularity of Venezuelan singers abroad has been helped greatly by the licensing of telenovelas to television networks around the world, because each telenovela usually includes one or more new musical themes that are disseminated via television. Sonográfica (affiliated with RCTV) has specialized in composer-singers, and some of their artists, including Yordano, Ricardo Montaner, Franco de Vita, and Carlos Mata, have become popular throughout the Spanish-speaking world mainly through their themes in telenovelas licensed abroad by Radio Caracas Televisión. Sonorodven, affiliated with Venevisión, usually separates the composer and performer roles, and has promoted such telenovela performing artists as Kiara and Guillermo Dávila.

Advertising is another related industry where Venezuelan talent plays an important role. As of 1994, local industry executives rate the quality of Venezuelan television advertising overall about on par with that of Argentina and Brazil and above that of Mexico, Colombia, and the rest of Latin America. These executives believe Venezuela leads Latin America in one aspect of television commercials, the quality of production. Advertising agencies generally develop a commercial's story line and then outsource its production to independent producers. In 1993, local production capabilities at their best were comparable to those in the medium tier of the U.S. market, at a fraction of the cost. A top-quality TV commercial could cost up to $1 million in the United States, while an equivalent but slightly less sophisticated commercial might cost less than $200,000 in Venezuela.

The story lines of Venezuelan TV commercials tend to be less sophisticated than the production. This reflects the advertising tastes of the Venezuelan firms that commission the commercials and the fact that many local firms are still family-held companies whose advertising decisions are not in the hands of trained marketing professionals. (Multinational firms with local headquarters, in contrast, are more sophisticated consumers of advertising.) During the decades of protectionism and price controls, there was relatively little pressure on local firms to maximize the effectiveness of their story lines, a fact that has slowed the development of Venezuelan advertising. The ad agencies in Venezuela include the best-known multinational advertising firms, such as J. Walter Thompson, McCahn-Ericcson, and Saatchi & Saatchi, and a number of domestic firms, including CORPA and Ars.

Although Venezuela is a Latin American leader in production technology for television commercials, it will be difficult for the nation to use this advantage to improve its position in industries that are heavy users of advertising. The main reason is that the industries supported by such activities, such as consumer packaged goods, are dominated by multinational firms, which make their location decisions as part of global and regional strategies. On the other hand, Venezuela's advantages in this area might be a reason for a multinational firm to locate Andean Pact or Latin American operations in the nation.

One mass media industry in which Venezuela has not been successful is the motion picture industry. In contrast to the tough competition and private-sector funding of the television production industry, the Venezuelan motion picture industry has followed a different path. The history of filmmaking in Venezuela dates back to the early twentieth century, but it started without the benefit of a well-developed theater movement. For decades, leaders of the Venezuelan cinematic sector have believed that a movie industry could be created through government programs, regulations, and public funds. In the 1980s, they obtained generous public funding through Foncine, a cinematic institute funded primarily by the state.[55] They also won a decree that required the showing of Venezuelan films and imposed a tax on the revenues earned by movie houses to provide additional funds to Foncine. In 1993, Foncine still received funding, at reduced levels. In the early 1990s, only a few movies were produced in Venezuela per year. According to the movie distributors, the 13 Venezuelan-made movies shown at home between 1990 and

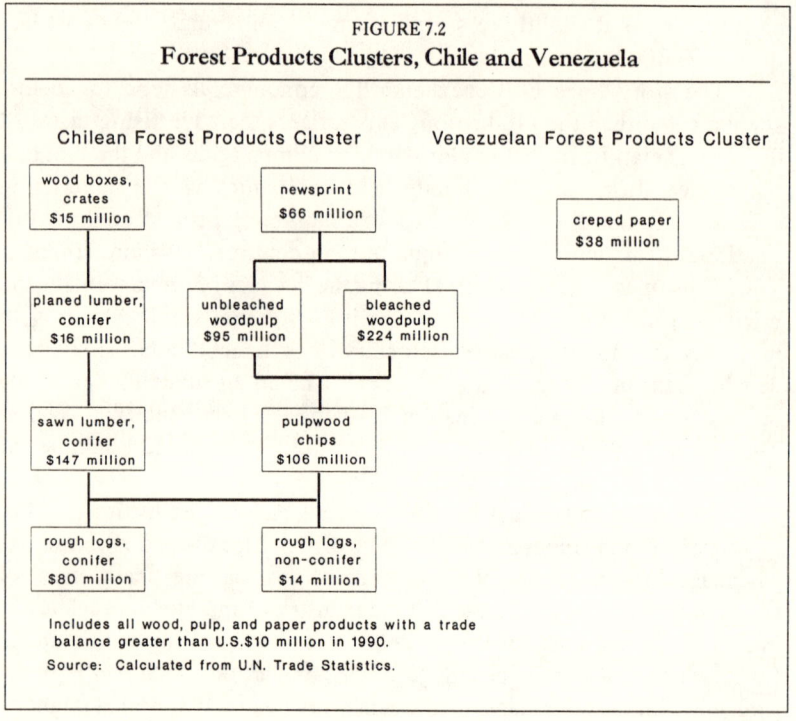

FIGURE 7.2
Forest Products Clusters, Chile and Venezuela

Includes all wood, pulp, and paper products with a trade balance greater than U.S.$10 million in 1990.
Source: Calculated from U.N. Trade Statistics.

1993 were commercial failures, although some were critically acclaimed.[56] The absence of a viable, self-sustaining motion picture industry may place long-run limits on the development of the Venezuelan entertainment cluster.

Other sectors of the performing and fine arts, in contrast, have been a source of talent and know-how for the commercial entertainment cluster. Venezuelan theater has developed strongly since the 1960s, due in part to an influx of exiled directors and producers from other South American countries. Painting and architecture are strong and have influenced the evolution of graphic and interior design, as well as fashion. (See Chapter 6.) Music is part of everyday life in Venezuela, and popular singers become national figures. Overall, the arts, and an appreciative public, provide a foundation for Venezuela's robust entertainment industry that has substantial export potential.

Pulp and Paper. The pulp and paper industry provides an example of how most industries in Venezuela currently lack the benefit of a cluster of related and supporting industries. As was discussed in Chapter 4, Venezuela possesses what are perhaps the most favorable conditions in the world for growing trees for conversion into pulp. However, an inadequate regulatory framework and years of state control of the nation's forest plantations have stymied the growth of forestry as a supporting industry. Most pulp and paper plants are located in the central area of the country, in Valencia, Maracay, and Morón. The industry is vertically integrated downstream into a diverse array of end products, including crepe (tissue) paper, packaging, and stationery.[57] While Venezuelan paper producers do produce some pulp in private plantations, they import a substantial percentage of their needs. As of 1993, all of the machinery and equipment used for logging and pulp and paper manufacturing was sourced abroad. The contribution of supporting industries at home has been limited to certain chemical products and the provision of civil construction and some engineering services.

Chile provides an instructive example for Venezuela. Chile has succeeded in international competition in a variety of forest products industries without having developed a strong position in machinery, equipment, and related technologies. As Figure 7.2 shows, Chile enjoys a substantial trade surplus in a number of forest products industries, including rough logs, pulpwood chips, pulp, paper, lumber, and lumber products. It has a substantial trade deficit in processing machinery and equipment. It is clearly importing technology to exploit its factor advantages in tree growing. As noted, Venezuela has a very limited export position in the sector at present. This should be viewed as an opportunity for the future, since there is no reason why Venezuela should not be able to match Chile's forest products cluster, given a stable macroeconomic environment and prudent public policy.

Although Chilean forest products, for example, have been successful with only a shallow cluster, the presence of a deeper cluster confers even stronger competitive advantage in world markets. The Swedish pulp and paper industry is a good example.[58] Sweden is a world leader in forest products, pulp, and paper. It also is a world leader in pulp and paper machinery and is competitive in soda recovery boilers, conveyor systems, wood handling machines, energy-saving equipment for pulp plants, chain saws, and some chemicals related to pulp and paper production. Sweden is renowned for its strengths in transportation (including specialty trucks for pulp and paper) and logistics. Proximity to these clusters is an important advantage for Swedish paper producers. (See Figure 7.3.)

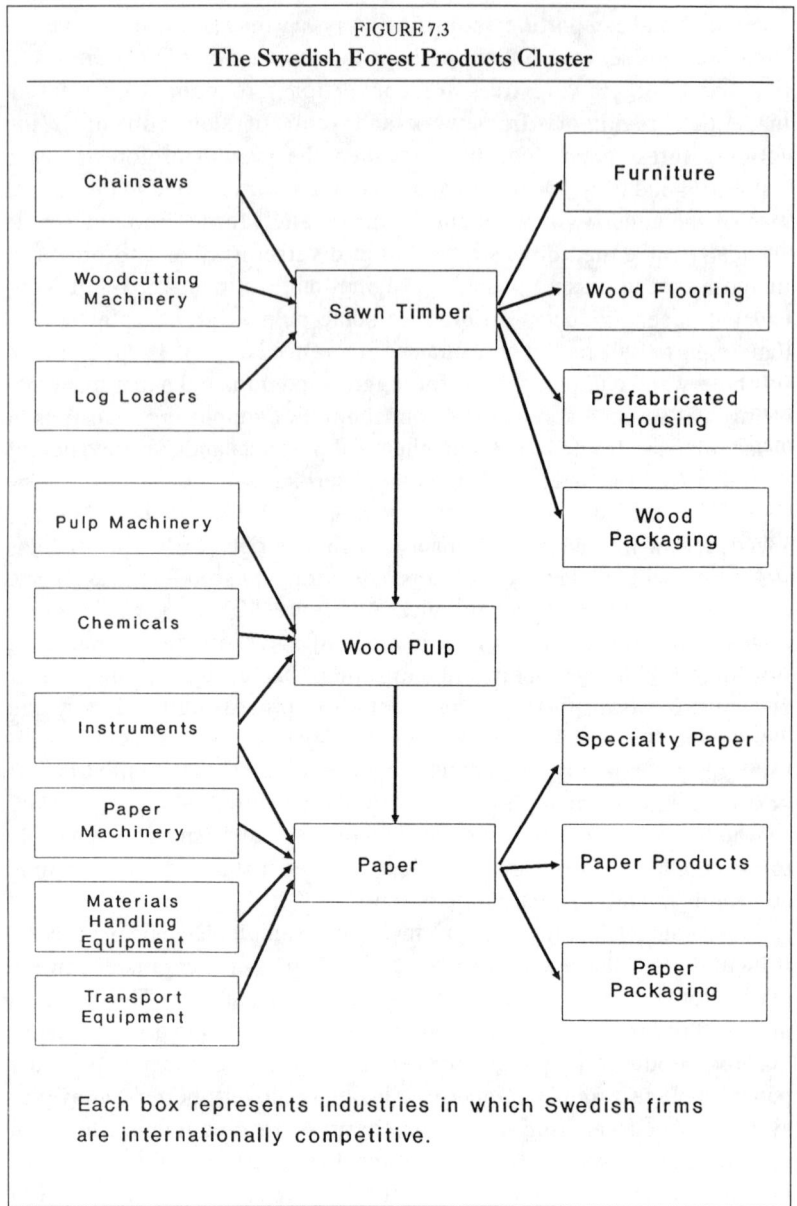

FIGURE 7.3
The Swedish Forest Products Cluster

Each box represents industries in which Swedish firms are internationally competitive.

Venezuelan Demand Conditions, Related Industries, and Supporting Industries in Context

This chapter has explored the demand conditions, related industries, supporting industries, and industrial clusters found in Venezuela. Again, it is useful to place the Venezuelan situation in the context of other developing nations. Clearly, there are many similarities between the Venezuelan situation and that found in a variety of developing nations.

Limited Demand Advantages

In most industries, Venezuelan demand conditions are unlikely to provide a competitive advantage in the global marketplace. In most cases, local demand sophistication lags behind developed countries, and the Venezuelan market can hardly be considered an incubator for highly refined goods and services. In only a few industries do we find Venezuelan demand that is on the cutting edge in international terms. Instead, in industry after industry, Venezuelan firms must make additional efforts and investments to bring their goods up to international standards in order to export.

In many industries, however, Venezuelan demand is more sophisticated than in other Latin American countries. Thus, Venezuelan demand could be an advantage in industries where competition is regional rather than global. In the past, trade restrictions within Latin America and the Caribbean made it difficult or impossible to translate regional demand advantages into exports. Nor will it be straightforward to do so in a more open trading environment. Many of the industries in which Venezuela might have more sophisticated demand than other nations in the region, such as autos and personal care products, are dominated by multinational companies with production sites throughout the region. The location and expansion decisions of these companies will depend on their long-term strategies and many aspects of the environment in addition to the sophistication of local demand. Furthermore, specific aspects of Venezuelan demand, such as language, culture, and local challenges, can be a source of advantage for firms exporting within the region, to nations with similar language and culture, and to other developing nations.

Venezuelan industrial demand is rather small and volatile in international terms. This lack of size and certainty impedes the development of local suppliers of capital goods and inputs with substantial development or lead times. Venezuela has a large and relatively sophisticated energy sector that has worked to develop the capabilities of local firms to compete in international markets. The energy sector, leading local companies, and local subsidiaries of multinational companies are the most likely to be sources of sophisticated demand that might help Venezuelan suppliers.

Potential for Venezuelan Clusters

At present, Venezuelan firms generally lack the support of vigorous, innovative, and responsive supplier industries. Outside the petroleum and entertainment sectors, there is little synergy among related industries or sharing of complementary pools of talent and expertise. The clusters that do exist tend to be relatively isolated and shallow. This is not surprising given the history of weak linkages between buyers and suppliers, high levels of vertical integration, and lack of market incentives in the Venezuelan economy. There is substantial potential for the Venezuelan economy to develop vibrant clusters in a number of areas.

In the days of import substitution, Venezuela's economic structure actively discouraged the formation of clusters in several ways. Clusters tend to develop through the interaction of buyers and suppliers in the marketplace. Suppliers and buyers learn to work together when forced to do so by competitive pressures. In the early 1990s, distortions that limited the potential for cluster development have been reduced. Potential clusters of export industries in tropical crops, pulp and paper, and communications are beginning to emerge. Changes that should improve the prospects for the development of competitive clusters in aluminum, steel, and petrochemicals are also beginning. It will perhaps take somewhat longer for Venezuelan firms to realize that local suppliers and buyers both can benefit from working together to improve productivity.

Unfavorable Demand Conditions in Developing Nations

Developing nations often are faced with domestic demand conditions that are less favorable than those found in developed nations. Demand in developing countries often is not very large or sophisticated in world terms. Even developing nations with large populations have relatively low per-capita incomes (by definition) and small economies when compared to the industrial countries. The relatively small volume of demand in developing nations means that such nations find it difficult to export large quantities to nations with similar demand conditions. The latter often lack the income levels to support substantial levels of imports, making it difficult for firms to use knowledge of local demand conditions to succeed in international markets. In developed nations, demand is generally more exacting than that found in developing nations. Thus, firms from the developed nations often have significant advantages in terms of their proximity to sophisticated demand. Nonetheless, many developing nations contain pockets of sophisticated demand. In addition, the segment structure and special characteristics of demand in some developing nations can prove to be an advantage for the nation's firms in exporting to other nations with similar demand characteristics.

The absence of large or sophisticated local demand is not a disadvantage for firms that compete in commodity markets. Commodity products tend to have well-defined characteristics and well-defined markets. The producer has little need even to have contact with the ultimate customer. Instead, traders and trading companies act as intermediaries to match supply with demand. The lack of sophisticated home demand, on the other hand, does make it difficult for developing nations to supply industrialized countries with products geared toward sophisticated demand. In order to compete successfully in such industries, firms from developing nations often need a window into the sophisticated demand found in industrialized nations. Without such a window, firms from developing nations find it difficult to move from exporting commodities to exporting processed goods, where knowledge of the specific characteristics of demand in industrialized nations is required. In a variety of industries and countries, foreign multinationals or distributors provide a window into demand in their home nations. The first exports of television sets from Asian countries to the United States, for example, relied on American companies to provide designs, insights into the marketplace, and distribution.

Lack of Industry Clusters in Developing Nations

Most developed nations have achieved international competitiveness in a range of industries. These nations are not competitive in isolated industries, but rather in clusters of industries related by vertical linkages (buyer and seller relationships) or horizontal relationships (common technologies, channels, or customer bases). Many developing nations, on the other hand, export in a relatively limited number of isolated industries. The absence of well-functioning markets makes it difficult for related and supporting industries to develop around the isolated pockets of success. Developing nations often lack the technological and marketing infrastructure and expertise to use natural resource advantages to compete in downstream industries. These nations usually import, rather than produce and export, the equipment and machinery necessary to process their natural resources. They also tend to import the equipment they use for low-wage manufacturing. In nations such as Germany and Switzerland, on the other hand, expertise in production machinery has been an important component of cluster development. This is not to say that developing nations should try to export capital goods; it just means that most developing nations do not have the same access to this source of growth of clusters as do developed nations. Alternatives to importing foreign technology, such as low-technology techniques developed in India, have generally not been successful. The absence of successful industry clusters in developing nations is of particular note given the importance of cluster formation to the process of economic development.

Limited Spillover of Local Technology and Skills

In the industrialized nations, industrial clusters tend to form around particular technologies that are developed and enhanced over time, or around particular pockets of world-class expertise. The nation in which a new technology is developed first often gains a significant "first-mover" advantage in related industries that can utilize the new technology. The growth of biotechnology and its application in pharmaceuticals, agroindustry, animal husbandry, medical testing, and related industries in the United States is a good example of the first phenomenon. The machinery industries of Germany and Switzerland, which draw advantage from the mechanical engineering skills present in those two nations, are examples of the second. Success of the nation's machinery and process equipment industries also brings benefits to industries that use the machinery and equipment. These industries often serve as test sites for new equipment and obtain new generations of machinery before firms in other nations. Since firms from developing nations do not in general develop new technologies, they are unlikely to develop unique technological skills that can be shared across industries. Since they lack advanced markets and international sales networks, they usually are unable to share channels or distribution across industries.

The Challenge of Competitiveness

Most developing nations are relatively disadvantaged in demand conditions, related industries, and supporting industries. One way to try to minimize these disadvantages is by seeking out leading edge buyers in foreign markets or by attracting foreign investment of sophisticated and demanding companies. Another way is for firms in such nations to focus their efforts in industries in which advanced demand or ongoing technological improvement are not vital to competitive success. Still another way is to create conditions that promote the development of local demand and positive relationships among firms in related and supporting industries.

Meeting the challenge of competitiveness in Venezuela will involve further developing and exploiting advantages that have been identified in local demand, related industries, and supporting industries. It will involve using capabilities developed in serving existing local demand that is either relatively large in size or relatively sophisticated to expand in both domestic and foreign markets. It also will involve a gradual increase in the sophistication of local demand. Venezuelan consumer demand will become more sophisticated if the economy is characterized by open competition and increased consumer choice. Venezuelan industrial demand will become more sophisticated if firms are forced by competitive pressures to become more careful and demanding purchasers.

Meeting the challenge of competitiveness in Venezuela will involve buyer and supplier relationships in which both parties recognize their common interests and in which both are under competitive pressures constantly to innovate and improve, rather than a situation in which buyers and suppliers are competing against each other for protectionist rents. It also will involve the expansion of industry clusters through market-mediated buyer and supplier relationships and the spillover of technology from Venezuela's leading firms. These issues will be taken up in chapters 11 and 12.

8

Firm Strategy, Structure, and Rivalry in Venezuela

The national environment influences a firm's choice of strategies and the way in which companies are organized and managed. It also shapes the goals of individuals and firms in ways that influence investment and productivity. In Venezuela, firm strategies have not, in general, fostered the improvement and efficiency that leads to competitiveness. An environment created by inward-looking development policies and government-sponsored industrialization led Venezuelan firms to focus on supplying a captive and relatively undemanding domestic market. The pressures to innovate and improve were largely absent. Many industries became highly concentrated. Many Venezuelan firms had no serious competitors in some, or even any, of their lines of business. Few firms adopted outward-looking strategies, such as exporting, or direct foreign investment.

One of the most important findings of the ten-nation study reported in Porter (1990) was the importance of domestic rivalry in stimulating firms to innovate and improve. World-class industries repeatedly exhibit rivalry that forces firms constantly to improve and to innovate. In Venezuela, prior to 1989, governmental policies dampened competition, particularly through price controls and barriers to entry. Competition did take place, but it was channeled to achieve control over strategic resources and distribution channels rather than toward improvements and innovations leading to higher quality and lower prices. The lack of rivalry does not appear to be an inherent trait of Venezuelan firms but rather a consequence of a system of incentives that muted or distorted market signals and often made collusion and imitation more profitable than competition and improvement.

The economic opening upon which Venezuela embarked in 1989 had a profound effect on the strategies and structures of its firms and on rivalry in its marketplace. For the first time, many Venezuelan firms found themselves competing on the basis of price and quality. They had to look to themselves rather than to government for sources of competitive advantage. Many firms were ill-prepared for the new environment. By early 1994, most Venezuelan firms seemed to be engaged in reactive survival strategies. Nevertheless, some firms were moving quickly to meet the challenges of a more competitive marketplace.

Strategy and Structure: Venezuelan Private-Sector Firms

Family-Owned Firms

Most Venezuelan firms, even the nation's largest firms, are privately owned and managed, often by members of one or a few families.[1] In many instances, the company's identity is that of its family ownership and leadership. This ownership structure has influenced the firms' goals and strategies. Many of the family-owned firms obtained financing through friendly banks rather than by issuing new stock. In some instances, this has been the result of valuing control over growth. The traditional mechanisms of management control and internal communications within the family-owned firms tended to be informal.[2] In many firms, authority and responsibility have been concentrated at the top, with management selection based more often on loyalty and family ties than on ability and training. The selection of suppliers, contractors, and partners often rested on considerations of kinship or loyalty rather than intrinsic quality or cost. Family ownership also made it more difficult for unrelated firms to achieve efficiencies through mergers or consolidations.

Government-Oriented Strategies

In the 1970s and 1980s, the strategies of Venezuelan firms reflected their protected and subsidized business environment. The country was largely closed to imports and foreign investment, and the state provided a wealth of incentives and subsidies, including soft loans, cheap foreign currency, and tax holidays. Effective government access was crucial because of the state's pervasive controls on business. Permits were required to open a plant or produce a new model in certain industries.[3] The government controlled the price and supply of many important inputs and in many cases determined the price at which a firm's output could be sold. For example, firms in the same sector often paid different prices for an identical import, or received different import quotas for the same product, different rates on loans, or different sums of subsidized foreign exchange.[4] Since the decisions of ministries and agencies often varied by company, it was essential to try to get the best terms.

In this environment, the differences between the market shares and profitability of Venezuelan firms often depended on the skills and connections of their lobbyists.[5] As a result, many firms centralized power and authority in designated senior executives with the best ties to decision makers. Because business conditions could change at the whim of a politician or bureaucrat, most firms focused on short-term strategies. Many were, in essence, improvisors,[6] firms that were skilled at responding to political changes and to new opportunities offered by state policies but were less skilled at identifying and pursuing market opportunities independent of government policy.

Lack of Pressures for Competitiveness

The lack of competition from domestic or foreign sources meant that Venezuelan firms had little incentive to improve efficiency, products, or workforce. Efficiency was not a major concern in an environment in which cost increases, no matter what the cause, were justifications for negotiated price increases. Because the customer often had no alternative, pleasing him or her with new products, with high quality, with timely delivery, or with lower prices was not a major concern. As a result, most Venezuelan firms had little understanding of markets, technology, or cost efficiency. The debates and discussions about industrial competitiveness that went on in North America, Asia, and Europe in the late 1970s and early 1980s were simply not part of the Venezuelan scene.

In the 1980s, Venezuelan firms invested relatively little in developing or adopting new technology.[7] As Viana (1993) has found, "the 'technological behavior' of a firm may be seen as a series of responses to stimuli coming from its environment. In general, it may be said that protectionist policies reduced the stimuli that would give rise to technical change, due to the creation of a non-competitive environment and excess capacity."[8] During the 1980s, Venezuelan firms tended to import technology already incorporated into capital goods but neglected to invest in the creation of the know-how and skills needed to use and to assimilate the imported technology effectively. For example, in 1985, Venezuela's imports of capital goods were equal to 17 percent of GDP, a high percentage that, given statistics on industrial performance at the time, suggests that "these investments in new technologies were not assimilated adequately."[9] In the highly protected market of the 1980s, the combination of state intervention in the marketplace and protectionism meant that "the Venezuelan manufacturing industry never had to place a value on producing better."[10]

Venezuelan firms also tended to make minimal investments in training and personnel management. Granell and Parra (1993) found that firms that are not subject to competitive pressures "do not perceive their human resources as indispensable elements for increasing productivity and the quality of products manufactured," and therefore do not concern themselves with improving the skills and knowledge of their workers.[11] At the same time, outdated technologies tend not to require workers with specialized knowledge and skills, which further discourages investments in training.

Venezuelan firms focused on the domestic market during the 1970s and 1980s. Between 1980 and 1990, the average annual growth rate of Venezuelan exports was only 1.8 percent, far lower than those of South Korea (12.8 percent), Colombia (10.6 percent), Chile (4.8 percent), Brazil (4 percent), and Mexico (3.4 percent).[12] An overvalued currency made it very difficult for Venezuelan firms to compete in world markets. In addition, protection and monopoly or oligopoly rents made the domestic market immensely profitable for firms with the right skills and connections. In most cases, export businesses were complements to domestic operations rather than the mainstay of corporate strategy. There were, of course, some exceptions. Química Venoco (petrochemicals), Sural (aluminum wire), and Grupo CNV (Constructora Nacional de Válvulas) (cast steel and valves) were all export-oriented.[13]

Under the import substitution regime, many Venezuelan businesses tended to take large profits for granted. There was a low level of reinvestment, and by the 1980s, many large Venezuelan firms were undercapitalized.[14] When the crisis in confidence over economic and social stability arose in the 1980s, private fortunes were reinvested abroad, depriving local firms of equity capital. Instead, many large companies took advantage of negative real interest rates to amass substantial debts.

Excess Diversification and Vertical Integration

In the 1970s and 1980s, many of Venezuela's leading firms became highly diversified. In an economy in which an overvalued currency and the protectionist policies of neighboring nations made exporting difficult, the natural outlet for growth of Venezuelan firms was through diversification in the home market. In addition, abundant opportunities under import substitution policies promoted rapid and broad diversification.[15] In Venezuela, conglomerates were able to take advantage of the exclusion of imports and foreign investment as well as the government's policies of promoting domestic private investment. Soft loans, tax holidays, and exemptions from import duties made it relatively easy for firms with managerial skills and political connections to enter one industry after another, leading to a proliferation of conglomerates, both large and small.[16] Diversification also allowed firms to limit exposure in any one industry and to take advantage of new promotion schemes, since existing firms often were given preferential access to new government development schemes.

In an uncertain environment, many Venezuelan firms sought to protect themselves through both backward and forward integration.[17] In many industries, firms backward-integrated in order to gain access to imported inputs. Food product companies sometimes had to backward-integrate into farming to ensure supplies and import quotas, for example. In addition, dependence on a few suppliers in a closed and protected market frequently led to defensive backward integration. Beer and soft drink bottling companies, for example, invested in bottle and can manufacturing. The absence of well-functioning markets in general and the lack of enforcement of contracts in the legal system also promoted backward integration. Similarly, Venezuelan firms forward-integrated into distribution to make sure that their products were distributed properly and so that they could exercise market power in distribution (or prevent others from exercising such power against them).

In some industries, the closed market and its unique set of dynamics induced businesses to diversify into product areas where the domestic market was too small to support scale-efficient plants. One result, in such sectors as petrochemicals and textiles, was inefficiency.[18] Another was diversification by firms before they reached organizational and management maturity.[19]

Responses to the Economic Opening

The economic opening took important steps toward correcting the distortions that had influenced firm strategy in Venezuela. The state eliminated cheap dollars and many producer subsidies. It freed exchange rates, interest rates, and most prices. It largely got out of the business of granting favors, such as import or manufacturers' licenses. It also lowered barriers to imports, which created competition for many Venezuelan firms.

Most firms were surprised by the market's opening. Even those that thought it might happen were not truly prepared for the speed and extent of the changes.[20] Many Venezuelan industries and firms never before had been expected to compete with foreign goods. Firms that thought their letters of credit would be guaranteed by the government were hit particularly hard when the new government decided that they would not be honored. Although the wave of bankruptcies that some predicted did not occur, many Venezuelan firms found themselves in financial difficulties. Short-term survival was the first objective for many firms, profit was a distant second, and long-term competitiveness was farther down the list. This fact was in large part responsible for the decrease in investment in technology and in human resource development by many firms in the years immediately following the economic opening.

Ways of thinking about and doing business do not change across an entire economy overnight, in Venezuela or anywhere else. By 1994, many of the features of the closed Venezuelan economy remained, including family ownership, diversified firms, highly concentrated industries, and a heavy presence of state-owned companies. Many Venezuelan firms had not moved beyond survival strategies. Other firms, however, were more proactive. They looked at the brave new world, looked at themselves, and found new ways to address the challenges and opportunities present in the newly opened marketplace.

Reactive Strategies and Short-Term Thinking

Venezuelan firms still tend to adopt reactive strategies, adapting in response to changes in the national and international environment rather than trying to forge ahead to anticipate and to shape their future through investments. Venezuelan firms in general suffer from a lack of strategic thinking. In the Viana survey, 44 percent of the Venezuelan manufacturing firms surveyed reported that they did not have business strategies.[21] Granell and Parra (1993) have found a lack of strategic thinking in the personnel management and personnel planning practices of many Venezuelan firms.

For the most part, Venezuelan firms still suffer from an excessive short-term orientation in their business strategies. Many managers who were interviewed for this project claimed that the conditions for long-term planning and investment programs still do not exist in the nation. The macroeconomic and political uncertainties of the early 1990s have made many firms reluctant to plan and to invest. In addition, Venezuelan firms in general seem to wait until the very last moment before accepting that change is occurring. Perhaps they hope that someone or something will help them out of their difficulties. Government protection of domestic firms has been taken for granted for a long time in Venezuela.

In the Viana survey, 35 percent of the Venezuelan manufacturing firms surveyed did not know the market share of their largest competitor.[22] Viana also found that most Venezuelan firms invest little, or not at all, in employee training, expecting workers to learn by example. Most firms give little thought to their acquisition of technology, buying from catalogs and neglecting to build up an institutional memory of technical adaptations. In the early 1990s, more Venezuelan firms reduced rather than increased expenditures on training and technology development. Many firms invested in improving quality and cutting costs, but relatively few developed formal marketing programs. Only about one-quarter of Venezuelan firms engage in systematic market research. One manager of a foreign-owned firm in Venezuela said, "Venezuelan firms are investing in TQM, but what they really need to learn is marketing."[23]

New Strategies for an Open Environment

While many Venezuelan firms found it difficult to change their ways or to move proactively into the future, others moved aggressively to compete in the newly opened marketplace. During the early 1990s, these firms cut costs, improved product quality and marketing, rationalized activities, and found new sources of capital. They developed a new focus on efficiency and cost reduction. Because prices were set in market competition, Venezuelan firms found it imperative to control their costs as they never had before. Many firms improved their efficiency by restructuring their operations and reducing administrative overhead. Many firms adopted Total Quality programs to improve their efficiency and quality. Some firms stepped up their efforts to develop new products and placed greater emphasis on marketing and distribution to serve their customers better.

In the closed market of the 1970s and 1980s, diversifying and integrating vertically often made good business sense. After the opening, firms reconsidered and exited certain product areas. In 1993, several firms were exiting businesses that they entered in order to have access to inputs and to import quotas. Other firms were focusing their efforts on a few core businesses, preferring to specialize and to grow in international markets rather than to continue diversification in the domestic market. Corimon, for example, which was active in seven different lines of business—paints, chemicals, petrochemicals, packaging and graphic arts, processed foods, construction materials, and distribution—was considering "getting back to basics."[24]

Competitive forces also pressured firms to find new ways of raising capital. Madosa issued stock in a public offering on the Caracas Stock Exchange, paving the way for others to do the same. In 1990, Corimon and Sivensa successfully placed dollar-denominated notes outside Venezuela. Other firms soon followed suit. In 1991, Sivensa, Corporación Cerámicas

Carabobo, and Corimon placed shares (American Depository Receipts) in the United States. In 1992, Sivensa, Corimon, and Venepal issued Global Depository Receipts (GDRs). These financial strategies would have been "almost unthinkable" in the 1980s.[25]

New International Strategies

Most Venezuelan firms remain focused on the domestic market. In the Viana survey, 37 percent of the manufacturing firms surveyed reported selling in "regional" markets, but only 2 percent (mostly large firms) reported selling in "international" markets. The firms identified their three principal marketing objectives, prior to 1988, as increasing market share in existing domestic markets, developing new products, and entering new domestic markets. They also indicated that since 1988 (and the economic opening), these principal objectives had not changed. Only a small percentage had as an objective to increase their market share in existing or new international markets.[26]

There were, however, major changes in the export strategies of some Venezuelan firms. Before the economic opening, exporting was often a way to dispose of "excess" products that could not be sold on the home market. Only a few firms actively pursued export markets in order to grow and to become stronger competitors. In the early 1990s, the market opening and exchange rates that were closer to market rates stimulated firms to identify and to seek out foreign markets and to identify new business opportunities at home. Venezuelan firms were forced to improve and to innovate in order to succeed in export markets.

Many Venezuelan firms have entered the Colombian market, and many no longer consider Colombia to be a "foreign" market.[27] One strategy is exports, in products such as aluminum, steel, chemicals, minerals, autos, rice, paper, and processed foods. There are more complex strategies as well. In 1993, sugar was being imported into Venezuela from Colombia, refined and reexported, to take advantage of Venezuela's superior refining capacity. All of the Colombian banks privatized in 1992 were purchased by Venezuelan financial institutions.[28] In products such as paper, Venezuelan firms are forming partnerships with Colombian firms in order to strengthen their market positions in both countries. Even firms that have been fighting for protection, such as some auto parts makers, are willing to expand the home market to include the Andean Pact. Moreover, according to a former vice minister of the ministry of development, trade between Venezuela and Colombia is exposing both sides to new business skills and techniques. Venezuelans are already learning from the Colombians' ways of doing business, and they also are introducing methods that Colombians did not know in areas such as marketing and design.[29]

Some Venezuelan firms have expanded their positions through foreign investment. Empresas Polar has acquired food processing firms in Colombia, Ecuador, Peru, Jamaica, Guatemala, Honduras, and Panama. Although production tends to be undertaken on a nation-by-nation basis, some administrative functions are being centralized in Venezuela. The ODC Group has been active outside of Venezuela since the 1970s. Its main foreign activities have been in beverages, supermarkets, department stores, entertainment, consumer goods, and real estate. Corimon has expanded its foreign holdings in the paint industry. Other Venezuelan firms have invested abroad, primarily in Colombia, for the first time.

Firm Examples

The following are only a few examples of Venezuelan firms that responded quickly and decisively to the economic opening.

Alfonzo Rivas & Cia. In 1988, the agroindustrial firm Alfonzo Rivas & Cia. foresaw that the Venezuelan market would open and that the firm soon would find itself in a competitive environment.[30] The firm hired consultants, reviewed its strengths and weaknesses, identified new opportunities, and began to restructure. Alfonzo Rivas made changes in every area of its activities. It decided to expand its focus from agroindustrial inputs to inputs and consumer products. In just a few years, the firm introduced over 50 new consumer products, some developed in-house, others imported. It decentralized publicity and marketing, boosted spending on commercials and supermarket promotions, improved the effectiveness of its distribution system, made major investments in capital goods, and instituted statistical process controls. In 1988, inputs for the food, pharmaceutical, chemical, and textile and other industries accounted for 80 percent of the company's production. By 1993, it had developed a healthy and diversified consumer products division that accounted for 50 percent of its total capacity.[31] It also had boosted exports, particularly to regional markets.

Chocolates El Rey. At the time the economic opening was announced, management at Chocolates El Rey decided that changing events required them to redefine the company's mission.[32] Since then, the firm has changed practically every aspect of its business. It has integrated vertically into cocoa production. In 1993, Chocolates El Rey was trying to stimulate new production areas within Venezuela in order to generate a continuous supply of high-quality cocoa beans. It was working to create its own specialty cocoa niche in foreign markets, had designed a new factory, and was in the process of upgrading its technology to world standards. The company also made considerable efforts to change the attitude of the workforce through a total quality program and a company code of ethics, and had transformed its administrative systems.[33]

Madosa. In the 1980s, Madosa had what it believed to be a secure position in the high end of the domestic market for consumer appliances.[34] The market opening in 1989 brought a sudden shock as imports from the United States quickly became formidable competitors. Madosa responded by challenging its engineers and workers to meet the cost and quality of U.S. goods sold in Venezuela. The company also set out to compete on design, studying and copying the best ideas worldwide and finding ways to take advantage of particular conditions found in Venezuela that do not exist in the United States. Madosa developed motors tolerant to a wide range of voltages, downsized appliances to suit local requirements, and developed a purification system to ensure the purity of ice water in home refrigerators. In order to improve its balance sheet, Madosa issued stock on the Caracas Stock Exchange, something many observers thought would be impossible. In 1993, the company planned to export its appliances throughout the Caribbean and to set up production in Colombia and Ecuador.

Mavesa. Mavesa responded to the economic opening by cutting costs, rethinking its vertical integration, and expanding its geographic scope.[35] In 1993, the company was investing in new plants and upgraded equipment. Mavesa also was focusing its promotional efforts more directly at the final consumer, including advertising to increase brand recognition, and was working to boost the sophistication of its promotions. Mavesa exited some businesses, such as animal feed and edible oils, and was searching for new market niches in others.[36] Since 1988, Mavesa has identified and invested in new startups oriented toward export markets involving new products such as shrimp and dehydrated egg yolks.[37] The firm also has begun to penetrate the Colombian market.

Sivensa. After the market opening, Sivensa's steelmaking division (Sidetur) reorganized its operations. The number of employees in its divisional office was reduced from 220 to 70, with many moving to strategic business units. Overheads have been reduced substantially, financial information and control systems have been improved, and compensation systems have been changed to reflect individual and unit performance.[38] Since 1989, Sidaven, a manufacturer of auto parts, has altered its production processes to meet the requirements of its new foreign customers. Since becoming an exporter, Sidaven has been immersed in a continual process of acquiring equipment, adapting technology, and training workers.[39] Sivensa also has accessed foreign markets for capital, placing dollar-denominated notes outside Venezuela starting in 1990 and issuing American Depository Receipts (in 1991) and Global Depository Receipts (in 1992).

Strategy and Structure: The State-Owned Companies

Multiple Goals

Prior to the economic reforms, most state-owned firms had multiple, even conflicting, goals. They were supposed to develop industries, to provide employment, to foster regional and industrial development, and to provide services to local communities.[40] PDVSA, in addition to providing the vast majority of government income, became a major source of technical and scientific training. The CVG, in addition to operating a number of industrial companies, also served as the economic development agency and provided many social services in Bolívar state. The goals just mentioned were the official goals of the state-owned enterprises. Unofficial goals often included funding political campaigns and providing patronage jobs. During the Lusinchi administration, state-owned enterprises were ordered to increase employment by 10 percent, at a time when many enterprises were already overmanned. These conflicting goals and pressures are in part responsible for the unsatisfactory performance of most state-owned firms in Venezuela.

Patronage and Poor Results

Some state-owned firms seemed to be run more for patronage than to provide goods or services. Under state control, CANTV was notorious for its lack of quality service. Top management personnel, almost all political friends of the government, were rotated frequently. By the early 1990s, more than 75 percent of the company's workforce consisted of managers or administrative staff.[41] The Ports Administration had a similarly poor reputation for service. The unions in the ports were able to ensure payment, whether the workers actually did their jobs or not. State-owned firms other than PDVSA rarely generated profits, although in the aluminum industry Venalum did generate positive results until international aluminum prices fell and export subsidies were eliminated. Generally, state-owned firms regarded themselves as successful if they managed to generate a positive cash flow. State-owned firms almost never presented their results as return on invested capital.[42]

The state-owned firms often deeply influenced the strategies of private firms active in the same area of business, but in a way that discouraged rather than promoted efficiency and improvement. When the state set the price of a product produced by the public and private sectors, it based the price on the cost structure of the state-owned firm. This produced a windfall for the private firms, which tended to have significantly lower costs.[43]

Weak Control Structures

The control structure of many state-owned firms had serious weaknesses. These firms often lacked concerned shareholders. The boards of directors tended to change with each change in government, and sometimes even with a change in ministers. With the exception of PDVSA and the CVG, in many cases directors held part-time posts and relied excessively on results provided by the firm's president. According to Kelly and González (1993), in some cases their objective was to ensure the survival of the firms and maintenance of operations, rather than optimizing firm performance.[44] The policies and strategies of state-owned companies also have been the constant subject of congressional "oversight," which has limited the ability of these companies to plan and to carry out long-term strategies.[45]

Privatization and Restructuring

The economic reform program brought with it plans for the privatization of many state-owned enterprises. Whereas a number of obstacles have been put in the path of privatization, for the companies that have been sold, privatization has brought profound changes in strategy and structure. The leading example is CANTV, which has been restructured and set on a path of ambitious growth. After the new management took over in December 1991, CANTV cut out inefficiencies, boosted employee productivity, and made significant improvements in service. In 1993, it was in the process of changing from a passive public enterprise into an active company that would market products and services. CANTV was working to cut administrative staff and to replace old employee attitudes with a proactive approach to helping the customer. In 1992, GTE and other shareholders invested $510 million in service and network improvements and expansion. The total investment for 1993 was estimated at an additional $650 million.[46]

Reforming the CVG

In the early 1990s, the CVG leadership assumed the formidable challenge of transforming the conglomerate into a financially viable business. This task entailed redefining corporate and business strategies at every level and in every business activity. In 1993, management was asking hard questions about the purpose and prospects of each CVG company, what its capital needs were, and where the capital must come from. Most of the CVG's subsidiaries in aluminum and aluminum inputs were being restructured into a single company, and more foreign capital was being sought. Negotiations over rights to forests and mining concessions were expected to become more transparent than they had been in the past.

Sidor has implemented strategies to boost efficiency and cut costs. In 1993, the company took steps to transfer to the private sector no less than 100 different services formerly performed in-house, such as transportation, maintenance, industrial, personnel, financial and administrative services, which in turn was expected to stimulate private-sector growth.[47] In 1993, the new head of CVG (who was himself replaced in early 1994) hoped that the CVG would become more of an investment promotion and regional development agency and less of an operating company.[48]

Political Constraints

Despite these changes, the ability of the state-owned firms to define and to pursue business strategies is still handicapped in several respects. The single greatest constraint has historically been the Venezuelan Congress and parliamentary debate. Some in Congress have seemed to have little understanding of the benefits of economic or private-sector growth. Some have little understanding of business and why certain basic strategies are essential to the performance of firms in which the state has ownership interests. Congressional "oversight" has hindered the Venezuelan Investment Fund from making share offerings abroad.[49] It converts straightforward decisions, such as PDVSA's contracting out the reactivation of marginal fields, into drawn-out political struggles, and it remains an obstacle to much-needed privatization.

In some instances, there is also resistance to change at the directorate level. The quasi-familial ties among state firms in different related and supporting industries sometimes leads to practices that damage the competitiveness of Venezuelan industry. These quasi-familial ties facilitate the survival of inefficient firms, whose flaws can be hidden behind accounting mechanisms.[50] The use of transfer pricing to cover up deficiencies in financial performance can lead to the poor distribution of investment resources.

Strategy and Structure: Multinational Firms in Venezuela

Multinational firms, particularly those from the United States, played an important role in Venezuela's industrialization in the 1950s and 1960s, but these activities were sharply curtailed when Venezuela joined the Andean Pact in 1973. In 1989, the economic opening swept away many of the restrictions on foreign investment dating from the 1970s, and the macroeconomic reforms set the bolivar at more realistic values. The Andean Pact Free Trade Area opened up new opportunities for regional trade. These forces combined to increase the attractiveness of Venezuela as a site for production and sales operations of multinational companies in the period from 1990 to 1992. During this time, there was relatively little disinvestment and plenty of new investment. Political and economic uncertainties and difficulties limited foreign investment in 1993 and the first part of 1994.

Worldwide, foreign direct investment (FDI) tends to fall into three types: "factor sourcing" investments, which seek access to basic factors, such as cheap labor or abundant natural resources; those oriented toward market access (national or regional); and those that are designed to take advantage of higher-level competitive advantages found in the host country by establishing a home base there. Each of these types of FDI tends to reflect a different mix of competitive advantages between the host country and the home country of the multinational firm. (See Chapter 3.) While foreign investment of all types generally promotes economic growth, it is the third category, investment based on local competitive advantage, that generates the greatest benefits to the local economy.

Factor sourcing investments seek access to natural resources or other basic factors. In the early 1990s, investment of this kind was occurring in Venezuela in the pulp and paper, petrochemical, petroleum, and mining sectors.[51] In 1993, Louisiana Pacific and Stone Container were making large new investments in forest products, for export. Smurfit was spending about $80 million to expand its paper-making capacity and another $20 million on its forest plantation program, to address both Venezuelan and export markets.[52] In petrochemicals, the economic reforms induced foreign companies to invest heavily in new projects. As the president of Mitsubishi Venezolana, C.A. explained, "We've had a presence in Venezuela since 1964, but it wasn't until 1988, when Venezuela's economy began to open up, that we began to invest heavily here."[53] Since then, Mitsubishi Corporation and Mitsubishi Gas Chemical Corporation have invested in the Metanol de Oriente (Metor) Project. Mitsubishi also has invested in the Cristóbal Colón project. Other foreign partners in local petrochemical projects include Atochem (France), Combustion Engineering (USA), Dow Chemical (USA), DSM (Netherlands), Ecofuel (Italy), Ecopetrol (Colombia), Foret (Spain), Instituto de Fomento Industrial (Colombia), Olin Corporation (USA), Mitsui Petrochemical (Japan), Repsol Derivados (Spain), and Shell Chemical (Netherlands).[54]

Market access investments occur when firms establish a presence in a country in order to get access to its domestic market or to a protected regional market. In the early 1990s, new investments of this type were taking place in the Venezuelan beverage and automotive assembly sectors. In beverages, several multinational companies, such as Prestige Beverage, Universal Breweries, and Guinness Distillers, have acquired equity holdings in local firms. Although some of these multinational companies planned to export Venezuelan products, in most cases, the investments were aimed at using local firms and their distribution networks to place products, such as whiskeys, in the domestic market.[55] Chrysler and other automakers invested in their Venezuelan assembly operations with an eye toward the Colombian and Ecuadorian markets. Chrysler, for example, started exporting to Colombia in the fourth quarter of 1992.[56]

Home-base investments occur when multinational firms set up regional or general headquarters in the host nation for specific product lines or business units, not because of preferential market access but rather because of the existence of competitive advantages in the host country. Often this type of investment involves sophisticated production and capabilities in the host country. Foreign investments of this nature are not common in Venezuela. Nevertheless, Adolfo Taylhardat (1993), in his study of foreign investment and competitiveness in Venezuela, identified several examples that suggest that, in 1993, certain international firms were looking to Venezuela as a regional production center.[57] Procter & Gamble, which has its Latin American headquarters in Caracas, was in the process of establishing a Latin American Research and Development Center. This R&D center, also to be located in Caracas, was planned to develop products to meet the needs of consumers throughout Latin America.[58] Warner-Lambert was expanding its production facilities of Schick Interamericana and planned to use these Venezuelan production operations as a base of supply for markets in Chile, Peru, Ecuador, and Mexico as well as the Russian republics and Eastern Europe.[59] Warner-Lambert estimated its 1993 exports at $30 million.[60]

The presence of multinational firms in Venezuela has been the source of positive spillover effects for local companies. Foreign investment will be necessary to support the growth of industries such as steel and petrochemicals in the short and long term. Foreign joint venture partners also are often a source of advanced technology and foreign market access.[61] In addition, Granell and Parra (1993) have found positive spillover effects from the local operations of multinational companies in the area of worker education and training. In their words:

> Multinational firms installed in Venezuela—such as Ford—that adhere to Total Quality Principles demand from [their] supplier firms high levels of product quality and, in particular, the application of statistical process controls. Initially, this requirement requires workers to be trained in statistical tools. But, due to the educational deficiencies present in the workers, the training activities have to be extended further and have to cover more basic training needs.
>
> When the foreign firms ally with the national firms, they can transfer to the latter their vision of the business, work systems, elements of organizational culture and their concept of human resources. If they possess structured training programs, in general, they send managers and professional technicians to perfect themselves in their training centers, who, in their turn, become facilitators and multipliers of this educational experience in the national plants. This is illustrated by the success of programs such as inventory control and excellence in manufacturing implanted in some of the firms of the metal mechanics sector (Gates and Ejeven of Sivensa), following the model of Dana University.[62]

Strategy and Structure: Business Chambers and Industry Associations

Venezuelan business and industry associations have played an important role in representing business in negotiations with government and labor. For decades, Venezuelan industry associations served as intermediaries, or brokers, between the government and private firms in the all-important business of government regulation.[63] During the import substitution decades, many hundreds of business federations, associations, and councils were formed, ranging from sector-specific associations to national umbrella organizations. Fedecámaras, the Federation of Chambers of Commerce and Production, founded in 1944, was recognized as the representative of business in all laws that formally establish business and labor participation in policy formulation or decision making. Other major business umbrella organizations include

Conindustria for manufacturing firms, Fedeindustria for small industrial firms, and the Asociación Bancaria for banks.

Prior to the economic opening, business chambers played a major role in setting prices, controlling entry to industries, controlling import licenses, and pushing special protections into law.[64] Government intervention promoted the formation of cartels in order to facilitate bureaucratic decision making. Industry councils, which included representatives of industry associations, controlled entry and imports in many industries. Thus, existing companies had a large say over whether they would have to compete with additional firms or imports. At the height of government price fixing (1986-1989), they provided the government with cost structures agreed to by their members and negotiated profit margins on thousands of products with controlled prices. Allocation of currency under the differential exchange rate system, in place for much of the decade, also took place ostensibly through industry associations.

The economic opening removed many of the traditional contexts for chamber action. Reduced government intervention in the economy eliminated the need for concerted action. When the government stopped setting prices, granting import and manufacturers' licenses, and allocating quotas, credits, and foreign exchange, the associations lost much of their power as intermediaries and lobbyists. The reaction to these changes was mixed. Some traditional groups represented firms that were not happy with the new rules of the game. In the early 1990s, these groups were lobbying vigorously for a return to the past. For example, national associations of agricultural producers pressured the government to return to the old ways of setting prices.[65] Other groups, such as the pharmacists' association, lobbied to uphold old laws and regulations that restricted competition or guaranteed monopolies.

In contrast, other chambers and associations redefined their mission. Conindustria, for example, changed its focus following the economic opening.[66] In the 1980s, its primary purpose was lobbying. Members used to attend its functions to put in a word with prominent public officials. In the early 1990s, Conindustria offered symposia on such topics as total quality management in order to educate all industries about what firms must do to compete in open markets.

The focus of the chamber of the Venezuelan petrochemicals industry, ASOQUIM, also changed. Under the old regime, ASOQUIM largely occupied itself with lobbying for government favors, such as exemptions and permits. By the early 1990s, the chamber's mission was to enhance the competitiveness of the national petrochemical industry. Toward this end, ASOQUIM was creating a data base with information on foreign trade and other statistics intended to enhance the industry's knowledge of foreign markets. It was working to strengthen chemical education within Venezuela to meet the industry's needs, through the Vicente Marcano Institute.[67] It held courses to keep managers up to date, primarily in areas related to management and productivity improvements. It participated in conferences overseas and sponsored conferences at home. ASOQUIM's second congress in 1991 brought together industry participants and experts from around the world to discuss competitiveness. Topics included human resource development, total quality management, and the drivers of competitiveness in the industry. ASOQUIM also has been active in trying to ensure long-term supplies of key inputs and adequate infrastructure for the industry. Fifty-five members of ASOQUIM have adopted the *Responsabilidad Integral* program for environmental responsibility, which sets forth a series of environmental protection practices and guidelines for the chemical industry.[68]

In agribusiness, the Venezuelan Association of Industrial Millers (Asotrigo) has taken the lead role in designing and managing a new regional training center for Latin America (La Escuela Latinoamericana de Molinería), under construction in 1993 in the industrial zone of Puerto Cabello. The program was financed by the industries of the 11 member countries of the Latin American Association of the Milling Industry (ALIM) and also had the support of U.S. Wheat Associates. Course instruction would be provided by experienced workers who would complete courses on instruction techniques in coordination with the University of Kansas in the United States. As Granell and Parra (1993) have observed, a regional training center for Latin America would offer its participating industries several advantages, including lower costs, geographic proximity, a shared language, and commonality of identity and concerns.

In the rice sector, there has been a shortage of technical personnel. No school in Venezuela graduates workers with the skills necessary to work in modern rice plantations. The Association of Certified Seed Producers of the Central Western Plains (APROSCELLO) has carried out a wide range of activities directed at improving the productivity of local rice farms, including R&D, training, technical assistance, and financing programs. APROSCELLO's efforts, which received the backing of the International Center for Tropical Agriculture, have helped to boost the technological level of rice cultivation in the country.[69]

Competition and Rivalry

Local rivalry has been found to be an important stimulus to improvement and innovation among a nation's firms. (See Chapter 3.) The nature of competition and rivalry in Venezuela has undergone a number of changes during the early 1990s. Changes in policies and laws dealing with local rivalry have promoted change in a number of Venezuelan industries.

The 1970s and 1980s: Limited Competition

While the Venezuelan market was closed, there was relatively little rivalry on price, quality, or service in the economy. In most industries, firms negotiated retail prices (price to the public, or PVP) with the ministry of development. To do this, the firms got together and shared information on their costs. As was to be expected, the price presented to the ministry of development often was based on the cost structure of the least efficient firm. In the case of many consumer goods, the producers marked the final resale price on the product itself; in other cases, they published lists of identical prices, good for identical time periods, for many industrial goods and services. Then the producers and retailers negotiated distribution margins, which were typically on the order of 60 percent of PVP, 30 percent for the wholesaler and 30 percent for the retailer.[70] In many industries, firms divided up the market, either on their own or at the prompting of government. In the steel industry, Sidor held a de facto, though not de jure, monopoly in some product segments and shared others with Sivensa. In steel reinforcing bar, for example, Sivensa focused on small rebars, Sidor on longer ones.[71] Alcasa and Venalum, both under the guidance of the CVG, divided aluminum markets by product and geography to avoid competition.[72]

Rivalry for Oligopoly Rents and Governmental Favors

Behind industry agreements, often rivalry existed between firms of similar size competing for oligopoly rents. Firms were affected to a much greater degree by the decisions of other firms than by consumer choice. As a result, they focused their rivalry on outdoing other firms instead of serving consumers.[73] Firms competed with each other for government favors, scarce supplies, preferred locations, distribution channels, and customers. From time to time, all-out confrontations in some industries, including soft drinks, mayonnaise, and cigarettes, resulted in substantial changes in the market position of the major firms.[74] Rivalry also was motivated by personal feuds and dislikes, which served no constructive business purpose and tarnished the reputation of the private sector as a whole. This form of competition often did not benefit the general public because as a rule it did not translate into better products, wider selections, or lower prices. It was competition over who was going to get the monopoly or oligopoly rents, rather than competition that would reduce the rents to benefit the consumer. This type of rivalry did not generate pressures for firms to innovate and to improve in ways that would enable them to become better competitors in international markets.

Venezuelan industry did not lack inherent rivalry or the urge to compete. Competition did occur, but in ways that did not develop the capabilities to compete in the international marketplace. For example, firms competed for access to government credit via Corpoindustria, the Venezuelan Development Corporation, and the Industrial Bank of Venezuela. Rivalry was very politicized, with certain groups exploiting their ties to political parties.[75] At the same time, firms cooperated in seeking protection from imports. The mix of competition and cooperation in each industry depended on industry conditions and the degree of governmental intervention in the industry in question.

Responses to the Economic Opening

The economic opening introduced new competitive pressures to the marketplace. Prices were deregulated. Tariffs were lowered to internationally accepted levels. The ministry of development ceased fixing prices and promoting industry agreements. Pro-competition legislation was enacted and enforcement authority in antitrust matters granted to a newly created Pro-Competition Superintendency. These reforms evoked several changes in the Venezuelan business and economic landscape, which unfroze existing structures.

Battles among the Conglomerates

Following the economic opening, a series of battles erupted as the major business groups rushed to make acquisitions and to enter industries from which they previously had been barred by high barriers to entry or outright prohibitions. Some of the moves represented expansion into industries closely related to industries in which the groups already had a presence. Others represented offensive attempts to extend market power or defensive attempts to break or to limit the market power of others. Still other moves were directed against specific rivals. The Polar Group, Venezuela's leading beer supplier, invested with Makro (Holland) in a discount retailing chain. The Cisneros group (ODC), owner of the leading retail chain, entered the beer industry. The Banco de Venezuela was acquired by the Banco Consolidado in a hostile takeover. Rivalry escalated in broadcasting between the Cisneros and Phelps groups.[76] Many of these competitive moves represented the type of rivalry that had occurred within the closed market.

New Forms of Rivalry

At the same time, the new forces introduced by the economic opening started to change the nature of rivalry in Venezuelan industry. New pressures started to stimulate new ways of competing. Some firms began to redirect their competitive energies toward innovation and improvements in products, processing, and marketing. Productivity improved and product variety increased, as new opportunities and market niches were explored.

The new forms of competition gave rise to new types of products. Product introductions stimulated by competition in the early 1990s included new flavors of fruit juices, new types of ice cream, new types of pasta (spinach, carrot, and even shrimp flavored), new chocolate bar combinations (with peanuts, nuts, coconut, and fruit), and candies of higher quality. In mass consumer goods, new types of paints in a variety of colors and textures, new varieties of notebooks and paper products, new sanitary pads with lining, and new models of automobiles were introduced. In the financial sector, new types of bank accounts offering competitive rates, including combined checking and savings accounts, and certificates of deposit were introduced.[77]

In some cases, competitive pressures resulted in immediate and dramatic gains for the consumer. In the 1980s, when price agreements were the norm in the paper industry, the selection of stationery goods within Venezuela was very limited and quality was poor.[78] At the time, one of the leading Venezuelan firms produced only two types of notebooks. After 1989, the Colombian firm Carvajal & Cia. entered the Venezuelan market, offering students a wide range of high-quality notebooks in different colors and sizes. By 1993, the same Venezuelan firm that used to produce two types of notebooks produced more than 200 different kinds and had entered the Colombian market, in alliance with a competitor of Carvajal.

Prior to the market opening, there was little rivalry in the Venezuelan market for chocolates. Venezuelans were restricted to a limited assortment of chocolate bars and their per-capita consumption was low by regional standards. Following the economic opening, there was an explosion in head-to-head competition in chocolate candies as domestic producers raced to compete with imports and each other. In the words of the president of the association of cocoa processors, "fear of losing market share translated itself into innovation in products, packaging design, the strengthening of distribution channels and greater aggressiveness in publicity and marketing campaigns."[79] The result was unprecedented consumer choice in chocolate candies (as of 1993, over 100 chocolate products were marketed in Venezuela) and increased Venezuelan chocolate consumption. Imports stimulated rivalry in many other sectors, including wire rod, petrochemicals (polypropylene, polyethylene, polystyrene, and ethylene glycol) and petrochemical endproducts, home appliances, wool textiles, foods, and clothing.[80]

Little Change in Some Areas

In certain areas of the economy, however, there was little or no change. In some industries, existing monopolies and cartels continued to fight to protect their rents. Many laws that restricted competition and granted privileges remained in force. In some instances, weaknesses in distribution chains prevented the benefits of competition from being passed to the consumer. As Jatar (1993) observed in her study of competition and rivalry in Venezuela, there also was the legacy of a business culture in which agreements were the route to prosperity. For many years, meetings among businessmen had been carried out in an atmosphere in which "we have to arrive at an agreement" because the custom was to make joint decisions.[81]

According to Jatar, for many Venezuelans, the transition from cooperation to competition during the early 1990s was "difficult and painful.... Firms recall with nostalgia the days of the 'gentleman's pacts' to maintain price agreements and do not understand why, overnight, what they have done for years is suddenly illegal."[82] For some, the change in rules was at first beyond comprehension. In the first case of cartelization brought by the Pro-Competition Superintendency, a manager of one of the firms under investigation was asked to discuss how his firm used to fix prices. He defended himself by responding, "we always respect the price agreement, the people who violate it always are those of the [other] firm, they always do whatever they feel like."[83] Likewise, in other price-fixing investigations, a very common response of firms was to say "we only concertedly fix a nominal price, from which everyone competes in discounts and service."[84]

One sector that resisted pro-competitive change was pharmacy retailing and distribution.[85] Over the years, the Venezuelan pharmacy sector had obtained legal protections that assured them monopoly power and erected high barriers to entry. For example, by law only pharmacies were permitted to sell medicines, including over-the-counter items such as aspirin and antacids. Pharmacies had to be "independent," which meant that no other type of commercial establishment could enter the business.[86] Only one pharmacy per urban district was allowed to operate at night, on weekends or holidays. By ministerial decree, there had to be a minimum distance of 250 meters between pharmacies. New products to be introduced by pharmaceutical firms were required to receive prior state approval, and delays in the review process constituted a major barrier to entry. Moreover, new pharmacies also had to be approved by the chapter of the Pharmaceutical College operating in the locality of the proposed store. Following the market opening, when the Pro-Competition Superintendency tried to open the pharmacy sector to competition, it encountered a concerted lobbying, public relations, and legal campaign on the part of the pharmacists' association.[87]

Concentration and Rivalry in Venezuela

Venezuelan industries on the whole tend to be concentrated. In many industries or product segments there is only one firm present—for example, one producer in each of several petrochemical products, or one producer in each of many auto parts. In many other industries, including aluminum, beer, steel, and batteries, the two largest firms account for more than 90 percent of total industry sales.[88]

Industry concentration and rivalry tend to be related, but the relationship has not always been a straightforward one, at least not in Venezuela.[89] While it is generally easier to collude where there are few competitors, the presence or lack of competitive behavior, rather than concentration, determines the contribution of rivalry to the competitiveness of a nation's firms. In Venezuela, in some industries there are few firms and fierce competition, and in others there are many firms but little competition. In some highly concentrated sectors, there is little rivalry. These industries tend to be near monopolies, at least by product or market segment. In several petrochemical products, for example, one plant was adequate to meet local demand.

On the other hand, rivalry is intense in some sectors where only two or three major firms exist, such as television broadcasting, music recording, batteries, tobacco, sanitary fixtures, and ice cream. In a few industries, including telenovelas (soap operas), such rivalry has been extended to the international market. Less concentrated industries, with four or more principal participants, also can present a high degree of rivalry. Examples include paints and pasta. In contrast, less concentration, but also less rivalry, is to be found in the textile, chemical, and banking industries. The relationship between concentration and rivalry in selected Venezuelan industries is shown in Table 8.1.

Venezuelan Strategy, Structure, and Rivalry in Context[90]

As with the other determinants, strategy, structure, and rivalry in Venezuela have had similarities with those found in many developing nations. In particular, the distinctive economic actors, uncertainty, opportunistic strategies, and limited rivalry found in Venezuela have parallels in other developing nations.

TABLE 8.1
Levels of Concentration and Rivalry in Venezuela,
Selected Sectors, 1991–1992

Sector	Concentration Index (%)[a]	Level of Rivalry
Steel	CR2=100	Low
Batteries	CR2=98	High
Beer	CR2=92	Low
Sanitary Fixtures	CR2=91	High
Chocolates	CR2=91	High
Ice Cream	CR2=90	High
Rum	CR3=90	High
Tobacco	CR2=84	High
Automobiles	CR4=80	Medium
Sanitary Napkins	CR2=70	High
Paints	CR4=73	High
Chemicals	CR4=60	Low
Textiles	CR4=47	Medium
Banking	CR4=42	Medium
Computation Services	CR4=30	Low

[a] The "Concentration Index" CRX measures the market share of the X largest firms in the industry, taken as a group.

Source: Jatar (1993).

Distinctive Economic Actors

The relative importance of different economic actors in developing nations often differs from that in industrialized nations. In particular, large industrial groups, state-owned enterprises, foreign-owned multinationals, and informal microenterprises often represent a larger portion of developing economies than industrialized economies. Well-connected local business groups dominate large portions of the economies of many developing nations. Some large business groups, such as the Korean *chaebol,* have worked closely with government to promote economic development. Others have become virtual states within states, promoting their own interests. The strategies of many large business groups in developing nations tend toward preserving their position and perquisites rather than profit maximization and nation building.

Multinational firms are another major presence in many developing nations. Multinational firms from industrialized nations generally employ skills and capabilities developed in their home markets and are therefore not as tied to local economic conditions as indigenous firms. Foreign multinationals generally have access to foreign capital, foreign technology, foreign market intelligence, and expertise sourced through their international networks. Since the multinational's overall corporate strategy usually is set outside the developing nation, it need not correspond to the development needs of the host country. Actual and perceived exploitation of local resources by multinationals has created local opposition to them in many developing nations. In addition, some nations fear that foreign firms will crowd out the nation's own firms.

The state-owned enterprises (SOEs) that figure prominently in many developing nations have been created for a number of reasons, including the desire to exercise control over natural resources, to take an active role in economic development, to control "strategic" industries, to take over failing firms, and so on. SOEs often have noneconomic, and sometimes conflicting, goals. Many state-owned enterprises become poorly performing outlets for political patronage. Their performance often is difficult to assess. Accounts tend to be spotty, and frequently it is difficult to tell whether profits come from efficiency or protection and subsidies. Since they often do not need to turn a profit, SOEs sometimes buy market share. Recently, the viability of SOEs has been questioned in a number of nations. The late 1980s and early 1990s have seen a wave of privatizations in developing nations, particularly those of Latin America. The goals of privatization have been to depoliticize industries, to reduce subsidies to failing state-owned firms, to reduce inefficiencies, and to raise money to offset government deficits.

Informal microenterprises represent a significant portion of total employment in most developing nations. These enterprises operate at the fringes of the economy. The primary goal of such firms is to survive and to provide the proprietor with at least a minimal standard of living. Such firms are unlikely to develop real strategies or to invest in developing new skills and capabilities.

Opportunistic Strategies and Firm Structures

The nature of firm strategies in developing nations often differs substantially from that in industrialized nations. Firms in developing nations often adopt political, opportunistic, and risk-averse strategies.[91] In many developing nations, the dominance of government in economic and business affairs means that a company's political strategy is far more important than its business strategy. A company can develop excellent products and services, but if it is not allowed to compete, is not given access to inputs or foreign exchange, cannot obtain import or export licenses, or cannot obtain financing from state dominated capital markets, it cannot survive. In many developing nations, whom you know is much more important than what you know. The thrust of company strategy then becomes cultivating the right friendships with high officials and covering one's bets in the face of political uncertainties. Firms engage in opportunistic efforts to take advantage of regulations, loopholes, exemptions, and connections.

Many things that firms in industrialized nations take for granted cannot be taken for granted in developing nations, where markets do not function well and firms cannot assume that contracts will be enforced. Anticompetitive behavior often is tolerated or even supported. Distribution channels often are controlled by tight-knit oligopolies or cartels that limit access to outsiders. The result is often excess vertical integration and diversification, or at least greater levels of vertical integration and diversification than economic efficiency would warrant. Firms engage in vertical integration in order to ensure supplies of materials and inputs. Diversification is used to spread risks across industries and to ensure firms are not too exposed to a single industry that might fall out of government favor. Thus, what might be considered excess diversification or vertical integration is a rational response to existing circumstances.

Uncertainty Influences Business Strategy

The uncertainty present in many developing nations goes far beyond that found in most developed nations. In some parts of the world, one cannot assume that access to international markets will remain uninterrupted by hostility or wars. Many developing nations have unstable political structures with rival factions contending for power. Even in nations with relatively stable governments, economic policy can be extremely unstable. Developing country governments have been known to change policies quickly and unpredictably. Finally, developing countries are particularly vulnerable to fluctuations in commodity prices, economic shocks, and macroeconomic conditions, thus increasing the uncertainty surrounding business decisions.

Uncertainty and instability lead to risk-averse behavior. In contexts where the stability of trading relationships cannot be assumed, self-sufficiency might be a better policy than specialization and international trade. In uncertain environments, self-preservation might be a more common firm strategy than profit maximization. Uncertainty in policy regimes leads to greater efforts on the part of firms to control outcomes through their political connections. Uncertainty increases the risk premium placed on investments and shortens the time horizon of firms and capital markets, making long-term investments particularly difficult to justify.

Limited Domestic Rivalry

In many developing nations there is limited domestic rivalry. A combination of small domestic markets, few or no pro-competition policies, state ownership, and control by large indigenous industrial groups tends to reduce domestic competition in many developing nations. State-owned enterprises often dominate the industries that are considered strategic. Many governments in developing nations find it far easier to negotiate with, or exert control over, a limited number of firms in a given industry. In addition, such countries often lack an appreciation of the benefits of competition in terms of the pressures to improve and innovate.

The Challenge of Competitiveness

In recent years, a number of developing nations, particularly in Latin America, have begun to change their economic and business environments. Trade barriers have been reduced, as free trade has begun to replace import substitution as a dominant ideology. Foreign investment has been encouraged rather than discouraged. Privatization has reduced the direct role of the state in the economy. Increased emphasis has been placed on the role of domestic competition. The goal has been to promote economic growth through a more open, outward-looking policy regime. These changes have resulted in substantial changes in firm strategy, structure, and rivalry within nations. Venezuela, of course, has moved in the same direction, though not as early or completely as some of its neighbors.

Meeting the challenge of competitiveness in Venezuela will involve further progress in firm strategy, structure, and local rivalry and in the forces that influence them. After all, Venezuelan firms have tended to adopt strategies and structures suited to the environment in which they have had to operate. Meeting the challenge of competitiveness will involve developing firm strategies and structures that are geared to competing in the international marketplace and with international competitors. Doing so will involve an economic environment in which firms respond to signals from the market, but in which monopolistic or monopsonistic practices are regulated. It will involve a greater focus on business strategies that serve consumers and compete with other firms in the marketplace, instead of political strategies that serve a privileged few and compete for protection and favors. It will involve a pro-competition framework that provides pressures for firms to improve and innovate. Meeting the challenge of competitiveness in Venezuela also will involve the creation of a more stable economic and business environment in which medium- and long-term planning can better supplement and direct short-term action. Suggestions for improvements in these areas are found in chapters 11 and 12.

9

Government Policy and Competitiveness in Venezuela

Government policy has an important influence on competitiveness in any country. As we have seen, in Venezuela, government policy has influenced the factor conditions; demand conditions; related and supporting industries; and firm strategy, structure, and rivalry present in the nation. It is through its impact on these determinants that government exerts its influence on competitiveness. Government policy affects factor conditions through its resource, agricultural, and macroeconomic policies, as well as through its investments in education, training, science, and infrastructure. It affects demand conditions through its role as a purchaser and through regulation of product markets. It affects related and supporting industries through industrial policies and trade policies. It affects firm strategy, structure, and rivalry through its tax policies, regulatory policies, trade and industrial policies, competition policies, and ownership of firms.

Just as government policy in general affects each of the determinants, specific policies or types of policies can influence several if not all of the determinants. This reflects the systemic nature of the framework developed in Chapter 3. Competition policy, for example, not only influences firm strategy, structure, and rivalry, it also influences the incentives for firms to engage in factor creation (through investments in training or research and development) as well as demand conditions (firms under competitive pressures often become more demanding buyers). Policies toward capital markets affect factor conditions (availability and price of capital), which, in turn, influence firm strategies and rivalry within industries. Natural resource policies influence the degree to which factor conditions are exploited, the extent to which resource-based industries develop into vibrant clusters of related and supporting industries, and the nature of firm strategies in resource-intensive industries. In fact, every major policy area will influence several determinants. The impact of individual policies on particular determinants has been described in earlier chapters. For convenience and ease of exposition, in this chapter, we have grouped policies together by types (economic policies, human resource–related policies, etc.), instead of determinant by determinant. The links between the policy areas and the determinants should be clear from earlier chapters.

Economic Policy

The impact of the Venezuelan government's economic policies on the determinants of international competitiveness has been described in previous chapters. There is no need to revisit these matters in detail here. Instead, the purpose of this section is briefly to organize and to summarize the main aspects of Venezuelan economic policies and administration that have influenced the nation's competitiveness.

Macroeconomic Policies

Macroeconomic policy has had an important influence on the overall competitiveness of the Venezuelan economy. For decades, the Venezuelan government followed a policy of fixed exchange rates, fixed interest rates, and a balanced budget. Revenues from oil supported these policies in the 1960s and 1970s. The oil industry has provided the major share of government revenue and foreign exchange in Venezuela for decades. Taxes on oil income typically accounted for more than 80 percent of the Venezuelan government's revenue. Revenues from personal income taxes, corporate income taxes, and indirect taxes, on the other hand, were extremely low by world standards. Oil income also accounted for roughly 80 percent of Venezuela's foreign exchange earnings. Given government control of the oil sector, the Venezuelan government directly controls the vast majority of the nation's foreign exchange earnings.

Fixed Rates. In the 1960s and 1970s, rising oil income allowed the Venezuelan government to invest in infrastructure and industrial development. Gross fixed capital formation, led by government investment programs, reached 42.5 percent of GDP in 1978. During this time, Venezuela sustained a constant fixed exchange rate, with the bolivar pegged to the U.S. dollar. As oil prices fell in the early 1980s, the revenue available to the Venezuelan government was sharply reduced. Real per-capita government spending fell by 50 percent between 1981 and 1984. Investments were curtailed, and expenditures on maintenance of infrastructure and government property were reduced, as were expenditures on supplies. Public sector wages failed to keep up with inflation. Spending cuts, however, did not keep pace with falling government revenues, resulting in substantial budgetary imbalances and a mounting debt. This, in turn, meant that an increasing portion of government spending went to pay interest on external debt.

Mounting Pressures. Through most of the 1970s and 1980s, the bolivar was overvalued. This overvaluation sent distorted signals to Venezuelan firms and consumers. Few Venezuelan industries, outside the oil sector, could overcome the cost disadvantages imposed by the overvalued currency to sell in international markets. Development of other resource industries, such as forest products, tourism, and mining, which should have been able to compete on world markets, lagged. Venezuelan manufacturing, which would have been hopelessly uncompetitive at the fixed exchange rate, relied on protection for survival. Venezuelan firms and individuals bought low-priced imports whenever they could. Macroeconomic imbalances forced a 50 percent devaluation of the bolivar in 1983. That year, a differential exchange rate system was established in which foreign exchange could be obtained at preferential, subsidized rates for certain uses. Even with subsequent devaluations in 1986 and 1988, the official bolivar rate generally remained overvalued.

The inflationary pressure created by mounting budget deficits combined with a fixed interest rate regime resulted in negative real interest rates in Venezuela for much of the 1970s and 1980s. These negative real interest rates, in turn, distorted credit and capital markets. Credit was rationed. Those with access to friendly house banks and to government-backed financing tended to borrow as much as they could. Many Venezuelan firms became highly indebted as a result. Credit rationing meant that those without access to friendly bankers or government credits were in essence excluded from the financial markets. Needless to say, this system resulted in gross distortions of investment decisions and capital allocation.

The dual exchange regime in effect between 1983 and 1989 allowed for manipulation and profiteering on a scale previously unknown in Venezuela. Many Venezuelan firms were able to obtain dollars at preferential rates and then either ship the dollars overseas through false invoicing or use them to buy bolivars at the free rate (roughly twice the preferential rate) and pocket the difference. The combination of dual exchange rates, interest rates fixed below those available in the United States and elsewhere, and free convertibility was a clear invitation to capital flight.

Policy Changes. Venezuela's macroeconomic policies proved to be unsustainable in the face of falling oil revenues. A reluctance to accept the changes in the world economic environment delayed further action until 1989, by which time international operating reserves were low and international credit was exhausted. The budget deficit ballooned as the government could not cut expenditures to match falling revenues. The nation's reserve position weakened. One of the first tasks of the Pérez government, which took office in 1989, was to restore some semblance of macroeconomic order. Under the new regime, interest rates, exchange rates, and most prices would be set by markets rather than by government intervention. Venezuela's foreign debt was rescheduled and attempts were made to balance the national budget. These moves prevented the onset of hyperinflation, but the failure to get the entire economic reform program through Congress made restoring the macroeconomic balance extremely difficult.

The government attempted to put public finances on a firmer footing. It hoped to cut government spending by reducing direct expenditures, downsizing government, privatizing state-owned enterprises, eliminating government subsidies, and renegotiating its foreign debt. It hoped to raise and to diversify government revenue by increasing the prices of government-supplied goods and services. An asset tax and a value-added tax were proposed to widen the tax base. Real per-capita government spending was cut in half from 1988 to 1990. Government was downsized to a certain extent, many subsidies were removed, and the foreign debt was renegotiated. The privatization program, however, was stalled after the sales of majority stakes in CANTV and Viasa in 1991. The government was unable to enact the rest of its fiscal program. Prices for gasoline and electricity were not raised as had been planned after the February 1992 coup attempt. The value-added and asset taxes were approved only in late 1993, after Pérez had left office.

In February 1989, Venezuelan exchange rates were unified and a floating exchange rate, with heavy intervention by the Central Bank, was adopted (the so-called dirty float policy). Interest rates also were freed as part of the economic reform program. Access to preferential loans was curtailed sharply. Real interest rates soon became positive for the first time in years. Distortions in investment decisions were reduced substantially. Removal of distortions paved the way for substantial increases in investment in a number of industries in which Venezuela has natural advantages, such as forestry, tourism, and tropical crops, but which had been uneconomic to develop under the previous regime. Interest rates rose to reflect inflationary expectations and the political and economic uncertainty brought about by opposition to the economic reform program. Calls for a return to controlled interest rates came from some quarters. High interest rates, however, were a symptom of an underdeveloped financial sector and fundamental macroeconomic problems, particularly the fiscal deficit, that had not been solved.

During the 1970s and early 1980s, the Central Bank of Venezuela was effectively controlled by the Venezuelan government. At the time, the Central Bank engaged in a passive and accommodating monetary policy that created money to fuel the rentist economy.[1] As mentioned, in 1989, the Central Bank adopted a dirty float policy. In the early 1990s, the bolivar was devalued more or less in line with differential inflation with the United States. It was somewhat undervalued immediately after exchange rate unification but became somewhat overvalued in 1991, after the Persian Gulf War oil income windfall.

The Central Bank Law, passed in 1992, made the Central Bank of Venezuela largely independent from governmental intervention. It freed the Central Bank of responsibility for saving failing banks (limiting it to short-term financing) and from other functions inconsistent with its monetary role. In addition, the law eliminated the possibility of the bank granting direct financing to the government, and modernized its instruments of monetary policy.[2] In 1992 and 1993, the Bank endeavored to promote monetary stability, to protect international reserves, to improve the stability of financial markets, and to strengthen confidence in the bolivar. During this period, it generally proceeded with a medium-term time horizon, attempting to maximize its stabilizing effect while minimizing the social costs of adjustment. Overall, the Bank under the leadership of Ruth de Krivoy received high marks for helping to maintain economic stability in the midst of political and fiscal uncertainty.

The value-added tax (VAT) entered into effect at the retail level on January 1, 1994. On January 18, implementation of the VAT was suspended at the retail level, though it remained in force at the wholesale level. The clearing privileges of the Banco Latino were suspended on January 14 due to its failure to meet reserve requirements. These developments had an important impact on the capital markets. In two weeks, the value of Venezuela's Brady Bonds dropped nearly five points (from 75 to 70 percent of par value), roughly half as much as the decline that followed the unsuccessful coup attempt of February 1992. According to one report, Venezuelans transferred approximately $500 million out of the country in a single week.[3]

The banking sector crisis, concern over the public sector deficit, and the resignation of the Central Bank's president due to sharp disagreements over the new administration's economic policies resulted in a sharp decline in the bolivar, which fell from 106 to the dollar at the end of 1993 to nearly 200 to the dollar in July 1994. In order to stop the decline, the Venezuelan government adopted a fixed exchange rate of 170 bolivars to the dollar and instituted foreign exchange controls in July 1994. Individuals and firms had to apply for foreign exchange for international travel and transactions. Venezuelans were forbidden to use credit cards that had been issued in Venezuela outside the country. Foreign currency holdings were mostly outlawed, and stiff penalties were adopted for anyone found holding illicit currency.

In September 1994, Planning Minister Werner Corrales proposed a series of measures to improve the government's fiscal position. These proposals included increased revenues from the wholesale tax, increased personal and corporate income taxes, and "rationalized" (or "raised") gasoline prices. (A debit tax on banking transactions had been implemented earlier in the year partially to defray the costs of reimbursing depositors in failed banks.) Government spending was to be reduced by reforming the public administration, and the government's internal debt was to be refinanced through the issuance of long-term treasury bills, instead of the short-term zero-coupon bonds used in the early 1990s. The proposals generally were warmly received by the business and economic communities, though it was unclear which provisions would actually be enacted.

Industrial and Trade Policy

The industrial and trade policies prevailing in Venezuela in the 1970s and 1980s can be summarized as investing in state-controlled heavy industry and protecting private import-substituting manufacturing initiatives. The combination allowed for the relatively rapid development of an indigenous industrial base in the 1970s. The absence of competitive pressures and the politicization of the operations of individual state-owned companies, however, resulted in a rather inefficient industrial base that required protection and subsidies to ensure its viability. Falling oil revenues in the 1980s made it increasingly difficult to subsidize an industrial base that had grown rife with distortions and inefficiencies when compared with those in much of the rest of the world.

State-Led Development and Protection. Historically, the Venezuelan state assigned itself the primary role in industrialization, particularly with regard to heavy industry. The Pérez Jiménez government (1948-1958) set the basis for state enterprises in steel, hydroelectricity, and petrochemicals. The 1961 Constitution reserved the development of heavy basic industries to the state. Beginning in the mid-1970s, massive government investments were made in oil, iron, steel, petrochemicals, and aluminum. The government also took control of tourism development, mining, forestry resources, and part of the financial sector. A large portion of the oil windfall of the 1970s was invested in these industries by state-owned enterprises. The architects of the system believed that the government was the only actor that could muster the resources to develop heavy industry while preventing domination by foreign multinationals.[4]

In the 1970s and 1980s, the Venezuelan market was heavily protected through tariffs and administrative restrictions preventing imports of many consumer goods. Capital goods and raw materials generally were excepted from import duties. Soft loans and tax holidays were available for industrial projects aimed at substitution of imports. Approval was denied to projects when they would compete with existing established producers.[5] Such policies resulted in rapid industrialization but offered little incentive for firms to improve efficiency or quality. A similar situation emerged in agriculture, where subsidies and market protection resulted in an oil-subsidized "green revolution."[6] Production was increased in many agricultural products, but at prices several times those prevailing in international markets.

Government procurement also followed the import substitution policy. "Buy local" policies directed government agencies to purchase local goods and services as long as the price was less than 20 percent higher than the imported alternative. In practice, many agencies purchased goods and services that were produced locally with little regard to price differentials. Although government procurement was legally mandated to follow competitive bidding processes, purchase decisions often were made on the basis of personal contacts or even corruption.[7] Exceptions to this tendency were found in the oil industry, the Metro de Caracas, Edelca, and a few other agencies known for their demanding acquisition procedures. These agencies and companies tended to purchase on the basis of the quality and price of goods and services.

Artificially low input prices distorted firm purchasing decisions. In some cases, this led to wasteful use of resources. In other cases, industries were allowed to import inputs at artificially low prices which made it uneconomical to develop sources within Venezuela. Excess regulation and limited competition meant that firms had to worry more about pleasing politicians and bureaucrats than about pleasing consumers and beating their competitors. Competition and competitiveness were discouraged. The efficiency of investment (in terms of output per unit of invested capital) in Venezuela plummeted during the 1970s and 1980s. While a certain drop in investment efficiency might have been expected, (after all, large government investments were being made in heavy industries that were supposed to have long-term returns), the magnitude of the reduction was surprising.[8]

Reform of Industrial and Trade Policies. The economic reform program of 1989 called for a reduced role for the Venezuelan government in the economy. The new industrial policy focused largely on promoting large export-oriented investment projects in oil, petrochemicals, aluminum, pulp and paper, and tourism. Some of these projects were meant to be carried out through strategic alliances between state-owned enterprises and private investors. Such projects were expected to generate up to $4 billion in exports in the medium term and thus reduce Venezuela's dependence on oil revenues.[9]

Unfortunately, each of the industries in which the investments were to be made faced falling demand and/or falling prices in world markets in the early 1990s. In 1993, real oil prices reached their lowest levels since the 1970s. The prices of some petrochemicals and aluminum reached historic lows at roughly the same time. Pulp and paper prices reached new lows in 1991 and rebounded somewhat by 1993. Venezuelan tourism revenues were hurt by the world recession of the early 1990s, but much more so by the political unrest and attempted coups of 1992. The downturns in the aluminum, petrochemical, pulp, paper, and tourism markets, along with unstable political and macroeconomic conditions, delayed the expected growth of these industries in Venezuela, at least temporarily. In early 1994, the world market outlook for several of these industries was improving somewhat.

The economic reform program represented a total change in Venezuela's trade environment. The program opened the nation to foreign competition and placed a much greater emphasis on exports than had been the case in the days of import substitution industrialization. The new trade policy progressively reduced tariffs and eliminated administrative import restrictions. Average tariffs were lowered from 37 percent overall and 61 percent for finished consumer goods to 19 percent overall and 33 percent for consumer goods in 1990, and 16 percent overall and 25 percent for consumer goods in 1991.[10] Import liberalization was intended to increase competition in the domestic market and to force local firms to upgrade their competitiveness. Venezuela also became a signatory to the General Agreement on Tariffs and Trade (GATT). It negotiated a landmark agreement to reduce trade barriers with Colombia and to effectively integrate the two economies. By

1993, Colombia was the leading destination for Venezuela's nontraditional exports, and total trade between the two nations approached $2 billion a year. Venezuela also passed an antidumping law, based on the European Community's law, to limit unfair foreign competition.

The nation also entered into a series of trade negotiations within the Andean region, the Group of Three (Colombia, Mexico, and Venezuela), and with the Central American Common Market (MCCA), the Caribbean Common Market (CARICOM), and Chile. It was hoped that Venezuelan firms would get full access to the nations of the Andean Pact (with a total population of 94 million in 1991) versus Venezuela alone (20.3 million), Mexico (88 million), and MCCA and CARICOM (32.7 million). There also was talk in 1992 and 1993 of Venezuela eventually joining the North American Free Trade Agreement (NAFTA) negotiated by the United States, Canada, and Mexico.

The years 1993 and 1994 showed a continuation of regional trade negotiations, something of a return to protectionism in some sectors, and calls for a more active industrial policy. President Caldera signed an accord with Colombia and Mexico to reduce trade barriers between the three nations in mid-1994. Agricultural and automotive interests were able to obtain somewhat higher levels of protection in 1993. Members of the administration called for direct government involvement in supporting the development of a limited number of export industries.

Privatization. The first moves toward privatization in Venezuela were made in the early 1980s. With the financial and fiscal crisis of 1989, this policy began to be pursued seriously.[11] Under the reform program, majority stakes in CANTV and Viasa were sold to foreign and Venezuelan interests, though the government retained a substantial stake. The ports system was regionalized and put under private operation. The government also sold off banks and sugar mills. After the coup attempt of February 1992, however, the Pérez administration's privatization program was virtually stopped by members of the Congress who refused support to a weakened president.

Privatization seemed to regain some momentum in 1993, after President Pérez was removed from office, although little was sold except for Banco Popular and one sugar mill. New management at the CVG announced plans to privatize several CVG companies. Other obstacles to privatization, however, emerged. The privatization of the water system in Caracas did not go forward, as a result of flaws in the privatization plan and the opposition of insiders who were against the sale. In late 1993, a Venezuelan judge ordered the president of CANTV arrested after a subcontractor ruptured a gas line, resulting in the death of 53 people. Many believed that the judge's order, widely viewed as arbitrary, would frighten away foreign investors. Sales of the Enelbar and Enelco electricity generating plants scheduled for late 1993 were delayed in part as a result of the CANTV incident.

Economic Regulation

During the 1970s and 1980s, the Venezuelan economy was heavily regulated. Although the Venezuelan Constitution had assured freedom of economic action, these economic freedoms were suspended from 1961 (when the Constitution took effect) until 1991. This suspension allowed the Executive Branch of the government to regulate in economic matters, through a myriad of decrees and resolutions. Almost every aspect of economic life was subject to some form of regulation. Prices were controlled to protect consumers. Plant openings were subject to numerous regulations. Permits were required for the most mundane of company activities. It was not uncommon for companies to employ people whose only job was to stand in line at the ministry of development for permits. Companies needed government approval to import and export, change prices, add capacity, change employment conditions, and enter new industries. A government agency's failure to approve a request was the equivalent of disapproval. Many firms found themselves subject to the "administrative no" in which they might never receive a formal decision on a petition.

The Venezuelan government had a substantial influence on industrial input prices. In addition to its direct role in setting prices across the economy, the state influenced input prices through its role as regulator and through state-owned enterprises. The Venezuelan government also set prices for natural resources and energy directly through state agencies and state-owned enterprises.

The Pérez administration instituted a massive reduction in economic regulation. The economic freedoms guaranteed by Venezuela's Constitution finally were granted. Most prices were decontrolled. Permission was no longer required to enter most industries. It was no longer necessary to spend hours in line at the ministry of development in order to get permits to carry out basic firm activities. In fact, the entire function of the ministry changed from controlling and administering the economy to supporting private-sector development. In the process, the ministry was downsized substantially.

Pent-up inflationary pressures resulted in a sharp rise in prices of many goods in 1989. After the market was opened to foreign competition, domestic prices for steel, aluminum, chemicals, and other products subject to international competition tended to approximate international prices. For the most part, Venezuela's state-owned enterprises stopped selling intermediate products at prices below international levels, except where vertical integration or long-term contracts established special transfer prices and other support programs. The agricultural sector lost most of its fertilizer subsidies but still had access to concessionary loans.

In early 1994, the Caldera administration suspended the economic freedoms guaranteed by the Venezuelan Constitution. Although in theory this gave the administration broad powers to regulate economic affairs, in practice the government intervened to try to shore up the banking sector, instituted price controls on a limited (but expanding) range of goods and services, and instituted foreign exchange controls. Although the goal of heightened regulation was to limit the impact of the economic crisis on lower- and middle-income Venezuelans, there were a number of unintended consequences.

The pharmaceutical industry represented an extreme case of such unintended consequences. Venezuelan pharmaceutical prices were frozen, even though devaluation and inflation meant that the price of imported inputs was rising rapidly. Soon the pharmaceutical manufacturer's association claimed that the controlled prices were below the cost of inputs. Several firms curtailed production rather than producing and selling at a loss. The government responded by issuing arrest warrants for the presidents of several pharmaceutical firms operating in Venezuela and announced plans to import bulk pharmaceuticals from Bulgaria.

Competition Policy

The Venezuelan government had no real policy to promote competition in the marketplace in the 1970s and 1980s. In fact, it tended to do just the opposite. Industrialization was viewed as a means to "sow the oil rent," to share wealth rather than to create it. In this context, competition was considered wasteful and competitiveness was not even on the list of policy priorities. Industry after industry was induced to cartelize to allow more effective control. Import restrictions prevented competition from abroad. Some industries were reserved, de jure or de facto, to state-owned monopolies. In others, state-owned firms engaged in market-sharing arrangements with private-sector firms.

Government felt the need to regulate prices throughout the economy on behalf of the consumer and in the process further encouraged cartelization and reduced competition. Restrictions on entry often gave existing competitors the right to veto entry by new competitors. Many of the laws regulating business and finance were designed to foster cooperation and distributive behavior. The Insurance Law, for example, established price fixing by the

Insurance Authority. The Capital Markets Law assigned to stock exchange boards the task of fixing brokerage fees. The Agricultural Marketing Law established a scheme to fix prices for agricultural products through agreements between the government and producer's representatives.[12] Hundreds of other arrangements between the government and industry associations served to reduce competition based on price, quality, or new entry.

The new economic policies introduced in 1989 were designed to foster competition mainly through the removal of price controls and other mechanisms of government intervention, by reducing protection and by encouraging competition in the domestic market. The Pro-Competition Law enacted in 1991 was designed to promote and to protect competition on behalf of producers and consumers. Its main thrust was the prohibition of monopolistic and oligopolistic behavior that restricted or limited the exercise of economic freedom. Both horizontal and vertical agreements restricting competition were forbidden, as was the abuse of market power. The law sought to limit industry concentration through ex-ante control of mergers and acquisitions. It also established a Pro-Competition Superintendency, which has faced several difficult cases, including an attempt to break a monopoly held by pharmacies on sales of nonprescription medications.

Under the leadership of Ana Julia Jatar, the enforcement objectives of the new superintendency were the regulation of firm conduct, legal changes to remove barriers to entry, and emphasis on education on the advantages of a market economy. Lesser priority was placed on vertical restrictions, penalizing of price fixing, and market-sharing agreements. The superintendency generally did not seek to break up monopolies, near monopolies, or oligopolies in industries subject to substantial barriers to entry. Instead, it relied on reduced protection and reduced restrictions on entry to ensure some level of competition, or potential competition, should prices be set artificially high. The Pro-Competition Superintendency has been hampered by long-held attitudes toward competition, existing collusive arrangements, and the fact that old laws favoring collusion remain on the books and have been invoked by those affected by the new law.[13] In late 1993, the government of Provisional President Ramón J. Velásquez took steps to exempt agricultural price setting from the Pro-Competition Law, resulting in the resignation of Superintendent Jatar.

Foreign Investment

As part of the economic opening, the government liberalized the rules governing foreign investment in an attempt to provide foreign investors with an adequate and attractive regulatory regime. It eliminated restrictions on the payment of dividends and the repatriation of capital, on reinvestment, and on access to external financing. It opened new sectors of the economy to foreign investment. It eliminated the requirement that contracts for the transfer of technology receive government approval and ended the prior authorization and registration requirements for contracts for external credit entered into by firms that operate within Venezuela. Overall, it sharply reduced the bureaucratic hassles involved in making foreign investments and operating in Venezuela. Venezuela was not, however, unique in making these changes, which fall within the new normative framework approved by Decision 291 of the Andean Pact.[14]

Venezuela also made additional changes in the environment for foreign investment. A new income tax law lowered the tax rate to 30 percent and allowed tax credits for new investment. The process of subregional Andean integration widened the markets to which investors have access. Venezuela entered into agreements with the Multilateral Investment Guarantee Agency (MIGA) and the Overseas Private Investment Corporation (OPIC) as well as agreements for the promotion and protection of investment with Italy and the Netherlands, which established mechanisms to reduce the risks of foreign investors and to permit mediation of contractual disputes via international arbitration.

In the early 1990s, many foreign investors gave Venezuela their vote of confidence by significantly increasing the flow of investment into the country. Much of the new investment flowed to sectors that were attractive for the first time in Venezuela's modern history, due to changes in the regulatory framework that corrected market signals and to the rise of an integrated Andean market, which expanded the market for goods and services produced in Venezuela. The sector that stands out the most is telecommunications. The privatization of CANTV laid the foundation for an extraordinary expansion and development of telecommunications in Venezuela. CANTV committed itself to an ambitious eight-year investment plan, and additional investors began to get involved in new areas such as private networks, data transmission, public telephone systems, cellular phones, teleservices, and radio locators. There were also large new investments in sectors such as pulp and paper, beverages, tourism, and petrochemicals.[15] In addition, the Venezuelan Congress approved private foreign investment in the Cristóbal Colón project as well as strategic associations between Maraven and Conoco and between Maraven and the Itochu-Marubeni consortium in the petroleum sector.

Foreign investment dropped sharply in 1993 as privatization slowed and economic uncertainty increased. In September of 1994, the planning minister called for the participation of private investors in the oil sector and in the CVG companies. If carried out, this would represent a substantial revision of previous policy.

Natural Resource, Agricultural, and Infrastructure Policies

In addition to its direct economic policies, policies toward natural resources, agriculture, and infrastructure have a substantial impact on the competitiveness of a nation's economy. Natural resource policy is particularly important in Venezuela, given the prominent role of such resources in the economy. Agricultural policies affect the management and uses of land resources. Infrastructure, of course, is an important consideration in any industry.

Natural Resource Policies

Many of Venezuela's policies concerning natural resources have been described earlier in this book. Here we give only a brief overview of these policies and some of their consequences. As stated, policies that govern the ownership, development, and pricing of natural resources are particularly important in Venezuela.

Development Policies. In Venezuela, in keeping with the Spanish tradition, all underground resources, such as oil and minerals, are regarded as the property of the state. The state exercised its control over many of these resources by the direct involvement of state-owned companies. Much of the state-led industrialization of the 1970s, in fact, was designed to build heavy industry to utilize Venezuela's iron ore, bauxite, hydroelectrical potential, hydrocarbon deposits, and other resources. Still other resources were developed through concessions granted by the state.

This strategy did result in growth in the oil, steel, and aluminum industries, but it also hindered development in certain areas. State agencies often acted under political pressure and sometimes in less than transparent ways. As discussed in Chapter 4, the Venezuelan state controlled forestry development, but for years it was unable to reach agreements to utilize the resource. Development of the mining sector was held back by confusion over the management of mineral resources. In some cases, it was not clear whether the ministry of energy and mines or the CVG had jurisdiction over mineral deposits. Forestry and mining also were affected by an uncertain land tenure system.

Resource Pricing. Resource pricing has been a major issue in Venezuela. Low energy prices, designed to stimulate development, have been part of the nation's industrial policy for decades. Gasoline for both commercial and private use was sold in the domestic market at prices covering production costs but well below prevailing export prices. Until 1989, electricity rates were subsidized at levels that did not allow for the recovery of investment costs. Public sector enterprises sold certain aluminum, steel, fertilizer, and petrochemical products at below-market prices. Agriculture enjoyed low-interest loans subsidized by banks, along with cheap fuel and subsidized fertilizer.

Beginning in February 1989, domestic prices for fuel were increased. Internal prices for gasoline reached 60 percent of export price in February 1992, while prices for related products reached 90 percent of export prices. These price increases, however, were accompanied by riots in February 1989 and by denunciations in the press thereafter. After the coup attempt of February 1992, the price of gasoline was frozen in nominal terms. By February 1993, with inflation, the price of gasoline was roughly 40 percent of the export price. PDVSA, and by extension the Venezuelan government, lost 40 billion bolivars in 1993 when prices were not raised as planned. Artificially low gasoline prices primarily benefit middle- and upper-class car owners and providers of transportation services.

The price of natural gas for industrial use in Venezuela was 350 bolivars per 1,000 cubic meters in 1990, 700 in 1992, and 1,400 after January 1993, or approximately one-third of the U.S. price.[16] PDVSA estimates that costs were covered, on average. Private industries that use natural gas are handicapped by the absence of a stable, long-term policy for natural gas pricing, which makes it difficult for them to predict their own future cost structure, to enter into long-term sales commitments, and to attract foreign capital.[17] Liquefied natural gas has been provided to Pequiven at transfer prices somewhat below cost, producing a 15 billion bolivar loss in 1993 for PDVSA. Electricity rates for Venezuelan industrial users were increased 300 percent from 1989 to 1990, and another 100 percent increase was approved at the end of 1992. Industrial electricity rates in Venezuela were set in 1993 near the long-term marginal cost of the service. The new tariffs were designed to encourage energy conservation for users and operational efficiency for distribution companies, although industrial electricity users continued to subsidize residential users. (See Chapter 6.)

Agricultural Policy

Agriculture is a politically charged topic in many if not most countries. In many nations, farmers have won relief from fluctuating markets, concentrated buyers, and foreign competition through subsidies and protection. The agricultural sector provides a good example of Venezuelan economic policy in action. This example shows how policy fostered and encouraged the development of inefficient industries and how difficult the reform process has been in Venezuela. It also shows signs of a return to protection and a reversal of much-needed reform.

Agricultural Protection. For decades, the Venezuelan government intervened heavily in domestic agricultural markets. The state protected farmers from agroindustrial buyers by setting minimum prices and, in some sectors, by guaranteeing that state marketing boards would purchase crops. When domestic prices climbed above the price of imports, the state erected trade barriers. It also introduced price controls on food in an effort to help the poor. This created distortions in agroindustry, which required state-subsidized agricultural inputs in order to sell at a profit in the domestic market. One distortion led to another, until the entire chain of production and consumption within Venezuela was insulated from external market forces.[18]

By 1990, Venezuelan agriculture had ceased to work by the laws of the market. As Coles (1993) observed, setting the annual price for a crop and "deciding who would buy how much and when" involved political lobbying and state action.[19] Farming could be profitable as long as lobbyists were powerful and well-connected. Farmers and agroindustry had little incentive to improve efficiency, because profits depended on government favors, permits, policies, and prices. Import barriers permitted the rise of new sectors, such as animal feed and vegetable oil, that were based on temperate-zone production systems unsuited to Venezuelan conditions. Insecurity regarding property rights also plagued Venezuelan agriculture. The Agrarian Reform in the 1960s won the peasants' loyalty to the democratic regime by allowing farmers to settle on "unused land," but it further encouraged the incursion of farms and heightened other landowners' insecurity.

A substantial portion of the nation's wealth was redistributed to agriculture. In 1990, agricultural subsidies were estimated at the equivalent of U.S. $1 billion, nearly 2 percent of GDP, at a time when agriculture produced less than 6 percent of total GDP.[20] Subsidies accounted for one bolivar for every three bolivars of agricultural "output." In most sectors, Venezuelan productivity lagged far behind that of world leaders. In 1990, Venezuelan corn yields averaged 2,160 kilos per hectare, compared to average yields of 7,430 kilos per hectare in the United States. Venezuelan sorghum farmers harvested on average 2,140 kilos per hectare, compared to the U.S. average of 3,950 kilos per hectare.[21] The average yield of Venezuela's cocoa farms was between 160 and 300 kilos per hectare, compared to yields of 700 kilos per hectare in the Ivory Coast and higher yields in Malaysia and Indonesia.[22] Coffee yields were far below those of Colombia and Costa Rica.

Changing the Rules. Starting in 1990, the Venezuelan government tried to dismantle the old agricultural regime. It reduced tariffs, eliminated import licenses, and stopped the supply of subsidized foreign exchange. It eliminated state monopolies, such as those held by the cocoa and coffee marketing boards, deregulated prices, and phased out many producer subsidies. The idea was to staunch the flow of public monies into agriculture, which the country could no longer afford, and to rewrite the rules of the game so that the market, not politics, would govern the sector. According to the then minister of agriculture, the planners hoped that once market signals were corrected and the market set prices, the food sector would become more dynamic and productive. They believed that Venezuelan agriculture could realize its potential in both local and export markets only if the "clutter" (distortions, special deals, and inefficiencies) was cleared away so that investors would pursue new opportunities.[23]

Changing the rules of the game, in this case, meant going from a system of arbitrary preferences to one that operated on general rules.[24] Change of this sort threatened the sectors that had been most privileged as well as the power of the traditional political brokers who negotiated special deals for agricultural interest groups. Predictably, it was the producers who had received the most protection who voiced the loudest opposition. The price support policies of the Lusinchi administration (1983-1988) had greatly stimulated the cultivation of sorghum, giving rise to a group of farmers with vested interests in state protection. Cheaper imports were kept out via import licenses. When the government announced that the licensing scheme would be replaced by a system that allowed imports subject to tariffs, the sorghum producers organized a protest that became known as the Cherokee March, because of the Cherokee Jeeps the farmers drove to Caracas.[25]

The attempt to replace government mediation with market mediation in agriculture was a shock to farmers. In the early 1990s, however, there were signs that the agricultural sector was responding. New investments were flowing into areas where entrepreneurs saw potential advantage, such as cocoa, coffee, yucca, African palm, bananas, other fruits and vegetables, cattle, and aquaculture. At the same time, production and profitability dropped in areas that showed less promise independent of government support, such as sorghum and corn.[26] Under competitive pressure, some farmers made important gains in productivity. Venezuelan food companies began to restructure and to develop new marketing strategies, and Venezuelan consumers enjoyed greater selection than before.

Backlash. The protests from organized agricultural interests continued. By mid-1993, there were signs that the tide of reform was turning. The government approved a new duty on imports of yellow corn, which boosted the domestic price for sorghum, a competing feed grain, by nearly 20 percent over the year before. It banned poultry imports from the United States because of reports of avian influenza, possibly legitimate but possibly an attempt to use sanitary requirements to block competition from imports.[27] President Velásquez appointed a leader of the national farmers' federation, which had bitterly fought the reforms, as minister of agriculture. There was talk in official circles of charting a "middle course," one that somehow would achieve the benefits of free market competition while granting increased protection and subsidies. In late 1993, the government announced that agricultural price setting would be exempt from the Pro-Competition Law.

While it often is argued that almost every country protects its agricultural sector, in Venezuela protection resulted in substantial distortions and inefficiencies. In addition, the poorest citizens often pay the cost of protection for agriculture, as they usually are hit hardest by price increases. Relatively little consideration appears to have been given to the costs of agricultural protection.

Infrastructure Policy

Venezuelan governments have prided themselves on ambitious new infrastructure projects, projects that would leave their mark on the country. Generally, they have been less enthusiastic about following through with projects already begun or maintaining those already completed. As a result, major highways have lain near completion for years, and there are two large, unfinished bus terminals on the outskirts of Caracas. Starting in 1990, reforms began to transform Venezuelan infrastructure by injecting a new dynamism into several areas of the economy, by allowing new entrants, and by stimulating competition.

Development and Control. For many decades, government policy reserved the development and administration of most of Venezuela's infrastructure to the central public administration. The main elements of Venezuela's present-day infrastructure were built under central government direction in the 1950s through 1980s. Public entities were created to manage the nation's telecommunications system, highways, ports, water, and electricity supplies as well as waste collection for Caracas and other cities. Many of these agencies were set up outside the main arms of government, as quasi-independent public entities, and were allowed to operate with little or no oversight or control. The government tended to keep down the rates charged to the public. At the same time, many public entities adopted a bureaucratic mentality that did not value efficiency or service to the customer, such as the old CANTV's "mindset of no." They also fulfilled unofficial functions, by providing political patronage posts and privileges to the well connected.

During the 1980s, public agencies proved unable to fulfill their basic obligations. Lack of effective oversight and political clientelism took a heavy toll on their performance. Roads and aqueducts fell into disrepair. The telecommunications system stagnated. The electricity system failed to grow to meet the needs of the country. Rates and fee structures, which had been kept artificially low for decades, failed to generate the revenues necessary for upkeep, much less expansion, and Venezuelans grew accustomed to paying little or nothing for unacceptable services. Public dissatisfaction with waste collection in Caracas led to the transfer of the trash collection function from the Metropolitan Institute of Urban Cleanliness (IMAU), the public entity previously responsible for the service, to private firms.[28]

Changing Policies. In 1990, the Pérez government embarked on a program to dismantle the centralized public agencies and to devolve their duties to the states and the private sector. For example, the government transferred responsibility for managing most of the maritime ports from the National Institute of Ports to the states in which they are located; in turn, most states contracted their management to the private sector. The state governments also began to assume management of the airports, highways, roads, and bridges within their territories. The Maracaibo Bridge came under the authority of the state of Zulia, which contracted management to a private firm. Management of the Porlamar Airport in Margarita was turned over to the government of Nueva Esparta. The public telecommunications network, CANTV, was privatized outright at the national level. An unsuccessful effort was made to privatize management of the Caracas water supply.

In the early 1990s, a series of privatizations improved the quality of infrastructure and basic services. We already have seen as examples the maritime ports and the telephone system. Privatization also opened up new business opportunities and was starting to stimulate competition and rivalry in new areas of the economy.[29] Hundreds of service firms sprang up around the maritime ports. Waste management firms started to compete for contracts with municipalities. Telecom firms started to offer new telecommunications services. Rivalry of this nature showed promise of upgrading the efficiency and quality of infrastructure throughout Venezuela.

In addition to privatization, the government opened certain areas of infrastructure to multiple private actors in order to stimulate rivalry.[30] For example, in the early 1990s, the minister of transportation and communications supported the privatization of Viasa, the opening up of international air routes to Venezuela, the approval of new national airlines, and the expansion of domestic airlines to foreign destinations. Controls on airfares were in effect removed. In telecommunications, in addition to the privatization of CANTV, the ministry approved the entry of private firms into the domestic markets for cellular phones, data transmission, and other value-added services.

Challenges Remain. At the same time, some privatizations, such as the Caracas aqueduct, Enelven, and Enelbar, have been blocked by entrenched interests and by bureaucrats who are not committed to reform. In addition, the Venezuelan government still faces the challenge of mustering the financial and human resources needed to invest in and maintain basic public goods, such as streets, sewers, and sidewalks, which are not suitable for privatization. In 1994, a statute was enacted to permit the construction of public works under concession that, it was hoped, would create new opportunities for infrastructure development.

Human Resource–Related Policies

Increasingly, the standard of living achieved by a nation depends more on its human resources than its natural resources. Policies related to human resources include labor and social policies as well as policies toward education, training, science, and technology.

Labor Law and Labor Policy

The liberalization of the Venezuelan economy in the late 1980s and early 1990s was far from complete. A more liberal regime did free interest and exchange rates, open up competition in a number of industries, privatize a number of state-owned enterprises, and free most prices. However, several other aspects of economic life were not liberalized. Perhaps the foremost examples were the policies and institutions that shape the labor market in Venezuela.

Since the 1930s, the Venezuelan state has assumed an active and pervasive role in regulating labor relations. Although the state has failed to provide a viable system of social security and retirement funds for its people, it has intervened extensively in the relationship between employer and employee, in such areas as hiring, remuneration, other terms of employment, dismissal, and labor disputes. For decades, the driving purpose of this intervention has been to improve the labor conditions and standard of living of the Venezuelan workforce. However, some of these regulatory provisions, originally intended as safeguards for labor, have had unforeseen results detrimental to competitiveness.

The ideal of protecting the worker through labor regulation became enshrined in Venezuelan labor legislation in the Labor Law of 1936.[31] The law drew its inspiration from the Labor Codes of Mexico and Chile, both adopted in 1931, and from the principles espoused by the International Labour Organization. It laid down many of the basic tenets of today's Venezuelan labor law, including severance payments upon dismissal from employment, the participation of employees in firm profits, and union leaders' immunity from dismissal.

The reformers of the 1930s did not adopt liberty of action between employer and employee as a basic tenet of their labor regime. Instead, they adopted a regime founded on regulatory authorizations and prohibitions, where certain employer actions were justified only if expressly allowed by law. The result, after years of legislative amendments, is a regime that purports to regulate the very fabric of the labor relationship and to establish legal presumptions in favor of the worker. During the 1930s, the concept of a strong, interventionist state held sway in Western Europe, the Soviet Union, the United States, and Latin America. Within Venezuela, the state itself and the multinational oil companies were major employers. The Labor Law of 1936 reflected a desire to protect Venezuelan workers from potential exploitation by foreign firms. It also reflected a pledge by the state to regulate its future actions vis-à-vis its own employees.

During the years of import substitution and closed markets, labor laws and labor policies served to redistribute rents from firms to workers. This was part of doing business in a market environment characterized by protection, low levels of competition, and, in many sectors, monopoly or oligopoly rents. In such a closed system, labor policies had a limited impact on the relative positions of firms. In the more open environment that began in 1989, in contrast, labor policies had a much greater impact. For the first time, many Venezuelan firms faced competition at home from foreign firms that operated under different labor arrangements. The Venezuelan firms that ventured into export markets faced the challenge of meeting fluctuating international demand, a new phenomenon for firms accustomed to monopoly or near-monopoly conditions in the domestic market. Labor costs and labor productivity can make or break a firm in such competitive, rapidly changing environments. As Gustavo Márquez (1993b) has explained, "in this sense, the adaptation of the legal and institutional framework of the labor market to the new conditions in which the economy functions are as or more crucial than the reforms of the monetary exchange and financial regimes that generally account for a disproportionate part of the debate."[32]

Nevertheless, in 1991, Venezuela enacted a statute that to a large extent codified preexisting labor laws. Instead of liberalizing the labor market, it cemented preexisting rigidities. Whereas it is understandable that labor would wish to protect its position against the uncertainties inherent in an open economy, the rigidities have made it more difficult for Venezuelan firms to respond to new competitive pressures and for firms and workers alike to improve their productivity.

Mandated Wage Increases. The practice of implementing across-the-board increases in salaries and benefits by executive decree increased in frequency starting in the mid-1970s and has continued through the early 1990s. Across-the-board benefit increases have a negative impact on the competitiveness of an economy. They decouple the wage-setting process from firm-based or individual-based productivity and thereby weaken the incentives to invest in the capabilities of a nation's workers. Escalante (1994) has observed that, in part as a result of repeated across-the-board salary increases, factors key to improving a worker's productivity, such as skilled or professional expertise, advanced education, and work experience, are not the ones that determine earning power in Venezuela. This, in turn, discourages workers from investing in improving their own productivity through education and training. Across-the-board salary increases also feed inflation, which in turn erodes a nation's quality of life. (Since the mid-1970s, the purchasing power of the minimum wage has declined.) Venezuela needs a greater public awareness of the detrimental effects of such policies.

Collective Contracts. Venezuelan law restricts the substantive terms of collective contracts in various ways.[33] No new collective contract may result in "worse" terms for labor than its predecessor, and the law does not provide a method of making this comparison. By law, changes to the conditions of employment may be made only if the parties agree "that the new conditions are more favorable for the workers."[34] A proposal to change the conditions of employment must be made to the official labor inspector, and, if an agreement is reached, the workers cannot be dismissed until the collective contract expires.

Among the types of collective contract established by Venezuelan law is the industry-wide collective contract *(reunión normativa laboral)*. This type of contract is binding on all employers and unions belonging to a specific sector, whether they have participated in the collective negotiation or not. The contracting parties may request that it be binding on a sector-wide basis, or the ministry of labor may decide that the participants represent the majority of the unionized workers and employers in the sector. According to Márquez (1993a), the centralized union movement in Venezuela prefers this type of contract. However, as he also points out, "it is not clear that the concentration of decision making power in the hands of the administrative authority leads to the greater well-being of the workers involved."[35] For example, a "generous" collective contract might be within the means of larger employers but might be onerous for smaller firms. Employees of the latter firms might be willing to accept a less "generous" contract "in order to preserve their jobs."[36]

Dismissal and Severance Provisions. Venezuelan workers have the right, upon dismissal, to a severance payment equal to one month's salary (based on their average monthly wage during their final year of employment) multiplied by the number of years of employment (that is, a retroactive severance). Workers dismissed for unjust cause are entitled to collect a double indemnity. In fact, many employers pay double indemnity as a matter of course, because of numerous pro-labor biases in the law.[37] Employers must maintain their employees' severance funds in trust (either within the firm's own accounts or in the banking sector) and are required to pay interest on the funds once annually. This annual payment of interest combined with retroactive application of future salary increases results in a double indexation of severance payments.

The Labor Law of 1936, as amended, attempted to define comprehensively the causes or reasons for which an employer could dismiss an employee "justly" as well as the "just causes" for employee resignations, and mandated a formula for compensating employees who resigned with just cause. In 1974, social severance payments were declared an "acquired right," regardless of the cause for termination of employment. In practice, this system has served as a partial substitute for unemployment insurance, as the nation lacks an effective unemployment insurance system. However, it introduced disincentives to productive performance into the workplace: Employees are guaranteed a lump-sum payment upon dismissal even if they perform unsatisfactory work. The provision for double indemnity in the case of unjust dismissal, introduced in 1974, introduced additional disincentives to good job performance. It places a premium on being dismissed without just cause, even if the employee wishes to resign, because dismissal without just cause doubles the severance payment. This can motivate misbehavior on the part of either the employee (to try to instigate an "unjust" dismissal) or the employer (to try to find a "just" pretext for terminating employment).[38] Even under the best of circumstances, the double indemnity provision introduces an element of tension into labor-management relations on the job.[39]

The retroactivity of severance payments influences firm decision making with respect to hiring and salaries. An example set forth in Escalante (1994) shows the financial consequences of a decision to increase a worker's salary under the retroactive severance system. A worker earns 20,000 bolivars per month and has worked for one employer for ten years. At today's prices, this salary does not go far toward meeting a family's needs, and for this reason the worker requests a wage increase of 10,000 bolivars per month (50 percent increase). As Escalante observed, it is possible that the employer might be willing and able to grant the salary increase requested, in the absence of retroactive obligations. However, the retroactivity provision greatly increases the cost of this salary increase to the employer. After ten years' employment, the worker has a severance fund valued at 200,000 bolivars. If the employer grants the raise, the firm must contribute an additional 100,000 bolivars to the worker's severance fund (10,000 bolivars multiplied by ten years of employment), plus annual interest payments going forward. The employer must meet this obligation immediately by drawing from cash flow, incurring debt, or other means. If instead of a single worker, a large number of workers make this type of request, the immediate financial impact of a single wage increase on the employer can be severe.

According to Escalante (1994), in practice the retroactivity provision typically results in lower wage increases than requested by labor in their collective contract negotiations, as has occurred at CANTV, PDVSA, the ministry of education, and the Metro de Caracas. The provision entails many costs to the worker, the firm, and the competitiveness of the economy overall. The worker receives a lower salary than otherwise would be the case, which hurts the family's purchasing power on a day-to-day basis. The firm incurs substantial financial obligations that often must be funded out of cash flow, diverting capital from reinvestment. Productivity suffers as a result of protracted contract negotiations and, sometimes, labor disputes. Less is spent on training and educating workers, because education and training would lead to costly salary increases. Escalante has observed that, because of retroactive social severance obligations under the Labor Law, firms that do grant wage increases sometimes dismiss personnel afterward, in an effort to balance their accounts.

Márquez (1993b) has shown that the dismissal and severance payments of the labor laws end up hurting many of those whom they were intended to help. Firms will employ an additional worker only up to the point where the marginal cost of employing him or her equals the value of the worker's output. The severance and dismissal provisions have forced up marginal costs to the point that many workers are not hired who otherwise would be. The workers who find themselves shut out of the system are precisely those with greatest need, unskilled workers with limited bargaining power.[40]

Additional Mandated Benefits. Venezuelan labor legislation provides such benefits as paid vacations and vacation bonuses, day care, yearly profit-sharing bonuses, food and transportation bonuses, and employers' contributions to the national housing fund, work stoppage insurance, social security, and INCE (for vocational training). Venezuelan managers often refer to these benefits as a heavy burden, although they are comparable to those in other Latin American countries.[41] The labor laws guarantee workers 15 days of paid vacation in their first year of employment, increasing to a total of 30 days' paid vacation over time. In addition, the employer must pay a vacation bonus, over and above salary, ranging from seven to 21 days' salary, depending on seniority. According to one Venezuelan manager, many Venezuelan firms determine the total compensation, including benefits, that they can pay and then subtract out the value of benefits in order to determine salaries and wages.[42] In such situations, mandated benefits do not really leave the worker better off. Other Venezuelan firms hire fewer workers than they would in the absence of some of the mandates. The underlying question for the economy is whether the Venezuelan workforce is sufficiently productive to support benefits comparable to those of Western European nations.

Labor Policy and Competitiveness. Venezuela's labor policy was designed to protect the worker in the formal sector rather than to promote employment, economic growth, or competitiveness. Businesses in open economies need the flexibility to respond quickly to pressures and opportunities and to cut back when necessary. In the short run, this may translate into the loss of jobs, but in the long run, it may mean survival and growth for firms and for industries. Workers in open economies benefit from labor markets that place a positive value on investing in the individual worker and his or her productive capacity through training and education, which in turn help achieve a higher standard of living. Pro-competitive labor policies promote investing in people in ways that build stronger workers. However, government policies toward labor are only part of the government input side of the human resources equation. The competitive impact of Venezuelan government policies toward education, training, science, and technology are addressed in the following sections.

Education and Training Policy

Despite many conflicts and about-faces in educational policies over the past 30 years, Venezuelan public policy toward education has been characterized by certain basic continuities. The government has expanded the reach of education to ever-growing numbers of Venezuelans and has extended the number of years of obligatory schooling. For the past 30 years, efforts also have been made to improve the quality of education. Although there have been sporadic efforts to develop the productive skills necessary to contribute to the competitiveness of the economy, this has never been one of the primary goals of education in Venezuela.

Universality. Since the early 1960s, the main goals of Venezuelan education policy have been to build a human foundation for democracy and economic development.[43] At that time, education was seen as a means of consolidating democracy and promoting growth. The situation was urgent: More than one-third of the adult population was illiterate and the primary school system reached only 73 percent of the country's children. The state responded with an ambitious effort to construct a modern, universal education system that would incorporate youth from all geographic regions and all socioeconomic backgrounds. It would eliminate illiteracy. It was intended to be universal at the primary school level and to provide opportunities for a university education to all students who were interested, regardless of socioeconomic background.

The goals of education policy also reflected political realities. In its earliest days, the survival of the new democratic regime depended on the incorporation of politically powerful groups, such as teachers, university students, and the intelligentsia, and the ability to reward armies of political supporters with public posts. The process of appointing teachers and other education personnel, and the reward structure of contract negotiations, became politicized in the earliest years of Venezuela's democratic period. The system's subsequent evolution has been shaped to a large extent by its political functions and constraints. Government also has depended on the education and socialization of new generations of public officials and bureaucrats. In many years, most university graduates went on to work in the public sector.

El Estado Docente. The administration of education in Venezuela has been shaped by a unique set of guiding principles.[44] Foremost has been the notion of *el Estado Docente,* (the teacher state), under which the state is the primary agent of education. The national government has been the primary actor in building schools, educating and hiring teachers, and formulating educational policies. Although private educational institutions have made important contributions at all educational levels, they have been relegated a secondary role in the system at large.

The second guiding principle is that Venezuela's education system must provide equal educational opportunities to Venezuelans from diverse socioeconomic backgrounds and that equality of opportunity means the number of students served, not the quality of education offered. The perceived conflict between expansive educational policies and meritocratic education dates back to the 1940s, before Venezuela had made a commitment to universal education. As of 1994, there was no thought of rolling back universal public education at the expense of the less privileged. However, many Venezuelan educators still believed that seeking academic excellence was incompatible with the "democratization" of education and that raising academic standards would hurt, not help, the majority of the nation's students.

Uniformity and Centralization. For decades, Venezuelan educational policy at the primary and secondary school level has been biased strongly in favor of uniformity. Since the 1960s, the concern for uniformity has been fostered by the rapid growth of new schools and institutions and the growing complexity of educational administration, which sparked worries that the system lacked coherence. There also has been a pervasive belief that uniformity in content, methods, quality, and organizational methods is necessary to build an educational system that upholds the values of democracy and equality in education.[45] These factors fostered centralization, with primary and secondary schools throughout Venezuela administered by the ministry of education from its Caracas headquarters.

As of 1993, the ministry in Caracas directly administered public schools that accounted for more than one-half of the national student body.[46] It assigned and allocated school budgets and controlled the hiring, promotion, and dismissal of individual teachers and principals. Centralized policies tied the hands of most school principals, who lacked the power to name, promote, or dismiss teachers and other school workers, and who were authorized to manage only a small portion (less than 10 percent) of their schools' operating budgets. Concern over the degree of centralization of the schools had led to certain reforms, most notably the creation of "educative zones" within the ministry of education, but this administrative reorganization did not result in any substantial redistribution of power or decision making.[47]

In 1993, efforts to decentralize government were still at early stages and were only starting to have an impact on the public schools in Venezuela.[48] Education was included among the public services transferrable to state governments under the Decentralization Law. In practice, this means that the transfer of public schools from the ministry of education to state governments will be a lengthy process. As of 1993, no state had obtained the transfer of authority over public schools within its borders, although governors of Bolívar, Miranda, and Falcón had submitted requests. Uncertainty over mechanisms for funding the transferred schools was further delaying the process. At the same time, the revitalization of state governments had a positive impact on many public schools that by law were under state, rather than national, jurisdiction, and therefore were free of the ministry of education. Several states started to reorganize these schools, sometimes in direct confrontation with the teachers' unions. In many cases, the results at first evaluation have been exceptionally good in terms of the efficient use of public resources and of students' achievements and well being.[49]

Politics Rather than Performance. Personnel policies in Venezuelan schools have traditionally been based on considerations of politics, not performance.[50] Many Venezuelans believe that party influence long has played a determining role in the teacher selection process. The teachers' unions often have controlled the movement of teachers through the system (naming, promotion, and dismissal). Under the union's terms of employment, teachers' classroom performance and productivity have not been taken into account in promotion decisions. Instead, employment contracts have contained incentives for teachers to involve themselves in union activities (union officers have been absolved of teaching duties and guaranteed full pay) or to obtain advanced education regardless of how they perform on the job. Removing a teacher from a teaching post, for any reason, has been extremely difficult, and school principals have held office for life. Retirement has been the most common reason for a change in school principals in Venezuela.

Navarro's 1993 report of a visit to a technical school showed this incentive (or disincentive) structure in action. The director was elderly and on the verge of retirement. One subdirector was "preretired," a condition that excused him from working while guaranteeing full pay. Another had been elected to the State Legislative Assembly. Out of a total of 172 teachers, 14 were excused from duties. Another 41 teachers were working part time. Nevertheless, the school suffered from an overabundance of teachers, because it was not possible to dismiss excess personnel. Many never got to teach in a classroom. According to experts on the Venezuelan education system, this is a "very real example" of the overstaffing in the public schools.

Few policies exist to set nationwide performance standards for students. Venezuela has had no policies in the area of nationwide academic testing and standards.[51] The education system applies no test of skills or knowledge in standardized fashion to students at specific grade levels, except for the test administered to graduates of the diversified cycle (high school) who wish to apply to a postsecondary institution. Throughout the primary and secondary levels, the government has not set quality standards for academic achievement. Due to this fact, parents and students cannot measure the students' achievement or evaluate the quality of the education local schools are providing. Nor has the government formally evaluated the performance of the institutions of higher learning responsible for training the nation's teachers.

Bottlenecks and Inefficiencies. The extreme centralization of administration of the national school system has created continual bottlenecks and inefficiency. It also has weakened the ministry's capacity for planning and policy formulation. As part of this project, the ministry was asked to supply a breakout of central government educational spending by state; it replied that such data was not available, and that, in any case, the ministry's central computer system was burdened to capacity with the processing of school paychecks.[52] Centralization, plus a tradition of padding the payroll with political appointees, has bloated the ministry's administrative ranks, which, in the early 1990s, included one worker or administrative employee for every two teachers. Internationally, one worker or administrative employee for every eight teachers was considered the appropriate standard. Centralized control has distanced schools from their local communities: Because communities have no input into school administration, schools have no incentives to reach out to their communities, and centralized controls prevent the schools from adapting programs or curricula to the needs of the neighborhoods that they serve.[53]

Privileged Universities. At the postsecondary level, the dominant goal has been to maximize admissions opportunities for Venezuelan students. Over the past 30 years, the state has built a system of mass postsecondary education that is for the most part publicly funded, has low admissions standards, and is free of charge. Venezuelan budget priorities have favored higher education over primary and secondary education. Since the early 1980s, postsecondary education has consumed more than 40 percent of the budget of the ministry of education. Postsecondary students have accounted for only 10 percent of the national student body, and they have come largely from the middle and upper classes of society. This is an ironic outcome for an educational system whose avowed purpose is equality of opportunity. Funding of public higher education in Venezuela actually increased in real terms through the 1980s at the same time as the rates of return to higher education declined.[54]

Another constant over the years has been a policy of university autonomy. During the 1980s, direct payments by the government accounted for more than 90 percent of public university recurrent expenditures. Whereas the ministry of education and the Venezuelan Congress set the overall budgets for higher education, they have had little say in how higher education funds were used. Traditionally, leaders of the various public universities, represented on the National Council of Universities, have negotiated among themselves to distribute the funds allocated to higher education. The share of any one institution was determined primarily by its traditional allocation of funds, without any regard to performance criteria.[55] If a particular university overspent its budget, the government paid its debts. Government has exerted relatively little influence on public universities' curricula. At the same time, it has permitted and even encouraged the politicization of the postsecondary education system as a means of co-opting radical students and faculty and defusing violent dissent. For decades, to major in economics or other branches of the social sciences was to learn that Venezuela was a dependent nation, exploited by first-world, capitalist nations and companies.[56]

While there have been attempts to reform higher education over the past decade, there have been few results. Sporadic government efforts to increase oversight of the universities, to raise admissions selection criteria or to enforce standards of academic performance have been far less successful. The students themselves have been a powerful opponent of attempts to impose even minimal academic standards. For example, student leaders, backed by political parties, have opposed the implementation of rules that established very modest requirements of academic performance at the universities.[57]

Two education ministers proposed modifying the zero-tuition system. In both instances, they abandoned their proposals in the face of opposition from interest groups. The ministry of education, through its Central Planning Office for higher education, tried to introduce a formula-based system for allocating funds among institutions of higher learning but was defeated by university administrators.[58] Decades of easy funding and lax controls have nourished the growth of entrenched and vocal elites within the university sector, including faculty and workers' unions, administrators, and students. Each group has a vested interest in current patterns of spending. Each group has vigorously opposed, through political pressure and the press, attempts at reform. These interest groups have argued that reforms (aimed at improving efficiency) would have an inequitable impact on less-privileged Venezuelans. However, educational experts have suggested that the Venezuelan system of higher learning is so inefficient that efficiency gains should be possible without any efficiency-equity trade-off and that social equity would be promoted, not hindered, by rerouting financial resources from the postsecondary sector to the primary and secondary schools.[59]

Limited Technical Education and Training. While Venezuelan governments have tried for decades to provide mass opportunities for technical training at the secondary school level, this has never been one of the primary goals of the system. In the early 1970s, technical schools were closed in favor of the introduction of a technical course of study at the diversified cycle (high school). The government reopened the technical schools with a redesigned curriculum in 1977, but their temporary closing dealt a further blow to their prestige in a society that places a premium on a liberal arts education.

Starting in the 1970s, the government adopted policies designed to bring the higher education system into line with the needs of the workforce and industry. In the 1960s, the higher-education policy focused on maximizing opportunities to enter universities and to pursue a liberal arts education. The explosion in university enrollments soon led to high rates of attrition and to a massive supply of university-level dropouts and graduates who lacked economically useful skills. In response, policy shifted toward the creation of postsecondary educational alternatives to four-year universities, such as technological institutes based on the French model and three-year university colleges based on the U.S. community college model. These institutions have accounted for less than 30 percent of higher-education graduates.[60] They also have encountered resistance from many teachers and students at the public universities.

In the area of training, the Venezuelan government's central instrument has been the National Institute for Educational Cooperation (INCE).[61] Since 1959, INCE has carried out training and apprenticeship programs by providing courses directly, by contracting with other institutions for the provision of courses, and by directing apprenticeships and intern programs in coordination with employers. Its funding has come from the state, a payroll tax paid by employers, and mandatory employee contributions. In 1989, the National

Executive ordered a reorganization and modernization of the institute, which had come under criticism for failing to keep pace with the dynamics of the workforce. Since 1991, INCE has been decentralized into 21 civil associations made up of worker, employer, state, and business representatives charged with identifying and satisfying the training needs of each region of the country. INCE has introduced innovative apprenticeship programs designed to accelerate the incorporation of trainees into the workforce and to increase on-the-job training.

Education and Training Needs. In most nations, the average standard of living depends on the average productivity of workers in the workforce. The level of education and training, and their applicability to economic activity, found in the workforce is a major determinant of its productivity. In Venezuela, the challenge will be to make public spending on education and training more effective, more efficient, and better targeted both in terms of the needs of the economy and social equity.

Science and Technology Policy

Venezuelan science and technology policy has focused on state-owned investigation centers as generators of domestic technology and the design of mechanisms to link that technology with the productive sector. The challenge of building the internal technological capability of local firms (defined as the capacity to select, negotiate for, assimilate, and adapt technology) has received relatively less attention. In particular, Venezuela has never had an official policy aimed at promoting the assimilation of technology by local firms.[62]

Focus on Science. Government support for research and development in Venezuela has been limited.[63] Those resources devoted to research and development have been directed mainly toward basic sciences and medical research. In 1967, the state formalized its role as a promoter of scientific research by founding the National Council of Scientific and Technological Research (CONICIT), which was based on the premise that science carried out in the laboratory was the principal source of technological innovation. Its major objective was to achieve more and better applied science. The technology component of its policy was limited to seeking ways to link the business community with the technologies developed inside CONICIT. CONICIT did not address the specific technological problems faced by a nation in the position of Venezuela, which was building its industrialization process on foreign technology. The private firm entered into its equation only as the end recipient of the fruits of public research.

During the 1970s and 1980s, state science and technology policy focused on the creation of additional research centers, some affiliated with state-owned companies (such as INTEVEP of PDVSA), others with ministries (such as the Foundation Institute of Engineering, under the ministry of development). At the same time, import substitution policies created a protected home market, in which mastery of technology by private firms was not important to business success. In the second half of the 1980s, when budgetary pressures began forcing cutbacks in traditional R&D expenditures, universities began to set up new types of R&D centers oriented toward the needs of private and public firms, such as the Foundation for Research and Development (FUNINDES), of the Simón Bolívar University. The Projects and Services of the Faculty of Sciences (PRO-SERVIFACICA) of the Central University of Venezuela is another successful initiative, the result of a faculty, rather than university, endeavor.

In the early 1990s, there was a concerted effort to bolster the so-called science and technology sector and to create closer ties between the research efforts of public organizations and private firms. The government obtained financing from the Inter-American Development Bank with the aim of bringing resource levels back to those of 15 years ago. It also fostered a series of negotiation roundtables between CONICIT, public R&D centers, and businesses to put the resources of the public R&D centers to work to serve the needs of industry, with financial assistance from CONICIT to the firms. However, the basic tenets of national science and technology policy were largely unchanged. Public R&D centers were still seen as the prime motors of innovation. Private firms were still seen as the recipients of publicly generated technology. There has been little focus on the need of private Venezuelan firms for a technological education to strengthen their capacity to assimilate, adapt, and innovate.

Limited Technological Sophistication in Firms. The results of Venezuela's science and technology policy are seen most clearly in the low level of technological sophistication characteristic of Venezuelan firms.[64] Under the import substitution regime, private business adopted a passive attitude toward technology. Technological learning was not regarded as an essential element of competitive strategy. Firms tended not to understand that such learning played an essential role in the acquisition and use of foreign technology. The official science and technology policy reinforced this view by promoting technological innovation within the public sector, not within private firms.

Relatively few Venezuelan firms have availed themselves of CONICIT's technology roundtables. One reason is that many firms lack a basic understanding of technology. Large and sophisticated Venezuelan firms have been availing themselves of the new opportunities for collaboration with public sector and university researchers. However, they are not the norm. The average Venezuelan firm lacks the basic technological capabilities required to understand, much less pursue, its technological requirements and as a result does not avail itself of public R&D resources.

Developing New Technologies. As of 1993, CONICIT was scheduled to receive $90 million over four years to finance a program for the development of new technologies.[65] Half of the financing was to be provided by the Venezuelan state and the other half by a loan from the Inter-American Development Bank (IDB). Its purpose was to stimulate the development of microelectronics, biotechnology, new materials, and alternative sources of energy, giving support to scientific and technological projects as well as training. The program was similar to those formulated in several other Latin American countries.

Many countries around the world, not just in Latin America, are trying to become leaders in new technologies as a way of ensuring their competitiveness in future markets. Many of these countries are focusing their efforts on the same technologies, such as microelectronics, biotechnology, and new materials. By definition, the vast majority of these countries will fall short of their goal, because all countries cannot be "leaders" in the same areas. Venezuela's most pressing need is to boost the technological capabilities of private firms, not just the nation's leading firms but the great majority of firms of all sizes across the economy.

In an ideal world, funding would be available for both types of policy initiatives, but given current budgetary constraints, it will be necessary to choose policy aims carefully. Improving the technological capabilities of local firms is likely to provide much greater leverage for the development of competitive industries in Venezuela than large-scale public research in areas that are attracting R&D investments around the globe. Public research does have a role, but it will be most effective if it is focused and supports the private sector.

Weak Intellectual Property Protection. A strong intellectual property regime can promote specialized factor creation and provide firms with incentives to innovate and to improve products and processes. Patent protection, for example, creates incentives for firms to invest in developing new technology. Copyright protection creates incentives for producing, distributing, and marketing new intellectual creations in a broad range of industries and service sectors.[66] Some developing countries, such as Singapore, have adopted strong intellectual property regimes in order to promote technological development and economic growth.[67] In contrast, many developing nations, including Venezuela and other Latin American countries, chose not to adhere to international standards for intellectual property protection. With respect to patent protection, for example, in the 1960s, it was widely believed that patent protection within developing nations served to benefit foreign firms and that, if patents were registered locally but not practiced, they amounted to "sterile monopolies" that impeded the flow of technology into the country.[68]

For 40 years, Venezuela gave weak legal protection to intellectual property. Government policy was to attract intellectual property into Venezuela free of legal protections and to minimize the amount spent by local firms on foreign licenses.[69] The laws, administrative enforcement agencies, and the courts all were lax in protecting intellectual property. For years, the Industrial Property Law of 1955 offered protection only in vague and general terms. By 1992, it was reported that the Industrial Property Register, responsible for registering and enforcing intellectual property rights, had a backlog of approximately 50,000 trademark and 5,000 industrial patent applications.[70] Lawsuits to enforce intellectual property rights in the courts tended to be expensive, lengthy, and of uncertain outcome. For example, between 1960 and 1993, an estimated 35,000 to 45,000 patents were issued in Venezuela, but as of 1993 only five court cases involving patents had been brought, and the Venezuelan courts had found only a few patents valid and enforceable.[71]

In 1992, intellectual property piracy in Venezuelan cost U.S. companies alone more than $100 million[72] and cost untold millions more to Europeans trying to do business in the country. Companies that have had problems with intellectual property piracy in Venezuela include Louis Vuitton (France), BMW (Germany), BHV Holdings, N.V. (Netherlands), HOLA (Spain), Mazda (Japan), and Reebok (United States).[73] For example, the Dutch company BHV Holdings, the owner of the Makro chain of wholesale stores, announced that it would invest 4,500 million bolivars to enter the wholesale market in Venezuela. A Venezuelan firm claimed already to own the Makro trademark there, despite never having operated a business under that name.[74] Under international legal standards, Makro's case would have been straightforward. However, Venezuelan trademark law required Makro to demonstrate that the Venezuelan firm had not used the trademark, a burden of proof contrary to international trademark law.[75]

The well-known Spanish magazine *HOLA* was banned by a Venezuelan court from circulating in Venezuela, after being sold in the country for years, after Venezuelan applicants were awarded an identical trademark. The Spanish firm recovered its marketing rights, and editions of the authentic *HOLA* reappeared in Venezuelan stores, only after a protracted legal battle. A national footwear manufacturer produced shoes under the Reebok brand name without entering into a licensing agreement with Reebok. The Venezuelan firm was willing to sell its local trademark to Reebok, but Reebok concluded that the asking price represented too large an investment given the small size of the Venezuelan market.[76] As a result, Reebok decided not to sell its merchandise in Venezuela. Incidents of piracy such as these are well known to potential investors abroad and have damaged Venezuela's reputation as a place to do business.

In an integrated world economy, access to markets and to inbound foreign investment are tied increasingly to intellectual property protection. Like many other Latin American countries, Venezuela has taken steps to strengthen its intellectual property regime. The early 1990s saw signs of a stronger commitment to intellectual property protection. Venezuela adopted three Andean Pact decisions that strengthened intellectual property rights and, in 1993, enacted a stronger copyright law. The Industrial Property Register has undertaken a campaign to modernize and to automate procedures and has made progress on its backlog. In August 1993, the register published about 20,000 trademarks, many of which had been pending for years, thereby giving the public an opportunity to oppose the proposed marks. Police confiscations of counterfeit merchandise increased in the early 1990s.[77] Venezuela was in the process of laying the ground rules for effective protection of intellectual property, although many changes remain to be made if the nation's intellectual property regime is to become a positive force for competitiveness.

Social Policy

The competitiveness of an economy has a large impact on the social policies that can be carried out in the nation. A competitive, productive economy generates the resources necessary to provide the less fortunate with sufficient nutrition, adequate housing, a decent education, adequate health care, and access to basic social services. Developing a vibrant, competitive economy raises the standard of living of a nation's workers and also provides the wherewithal to address the nation's social problems. Thus, those Venezuelans who are most concerned with the nation's social problems should be at the forefront of efforts to improve the competitiveness of the nation's economy.

The social policies that a nation adopts also influence its competitiveness in a number of ways. Social policies can affect the ability of individuals to be productive. It is, for example, extremely difficult for people without access to at least a minimal social safety net to provide for themselves and to become productive members of society. The purpose of this section is not to provide a detailed exposition or critique of Venezuelan social policy but rather to identify some of the key issues in social policy that have influenced or will influence the nation's economic development.

High Priority

Social policy has been the highest priority of Venezuelan governments during the democratic period.[78] For decades, the main goal of Venezuelan social policy has been to provide an acceptable standard of living for the population as a whole. This long has been regarded as necessary to ensure public confidence in the democratic system. Traditional social policy has been based on the premise that the state is responsible for guaranteeing the well-being of the population, especially the less fortunate, and that oil revenues would make this possible. At the same time, the basic mechanisms for the direct distribution of social benefits operated to distribute oil rents among political parties, unions, interest groups, and society at large. There was relatively little focus on efficiency or on targeting the truly needy. Over the years, these programs bought support for democracy but were highly inefficient as a means of income redistribution to the poorest sectors of society.

Certain types of social benefits were administered directly by centralized government agencies. For example, public hospitals were managed by the ministry of health and the Venezuelan Social Security Institute (IVSS). In the 1960s, their level of service was considered relatively high. However, later it declined as the administering agency succumbed to the ills of clientelism and weak controls. Another redistributive policy widely enforced throughout the 1970s and 1980s was that of price controls at the consumer level. The government set price controls for 12 basic food products, including precooked corn meal, vegetable oil, cheese, and sugar. Price controls provided an indirect subsidy to all consumers of these food products, whether they were needy or not, and as a result, the middle- and upper-income sectors received heavy subsidies. This subsidy imposed a severe burden on the public purse while benefiting many who did not need it. It sometimes was justified on the grounds that targeted subsidies were difficult or impossible to administer in Venezuela.

Pressure for Change

By the late 1980s, several years of economic hardship had worsened the lot of millions of Venezuelans, many of whom sank beneath the poverty line for the first time. At the same time, budgetary constraints made it imperative to find more efficient means to deliver social services and support to the poor. The government responded by reorienting efforts at poverty relief, replacing the indirect subsidies of the past with a targeted approach designed to identify individuals in need and to deliver benefits directly to them.

The new focus in social policy sought, above all, to help poor families with children in ways that would make a difference. During the 1980s, declining incomes had taken a toll on the calorie and protein consumption of the poor, and there had been a resurgence in certain diseases related to poor nutrition. The government undertook an ambitious effort to boost the diet and nutrition of needy children, through cash vouchers and stamps redeemable for food and through the provision of milk and meals at school. It expanded the existing network of home day care providers in low-income neighborhoods. It stepped up the delivery of health, nutritional, and educational support to expectant mothers, nursing mothers, and infants. It expanded the reach of preschool programs. In addition, there were initiatives in employment and social protection programs, including programs designed to promote small businesses and to assist low-income consumers in forming cooperatives; and programs for social investment, in such areas as public sanitation, education, health, recreation, and housing.

The government also enacted new social benefits for workers by imposing additional obligations on employers. Following the unrest of February 27, 1989, workers' salaries, as well as food and transportation compensation, in the private and public sectors were raised by presidential decree. As of August 1992, employers with more than 20 employees were required to provide or to pay for day care for employees' children. In addition, the government required both employers and employees to contribute to a work stoppage insurance *(seguro de paro forzoso)*.

Tangible Gains

Within a short period of time, the social policy initiatives succeeded in providing tangible benefits to large numbers of poor Venezuelans. An estimated 1.2 million poor families with children received benefits under the School Network program, such as vouchers for milk and for cereals (rice and corn flour) redeemable at food stores, money coupons, or glasses of milk at school. In other areas, smaller programs were expanded to many times their original size. In 1991, 671,000 households received nutritional support or medical care under the Program of Attention to Mother and Child (PAMI).[79] The number of homes providing day care in poor neighborhoods under the Day Care Homes Program increased from 1,795 homes in 1988 to nearly 15,000 homes, serving 145,000 children, in 1991. The value of the contribution made by the direct subsidy programs was estimated at roughly 16 percent of income for the lowest-income homes and 8 percent for the next tier.[80]

Despite the gains, the direct subsidy programs were unable to reach a large portion of the target families, and overall poverty levels remained very high. A significant number of extremely poor children have escaped the reach of the School Network programs, most commonly because they are less likely than other poor children to be enrolled in or live nearby the schools. The programs that were administered by existing centralized agencies fell prey to the types of problems that traditionally plagued social service delivery in Venezuela. After the implementation of some School Network Programs was placed in the hands of the ministry of education, the programs soon began to suffer from deficiencies in social information systems, oversight, evaluation, and control. Schools have complained that it was nearly impossible to get the ministry to correct errors in its lists of children eligible for assistance.[81]

At the same time, the government experimented with new, more flexible administrative structures. One example was the Program of Support to the Popular Economy, which enlisted the efforts of state and local governments as well as the Fundación Mendoza, the Center at the Service of Popular Action (CESAP), the Cooperatives Central of Venezuela (CECONAVE), the Fundación Fé y Alegría, and other nongovernmental organizations.[82] Between 1990 and the first half of 1992, this initiative provided technical and other support to more than 10,300 microenterprises, mostly in urban areas, as well as a number of cooperative projects aimed at lowering the cost of basic foodstuffs *(canasta básica)* to low-income consumers. Equally important, it succeeded in involving nongovernmental organizations in the provision of social services on a large scale, and the experience helped identify several challenges that future efforts of this type will have to address in the areas of oversight, targeting, and systematization.[83] Malavé and Piñango (1993), in their study on social conditions and competitiveness in Venezuela, found that some public/private partnerships in the social services have succeeded in delivering high-quality health and education services to the poor.[84]

Public Administration and the Judiciary

Public administration underlies all areas of government policy. Even the best policies will fail to have a positive impact unless they are administered effectively. The quality of the Venezuelan bureaucracy is generally considered lower than those in neighbors and competitors such as Colombia, Mexico, and Chile. In these countries, a well-trained, well-paid, professional government bureaucracy exists in most areas of public administration. In Venezuela in the early 1990s, only a few pockets of efficient bureaucracy survived, specifically the Central Bank, the National Library, and a few others.

The impact of Venezuela's weak public administration touches virtually every aspect of economic and social regulation. The sources of greatest popular discontent, such as low-quality schools and hospitals, bankrupt social security funds, and corruption in high places, can be traced in part to deficiencies in the administration of government. The problem is not one of knowing what to fix or how to fix it. Numerous commissions and experts have studied Venezuela's public administration over the past 20 years and have proposed plans of action. The problem is mustering the political will to rebuild the system, which would require numerous interest groups to give up old privileges and modes of behavior in exchange for a healthy government.

A number of structural features make it difficult for Venezuela's public agencies to implement public policy. They also make it relatively easy for the political parties and other interest groups to block the implementation of new policy directives with which they disagree.[85]

Lack of Organizational Strength and Technical Support

The formulation of policy at the highest levels of Venezuelan government has been hindered by problems of organization and inadequate technical support. The presidency, which for many years has taken the leading role in lawmaking, often has operated on the basis of incomplete factual knowledge. Its principal supporting office, the ministry of the secretariat, has lacked reliable data bases or computerized information systems and has provided only limited technical assistance. The Council of Ministers has been similarly hampered by weak support. The flow of reliable information has been sporadic at best. There has been little exchange of information among different ministries. Top officials, because of lack of competent support staff at middle-management levels, often have had to divert their attention to matters that should have been handled at lower levels within their ministries. As a result, decisions often have been based on insufficient information and poor or incomplete analysis.[86]

Congress has suffered from the same types of obstacles to effective policy making, only magnified. It traditionally has played a secondary role to the executive in the formulation of policy and lawmaking. This situation is due in part to a political tradition of a strong executive and in part to pervasive weaknesses in technical ability and leadership that limit its ability to analyze problems and to make independent decisions. Under the traditional system, individual deputies to Congress were named not by the voters but by party leaders. As a result, delegates tended to follow the party line rather than to demonstrate independence and initiative. At the same time, the principal congressional committees, in both chambers, have operated with very small staffs and only a few experts in policy matters, who in turn have had very little technical support. In practice, the political parties themselves have tended to contract for consulting support, a process that has thoroughly politicized the analytical process and the resulting debate.[87]

For the past decade, the Venezuelan public agencies have been losing many of their best and brightest employees at the managerial, supervisory, and technical levels. In part this has been a function of a widening gap in pay between the public and private sectors, a gap that has been particularly serious at the higher levels of government. The loss of capable workers also results from the realities of the public workplace. For many people, there are no career paths or opportunities for professional development. Advancement has seldom been based on merit. Instead, employees often have been subject to shifting, informal chains of command. Many agencies have tried to make up for the loss of qualified permanent staff by hiring outside consultants on a contractual basis.

Weak Bureaucratic Controls

The Venezuelan public administration has lacked the ability to implement policies efficiently and effectively, largely because it has been unable to regulate its own operations. In the early 1990s, between the top policy makers and lower-level staff were 38,000 supervisors and managers entrusted with the critical role of communicating policy decisions to the troops.[88] These posts were largely free from basic personnel controls. The duties and responsibilities of most of these posts were not formally defined. In many cases, there were no qualification requirements, no performance standards, and no systems for performance evaluation. Over the years, positions of this kind have been the province of political party and union activists, who have answered to their de facto bosses in their sponsoring organizations and have carried out objectives foreign to the government agency that employed them.[89]

While regulating the centralized public agencies has been difficult, regulating the hundreds of autonomous institutes, state-owned enterprises, public foundations, and other quasi-independent public entities has proven next to impossible. This is a very large sector of the government, accounting for an estimated 300,000 to 400,000 employees in contrast to 130,000 employees in the central public administration.[90] The decentralized entities, including the state-owned enterprises, have operated largely free of effective control. Sporadic efforts have been made to monitor the performance of the state-owned companies, but they generally have come to naught due to frequent personnel changes, lack of interest on the part of the state-owned firms themselves, and lack of pressure from the overburdened ministries.[91]

Legal Rigidities

The ability of Venezuelan public agencies to implement policy also has been hindered by a complex and inconsistent set of laws governing public personnel, which makes it difficult to dismiss workers for any reason. Blue-collar public employees generally belong to unions and fall within the sphere of the Labor Law, including its provisions governing termination of employment. Higher up the ladder, the terms of employment and dismissal of many professional employees are governed by the Law of Administrative Career, which guarantees "stability" in employment and makes dismissal next to impossible.[92] These factors have made restructuring an agency a complex and costly proposition. In some instances, reformers have had no other option but the wholesale dismissal of thousands of workers and the payment of prohibitive severance payments. In many other situations, legal obstacles to dismissal have prevented much-needed reforms.

A Troubled Judiciary

Despite various policy initiatives to strengthen the Venezuelan judiciary, the judiciary traditionally has shown a low degree of institutional independence. Venezuela has not been successful in insulating the naming and promotion of justices and judges from the influence of political parties. In 1988, the Law of the Judicial Council *(Ley Orgánica del Consejo de la Judicatura)* finally gave the judicial branch powers of self-governance, as provided in the Constitution of 1961. However, formal autonomy has not been a cure. In the *1993 World Competitiveness Report*, Venezuela ranked last among 15 developing nations in terms of "confidence in fair administration of justice in the society," below such nations as Brazil, Mexico, and Pakistan.[93]

A strong judicial system that defines and enforces the rules of the game provides the best environment for the development of competitive firms and industries. Consider a businessman weighing the potential risks and benefits of a new venture. He must make and rely on promises if his firm is to grow. In many countries, contract law spells out the rights and obligations of each party as well their liability in the event that they do not comply. It provides courses of action for restitution, which can be relied upon. Because contracts are enforced by the courts, they are a powerful business tool, opening up new universes of potential deals and business associates.

In Venezuela, many businessmen do not view contracts as enforceable. Many avoid the courts altogether. For example, it has become common for foreign investors, in their investment agreements, to specify that future disputes be decided by arbitration outside the judicial system.[94] The de facto unenforceability of contracts inflicts a heavy price on Venezuelan firms. Often it restricts business transactions to a small circle of family, friends, and trusted associates. It sharply reduces the number of business transactions and opportunities for growth.[95] It discourages business initiative and investment to the detriment of the whole economy.

A level playing field also means basic protections from unfair practices, such as predatory pricing or industrial sabotage, and from outright political attack. In Venezuela, the rule of law is so weak that the judicial system itself sometimes is used as a weapon. There have been several reports of "judicial terrorism," in which judges, for a price, convert civil proceedings into criminal ones.[96] In such instances, unfortunate parties to business deals or civil suits are forced to agree to unfavorable terms imposed by their adversaries in order to avoid imprisonment or criminal conviction.

Firms in Venezuela have adopted strategies for operation in the uncertain legal environment. For example, business owners often distribute their assets among various companies and entities in order to shield them from the risks posed by the judicial system, at the cost of lost productivity.[97] It is more difficult for business owners to protect themselves from seemingly arbitrary applications of the criminal law. Present and potential foreign investors are very sensitive to the risks posed by the judicial system in Venezuela, and although its impact in terms of foregone investments has not been quantified, it is very real. International companies have identified an "inefficient and corrupted judicial system" as one of Venezuela's main disadvantages as an investment location.[98]

Political Capture

Political capture of Venezuelan social programs has occurred again and again across the spectrum of public services. In Venezuela, even narrowly targeted, well-designed programs have been derailed by interference by political parties and other interest groups. The "academic grant" program is one example of a program that, despite its simple and transparent design, has failed to achieve its intended purpose due to political capture.

The academic grant program *(becas educativas)* was designed to provide grants to economically disadvantaged students.[99] A multitiered system was established within the ministry of education to review studies of applications submitted by students throughout the country. On paper, the education scholarship program appeared to be relatively simple and well thought out. However, one small but important detail was omitted. In order to apply, each student was required to complete an official application form. The program did not establish any controls over distribution of the application forms. No quotas for application forms were specified for different geographic regions. Special interests within the local power structures and political parties took control of the distribution of application forms and, in so doing, took effective control of which students had access to the grants. Many schools never received application forms for their students, and most of those that obtained forms did so through the informal power structure that in fact managed the program.[100]

Calzadilla (1993) observes that political capture is pervasive within public administration in Venezuela and often is the root cause of administrative difficulties that, on the surface, appear technical in nature. In his words, "the technical weaknesses of a project, program, or plan of the State usually represent a manifestation of a political contest; they represent ambiguities deliberately created in order to make possible the penetration by certain interests that seek to profit from the situation. Thus, the institutional weakness of the State is certainly associated with deficiencies of a technical-administrative, organizational, and management nature, but behind this there are deeper and more powerful reasons which constitute an important, inertial force in the process of modernizing the State apparatus."[101]

Outright Corruption

In the 1980s, the ways in which the Venezuelan government intervened in the economy fostered opportunities for corrupt conduct in the public sector. The dynamic was simple: Each time that the government operated as a broker—that is, engaged in buying or selling or granted privileges with a market value—an opportunity for corruption arose.[102] In Venezuela, the government operated, subject to few controls, as a broker throughout the economy. Subsidies, price controls, and an endless array of manufacturers' and import licenses meant there was an army of officials ready to turn discretion into cash.

For example, at the ministry of agriculture and livestock in the 1980s, it was reportedly commonplace for employees to charge for permits and licenses. This was not a small matter, considering that the agency had 30,000 employees and regulated every conceivable aspect of agricultural activity.[103] The export bonds program, which was supposed to encourage sales abroad, became an opportunity for bribery on a large scale. The program for making cheap dollars available to businesses (RECADI) became an opportunity for all-out fraud. INDULAC, the state-owned milk company, became a source of political campaign funds.[104] The larger the public sector and the more pervasive the state's role, the greater was the scope for corruption. In pruning back existing ministries, privatizing state enterprises, and reducing the scope of state regulation, the Pérez administration considerably reduced the potential for illicit dealings. This was a positive, and somewhat ironic, achievement for a president later to be undermined by corruption charges.[105]

A History of Central Control

For decades, the policy of the national government regarding state and local public administration has been one of preemption and control. The Constitution reserves the lion's share of responsibilities and authority to the national government, a much smaller sphere of authority to the municipalities, and the rest to the states. The chain of command, personnel assignments, and money flowed downward from the national government and political party directorates. Until 1989, the president of the republic designated the state governors, each of whom in turn named the presidents of municipal councils within his state.

The national government also controlled state and municipal funding and spending. The states received funding from the national government in the form of the *situado,* or share of the ordinary revenues of the national budget. Part of this funding was passed down to the municipalities, most of which supplemented their *situado* with local tax revenue. The national monies came with strings attached. By law, 50 percent of the state's quota had to be spent in coordination with national programs. The minister of Interior Relations issued directives for investments to the state governors. In order to put their hands on the restricted funding, the governors were required to sign legal agreements with the national ministers to ensure the "coordination" of policies. Similar restrictions were attached to 50 percent of the quota assigned to the municipalities.

Between 1988 and 1992, laws were approved that laid the foundation for the decentralization of the state and local governments. The goal was to strengthen state and local governance through the introduction of direct elections and the transfer of authority from the national to the state and local levels. The cutting edge of the reform was a restructuring of electoral policy, which took effect starting in 1989. Governors now are elected by direct popular vote, not appointed by the president. At the municipal level, an executive authority (mayor) has been set up in addition to the legislative municipal council. Both the mayor and municipal council members are elected by direct, uninominal vote.

The scheme for transferring power to the states and municipalities, in contrast, has been set up as a multistage process. The laws have defined the types of powers that may be transferred and have set up the formal processes by which the transfers may take place. For example, the Decentralization Act defines certain "exclusive" powers that may be transferred to the states, but only if their legislatures pass a law to allow the transfer. These "exclusive" powers include authority to administer ports and airports and to manage certain nonmetallic mineral deposits. The act also defines the so-called concurrent powers, which may be transferred only through agreements between the state governor and the national government, at the approval of the Senate. These include the power to administer social programs (such as education and health), to construct and manage certain types of infrastructure (such as highways), and to administer economic and other development programs.

Under the reforms, states will receive larger allocations of the national budget *(situado)*, which will remain their principal source of revenue. Although the Decentralization Act does keep the requirement that 50 percent of each state's *situado* be devoted to investment, it gives the states more liberty to formulate their investment plans, subject to presidential approval. The act also specifically authorizes the states to raise certain types of taxes (such as the stamp tax), to collect certain user fees, and to raise money through public financing. It also provides that when social services are transferred to the states from the national government, they will be accompanied by the funding allocated for those services at the national level.

The reforms set up a framework for the process of decentralization. They leave open-ended which states receive what powers, or when. This will be determined through political and legal negotiations over the next several years, negotiations that in turn will depend largely on the initiative shown by individual states to exert control over powers now in the hands of the national government.

Positive Change

As of early 1994, many positive changes were under way in public administration as a result of the recent electoral reforms and decentralization process. Venezuelans were learning quickly how to reward and to punish incumbents at the polls, commensurate with their performance in office.[106] This was demonstrated in the 1992 state and local elections, when many officials who had not responded to the needs of their communities found themselves suddenly out of office. Political accountability was stimulating state and local governments to raise their standards and to exert new leadership. At the same time, the transfer of authority was providing a basis for new leaders to formulate their own programs and goals. The state of Carabobo was rebuilding its infrastructure. The state of Zulia was carrying out ambitious economic development plans. At the municipal level, the municipality of Caroní, in Bolívar state, in a few years' time proved itself effective at revenue raising and reduced its financial dependence on the national government.[107] The seeds of a new public administration, less centralized and more responsive to local needs, have been planted.

Venezuelan Government Policy in Perspective

Governments play an important role in the economies of all nations, but they tend to play a particularly active role in economies of developing nations.[108] Government intervention can take many forms, including control of natural resources, direct ownership of enterprises, wage and price controls, restrictions on entry in some industries, trade restrictions, subsidies for preferred industries, preferential access to capital and foreign exchange, and restrictions on imports and foreign investments.

There are several reasons for the level of governmental involvement in the economies of developing nations. In some nations, there is an ideological predisposition to government intervention. The state is seen as the only entity able to protect consumers and workers from rapacious local industrial groups and multinational corporations. Governments also intervene to allocate the nation's scarce resources to foster development. Many of the actions of governments in developing nations, for example, are taken under the belief that local markets are too immature or "do not work" in a way that promotes national economic development. Finally, in some nations, governments view independent economic activity as a potential source of political challenge. Controlling key portions of the economy and society is seen as necessary to the preservation of the political status quo.

While governments in developing nations often take on responsibilities beyond those taken on by the governments of developed nations, they frequently are too weak to carry out the responsibilities that are taken as a matter of course in developed nations. Many states are unable to provide the basic levels of public safety, rule of law, infrastructure, and social services that are assumed in the industrialized nations. Many governments are unwilling or unable to enforce contracts and regulate markets. The very weakness of the state brings on intervention in order to stop abuses. A government that cannot effectively police markets, for example, is more likely to intervene to correct what it views as market failures than a government that can police markets.

Policies and Consequences

Over the last few decades, economic policy in Venezuela was based on the premise of an ever-increasing oil rent. Capturing and distributing this rent to social services, to infrastructure, to industry, to agriculture, and the like, was its principal aim. As a result, virtually every economic activity enjoyed a degree of protection and/or subsidy. After an initial period of rapid industrialization, however, such policies served to reduce rather than increase productivity and competitiveness. In many cases, poor administration or even corruption accompanied the implementation of policies that often either were ill-conceived or had outlived their usefulness. Venezuelan industry, agriculture, infrastructure, and social services became ridden with inefficiencies and increasingly unable to provide citizens with the quality of life they desired.

The decline in the price of petroleum after 1982 rendered the rentist model obsolete, but Venezuelan governments did not substantially change their approach until they could hold out no longer. Several economic and social sectors that had benefitted from subsidies and protection resented economic adjustment and policy changes, reading them as arbitrary and unjustified hardships. Political turmoil and social unrest ensued and two military coups were attempted. The Pérez government lost legitimacy and was ousted from power.

As indicated in previous sections, the trade and industrial policies instituted as part of the economic opening have resulted in an increase in competition for the vast majority of Venezuelan industries. By 1993, there was greater pressure to satisfy consumers, greater pressure to improve quality, and greater pressure to reduce costs. The flood of imports that some predicted when the market was opened did not occur. Economic recession, distribution channels largely controlled by domestic industry, and temporary currency undervaluation served as barriers to imports into Venezuela in 1989 and 1990. By 1993, real competition from imported products was felt in the garment, textile, appliance, and automotive sectors. Under the new trade policies, some multinational firms shifted from local assembly to importing finished products. Local parts manufacturers who could not compete with foreign firms on cost and quality were hurt by the elimination of mandated incorporation of domestically produced parts. Integration with Colombia brought increased competition in clothing, footwear, food, furniture, and other items and increased exports for rice, glass, tires, primary metal products, and petrochemicals.

The effective size of Venezuelan demand increased through integration with Colombia as did the sophistication of Venezuelan demand. Competition from Colombian firms stimulated improvement and innovation, and pressured firms to create effective firm strategies and structures.[109] Obstructions, however, remained. Oligopolies in distribution prevented Venezuelan consumers from obtaining the full benefit of increased competition. Macroeconomic difficulties and political uncertainty created a difficult investment climate. Many distortions remained in input markets. Signs of a return to a more restrictive, controlled economic environment in 1993 held out limited hope of further progress in the short run.

The economic reform program in Venezuela in the late 1980s and early 1990s reflected a change in focus from state-oriented development to market-oriented development. Perhaps the greatest change was an increase in the scope for private-sector initiative. Venezuelan firms now had to compete in the domestic and international markets in order to survive and prosper. The new system reduced the distortions of the old regime by replacing government incentives with market incentives. The existence of a market, however, does not instantly provide firms with the capabilities required to succeed in open competition. Most Venezuelan firms reacted to the opening of the economy by employing defensive strategies. The 1992 backlash occurred before they were able to adapt to the new environment. The market might provide the pressures and incentives to improve and innovate, but it does not provide the capabilities to do so. The more open economic environment in the period from 1990 to 1994 placed a premium on factor creation in terms of education and training that was not present before.

The Challenge of Competitiveness

Once the Venezuelan market was opened to outside competition and firms began to compete in international markets, attention began to focus on the impact of natural resource policy, agricultural policies, labor policy, education, training, science, technology, and social programs on the competitiveness of Venezuelan firms. In the days of import substitution, competitiveness was not an issue, so there was little reason to worry about how Venezuela stacked up against other nations in these areas. When Venezuelan firms began competing with foreign competitors in both foreign and domestic markets, it soon became apparent that the nation's ability to meet the challenge of competitiveness, and its economic performance, would be heavily influenced by its relative position, and government policies, in all these areas.

The changes in economic policy undertaken in the 1980s and early 1990s, and the nation's social and economic performance since those changes, have shown that prosperity for the Venezuelan people cannot be achieved through economic policy alone. Instead, a whole series of policies, guided by the quest for competitiveness, will be necessary if the Venezuelan economy is truly to meet the expectations of the Venezuelan people. The challenges that the Venezuelan government faces in this regard are addressed in Chapter 11.

10

Prospects for Venezuelan Firms and Industries

The previous chapters have described the determinants of national competitive advantage in Venezuela and the dynamics that promote or impede competitiveness across the economy. On the basis of the discussions found in those chapters, here we try to identify types of companies and industries that might contribute to Venezuela's future economic growth. Such an analysis provides additional insights into the changes in government policies and firm strategies that will be necessary to achieve this growth.

What Types of Firms?

As indicated in earlier chapters, Venezuela has many different types of firms. Given present circumstances within the nation, one might expect that these different types of firms would have different potentials for growth.

State-Owned Companies

The state-owned enterprise with the greatest potential for growth is PDVSA. Large current and planned investments (amounting to an estimated $37.8 billion over ten years) are expected to increase PDVSA's output substantially. We describe the prospects for the oil industry below. Outside of the oil industry, it is unlikely that substantial growth will come from enterprises that will remain in the hands of the state. The Venezuelan government will be in difficult financial circumstances for the foreseeable future. In the absence of a dramatic, unanticipated rise in oil prices, the state will not have the funds necessary to reinvest in existing companies, much less to make substantial new investments.

As a result of its financial situation, the Venezuelan state is slowly reducing its holdings in industrial and service companies.

Privatization appears to be the key to the long-term growth of many enterprises currently owned by the state. Privatization would alter the incentives and strategies of many of the state-owned enterprises. Many of the state-owned enterprises involved in infrastructure have been starved of investment for more than a decade. Substantial growth can be expected from the privatization of such operations, assuming that investors are allowed to charge prices that will allow them a reasonable return on their investment. CANTV's investments have been described in Chapter 6. Additional investments in roads, water, and other services are to be expected by private entities, if they are allowed to invest in these industries. This assumes, of course, that privatization actually will go forward and that privatized companies will be able to set prices that will allow them to recover their investments. Neither situation has always been the case in Venezuela to date.

The future in the short and medium term for state-owned industrial enterprises is less certain. Several overexpanded in the past and need to be restructured. Alcasa and Sidor in particular will be downsizing rather than expanding, at least in the short to medium term. It will take time for private capital and market incentives to produce growth in the steel and aluminum industries. Developing and exploiting Venezuela's mining and forestry industries, in which basic resources remain largely under state control, also will take time.

Large Indigenous Industrial Groups

The strategies of Venezuela's existing large indigenous industrial groups will have an important influence on the pace and direction of the nation's economic development. These groups should be well positioned to take advantage of the new opportunities present in the Venezuelan economy, particularly in areas newly opened to the private sector. They tend to have better access to materials, inputs, distribution, capital, and managerial talent than other Venezuelan firms. Some of them have been taking advantage of new opportunities in areas such as communications, food, and retailing, either alone or in conjunction with foreign partners. On the other hand, these groups grew up in a protected import substitution environment, which had an enormous impact on their strategies and structures. Some have large holdings in what can only be termed a shaky financial sector. While some will make the transition to a more open competitive environment, others will find it difficult.

Most of Venezuela's industrial groups are in industries that are inherently non-traded due to high transportation costs with respect to the value of the product (such as consumer packaged goods, foods, beverages, and some building materials) or by the local nature of the business itself (such as retailing, media, insurance, and local airlines). While the output of these firms should be able to grow with the Venezuelan domestic market or, in some cases, with the Andean Pact market, it is unlikely that most of these firms will become major exporters of Venezuelan-produced goods. Instead, they will tend to exploit opportunities outside Venezuela or the Andean Pact through foreign direct investment rather than exports. Thus, the traditional strategies and structures that resulted from growth in a closed economy could limit the contribution that indigenous industrial groups can make to economic growth.

The firms themselves might become more international, but the contribution of their internationalization to the local economy is likely to be limited to increases in headquarters operations and repatriated earnings. Substantial growth in exports is not likely to come from the large Venezuelan industrial groups unless they enter new, export-oriented businesses. In addition, some of the groups are reluctant to expand further within Venezuela due to concern about the economic and political environment and the fear that they will be subject to criticism for being too dominant in the local economy.

New Venezuelan Firms

Venezuela's prosperity also will depend to a large extent on the nation's ability to create an environment in which new firms can develop and prosper. New business formation energizes the determinants of competitiveness. It allows for entry to heighten local rivalry and to develop clusters of industries. The ability of a nation to generate new businesses also is a good barometer of its overall economic health. In any nation, there are some industries that inevitably decline. If the national environment is not conducive to new business formation, the nation will find it difficult to replace declining industries and expand healthy ones.

A number of factors make it difficult for new companies in Venezuela. Perhaps the most important is limited access to capital. Public and private financial institutions are risk averse and generally will not provide unsecured loans for new business ventures. Venture capital operations are essentially nonexistent in Venezuela. As a result, the financial risk arising from the founding of a new enterprise must be assumed entirely by the entrepreneur, committing family savings, unless he or she surrenders control to an established group and becomes a minority partner in the new venture.

For this reason, new ventures in the formal or modern sector often are created by established groups with access to capital, management, government contacts, and other critical resources. Shortcomings in factor conditions, such as the lack of a modern financial system, macroeconomic problems, and a shortage of skilled labor, make it extremely difficult to start a new firm and to grow existing firms in the formal sector. Limits on firm strategy, structure, and rivalry due to bureaucratic and regulatory constraints, and to less-than-free competition in many industries, add to the difficulties. The result of this combination is that many of the people who might be expected to start their own firms instead find employment with leading local firms or multinational corporations.

The informal economy is unlikely to be a source of sustained growth in Venezuela. Productivity in the nation's informal sector lags well behind that of the formal sector. On average, these firms simply lack the resources to improve their productivity to the point where they can provide more than marginal levels of growth.[1]

Overall, a dynamic economic environment would foster the development of new small and medium-size firms through its impact on demand conditions, but their potential will be limited for the foreseeable future. These firms are more likely to be followers in this process than leaders. The exception could well be small professional service firms, which generally require little in the way of fixed investment. The growth of consulting, financial, and engineering firms in Venezuela over the last several years is evidence that there is potential for firms that can avoid major capital investments.

Foreign-Owned Companies

The economic growth necessary to improve standards of living in Venezuela will require very substantial investments of capital in the very near future. Many Venezuelan industries, such as petroleum, petrochemicals, steel, aluminum, and pulp and paper, will require large investments if they are to achieve their potential. The capital requirements of these five industries alone are estimated at $50 billion during the period from 1993 to 2003. (See Table 10.1.)

As of 1994, the Venezuelan state is in financial difficulty, Venezuelan banks are in disarray, large indigenous groups are cautious, the rate of indigenous new business formation is low, and the domestic capital markets, in the absence of viable pension funds, are limited. Foreign-owned companies represent one of the few sources of ready investment capital. Foreign multinationals could make substantial contributions to the growth of the Venezuelan economy. In addition to capital, foreign firms can be sources of expertise, personnel, and technology that are needed to build a more productive

TABLE 10.1
Projections for Selected Venezuelan Industries

	1992 Internal Sales ($ million)	2003 Projected Internal Sales ($ million)	1992 Exports ($ million)	2003 Projected Exports ($ million)	1992 Employees (000)	2003 Projected Employees (000)	Capital Required ($ million)
Petroleum	1,057	2,290	11,209	23,360	84	110	37,767
Petrochemicals	505	1,618	260	1,457	7	12	3,994
Bauxite and Aluminum[a]	538	888	539	1,063	10	10	3,000
Iron and Steel[b]	853	1,245	674	1,246	20	15	4,590
Pulp and Paper[c]	545	900	45	230	8	16	783
Five Industry Total	3,498	6,941	12,727	27,356	129	163	50,134

[a] Bauxite and aluminum does not include aluminum manufactures.

[b] Iron and steel includes iron ore and pellets, direct reduction iron, and steel products.

[c] The historical figures for pulp and paper refer to 1991, not 1992.

The projections for the petroleum, petrochemical, bauxite and aluminum, and iron and steel industries are based on the plans of state-owned enterprises with the participation of private capital.

Conversion into U.S. dollars was made at an average 1992 rate of 66.22 bolivars per dollar, except the figures for pulp and paper, which were converted at an average 1991 rate of 57.21 per dollar.

Source: Venezuela Competitiva Project.

Venezuela. Thus, foreign multinationals can fill some of the gaps in Venezuela's factor conditions (capital and technology resources) that were identified earlier. The Cristóbal Colón Project is just one example of the types of investments that foreign firms could make in the hydrocarbon sector.

In other industries that make use of Venezuela's factor advantages in natural resources, such as chemicals, aluminum, forestry, pulp, power generation, and tourism, more transparent negotiations, clear regulations, long-term contracts, and reduced restrictions on foreign companies could bring substantial new multinational investments. Foreign investors have exhibited substantial interest in all of these industries.

There also are a number of existing multinationals whose growth within Venezuela will be influenced by the dynamism of the local economic environment, the comparison between the Venezuelan environment and that of its neighbors, and the overall regional and global strategies set by headquarters. A growing economy would allow existing multinationals to grow, just as it would allow indigenous firms to grow. In addition, a number of firms are beginning to consolidate their Andean Pact or Latin American operations, and Venezuela has succeeded in attracting some of these operations. They will tend to focus more of their operations in nations that provide the best business environments. Venezuela will succeed in capturing a larger share of the activities of existing multinationals only if it provides a better environment than its neighbors. Foreign investment represents a large opportunity for the Venezuelan economy, but again, such investment will come only if business conditions are favorable.

New Engines of Growth

The legacy of Venezuela's past, the incomplete reform process, and an unfavorable investment climate leave some types of firms more likely to be engines of economic growth in the nation than others. In the short to medium term, the types of firms that are likely to provide the greatest sources of growth would seem to be privatized entities, multinational firms, and mixed foreign-domestic companies. Privatized entities could start making investments that have been lacking under state control. Foreign multinationals have access to the capital and other factors necessary to help to develop Venezuelan industry. Mixed companies can combine foreign and Venezuelan resources.

Therefore, privatization and foreign investment promotion should be key priorities going forward. In addition, it is extremely important that the barriers to new business formation, in product markets, capital markets, and labor markets, be removed as quickly as possible so that a new generation of Venezuelan firms can come to the fore. In all likelihood, a new generation of

Venezuelan firms will develop only if there is a deep and abiding commitment to make these markets work in the national context. Privatization, foreign multinationals, and mixed foreign-domestic companies can be the engines of growth in Venezuela *only* in the short to medium term. The long-term prosperity of the economy and the country will depend in large part on the emergence of *new* Venezuelan firms and of *new* strategies in existing firms.[2]

What Types of Industries?

Another question that we might ask is: What types of industries are likely to be the main sources of economic growth in Venezuela over the next several years? Venezuela's experience with the oil industry has led some to think of economic development as finding the next oil industry. Some people seem to believe that a limited number of industries will be able to provide for a higher standard of living in Venezuela. This was one of the beliefs that triggered the state-led industrialization program of the 1970s and 1980s. In addition to petroleum, the industries usually mentioned as the potential "winners" include petrochemicals, aluminum, steel, and pulp and paper. All of these industries were studied as part of this project. Profiles of the industries, along with a discussion of their advantages and disadvantages, appeared earlier in Chapters 4 and 5. As we have seen, Venezuela has substantial existing or potential advantages in each of these industries.

A question arises, however, as to how much these industries will add to national income over the next ten years and whether supporting these industries will be enough to ensure a prosperous future for the Venezuelan people. Due to uncertainty over future policy regimes, economic conditions, and investment climates, it is difficult to develop projections for industries in Venezuela. Many plans that are announced with much fanfare are never carried out, or are carried out on a smaller scale as business and economic conditions change. Nevertheless, projections can provide insight into the growth potential of these industries over the next ten years.

Table 10.1 summarizes projections for the five industries just mentioned. It should be taken as a best-case scenario for this set of industries, because it makes a series of optimistic assumptions. It assumes that macroeconomic conditions will be relatively favorable, that investment programs go ahead on schedule, that capital will be available at reasonable prices, that the administrative and bureaucratic problems faced by some of the industries will be solved, and that privatization or injections of private capital take place in industries controlled by state-owned enterprises.

The Petroleum Industry

The oil industry has substantial potential over the next several years if it is not forced to cut back on its investment programs.[3] The official projections for the industry estimate an output of 4 million barrels per day by 2003. Export sales are projected to increase to 3.2 million barrels per day in 2003. With expected price increases to $20 per barrel, in 1992 dollars, this would raise export sales from over $11 billion in 1992 to more than $23 billion in 2003. Employment is projected to increase from approximately 84,000 persons in 1993 to 110,000 persons in 2003, with most growth to be generated by private contractors. The total investment required between 1993 and the year 2003 to support these levels of growth is estimated at $37.8 billion. These projections assume that PDVSA will be able to proceed with its ten-year investment plan.

However, these official projections are probably too optimistic. Growth in the oil sector will be limited by world prices, OPEC quotas, and PDVSA's ability to generate investment funds and to form new ventures. In addition, by mid-1994, the exploration and investments necessary to bring capacity to 4 million barrels per day had not yet been started. PDVSA's capacity in 2003 may well be closer to 3 million barrels per day. If export sales reach 2.9 million barrels per day at a price (in 1992 dollars) of $18 per barrel, then export sales will be in the $19 billion range rather than $23 billion range.

Other Resource-Based Industries

Venezuela's other natural resource-based industries, such as petrochemicals, iron and steel, aluminum, and pulp and paper, show substantial potential in the long term (ten years or more). Growth will be moderate in the short and medium term. It will take time for these industries to recover from decades of import substitution policies and state interference. Changes will be required in their management, employment practices, and marketing programs, as well as substantial investments to build and modernize facilities. Many of these industries face historically low prices that probably will remain depressed in the near term. In pulp and paper, Venezuela will not reach its full potential until private firms have been managing their own forests for at least a generation of trees. The chemical industry will require a resolution of feed stock pricing issues, an increase in worldwide prices, and substantial investments in order to grow. The Venezuelan aluminum industry will require transparent negotiations, long-term supply contracts, and an increase in world prices before firms will be willing to make the investments necessary for the industry to reach its potential. Projections for these industries are as follows.

If planned investments in the petrochemical industry are made according to schedule, domestic sales of the Venezuelan petrochemical industry could increase from $505 million in 1992 to $1.618 billion in 2003.[4] Export sales could rise from $260 million in 1992 to $1.457 billion in 2003. The greatest growth is expected in methanol and in aromatic products. The total investment required between 1993 and 2003 to support these levels of growth would be roughly $4 billion. The projections assume that there will be no major changes in the ownership or structure of Pequiven and the mixed state-private enterprises, and that Pequiven receives sufficient funding to proceed with its current expansion plans. These projections probably are optimistic, given the economic uncertainties present in 1994, Pequiven's financial position (which will make it difficult for the company to obtain the capital required for its planned investment program), depressed prices, and high capital costs in Venezuela. It is likely that Pequiven's investment program will be scaled back or slowed down.

Under best-case conditions, domestic sales of iron and steel products could grow from $853 million in 1992 to $1.245 billion in 2003.[5] Export sales could grow from $674 million in 1992 to $1.246 billion in 2003. Total investments to reach these levels of output would be approximately $4.59 billion. These projections are based on an optimistic scenario in which Sidor and Ferrominera Orinoco would be privatized, future investments would come primarily from private investors, and substantial internal changes would be made within the companies that would permit higher product quality, lower prices, and improvements in labor productivity. In the absence of such changes, we would expect to see lower growth.

Domestic sales of bauxite and aluminum products (not including aluminum manufactures) could increase from $538 million in 1992 to $888 million in 2003.[6] Export sales of bauxite and aluminum products could increase from $539 million to $1.063 billion during the same period. These projections assume that two new aluminum reduction plants are constructed, reflecting a substantial increase over the nation's present capacity. However, this might prove to be an extremely optimistic projection. The new facilities would require investments on the order of $3 billion. These investments would require improvements in world prices, an improved investment climate within Venezuela, the successful negotiation of power and input contracts with private investors, and large infusions of private capital.

Domestic sales of pulp and paper could increase from $545 million in 1991 to $900 million in 2003.[7] Export sales could increase from $45 million in 1991 to $230 million in 2003. The investments required to reach such figures would be on the order of $783 million. These projections, which assume the construction and startup of one Kraft pulp mill, are based on a cautious reading of future market trends. It should be noted that in terms of basic factor endowments, the potential of pulp production in Venezuela is much larger in the longer term (longer than ten years) than is projected here.

The Projections in Perspective

If the projections in Table 10.1 are accurate, then these five industries would account for $34.3 billion in sales in the year 2003. This would be more than twice their 1992 level. Thirty-four billion dollars appears to be a large number, and in the Venezuelan context, it undoubtedly is. However, if we assume that the Venezuelan population grows at roughly 2.5 percent per year from its 1992 level of 20.7 million, the incremental $18.1 billion that these industries would contribute to GDP in 2003 comes out to around $350 per person, or around 12 percent of Venezuela's 1992 per-capita GDP. Thus, even in a best-case scenario, this set of five major industries will not provide enough incremental income to raise per-capita GDP to the levels experienced in Venezuela in the late 1970s or early 1980s. In addition, by 2003, the optimistic projections predict that these industries will employ on the order of 163,000 workers, only a small fraction of the Venezuelan workforce. Even if one assumes a multiplier effect, this set of industries, which many view as the key to Venezuela's future, will not generate enough income to increase living standards substantially.

Given the budgetary, financial, and economic crisis that Venezuela faced in 1994, and the fact that many of the investment plans described were already behind schedule by mid-1994, one might safely assume that the optimistic projections would not be met. If the incremental contribution to the economy of these industries is a third lower than the optimistic figure of $18.1 billion, then the incremental contribution to real per-capita GDP would be on the order of $230, or around 8 percent of 1992 per-capita GDP. If these projections also proved overly optimistic, the incremental contribution to per-capita GDP would be even lower.

From this analysis, we can conclude that there is no single industry or small set of industries that will provide "the answer" for Venezuela's economic problems. It follows that policies that target or focus on a small set of industries, instead of on issues that affect the whole economy, cannot result in the substantial improvements in average living standards that most Venezuelans desire. Venezuela will need growth across a broad range of industries if it is to generate substantially higher standards of living.

Thinking More Broadly

In Venezuela there appears to be a tendency to equate economic development with the development of particular sectors in heavy industry or manufacturing. This is reflected in calls or policies to promote "industrialization." Many in Venezuela seem to forget that, if the primary economic goal for the nation is a high and rising standard of living, as was suggested in Chapter 3, then industrialization can be a means to that end but cannot be the end itself. This fact suggests that there are other means that might contribute to achieving the desired end. It also suggests that there are other types of industries that can add to national income. Table 10.2 provides a number of examples of Latin American nations that have added to national income through development for export of certain food and agricultural products. The table reports the exports of selected nations for each of several different products. It is not meant to suggest that Venezuela can or should duplicate the exports of other nations in all of those particular industries. Instead, it is meant to suggest that other nations, with conditions perhaps not so very different from those found in Venezuela, have been able to add to national income in industries outside the "industrial" sectors.

For example, in 1992, Colombia earned more in coffee exports ($1.26 billion) and Costa Rica earned more in banana exports ($804 million) than Venezuela earned in exports of aluminum and related manufactures ($710 million) or iron and steel exports ($674 million). Ecuador's $529 million in shellfish exports, Chile's $511 million in fresh fish exports and $451 million in pulp exports, Colombia's $341 million in fresh cut-flower exports, and Guatemala's $321 million in exports of coffee were more than Venezuela's exports of petrochemicals ($260 million). Colombia earned more in exports of fresh cut flowers ($341 million) than Venezuela earned in exports of auto parts, automotive vehicles, textiles, and apparel combined ($177 million).

The table is not meant to suggest that Venezuela can or should match the Latin American leaders in these export categories. However, it does show that there are substantial gains to be made in matching the export performance of smaller regional exporters with comparable natural factor endowments. Venezuela, with $18 million in exports of fresh fish, might not be able to match Chile ($511 million) in this export category, but perhaps it can come closer to Uruguay ($91 million). Venezuela, with $12 million in coffee exports, might not be able to match Colombia's coffee exports ($1.26 billion), but perhaps it can come closer to Guatemala ($321 million), Costa Rica ($225 million), or El Salvador ($191 million). In cocoa and cocoa products, Venezuela ($10 million) might not be able to match Brazil ($258

TABLE 10.2
Exports of Selected Commodities, Selected Latin American Nations, 1992

Millions of U.S. $

Meat of Bovine Animals
(SITC R2 0111)

Argentina	338
Brazil	285
Uruguay	146
Costa Rica	48
Nicaragua	41
Colombia	14
Venezuela[a]	**0**

Fresh Fish
(SITC R2 034)

Chile	511
Argentina	280
Uruguay	91
Ecuador	56
Colombia	51
Costa Rica	20
Venezuela	**18**

Shellfish
(SITC R2 036)

Ecuador	529
Cuba	281
Bahamas	264
Argentina	219
Mexico	202
Colombia	77
Venezuela	**36**

Rice
(SITC R2 042)

Uruguay	106
Argentina	53
Venezuela[a]	**14**

Bananas and Plantains
(SITC R2 0573)

Costa Rica	804
Ecuador	676
Colombia	407
Honduras	293
Panama	213
Martinique	108
Venezuela	**24**

Fruit and Vegetable Juices
(SITC R2 0585)

Brazil	1,100
Argentina	198
Chile	81
Mexico	35
Colombia	31
Venezuela	**5**

TABLE 10.2 (Continued)

Coffee (SITC R2 0711)		Cocoa (SITC R2 072)	
Colombia	1,260	Brazil	258
Brazil	971	Ecuador	69
Guatemala	321	**Venezuela**[b]	**10**
Mexico	266		
Costa Rica	225		
El Salvador	191		
Honduras	168		
Venezuela[a]	**12**		

Tobacco (SITC R2 121)		Pulpwood (SITC R2 246)	
Brazil	804	Chile	265
Argentina	137		
Cuba	110		
Guatemala	39		
Colombia	34		
Venezuela	**2**		

Sulphate Wood Pulp (SITC R2 2517)		Cut Flowers (SITC R2 29271)	
Brazil	740	Colombia	341
Chile	451	Ecuador	26
Argentina	42	Mexico	19
Venezuela	**0**	Costa Rica	17
		Venezuela[a]	**1**

[a] OCEI, *Anuario del comercio exterior de Venezuela*.

[b] Instituto de Comercio Exterior de Venezuela. OCEI's export figure is slightly higher, $12 million.

Source: United Nations (1992).

million), but perhaps it can come closer to Ecuador ($69 million). In sulphate wood pulp, Venezuela ($0) might not be able to match Brazil ($740 million), but perhaps, with large-scale private investment, it can come closer to Chile ($451 million).

Just as agricultural and food-related industries can provide sources of income, other industries outside the "industrial sectors" can do so as well. In the Venezuelan context, industries such as tourism, entertainment, communications, services, and others will present opportunities if the nation's basic economic conditions are favorable. In 1991, Venezuela's international tourism receipts ($365 million) lagged far behind those of Chile ($700 million), Jamaica ($764 million), and the Bahamas ($1.2 billion), suggesting substantial undeveloped potential. (See Table 4.7.) The telecommunications industry provides another example. The privatization of CANTV and the opening of competition in telecommunications services created a revolution in Venezuela's telecommunications sector. Under the regime that was in place in 1992 and 1993, it was expected that billions of dollars would be invested in telecommunications over the next several years. This sector was expected to grow from roughly 2 percent of GDP in 1988 to 6 percent by the late 1990s. Opportunities to expand coverage and introduce new services would result in substantial growth well into the next century.

The Need for Improvements in Productivity

"Industrialization" is only one of various ways to add to national income, and all industrializations are not the same. Venezuela's industrialization of the 1970s created new industries, but these industries were inefficient. Several were not, nor are they likely to be, able to compete effectively in international markets or against international competitors. A number of these industries suffered after the Venezuelan economy was opened in 1989, prompting worries and political speeches about "deindustrialization." Similar concerns were voiced in Chile in the years immediately following its economic opening. Books even were written about the "deindustrialization" of the Chilean nation.[8] They were right in that manufacturing industries contracted in the period immediately after the economic opening. However, just as such books were being published, the nation was experiencing a reindustrialization, based not on protected industries but rather on industries that exploited Chile's natural and created advantages, industries that used local resources productively.[9]

The process of state-led industrialization in Venezuela was accompanied by a dramatic decline in productivity across the economy. As mentioned in Chapter 2, Paredes (1993) has calculated that total factor productivity fell by 2.11 percent per year in the period 1974 to 1982. Capital productivity fell 4.16 percent per year in that period. From 1983 to 1989, total factor productivity fell 1.57 percent per year, while labor productivity fell 3.25 percent per year. Paredes concludes that if Venezuela had been able to maintain marginally positive total factor productivity growth (on the order of 1.5 percent per year), per-capita GDP in 1992 would have been 33 percent higher than the level actually registered, or 6 percent higher than the historic high of 1978. In the 1990 to 1992 period, on the other hand, total factor productivity, labor productivity, and capital productivity all increased substantially.[10]

Looking to the future, Paredes concludes that even under optimistic assumptions about the growth of the labor force and capital expenditures, any appreciable increase in per-capita income or standards of living will require substantial increases in productivity across the economy. He also concludes that in order to increase productivity, the Venezuelan economic system must provide the opportunity for capital and other resources to find their most productive uses. In order for an economy to grow, either more resources need to be invested, or the resources invested have to be used more productively, or both. In Venezuela, both will be needed.

The Challenge of Competitiveness

During the course of the research reported in this book, we repeatedly were asked, "In which industries is Venezuela competitive?" or "In which industries can Venezuela become competitive?" In all honesty, there are few industries today in which Venezuela can be termed "competitive." There are a number of industries, however, in which Venezuela has potential. There is clear potential in the industries just described, as well as potential for additional growth in engineering, entertainment, and some specialty agricultural products. This potential, however, does not mean that a small set of industries should be picked and supported as "potential winners." This study did not identify any single industry, or small set of industries, that will magically transform the Venezuelan economy. Rather, the research has shown that improvements need to be made on a broad front.

The nation's potential will require government policies and firm strategies that provide a good business climate for all Venezuelan industries.

Policies to promote a small set of industries will not provide the solution to Venezuela's economic difficulties, even if such policies could be effective in the nation's context, which is at best unclear. What is needed is an across-the-board improvement in productivity and competitiveness that will be felt in many Venezuelan industries. If we asked, "In which industries can Venezuela improve its productivity?" the answer would be *many if not most* industries.

The development of export industries is not an end in itself, especially if these industries need ongoing subsidies or protection in order to export. For a nation, it is a means to achieve a higher standard of living. For industries and firms, it is a means to be able to compete and to prosper in the world economy. At the national level, an important part of improving productivity is allowing resources (including human talent) to find their most productive uses so that they may generate competitive industries and firms. The biggest potential economic gains in Venezuela can be had through the creation of a flexible industrial and financial system that allows resources to seek out their most productive uses. The conclusion is that the challenge of competitiveness for both government and firms involves issues that cut across the economy. The challenge of competitiveness for the nation involves improving the national environment so that all, or at least many, industries have a chance to become winners. These challenges are the subject of the next two chapters.

11

The Challenge of Competitiveness for the Venezuelan Government

The Venezuelan government can help improve standards of living in the nation by meeting its own challenge of competitiveness. This will involve making competitiveness the underlying philosophy and the overriding goal of economic policy. There is a single question which Venezuelans should ask regarding all existing and proposed government policies and programs that affect the economy. The question is, Does this policy increase or reduce the pressures, incentives, or capabilities of Venezuelan firms to improve and innovate? If the policy increases the pressures, incentives, or capabilities to improve and innovate by improving factor conditions, by increasing the size or sophistication of local demand, by fostering the development of related and supporting industries, by giving rise to more effective firm strategies and structures, or by increasing local rivalry, then it is likely to contribute to the development of a more competitive economy and ultimately to a higher standard of living. If the policy reduces the pressures, incentives, or capabilities to improve and innovate, then it probably will hurt the nation's overall competitiveness. If the policy does neither, then it probably will have a limited impact on the nation's competitiveness. If this simple test had been applied over the last two decades, Venezuelans might well be enjoying a higher standard of living today.

Conclusions from the Study

Before providing a list of suggestions as to how the Venezuelan government might act to improve the competitiveness of the Venezuelan economy, it is useful to summarize some of the conclusions that have emerged from analysis of the preceding chapters. The first is that Venezuela's natural resources will not, by themselves, provide a high and rising standard of living for its citizens. Resources provide wealth when they are developed through prudent policies and effective strategies in an environment in which it makes economic sense to make the investments and develop the skills necessary to exploit natural advantages. In today's volatile commodity markets, it cannot be assumed that resource prices will sustain high standards of living on their own.

A second conclusion is that there is no single industry or small set of industries that will be the salvation of the Venezuelan economy. In order to achieve a substantially higher standard of living, it will be necessary to improve productivity throughout the economy. This was precisely the challenge of competitiveness at the national level that was identified in Chapter 3. The best way to meet this challenge and improve productivity is to improve conditions within the national diamond.

The world has changed substantially since the 1960s and 1970s. International competition, world markets, and resource prices have changed dramatically over the last two decades. Venezuela is a different country in the 1990s from what it was in the 1970s, in terms of its state of economic, social, and political development. It is therefore not surprising that assumptions and beliefs developed in Venezuela during that period might no longer be accurate. It is not surprising that policies and strategies that might have been effective or even necessary in earlier times might not succeed today. It is not surprising that changes in policies and strategies might be in order. It is also not surprising that a national environment in which policies and strategies can change to respond to new challenges would provide for greater dynamism and growth than an environment in which rigidities prevent such responses.

One striking conclusion from this study is that there is nothing inevitable about Venezuela's present economic condition or its economic future. Many of the obstacles to development identified in the previous chapters have been created within Venezuela as the unintended consequences of actions undertaken by well-meaning people that probably appeared reasonable at the time. They have not been the result of the forces of nature or the actions of outsiders. They generally have been, and generally will be, within the power of Venezuelans to change. This conclusion is of fundamental importance, because it means that Venezuelans have far greater power to shape their own economic future than is generally realized within the nation. It is in some ways an extremely positive conclusion, because it places Venezuela in a much more favorable position than many other nations.

Finally, the study has concluded that there are many ways in which the Venezuelan environment can be improved so that the Venezuelan economy and its firms can better meet the challenge of competitiveness. Government, firms, other organizations, and individuals can take many concrete actions to improve the competitiveness of the national economy and thereby improve the standard of living found in the nation.

The Need for Priorities

This study has identified many areas in which Venezuela's economic environment can be improved. Progress, indeed, can be made on many fronts. This chapter and the next describe some specific steps, as well as an underlying thought process, that would contribute to the growth and development of the Venezuelan economy. The aim is not to provide a detailed program for government or specific strategies for individual industries or firms, but rather to provide a set of guidelines that can be used to help in the formulation of policies and strategies. Although these chapters cannot be exhaustive, they attempt to convey the range of areas in which positive action can be taken.

It is clear that all of the actions suggested cannot be undertaken at the same time. Developing a more competitive and productive economy is a long-term proposition. Venezuela is a developing nation, with the scarcity of human and financial resources that developing status implies. It will therefore be necessary for the Venezuelan government and Venezuelan firms to prioritize their efforts and to focus their resources. While it will be important to build momentum one step at a time, we should not forget that competitiveness is systemic. The determinants of national advantage interact. Thus, as one constraint to developing a more dynamic economy is eased, another will bind. The following sections suggest some priorities for economic policies, natural resource policies, and human resource–related policies. In order to achieve maximum benefit from these policies, it also would be necessary to reform Venezuela's legal system, to improve its public administration, and to communicate to and educate the public about the need for such programs. A critical part of the challenge is how to avoid policies that, although politically attractive, are counterproductive in terms of competitiveness.

Improving Economic Policies

A number of economic policy issues should be high priorities for the Venezuelan government. As seen in earlier chapters, meeting the challenge of competitiveness will involve creating a sound macroeconomic environment, privatizing state-owned enterprises, championing free trade, making markets work, committing to competition as a means of stimulating improvement, and attracting both domestic and foreign investment.

Creating a Sound Macroeconomic Environment

A sound macroeconomic environment will be necessary if Venezuela is to preserve the purchasing power of its citizens and to attract the type of investments necessary to build a more productive economy. Progress in solving the crisis of public finance is the logical first step toward restoring a sound macroeconomic environment to Venezuela. In order for the government to carry out the tasks of government and to provide basic public services, it must solve its crisis of public finance. This is probably the most important problem of Venezuelan economic policy today. The public sector deficit was listed officially at just over 6 percent of GDP in 1992. If the unfunded liability, both principal and interest, that the government has under the present labor law had been included, the figure would have been 10 or 12 percent of GDP. In 1993, the figure was 3.7 percent of GDP before the liabilities. In early 1994, some observers believed that the budget deficit could reach 11 percent of GDP[1] (with unfunded liabilities equaling another 3 to 4 percent) by the end of the year. By the middle of the year, some believed the deficit actually would be closer to 20 percent of GDP.

Unless this gap is closed, inflation will continue to erode the purchasing power of the average Venezuelan and will remain a drain on the entire economy. Venezuelans cited inflation as the most important cause for concern in the early 1990s.[2] And that was before the budgetary and financial crisis of 1994. The best way to control inflation would be through prudent fiscal and tax policy, rather than through price controls that subsidize the upper- and middle-income classes as well as the lower-income classes, and limit incentives to produce and to invest.

The public sector deficit can be reduced by action on the spending side or the revenue side. On the spending side, it is not clear that there are major savings to be had, other than those that might be achieved through privatization. On the revenue side, there are several steps that the government can take to enhance its revenue, including accelerating privatization, increasing tax revenues, and increasing prices for energy and public services, which would place government finances on a firmer footing and reduce the inflationary pressures within the Venezuelan economy. If these steps or similar ones are not taken, it is likely that Venezuelans will continue to pay a high price in terms of inflation and foregone economic growth.

The results of this study strongly suggest that market-oriented macroeconomic policies would provide the best prospects for growth and development in Venezuela. In the early 1990s, some in Venezuela argued that the Pérez administration had "subordinated" Venezuelans to the macroeconomy. In reality, a nation's people become "subordinated" to the macroeconomy when the macroeconomy seriously malfunctions as a result of a failure to implement responsible economic policies. Recent experiences of Venezuela's neighbors in the Southern Cone bear this out. One might ask the Argentines and Chileans when they felt more "subordinated" to the macroeconomy: under hyperinflation, which stripped away their purchasing power, or under the economic recovery that followed the adoption of responsible macroeconomic policies?

The following specific steps would help restore a positive macroeconomic environment in Venezuela.

Accelerating Privatization. One way to reduce the public sector deficit would be to accelerate the privatization process that nearly came to a halt in 1992 and 1993. Privatization has a twofold impact on government finances. The sale or closure of loss-making state-owned companies reduces the ongoing drain on the public treasury. In addition, the proceeds from privatization can be used, as they have been in Mexico, to pay back debt and to reduce ongoing interest payments. This would be a fitting use for the funds, since much of Venezuela's debt was incurred initially by state-owned companies. Privatization proceeds also might be used to pay the one-time costs of a major restructuring of the Venezuelan state.

Increasing Tax Revenues. Without increased tax revenues, the Venezuelan government will not be able to deliver public services, provide for the country's neediest, and balance its budget. At the same time, rising costs, falling prices, and large investment requirements will make it very difficult for the oil industry to pay the same level of taxes as it has in the past without placing its future at risk. A wider tax base, with fewer loopholes, and better enforcement will be necessary to finance government spending. Venezuelans are among the least taxed people in the world. A number of tax loopholes exist, such as those that allow Venezuelan firms to channel profits through offshore subsidiaries to avoid taxes, and the enforcement of tax laws in Venezuela has been anything but strict. Increasing tax revenues from individuals and business to even one-half of the percentage of GDP typical in other Latin American nations would ensure a firm foundation for public finance that would be less subject to the vagaries of the oil market. Value-added and asset taxes, such as those enacted in 1993, might well be more effective, less distortionary, and easier to collect in Venezuela than other forms of taxation.

Chile, Argentina, and Mexico all have reformed their tax systems to increase collections and to provide a more favorable environment for business. In Argentina, simplification of the tax system and the institution of computerized collections has increased tax collections dramatically. Other tax reforms have improved the climate for investment. Mexico's tax reform program reduced the maximum tax rates for individuals and corporations and eliminated the capital gains tax on publicly traded firms. The changed tax code and stronger enforcement, which have led to the imprisonment of hundreds of tax evaders, increased government tax revenues by 33 percent in real terms between 1988 and 1991.[3] If these countries can improve tax collections, Venezuela should be able to do so as well.

Raising Prices for Energy and Public Services. Artificially low prices for gasoline, electricity, and water cost state-owned entities the equivalent of approximately 2 percent of GDP, or 10 percent of the national budget, each year. The price of gasoline in Venezuela is probably the lowest in the world. In late 1993, Venezuelan gasoline prices, in dollar terms, were one-half of those in Abu Dhabi and around one-third to one-quarter of those in Saudi Arabia. While Venezuelans outwardly pay some of the lowest gasoline prices in the world, the impact of low prices on government finances and inflation makes the present price structure for gasoline very expensive indeed. Higher prices for gasoline would be the equivalent of a tax that would be easy to collect and that would encourage the efficient usage of fuel. Although Venezuelans might prefer low gasoline prices to the government services and investments that higher prices could fund, it must be asked whether prices so much lower than those found in other nations make sense, particularly given the state of government finances and the current rate of inflation.

Electricity, water, and other public services are generally underpriced in Venezuela. Having the user pay a price that at least covers the cost of production, distribution, maintenance, and reinvestment would help end the vicious circle in which artificially low prices lead to wastage, limited investment, and poor services. Although there are arguments that such adjustments are best done gradually, the sooner prices reach the levels described, the sooner the vicious circle would cease, and the sooner the government, or government agencies or enterprises, would receive the revenues. In any case, in the absence of a firm commitment to a schedule of price increases and the indexation of such prices so they are not eroded by inflation, it is hard to imagine that public services will receive the investments that they will require to maintain or expand coverage.

Raising the prices of gasoline, electricity, and other public services has been very difficult politically in Venezuela. In order for such policies to succeed, the government would have to continue the efforts it has made in the past to convince people that they ultimately will be better off paying higher prices for better services and for a financially stable government. One way to reduce the impact of the increases on the truly needy would be to earmark part of the proceeds from the price increases to direct subsidies to the poorest Venezuelans.

Promoting Market-Oriented Macroeconomic Policies. Progress in reducing the public sector deficit should be coupled with a floating exchange rate and market-determined interest rates. As we have seen, the introduction of such rates reduced distortions in financial markets and opened up new opportunities in a number of industries in the early 1990s. Those persons who believe that the high interest rates experienced in Venezuela in the early 1990s were caused by the existence of the market are wide of the mark. The high interest rates were caused by macroeconomic imbalances and a shaky financial sector, not by the existence of a market. Calls for controls on exchange and interest rates usually confuse the symptoms (high interest rates and depreciating currency) with the disease, which has been inflation caused by government deficits, political disputes, and economic uncertainty as well as a history of relatively lenient banking regulation. Fixing interest rates in an inflationary environment will most probably result in negative real interest rates and capital rationing. As one writer has put it, fixing interest rates is like "trying to lower the temperature by breaking the thermometer."[4]

Similarly, those who have claimed that the devaluation of the bolivar caused the inflation of the early 1990s have had the logic reversed. Pent-up inflation was a major cause of price increases in 1989 and 1990. The government's inability to close its budget deficit has fueled inflationary expectations since then. The devaluation of the bolivar against the dollar has been the result of inflation higher than that in the United States, Venezuela's main trading partner, not the other way around. In this context, a fixed exchange rate would be an effective option only as part of a much larger program of spending cuts and tax increases that would reduce government deficits and inflation. Otherwise, a fixed exchange rate would result either in capital flight or in exchange controls that would create administrative barriers to international trade, international investment, and personal travel. It is hoped that Venezuela would not repeat its experience with the RECADI exchange system in the 1980s, in which a multiple, fixed exchange system became the basis for massive profiteering.

Market-oriented macroeconomic policies, in the Venezuelan context, are best coupled with a professional, independent Central Bank. In 1992 and 1993, the Central Bank of Venezuela was considered by many to have been the main force for economic stability in the nation at a time when the legislation needed to improve the government's financial position remained bottled up in Congress. An independent Central Bank was able to force the government to start to face up to its fiscal responsibilities in a way it never had to before. Only an independent Central Bank can hold the government accountable for its fiscal policies by refusing to supply easy money to fund deficits. An independent Central Bank also can work to educate the public in general, and policy makers in particular, in the fundamentals of public and monetary economics.

Modernizing Financial Markets. Venezuela will need modern financial markets if it wishes to create a more competitive economy. The collapse of the banking sector in early 1994 provided ample evidence of the nation's need for a modernized financial system. Clearly, the first order of business is to deal with the current crisis in order to salvage as much of the banking sector as possible within reasonable budgetary limits. In the longer run, clear rules of the game will be required in order for Venezuela's financial markets to work to the benefit of firms, investors, and workers. The Banking Law passed in 1993 should provide a reasonable basis upon which to rebuild the banking sector. New capital adequacy rules and more active oversight from a well-funded, independent Banking Superintendency will be necessary to reduce the abuses that were common in the old system.

Venezuelan capital markets will remain thin and risky until the clearing and settlements process is modernized, insider trading and market manipulation are outlawed, and the oversight of the capital markets is strengthened. A modern, electronic system of clearing and settlements will be necessary if the equity markets are to grow to any reasonable size. Investors will not risk large amounts of money in a stock market subject to insider trading and market manipulation. Unless these activities are made illegal with criminal penalties for violators, it is unlikely that they will be greatly reduced. A stronger Capital Markets Superintendency, with the ability to impose sanctions that can deter abuses instead of the meager fines it now can impose, would be the best guarantee that the capital markets work to the benefit of companies and investors alike.

Modernized capital markets could bring back some of the capital that Venezuelans have invested abroad. As of 1994, Venezuelan citizens own foreign assets worth on the order of $90 billion. If these assets are earning 5 percent per year, the returns are worth $4.5 billion per year. Thus, if just the interest on this money were to return to Venezuela, it would mean an additional capital inflow of $4.5 billion per year. At Venezuela's gross capital formation to GDP ratio of one to five, this would translate into an extra $22.5 billion in GDP each year, or more than 30 percent of present GDP. While some of this capital probably is finding its way back to Venezuela through the placement of the commercial paper of Venezuelan companies in foreign countries, more should return if capital markets were improved.

Modernized capital markets also would attract foreign portfolio funds that have stayed away from the Venezuelan market to date. If even a small number of U.S. money managers placed funds in Venezuela, it could mean hundreds of millions of dollars in capital for Venezuelan firms. Modernized financial markets could provide substantial stimulus across the Venezuelan economy as well as stimulate substantial growth in the financial services sector within the nation.

Modernized capital markets would be necessary to support a strong pension system. In Chile, by early 1993, the private pension system had assets of $15 billion. The forced savings that the program requires had given Chile the highest private savings rate in Latin America, which resulted in the lowest real interest rate in the region, stimulated the development of domestic capital markets, and allowed Chile to achieve a nearly balanced current account. Since 1984, the Chilean stock market has appreciated 2,800 percent in dollar terms. By 1993, total market capitalization had reached $31 billion, up from $13 billion in 1990. Overall, Chile funded approximately 90 percent of its investment needs with local capital.[5]

In the past, Venezuelan governments have tried to fill the gaps in weak financial markets with special programs and agencies that often appear to have been captured by special interests and generally have been ineffective. Stronger financial markets would reduce or eliminate the need for government programs to compensate for weak financial markets. In such an environment, banks and financial service companies would seek to fill profitable niches and to fund attractive projects.

Economic Impact. A wide range of policy options have been described here. Taken together, they would have a profound impact on the way business is transacted in Venezuela. This set of policies would provide incentives and pressures for Venezuelan firms to invest and improve. The deficit reduction measures suggested could result in reductions of the public sector deficit in the range of 8 to 10 percent of GDP (4 to 6 percent from greater tax collections, 2 percent from reductions in subsidies, plus reduction in debt service due to debt paid down out of the proceeds of privatization and better debt ratings). This would go a long way toward eliminating the public sector deficit. The economic impact of placing government finances on a firmer footing is likely to be substantial. Past failures to solve the problems of public finance have resulted in high interest rates, eroding purchasing power, devaluation, reduced investor confidence, and a downrating of Venezuela's debt, which in turn results in higher interest payments. Making headway on the problems of public finance would improve Venezuela's outlook substantially in all these areas.

Market-oriented macroeconomic policies and modern financial markets would allow investors to make clear choices based on the potential return on investment of various projects. Industries that showed the most promise would receive investment funds. Venezuelan exporters would not be disadvantaged by the exchange rate, which, if fixed, would become severely overvalued. The scope for patronage and abuse would be substantially less than in a system where fixed interest and exchange rates resulted in rationed capital and foreign exchange.

Privatizing State-Owned Companies

This study has shown that the Venezuelan government should accelerate the pace of privatization. State ownership has outlived its usefulness for most Venezuelan state-owned companies. State ownership allowed the development of heavy manufacturing industries in the country, but that job was finished a long time ago.[6] If many of these companies are not allowed to succeed or fail on their own, they will continue to be a drain on the treasury and will be managed as much for political as for economic gain. Privatization is a way to open up new areas to the creativity and entrepreneurship of the private sector and a way to reduce the potential for corruption and inefficiencies that have been present in some state-owned firms. As the case of CANTV shows, privatization is also a way to encourage investment in sectors that have been starved of investment capital.

Privatization of all or virtually all state-owned operating companies and many public utilities probably would result in substantial net gains in efficiency and quality. The only major exceptions to this policy would be PDVSA and Edelca, which arguably are too large and important to be placed in private hands at this time. However, partial ownership of these companies might be floated on local and foreign stock exchanges in order to obtain much-needed investment capital and to ensure that the performance information demanded by private capital markets is widely available. The CVG companies should be privatized and the CVG itself transformed from the operator of industrial companies to a regional development and investment promotion agency.

Dispelling the Misconceptions. There are a number of misconceptions surrounding privatization in Venezuela. Many of these will have to be dispelled if privatization is to be successful. Some people in Venezuela claim that privatization despoils the state and involves selling the "national jewels." Yet many of the "national jewels" are inefficient and money-losing companies that will not bring a high price in the marketplace. In fact, some Venezuelan state-owned firms should have sales prices that are zero or even negative—not because of privatization, but because they really are not worth anything. What many people see as the "costs of privatization," such as paying old debts and severance benefits for surplus workers, are actually the costs imposed by decades of state management and ownership. These costs will have to be borne eventually no matter who owns the companies. In several Venezuelan privatizations, such as Banco Italo, Viasa, and the Cumanacoa and Tacarigua sugar mills, debt payments and severance benefits exceeded 50 percent of the sales price of the privatized entities. The technical costs associated with privatization, on the other hand, have been estimated at less than 5 percent of the sales price.[7]

The large privatizations that have taken place in Venezuela up until now have been justified on the basis that the entities involved were either losing substantial amounts of money, providing extremely low levels of service, or both. This is correct, but it partially misses the point. Privatization is appropriate for other state-owned companies as well, even if they do not lose money or provide unacceptable levels of service. Additional privatization would allow the Venezuelan government to focus its efforts on social programs and on creating the conditions under which the private sector can flourish. Additional privatizations actually would strengthen the state by limiting its scope, allowing it to focus on providing essential government services, and reducing its deficit.

Some Venezuelans claim that privatization raises consumer prices and boosts unemployment. If privatization raises prices, it does so because the prices that had been charged in the past were not sufficient to cover the costs of operation and reinvestment. At the same time, it is difficult for citizens to know how much they are really paying for goods or services purchased from state-owned enterprises. They pay part of the "price" in the form of higher inflation and deficit-financed subsidies that reduce the amount of funds available for services such as health and welfare. Privatization increases unemployment when the privatized entity was grossly overmanned in the first place. The problem here is not privatization; the problem is that under state control, many companies and agencies hired people for political rather than business reasons and failed to maintain their payrolls at healthy levels. Privatization can increase employment through stimulating increased investment. In 1993, for example, it was estimated that CANTV would need another 10,000 workers to meet its expansion goals.[8]

Managing the Privatization Process.   As the case of CANTV has shown, privatization can succeed in Venezuela if certain conditions are met. It can succeed if it is managed in a transparent fashion. It can succeed if diverse political actors pull together for the common good and if special interests adverse to privatization are held in check. Part of managing the privatization process is to recognize and deal with opposition to privatization. Some people oppose privatization out of a conviction that private interests, particularly foreign private ones, cannot be trusted to manage privatized entities in a way that benefits the nation as a whole. Clear privatization agreements with specific performance targets can be used to allay such fears. Others oppose privatization because they do not have all the facts about it. This situation can be addressed only by better communication of the details of privatization processes, including the past performance of entities to be privatized.

In Venezuela, as in other nations that have instituted privatization programs, however, the main opposition to privatization often comes from vested interests trying to protect their own positions and privileges. Such privileges often inflict huge costs in terms of inefficiency and corruption. One way to meet this form of opposition is to try to separate the legitimate concerns of affected parties from unreasonable demands. The importance of privatization needs to be communicated effectively to the Venezuelan people.

Privatization in Other Nations.   Privatization has been, and will continue to be, a major factor in the world economy. In Eastern Europe, privatization has become a cornerstone of economic reform programs, whereas in Western Europe, mounting losses at state-owned companies and budget deficits are pushing even the most interventionist of states to sell state-owned companies. Several Latin American nations have begun major privatization programs. *Euromoney* has estimated that worldwide, the proceeds from privatization will reach $120 billion in 1993 to 1995, with Latin America accounting for $30 billion.[9]

Chile privatized 550 companies between 1974 and 1978. A second round of privatization in the late 1980s further reduced the Chilean government's role in industry. In the four years after its privatization in 1988, the Chilean phone company doubled its sales and profits. Chile's foreign debt was reduced from approximately 100 percent of GDP to less than 30 percent over the last decade. Between 1989 and 1991, the World Bank estimated that the deficits of Argentine state-owned enterprises equaled 9 percent of GDP. Since the late 1980s, Argentina has sold off companies in the oil, telecommunications, airline, gas, electric power, steel, and water industries. Railroads, roads, and government-owned real estate also have been privatized. The program netted the Argentine government more than $9 billion through July 1993, including $2.66 billion from the sale of 50 percent of the state oil company. In addition, Argentina became the first Latin American nation to auction off gas and oil exploration rights, a move that has sparked an increase in investment and output.[10] Argentina also plans to sell companies in the defense, energy, banking, and transportation sectors as well as privatizing the national mint.[11]

Mexico's privatization program has resulted in the sale of more than $33 billion in assets from the mid-1980s to 1993. Additional sales planned for completion before the end of 1995 could be worth $4 billion to $5 billion.[12] Mexico also has undertaken an ambitious program to promote private investment in infrastructure, and has opened communications, highways, ports, airports, power plants, water recycling projects, and even prisons to private investment. Concessions to build approximately 4,000 kilometers of toll roads at a cost of more than $10 billion already have been awarded. Several ports and airports were scheduled to go on sale in late 1993 or early 1994.[13] There even has been speculation that Pemex, the state oil company, might be privatized under the next administration.[14] The Mexican government has used the proceeds from privatization to pay down its debt. In the process, it reduced its public debt to less than 15 percent of GDP and reduced the share of interest payments in its national budget from 50 percent to under 25 percent.[15] The cash stream freed from debt service has been earmarked for the expansion of health care and investments in education under the Solidarity Program.

Other Latin American nations also have embarked upon privatization programs in recent years. Brazil plans to sell companies in the power, telecommunications, petrochemical, steel, and transportation industries. Colombia will privatize petrochemical, fishing, textile, communications, forest products, and financial service operations. Peru plans a far-reaching privatization program to include companies in the cement, mining, agriculture, utility, port, financial services, and telecommunications industries.

Championing Free Trade

Much of the progress made by Venezuelan firms in the last few years can be traced to increased competition from imported goods. Many Venezuelan firms have found themselves pressured to compete with foreign firms. It is this pressure that has created improvement and it is this pressure that must be maintained. The failure of some Venezuelan firms and industries in the process is to be expected. It is only through such failures that resources can be freed for use by more efficient firms and more competitive industries. Venezuelan firms increasingly have seized new opportunities to enter foreign markets. Nontraditional exports continue to grow, although it will take some time for more Venezuelan firms to learn how to compete in international markets. The benefits of freer trade to Venezuelan consumers in terms of the price, quality, and availability of goods are clear.

If the Venezuelan government maintains low-tariff and nontariff barriers to imported goods, it will be placing the interests of consumers on par with those of domestic producers. It will be giving consumers the rights that they have had difficulty claiming for themselves. It must be remembered that the companies and industries that call the loudest for protection tend to be those that are the least able to compete with foreign firms. These are precisely the companies and industries that inflict the highest costs on the Venezuelan people. Venezuela should limit the ability of firms and industries to use the antidumping law and other mechanisms to erect protectionist barriers. For example, initiatives to authorize the ministry of agriculture to order countervailing duties on imports without the involvement of the Antidumping Commission invite abuse by protectionist interests.

Pushing Ahead on Regional Trade Pacts. Venezuela has pushed ahead in its negotiations with Mexico, other Latin American nations, and North America to open trade further within the region. Much of the growth in the world economy over the last several decades can be traced to freer trade. The EC 1992 Program was designed to improve Western European economies by reducing barriers to trade. Venezuela's economic integration with Colombia has shown that there are large, and often unexpected, benefits from more open trading relations. Some fear that many Mexican firms are more advanced than their Venezuelan counterparts. One reason this might be true is that they have closer links with North America. However, Venezuela could try to use its links with the Mexican economy as a stimulus to improvement and growth, just as the Mexican economy has used links with the U.S. economy as a stimulus to improvement and growth.

There is always a danger that narrow interest groups will attempt to co-opt international agreements for protectionist purposes. While the stated purpose of the Auto Pact with Colombia and Ecuador, signed in September 1993, was to promote competition and efficiency, in fact it did the opposite. It set up a common external tariff and regional "minimum percentage of integration" requirement for autos that in effect raised barriers to trade with nations outside the pact. The minister of agriculture followed suit in October 1993 by signing an agreement with the other Andean Pact nations effectively to boost tariffs on imports of a wide variety of agricultural products from outside the Andean region and thereby raise the prices that Venezuelan consumers pay for food.[16] Some Venezuelan interests are trying to promote similar "free-trade" agreements in other industries. They seem to believe that competition within the Andean Pact is somehow "enough." Perhaps it is enough for the protected interests, but it is unlikely to stimulate sufficient improvement on the part of Venezuelan firms or for Venezuelan consumers, particularly the poor, who pay a disproportionate share of the costs of protectionism.

Making Markets Work in Venezuela

The creation of a dynamic, competitive business and economic environment is a primary goal in many nations. The collapse of the centrally planned economies of the Soviet Union and Eastern Europe, the stagnation of the import substitution economies of Latin America, the anti-Socialist movements in Scandinavia, the rethinking of Japanese economic policy in the face of recession, and the difficulties experienced in Western Europe prompted a resurgence in reliance on markets to provide such dynamism throughout the world in the 1980s and 1990s. In Venezuela, making markets work would generate substantial growth and well-being.

It has been said in Venezuela that markets do not function properly in the national context and that the required response to market failure is government intervention. Such failures, however, often have been caused by a lack of a clear framework to govern market transactions. They also have been caused by a lack of commitment to make markets work on the part of political parties, firms, and unions that profited under the interventionist system. Markets do not work by themselves. Markets work when government sets clear and stable rules of the game, enforces contracts, protects consumers, and prevents the abuse of market power. Markets work when government acts as a rule setter, impartial arbiter, regulator, and monitor of markets. This is true for product markets, capital markets, and labor markets. The benefits of the markets will be realized fully only when companies doing business in Venezuela are confident that contracts will be enforced, when consumers are confident that they will be protected, and when collusive, monopolistic, or monopsonistic behavior is limited.

Some of the legal framework to make product markets work is already in place, but, as we saw in Chapter 8, laws alone will not magically change decades of practice and deeply held beliefs. What is needed is the clear and stated commitment of the Venezuelan government to use these tools as they were intended, to create new ones as needed, and to engage in an active process of education of firms and individuals on the benefits of market-based competition.

Supporting Free Prices. Perhaps the clearest signal the Venezuelan government could send regarding its commitment to make markets work is support of free prices throughout the economy. In a market-oriented economy, prices send strong signals that influence the investment, production, and consumption decisions of producers and consumers. Price controls replace the action of the market with the action of government. When it set prices in the 1970s and 1980s, the Venezuelan government often fixed prices that allowed even the most inefficient producer to make a profit. This meant that controls did not stop price increases even on the most basic of goods. When prices were not fixed at high levels, they were often too low, as was the case for public services. (Many countries have had similar experiences; as a result, they have concluded that setting prices is too difficult to carry out in practice.) By definition, price controls favor some at the expense of others. They also provide the opportunity for corruption. In Venezuela, past price controls resulted in a tremendous amount of lobbying for special treatment. Those with influence prospered while everyone else paid the price.

Many in Venezuela fear that, in the absence of price controls, companies and shopkeepers will increase prices unfairly. This was in fact the reason given for instituting price controls on a limited set of goods in early 1994. More generally, there is a concern that many industries in Venezuela are oligopolies and that the oligopolists abuse their market power. The solution to this problem is to promote competition, to punish price gouging, and to regulate firms and industries with too much market power. Price controls are generally not the answer, except perhaps in the rarest and most extreme of circumstances, or in clear cases of monopolistic supply, such as certain public services.

Providing Timely and Accurate Economic and Business Information.
Good information and statistics about the Venezuelan economy are often very

difficult to come by. An often-overlooked fact is that it is very difficult for markets to function well, or for governments to make informed policy, without good information. An important task for the Venezuelan government would be to use some of its resources to obtain modern industrial and agricultural statistics. This might be done in conjunction with, or subcontracted to, private firms as a complement to OCEI (the government statistical office). As of 1994, efforts in this area already were under way. The National Center for Competitiveness was working with OCEI to strengthen the nation's informatics base. This important effort should be expanded and amplified.

Committing to Competition

Competition policy is one of the most important ways in which government can influence competitiveness. Increased competition in the Venezuelan economy during the early 1990s forced companies there to make much-needed improvements and has provided far more variety and choice to the Venezuelan consumer. The Pro-Competition Law of 1991 outlawed anti-competitive practices. In the early 1990s, the Pro-Competition Superintendency was vigorous and independent, but the task that it faced—changing the way business is done throughout the economy—could not be accomplished within only a few years. Continued commitment to going forward is needed. Only a strong, independent Pro-Competition Agency that receives the active and ongoing backing of the government, combined with effective enforcement of the Pro-Competition Law by the judiciary and the repeal of prior laws that conflict with the more recent legislation, will bring healthy competition to the Venezuelan economy.

In Venezuela, professional associations are allowed to limit entry according to their own criteria. A better solution would be for independent licensing boards to be set up to license and qualify doctors, lawyers, and other professions where special qualifications are required and for open entry into professions, such as journalism, for which special qualifications should not be necessary. Associations of retailers, which have effectively cartelized the distribution of pharmaceuticals, hardware, and other items, should be monitored carefully in order to ensure that they do not use their market power against suppliers or buyers.

The focus on competition here is not competition strictly for competition's sake. Instead, a focus on competition will provide pressure for firms to improve, greater consumer choice, and better prices. Whether we like it or not, competition is a fact of modern life. In Japan, Korea, the United States, Italy, Germany, Switzerland, and elsewhere, nations succeed in industries in which there is tough local competition. In Japan and Korea, students learn to compete at a young age in the school system. Later on they are taught how to engage in active business competition. If local competition can improve the capabilities of Venezuela's beauty pageant contestants, it can improve the capabilities of local firms.

Attracting Foreign Investment

The influx of foreign investment in the early 1990s into sectors of the Venezuelan economy, including many sectors that had lain stagnant for decades, was proof of the powerful stimulus that regulatory reform exerted on foreign investment. Many large investments were made that otherwise would not have been made. These investments have created new jobs and new business opportunities across the economy. At the same time, Venezuela is still handicapped by laws, bureaucratic practices, and an international reputation that raise doubts in the minds of foreign investors and, often, Venezuelan investors. Foreign investment represents one of the largest opportunities for economic growth in Venezuela in the next five to ten years. Due to the lack of sufficient local capital markets and the government's budgetary problems, foreign investment will have to be attracted if Venezuela is to develop its resources, to improve its services, and to build a more vibrant economy. Improving the level of awareness within the Congress and the general public regarding foreign investment and its actual and potential contributions to Venezuelan welfare therefore is extremely important.

Reforming the Legal Landscape. Although many restrictions on foreign investment have been lifted, Venezuela's legal system sets up a number of barriers and disincentives to foreign participation in the economy. Foreign participation is limited in the petroleum, television, radio, publishing, and professional service sectors. In other industries, such as mining, complex and changing regulations hamper investment. Weak intellectual property protection discourages innovation, promotes piracy by unlicensed users, and puts off potential investors. Venezuela offers a wide variety of opportunities in tourism but suffers because the country is not adequately publicized and promoted abroad. The Tourism Law of 1993 introduced a Fund for Promotion and Training, which has not been implemented due to lack of financing. Venezuela has great potential in telecommunications, but the Telecommunications Law is antiquated and the regulatory agency, CONATEL, needs greater autonomy to ensure long-term independence in its decision making. Venezuela has strong potential in forest plantations but is still having problems guaranteeing land ownership and long-term contractual regimes for resource use. The capital markets regime impedes business formation and growth. The judiciary, which creates uncertain and in some cases treacherous conditions for business, has not been reformed.[17]

These shortcomings are no secret abroad. Potential foreign investors already have a distinct image of Venezuela. The obstacle that foreign firms most often associate with Venezuela is its lack of "juridical security"; that is, they perceive that the judicial system does not provide an impartial administration of justice. Other commonly cited obstacles to foreign investment include lack of personal safety, the difficulty in exploiting natural resources, and the country's unattractive labor law.[18] All of this adds up to a large and complex agenda for policy makers. Much work is left to be done if Venezuela is to compete successfully with other nations that are engaged in the continual improvement of their investment climate.[19]

Building Trust and Changing Attitudes. There are many ways to build trust in Venezuela's investment environment. International agreements on double taxation, intellectual property, and foreign investment protection can be honored and amplified. Equally important is the task of reforming the many problem areas just mentioned, that plague investors who invest or seek to invest in Venezuela: the enforceability of contracts, the labor law, the rules governing the mining sector, and the protection of private property rights, to name just a few.

Many Venezuelans view foreign investment as exploitative, unnecessary, or in some way an infringement on national sovereignty. Debates about foreign investment often wind up focusing on the potential or imagined evils of the multinational company, based perhaps on old resentments toward foreign oil companies or perhaps on memories of scandals of years ago. Despite the work of the National Council for Investment Promotion (CONAPRI) and several binational chambers of commerce, the prevailing attitude often seems to be that the best policy is to extract the maximum possible from foreign-owned companies rather than to work with them to maximize investment, employment, and growth. Nations such as Singapore and Ireland have openly courted foreign investment to build their economies, with no apparent loss of sovereignty or other ill effect. Other Latin American nations, such as Chile, also are becoming far more aggressive in their efforts to attract foreign capital. As Taylhardat (1993) explains, Venezuela can try to encourage and promote foreign investment, through aid with planning and site selection, through the provision of infrastructure, and through joint provision of training.

Exploiting the Window of Opportunity. Latin American nations face a window of opportunity in the area of foreign investment. Investors, frustrated by recession and low rates of return in the capital markets of developed countries, are looking for new opportunities abroad, and many are showing unprecedented willingness to invest heavily in Latin American equity and debt instruments. However, this opportunity might not last forever, and there will be definite winners and losers among the Latin American nations in the contest to capture foreign investment flows. Chile, Argentina, and Mexico already are ahead of Venezuela in building modern economies and are the frontrunners in this race to win large sums of capital. Investments made in this period will bear fruit for many years, fruit that cannot be recaptured if lost.

Developing Natural Resources

Venezuela has abundant natural resources, but these resources do not provide wealth in and of themselves. The contribution that these resources make to the economy as a whole could be increased through their more effective management. Improving the management of Venezuela's resources would involve greater transparency in the operations of some of the state agencies that manage resources, greater clarity in jurisdiction over resources, a clearer regime of property rights, and a greater willingness to engage in long-term supply and development programs. It also will be necessary to meet the very real and legitimate concern that Venezuela's resources be managed for the good of the country.

Long-term contracts provide natural mechanisms to develop industry based on Venezuelan resources. Domestic and foreign private investors generally will not invest in facilities to process resources in Venezuela unless they are assured of continuous supply at reasonable prices. Long-term contracts with prices indexed to local costs or to world prices would allow Venezuela to gain from the development of its resources. The reluctance of the Venezuelan government and state-owned entities to sign such long-term contracts in the past hurt the development of local industries based on natural resources.

Some people in Venezuela wish to continue to use low hydrocarbon and electricity prices to promote the development of downstream industry. They point out that monopoly pricing of these resources does not help the development of resource-based industry. Instead, it maximizes profits upstream and limits the potential of downstream industry. On the other hand, concessionary pricing can lead to rent-seeking behavior, ineffective subsidies, and secret negotiations that could lead to favoritism. Natural resource pricing can be used to promote industry, but this must be done very carefully. The key point here is that to be effective, such pricing must be low enough to foster development, high enough to foster efficiency, and transparent enough to prevent favoritism. One way to meet these conditions would be to set resource prices at a fixed percentage of international prices for an entire sector. A further restriction would be that prices for resource inputs should never be set at levels lower than the full cost of production.

Improving Human Resources

The Venezuelan government can act in a number of ways to help improve the nation's human resource situation: It can reform labor legislation, improve education and training systems, and develop realistic science and technology programs. The idea is to create an environment in which Venezuelan firms and workers have the incentives to invest in the skills and capabilities they will need to succeed, both at home and abroad.

Reforming Labor Legislation

Venezuela's labor legislation places substantial barriers in the way of needed restructuring and improvement on the part of the nation's firms and the state. Although a number of aspects might be considered, we will focus on the severance system. The double indexation of severance liabilities through the combination of payment of interest at market rates and retroactivity is financially unsound (though either taken individually would not be). The turnover mentality, rigidity, and counterproductive actions that double indexation encourages are competitively unsound. Providing benefits for those with long tenure in the formal sector, while making it more difficult for others to achieve long tenure with a company and for still others to obtain formal sector employment, is questionable from an equity standpoint.

Notwithstanding its human aspects, the labor market is a market subject to the laws of supply and demand. In any nation, the productivity of that nation's workers and firms places an upper limit on wages and employment. In this context, higher costs of mandated benefits often are translated directly into lower salaries. The inflexibility and uncertainty associated with the labor regime in Venezuela often translate into lower take-home pay and lower levels of formal sector employment.

In the early 1990s, there were several proposals for reforming the system of severance payments.[20] Some have been the source of friction among employers, labor unions, and government. A detailed proposal is beyond the scope of this book. However, certain overall guidelines are in order. Reform of this system must take into account the legitimate needs and concerns of employees. The present severance system takes the place of unemployment insurance and of retirement programs found in certain other nations. The interests of the Venezuelan workforce in unemployment insurance and retirement security should be safeguarded. On the other hand, parts of the present legal regime that are uneconomical, place excess obstacles in the path of restructuring, and encourage counterproductive behavior are prime candidates for modification.

One could envision a system in which company payments were divided into two components: a trust that would fund a lump-sum severance payment (as a form of unemployment insurance) and an independently managed pension program that would provide old age and retirement benefits. The timing and frequency of the payments, as well as the mix of payments to the severance and pension funds, would have to be worked out through a process of political debate and consensus-building. Such a system would abolish retroactivity in the calculation of severance payments.[21] It would treat termination and resignation symmetrically with a single indemnity, or if the provision for double indemnity in the event of unjust dismissal were retained, it would be limited by tightening enforcement to cut down on its abuse and by recognizing the financial distress of firms as grounds for justified dismissal. A regime of this nature doubtless would be the subject of intense negotiation between labor and management. Both sides must be prepared to make concessions. For example, employers claim that the retroactivity provision prevents them from increasing wages and salaries as much as they could otherwise. If we assume other payments remain the same, an increase in current wages would be a logical part of an agreement for reform.

There could be a number of winners in such a system. On the surface, workers would have less protection against unemployment in the short term due to a smaller lump-sum payment than in the present system. However, this would be balanced somewhat by the fact that companies would have less of an incentive to terminate workers to save on future liabilities and that additional flexibility would allow employers in the formal sector to hire more employees. There would be provisions for retirement and old age benefits that do not exist in the present system, and current wages could be increased somewhat. Employers would gain greater certainty in their wage bills, would receive greater flexibility to undertake financially induced restructuring, and would be protected against counterproductive behavior. In return, they would be expected to increase current wages and set aside funds for the pension programs. The government would gain in its role as the nation's largest employer, through the creation of a viable retirement program and through a reduction in the political, legal, and economic difficulties created by the present system. The economy would benefit by a reduction of the disincentives to keep and invest in employees and from the pools of long-term capital that the pension fund portion of the program would generate.

Several Latin American nations have reformed their social insurance systems to provide an economically sound program for workers, more flexibility for firms, and more investment capital for economic growth. The Chilean social insurance system, privatized in 1981, is a defined contribution pension plan based on mandatory contributions of 10 percent of earnings for most employment categories. By 1990, nearly 80 percent of the workforce was enrolled in the system. The new system has provided superior levels of benefits at lower levels of contribution than the old state-run system.[22] Argentina, Colombia, Mexico, and Peru are in the process of adopting social insurance systems that are similar to the Chilean model. Argentina passed a law allowing the creation of private pension funds in April 1993. By early 1994, these had received relatively little interest from potential subscribers. Peruvian president Alberto Fujimori issued a decree allowing the formation of private pension funds in 1992.

Reforming Education and Training

Increasingly, a nation's standard of living depends on the productivity of its workforce. This productivity, in turn, is heavily influenced by the education and training received by workers of all sorts. A restructured education system could become a major contributor to Venezuela's economic well-being. However, the Venezuelan school system as it now exists is incapable of educating an internationally competitive workforce. This is not for lack of diagnoses or expert analysis. The diagnoses have been made and very specific proposals have been formulated for the most pressing problems by educational experts. What is needed now is the will to act to improve the system.

Rationalizing and Decentralizing Education.[23]   The principal challenge facing the Venezuelan primary and secondary school system is to improve its use of resources in order to deliver a higher-quality education. The first step should be to rationalize school operations and management. Venezuela cannot afford to pay teachers who do not teach, administrators who do not administer, or support people who do not support. A streamlined system that employed only the number of teachers and support personnel required would allow for better cost controls and higher pay for remaining staff. A system in which hiring and promotion were controlled by principals selected by locally elected officials would provide greater local responsiveness than the present system in which political parties and teachers' unions control appointments and advancement. It is not surprising that state governments that have made efforts to improve the performance of schools under their jurisdiction have run into opposition from teachers' and employee unions, and it is no accident that nationwide, the teachers' unions are the principal opponents of decentralization.[24] Venezuela's children are its future. It would be a shame to see this future sacrificed to an entrenched system of political, managerial, and union perquisites.

Among the more specific policies that should be considered are standards for classroom time. Venezuelan public school children spend too few hours in the classroom to learn the basics, no less to receive an education that will allow them eventually to compete with students from the rest of the world. A greater number of classroom hours, with time lost due to strikes and other stoppages made up at the end of the year, would give Venezuelan students a greater chance to obtain an adequate education. Similarly, it is difficult to find many investments worthier than those that would provide books and adequate classroom supplies.

Decentralization, though not a panacea, could be an important step in improving education. Decentralizing the public schools, by granting greater local autonomy and allowing for a higher level of community participation in decisions relating to the schools, is probably the most effective means available to bring them closer to local needs. Decentralization also would allow room for flexibility and innovation in a system that now suffers from excess uniformity and institutional obstacles to change. As indicated in Chapter 9, a number of successful experiments already have been carried out in schools under the control of local state governments. Decentralization also would allow the education ministry to set overall policies, engage in long-term planning, gather information, perform educational research, set standards and teacher qualifications, and monitor the performance of the school system through a series of achievement examinations or other means.

Reallocating Resources.[25]   Much literature on developing nations in general and Latin America in particular indicates that investments in primary education have the highest social returns.[26] The current state of primary education in Venezuela dooms a large number of young people to a lifetime of economic marginality. Venezuela should reorient its efforts and resources to focus more on primary education. Some in the nation claim that free university education is the most important opportunity for social equality.

The theoretical access to universities for all, however, is tempered by a reality in which most children of poorer families drop out of school well before reaching the university level. The absence of high-quality primary, secondary, and vocational education often keeps children from low-income backgrounds in poverty, because most children who leave school do not have a useful skill. In Venezuela, the road to social equality will depend on the existence of high-quality alternatives to universities that will allow students to develop skills that make them strong contributors to society, not on free tuition to universities that most will never attend. The current Venezuelan system is an elitist one wherein the illusion of equality hides a system that perpetuates inequality.

One way to effect a reallocation of resources would be to require students from well-to-do families to pay part of the costs of their education in a needs-based tuition system. The less affluent could be given access to a system of educational loans. This would have the effect of placing a value on the education and would allow the truly needy continued free university education. The universities also should be encouraged to raise funds from private sources to supplement tuition fees and grants. Doing so would require that the universities, and their courses of instruction, become more closely linked to the needs of business. Such reforms probably would provoke protests by university professors and university students. Such protesters might be asked why they should be favored at the expense of poor children attending elementary school.

Promoting Private-Sector Involvement.[27]   A cost-effective way to improve the education system would be to promote the involvement of the private sector in education. Some private institutions, such as Fé y Alegría, already have shown that they can manage schools more effectively than the ministry of education. The government should make it easier for nonprofit institutions to provide education and also for businesses and nonprofit groups to become involved in the schools. A number of businesses have donated funds for school construction and supplies; others have encouraged employees to teach in local schools and colleges. Clearly much greater scope exists for business involvement in education funding and operations. Such involvement, of course, is not a substitute for furthering educational excellence in the public schools.

Meeting Training Needs.   Venezuela faces a staggering deficit in workforce training. INCE does not, and never will, have the infrastructure and resources necessary to satisfy the nation's training needs, nor does it have the ability to identify and serve the many and evolving needs of business. Hands-on facilities and teaching potential do exist—inside private plants and offices across the country. Many owners of these businesses criticize INCE and argue that the money that they are required to contribute to public training efforts could be put to better use directly by the firms. At the same time, most Venezuelan businesses still believe that the state bears the primary responsibility for training, and most prefer to pay a fine rather than provide in-house apprentice programs.

In the last analysis, the private sector must assume responsibility for the lion's share of training efforts in Venezuela. The government never will be able to supply the resources and expertise that business has. Equally important, the government never will be able to supply the motivation, the spark of commitment that is essential if business is to devote itself to the task at hand. While the government must play an important role in national training efforts, in the end the success or failure of training in Venezuela lies with the private sector.

"Leveraging" INCE. INCE should be supported in its efforts to become a more efficient and flexible organization. In the early 1990s, the decentralization of INCE's management has encountered some problems, but it is a positive step because it involves local actors, who are better equipped to identify the needs of their region than the central government. It also will be important that INCE continue to find ways to maximize the efficiency and effectiveness of its use of resources. Over the years, the Venezuelan experience in training has shown that the more private businesses get involved, the greater the success of the training program. One solution for INCE is "leveraging" the private business and nonprofit sectors by drawing them into ever closer collaboration. INCE has taken positive steps in this direction during the early 1990s and, in the process, has shown considerable talent for innovation. Recent changes in its National Program for Apprenticeship put the principle of leverage into action. An innovation with very promising results to date is the Program for Development of Learning in the Firm (DAE), which places responsibility for selecting and training applicants directly with the firms, subject to INCE's supervision. INCE provides value added in a very cost-effective way by training employees of the firm how to give hands-on instruction in the workplace.

Leveraging also means making training a national effort that involves the civil society. Nonprofit organizations, especially those affiliated with the church, already have made very strong contributions. There exist 281 training centers nationwide under INCE-church partnerships, and the church has developed large education and training efforts of its own, through the Association for the Promotion of Popular Education (APEP), which runs more than 181 training centers, the Technical Institute Jesús Obrero, Fé y Alegría, the Don Bosco Salesians, and the Brothers of the Christian Schools. Many of their programs have achieved high levels of quality and excellent results, with very limited resources.[28] The government should continue to encourage these efforts, through contracts with INCE, grants, and other means.

Strengthening Technical Schools and Curricula. Steps should be taken to strengthen the technical schools and technical studies curricula administered by the ministry of education. To a large extent, the technical schools and programs need the same medicine as the public schools in general, but they also have specific needs of their own. In the 1992-1993 school year, several efforts were begun to give greater emphasis to the technical schools and to deemphasize or eventually eliminate *bachillerato* (high school) degrees in the sciences and humanities. For the first time, representatives of the private sector were participating directly in reform of this sort.[29] New, decentralized schemes for reforming high school curricula have been proposed. Some of these efforts have run into political opposition as well as organizational and legal difficulties, but, as in the case of INCE's Civil Associations, they are steps in the right direction and should be encouraged. Delegating these efforts to the state governments, an alternative under study in 1993, might give them a better chance for success in the political arena.

Reforming Science and Technology Policy

There is increasing awareness in Venezuela of the need for science and technology policy to focus on raising the level of industrial competitiveness and to strengthen the technological capacity of the productive sector. In the short and medium term, a policy to identify and disseminate foreign and domestic technologies that could improve the operations of Venezuelan firms would be the best match to the nation's needs. Most Venezuelan firms are far enough behind the world leaders in technology to make technology scanning and adoption high priorities. This could be achieved by setting up a service that would work with Venezuelan industry associations to identify and disseminate best-practice technology, and research and development programs that would focus primarily on applied research that is of immediate interest to Venezuelan firms.

Universities and research centers also have an important role to play, particularly if their work is directed to projects that Venezuelan companies find useful. Otherwise, we will see a return to the days when research in Venezuela was carried out apart from the needs of local industry. One way of encouraging universities and research centers to create direct linkages with companies would be to fund certain types of university and research center programs only if firms were willing to pay a substantial portion of the costs. Such a process would ensure that the programs were considered economically useful.

Use the Concept of "Clusters." The concept of clusters can be used to identify key technologies that influence major sectors of the Venezuelan economy. Working groups consisting of members from government, research organizations, firms in a given industry, their buyers and suppliers, distribution companies, academia, consulting organizations, firms from related industries, and financial organizations all are possibilities. The goal would be to identify the key technologies that would enable an entire cluster to become more competitive.

Additional sector- or industry-based programs might include research efforts in the areas of product and quality standards, grading systems, intellectual property protection, basic and technical training, industry specific financing mechanisms, international marketing activities, and infrastructure support. Programs aimed at firms would include the provision of information and technical assistance, technological management, consulting, and human resource development directly linked to the concrete needs of the firms through on the job training and technological advice. These programs would help promote the development and expansion of clusters of Venezuelan industries.

Building Human Resources. Venezuelan programs will be more effective if they move beyond the notion of technology as something divorced from human resources. If Venezuelan firms are to improve their technological capacity, human resources at all levels will require improvement. The Venezuelan government can play an important part by renewing its commitment to technical training for both workers and managers through investments in the technical schools, science and engineering education at universities, and managerial training.

Protecting Intellectual Property. Despite some recent progress, including enactment of a new copyright law, Venezuela's intellectual property regime is still deficient. The regime needs to be strengthened through effective implementation of the 1993 Copyright Law and Andean Pact Decisions 344 and 345. It will be necessary to enforce the penalties provided by the new copyright law, set up the copyright registry, as provided by the law, and provide training in the law to judges and lawyers.[30] In trademarks, patents, and trade secrets, Andean Pact Decisions 344 and 345 do make important improvements in many areas. However, rules regarding the free flow of trademarks, the exhaustion of rights, and parallel imports within the Andean Region need to be clarified.[31] The Industrial Property Register, which published thousands of marks for public review and opposition in 1993, needs to push ahead with the examination of these marks and to strengthen its procedures.[32] For example, rules that would allow legitimate trademark owners adequate time to oppose applications for notorious trademarks would be desirable. Rules on admissibility of evidence could be changed to make it easier to introduce business invoices and newspaper and magazine articles into evidence.[33]

Action of this kind will be necessary if Venezuela is to promote internal R&D and attract modern technologies developed abroad. It would be a shame if Venezuela's development were to be held back by an intellectual property regime that catered to shortsighted special interest groups rather than one that promoted investments in research and jobs.

Reforming the Public Administration and the Judiciary

Policies toward the economy will not achieve their goals fully unless they are administered by an effective public administration. Venezuelan experts already know what needs to be done to reform the public administration. What has been missing is not analysis but rather the political will to attack the problem at its root. Venezuela's judiciary is a competitive disadvantage for Venezuelan firms. New opportunities for economic growth can be created by removing the inefficiencies and barriers to productivity that remain embedded in the nation's legal system. The full benefit of the policies suggested earlier in this chapter will be felt only if they are supported by an improved legal environment.

Reforming the Civil Service[34]

The Presidential Commission for the Reform of the State (COPRE) has studied the problem of administrative management thoroughly and formulated a detailed and comprehensive reform proposal. In 1989, COPRE proposed the formation of a body of public managers that would be administered under a special regime based on merit and an effective civil service career program. The COPRE proposal addressed one of the key problems of public administration, the naming of party and union activists to public managerial posts. Public managerial and supervisory posts would be defined by law. At least 60 percent of all management posts would be permanent positions, and the vast majority would be reserved for career civil servants. The COPRE proposal also suggested an important element of control and rationality for the public posts that would be open to free naming and dismissal, by specifying qualification requirements for many such posts and defining the posts open to unconditional appointments. However, the COPRE proposal was consigned to legislative limbo.

The Venezuelan public administration has many supervisors and workers without well-defined tasks or duties. At the same time, there is a substantial gap in pay between the public and private sectors at the managerial and supervisory level. Ultimately, the government will have to pay salaries that approach those in the private sector if it is to attract and retain able professionals. There is scope for a smaller, more professional, and better-paid civil service than is the case at present. Defining such a service would involve deciding which functions are better done by the central government, which are best left to the states, and which might be eliminated.

Training the Civil Service

Training Venezuelan civil servants is another key priority for public administration. The fact that Venezuela is negotiating more trade and other agreements with its Latin American neighbors than before has highlighted the relative lack of training and experience of some of its civil servants, who do not receive adequate institutional training. Colombia has strong educational programs specifically for its civil servants, while to date, despite fragmented efforts, Venezuela does not. In the early 1990s, there were initiatives to coordinate and to set quality standards for existing training and education programs for civil servants, which were a step in the right direction.[35]

Decentralizing as a Force for Reform

Decentralization has the potential to be a powerful force for improvement in Venezuelan public administration. Local governments have more pride in their communities than the national government and in general have more at stake in the growth of their communities, and they are also far more responsive and accountable to community pressures.[36] Moreover, the states and localities may prove to be more auspicious arenas for reform. In areas such as education, reformers may have a better chance of making positive changes at the local level than the national level, because centralization has provided interest groups with the power to block reform nationwide. The nation has seen that successful local experiments soon come to national attention and have ripple effects throughout the country.

The decentralization process now under way, if handled properly, could provide an opportunity to redress some of the major deficiencies in the central administration.[37] It provides an excellent opportunity to refocus the central government on basic functions that must be performed at the national level. What matters is that the reforms introduce into the public administrative system incentives and pressures for productive performance.[38] Education will be required to prepare state and local employees for their new duties and to teach new skills to central government workers whose prior duties have been transferred. It also will be necessary to delineate clearly among the powers and authorities of each level of government.[39] Under the Ramón Velásquez administration, a detailed set of plans and mechanisms for decentralizing governmental functions was developed. Although some provisions, such as those that will make it difficult to reduce employment in decentralized agencies, need revision, the plans provide a much-needed blueprint for the decentralization process.

Modernizing the Commercial and Civil Codes[40]

The legal regulations under which business is transacted in Venezuela are in need of modernization. The Venezuelan Commercial Code dates in part back to 1919 and is in need of updating. Among the modifications should be provisions to allow electronic transfers of shares and other tradeable financial instruments. The Commercial Code does not recognize computerized accounting records and instead gives probative value to hard-copy books only. The Code requires stock transactions to be recorded manually and requires companies to provide sealed, manually prepared books when they are audited. Nor does the Code grant probative value to accounting information coded on microfilm or in electronic images. If this is not changed, Venezuelan firms will have to keep on storing papers and maintaining huge, costly archives. Legislative action is needed urgently to reform many of the rules that govern judicial decision making. The Civil Code and Code of Civil Procedure need updating to modernize Venezuela's rules of evidence. The further development of mechanisms for alternative dispute resolution, such as arbitration, conciliation, and mediation, would reduce the burden on the judicial system.

Reforming the Judicial System

Some of the best legal talent in Venezuela already has studied the problems of the nation's judicial system and what needs to be done to correct them. A few clear-cut steps would go a very long way toward transforming the Venezuelan judiciary. Choosing judges on the basis of professional merit and changing the appointment process, which is now secret, to an open one geared to choosing the best and most upright jurists in Venezuela would be welcome improvements.[41] Judges should be appointed on the basis of academic credentials, professional experience, and personal integrity. The law should prohibit judges from belonging to political parties, not just from engaging in public acts of party activism as is now the case, and should enforce this proscription with penal sanctions.[42] Spain, which inherited a weak judiciary, has strengthened its system of justice by making it a crime for judges to be members of political parties or unions and by prescribing fines and imprisonment as deterrents.[43]

Avoiding Counterproductive Policies

Just as there are a number of policies that would benefit the Venezuelan economy, a number of policies would either hurt the economy or would use valuable resources that might be better used elsewhere. Avoiding counterproductive policies is an important, and often difficult, part of the challenge of competitiveness.

Being Cautious When Using Foreign Models

The Venezuelan government should be cautious in adopting foreign models of policy or development. Often it is tempting to adopt one part of a foreign model without understanding the extent to which its success or failure depends on the local context in the country of origin or the extent to which that local context differs from that found in Venezuela. Two examples will suffice to explain.

Many in the Venezuelan agricultural and textile sectors have cited protection and/or subsidization in agriculture and textiles in the United States and other nations as support for their own calls for protection and subsidies. For those in the sectors this might make perfect sense. After all, if the competition is protected and/or subsidized, why not ask for a level playing field? It is not so clear, however, that this is the right question for the policy maker. One might ask if the United States is a wealthy nation because it subsidizes and/or protects agriculture and textiles, or if it subsidizes and/or protects agriculture and textiles because it is a wealthy nation? If the latter is true, then the policy maker might ask if Venezuela has the resources with which to subsidize and protect, and if it does, is that the best possible use to which those resources can be put? Consumers in the United States spend between $36,000 and $82,000 each year in artificially high prices for every textile job "saved."[44] A large portion of U.S. agricultural subsidies go into the pockets of Archer-Daniels-Midland, Cargill, and other large agroindustrial companies. It is not clear that either example should be copied, particularly in a nation where roughly 40 percent of the population is below the poverty level, in which more than 25 percent of the population is in critical poverty, and in which the average family already spends approximately 68 percent of its income on food and drink.[45]

Some in Venezuela point to the development of Japan and the East Asian newly industrialized countries (NICs) and claim that since these nations have targeted, subsidized, and protected industries, Venezuela should do the same. There are faults in this outwardly logical line of reasoning. The local environments that allowed some of these policies to succeed in the Asian countries had several characteristics that are not present in Venezuela.[46] These nations had consistent leadership that allowed governments to plan for the long term without fear of losing a political majority. Each nation had a tradition of a strong bureaucracy that planned and executed economic policy largely outside the political sphere. The relative weakness of organized labor allowed these nations to increase wages at rates lower than increases in productivity to free up funds for investment. In these nations, thousands of years of Confucian tradition instilled a deep belief in education as the road to advancement for the individual and the nation. In Japan and Korea, protection of the local market often went hand in hand with fierce competition within that market. It is not clear that nations without strong states can carry out effectively the types of policies that Japan and the East Asian NICs carried out. In fact, some researchers—Biggs and Levy (1988), for example—have concluded that in nations with weak states, having no policy at all might be preferred to having an activist policy that can invite rent-seeking behavior.

Avoiding Protectionism

Protection of Venezuelan industry did help create an industrial base within the nation in the 1970s and 1980s. However, this protection also left the nation with a series of inefficient firms and contributed to low productivity. In this regard, signs that Venezuela is beginning to slip back into protectionism should be cause for concern. While there are arguments for protecting infant industries, one can legitimately ask when such industries will finally grow up.

If the Venezuelan government starts down the road of protectionism, it will be difficult to stop. Industry after industry will plead its "special case." Many of the loudest proponents of raising tariffs are the firms that are least able to compete against efficient producers. Some appear to find it easier to complain and lobby than to improve and compete. Protectionism in Venezuela is a process in which only a favored few will win. Jonathan Coles's observation on Venezuelan agricultural reform is applicable for other industries and countries: "The more discretionary and selective the protection, the greater the cost, the injustice, and corruption."[47] Protection would reduce the pressure on firms to invest and to change, while firms in other nations move ahead. It would keep infant industries in their childhood, while industries in other nations grow up. The greater the delay, the worse the problem. Arguments that local firms need more time to prepare for open competition are suspect in Venezuela, since the time supposedly set aside for preparation often seems to be used to lobby or to build opposition to change rather than to adjust to it. As long as there is an opportunity to persuade the government to step up protectionism, many Venezuelan firms will not focus on the tasks of making themselves competitive in international markets, and other firms will not have the certainty that they need in order to redesign their strategies. The adjustment of the whole economy to the realities of international competition would be delayed.

A return to large-scale protection would hurt Venezuelan consumers and reduce the pressures and incentives for its firms to improve their competitiveness. Venezuela should take every opportunity to try to get the industrialized nations to open their markets, but closing its market or raising trade barriers around the Andean Pact nations is not the answer. Dumping or unfair subsidies by foreign nations should be dealt with through the antidumping laws that Venezuela already has on the books, not through protection. The Venezuelan economy was not opened as a concession to foreign companies. It was opened because Venezuelan firms were inefficient and the nation's consumers had little choice. A return to protection will only protect the inefficient, reduce consumer choice, and raise prices for all Venezuelans.

Avoiding Interventionist Industrial Policy

Some people in Venezuela are calling for the government to target particular industries with an active industrial policy. In the nation's current political and economic climate, it would be counterproductive for the government to attempt an interventionist industrial policy (defined here as incorporating protection, subsidies, or subsidized finance). Such policies would distract the government from other higher priorities, and in a very real sense, Venezuela does not need to engage in such policies to develop the industries in which it has inherent advantages.

The Venezuelan state does not have the financial, human, or administrative resources to formulate and to execute an active, interventionist industrial policy successfully. In the Venezuelan context, an active industrial policy means choosing to favor particular industries and industrial groups at the expense of others. The Venezuelan state is too weak to prevent such a policy from falling victim to favoritism and capture by special interests. If the government tries to target industries, it probably will get bogged down in patronage politics and will be distracted from more important tasks, such as controlling the public sector deficit, making markets work, and reforming the nation's education and training system.

In the current situation, eliminating government-imposed barriers to effective operation of the economy will result in greater benefits than any active industrial policy. Instead of a policy for individual industries, the Venezuelan government needs to formulate policies that support all industries. Instead of providing subsidized financing to specific industries in an attempt to mitigate a poor investment climate, for example, the government might focus on creating a favorable macroeconomic environment that would improve the investment climate for all industries. Just as no one could have predicted the patterns of trade that developed when trade barriers between Venezuela and Colombia were reduced, no one can predict the range of industries that will develop in Venezuela if they are given the opportunity.

Some of the industries that have the potential for being larger contributors to the Venezuelan economy are well known. Several were identified (certainly not for the first time) in earlier chapters of this book. The list of industries generally proposed for targeting in Venezuela include petroleum, petrochemicals, steel, aluminum, tourism, mining, and pulp and paper. When the needs of these industries are looked at, however, it is not clear that they need to be targeted. These industries, and their potential advantages, are well known to investors both in Venezuela and abroad. They do not need protection, government subsidies, or special financial arrangements in order to become more successful.

The oil industry needs to be able to reinvest more of its earnings or receive injections of private capital. The petrochemical industry needs transparent, long-term supply arrangements, adequate infrastructure, and access to long-term capital. The steel and aluminum industries need restructuring, injections of private capital (and probably private management), and adequate supply arrangements. Tourism needs better promotion, a better investment climate, some industry-specific infrastructure, and management that can instill a high level of service. The mining industry needs a clear governing legal framework, transparent jurisdiction, well-defined land rights, and some infrastructure. The pulp and paper industry needs long-term supply arrangements, well-defined land rights, access to long term capital, and private management.

Government clearly does have an important role to play in the development of these industries—it must create a favorable macroeconomic environment, modernize financial markets, join with industry to make infrastructure investments, create a transparent regulatory environment, invest in general and industry-specific educational and training programs, attract private investors, and support these industries through promotional campaigns. Many of these efforts should be carried out through public-private partnerships in order to ensure that they have a commercial basis and that government does not end up subsidizing investments that can be made by the private sector alone. Otherwise, these industries would benefit more from government efforts to remove obstacles to growth than from active government intervention.

Communicating and Educating[48]

One of the major challenges of creating a more competitive economy is that of communication and education. To implement even part of the agenda suggested in this chapter, a big effort to communicate the reasons for the agenda and to educate the public about its specifics will be required. The suggestions would impact the lives of many, if not most, Venezuelans. In order to gain support for such an agenda, it will be necessary to communicate a clear and correct explanation of the basic problems facing the economy. It will be necessary to communicate that falling natural resource revenues, inefficiencies generated by past government intervention, and the corruption generated by protection, subsidies, and special favors for special interests have created the present problems.

It will be difficult, but necessary, to communicate that there is no easy answer and that no sudden, magic return to prosperity is around the corner. Venezuela can meet the challenge of competitiveness, but it will not be easy. The nation has enormous potential, but reaching it will take hard work, realistic government policies, and business-oriented firm strategies. It will be necessary to communicate that Venezuela can become a rich country but only when it learns how to develop its natural and human resources in order to compete in the modern world economy.

Clear communication and education will be particularly important for the types of policies that have been recommended herein. Policies that focus on providing a good environment for all industries are more difficult to explain and to justify than policies that target particular industries.[49] The public and the press tend to want specific programs with specific guarantees for growth in specific sectors. Governments that take a less interventionist approach often cannot say precisely where the growth will come from. While this might make such policies difficult to sell to the public, it is precisely because no government can identify and support all the potential areas for growth that it is essential for government to ensure that private initiative is allowed to seek out and explore all new opportunities.

The mechanisms for political and policy communication in Venezuela have undergone a revolution. Today, the traditional leaders of business, labor, and the parties have much less influence than they used to have and are far less able to keep their constituencies in line. Furthermore, the media and the general public are far more interested and involved in the political process than ever before. Governmental leaders now must reach the general public through the mass media rather than reach a small elite through one-on-one meetings. The communication strategy surrounding the suggestions contained in this chapter will be as important as the suggestions themselves. Only through an effective communication strategy will the Venezuelan government ever be able to enact the reforms urgently needed to promote competitiveness.

Other Nations Are Not Standing Still

The governments of other nations are moving quickly to improve their competitiveness. Venezuela already is behind other Latin American countries in some respects. Argentina has put aside nearly 50 years of central planning in favor of a market economy. It has sold off a variety of state enterprises and has managed to reduce inflation to 10 percent and unemployment to 6.5 percent.[50] Chile, after 18 years of sometimes difficult market-oriented economic reform, has been growing rapidly. In 1992, its economy grew by 10.4 percent with unemployment of 4.2 percent.[51] In 1993, the Chilean economy grew another 6 percent. In Colombia, a $2.1 million consulting study has focused on increasing the export competitiveness of seven Colombian industries. The Colombian government and private sector are increasingly emphasizing competitiveness as the key to economic growth. In Mexico, the Salinas government has tied the future of the Mexican economy (and the political fortunes of the ruling political party, the PRI) directly to export competitiveness through the free trade agreement with the United States and Canada.

These Latin American nations already are Venezuela's direct competitors in a wide range of product markets. In addition, they are competitors for foreign investment funds. The economies of North America, Western Europe, and Japan have stagnated. Investment in Eastern Europe is still too risky for most investors. At present, Southeast Asia and Latin America are the obvious places for investors to look for opportunities. The Latin American nation or nations that provide the best business environment over the next few years will receive the investment necessary to modernize infrastructure and to build more productive economies. As trade barriers are reduced within Latin America, foreign multinationals will consolidate their operations in the countries that offer the most dynamic and competitive environments.

The governments of other Latin American nations have been moving decisively to help create more productive and competitive economies. They have been pushing forward with reform of social security, labor, and tax systems. They are increasingly unleashing the private sector, reducing the direct role of government in the economy, and seeking new investment at home and abroad. Several of these nations have realized that increased productivity and competitiveness are essential to their economic and social futures. The path has not been easy for any of them, and many mistakes have been made, but these nations still seem to prefer a difficult path to potential prosperity over an easy path to stagnation or poverty. Meeting the challenge of competitiveness in Venezuela will involve difficult decisions by the Venezuelan government as well.

12

The Challenge of Competitiveness for Venezuelan Firms

Most discussion of competitiveness in Venezuela, and in Latin America as a whole, focuses on government policy, but that is only half the story. In many Latin American nations, the state is withdrawing from the direct control of production and the tight regulation of private firms and is concentrating its efforts on macroeconomic and social policy. Production of goods and services is more and more under the control of the private sector. This means that firms have a more important role in determining their own and their nations' futures than ever before.

Sources of national advantage provide advantages in the marketplace only if they are identified and developed by private and public investment and then used as part of creative firm strategies. The firms that succeed in international competition are those that constantly seek out, develop, and exploit new advantages. They make their national environments better through investment in education, training, supplier development, and technology development or adaption, and by educating their local customers. They meet the challenge of competitiveness by combining nation-specific advantages with strategies that develop firm-specific advantages.

In Venezuela, business has a particularly important role to play. The Venezuelan state will in all likelihood have to devote its scarce resources to social programs and to setting the rules of the game for the private sector. Even so, the Venezuelan political establishment largely looks backward to a "golden age" of bountiful oil income and pervasive state control. At present, the political establishment is unlikely to take the lead in adopting the future-oriented, outward-looking mind-set that will be necessary for the economy to prosper on its own. Therefore, the Venezuelan business community must take the leading role, not only in improving the competitiveness and productivity of their own firms in order to compete in local, regional, and international markets but also in showing the way to other sectors of Venezuelan society.

Each firm and each businessperson faces a unique set of challenges. The competitive dynamics of one industry often contrast sharply with those of another industry. It is therefore not possible to provide a single detailed strategy for each Venezuelan firm or industry. It is possible, however, to provide a series of guidelines that can be used to formulate strategy in the Venezuelan context. Some Venezuelan firms already have started down the road suggested by our research. They will find many of the recommendations that follow familiar. Other firms can use these recommendations as a starting point for their own process of self-assessment and revitalization.

Most of these recommendations refer to aspects of firm strategy, structure, and rivalry. Given the systemic nature of the framework developed in Chapter 3, however, firm actions also have a major impact on the other determinants. Human resource, technology, and infrastructure decisions affect factor conditions. A firm's size and sophistication as a buyer affect demand conditions. Its relationships with firms in other industries influence related and supporting industries. Firms can even work to influence government policy. Thus, decisions made by Venezuelan firms will have a profound impact on all parts of the Venezuelan diamond.

Reassessing Firm Structures and Corporate Strategies

Venezuelan firms must reexamine their structures and corporate strategies. As described earlier, the structure of many Venezuelan firms has been shaped (or distorted) by relations with government. Today's different circumstances require different responses and different firm structures. In a closed economy, many Venezuelan firms could grow only through diversification or vertical integration within the nation's market. In an open economy, Venezuelan firms can specialize and achieve greater productive and managerial efficiency through exports and foreign investment. They no longer have to produce complete product lines themselves but can afford to specialize in some product lines and import others. A number of leading Venezuelan firms already have implemented extensive changes in this regard. (See Chapter 8.)

Reassessing Diversification and Competitive Scope
The globalization of industry has coincided with reduced diversification in many firms throughout the world. Venezuelan firms should look carefully at the businesses they are in to determine in which businesses they can be competitive and in which ones they cannot. Reducing diversification will be advisable in many cases. Some Venezuelan firms and conglomerates, or *grupos económicos,* already are doing this. Many Venezuelan firms also will need to reassess the competitive scope of their individual business units. Many firms supply a broad range of products within a given industry. Under import substitution, a firm often produced all these goods itself. After the economy was opened, Venezuelan firms were able to specialize in particular product segments, for national, regional, or even international markets. If they wish to continue to supply a broad range, they can import or buy goods from outside the firm to cover other segments.

Reassessing Vertical Integration
It also is time for Venezuelan firms to reassess their level of vertical integration. Old rules that forced firms to integrate vertically in order to ensure adequate supplies or import quotas have changed, and it would only be natural for structures that depended on those rules to change as well. After all, defensive vertical integration can lead to a loss of focus and competitiveness. Venezuelan firms can determine which activities must be controlled inside the firm and which can be left to suppliers or related firms. Key sources of competitive advantage normally would be controlled by the firm, but activities that have less of an impact on the firm's competitive position might be left to others. Venezuelan firms also have an interest in ensuring that markets, including product markets, input markets, labor markets, and financial markets, function so that the firms can restructure in a way that improves their productivity and competitiveness. They will be able to adopt effective and efficient firm structures only if markets operate well enough to ensure adequate supplies of inputs at reasonable prices.

Adopting New Corporate Strategies
Venezuelan firms traditionally have had relatively unsophisticated corporate strategies. These strategies, the common threads that ran through the different business units of the firm, often revolved around the use of connections and access to capital, to distribution, or to inputs. The firms tended not to develop corporate strategies that improve productivity by sharing activities or productive resources across business units. In a more open economic environment, there is a premium on creating corporate strategies that develop

synergies within the corporation that allow it to be more than the sum of its parts. Venezuelan firms will be forced to share activities and resources across business units in a way they have not had to historically, if they are to succeed. This also suggests that for Venezuelan firms, diversification in related industries will be more preferable than diversification in unrelated industries.

A New Role for Small Firms

Small and medium-size firms play a significant role in developed economies, accounting for large portions of total output and employment. In Venezuela, the role of small and medium-size firms has been shrinking, and many barriers to their growth have been identified. The costs of entering the formal sector keep many small firms in the informal sector, which in turn makes it difficult for them to grow. Removing official red tape and costly labor law provisions would allow more firms to enter the formal sector and play a greater role in the economy. Small and medium-size firms also would benefit from government action to prevent existing firms from using exclusionary practices to prevent the growth of nascent firms. The private sector also has a role in fostering the development of small and medium-size firms. Efforts to develop industry clusters through the creation of networks of suppliers and distributors would create new roles for these firms. Efforts will be needed to foster entrepreneurship and provide the expertise and support systems that would help small firms succeed. In addition, industry associations need to support newcomers, instead of acting as defenders of established firms.

Developing New Business Unit Strategies

The business unit strategies of many Venezuelan firms once focused on gaining market power, often through governmental favors or dominance over inputs or distribution. These strategies were profitable for many firms and their owners, but left companies unprepared for today's fierce international competition. They also dampened the impact of competition from imported goods when the economy was opened. Business strategies that emphasize satisfying customers and outdoing competitors will be required if Venezuelan firms are to prosper in the future. Many Venezuelan firms have started to make changes to improve their competitiveness, changes that, it is hoped, will be continued and extended.

Seeking Competitive Advantage

Competitive advantage stems from achieving lower costs or receiving higher prices than competitors in particular industries and industry segments. Lower cost stems from low-cost inputs, greater efficiency in the firm's productive activities, or greater productivity in the firm's supporting activities. Higher prices are obtained by providing superior value that customers are willing to pay for. Drivers of cost include scale, scope, and learning economies, use of the most up-to-date technology, and superior linkages among firm activities, among others. Drivers of value include product quality, brand equity, customization, timely delivery, and after-sales service, among others. Note that the source of lower costs or greater value can be in any of the firm's activities (such as marketing, inbound or outbound logistics, service, technology development, and firm infrastructure), not just in manufacturing or production.[1]

Adopting Regional or Global Strategies

Most Venezuelan firms have focused almost exclusively on the Venezuelan market. In the past, overvaluation and import substitution made it very difficult for these firms to serve foreign markets. Similar policies in neighboring nations closed their markets to Venezuelan goods. Since the economic opening, both in Venezuela and elsewhere in Latin America, relatively few Venezuelan firms have taken advantage of the opportunities presented by market exchange rates, entry into the GATT, and economic integration with Colombia. Colombian firms, in fact, seem to have seized the initiative to a greater extent than Venezuelan firms. Venezuelan firms should look to regional or global markets for new customers and growth. They can mitigate fluctuations in the domestic market by serving wider markets. The natural starting point for most Venezuelan firms will be Colombia. After penetrating the Colombian market, Venezuelan firms can look to expand their sales to the Caribbean, other Latin American nations, and the United States. Ratification of NAFTA and the prospects for further economic integration in Latin America make it even more important for Venezuelan firms to expand their outlook. Latin American economies have been growing rapidly in the last few years. If Venezuelan firms do not position themselves to take advantage of this growth, they might well be left behind as the region grows.

Learning to Sell in Foreign Markets

It is perhaps not surprising that relatively few Venezuelan firms have the knowledge and marketing skills to sell their products outside of Venezuela (see

Chapter 8), but this situation clearly needs to be remedied. Venezuelan firms can hire consultants, invest in foreign market research, find individuals with overseas experience, or work with agents and distribution organizations in foreign markets. They also can use domestic or foreign trading companies. A substantial percentage of the exports of Japan, Korea, and Brazil are channeled through such companies. Joint ventures and other partnership arrangements also could provide relatively quick entry into foreign markets. Some of Venezuela's state-owned companies, such as Pequiven and Venalum, and some private-sector firms, such as Sivensa, have entered export markets through this path. Venezuelan firms should remember, however, that joint ventures and partnerships are not panaceas. While they might be good short-term strategies, Venezuelan firms will not be able to rely on foreign partners forever. They will need to develop their own expertise in addressing foreign markets and foreign competition as well as their own sense of what the foreign customer wants and the strengths and weaknesses of foreign competitors. Venezuelan firms eventually will have to develop the capabilities to sell in foreign markets, or they always will be at the mercy of others.

Developing Niche Strategies

In a closed economy, Venezuelan firms often developed strategies to serve the entire Venezuelan market. Given the limited size of this market, it often was difficult or impossible to serve individual niches efficiently. Today, Venezuelan firms should view the world as their market. As a result, it is possible to obtain efficient scale by serving niche markets on a regional or global basis in ways that were not possible under the import substitution regime. Agriculture is a prime example of a case in which the past strategy of focusing on high-volume products for the local market resulted in the misallocation of national and firm resources. Instead, Venezuelan agriculture should focus more on niche markets in which Venezuelan firms can compete internationally. Other Venezuelan firms also could benefit from serving niche markets on a regional or global basis in their own industries.

Getting the Business Basics Right

Many Venezuelan firms need to improve their execution of the strategies that they select. Doing so involves getting the business basics right to a greater extent than ever before. Many Venezuelan firms do a very professional job in marketing, production, finance, purchasing, and human resources management. As we have seen in Chapter 8, however, a majority of

Venezuelan firms, including many large ones, still are dangerously weak in performing what might be considered basic functions. Within a protected environment, where little competition or consumer power existed, even the amateurish and inefficient had a chance to thrive. In a competitive environment, such weaknesses can put survival at risk.

Becoming More Effective Competitors

Venezuelan firms will become more effective competitors as they become better at identifying and satisfying consumer needs and at identifying and beating foreign and domestic competitors. In an open market, competition is dynamic, not static. Foreign competitors will improve their products and processes on an ongoing basis. Local firms must improve each day if they are to succeed. Effective competitors look to themselves rather than to others to make the investments and strategic choices necessary to achieve success. Effective competitors seek to determine their own futures rather than have their futures determined for them. Venezuelan firms need to develop the skills and proactive strategies that help the firm control its own future, rather than relying on reactive strategies that put them at the mercy of others.

Restructuring Earlier, Not Later

Several Venezuelan firms have undergone a painful, but necessary, process of restructuring. A number of them, primarily in financial and service industries, have adopted business process reengineering approaches to trim their organizations. Sidor has closed old production lines, reduced its labor force substantially, and contracted out a number of services that were formerly performed within its organization. Some Venezuelan firms already are benefitting from the difficult decisions that they have made. Many other Venezuelan firms, however, have not yet begun the process of exiting unprofitable businesses, reducing unnecessary overheads, trimming workforces, and repositioning their products. Restructuring is always difficult. The longer it is delayed, however, the more difficult it becomes. If Venezuelan firms do not move quickly to restructure their operations, they might become mired in the past, while competitors move into the future. The hard work does not end with restructuring. Restructuring itself is not a strategy, it is the transition between a failed or obsolete strategy and a new strategy. It should be done quickly so that the firm can get on with its new strategy.

Improving Quality and Efficiency

Market pressures are forcing Venezuelan firms to improve their product quality and productive efficiency. Venezuelan consumers are learning that they do not have to accept poor-quality goods and services. Venezuelan firms will have to reach international quality standards if they expect to compete against imports, or if they hope to penetrate international markets. Several Venezuelan firms are striving to meet the standards required by international customers, while others are attempting to meet ISO 9000 standards. Venezuelan firms should increase their efforts to meet international standards, not complain about them as some have done.

Many Venezuelan firms also need to improve their efficiency in order to compete in international markets, or even to maintain their positions in the nation's marketplace. In the 1970s and 1980s, prices in Venezuela were set so that relatively inefficient firms could make a profit. In a more competitive environment, Venezuelan firms will have to improve efficiency and to get their costs under control. This will require a detailed understanding of the firm's cost structure and the ability to identify potential gains throughout the organization.

Improving quality and efficiency will require that Venezuelan firms take a different approach to human resources and to technology than they have in the past. Human resource systems in which employees are encouraged to suggest improvements and feel they have a stake in improved efficiency will ultimately be required. Venezuelan firms have tended to view technology as a black box, something to be purchased off the shelf with little or no modification or customization. Venezuelan firms will have to take a more hands-on approach to technology, including adaption and in-house modification, if they are to achieve the highest quality and lowest cost possible with purchased technology.

Increasing Sophistication in Finance and Control

Many Venezuelan firms are relatively unsophisticated in their finance and control functions. This has been a particular problem in periods of high inflation. The Venezuelan capital markets are becoming more sophisticated despite, or even in some cases because of, the financial and banking crises of the early 1990s. Eventually, after the crises are overcome, local capital markets will provide more options to Venezuelan firms than they do today. Venezuelan firms will profit from a more sophisticated financial sector only if they develop the requisite financial expertise. Many Venezuelan companies lack control systems that can provide good internal records of sales, inventories, and costs that could be used to support managerial decision making. Many are not audited. In Venezuela, it is difficult to get information from outside the firm (on competitors, markets, and potential customers). Venezuelan firms cannot afford to handicap themselves by failing to obtain information from within the firm. The expertise to set up modern accounting and control systems exists within the nation. It is up to firms to take advantage of this expertise.

Improving Marketing

Relatively few Venezuelan firms are known for their sophisticated marketing capabilities. Within a closed economy, limited competition meant that consumers usually were forced to accept the products that companies supplied. Under price controls, firms often had little pricing flexibility. In this environment, firms often did not have to understand consumer preferences or convince them to buy products that directly competed with those of other firms. Marketing was usually not a source of competitive advantage. Since the economic opening, many Venezuelan firms have instituted total quality programs to improve their manufacturing capabilities. Relatively few firms have made the same effort to improve their marketing skills. Often they appear to possess less marketing savvy than their Colombian or other Latin American competitors. Venezuelan firms would benefit from an improved knowledge of consumers, from a better understanding of the use of price as a competitive weapon and a signal of value, and from improvements in the information that they provide to potential customers. They need to become sellers as well as producers.

Improvements in marketing will come as part of a larger transition within Venezuelan firms. Under the import substitution regime, the customer was not king, the producer was. As a result, Venezuelan firms never really learned how to satisfy the customer with new products or first-rate service. In a more competitive environment, Venezuelan firms should recognize that the customer is king and it is the obligation of the firm to convince the customer to buy its products and services. Once this change in philosophy is understood, the need for improvement in marketing in most Venezuelan firms will be clear.

Never Resting

Improved productivity and innovation at all levels of the organization should become the focus of Venezuelan firms. Under the import substitution regime, profits were determined by levels of protection and special treatment given by government. In the future, firm profitability will be determined by the firm's own productivity and its ability to innovate. This will require a constant focus on productivity improvements and on increased competitiveness. It is not sufficient, either, to look abroad for new products, processes, or marketing techniques in order to introduce them as innovations into a closed Venezuelan market. Venezuelan firms, even small ones, will need to come up with improvements and innovations generated inside the firm. After all, many of the world's innovative firms are small, and large size often hinders, rather than helps, innovation.

Many firms, in Venezuela and elsewhere, view strategic change and renewal as something that is carried out once a year or once every five years. Firms that ultimately succeed in the face of difficult competition, however, do not rest on past achievements. Instead, they challenge themselves on a daily basis and constantly look for new sources of advantage that make old sources of advantage obsolete. Because they know that if they do not, their competitors will. There is no secret to doing many of the things just mentioned. Expertise in most of these areas is readily available from consultants, accountants, academics, partners, or other sources. Systems and practices to improve the basic business operations of the firm are widely available. Venezuelan firms should not try to reinvent the wheel. They should seek out help in identifying and implementing needed changes so that management is free to tackle more pressing problems.

Using the Framework as a Strategic Tool

The framework described in Chapter 3 can be used by firms in formulating strategy. Firms that wish to exploit fully the conditions that are found in their home nations can take the following steps.

Doing Comparative Assessments

Venezuelan firms can use the type of analysis described in Chapter 3 to understand the sources of advantage and disadvantage present in the nation, and to understand the sources of advantage and disadvantage present in competitors' home nations. It is critical that Venezuelan firms know which nation has the best factor conditions for a given industry, which has advantageous demand conditions, which has the deepest set of related and supporting industries, which has the most creative firm strategies and structures, and which has the toughest local rivalry. Understanding the sources of advantage and disadvantage should be part of the normal analysis that the firm does of its own strengths and weaknesses as well as those of foreign competitors. The analysis also can be used to forecast the evolution of competitive positions of firms from different nations.

Identifying and Developing Factor Advantages

As we have seen in Chapter 6, Venezuela has factor advantages in a number of areas that were not traditionally turned into advantages in the marketplace.

In the early 1990s, floating exchange rates and more open markets allowed Venezuelan firms to begin to develop resources that were uneconomical to develop in the 1970s and 1980s when the bolivar was overvalued and many industrial inputs were subsidized. Tropical fruits, specialty agricultural products, aquaculture, forestry, mining, and tourism are only a few of the industries in which Venezuelan firms began to make investments. As long as exchange and trade policies are free and open, there will be opportunities in these and other industries in which Venezuelan resources can be turned into competitive advantages.

Similarly, Venezuelan firms might overcome certain factor disadvantages through investment and research. Direct reduction iron is a good example of a technology in which Venezuelan firms invested to overcome a factor disadvantage, the lack of metallurgical carbons. (See Chapter 4.) The resulting technology and the arc furnace steel manufacturing process that it feeds avoid the use of metallurgical carbons and use resources, particularly electricity, that Venezuela has in abundance.

Taking the Lead on Infrastructure Development

Venezuelan firms have an important role to play in developing the nation's infrastructure. Private-sector firms often are best placed to understand the infrastructure needs of industry. Firms should be willing to propose industry-specific infrastructure projects, pay at least part of their costs, and contribute to their management. Rural roads, irrigation systems, electrification, and pollution control in beach areas are but a few examples. While the appropriate forum for such action will often be an industry association, Venezuelan firms also can work directly with local or national governments to develop infrastructure projects beneficial to business. At the very least, private-sector firms should identify and communicate the need for industry-specific infrastructure projects to the proper planners and authorities.

Seeking Demand Advantages

Markets in which demand conditions are similar to those within Venezuela represent opportunities for the nation's firms. Specifics of Venezuelan demand, including Spanish language, tropical climate, and stage of development, can be sources of advantage, particularly if such demand is not common in industrialized nations. Spanish language has helped Venezuelan telenovelas penetrate the Spanish and Latin American markets. Some Venezuelan firms, such as Venoco in lubricant oils, Cindu in roofing, and Madosa in appliances, have tropicalized products and designs to create advantages in the marketplace. The point is that Venezuelan firms should seek out the unique aspects of Venezuelan demand that can be exploited in other markets.

Venezuelan firms also can benefit by finding and serving pockets of sophisticated demand within the nation. Demanding and sophisticated buyers provide an important stimulus for improvement. By learning to serve pockets of advanced demand in Venezuela, firms could learn how to serve such customers in other markets. The Venezuelan oil industry, for example, routinely demands international standards from its suppliers. The local subsidiaries of multinational companies could provide an important source of advanced demand. Venezuelan firms can try to serve these companies, not just at home, but as part of their international supplier networks. If there are no such customers in Venezuela, firms can seek out sophisticated customers elsewhere.

Seeking Out the Best Suppliers

The quality of a firm's suppliers has a major influence on the firm's ability to succeed in local or international competition. Venezuelan firms will benefit from finding the best suppliers available, no matter where they are located. Given a history of import substitution, many Venezuelan firms are not used to searching the world for the most economical and highest quality inputs available. In some cases, foreign suppliers also can be used as leverage to ensure that local suppliers improve their quality and costs to meet regional or international standards.

In the longer term, Venezuelan firms will be better off if they develop local suppliers. While obtaining supplies and inputs from other nations might be a competitive necessity, foreign suppliers will never provide a unique source of advantage for Venezuelan firms. Local suppliers will become an advantage only if Venezuelan firms work with them to improve quality, cost, and overall productivity. This will require a type of close, cooperative buyer-supplier relationship that has not been common in Venezuela to date. PDVSA is the best example of a firm that has worked with its suppliers to improve their capabilities, but other Venezuelan firms are starting to do so as well. More effective buyer-supplier relationships could involve training supplier personnel, synchronizing production schedules, working as a test site for local suppliers, or even joint development of new products. Venezuelan buyer-supplier relationships will become advantages rather than disadvantages when the traditional distrust and animosity between Venezuelan suppliers and buyers changes to one of mutual cooperation with standards imposed by the outside market.

The Challenge of Competitiveness for Venezuelan Firms 423

Seeking Opportunities through Cluster Development
Venezuelan firms can use the concept of cluster development to identify business opportunities. The Venezuelan industries that are most likely to succeed in international competition are those that are related to existing export industries through supplier-buyer relationships or through use of common resources, technologies, distribution channels, infrastructure, or customer bases. Venezuelan firms can seek out opportunities in existing clusters and to develop new clusters around particular factor advantages, demand advantages, related industries, and supporting industries. Scope for cluster development exists in petrochemicals, metal products, agribusiness, communications and entertainment, tourism, and many other sectors. Opportunities exist for firms that could become a supplier of goods or services to an existing export industry, take advantage of existing distribution channels, or utilize resource advantages in downstream industries.

Welcoming Tough Competition
Venezuelan firms should welcome tough competition from local firms. Competition makes firms sharper; it forces them to improve. Venezuelan firms will face tough competition from foreign firms in local and international markets if they have not already. To compete with foreign firms, they need other local firms to push them in the local market. In industry after industry during the early 1990s, local competition forced Venezuelan firms to improve. Competitors provide motivation, ideas that often can be copied, and can provide a critical mass that could help Venezuelan products penetrate foreign markets. Fierce domestic competition in television production and broadcasting, sanitary fixtures, graphic arts, rum, and other industries has spurred innovation and fostered export success.

Venezuelan firms also should seek out world-class competitors wherever they may be. Competing with these firms is an excellent way to learn and improve. If Venezuelan firms can compete against the best, they will be able to compete with anyone else. In detergents, mayonnaise, and baby food, Venezuelan firms have taken on multinational competitors in local and regional markets. In addition, if Venezuelan firms do not seek out world class competitors in other markets, those firms probably soon will appear in the Venezuelan market.

Locating Activities for Maximum Advantage
Venezuelan firms should work to improve conditions within the nation. Ultimately, however, Venezuelan firms will have to decide where to locate their activities. If the nation proves not to be an advantageous location for

particular activities, its firms should consider moving those activities outside the country. Since the elimination of trade barriers between Venezuela and Colombia, for example, firms can serve both markets from either nation. Venezuelan firms should keep a close watch on economic and political conditions in Colombia and should consider moving activities there if Venezuelan conditions deteriorate. Conversely, if Venezuelan conditions prove better than those in Colombia, one would expect that Colombian firms would move some activities to Venezuela.

Raising Human Resources to the Highest Priority

As we have seen, human resource development was not a priority in an environment in which profitability was determined by other factors. In an environment of active and open competition, human resources, at all levels, are vital to firm performance. The quality and productivity of a firm's human resources are fundamental to its competitive position and success.

Professionalizing Management

Many of Venezuela's leading firms are family-owned and managed. Family members are educated and trained to take over the family business. However, the most effective managers available might not be family members. In the past, in an environment with limited competition and where family ties and personal contacts were vital, this was perhaps not a major problem. As they face greater competition from both Venezuelan and foreign firms, however, Venezuelan companies will need the best managers that they can find, from outside as well as inside the owning families. Family-owned or -controlled firms will need to provide a career path for nonfamily members if they are to attract and retain the best managers available. Many Venezuelan firms have experienced turnover and disincentives among managers because of limited opportunities for advancement in family-owned firms. Ultimately, firms will be best served by attracting and keeping the most able managers they can find, whatever their background or family ties.

Looking for Different Types of Managers

A changing environment requires new management skills and, in many cases, new managers. As George Kastner of Arthur D. Little said recently, "Venezuelan firms must manage change, or change management."[2] The management ranks of many Venezuelan firms are populated by people with training in law or accounting, professions that have historically provided access to sources of power within the nation. This made sense in a system in which government relations was a primary activity. A different type of manager, one with a better understanding of technology, marketing, finance, and the international environment, will be necessary to lead many of Venezuela's firms into the future. Some Venezuelan firms already have well-structured training programs to upgrade their executives' skills. It is not surprising that management ranks in nations such as Singapore and Korea are populated with engineers, many with broad international exposure and experience, not accountants or lawyers. There are signs that Venezuela is moving in the same direction. Over 60 percent of the MBA students at IESA, Venezuela's leading school of administration and management, hold engineering or science degrees. This is a promising sign that Venezuela's future managers might place greater emphasis on creating wealth than on counting or distributing wealth.

Investing in Human Resources

As we have seen in Chapter 6, Venezuelan firms generally have not invested aggressively in human resource development. Instead, they have left it largely to others. In the modern world economy, human resources are far too important to leave to someone else. This means that Venezuelan firms must make greater efforts in educating and training their workers. Many Venezuelan workers enter the workforce without skills and without basic literacy and numeracy. Reform of the Venezuelan education system will take time to have an impact on the Venezuelan workforce. Instead of waiting for a reformed educational system to provide a more able workforce, Venezuelan firms should take it upon themselves to train, and even educate, their workers. Company training schools such as Fundametal (Sivensa), CEPET (PDVSA), CEN (Caracas Metro), and CEFORME (Polar) already are training personnel to high standards of performance. Investments in human resources can have immediate positive impacts on morale, attitudes, and productivity. Employees usually respond favorably when they are treated as integral parts of the firm.

Forging a New Labor-Management Relationship

Management-labor relations in Venezuela traditionally have been strained. Labor and management have vied for the rents created by protected markets and subsidies. Some provisions of the labor law have encouraged firms to treat workers as liabilities rather than as productive individuals. In the future, Venezuelan firms will have to work to develop their workforce. Training and retaining qualified people will be more and more important as time goes on. Better management techniques and relationships will be required in order to develop these people. The imperious management style of many Venezuelan managers will have to be changed if a firm is to develop a loyal and productive workforce. Management needs to find common ground with labor if both are to prosper in the current economic environment. If they are to improve both real salaries and firm performance, management and labor need to work together in improving productivity. Competition from domestic and foreign sources will create common interests on the part of a firm's management and workforce. Management should try to identify these common interests and work to fulfill them.

Improving the Local Environment

Venezuelan managers can work to improve the economic and business environment in areas such as education and training, infrastructure development, developing sophisticated buyers and suppliers, working to create vibrant clusters, and supporting a stronger state that can set and enforce clear rules to the economic game. In addition, due to their training and background, managers often can make substantial contributions to the nation on a personal level as private citizens. It is encouraging that a number of Venezuelan firms and individuals are becoming more involved in improving the local environment.

Getting More Involved in Education

Venezuelan managers are well positioned to understand the type of education that will provide students with economically viable skills. Many managers complain about the mismatch between the Venezuelan education system and the needs of the economy, but few actually get involved to improve the situation. Companies and industry associations can work with local governments to get the educational system to provide what is needed for a more competitive economy. Venezuelan firms can influence curriculum development, particularly in vocational education. They can provide teachers, instructors, and equipment to both technical and nontechnical schools. They can participate in apprenticeship and cooperative education programs. They also can form links with universities to support research projects or engage in joint research. Such cooperation can provide the firms with better basic foundations for their own research and can bring academic research into better alignment with the needs of industry.

Venezuelan managers also can play a role as individuals. They can contribute, as many do, some of their own time, as instructors or advisors, and resources to local educational institutions. They can work to ensure that education and educators are accorded the respect that they deserve. They also can ensure that they pay their fair share for the private or public education of their own children. The signal should be that the nation's elites highly value education for all Venezuela.

Getting More Involved in the Political Process

Venezuelan private-sector managers are in a unique position to understand the impact of government policy on business practice and the economy as a whole. They are on the front lines of competition with firms from other nations. Many of Venezuela's managers are highly educated and trained. Many have traveled extensively and are well aware of what is going on outside the nation. Venezuela's private-sector managers can be a source of valuable perspectives that could hasten the nation's integration into the world economy.

Venezuelan private-sector managers should get more involved in the political process, by serving in government, running for office, and expressing their views in public forums. Traditionally, Venezuelan businesspeople have largely stayed out of the public political process. This means that many of the best minds and most experienced people in the nation have not contributed to the political debate or to the management of the country and economy. Some have intervened in the political process to foster their own interests rather than the nation's. To enter the process, private-sector leaders can take a public-spirited approach that focuses more on the common good than on immediate self-interest. Private-sector leaders doubtless understand making the whole nation and the economy stronger is in their own self interest, as well as the national interest.

A New Role for Venezuelan Industry Associations

Historically, most Venezuelan industry associations saw their main roles as lobbying government and reaching and monitoring collusive agreements with other firms. In order to help their members in the future, Venezuelan industry associations will need to find ways to help them compete in both domestic and international markets. In the days of the closed economy, Venezuelan business was a zero-sum game. The search for protection and favors meant that profit for some came at the expense of others. In the future, what is good for one Venezuelan company can be good for others as well. Industry associations can work toward creating a self-sustaining positive-sum game that can benefit member firms and the country as a whole.

Making Human Resource Improvement a Central Priority

Human resource development should be a central priority for Venezuelan industry associations. Associations can work with educational and training authorities at all levels to set up industry-specific training programs tailored to their members' needs. Doing so can create pools of skilled individuals that all members can draw upon and limits the free-rider problems that occur when only a small number of firms invest in training their workforces. Industry associations play this role in many nations, such as Germany, Switzerland, and Italy. There is no reason why they cannot do so in Venezuela.

Coordinating Focused Infrastructure Investments

Industry associations can work with the government to coordinate industry-specific infrastructure investments. Infrastructure is an area with clear public goods features; its improvement should benefit all Venezuelan firms. Examples might include investments in water systems for chemical facilities, storage facilities for agricultural goods, electricity lines for industrial areas, waste treatment facilities, and investments in environmental control. Some Venezuelan industry associations already are undertaking activities in these areas. Others should follow their example.

Providing Business Services to Member Firms

Industry associations can provide a wide range of business services to their members, including providing market research and intelligence for foreign markets, undertaking generic promotion in foreign markets, and holding international trade fairs that feature the products of members. In some nations, industry associations also provide business infrastructure and service functions such as bookkeeping, payroll, bulk purchasing, and technology consulting. In Venezuela, these associations also can try to fill the gap in information that plagues the economy as a whole. The lack of reliable information makes it difficult for Venezuelan firms to make decisions. Firms can pool their efforts to compile industry-specific information for the use of members.

Setting High Product and Process Standards

Venezuelan industry associations should encourage their members to meet the world's best quality standards by collecting and disseminating information on international standards, technology, and the practices of the world's best firms. We should look forward to the day when it will not be news that a Venezuelan firm has reached world quality standards. "Venezuelan made" should become a hallmark of quality known throughout the region, if not the world.

Focusing on Upgrading Competition

Venezuelan industry associations need to strike a balance between fostering cooperation in infrastructure and supporting functions while maintaining vigorous rivalry among local firms. Industry associations can perform a variety of functions without reducing competition in product markets. Their focus should be on improving the competitiveness of the Venezuelan industry, not seeking to reduce competition or obtain protection. The associations must be on continual guard to prevent price fixing and special interest lobbying.

A Special Place for General Associations and Public-Private Organizations

Venezuela's general industry associations, such as Conindustria, Consecomercio, and Fedecámaras, have a particularly important role in the nation's economic future. These associations can and should take on a leadership role in promoting a more competitive and prosperous Venezuela. They can educate their members and the general public by sponsoring research and seminars as well as by their actions and public positions. Some associations have taken up the challenge. Conindustria has made improving members' managerial and technical capabilities a major priority. The Association of Venezuelan Executives (AVE) has organized many public events to promote competitiveness and excellence in management. PROMEXPORT is a private export-promotion agency affiliated to Fedecámaras, which provides invaluable information and support to exporters. The rest of the private sector should support and emulate these types of initiatives.

Public-private organizations, such as the National Council for Investment Promotion (CONAPRI) and the National Center for Competitiveness (Venezuela Competitiva), are in a privileged position to promote both the concept of competitiveness and actions directed to upgrade competitiveness at the firm, industry, and national level in Venezuela. These non-partisan organizations seek to improve the nation's economic performance by bringing together public and private-sector representatives to promote investment and upgrade competitiveness. CONAPRI's position gives it special access to foreign firms that allows it to see Venezuela through the eyes of others, something that is always valuable for a nation. It also is in a good position to assess the investment promotion schemes developed by other nations. In addition, if the Venezuelan economy is to prosper, it will require massive amounts of investment and expertise, both from within Venezuela and from abroad. Compiling information on Venezuelan investment opportunities and "marketing" these opportunities was a relatively low priority in the past. CONAPRI's role as an investment promoter and facilitator should become more important and take on a higher profile if such investment is actually to take place. As the Venezuelan state governments take on new responsibilities, they also should make use of the information and expertise developed within CONAPRI.

The National Center for Competitiveness is a nonprofit civil association sponsored by the public and private sectors, whose mission is to promote the continual growth of Venezuelan competitiveness in order to improve the quality of life of the nation's people. The center places particular emphasis on promoting the interest and active participation of civil society in issues relevant to competitiveness. It has sponsored a number of research projects on the competitiveness of the Venezuelan economy, including this project and a large and interesting survey of Venezuelan manufacturers.[3] In addition, it has sponsored contests for teachers and students to promote the dissemination of fundamental concepts of competitiveness. The center also has worked to improve the availability of statistics in the areas of industry, foreign trade, and prices by working to improve the capabilities of OCEI. It has undertaken to disseminate examples of positive, concrete examples of Venezuelan firms, industries, local governments, and other organizations and individuals in order to show the advantages of having a competitive attitude in the face of local problems. The center also has sponsored projects to bring the concepts of competitiveness to firms, managers, journalists, legislators, and the general public.

The National Council for Investment Promotion and the National Center for Competitiveness have begun to fill important gaps in Venezuela. The nation has needed a window into the thinking and operations of foreign companies, which nations that tend to distrust foreign investors often lack. It also has needed an organization to educate outsiders about a nation that is very much misunderstood in the outside world. In addition, Venezuela has needed an organization that can act to educate its citizens about the need for a productive, competitive economy and the means for achieving it, concepts that do not generally resonate with a public that has been taught that

Venezuela is a rich nation. It also has needed an organization that can provide the expertise and technical support necessary to guide the acquisition and dissemination of information that is vital to creating a more competitive economy. The two organizations have been extremely creative, dedicated, and professional in their efforts to meet those needs and to create a more competitive, prosperous Venezuela.

Learning More Productive Ways

Most of the suggestions found in this chapter revolve around the need for many Venezuelan firms to learn to become more productive than they have been. Doing so will involve new ways of thinking and acting for many firms. It also will involve rejecting some of the mind-sets and ways of thinking that prevailed in the days when the economy was closed and oil incomes were high. Most Venezuelan firms grew up in an environment of protectionism, governmental favors, and collusion. Many Venezuelan firms seem paralyzed into inaction by present economic and political conditions. Many seem to be waiting for a return to protection or the reinstitution of special governmental treatment. Venezuelan firms will have to learn new ways if they are to develop the strategies, structures, skills, and capabilities required to prosper in the modern world economy.

Many Venezuelan firms would benefit from putting protectionism behind them. There are signs that some Venezuelan senior managers might not be up to the task of showing the way to a more competitive Venezuela. Instead of getting down to the business of making their companies more competitive, some are trying to return to protection. They speak about the need to develop a greater degree of competitiveness and support the opening of the Venezuelan market in all industries except their own, which of course deserves special considerations due to its "unique characteristics." This behavior will be counterproductive. Venezuela has been behind other Latin American nations in its integration into the world economy. A return, even in part, to past practices will leave Venezuelan firms further behind those of Chile, Mexico, and even Colombia, not to mention firms in the industrialized and newly industrialized countries.

Similarly, while competition for market power might be appealing in the short run, it will prove counterproductive in the long run, because it reduces the stimulus for needed improvements. Some Venezuelan firms have taken their rivalry into the press and the media, competing by denouncing competitors. This type of competition is ultimately not very effective.

Denunciation leads to countercharges and further countercharges. The resulting spiral of denunciation usually benefits no one. In addition, such behavior gives the entire private sector a bad reputation and makes the public even more suspicious of entrepreneurs and businesspeople than they might have been before.

Venezuelan firms would be better off if they worked for a more transparent environment, devoid of special favors, subsidies, or exemptions, in which all firms were treated equally. The Venezuelan state traditionally has been too weak to resist the calls of industry for protection and special treatment. Powerful industrial groups have been able to put substantial pressure on any government. Use of power in this way, however, is ultimately counterproductive. While it might succeed in the short run, the costs such behavior inflicts on the economy eventually will hurt these same groups, since they themselves would profit from a more competitive economy and a higher standard of living. Any short-term gains obtained through government favors probably will be reversed, due to the limited resources the state has at its command and the opposition of public opinion. Finally, such favors will not solve the fundamental problems of productivity that plague Venezuelan firms.

It is vital that Venezuelan firms go forward rather than backward. Critical senior management time and effort should be spent making companies more competitive. If Venezuelan managers really desire the stable policy environment that they claim they do, they should work to create an environment in which no industry or firm gets special treatment. The fundamental question is whether Venezuelan firms wish to move forward into a future governed by transparent rules and evenhandedness or a future of opaqueness and favoritism. The former represents the best hope for a dynamic, growing environment for firms and individuals.

Policy Directions and the Venezuelan Private Sector

The suggestions made in this chapter hinge on the existence and persistence of a relatively open economic environment characterized by a market-oriented macroeconomic regime, a competition-based economic system, a relatively open trade regime, and a relatively noninterventionist government. The imperative for Venezuelan firms to improve, to innovate, to get the business basics right, to reassess firm structures and corporate strategies, to develop new business unit strategies, to use the competitiveness framework as a strategic tool, to raise human resources to the highest priority, to improve the local environment, to develop a new role for Venezuelan industry associations, and to learn new ways comes from the competitive pressures that Venezuelan firms have felt from local and foreign firms. If Venezuela returns to a closed economy with heavy government intervention, its firms will have much less incentive to carry out any of the suggestions made in this chapter. In fact, in many cases, there will be incentives to do the opposite. Firms will react to the signals they receive. They will become more productive and competitive only if the signals they see point in that direction.

13

Final Thoughts

The analysis presented in previous chapters indicates that there is substantial potential for growth in the Venezuelan economy. This analysis has pointed out the potential, as well as obstacles, for development in the Venezuelan environment. It has identified fundamental, well-defined opportunities for positive change in the nation. While the suggestions and recommendations made to government and firms in Chapters 11 and 12 might appear daunting, they represent several areas in which positive action can be taken. As this book goes to press, there is an ever greater need for positive action of this sort.

Venezuela: Looking to the Future

Events in 1993 and 1994 have highlighted the need for positive change for Venezuela to meet the challenge of competitiveness. Strong economic growth between 1990 and 1992 turned to stagnation in 1993 as political and economic uncertainty within the nation mounted. In the process, much of the optimism and energy present in the economy was lost, at least for the time being. The financial crisis of early 1994, and the accompanying economic instability, heightened the economic difficulties faced by individuals and firms within the nation. By September of 1994, the worst fears for the economy appeared to have been realized, and even an uneasy stability had become elusive.

While Venezuela experienced difficulties in 1993 and 1994, the economies of other Latin American nations exhibited substantial growth. The economic liberalization begun in several of these nations appeared to have taken hold. Chile continued its economic expansion. The popularity of President Carlos Menem appeared to ensure that Argentina would continue on a path of economic liberalization. The election of Ernesto Zedillo, one of the architects of Mexico's liberalization program, as the nation's president assured that the policies of his predecessor, Carlos Salinas, would be continued. The liberalization of the Peruvian economy, undertaken by Alberto Fujimori, had attracted international attention and investment. In Colombia, the new president, Ernesto Samper, promised to continue the liberalization begun under his predecessor, César Gaviria. Fernando Henrique Cardoso, the newly elected president of Brazil, promised to pursue economic liberalization.

In Venezuela, stability will be necessary but not sufficient to restore economic growth. As the nation emerges from its economic crisis, new efforts will be made to find a path to economic growth and prosperity. From an economic standpoint, the events of 1993 and 1994 showed that Venezuela has lacked an organizing framework, a set of overarching principles, that can help build a vibrant and dynamic economy. This book provides such a framework and set of principles. We believe that focusing government policy and firm strategy on meeting the challenge of competitiveness as set forth herein provides the best chance for developing a more prosperous economy in Venezuela.

Accepting the challenge of developing a more competitive economy would be an important step toward a more prosperous future for Venezuela. Earlier we showed what needs to be done in order to meet this challenge. Meeting the challenge of competitiveness in Venezuela means working to improve factor conditions through transparent and coherent natural resource policies, through reform of education and training systems, and through the development of realistic science and technology programs. It means working to improve demand conditions by becoming more sophisticated consumers and by learning to serve advanced demand in the nation. It means working to develop related and supporting industries through relationships between suppliers and buyers as well as open competition.

Meeting the challenge of competitiveness means developing firm strategies and structures better attuned to the requirements of local and international competition. It also means developing rivalry that stimulates improvement and innovation. It means pressing forward with market-oriented reforms and working to make markets work in the Venezuelan context. It means generating and collecting sufficient tax revenues, raising prices on public goods and services, speeding up privatization, and promoting the flow of private capital into all sectors of the economy. It means reforming the social security and labor systems. It means rejecting widespread price controls, large-scale government intervention, and protectionism.

The Challenge in Context

Although each nation faces its own challenge of competitiveness, the suggestions for Venezuelan government and firms in Chapters 11 and 12 are likely to be appropriate for a number of nations at a similar stage of development. Further lessons can be learned from the Venezuelan study, including ones concerning the sources of wealth in the modern world economy, the importance of consensus in taking steps to improve the competitiveness of a nation's firms and economy, the role of government and business competition in fostering competitiveness, and the systemic nature of competitiveness.

Sources of Wealth in the Modern World Economy

The Venezuelan case shows the importance of understanding the sources of wealth in the modern world economy. In many resource-rich nations, there is a belief that wealth is something that is inherited, rather than created. In many resource-rich nations, not just Venezuela, traditionally it has been more profitable to try to obtain a portion of the natural resource wealth than to create wealth through the productive efforts of individuals.

Wealth in the industrialized nations, on the other hand, is far more a product of the ideas and productivity of its people than the presence of natural resources. Countries such as Switzerland, Japan, and, recently, Korea, are prospering without major endowments of natural resources. Unfortunately, natural resource wealth can blind people to what is required to develop competitive industries and nations. According to one analyst, flows of natural riches create a false sense of wealth as natural resources, "whereas true wealth [lies] in productive investment and the development of industry, agriculture, and trade." The analyst was not a modern observer of the Venezuelan economy. It was González de Cellorigo, who, in the year 1600, was trying to explain the economic decline of Spain.[1]

The notion that wealth is created rather than inherited implies a very different view of the role of education, of government and firm strategies, and of the interaction of business and government than is often found in resource-rich nations. It implies an urgency for individuals and institutions to invest to become more productive and competitive rather than an urgency to distribute inherited wealth. At present, the idea of wealth as something created by productive efforts, rather than inherited in the form of natural resources, is gaining ground in many nations, though such a change of mind-set is difficult for some.

The Importance of Consensus

Another lesson is the importance of consensus in economic reform processes in democratic regimes. The first consensus that is necessary for a nation to undertake steps to improve competitiveness is about the economic problems the nation faces. There has been no consensus in Venezuela about the cause of its economic problems. Many people appear to believe that economic reform is largely responsible. Other Venezuelans know that a combination of falling world commodity prices and years of ineffective economic management that did not allow for the development of a healthy national economy are largely responsible for the decline in living standards. This discrepancy is important. Unless there is widespread understanding of the real problems, actions necessary to build a strong economy will be politically impractical.

However, consensus by itself is not enough. Consensus that is built on a false picture of the nation's economic situation will not result in policies and strategies that will bring about positive change. Without a consensus, a government can develop a creative and sound economic program but will be unable to obtain the political backing to carry out its program. With a misguided consensus, one that does not correctly identify a nation's true economic problems, a government might be politically popular, but will be unable to develop an economic program that delivers positive results. In Venezuela, many of the aspects of the program developed by the Pérez administration were economically sound, but a lack of political consensus prevented the program from being fully implemented. In its first few months, the Caldera administration and its economic policies were politically popular but the soundness of its economic policies was questionable. (Further complicating matters is the fact that Pérez's unpopularity was partially due to questions about the ethics of some members of the government and Caldera's popularity was partially due to his personal reputation for integrity.)

International competition actually can help bring different groups within a nation together. Closed economies help to create societies in which different groups vie for a larger share of an existing pie. In a closed system, often the only way for one group to increase its welfare is to take from another. This has been the case in Venezuela since oil revenues started to decline. International competition creates interests that are common among management, labor, and government within a nation. Nations succeed in developing a more prosperous economy when their focus is on making the pie larger for all members of society through increased productivity and efficiency that improves the competitiveness of firms and the nation. Nations succeed when different groups in society recognize their interdependence and work together in order to compete on world markets. In this way, gains by one portion of society are gains for many portions. Individual segments of society often can halt the development of a more competitive economy; only several segments of society working together will be able to promote it. Pressures from foreign competition and pressures to succeed in the international economy can become a great unifying force within a nation.

Chapters 11 and 12 set forth steps that the Venezuelan government and Venezuelan firms can take to improve the competitiveness of the nation's economy. In any nation, however, these groups will not be able to create a prosperous nation on their own. Labor unions, educational institutions, community organizations, and individuals also have essential roles to play. Many of the intangibles that nations need the most, such as better education, training, and stronger communities, are areas in which society as a whole plays the most important part. This points to the importance of the involvement of many segments of society in the process of change.

The Role of Government and the Role of Business Competition

Another lesson that emerges from the Venezuelan study is the importance of changing views of government and of business competition. In many nations, government is viewed as the principal provider of social and economic well-being. Government often is seen as an agent that could distribute wealth to the population through state-led development, direct employment, low prices for publicly provided goods and services, and other benefits. In Venezuela, government is still widely seen as an agent that must provide benefits of every kind.[2] Demands on government appear to be increasing as its resources decrease.

Our study shows that it is difficult for governments to create competitive industries out of thin air. Even with Venezuela's vast resource wealth and natural advantages, the government has had serious difficulties trying to build productive, efficient industries that can compete in the international marketplace without subsidies. This study has shown that government's most important influence on the competitiveness of a nation's firms can come from policies that affect the economy as a whole, such as its macroeconomic policies, its trade and industrial policies, and its policies toward competition. In particular, it has shown that in the absence of sound economic and business fundamentals, government policy is unlikely to create competitive industries or a competitive economy. The study also has pointed out the importance of government investments in education, training, and infrastructure.

In many nations, market economies and business competition are viewed with suspicion by the general public. In a 1992 survey, 55 percent of the Venezuelans surveyed were not supportive of free market values, 8 percent were definitely supportive, and the rest were indifferent.[3] Capitalism often is seen in Venezuela as exploitative. In a 1986 survey, more than two-thirds of the respondents agreed that "capitalism is immoral because it deprives workers of part of their rightful earnings."[4] According to Templeton (1995), the Venezuelan public places less confidence in the honesty of business management than in the honesty of the universities, the armed forces, and the press.[5] Competition has not been widely understood to be a force toward change and improvement because, historically, it did not work that way. The consumer seldom saw the benefits of competition in terms of better products, improved selection, or lower prices. This points out the importance of making markets work so that consumers can benefit from competition and so that rivalry can be a stimulus to improvement and innovation. As international competition becomes tougher, firms will increasingly have to learn to become capable competitors in the domestic market before they can succeed in international markets.

As in any nation, views toward the role of government and business competition found in Venezuela arose in response to a particular set of circumstances. One would expect them to change, albeit with a time lag, as the initial circumstances change. It will take some time for the realization that oil will not provide an adequate standard of living by itself to take hold. It will take some time for the realization that a government with limited resources cannot provide in quite the same way as it did before to become widespread. It also will take some time for the public to recognize the benefits that can arise from business competition and to focus on creating wealth through individual and firm initiative.

Competitiveness and Systemic Change

In most nations, there is no one industry or small set of industries that will meet the nation's need for growth. This means that competitiveness must be thought about across the economy and in systemic terms. One of the most important lessons that arises from the Venezuelan context is that competitiveness at the national level is systemic. Competitiveness involves the development of the capabilities to improve and innovate coupled with pressures and incentives to do so. All three often are necessary for an economy to progress. The determinants of competitiveness of individual

Final Thoughts

industries and of national economies act in concert. They mutually reinforce each other in positive or negative ways.

The framework described in Chapter 3 is a tool that can be applied in a variety of national contexts. This framework emphasizes the systemic nature of the sources of competitive advantage and disadvantage in a national economy, by helping to identify them in a particular industry or nation and highlighting the interaction among these determinants. As we have seen, many of the most important influences on national competitiveness are human ones that citizens can change or improve. In fact, in Venezuela and elsewhere, it is the nation's ability to support positive change that will determine its ultimate economic success.

Each nation must find its own path to economic prosperity. The process is a long and difficult one, as the experiences of Chile, Argentina, Mexico, and other nations have shown. Administrations will come and go, but Venezuela will remain in many ways a land of opportunity. It is a nation blessed with a number of underutilized assets, including abundant natural resources, a favorable location, and an energetic and dynamic population. It is a nation that has started down the difficult path toward developing a more prosperous and competitive economy. Venezuela has yet to make the breakthrough necessary to become more prosperous, but it is a young nation that can support positive change. One business executive said it best: "When I arrive back in Venezuela [from overseas], I kiss the ground. This is a country that is open to new ideas and where change can happen." In Venezuela, as in other nations, the potential for prosperity lies in its ability to make positive changes that help it meet the challenge of competitiveness.

Appendix

Recommendations for the Venezuelan Government and Venezuelan Firms Listed by the Determinants of National Competitive Advantage

The following tables provide a user-friendly overview of the recommendations of the study. The determinants of national competitive advantage are used to organize the major policy and strategy initiatives. Along with each initiative, the tables contain a subjective assessment of the extent of the positive impact the initiative might have on the economy and the likely time frame in which this positive impact would be felt.

TABLE A.1
Factor Conditions: Natural Resource Initiatives

	IMPACT ON THE ECONOMY	TIME HORIZON
Clear, long-term contracts for industrial users	very high	short term
Transparent and effective supply negotiations	high	short-medium term
Pricing that fosters development, covers costs, and promotes efficiency	moderate-high	short-medium term
Clear land tenure and property rights	high	short term
Clear mineral rights and jurisdiction	moderate	short-medium term
Actively recruiting private domestic and foreign investments	very high	short-medium term

TABLE A.2
Factor Conditions: Financial System and Capital Formation

	IMPACT ON THE ECONOMY	TIME HORIZON
Reduce budget deficit	very high	short term
Market-oriented macroeconomic programs	very high	short-medium term
Better banking regulation	high	medium term
Capital market reform	moderate-high	medium-long term
Actively recruiting private domestic and foreign investments	very high	short-medium term
Creation of viable pension funds	high	medium-long term

TABLE A.3
Factor Conditions: Human Resource Development and Technology Development

	IMPACT ON THE ECONOMY	TIME HORIZON
Viewing workers as assets	very high	short-long term
Greater emphasis on worker training	high	medium term
Reform of severance system	high	short-medium term
Better labor relations	high	medium term
Better technical training	moderate-high	short-medium term
Identification and adoption of existing technology	moderate-high	medium term
Public-private centers of excellence	moderate	medium-long term

TABLE A.4
Factor Conditions: Education System

	IMPACT ON THE ECONOMY	TIME HORIZON
Improvements in the effectiveness of operations and management of primary and secondary levels	high	medium-long term
Reduction of overstaffing and excess privileges	high	short-medium term
Decentralized administration and control	moderate-high	medium term
Objective evaluation of teachers and students	moderate-high	medium term
Reallocation of resources toward primary and secondary levels	moderate	medium-long term
Curricula more relevant to the needs of the economy	high	medium term
Technical track as a respected alternative	high	medium-long term
Greater participation of the private sector	moderate-high	short-medium term

TABLE A.5
Demand Conditions, Related Industries, and Supporting Industries

	IMPACT ON THE ECONOMY	TIME HORIZON
Foster more sophisticated consumer demand by ensuring open competition	moderate	medium-long term
Leading companies developing local suppliers	moderate-high	medium-long term
Using Andean Pact to extend the "home" market	high	short-medium term
Government procurement to stimulate improvements by suppliers	moderate	medium term
Closer buyer-seller relationships	moderate-high	medium term
Better networking among firms	moderate	medium term
Attracting investment to build clusters	high	short-medium term

TABLE A.6
Firm Strategy and Structure

	IMPACT ON THE ECONOMY	TIME HORIZON
Privatization	very high	short term
Optimize corporate structures	high	short-medium term
Getting the business basics right	high	short-medium term
Regional or global strategies	moderate-high	medium-long term
Greater focus on training and human resources	high	short-medium term
More professional management	high	medium term
Better marketing at home and abroad	moderate-high	medium term

TABLE A.7
Interfirm Rivalry

	IMPACT ON THE ECONOMY	TIME HORIZON
Business rivalry, not political rivalry	high	short-medium term
Rivalry to serve customers, not to control resources	high	short-medium term
Active pro-competition policies	moderate-high	short-medium term
Avoiding protectionism	high	short term
Emphasis on tough but fair competition	high	short-medium term
Selective cooperation through industry associations and between suppliers and buyers	moderate-high	medium term

TABLE A.8
Public Administration and Legal System

	IMPACT ON THE ECONOMY	TIME HORIZON
Impartial judicial system	very high	short term
Modernized commercial code	moderate	short-medium term
Streamlined public administration	high	short-medium term
Better-trained civil service	moderate-high	medium term
Better technical support for administration and legislation	moderate-high	short-medium term

Notes

Chapter 1

1. World Economic Forum (1994).
2. Pérez had been president from 1974 through 1978. The Venezuelan Constitution does not allow any president to serve two consecutive terms in office.

Chapter 2

1. The output of Venezuela's oil industry is captured in part under mining and quarrying and part under manufacturing. Processed metal products appear in the manufacturing category (which accounts for the lower than expected mining and quarrying figures of countries such as Chile and Peru).
2. OCEI (1991).
3. See Kelly and González (1993).
4. Kelly and González (1993).
5. Naím and Francés (1995).
6. See Betancourt and Freije (1993).
7. Betancourt and Freije (1993).
8. The Economist (1990).
9. PDVSA.
10. IMF Financial Statistics.
11. Economist Intelligence Unit estimates.
12. Ibid.
13. Kelly (1992) takes the average of several estimates of poverty in Venezuela.
14. Márquez (1995) (draft), cited by Rigobón (1993).
15. Rodríguez (1991) and Naím (1993).
16. VenEconomy estimate.
17. The Economist (1990).
18. Naím (1993).
19. Paredes (1993).
20. Rodríguez (1991).

21. Ibid. and private communications.
22. Rodríguez (1991) and Naím (1993).
23. Rigobón (1993), citing Oficina Central de Presupuesto, *40 años de presupuesto fiscal* and *Exposición de motivos del proyecto de ley de presupuesto* (various years).
24. Banco Central de Venezuela, *Informe económico*.
25. World Economic Forum (1993).
26. "BV Business Briefs" (1994).
27. Naím (1993).
28. Datos (1993). Figures taken from projections from the 1990 census.
29. Kline (1994), citing OCEI data.
30. Ibid.
31. Lordan (1993).
32. Cisneros (1993).
33. "Foreign Investment in Venezuela" (1992).
34. Wilson (1994).
35. Naím (1993).
36. Templeton (1995).
37. Malavé and Piñango (1993).

Chapter 3

1. In the mid-1980s, for example, Olivetti was considered a successful firm, but Italy's trade balance in office equipment was negative by billions of dollars. While the Italian firm might have been competitive, the Italian industry clearly was not.
2. There is increasing agreement over the definition of the term "competitiveness" with respect to nations. According to Bruce Scott (1985), p. 14-15, "National competitiveness refers to a nation's ability to produce, distribute, and service goods in the international economy in competition with goods and services produced in other countries, and to do so in a way that earns a rising standard of living. The ultimate measure of success is not a 'favorable' balance of trade, a positive current account, or an increase in foreign exchange reserves: it is an increase in the standard of living." According to the United Nations ECLAC (1990), p. 68, "... the economy as a whole is regarded as being competitive if, within the overall framework of macroeconomic equilibrium, it has the capacity to increase (or at least maintain) its international market share while at the same time raising the standard of living of the population." Dollar and Wolff (1993), p. 3, offer a similar definition, "... a competitive nation is one that can succeed in international trade via high technology and productivity, with accompanying high wages and income. Given this definition, the best overall measure of competitiveness is one that has long been used in international comparisons: productivity."
3. Porter (1990) and Krugman (1994) make similar points.

4. Barro (1990, 1991) found that the openness of the economy was positively correlated with growth in a sample of 98 nations.
5. This section draws upon Porter (1990) and Crocombe, Enright, and Porter (1991).
6. A similar focus on the need for incentives, pressures, and capabilities to innovate and improve can be found in Lall (1990) and ECLAC (1990, 1992a). Porter's version is adopted here because it provides a detailed framework to assess the concrete underlying influences on these features. This framework has been applied directly to a number of nations. In addition to Porter (1990), see Crocombe, Enright, and Porter (1991); Porter and the Monitor Company (1991); Borner, Porter, Weder, and Enright (1991); van der Linde (1992); and Sölvell, Zander, and Porter (1991).
7. See Enright (1992).
8. This section is based on Güerere (1993a).
9. This argument is consistent with those found in Vernon (1966).
10. See Enright (1993) for a discussion of the impact of local differences on competitive advantage.
11. Jatar (1993).
12. This section draws upon Porter and the Monitor Company (1991).
13. This is the rationale for the multinational firm given by Caves (1982).
14. Reich (1991) goes even further, claiming that nations should not be concerned with the nationality or ownership of firms, but rather should be concerned about the activities that they perform and the workers that they employ.
15. Smith (1993) calls Porter (1990) "potentially an extraordinarily important book for the development field."

Chapter 4

1. This profile is based on Güerere (1993b) and additional research by Edith Scott Saavedra.
2. Official government or industry figures are not available. Estimates by Venezuelan industry executives interviewed for this study range from $40 million to $60 million in revenues from foreign licenses in 1992.
3. Comparative statistics on telenovela exports are not available. Venezuela's international ranking is based on interviews with Venezuelan industry executives and industry market intelligence.
4. Reyes-Matta (1992).
5. For example, Marte TV's *Las dos Dianas* ("The Two Dianas") had 137 episodes, while the longest-running telenovela, *El derecho de nacer* ("The Right to Be Born"), was on the air for nearly two years. In January 1994, RCTV's *Por estas calles* ("On These Streets") was approaching this record, with nineteen months on the air (475 hours).

6. Their earliest origins can be traced back to the *folletines*, or serialized novels popular in the nineteenth century.
7. Today some telenovela authors, such as the successful Cuban-born writer Delia Fiallo, live in Miami.
8. Industry market intelligence.
9. Estimates are from Venezuelan industry sources. There are reports of Venezuelan telenovelas selling for as much as $15,000 per hour in Spain. Besas (1993).
10. Venezuelan expertise in telenovelas has roots that go back to the days of radio. Some of the leaders of the senior generation active in telenovelas today, including writers and coaches, got their start at that time and have continued to help build the talent on which this industry is based.
11. Datos (1993). Industry estimates are even higher.
12. Datos (1993).
13. Industry interviews.
14. Venezuelan television and advertising executives interviewed for this study estimated the Venezuelan advertising market (for measured media) in 1993 at between $450 million and $500 million, and estimated that television advertising accounts for 60 percent of that total.
15. Güerere (1993a).
16. No official government or industry figures are available. Estimates are by industry participants.
17. Reyes-Matta (1992).
18. Ibid.
19. This profile is based on Briceño (1993) and additional interviews.
20. Briceño (1993), citing Pulp and Paper International (1992).
21. Briceño (1993), citing OCEI, *Anuario del comercio exterior* (1991).
22. Briceño (1993).
23. Pulp & Paper International (1993).
24. Briceño (1993).
25. Ambrus (1992b).
26. Ibid.
27. Briceño (1993).
28. The Agrarian Reform Law makes no provision for the large land areas (50,000 hectares) necessary for forestry plantations. A property larger than 5,000 hectares is deemed to be a latifundium. The law allows farmers and landless peasants to occupy "idle" land. Because tree plantations often involve some land that is idle at any one time, the plantation owners are at substantial risk. Briceño (1993).
29. The Venezuelan cost advantage in tissue paper derives primarily from recycled fiber. Venezuelan paper producers have become low-cost recyclers and Venezuela has, after Mexico, the second-highest recycled fiber utilization rate in Latin America. Briceño (1993).

30. Briceño (1993), Graphic No. 14. Although world markets generally have been depressed, Latin America has been an exception. In 1991, the commercial opening of various Latin American nations fueled a seven percent increase in the consumption of paper and cardboard across the region, to 12 million metric tons. Pulp & Paper International (1993).
31. Briceño (1993).
32. Agroinvest Consultores, S.A. and J.E. Austin Associates (1993b).
33. Ibid.
34. Briceño (1993).
35. Ibid.
36. Ibid.
37. This profile is based on Boza (1993) and additional research by Edith Scott Saavedra.
38. World Tourism Organization (1993).
39. Raúl López Pérez, cited in Boza (1993), p. 61.
40. *Business Venezuela*, "Interview with Diego Arria, Former Minister of Information and Tourism" (1993).
41. Holder (1993).
42. Foote and Hawkins (1991), citing Wharton Econometric Forecasting Associates.
43. Caribbean Tourism Organization, cited in Foote (1992).
44. Ibid.
45. Ibid.
46. United Nations, World Tourism Organization (1993).
47. This paragraph is based on Betancourt and Jatar (1990) and industry interviews.
48. Industry interviews. See also Wilson (1993) and Oldham and Wilson (1993).
49. Mr. F. & Mrs. V. Davison, Tyne & Wear, England, Letter to the Editor, "Mira!—The Venezuela Traveler" (1993). The Davisons did receive reimbursement from the tour company for half the price of the tour.
50. Private communication.
51. Foote and Hawkins (1991), citing study by Opinion Research of Venezuela.
52. Corpoturismo, cited in Foote and Hawkins (1991).
53. Peter Schaepe, Hilton Division Director for Venezuela, quoted in Wilson (1993).
54. Industry interviews.
55. Betancourt and Jatar (1990).
56. In 1974 the newly created Corpoturismo invited bids from international hotel chains to manage the hotels run by CONAHOTU and awarded several contracts. However, the arrangement proved politically unpopular because private management curtailed perquisites traditionally granted to certain groups. One year later management was returned to the Venezuelan state. Private communication.
57. Industry interviews.
58. Rodríguez (1992), p. 43.

59. Caribbean Tourist Organization, cited in Foote and Hawkins (1991).
60. Berrol and Walker (1991).
61. Estimate of David Foote.
62. Information provided by the National Council for Investment Promotion.
63. Wilson (1993).
64. Navarro (1993).
65. Information provided by INCE-Turismo, Instituto de Capacitación Turística.
66. Boza (1993).
67. Estimate provided by the National Council for Investment Promotion.
68. For example, see Peter Schaepe, Hilton Division Director for Venezuela, quoted in Wilson (1993), and Diego Arria, quoted in *Business Venezuela*, "Interview with Diego Arria, Former Minister of Information and Tourism" (1993).
69. This profile is based on Balaguer and Segnini (1993) and additional interviews.
70. Balaguer and Segnini (1993), citing the Ministry of Energy and Mines. The estimate of petrochemical exports in 1992 does not include exports by firms that are owned 100 percent by private investors, for which statistical data are not available.
71. 1991 data. This percentage increased in 1992 with the start-up of the export-oriented MTBE plant. Balaguer and Segnini (1993).
72. As of 1993, Brazil was the only country in Latin America that produced engineering plastics (polycarbonates). Balaguer and Segnini (1993).
73. Balaguer and Segnini (1993).
74. Ibid. and private communications.
75. Balaguer, private communication.
76. Balaguer and Segnini (1993), citing Viana (1990).
77. Balaguer and Segnini (1993), citing Exxon 1991 Annual Report.
78. Balaguer and Segnini (1993).
79. This profile is based on Alvaray (1993) and additional interviews.
80. Banco Central de Venezuela. Exports of iron and steel products reached an estimated $674 million in 1992.
81. Alvaray (1993), citing the Latin American Iron and Steel Institute (ILAFA) (1992 figures).
82. Ibid.
83. De Sanctis (1993).
84. Alvaray (1993), citing the Venezuelan Steel Institute (IVES) and OTEPI Consultores.
85. De Sanctis (1993).
86. Sweeney (1992a).
87. Sweeney (1992a and 1992b).
88. Sidor also had an important social mission to provide housing, schooling and other social benefits to its workers and their families in the Guayana region.

Notes

89. Sweeney (1992b), p. 40.
90. Sweeney (1992b).
91. Sidor official, quoted in Sweeney (1992b). See also Alvaray (1993).
92. Alvaray (1993).
93. Sweeney (1992b).
94. Ibid.
95. Sidor official, quoted in Sweeney (1992b).
96. Alvaray (1993).
97. Viana et el. (1993).
98. Ibid., p. 32.
99. Viana et al. (1993).
100. Ibid., citing Viana (1984).
101. Viana et al. (1993).
102. Alvaray (1993).
103. Ibid.
104. Viana et al. (1993).
105. Alvaray (1993), citing Midrex and OTEPI.
106. Alvaray (1993), citing IVES and Paine Webber.
107. Alvaray (1993), citing Paine Webber, Sidor, and UEC Report.
108. Alvaray (1993), citing CVG, Fondo de Protección al Empleo.
109. Alvaray (1993), citing UEC Report.
110. Alvaray (1993), citing IVES.
111. Alvaray (1993), 1992 figures.
112. Alvaray (1993), citing IVES.
113. Industry interviews.
114. Ibid.
115. Alvaray (1993).
116. This paragraph is based on Alvaray (1993) and Silva (1993).
117. Granell and Parra (1993).
118. Alvaray (1993), citing Sidor.
119. Ibid.
120. Alvaray (1993).
121. Ibid.
122. Ibid.
123. Ibid.
124. Luis Alvaray, private communication.
125. Enright and Tenti (1990).
126. Viana et al. (1993).
127. Ibid.
128. This profile is based on Sánchez (1993a) and additional interviews.

129. Sánchez (1993a), citing Clemente (1993).
130. Sánchez (1993a), citing the Venezuelan Auto Parts Producers (FAVENPA) (1993). Percentage estimates are based on the aggregate production of the seven largest Latin American auto producers: Mexico, Brazil, Argentina, Venezuela, Colombia, Ecuador, and Peru.
131. Estimate provided by Francisco Vázquez, based on data from the Ministry of Development and industry chambers.
132. Estimate of Lino Clemente.
133. Clemente (1993) and private communications from industry members.
134. Sánchez (1993a).
135. Ibid. and additional industry interviews.
136. Sánchez (1993).
137. For a study on the foreign exchange savings effect of the Venezuelan automotive industry, see Villalba, project coordinator (1989a, 1989b, and 1989c).
138. Sánchez (1993a).
139. Ibid.
140. Karmokolias (1990)
141. United Nations (1991).
142. Sánchez (1993a), Appendix 2.
143. Pérez (1991).
144. Sánchez (1993a).
145. Industry interview.
146. Interviews with industry management.
147. "¿Qué tán fácil es convertirse en exportadores? Entrevista a Gianfranco Francesconi" (1993).
148. Ibid.
149. "*Convenio de complementación en el sector automotor,*" September 1993, Article 1.
150. For the estimate of 44,916 workers, see Clemente (1993). Estimate of 19,000 workers based on private sector interview.
151. Clemente (1993).
152. Estimate provided by Rodger Farrell.

Chapter 5

1. This summary is based on Vásquez (1993) and additional interviews.
2. Estimate for 1992 provided by Nelson Vásquez; estimate for 1991 provided by Balaguer and Segnini, citing Banco Central de Venezuela.
3. Balaguer and Segnini (1993), citing Banco Central de Venezuela.
4. Estimate provided by Nelson Vásquez.

5. Julián Villalba contributed this discussion of the challenges facing the Venezuelan oil industry.
6. The recent international financing operations of PDVSA, such as the bond issues by Bariven and PDVSA, have had substantial success, but they will be limited over time by the absence of guarantees. For example, for the issue of bonds in the amount of $1 billion by PDVSA in mid-1993, it was necessary to offer CITGO shares as a guarantee. Although other guarantees could be devised in Europe and North America, they all would be less than that already offered. Venezuelan law forbids offering reserves, which belong to the state, as a guarantee for any credit operation.
7. To finance these operations, it would be possible to resort to project financing, where company risk is insulated from project risk. In the worldwide petroleum industry, these operations have been carried out from time to time, especially in the North Sea.
8. This summary is based on González de Pacheco (1993) and additional interviews.
9. Banco Central de Venezuela, *Anuario estadístico*.
10. The eight nations with more primary aluminum production capacity than Venezuela are the United States (20.1 percent of the world total), the former Soviet Republics (17 percent), Canada (9.1 percent), Australia (6.2 percent), Brazil (5.6 percent), China (4.6 percent), Norway (4.3 percent), and West Germany (3.6 percent). González de Pacheco (1993) citing King (1991).
11. This paragraph draws upon Kelly and González (1993).
12. Recently Venalum has made improvements in its production standards to meet the requirements of its Japanese customers, in such areas as grades of purity, development of alloys, and fulfillment of delivery terms. González de Pacheco (1993).
13. Information provided by OTEPI Consultores.
14. Kelly and González (1993).
15. Alcasa's sales in 1993 equaled 21,637 million bolivars, or $240.67 million at an exchange rate of 89.9 bolivars per U.S. dollar (the exchange rate in effect as of June 1993).
16. González de Pacheco (1993) citing CVG President Francisco Layrisse.
17. González de Pacheco (1993).
18. The leading aluminum producers worldwide are working with customers to develop new products and process technologies. Alcan, for example, is developing new alloys for the air transportation sector adapted to recent advances in jet construction. In 1992, primary aluminum accounted for only 16 percent of Alcan's sales and a mere 7 percent of Reynolds' sales. González de Pacheco (1993), citing Alcan and Reynolds 1992 Annual Reports.
19. This paragraph is based on information supplied by OTEPI Consultores.
20. This summary is based on Rivas Acosta (1993b) and additional interviews.
21. Corimon (1992).
22. Rivas Acosta (1993b), citing Instituto de Comercio Exterior de Venezuela (ICEI). The total export value for 1992 given by the *Anuario del comercio exterior de Venezuela* was $12 million.

23. Rivas Acosta (1993b), citing International Trade Centre (1991).
24. Garip-Bertuol (1993a).
25. Ibid.
26. Rivas Acosta (1993b), citing "Operación chocolate" (1993).
27. International Trade Centre (1991).
28. Ibid.
29. Many Venezuelan cocoa farmers are 50 years of age or older and are illiterate. Often, their sons have migrated to the cities and no one remains on the farm to carry on production.
30. Rivas Acosta (1993b). Some believe that the average yield per hectare in Venezuela is as low as 167 kilos, which places Venezuelan productivity among the lowest in the world. Corimon (1992).
31. This summary is based on Cervilla (1993b) and additional interviews.
32. Cervilla (1993b), citing National Rice Consulting Council (CCNA) harvest data for 1992. Venezuelan production as a percentage of world production is based on FAO figures for 1990 and 1991.
33. Cervilla (1993b), citing CCNA export data for 1992.
34. Cervilla (1993b).
35. Cervilla (1993b).
36. Cervilla (1993b), citing FEDEARROZ and CCNA.
37. Cervilla (1993b).
38. Ibid.
39. This summary is based on Rosales Linares (1993) and additional interviews.
40. Estimate provided by Ramón Rosales Linares.
41. Rosales Linares (1993), citing Central Office of Statistics and Informatics (OCEI) (1992).
42. Rosales Linares (1993).
43. Ibid.
44. Marco Zarikian, executive president of Grupo Telares Maracay, quoted in "¿Viraje Textil?" (1992).
45. Ibid.
46. Rosales Linares (1993), based on interview with officials of INCE-Textil.
47. Rosales Linares (1993), based on interviews with production managers of Venezuelan textile firms.
48. Rosales Linares (1993), citing OCEI (1992).
49. Rosales Linares (1993), based on industry interviews.
50. This summary is based on Dallmeier (1993) and additional interviews.
51. Dallmeier (1993).
52. Nash (1993).
53. Huneeus (1993).

54. This summary is based on Francés (1993b) and additional interviews.
55. Francés (1993b), citing Venezuelan Chamber of Consulting Firms (CAVECON).
56. Francés (1993b), citing Paúl (1990).
57. Francés (1993b), citing CAVECON.
58. Ibid.
59. See Porter (1990) for an elaboration of this point.

Chapter 6

1. *Oil and Gas Journal Data Book,* 1993 Edition.
2. Calculated from information contained in ibid.
3. Vásquez (1993).
4. Data provided by PDVSA.
5. Vásquez (1993).
6. "Oil Giant Moves to Revert Weak Oil Prices" (1993).
7. One mill equals one-thousandth of one U.S. dollar.
8. CVG, private communication.
9. Corrales (1993) and Resource Strategies, Inc. (1989).
10. Fischer (1991a).
11. Fischer (1991c).
12. Fischer (1991b).
13. Alvaray (1993).
14. González de Pacheco (1993).
15. Gómez (1993).
16. In 1992, 150,000 hectares were under rice cultivation, and it is estimated that in Guárico and Portuguesa states alone there are an additional 179,090 hectares with good rice growing potential. The Orinoco Delta and Apure state also offer good growing conditions for rice. Cervilla (1993b).
17. Oficina Central de Estadística e Informática, *Anuario del comercio exterior de Venezuela,* except for cocoa estimate from ICEI data.
18. United Nations, ECLAC (1992b).
19. AgroInvest Consultores, S.A. and J.E. Austin Associates (1993b).
20. Briceño (1993).
21. AgroInvest Consultores, S.A. and J.E. Austin Associates (1993a).
22. United Nations, ECLAC (1992b).
23. Reynolds Metal Company (1992).
24. Briceño (1993).
25. Cervilla (1993b).
26. U.S. Department of Agriculture (1992), citing the Cocoa Merchants Association.

27. Balaguer and Segnini (1993).
28. Barker (1993).
29. U.S. Department of Agriculture (1992).
30. Tejera (1992).
31. Silva (1993).
32. Ibid.
33. Viana et al. (1993).
34. Silva (1993).
35. Cervilla (1993b).
36. Rosales Linares (1993).
37. Silva (1993).
38. Pantin (1993a).
39. Interviews with Venezuelan management.
40. Interview with textile industry executive.
41. Silva (1993).
42. Lozano Zorilla (1993).
43. Ponce (1993).
44. Lozano Zorilla (1993).
45. Silva (1993).
46. Francés (1993a), citing AT&T.
47. Francés (1993a).
48. Viana et al. (1993).
49. Francés (1993a).
50. Faber (1994).
51. Ibid.
52. Ibid.
53. Ibid.
54. Pantin (1993b).
55. Private sector interviews.
56. Kelly and González (1993).
57. For example, in 1990, IESA faculty and researchers encountered difficulties in gathering data for a study on human resource management practices in Venezuela. It was difficult to get "fairly simple financial and personnel information," and much of what was obtained turned out to be unreliable and contradictory. Private communication.
58. Interviews with Venezuelan management.
59. Granell and Parra (1993).
60. Alvaray (1993).
61. Malavé and Piñango (1993).
62. Viana et al. (1993).

63. Betancourt and Freije (1993).
64. National Council for Investment Promotion (1992), citing Organization for Economic Cooperation and Development and Euromonitor.
65. Datos (1993).
66. Granell and Parra (1993).
67. Ibid.
68. National Council for Investment Promotion (1992), p. 209.
69. José Malavé, private communication.
70. National Council for Investment Promotion (1992), citing the Union Bank of Switzerland (1992).
71. Union Bank of Switzerland (1992).
72. For further explanation of these provisions, see Maldonado and Rojas (1992), Chapter 5.
73. Márquez (1993a).
74. This paragraph is based on Márquez (1993b).
75. Interviews with managers of multinational companies in Venezuela.
76. Interviews with Venezuelan and multinational managers.
77. Malavé and Piñango (1993).
78. Interviews with Venezuelan management.
79. Malavé and Piñango (1993), pp. 5-6.
80. Navarro (1993).
81. Kelly (1992).
82. The highest post-secondary enrollment in Latin America is found in Uruguay, 50 percent.
83. Navarro (1993).
84. UNESCO.
85. Carvajal (1993).
86. Navarro (1993).
87. Prof. Elena Granell, private communication.
88. Navarro (1993).
89. Ibid.
90. Malavé and Piñango (1993).
91. Ibid., p. 5.
92. Navarro (1993).
93. Granell and Parra (1993).
94. Navarro (1993) and Granell and Parra (1993).
95. The popularity of engineering can be considered a plus for the nation's competitiveness, as this profession is at the core of most industrial activity, but decreasing capabilities in mathematics at the primary and secondary school levels raise concerns

for the future expansion and development of this profession. The low prestige of careers in education is also a cause for concern.

96. Murphy, Shliefer, and Vishny (1991).
97. Balaguer and Segnini (1993), citing ASOQUIM.
98. Navarro (1993).
99. Viana et al. (1993).
100. Navarro (1993).
101. Carlos Eduardo Vélez, coordinator, Public Expenditure Incidence Project, Social Mission, National Planning Department (NPD) of the Republic of Colombia, Panel Discussion, Massachusetts Institute of Technology, February 19, 1994.
102. Navarro (1993).
103. World Economic Forum (1993).
104. Granell and Parra (1993).
105. Navarro (1993).
106. This paragraph is based on Granell and Parra (1993), citing Brunicelli and Calzadilla (1994).
107. Héctor Riquezes, former INCE president.
108. Interview with Nestlé management.
109. Navarro (1993).
110. Viana et al. (1993).
111. Ibid.
112. Granell and Parra (1993).
113. Ibid.
114. Viana et al. (1993).
115. Granell and Parra (1993).
116. Ibid.
117. Ibid. and interview with Siemens management.
118. Interview with Siemens management.
119. Granell and Parra (1993).
120. Ibid.
121. Granell and Parra (1993), citing Center for Petroleum and Petrochemical Formation and Training (CEPET) (1991).
122. Márquez (1993a).
123. Ibid.
124. Ibid.
125. Interview with Venezuelan labor union leader.
126. Ibid.
127. Malavé and Piñango (1993).
128. Ibid.
129. Ibid., pp. 35-36.

130. Granell and Parra (1993).
131. Ibid.
132. Ibid.
133. Private-sector interview.
134. Larrañaga (1993), p. 23.
135. Venezuela is highly dependent on the importation of capital goods. Mexico and Brazil have had less dependency on the importation of capital goods, because they have developed diversified capital goods sectors. In the mid-1980s, Brazil and Mexico produced 74 percent and 62 percent of their capital goods requirements, while Venezuela only produced 23 percent of its requirements. (UNIDO, 1990). In 1985, Brazil and Mexico exported capital goods worth $2.538 billion and $2.192 billion, respectively, while Venezuela only managed to export $59 million. Viana et al. (1993).
136. Viana et al. (1993).
137. Ibid. Korean figure is for 1988.
138. Viana et al. (1993).
139. Ibid.
140. Ibid.
141. The most important scientific research institute in Venezuela is the Venezuelan Institute of Scientific and Technological Research (IVIC), which has focused on basic biomedical sciences with an emphasis on fields of local interest such as tropical diseases. Viana et al. (1993).
142. Viana et al. (1993).
143. Ibid.
144. Ibid.
145. Viana et al. (1993).
146. Viana et al. (1993).
147. Ibid.
148. Ibid.
149. Ibid.
150. Viana et al. (1993).
151. Information on Venezuelan design in this section was provided by Luis Alemán.
152. Central Bank of Venezuela.
153. At present, Citicorp, which was grandfathered when the present Banking Law was enacted, is the only foreign owned bank with full operations in Venezuela.
154. Sabal and Aguirre (1991).
155. Ibid.
156. Bauman (1993).
157. This discussion draws upon Austin (1990).
158. In the late 1980s, for example, the New Zealand forest products industry actually subtracted value from the natural resource. Some products processed in New Zealand actually sold for less than the raw timber. Crocombe, Enright, and Porter (1991).

159. In Korea, increases in wages were generally kept below the increases in productivity. The resulting surplus was invested to upgrade and improve the economy. Mexico has adopted a similar strategy in order to attract foreign investment and to generate funds for domestic investment.

Chapter 7

1. Sánchez (1993a).
2. Rosales Linares (1993).
3. Mixon (1993a).
4. Datos and Towers Perrin statistics are from Mixon (1993a).
5. Ibid.
6. Mixon (1993b).
7. Sánchez (1993a).
8. Ekvall (1992a).
9. Private-sector interviews.
10. Kelly and González (1993).
11. Ibid.
12. Rivas Acosta (1993b), Briceño (1993), and Rosales Linares (1993).
13. Ekvall (1993a), quoting John Werner, Alimentos Heinz de Venezuela.
14. Francés (1991).
15. Jatar (1993).
16. Güerere (1993b).
17. Interviews with industry executives.
18. Rosales Linares (1993).
19. Kline (1993).
20. Briceño (1993).
21. Ekvall (1993a), quoting John Werner, Alimentos Heinz de Venezuela.
22. Information provided by Procter & Gamble de Venezuela.
23. Brannigan (1994), quoting Ed McDonald, Procter & Gamble.
24. Brannigan (1994).
25. Ibid., quoting Richard McGowan, Valebrón.
26. Brannigan (1994).
27. Dallmeier (1993).
28. Rosales Linares (1993).
29. "Still Pulling Threads" (1994).
30. "¿Es la calidad una frase? Entrevista a Rafael Alfonzo Hernández" (1993).
31. Interview with Madosa management.
32. "¿Es la calidad una frase? Entrevista a Rafael Alfonzo Hernández" (1993).

33. Ibid. and interview with management of Alfonzo Rivas & Cia.
34. Interview with management of Venevisión.
35. Industry interviews.
36. This paragraph is based on an interview with management of Ediciones Ekaré.
37. Interview with management of Ediciones Ekaré.
38. Kelly and González (1993).
39. Ibid., p. 25.
40. Garip-Bertuol (1993a), p. 19.
41. This paragraph is based on Viana et al. (1993).
42. Viana et al. (1993), p. 20.
43. Viana et al. (1993).
44. Briceño (1993).
45. Interview with executive of a state-owned enterprise.
46. Alvaray (1993).
47. González de Pacheco (1993).
48. Viana et al. (1993), citing UNIDO (1990).
49. Viana et al. (1993).
50. Rosales Linares (1993).
51. González de Pacheco (1993).
52. This paragraph is based on Kelly and González (1993).
53. Alvaray (1993).
54. As of 1993, there were also 11 regional TV channels and one government-owned TV channel. Most upper-middle-class homes in the big cities received international channels by subscription.
55. Rodríguez (1993).
56. Lorenzo González Izquierdo, quoted in Rodríguez (1993).
57. Briceño (1993).
58. Porter (1990).

Chapter 8

1. This paragraph is based on interviews with the private sector, except as otherwise noted.
2. Naím (1989a).
3. Naím and Francés (1995).
4. Ibid.
5. This paragraph draws upon Naím and Francés (1995), Naím (1993), and Naím (1989b).
6. Naím (1989a).

7. Viana et al. (1994) and Viana et al. (1993).
8. Viana et al. (1993), p. 22.
9. Ibid., p. 17.
10. Ibid., p. 23.
11. Granell and Parra (1993), p. 27.
12. Viana et al. (1993), citing the World Bank (1992) and GATT.
13. Grupo CNV, for example, entered international markets with the purpose of strengthening itself by competing with the best firms in the world, in preparation for the day when Venezuela would open its markets. Sosa Pietri, quoted in Wade (1992).
14. Interviews with the private sector.
15. Naím (1989b).
16. Naím (1989a and b).
17. Interviews with the private sector.
18. Balaguer and Segnini (1993) and Rosales Linares (1993).
19. Naím (1989b).
20. Interviews with the private sector.
21. Viana et al. (1993).
22. Ibid.
23. Interview with executive of foreign-owned firm.
24. Interview with firm management. See also Erard (1993).
25. Mann (1993).
26. Viana et al. (1993).
27. "1993: ¿Crecer con inflación y devaluación? Entrevista a Juan Fernando Roche" (1992).
28. Sweeney (1992d).
29. Laura Rojas, former vice minister of the Development Ministry, quoted in Lozano Zorilla (1992).
30. This paragraph is based on an interview with firm management, and on "¿Es la calidad una frase? Entrevista a Rafael Alfonzo Hernández" (1993).
31. "¿Es la calidad una frase? Entrevista a Rafael Alfonzo Hernández" (1993).
32. This paragraph is based on an interview with firm management.
33. Interview with firm management.
34. This paragraph is based on an interview with firm management. See also Hillman (1993).
35. This paragraph is based on an interview with firm management and also on "1993: ¿Crecer con inflación y devaluación? Entrevista a Juan Fernando Roche" (1992).
36. Palacios (1993).
37. Ibid.
38. Interview with firm management.
39. "¿Qué tan fácil es convertirse en exportadores? Entrevista a Gianfranco Francesconi" (1993).

40. This paragraph draws upon Kelly and González (1993).
41. Ekvall (1993c).
42. Kelly and González (1993).
43. Naím and Francés (1995).
44. Kelly and González (1993).
45. Interviews with the Venezuelan Investment Fund.
46. Ekvall (1993c).
47. Alvaray (1993).
48. Interviews with CVG management.
49. Interviews with the Venezuelan Investment Fund.
50. Kelly and González (1993).
51. Taylhardat (1993).
52. "Smurfit Paper Division Shines" (1993).
53. Minoru Asakawa, President, Mitsubishi Venezolana, quoted in Ekvall (1993b), p. 10.
54. Ekvall (1992b).
55. Taylhardat (1993).
56. "Chrysler Is Back with a Bang" (1993).
57. Taylhardat (1993).
58. Interview with firm management. See also Rivas (1993).
59. "Warner Lambert Expands Its Production Facilities" (1992).
60. Taylhardat (1993).
61. Alvaray (1993) and Balaguer and Segnini (1993).
62. Granell and Parra (1993), pp. 29-30.
63. Naím and Francés (1995).
64. This paragraph is based on Naím and Francés (1993).
65. Jatar (1993).
66. Interview with Conindustria executive.
67. Balaguer and Segnini (1993).
68. "Asoquím responde a su compromiso comunitario" (1993).
69. Cervilla (1993b).
70. Jatar (1993).
71. Alvaray (1993).
72. González de Pacheco (1993).
73. Naím and Francés (1995).
74. Villalba (1991).
75. See, e.g., Rosales Linares (1993).
76. Naím and Francés (1995).
77. Jatar (1993).
78. This paragraph is based on Gómez (1993).
79. As quoted in "Operación chocolate" (1993).

80. See, e.g., Balaguer and Segnini (1993) and Rosales Linares (1993).
81. Jatar (1993), p. 35.
82. Ibid., p. 34.
83. Ibid., p. 35.
84. Ibid., p. 35.
85. This paragraph is based on Jatar (1993).
86. Hospitals and clinics were allowed to operate pharmacies, but only to supply the internal needs of the hospital.
87. Jatar (1993), p. 39.
88. Ibid.
89. This paragraph is based on Jatar (1993).
90. This section draws upon Austin (1990).
91. See Austin (1990) and Nelson (1990) for interesting discussions of firm strategies in the developing country context.

Chapter 9

1. de Krivoy (1993b).
2. Ibid.
3. Moffett (1994).
4. Kelly and González (1993).
5. This was the "supplied market" policy, which was based on the notion that only a few plants could operate at efficient scale in the small and closed Venezuelan market. In theory, it amounted to an infinite barrier to entry for latecomers. In practice, political pressure or personal influence could overcome the restrictions in some cases.
6. Coles (1993).
7. Kelly and González (1993).
8. The incremental capital-output ratio increased from three to nine during this period. The level of essentially nonproductive investment has been estimated at roughly $38 billion by Paredes (1993), a figure approximately equal to Venezuela's foreign debt.
9. Rodríguez (1988).
10. García (1993).
11. Kelly and González (1993).
12. Jatar (1993).
13. Ibid.
14. Taylhardat (1993).
15. Ibid.
16. Corrales (1993).
17. Industry interview.

18. Coles (1993).
19. Ibid., p. 11. This paragraph is based on Coles (1993).
20. Coles (1993), citing the World Bank (1991) and FAO (1991).
21. Cervilla (1993a).
22. Rivas Acosta (1993b) and Corimon (1992).
23. Coles (1993).
24. This paragraph is based on ibid.
25. Coles (1993).
26. Ibid. and Bottome (1993a).
27. Funaro (1993).
28. Kelly and González (1993).
29. Ibid.
30. Ibid.
31. Larrañaga (1993).
32. Márquez (1993b), p. 12.
33. This paragraph is based on Márquez (1993a).
34. Márquez (1993a), p. 311.
35. Ibid., p. 313.
36. Márquez (1993a).
37. Larrañaga (1993) and Márquez (1993a).
38. Rodríguez M. (1993).
39. Ibid.
40. Márquez (1993b).
41. Ibid.
42. Interview with Venezuelan manager.
43. This paragraph is based on Navarro and Piñango (1992).
44. This discussion is based on ibid. (1992).
45. Navarro and Piñango (1992).
46. Navarro (1993).
47. Navarro and Piñango (1992).
48. This paragraph is based on Navarro (1993).
49. Navarro (1993).
50. This paragraph is based on ibid.
51. Ibid.
52. Navarro (1993).
53. Ibid.
54. Navarro (1991), Navarro (1993), and Navarro and Piñango (1992).
55. Navarro (1991).
56. Ellner (1986).
57. Navarro and Piñango (1992).

58. Navarro (1991).
59. Navarro (1991), citing Birdsall and James (1990).
60. Navarro (1993).
61. This paragraph is based on Granell and Parra (1993).
62. Viana et al. (1993).
63. This discussion is based on Viana et al. (1993).
64. Ibid.
65. Viana et al. (1993).
66. Figuera Fortique (1993).
67. Sweeney (1992c).
68. Sweeney (1992c), quoting Richard N. Brown, and Brown (1991).
69. Ibid.
70. "Industrial Property" (1992).
71. Richard N. Brown, private communication.
72. Ibid.
73. "Industrial Property" (1992).
74. Ibid.
75. "¿No más piratería?," quoting Richard N. Brown.
76. Ibid.
77. Richard N. Brown, private communication.
78. This paragraph is based on Kelly and González (1993).
79. Gruson, Rodríguez, and Suárez (1993).
80. González Barreto (1992).
81. Kelly and González (1993).
82. Ibid. (1993).
83. Ibid. (1993).
84. Malavé and Piñango (1993).
85. Calzadilla (1993).
86. Ibid.
87. Ibid.
88. Ibid.
89. Ibid.
90. Ibid.
91. Ibid.
92. Ibid.
93. World Economic Forum (1993), p. 469.
94. Interviews with Venezuelan legal practitioners.
95. Naím (1989c).
96. García Montoya and Briceño (1993), and interviews with Venezuelan legal practitioners.
97. García Montoya and Briceño (1993).

98. Taylhardat (1993), citing National Council for Investment Promotion (1992).
99. This paragraph is based on Calzadilla (1993).
100. Calzadilla (1993).
101. Ibid., p. 25.
102. Naím (1993).
103. Coles (1993).
104. Kelly and González (1993).
105. Naím (1993).
106. Interviews with Venezuelan political analysts.
107. Calzadilla (1993).
108. This section draws from Austin (1990).
109. Competition from foreign firms does not provide Venezuela with a source of advantage in international competition (there is nothing unique to Venezuela about the pressures exerted by foreign competition), but it does eliminate the disadvantage of the old system, which sheltered Venezuelan firms from competitive pressures.

Chapter 10

1. Betancourt and Freije (1993).
2. The discussion of the determinants of national advantage in Venezuela in the previous chapters has pointed out some of the important features that will influence new business formation in the nation.
3. Petroleum sector projections provided by Nelson Vásquez.
4. Petrochemical sector projections provided by Antonio Balaguer. Due to lack of information, these projections do not take into account the 20 percent of the Venezuelan petrochemical industry which is 100 percent privately owned.
5. Iron and steel sector projections provided by Luis Alvaray.
6. Bauxite and aluminum sector projections provided by OTEPI Consultores.
7. Pulp and paper sector projections supplied by Magín F. Briceño.
8. See Gatica Barros (1989), for example.
9. The same pattern has been seen in New Zealand in recent years. See McLoughlin (1992).
10. Paredes (1993).

Chapter 11

1. Bottome (1993d).
2. Templeton (1995).

3. Forbes (1992b).
4. Rigobón (1993).
5. Ryser (1993).
6. See Kelly and González (1993).
7. Kelly and González (1993).
8. Ibid.
9. "Who's Selling What: The Global Picture" (1993).
10. Smith (1992).
11. Ryser (1991).
12. "Who's Selling What: The Global Picture" (1993) and Flint (1991).
13. Fraser (1993).
14. Torres (1994).
15. Forbes (1992a) and Flint (1991).
16. Bottome (1993b).
17. Taylhardat (1993).
18. Ibid., citing National Council for Investment Promotion (1992).
19. Taylhardat (1993).
20. See Escalante (1994).
21. Escalante (1994) makes the same point.
22. Myers (1992).
23. This section draws upon Navarro (1993).
24. Navarro (1993).
25. This section draws upon ibid.
26. Psacharopolous and Steier (1989) and World Bank (1992).
27. This section draws upon Navarro (1993).
28. Granell and Parra (1993).
29. Ibid.
30. Richard N. Brown, private communication.
31. Brown (1994).
32. Richard N. Brown, private communication.
33. Brown (1994).
34. This paragraph draws on Calzadilla (1993).
35. Calzadilla (1993).
36. De la Cruz (1993).
37. Ibid.
38. Ibid.
39. Ibid.
40. This section draws on García Montoya and Briceño (1993).
41. Ambrus (1992a), quoting Fernando Fernández.
42. Fernández (1993).

43. Ibid.
44. "Trade, the Uruguay Round, and the Consumer: The Sting—How Governments Buy Votes on Trade With the Consumer's Money" (1993).
45. Mixon (1993b).
46. Naím (1993) also makes this point.
47. Coles (1993), p. 28.
48. See Naím (1993) for a discussion of the importance of mass communication in modern-day politics in Venezuela.
49. Naím (1993) makes the same point.
50. McCrary (1993).
51. Ryser (1993).

Chapter 12

1. See Porter (1980) and Porter (1985) for an explanation of generic firm strategies, sources of competitive advantage, and the value activities of firms.
2. Speech given at the Fortieth Anniversary of Grupo Químico, Caracas, November 1993.
3. The results of this survey are reported in Viana et al. (1994).

Chapter 13

1. González de Cellorigo, paraphrased in Elliot (1989).
2. Francés (1990).
3. Consultores 21 (1993).
4. Consultores 21 (1986).
5. Answers to the question: Little or no confidence in the honesty of those who manage: Armed forces (28), Universities (33), Press (39), Television (43), Business in general (44), Police (52), Banks (54), Congress (57), State enterprises (60), Retail commerce (62), Trade unions (64), Public administration (67), Templeton (1995). Other surveys have shown similar results. Political parties, not included in this one, usually fare worst of all in ratings of public confidence.

Bibliography

AgroInvest Consultores, S.A., and J.E. Austin Associates, Inc. (1993a). "Investor Profile for Tilapia." Prepared for the National Investment Promotion Council, May.

———(1993b). "Investor Profile for the Venezuelan Forestry Plantations Industry." Prepared for the National Investment Promotion Council, May.

Alcan Aluminium Limited (1992). *Annual Report 1992*.

Almanaque Mundial (1993) (Miami, FL: Editorial América, S.A.).

Alvaray, Luis (1993). "Industria siderúrgica." Industry Study, Project Venezuela Competitiva.

Ambrus, Steven (1992a). "Re-balancing the Scales: New Reforms Aim to Correct the Judicial System," *Business Venezuela, 144*, October, 32-35.

———(1992b). "Unshackling the Pines of Uverito," *VenEconomy Monthly*, November, 25-27.

"Asoquím responde a su compromiso comunitario, responsabilidad integral: el paradigma de los 90," *Química Hoy, 48*, April 1993, 12.

Austin, James E. (1990). *Managing in Developing Countries: Strategic Analysis and Operating Techniques* (New York: The Free Press).

Balaguer, Antonio, and Ana M. Segnini (1993). "La competitividad de la industria petroquímica venezolana." Industry Study, Project Venezuela Competitiva, August.

Banco Central de Venezuela (1990). *Anuario de cuentas nacionales* (Caracas: Banco Central de Venezuela).

———(January 1984-December 1993). *Boletín mensual* (Caracas: Banco Central de Venezuela).

———(1985-1992). *Informe económico* (Caracas: Banco Central de Venezuela).

Banco Central de Venezuela–FINEXPO (1975-1991). *Anuario estadístico del sector exportador notradicional* (Caracas: Banco Central de Venezuela).

Barker, Randolph (1993). "The World Rice Market and the Potential for Burmese Rice Exports." Presented at the Harvard Center for International Affairs, April 15.

Barro, Robert (1990). "Discussion of W. Easterly, Endogenous Growth in Developing Countries and Government-Induced Distortions." Harvard University mimeo.

———(1991). "Economic Growth in a Cross Section of Countries," *Quarterly Journal of Economics, 106*, 407-443.

Bauman, Everett A. (1993). "World Bank Loans for Venezuela Aimed at Backing Economic Growth, Aiding Poor," *Business Venezuela, 153*, July, 48-54.

Berrol, Edward, and Jack Walker (1991). "Trends in Travel and Tourism Advertising Expenditures in United States Measured Media, 1986-1990, A Special Report for Ogilvy & Mather Based on Data from Leading National Advertisers, Inc." September.

Besas, Peter (1993). "Radio Caracas: A Novel Rise to the Top," *Variety*, October 11, 181-182.

Betancourt, Keila, and Samuel Freije (1993). "El sector informal en Venezuela." Key Issue Paper, Project Venezuela Competitiva, August.

Betancourt, Norelis, and Ana Julia Jatar (1990). "Los personajes del turismo: por qué un charter?" In Frank Briceño, ed., *Turismo: algo más que un charter* (Caracas: Ediciones IESA), 81-119.

Biggs, Tyler S., and Brian Levy (1988). "Strategic Interventions and the Political Economy of Industrial Policy in Developing Countries," Employment and Enterprise Development Division, EEPA Discussion Paper No. 23, December.

Birdsall, Nancy, and Estelle James (1990). "Efficiency and Equity in Social Spending. How and Why Governments Misbehave" (Washington, D.C.: PRE Working Papers, World Bank).

Borner, Silvio, Michael Porter, Rolf Weder, and Michael Enright (1991). *Internationale Wettbewerbsvorteile: Ein strategisches Konzept für die Schweiz*. (Frankfurt: Campus/NZZ).

Bottome, Robert (1992). "Bananas: A Traditional Product; Now a Non-Traditional Export," *VenEconomy Monthly*, November, 18-21.

——(1993a). "Meanwhile, Back at the Farm: Change is the Order of the Day," *VenEconomy Monthly*, February, 21-24.

——(1993b). "Neo-Protectionism: Now, the Farmers," *VenEconomy Monthly*, October, 25-26.

——(1993c). "The Gaviria Amendment: The Clock Turns Back," *VenEconomy Monthly*, November, 26.

——(1993d). "The Economy: Headed for a Crash?" *VenEconomy Monthly*, December, 4.

——(1993e). "Gaviria Wins Another," *VenEconomy Monthly*, December, 20-21.

Boza, María Eugenia (1993). "El turismo en Venezuela." Industry Study, Project Venezuela Competitiva, July.

Brannigan, Kathy (1994). "Beauty and Bucks," *Business Venezuela, 159*, January, 72-75.

Briceño, Frank (1990). *Turismo: algo más que un charter* (Caracas: Ediciones IESA).

Briceño, Magín F. (1993). "Análisis competitivo del sector de productos forestales, pulpa y papel." Industry Study, Project Venezuela Competitiva, May.

Brown, Richard N. (1991). "The Little Recognized Connection between Intellectual Property and Economic Development in Latin America," *International Review of Industrial Property and Copyright Law*, No. 3.

———(1994). "Venezuelan Trademark Law Expands," *Managing Intellectual Property,* March, 38-40.
Brunicelli, Josefina, and Víctor Calzadilla (1994). *Las escuelas técnicas en Venezuela* (Caracas: CINTERPLAN/Ediciones IESA).
"Business Venezuela Interview: Diego Arria, Former Minister of Information and Tourism," *Business Venezuela, 158,* December, 8-13.
"BV Business Briefs," *Business Venezuela, 160,* February, 41-48.
Caldera, Rafael (1993). "My Letter of Intention with the Venezuelan People," *VenEconomy Monthly,* November, 6.
Calzadilla, Víctor M. (1993). "La administracíon pública venezolana: características y tendencias." Background Paper, Project Venezuela Competitiva, June.
Carvajal, Leonardo (1993). "Apuntes para la transformación educativa." In *Encuentro y alternativas Venezuela, 1994,* vol. 2 (Caracas: Universidad Católica Andrés Bello), 575-603.
Caves, Richard E. (1982). *Multinational Enterprise and Economic Analysis* (New York: Cambridge University Press).
Central Bank of Venezuela (BCV). *See* Banco Central de Venezuela (BCV).
Central Office of Statistics and Information (OCEI). *See* Oficina Central de Estadística e Informática (OCEI).
Centro de Formación y Adiestramiento Petrolero y Petroquímico (CEPET), Gerencia de Planificación (1991). *Estudio de las tendencias en la formación y adiestramiento de personal: síntesis ejecutiva* (Caracas: Desarrollo Empresarial LTD, SRL, June).
Cervilla, María Antonia (1993a). "Estudio del sector cereales." Industry Study (first draft), Project Venezuela Competitiva, February.
———(1993b). "La competitividad de la industria del arroz en Venezuela." Industry Study, Project Venezuela Competitiva, July.
Chapman, K. (1991). *The International Petrochemical Industry, Evolution and Location* (Oxford: Blackwell).
Chelminski, Vladimir (1991). *La nueva ley del trabajo (diez falacias)* (Caracas: Editorial Panapo).
"Chrysler Is Back with a Bang," *Venezuela Now,* March, 5.
Cisneros, Imelda (1993). "La política económica internacional de Venezuela y la globalización y competitividad de las empresas venezolanas." Key Issue Paper, Project Venezuela Competitiva.
Clemente, Lino (1993). "Análisis de la industria automotriz a partir de los informes del PCD y la Encuesta Industrial: hacia los reportes sectoriales." Mimeo (Caracas).
Coles, Jonathan (1993). "Reforming Agriculture: The Venezuelan Experience." Mimeo (Caracas).
———(1995). "Reforming Agriculture." In Louis Goodman, Johanna Mendelson Forman, Moisés Naím, Joseph Tulchin, and Gary Bland, eds., *Lessons of the Venezuelan*

Experience (Baltimore: John Hopkins University Press and The Woodrow Wilson Center Press).

"Convenio de complementación en el sector automotor," September 1993, Article 1.

Consultores 21 (1986). "Estudio de la tipología del venezolano." Mimeo (Caracas: Consultores 21).

———(1993). "El escenario socio-político venezolano," May.

Corimon (1992). *Revista M*, 97, June.

Corpoven (1988-1991). *Indice de leyes vigentes* (Caracas: Corpoven, S.A.).

Corrales, María Elena (1993). "Energía." Key Issue Paper, Project Venezuela Competitiva, June.

Crocombe, Graham, Michael Enright, and Michael Porter (1991). *Upgrading New Zealand's Competitive Advantage* (Auckland: Oxford University Press).

De la Cruz, Rafael (1993). "Federalismo y descentralización: un nuevo pacto entre el Estado y la sociedad en Venezuela." In Carlos Blanco, ed., *Venezuela, del siglo XX al siglo XXI: un proyecto para construírla* (Caracas: Editorial Nueva Sociedad), 83-103.

Dallmeier, Carlos Enrique (1993). "La competitividad exportadora de la industria del software venezolana." Industry Study, Project Venezuela Competitiva, June.

Datos C. A. (1993). *Indice Económico 1993* (Caracas: Datos C. A., January).

Dávalos Tamayo, Lorenzo (1993). "Ambiente, política ambiental y competitividad." Key Issue Paper, Project Venezuela Competitiva.

Delpretti, Eduardo (1993). "Laura Rojas: el consumidor siempre ha sido el sacrificado," *El Globo*, July 10, 24-25.

De Sanctis, Bernardo (1993). "La industria siderúrgica." Industry Study (first draft), Project Venezuela Competitiva, April.

Dollar, David, and Edward N. Wolff (1993). *Competitiveness, Convergence, and International Specialization* (Cambridge, MA: MIT Press).

ECLAC. *See* United Nations, Economic Commission for Latin America and the Caribbean (ECLAC).

The Economist (1990). *Book of World Vital Statistics* (New York: Random House, Inc.).

Ekvall, Erik (1992a). "The Andean Pact. South America's Common Market," *Venezuela Now*, September, 5.

———(1992b). "Petrochemicals," *Venezuela Now*, September, 8.

———(1993a). "Agribusiness Firms Expanding," *Venezuela Now*, March, 9.

———(1993b). "Mitsubishi Pioneers Methanol Plant," *Venezuela Now*, March, 10.

———(1993c). "Privatized Phone System Ringing Clear," *Venezuela Now*, March, 9.

Elias, Victor J. (1992). *Sources of Growth: A Study of Seven Latin American Economies* (San Francisco: ICS Press).

Elliot, J. H. (1989). *Spain and Its World, 1500-1700* (New Haven, CT: Yale University Press).

Ellner, Steven (1986). "Educational Policy." In John Martz and David Myers, eds., *Venezuela: The Democratic Experience* (New York: Praeger), 296-328.

"Emerson expands in Venezuela," *Venezuela Now*, March 1993, 14.
Enright, Michael J. (1992). "Why Local Clusters Are the Way to Win the Game," *World Link*, July/August, 24-25.
———(1993). "The Geographic Scope of Competitive Advantage." Working Paper 93-060, Division of Research, Harvard Business School.
Enright, Michael J., and Paolo Tenti (1990), "La competitività della ceramica italiana," *Harvard Espansione*, September, 28-41.
Erard, Philippe, President of Corimon (1993), Address before the Global Management Development Forum, Sitges, Spain, June.
Escalante, Luis Manuel (1994). "Propuesta: como mejorar el salario sin perder las prestaciones ni crear pasivos en el sector empleador, método suma y sigue" (Caracas: Asociación de Industriales Metalúrgicos y de Minería de Venezuela).
"¿Es la calidad una frase? Entrevista a Rafael Alfonzo Hernández, Alfonzo Rivas & Cia.," *Gerente Venezuela*, 76, May 1993, 20-26.
Exxon Corporation (1991). *Annual Report*.
Faber, J. P. (1994). "Telecom: Latin America Goes Wireless," *U.S./Latin Trade*, February, 58-66.
Fabricantes Venezolanos de Partes Automotrices (FAVENPA) (1993). *Directorio de empresas venezolanas de autopartes* (Caracas: Fabricantes Venezolanos de Partes Automotrices).
FAO. *See* United Nations, Food and Agriculture Organization (FAO).
Fernández, Fernando M. (1993). "Crísis de la justicia en Venezuela, ensayo sobre la independencia del poder judicial. Análisis comparativo," *Mundo Nuevo Revista de Estudios Latinoamericanos*, 16, 2-3, April-September, 289-322 (Caracas: Universidad Simón Bolívar).
Figuera Fortique, Fernando (1993). "Intellectual Property: Protection at Last," *VenEconomy Monthly*, October, 19-20.
Finkel, Aaron (1992). "Goin' Down Under," *Business Venezuela*, 144, October, 43-45.
Fischer, Bernardo (1991a). "Dull Diamonds, Bright Gold," *Business Venezuela*, 136, November/December, 13.
———(1991b). "Hot Coals," *Business Venezuela*, 136, November/December, 15.
———(1991c). "Precious Non-Metals," *Business Venezuela*, 136, November/December, 20.
Flint, Jerry (1991). "Mexico's 'Piece' Dividend," *Forbes*, December 9, 50-56.
Foote, David L. (1992). "Tracking Tourism Trends, Venezuela Readies Itself for Industry Growth Explosion," *Business Venezuela*, 145, November, 13-30.
Foote, David L., and Donald E. Hawkins (1991). *Turismo Venezuela, invertir en calidad, Volumen 2, 1991-1992* (Caracas: VenAmCham, October).
Forbes, Malcolm S., Jr. (1992a). "We Don't Tax Capital Gains," *Forbes*, August 17, 67-68.
———(1992b). "We Had to React Quickly," *Forbes*, August 17, 64-67.

Ford, Doug (1992). "Don't Forget My 'Gift'—Wading through the Customs Payoff Nightmare," *Business Venezuela, 144*, October, 28-31.

"Foreign Investment in Venezuela," *Venezuela Now*, September 1992, 1, 11.

Francés, Antonio (1990). *Venezuela posible* (Caracas: Corimon IESA).

——(1991). "Viviendo en inflación: el comportamiento del venezolano en una economía inestable." In Antonio Francés and Lorenzo Dávalos, eds., *Inflación: economía, empresa y sociedad* (Caracas: Ediciones IESA), 235-273.

——(1993a). "Comunicaciones y competitividad en Venezuela." Key Issue Paper, Project Venezuela Competitiva.

——(1993b). "The Engineering Consulting Services Industry." Industry Study, Project Venezuela Competitiva.

Fraser, Damian (1993). "Private Ambitions on Public Priorities," *Financial Times*, August 25, 10.

Frischtak, Claudio R., with Bita Hadjimichael and Ulrich Zachau (1989). "Competition Policies for Industrializing Economies," *Policy and Research Series, 7* (Washington, D.C.: The World Bank).

Funaro, Rita (1993). "Agriculture: The First Domino?" *VenEconomy Monthly*, July, 1-4.

García, Elba Julieta (1993). "Política industrial y comercial: controles y regulaciones." Background Paper, Project Venezuela Competitiva, April.

García Montoya, Luis, and Francisco J. Briceño (1993). "¿Cómo afecta la legislación y el sistema judicial venezolano a la competitividad de las empresas?" Background Paper, Project Venezuela Competitiva, April.

Garip-Bertuol, Patricia (1993a). "Coffee and Cocoa: Rooted for a Renaissance," *VenEconomy Monthly*, May, 18-21.

——(1993b). "The Second Coming," *VenEconomy Monthly*, December, 1-5.

Gatica Barros, Jaime (1989). *Deindustrialization in Chile* (Boulder, CO: Westview Press).

Gómez, Henry with Carlos Suárez (1993). "La formación de nuevas empresas en Venezuela." Key Issue Paper, Project Venezuela Competitiva, August 1993.

González, Francisco and Magín Briceño (1993). "El mercado de capitales y el sistema financiero venezolano, factores que afectan la competitividad del país." Background Paper, Project Venezuela Competitiva, July 1993.

González, F., and John Kehoe (1993). "Venezuelan Cocoa. Change for the Better," *Coffee and Cocoa International, 3*, 52.

González Barreto, Bernardo (1992). "Programas de subsidios directos e indirectos para enfrentar la situacíon nutricional, trabajo elaborado para CORDIPLAN," March.

González de Cellorigo, Martín (1600). *Memorial de la política necesaria y útil restauración a la república de España* (Valladolid).

González de Pacheco, Rosa Amelia (1993). "La industria del aluminio." Industry Study, Project Venezuela Competitiva, July 1993.

Granell de Aldaz, Elena, and Matilde Parra (1993). "Formación de recursos humanos en Venezuela." Key Issue Paper, Project Venezuela Competitiva, May 1993.

Gruson, Alberto, Alberto Rodríguez, and Antonio Suárez (1993). "Apuntes sobre los subsidios directos." Mimeo (Caracas: Ministerio de la Familia, Fundación Escuela de Gerencia Social, April).

Güerere, Abdel (1993a). "El Miss Venezuela." Project Venezuela Competitiva.

———(1993b). "Industria de las telenovelas." Industry Study, Project Venezuela Competitiva, April.

Guía Mundial (1993). (Miami: Editorial Cinco, S.A.).

Helms, Paxton (1993). "The Hidden Key: Property Rights and Development," *VenEconomy Monthly*, December, 11-13.

Hillman, Leslie (1993). "Madosa Moving into the Global Arena," *Venezuela Now*, July, 6.

Holder, Jean, Secretary General, Caribbean Tourism Organisation (1993). "Quality Tourism, The Key to Success" In *Today, The Free Vacation Newspaper*, October 23, 1-2, 38.

Holman, Richard L. (1994a). "International World Wire: Venezuela Sets Price Controls," *The Wall Street Journal*, January 11, A7.

———(1994b). "International World Wire: Venezuela to Revise VAT," *The Wall Street Journal*, January 18, A13.

Hotelling, Harald (1931). "The Economics of Exhaustible Resources," *Journal of Political Economy*, 39, 137-175.

Huneeus, Alexandra (1993). "The Tiger Tackles Software," *U.S./Latin Trade*, April, 40-42.

IFC. *See* International Finance Corporation (IFC).

ILO. *See* United Nations, International Labour Office (ILO).

IMF. *See* International Monetary Fund (IMF).

"Industrial Property," *The Monthly Report*, December 1992, 27.

International Finance Corporation (1993). *Emerging Stock Markets Factbook 1993* (Washington, D.C.: International Finance Corporation).

International Monetary Fund (1993). *International Financial Statistics* (Washington, D.C.: International Monetary Fund).

International Trade Centre. *See* United Nations, International Trade Centre (ITC).

Jatar, Ana Julia (1993). "Rivalidad, competencia y políticas públicas." Key Issue Paper, Project Venezuela Competitiva, April.

Karmokolias, Y. (1990). "Automotive Industry: Trends and Prospects for Investment in Developing Countries," Discussion Paper No. 7 (Washington, D.C.: World Bank).

Kastner, George (1993). "Cambio de gerencia o gerencia de cambio." Address to Grupo Químico, Caracas, November 4.

Keller, Alfredo (1992). "Indicadores sociales y electorales como reflejo del grado de satisfacción de las reivindicaciones políticas." Speech presented before the 1992

Annual Scientific Assembly of the German Association of Research on Latin America, November.

Kelly, Janet (1992). "The Question of Inefficiency and Inequality: Social Policy in Venezuela." Mimeo (Caracas: IESA).

Kelly, Janet, and Keila Betancourt, Rosa Amelia González, Miriam Kornblith, and Matilde Parra (1993). "Estrategias para combatir la pobreza en América Latina: programas, instituciones y recursos, propuesta para el estudio nacional: caso de Venezuela." Mimeo (Caracas: IESA, July).

Kelly, Janet, and Laura González (1993). "Las empresas del estado y la competitividad en Venezuela." Key Issue Paper, Project Venezuela Competitiva, July.

Kielmas, Maria (1993). "Private Pensions Advance in Latin America," *Business Insurance*, May 31, 23-24.

King, James R. (1991). *Aluminum to 1995: The Path to Profitability*. The Economist Intelligence Unit, Special Report No. 2161, November.

Kline, Elizabeth (1993). "Dressing for Success," *Business Venezuela, 154*, August, 62-65.

——(1994). "The Widening Export Vista," *Business Venezuela, 163*, May, 16-23.

Kornblith, Miriam (1993). "Estado, políticos y empresarios: nuevas reglas de juego y democracia." Background Paper, Project Venezuela Competitiva, May.

de Krivoy, Ruth (1993a). "Annual Message of the President of the Central Bank," December.

——(1993b). "La política monetaria: su aporte al país, conferencia dictada en la XII Asamblea de la Federación de Economistas," July 1.

Krugman, Paul (1994). *Peddling Prosperity: Economic Sense and Nonsense in the Age of Diminished Expectations* (New York: Norton).

Lall, Sanjaya (1990). *Building Industrial Competitiveness in Developing Countries* (Paris: OECD).

Larraín, Felipe, and Marcelo Selowsky, eds. (1991). *The Public Sector and the Latin American Crisis* (San Francisco: ICS Press).

Larrañaga, Juan Carlos (1993). "Legislación, sindicatos y relaciones laborales." Background Paper, Project Venezuela Competitiva, May.

Lordan, Betsy (1993). "The Puzzle of Pacts," *U.S./Latin Trade*, April, 53-58.

Lozano Zorilla, Desirée (1992). "BV Interview: Laura Rojas, Vice Minister of Development Ministry," *Business Venezuela, 146*, December, 8-13.

——(1993). "BV Interview: Fernando Martínez Móttola, Minister of Transportation and Communications," *Business Venezuela, 151*, May, 8-12.

Malavé, José, and Ramón Piñango (1993). "La cuestión social y la competitividad en Venezuela." Background Paper, Project Venezuela Competitiva, July.

de Maldonado, María Luisa, and Mariela de Rojas (1992). *Legislación laboral venezolana, aplicación práctica* (Caracas: Ediciones LUI C.A.).

Mann, Joseph (1993). "Local Companies Eye International Capital Markets," *Venezuela Now*, March, 14.

Marcano M., Ninoska (1993). "Modern Biotechnology Key to Old-fashioned Farming Success," *Business Venezuela*, 152, June, 30-32.

Márquez, Gustavo (1993a). "Legislación laboral y mercado de trabajo en Venezuela." In Gustavo Márquez, ed., *Regulación del mercado de trabajo en América Latina* (Caracas: CINDE-Ediciones IESA), 289-326.

———(1993b). "Ley y mercado en el mundo del trabajo." In Gustavo Márquez, ed., *Regulación del mercado de trabajo en América Latina* (Caracas: CINDE-Ediciones IESA), 1-28.

———(1993c). "Cui-Bono: Regulation and Outcomes in the Labor Market" (Washington, D.C.: The World Bank).

———(1995). "Venezuela: Poverty and Social Policies in the 1980s." In Nora Lustig, ed., *Coping with Austerity: Poverty and Inequality in Latin America* (Washington, D.C.: Brookings Institution), 400-452.

Márquez, Gustavo, et al. (1991). "Gestión fiscal y distribución del ingreso en Venezuela." Study carried out for the Network of Research Centers in Applied Economics of the InterAmerican Development Bank (Caracas: Ediciones IESA).

"Mavesa Consolidates its Export Strategy," *Venezuela Now*, July, 11.

McCrary, Ernest S. (1993). "Argentina's About Face," *Global Finance*, May, 74.

McLoughlin, David (1992). *The Undeveloping Nation: New Zealand's Twenty-Year Fall Towards the Third World* (Auckland: Penguin Books).

Ministerio de Educación (1962, 1972, 1982, 1990). *Memoria y cuenta* (Caracas: Ministerio de Educación).

Ministerio de Energía y Minas (1970-1991). *Petróleo y otros datos estadísticos* (Caracas: Ministerio de Energía y Minas).

Mira!—The Venezuela Traveler, 105, July 1993.

Mixon, Laura (1993a). "The ABCDE's of Marketing," *Business Venezuela*, 149, March, 16.

———"In Search of Value," *Business Venezuela*, 149, March, 20-22.

Moffett, Matt (1994). "Bank Collapse and Political Fears Shake Venezuela Financial System," *The Wall Street Journal*, January 27, A10.

Murphy, Kevin M., Andrei Shliefer, and Robert W. Vishny (1991). "The Allocation of Talent: Implications for Growth," *Quarterly Journal of Economics*, 106, 502-530.

Myers, Robert J. (1992). "Chile's Social Security Reform, After Ten Years," *Benefits Quarterly*, Third Quarter, 41-55.

Naím, Moisés (1989a). "El cambio en las empresas venezolanas: una guía para la gerencia." In Moisés Naím, ed., *Las empresas venezolanas: su gerencia* (Caracas: Ediciones IESA), 457-489.

———(1989b). "El crecimiento de las empresas privadas venezolanas: mucha diversificación, poca organización." In Moisés Naím, ed., *Las empresas venezolanas: su gerencia* (Caracas: Ediciones IESA), 17-56.

———(1989c). "Viejas costumbres y nuevas realidades en la gerencia venezolana." In Moisés Naím, ed., *Las empresas venezolanas: su gerencia* (Caracas: Ediciones IESA), 493-520.

———(1993). *Paper Tigers and Minotaurs: The Politics of Venezuela's Economic Reforms* (Washington, D.C.: The Carnegie Endowment for International Peace).

Naím, Moisés and Antonio Francés (1995). "The Venezuelan Private Sector: From Courting the State to Courting the Market." In Louis Goodman, Johanna Mendelson Forman, Moisés Naím, Joseph Tulchin, and Gary Bland, eds., *Lessons of the Venezuelan Experience* (Baltimore: John Hopkins University Press and The Woodrow Wilson Center Press), 165-192.

Nash, Nathaniel C. (1993). "A New Rush into Latin America," *New York Times*, April 11, 3-1, 3-6.

National Council for Investment Promotion (CONAPRI) (1992). "The Venezuelan Advantage, Quantitative Comparative Analysis and Survey of Corporate Attitudes," October.

Navarro, Juan Carlos (1991). "Venezuelan Higher Education in Perspective," *Higher Education* 21: 177-188 (The Netherlands: Kluwer Academic Publishers).

———(1993). "La educación en Venezuela y la competitividad." Key Issue Paper, Project Venezuela Competitiva, April 1993.

Navarro, Juan Carlos and Ramón Piñango (1992). "La formación de los recursos humanos en Venezuela: realizaciones de la democracia y los costos de la ausencia de debate," Working papers *27* (Caracas: Ediciones IESA).

Nelson, Reed E. (1990). "Is There Strategy in Brazil?" *Business Horizons*, July-August, 15-23.

"1993: ¿Crecer con inflación y devaluación? Entrevista a Juan Fernando Roche, Presidente Ejecutivo de Mavesa," *Gerente Venezuela*, 71, December 1992, 66-70.

"¿No más piratería?" *Gerente Venezuela*, 75, April 1993, 28-32.

Número: economía, negocios, mercadeo. Edición XIII, 587, June 1993.

OCEI. *See* Oficina Central de Estadística e Informática (OCEI).

Oficina Central de Estadística e Informática (OCEI) (1970-1984). *Encuesta de hogares por muestreo* (Caracas: Oficina Central de Estadística e Informática).

———(1985-1992). *Anuario del comercio exterior de Venezuela* (Caracas: Oficina Central de Estadística e Informática).

———(1985-1992). *Anuario estadístico* (Caracas: Oficina Central de Estadística e Informática).

———(1985-1993). *Indicadores de la fuerza de trabajo* (Caracas: Oficina Central de Estadística e Informática).

———(1991). *Encuesta industrial* (Caracas: Oficina Central de Estadística e Informática).

Oficina Central de Presupuesto (1989). *40 años de presupuesto fiscal* (Caracas: Oficina Central de Presupuesto).

———(1992-1993). *Exposición de motivos del proyecto de ley de presupuesto* (Caracas: Oficina Central de Presupuesto).

Oficina de Presupuesto del Sector Universitario (OPSU) (1976-1990). *Boletín estadístico* (Caracas: Oficina de Presupuesto del Sector Universitario).

Ohkawa, Kazushi, in collaboration with Katsuo Otsuka and Bernard Key (1993). *Growth Mechanism of Developing Economies: Investment, Productivity and Employment* (San Francisco: International Center for Economic Growth and International Development Center of Japan).

Oil and Gas Journal Data Book, 1993 Edition (Tulsa, OK: Penn Well Books).

"Oil Giant Moves to Revert Weak Oil Prices," *New York Times*, Advertising Supplement, October 25, 1993, A10.

Oldham, Barry, and Peter Wilson (1993). "Paradise in Peril," *Business Venezuela, 158*, December, 52-59.

"Operación chocolate," *Producto, Publicidad/Mercadeo/Comunicación, 115*, April 1993, 30-34.

OPSU. *See* Oficina de Presupuesto del Sector Universitario (OPSU).

Palacios D., Rafael (1993). "Mavesa Consolidates Its Export Strategy," *Venezuela Now*, July, 11.

Pantin, Manuel (1993a). "Ports Projects Make Waves," *Business Venezuela, 151*, May, 38-42.

Pantin, Manuel (1993b). "Phone Rage," *Business Venezuela, 157*, November, 65-68.

Paredes, Carlos E. (1993). "Productivity Growth in Venezuela: The Need to Break with the Past." Key Issue Paper, Project Venezuela Competitiva, August.

Paúl, Luis Eduardo (1990). "Estado del arte en el diseño de ingeniería, conferencia pronunciada en el Primer Simposio de Ingeniería de Proyectos," December 6.

Pérez, Carlos Andrés (1991). "Decreto No. 1,878, Mediante el cual se dictan las normas para el desarrollo de la industria automotriz," *Gaceta Legal, 787*, Articles 861-865, October 14.

Perrottet, Tony, ed. (1993). *Insight Guides Venezuela* (Singapore: APA Publications [HK], Ltd.).

Ponce, Fabián (1993). "Airline Industry Flying in a Holding Pattern," *Business Venezuela, 151*, May, 68.

Porter, Michael E. (1980). *Competitive Strategy* (New York: The Free Press).

———(1985). *Competitive Advantage* (New York: The Free Press).

———(1990). *The Competitive Advantage of Nations* (New York: The Free Press).

Porter, Michael E., and the Monitor Company (1991). *Canada at the Crossroads: The Reality of a New Competitive Environment* (Ottawa: Business Council on National Issues and Minister of Supply and Services).

Psacharopoulos, George, and F. Steier (1989). "Education and the Labor Market in Venezuela," *Economics of Education Review*, 7.

Psacharopoulos, George, and Asad Alam (1991). "Earnings and Education in Venezuela: An Update from the 1987 Household Survey," *Economics of Education Review*, 10, *1*, 29-36.

Pulp & Paper International, 34, 7, July 1992, 36-37.

Pulp & Paper International (1993). *International Fact & Price Book 1993* (San Francisco: Miller Freeman Publications).

"¿Qué tán fácil es convertirse en exportadores? Entrevista a Gianfranco Francesconi, Gerente de Operaciones de Sidaven," *Gerente Venezuela*, 76, May 1993, 32-38.

Reich, Robert (1991). *The Work of Nations*. (New York: Knopf).

"A Reputation for Integrity," *Euromoney*, February 1992, Argentina Supplement, 8, 10.

Resource Strategies, Inc. (1989). "Limitations on Expanding World Primary Aluminum Smelter Capacity," Exton, PA, August.

Reyes-Matta, Fernando (1992). "Journalism in Latin America in the 90s: The Challenges of Modernization," *Journal of Communication*, Summer, 74-83.

Reynolds Metal Company (1992). *1992 Annual Report*.

Rigobón, Roberto (1993). "Política fiscal, monetaria y externa," Background Paper, Project Venezuela Competitiva, May.

Rivas, José Rafael (1993). "Procter & Gamble's Globalization Strategy Finds a Home in Venezuela," *Venezuela Now*, July, 7.

Rivas Acosta, Luis Manuel (1993a). "Estudio del sector cultivos tropicales." Industry Study (first draft), Project Venezuela Competitiva, February.

———(1993b). "Cultivos tropicales de Venezuela: el cacao." Industry Study, Project Venezuela Competitiva, July.

Rodríguez, Albor (1993). "Muchos actores y pocas películas," *Domingo Hoy*, August 1, 10-11.

Rodríguez, Luis Eduardo (1992). "El Fondo de Promoción Turística no debe ser manejado por el Estado," *Radar Turístico*, 72, 41-44.

Rodríguez, Miguel (1988). "Towards Renewed Non-inflationary Growth in Venezuela in the 1990's: A Blueprint of Macroeconomic Policy for the New Administration." Mimeo (Washington, D.C.: Institute of International Economics).

———(1991). "Public Sector Behavior in Venezuela." In Felipe Larraín and Marcelo Selowsky, eds., *The Public Sector and the Latin American Crisis* (San Francisco: ICS Press).

Rodríguez M., Leandro (1993). "A New View: The Unmasking of Prestaciones Sociales," *Business Venezuela*, 156, October, 70-75.

Rosales Linares, Ramón (1993). "La industria textil." Industry Study, Project Venezuela Competitiva, May.

Ryser, Jeffrey (1989). "Argentina Gets Ready for 'Surgery Without Anesthetic,'" *Business Week*, October 2 (Industrial/Technology Edition), 46, 50.

———(1991). "Argentina's 'Economic Takeoff'," *Global Finance*, December, 67-69.
———(1993). "Chile Is the Model," *Global Finance*, May, 77.
Sabal, Jaime, and Noris Aguirre (1991). "El mercado de capitales en Venezuela." Mimeo (Caracas).
Salinas de Gortari, Carlos (1992). "Economic Planning for Mexico: North American Free Trade Agreement," *Vital Speeches*, November 15, 69-71.
Sánchez, Rómulo (1993a). "La industria automotriz de Venezuela." Industry Study, Project Venezuela Competitiva, May.
———(1993b). Presentation on Venezuelan Automotive Sector, Project Venezuela Competitiva, IESA, August.
Scott, Bruce R. (1985). "U.S. Competitiveness: Concepts, Performance, and Implications." In Bruce R. Scott and George C. Lodge, *U.S. Competitiveness in the World Economy* (Boston, MA: Harvard Business School Press), 13-70.
Scott, Bruce R., and George C. Lodge (1985). *U.S. Competitiveness in the World Economy* (Boston, MA: Harvard Business School Press).
Silva A., Alberto, Consultores OTEC S.A. (1993). "Estudio de transporte." Key Issue Paper, Project Venezuela Competitiva, August.
Smith, Geri (1992). "How Argentina's Menem Touched Off a Gusher," *Business Week*, March 2, Industrial/Technology Edition, 94A.
Smith, Stephen C. (1993). "Book review of *The Competitive Advantage of Nations*," *Journal of Development Economics*, 40, 399-404.
"Smurfit Paper Division Shines," *Venezuela Now*, March 1993, 5.
Sölvell, Örjan, Ivo Zander, and Michael E. Porter (1991). *Advantage Sweden* (Stockholm: Norstedts).
Stanford Research Instititute (SRI) (1990). *Chemical Economics Handbook* (Menlo Park, CA: Stanford Research Institute).
Staubus, Janette (1990). "Argentina's Privatisation Aspirations," *Multinational Business*, Summer, 48-53.
"Still Pulling Threads," *Business Venezuela*, 161, March 1994, 42-43.
Sweeney, John (1992a). "Imminent Explosion at Sidor," *VenEconomy Monthly*, February, 33-38.
———(1992b). "Who Listens to Sidor's Viewpoint?" *VenEconomy Monthly*, February, 38-41.
———(1992c). "Intellectual Property: A Problem of National Attitudes," *VenEconomy Monthly*, August, 15-17.
———(1992d). "Venezuela and Colombia: Trade Partnership Flourishes," *VenEconomy Monthly*, November, 13-14.
Sweeney, John, and José Antonio Gil Yepes (1990). "Caldera's Labor Law: Requiem for the Venezuelan People," *VenEconomy Monthly*, November, 1-5.
Taylhardat, Adolfo (1993). "Las Inversiones Extranjeras." Key Issue Paper, Project Venezuela Competitiva, August.

Taylor, Lance (1991). *Varieties of Stabilization Experience: Towards Sensible Macroeconomics in the Third World* (New York: Oxford University Press).

Tejera, María (1992). "Legal Logjam: PDVSA Expects a Flurry of Lawsuits," *Business Venezuela, 140*, June, 26-28.

Templeton, Andrew (1995). "The Evolution of Popular Opinion." In Louis Goodman, Johanna Mendelson Forman, Moisés Naím, Joseph Tulchin, and Gary Bland, eds., *Lessons of the Venezuelan Experience* (Baltimore: John Hopkins University Press and The Woodrow Wilson Center Press), 79-114.

Torres, Craig (1994). "Mexico Plans to Sell Four Firms as Part of Privatization," *The Wall Street Journal*, January 21, A9.

"Trade, the Uruguay Round and the Consumer: The Sting—How Governments Buy Votes on Trade with the Consumer's Money," *VenEconomy Monthly*, October 1993, 27-30.

UEC Report. *See* USX Engineers and Consultants (UEC).

Ugalde, Luis, S.J. (1993). *La valoración del trabajo productivo* (Caracas: Fundación Sivensa).

UNIDO. *See* United Nations, Industrial Development Organization (UNIDO).

Union Bank of Switzerland (1992). *Prices and Earnings around the Globe* (Zurich: USB Publications).

United Nations (1991 and 1992). *International Trade Statistics Yearbook* (New York: United Nations).

United Nations, Economic Commission for Latin America and the Caribbean (ECLAC) (1990). *Changing Production Patterns with Social Equity: The Prime Task of Latin American and Caribbean Development in the 1990s* (Santiago: United Nations Economic Commission for Latin America and the Caribbean).

———(1992a). *Social Equity and Changing Production Patterns: An Integrated Approach* (Santiago: United Nations Economic Commission for Latin America and the Caribbean).

———(1992b). *Statistical Yearbook for Latin America and the Caribbean* (Santiago: United Nations Economic Commission for Latin America and the Caribbean).

United Nations, Educational, Scientific and Cultural Organization (UNESCO) (1992). *Statistical Yearbook* (Paris: UNESCO).

United Nations, Food and Agriculture Organization (FAO) (1980-1990). "Trade Yearbook." *FAO Statistics Series* (Rome: Food and Agriculture Organization of the United Nations).

———(1991). *1991 Annual Report* (Rome: Food and Agriculture Organization of the United Nations).

United Nations, Industrial Development Organization (UNIDO) (1990-1991). *Industry and Development, Global Report* (New York: United Nations).

United Nations, International Labour Office (ILO) (1989:4-1993:4). *Bulletin of Labour Statistics* (Geneva: Ed. Hazel Bennett).

United Nations, International Telecommunications Union (ITU) (1984). *The Lost Link: Report of the Independent Commission for World Development in Telecommunications* (Geneva: ITU).

United Nations, International Trade Centre (ITC) (1991). *Fine or Flavor Cocoa: An Overview of World Production and Trade* (Geneva: International Trade Centre, UNCTAD/GATT).

United Nations, Organisation for Economic Co-operation and Development (OECD) (1992). *Tourism Policy and International Tourism in OECD Member Countries* (Paris: Organisation for Economic Co-operation and Development).

United Nations, World Tourism Organization (1993). *Yearbook of Tourism Statistics* (Madrid: World Tourism Organization).

U.S. Department of Agriculture (1992). *World Cocoa Situation*, October.

USX Engineers and Consultants (UEC) (1992). "Recommended Restructuring and Investment Plan for Sidor, Siderúrgica del Orinoco S.A.," Project 2853, Final Report, January.

van der Linde, Claas (1991). *The Competitive Advantage of Germany: A Microeconomic Approach* (St. Gallen: H. Tschudy & Co. AG).

———(1992). *Deutsche Wettbewerbs Vorteile* (New York: ECON Verlag).

Vásquez, Nelson (1993). "La industria petrolera." Industry Study, Project Venezuela Competitiva, July 1993.

Venezuelan Auto Parts Producers (FAVENPA). *See* Fabricantes Venezolanos de Partes Automotrices (FAVENPA).

Vernon, Raymond (1966). "International Investment and International Trade in the Product Cycle," *Quarterly Journal of Economics*, 80, 190-207.

Viana, Horacio (1984). "International Technology Transfer, Technological Learning and the Assimilation of Imported Technology in a State-owned Enterprise: The Case of Direct Reduction in SIDOR Steel Plant." Ph.D. Thesis. Brighton, UK: SPRU. University of Sussex.

Viana, Horacio with Ignacio Avalos, Antonio Balaguer, María A. Cervilla, and Carlos Suárez (1994). "Estudio de la capacidad tecnológica de la industria manufacturera venezolana" (Caracas: Fondo Editorial FINTEC).

Viana, Horacio with Ignacio Avalos, María A. Cervilla, and Antonio Balaguer (1993). "El desarrollo tecnológico en Venezuela." Key Issue Paper, Project Venezuela Competitiva, May 1993.

Villalba, Julián (1991). "Menú estratégico" (Caracas: IESA).

Villalba, Julián, project coordinator (1989a). *La industria automotriz venezolana: análisis de su estructura, conducta y potencial* (Caracas: IESA-CAVENEZ-FAVENPA).

———(1989b). *Reporte de la segunda fase. Demanda de divisas de la industria automotriz* (Caracas: IESA-CAVENEZ-FAVENPA).

———(1989c). *Reporte de la tercera fase. Evaluación social de la industria automotriz* (Caracas: IESA-CAVENEZ-FAVENPA).

"¿Viraje Textil? Entrevista a Marco Zarikian, Presidente Ejecutivo de Telares Maracay," *Gerente Venezuela, 71,* December 1992, 92-96.

Vogel, Thomas T., Jr. (1994). "Politics Roil Developing Nation Debt," *The Wall Street Journal,* January 24, C1.

Voljc, Marko (1993). "Privatization and Economic Stabilization in Mexico," *Columbia Journal of World Business,* Spring, 122-133.

Wade, John (1992). "Steel Foundry Goes Global," *Venezuela Now,* September, 6.

"Warner Lambert Expands Its Production Facilities," *Venezuela Now,* September 1992, 4.

"Who's Selling What: The Global Picture," *Euromoney,* July 1993, 114-125.

Wilson, Peter (1993). "Return from the Depths," *Business Venezuela, 158,* December, 14-18.

———(1994). "Until the Gavel Falls," *Business Venezuela, 160,* February, 51-54.

Wood, Christopher (1993). "Mexico: A Latin Big Bang," *The Economist,* February 13, SS16-SS18.

World Bank (1991). Report No. 9631-VE: Venezuelan Agricultural Research, Extension and Education, July 31.

———(1992). "Education for Growth and Social Equity." Mimeo (Washington, D.C.: The World Bank).

———(1993). *World Development Report 1993* (Washington, D.C.: World Bank).

World Economic Forum (1993). *The World Competitiveness Report* (Lausanne: World Economic Forum).

———(1994). *The World Competitiveness Report* (Lausanne: World Economic Forum).

World Tourism Organization. *See* United Nations, World Tourism Organization.

Index

AD (Democratic Action Party), 4, 5, 6-7, 218
agriculture
    conditions for, 83-84, 90-92, 157-159, 185-186
    crops, types of, 185
    factor advantages, 173 table 5.1
    government policies, 162, 185-186, 321-324
    protection of, 162, 322-324
    specific sectors. *See* cocoa, pulp and paper, rice
    subsidies, 3, 49, 322-324
Alcasa (Aluminum of the Caroní, Inc.), 16, 151-154, 255, 258, 264, 297, 358
Alfonzo Rivas & Cia., 226, 250, 251, 252, 287
aluminum industry, 150-154, 155 fig. 5.2, 173 table 5.1, 258, 264, 361 table 10.1, 364-365
Andean Pact, 17, 118-119, 122, 130, 140-141, 144, 159, 161, 172, 190, 191, 196, 245, 251, 269, 286, 292, 315, 319, 342, 359, 362, 387, 400-401, 406
ASOQUIM (Association of Chemical Products Producers), 116, 295-296
attitudes toward
    business, 440-441
    competition, 440-441
    economic reform, 4
    foreign investment, 154, 391
    government, 440
    market economy, 440-441
    service sector employment, 98-99
    tourism, 98-99
    wealth creation, 438-439
automotive industry, 133-144, 135 table 4.9, 141 fig. 4.6, 173 table 5.1, 261
AVE (Venezuelan Association of Executives), 9, 11, 429

Banco Latino, 5-6, 32, 229, 231, 311
basic industries, 33, 312-313
    reserved to the state, 312-313
Bauxiven (Bauxite of Venezuela, Inc.), 16, 152, 154, 184

BCV (Central Bank of Venezuela), 196, 235, 244, 311, 380
    Central Bank Law of 1992, 311, 380
    independence of, 311, 380
    monetary policies during economic opening, 311, 380
    reform of, 311
beauty pageant sector. *See* Miss Venezuela
BIV (Industrial Bank of Venezuela), 236-237, 298
bolivar. *See* currency devaluations; exchange rate
Boulton Group, 16
Brady Bonds, 311
business chambers and industry associations
    activities, 294-296, 429-430
    economic opening, impact of, 295
    education and training, contributions to, 295-296, 428
    general associations, 429-431
    historical role, 294-295, 427-428
    individual chambers and associations, 295-296
    public-private organizations, 429-430
    recommendations for, 427-429
    response to economic opening, 295
CACM (Central American Common Market), 315
Caldera, Rafael, 5, 6, 7, 30, 42, 231, 315, 317, 438
capital flight, 27, 30, 230, 309-310, 311, 379-381
capital formation, 30, 31 fig. 2.3, 308
Caracas Metro. *See* transportation
Carbonorca (Coals of the Orinoco, Inc.), 16, 152
CARICOM (Caribbean Community), 315
CEPAL. *See* ECLAC
Cerámicas Carabobo Corporation, 237, 285-286
Central Bank of Venezuela. *See* BCV
chance events. *See* competitive advantage, specific industries
Chocolates El Rey, 157, 287-288
clusters

aluminum and steel, 264-265, 266
   table 7.2
Chilean forest products cluster, compared, 270 fig. 7.2, 271
definition of, 261-262
developing nations, 275-276
mass media entertainment, 55, 78-79, 262, 265-270, 267 fig. 7.1
petroleum and petrochemicals, 262-263, 263 table 7.1
policy recommendations, 400
potential for cluster formation, 274
pulp and paper, 270-272, 270 fig. 7.2
role in competitiveness, 53, 262, 423
spillover of technology and skills, 276
Swedish forest products cluster, compared, 271, 272 fig. 7.3
CNV Group, 282
cocoa industry, 155-158, 159 fig. 5.3, 173 table 5.1, 185-186, 188-189, 256, 368-369, 369 table 10.2
Coles, Jonathan, 322, 406
competition and rivalry
   and competitiveness, 52, 56, 60-61, 296-301, 387-388, 423, 447 table A.7
   concentration and rivalry, 301, 302 table 8.1
   conglomerates, battles between, 298
   developing nations, 302-305
   during 1970s and 1980s, 297-298
   economic opening, responses to, 298-301, 354-355
   product innovations, 299
   resistance to change, 300-301
   specific industries. *See* industry name
   Venezuelan competition and rivalry in context, 301-304
competition policies
   consumer gains from, 298-299
   economic opening, after, 298, 318
   import substitution, during, 317
   policy recommendations, 389-390, 447 table A.7
   See also Pro-Competition Superintendency
competitive advantage, patterns of
   in Canada, 175 table 5.3, 176
   in New Zealand, 174 table 5.2, 175, 177
   in Switzerland, 176, 177 table 5.4
   in Venezuela, 173-177, 173 table 5.1
competitive advantage, theory of
   chance events, role of, 52-53, 56
   determinants, defined
      demand conditions, 51, 54-55, 59-60, 243
      factor conditions, 50-51, 54

firm strategy and structure, 52, 55, 60-61
related and supporting industries, 51-52, 55
rivalry, 56-57
   domestic, nature of, 52, 60-61
   domestic, number of competitors, 61
   foreign, not a perfect substitute, 61-62
determinants, relative importance, 58-59, 64-65
government, role of, 52, 56, 307-308
location of advantage, in transnational industries, 63, 292
See also competition and rivalry; competitiveness; demand conditions; factor conditions; firm strategy and structure; related and supporting industries
The Competitive Advantage of Nations, 9, 50, 52, 57, 67
competitiveness
   analysis for nations, 64-67
   compare export subsidies, 48-49
   compare export success, 49
   compare low wage base, 49-50
   compare preserving industrial base, 49
   defined, for companies, 45-46
   defined, for industries, 46
   defined, for nations, 46-47
   developing nations, and, 67-68
   diamond, national, 65-66, 65 fig. 3.3, 66 fig. 3.4
   disadvantage, impact of, 51, 57-58
   drivers of competitive success, 59
   economic integration, impact of, 59-60
   extensions to framework, 57-68
   foreign demand, role of, 59-60
   geographic concentration and, 53
   illustration of, Miss Venezuela, 53-57, 57 fig. 3.2
   importance of, 47-48
   investment, foreign direct (FDI) and, 62-64
   nontraded sector, 48, 65-66
   sources of, 50-53
   standard of living, link to, 46, 47 fig. 3.1, 65-66, 66 fig. 3.4, 371-372, 373-374
   systemic nature of, 307-308, 375, 440-441
   traded sector, 65-66
   using framework as strategic tool, 420-424

Index

See also competitive advantage, patterns of; competitive advantage, theory of
CONAPRI (National Council for Investment Promotion), 9, 391, 429-430
Conindustria. *See* business chambers and industry associations
consensus, need for, 438-440
consumer demand, Venezuelan
    adaptation of products for export, 246-247
    advantage due to specific aspects, 252-253
    changes in consumer behavior, 247-248
    demand advantages in regional markets, 250-251
    demand advantages in world markets, 248-250
    distribution and retailing sectors, impact on, 246-247
    public goods and services, consumption of, 247
    size of, 133-134, 160, 244-245
    sophistication of, 54-56, 75-76, 157, 164, 244, 245-246, 273
    See also demand conditions; industrial demand, domestic
COPEI (Committee for Political Organization and Independent Election), 5, 6-7
Cordiplan (Central Office of Planning and Coordination), 149
Corimon, 16, 237, 285-286, 287
Cristóbal Colón project, 181-182, 292-293, 319, 362
currency devaluations, 29-30, 309, 379
CVG (Venezuelan Guayana Corporation), 15-16, 38, 86-87, 122, 125, 128, 151, 154, 183, 184-185, 255, 257, 258-259, 264, 289, 290, 291, 297, 315, 319, 320, 383

debt, public sector
    fiscal adjustment during economic opening, 310-311
    fiscal deficit as percentage of GDP, 27-28, 376, 381-382
    growth of deficit during 1980s, 27-28
    policy recommendations, 376-380
    state-owned enterprises' contribution to, 377
deficit. *See* debt, public sector
de Krivoy, Ruth, 311
Delfino Group, 87, 90
demand conditions
    and competitiveness, 51, 54-55, 59-60, 243-257, 273, 421-422, 447
    table A.5

    developing nations, 274-275, 276
    specific industries. *See* industry name
    See also consumer demand, domestic; consumer demand, industrial
design, capabilities in, 227-228
determinants. *See* competitive advantage
developing nations and competitiveness. *See* competitiveness
DRI (Direct Reduced Iron). *See* steel industry

EC (European Community), 61, 62, 117, 315
ECLAC (Economic Commission for Latin America and the Caribbean), 1, 194
economic freedoms, suspension of, 317
economic opening
    competition and rivalry, impact on, 298-301, 354
    demand conditions, impact on, 35, 247-248, 255
    historical background, 1-4, 7-8, 17-43, 308-310, 312-314
    industries. *See* specific industry name
    macroeconomic performance, following, 3-4, 21-23
    firm strategy and structure, impact on, 280, 283-286
    related and supporting industries, impact on, 261
    need for, 308-310, 377
    opposition to, 3-4, 300-301, 322-324
    partial nature of, 42, 138-140
    public attitudes toward, 4, 438
economic policies
    communication of, 408-409
    interventionist policies, consequences of, 406-408
    macroeconomic policies, 308-312
    See also specific policies by name
economic policies, recommendations for
    basic philosophy, 373
    business information, 388-389
    capital markets, 380-381
    competition, 389-390
    energy pricing, 378-379
    exchange rates, 379
    foreign investment, 390-392
    interest rates, 379
    markets, strengthening of, 387-388
    prices, freeing of, 388
    priorities, need for, 375
    privatization, 377, 382-385
    public services pricing, 378-379
    regional context, within, 367-370, 384-385, 391-392, 409-410, 435-436
    tax revenues, increase in, 377-378
    trade and trade pacts, 386-387

urgency of need for reform, 391-392, 409-410
economic reform program of 1989. *See* economic opening
economy, Venezuelan
    compared to other major Latin American nations, 1-4, 8, 14 table 2.1, 19 table 2.2, 23, 367-370, 368 table 10.2, 384-385, 391-392, 409-410, 435-436
    framework of analysis, 41-43
    Gross Domestic Product. *See* GDP
    Gross National Product. *See* GNP
    income per capita, 18-23, 19 table 2.2, 366, 371
    multinational firms, role of, 17, 292-294, 360-362
    oil income. *See* oil revenues
    performance of, 1970-1994, 2-4, 7, 17-18, 21-23
    population growth, implications of, 32, 33 table 2.7
    private-sector Venezuelan firms, role of, 16, 280-289, 358-360, 411-414
    size distribution of firms, 13-14
    social indicators, 24
    standard of living, 8, 24, 42, 366, 374-375
    state-owned enterprises, role of, 15, 289-291, 357-358
    structure, 13-17
    tax base, 28, 377
    See also related topics
Edelca, 16, 128, 152, 154, 254, 255, 264, 313, 382
education
    and competitiveness, 51, 188-189, 395
    Fé y Alegría schools, 210, 345, 397, 399
    higher education sector, 211-213
    misallocation of resources, 212, 396-397
    needs of industry, mismatch with, 126-127, 211, 213-214, 397-399
    performance indicators, comparative, 209
    primary and secondary sector, 208-210
    public education system, historical expansion of, 207-208, 211, 213
    public spending on, 206-207, 207 table 6.5, 208 table 6.6, 209
    teacher salaries, comparative, 209
    See also training
education policies
    centralization, 333-334

El Estado Docente, concept of, 332-333
    goals of education policies, 332
    inefficiencies in, 335
    performance standards, academic, 334-335
    politics, influence of, 332, 334, 336-337
    policy recommendations, 395-397, 446 table A.4
    post-secondary sector, 335-337
    primary and secondary schools, 333-334, 337
    See also training
electricity
    generating capacity, 182, 182 table 6.2
    pricing, 182 table 6.2, 183
    quality, 183
    See also Edelca
El Tablazo petrochemical complex, 112, 114, 189
employment and unemployment, 4, 24, 25 table 2.4, 26, 200 table 6.3
energy sector
    energy pricing, policy recommendations, 378-379
    energy reserves, 180 table 6.1, 181-182
    energy resources, 180-183, 180 table 6.1
    energy sector demand, 253-254, 274-275
    Guri hydroelectric complex, 182, 254
    Macagua hydroelectric complex, 170, 182, 254
    See also economy, Venezuelan; electricity; natural resources; petrochemical industry; petroleum industry
engineering consulting services sector, 169-172, 172 fig. 5.7, 173 table 5.1, 254
exchange rate
    dirty float, 30, 310, 311
    dual regime, 30, 309-310
    fixed regimes, 308-309, 312, 379-380, 382
    policy recommendations, 379-380
    unification of, 310
exports and export performance, 33-35, 34 fig. 2.4, 35-36, 36 table 2.8, 38 table 2.10, 39, 71-72, 73 table 4.1, 83-84, 105, 121, 129-130, 133, 150, 155, 158, 162, 167-168, 171, 367-370, 368-369 table 10.2
    See also imports; trading partners

factor conditions

Index

and competitiveness, 50-51, 179, 241-242, 420-421
competing on natural resources, 240
definition of, 50-51
design capabilities. *See* design capabilities
financial markets. *See* financial markets
human resources
    education. *See* education; training
    informal economy. *See* informal economy
    labor force. *See* labor force
    labor/management relations. *See* labor/management relations
    low-cost labor, reliance on, as national strategy, 241
information resources. *See* information resources
infrastructure, telecommunications. *See* telecommunications
infrastructure, transportation. *See* transportation
natural resources. *See* natural resources
scarcity of factors, 239
technological resources. *See* technological resources
Venezuelan factor conditions in context, 239-242
Ferrominera Orinoco, 128, 131, 184, 258, 365
financial markets
    and competitiveness, 228-229, 238
    banking sector, crisis, 1, 5-6, 32, 103, 231, 312, 380
    banking sector, generally, 228-231, 380
    Caracas Stock Exchange, 32, 232-234, 235, 285, 288, 318
    disintermediation, trend toward, 234-235
    equity markets, 232-235, 232 table 6.8
    insider trading, 233, 238
    international capital, access to, 237-238, 285-286, 289
    oversight, regulatory, 231, 234, 238, 318, 380
    policy recommendations, 380-381, 444 table A.2
    state financing, 236-237, 298
    venture capital, scarcity of, 228, 235, 359
FINTEC (Fund for the Promotion of Technological Innovation), 9, 224

FIOR (Fluidized Iron Ore Reduction). *See* Sivensa; steel industry
firm strategy and structure, by type of firm
    family-owned firms, 280, 424
    industrial groups, 358-359
    informal firms, 302-303
    microenterprises, 302-303
    multinational firms, 302-303
        foreign direct investment, categories of, 292-293
        historical role, 17, 292
        spillover effects for local companies, 293-294
    private-sector domestic firms, 280-289
        government orientation of, 280-281
        international strategies, 286-287
        reactive thinking, 284-285
    state-owned enterprises, 289-291
        control structures, weakness of, 290
        patronage, political, 289-290, 303
        political constraints on strategy, 291
        privatization and restructuring, 290, 303, 315-316, 357-358, 382-385
        reforming the CVG, 154, 291, 315, 382-383
firm strategy and structure, generally
    and competitiveness, 52, 279, 411-426, 448 table A.6
    business unit strategies, developing new, 414-416
    definition of, 52
    developing nations, in, 301-304
    diversification, 282-283, 304, 413
    economic opening, responses to, 280, 283-284, 285-289
    framework as strategic tool, use of, 420-424
    opportunism, role of, 303-304
    pressures for competitiveness, lack of, 281-282
    uncertainty, influence of, 283, 304
    vertical integration, 2, 16, 117, 282-283, 285, 287, 288, 297, 304, 413
firms, recommendations for, 412-427
foreign direct investment
    and competitive advantage, 62-64
    future needs, 131, 360-362
    levels of, 3, 30-32, 39-40, 40 table 2.11, 292-293

lifting restrictions on, 1980s and 1990s, 292-293, 318-319
policy recommendations, 390-392
restrictions on, 1970s and 1980s, 39, 318-319
specific industries. *See* industry name
types of FDI in the Venezuelan economy, 40, 292-294
foreign models of development, caution using, 404-405

GATT (General Agreement on Tariffs and Trade), 3, 18, 415
GDP (gross domestic product), 14 table 2.1, 15, 18-23, 19 table 2.2, 20 fig. 2.1, 23 table 2.3, 27-28, 31 fig. 2.3, 97, 97 table 4.5, 129, 195, 199, 223, 308, 322, 366, 371, 376, 378, 381, 382
geographic concentration. *See* competitiveness
government. *See* competitive advantage; public administration
government expenditures, *See* public spending
government procurement policies, 169-170, 254-256, 313
Great Turnaround (*el gran viraje*). *See* economic opening
Grupo Químico, 237
GTE (General Telephone and Electronics), 39, 40, 194, 290

Hausmann, Ricardo, 149
Herrera, Luis, 6

IDB (Inter-American Development Bank), 339, 340
IDEC (Institute for the Defense and Education of the Consumer), 248
IESA (Institute for Advanced Administrative Studies), 9, 217-218, 248, 425
IMF (International Monetary Fund), 3, 198, 237
imports, 33-35, 34 fig. 2.4
See also exports and export performance; trading partners
import substitution, 2, 162-163, 186, 193, 313, 327, 339, 355, 364, 385, 419-420
demand conditions, impact on, 25-26, 33, 88-89, 92-93, 109-110, 122-123, 136
related and supporting industries, impact on, 244, 245, 253, 254-255, 258, 259, 260-261

strategy, structure, and rivalry, impact on, 281-283, 294-295, 297-298, 305, 319, 339
See also protectionism
Industrial Bank of Venezuela. *See* BIV
industrial demand, domestic
energy sector demand, 253-254
multinational firms as a source of demand, 257
private-sector demand, 256-257
state-owned enterprises as a source of demand, 255-256
uncertainty, impact of, 253
See also consumer demand, domestic; demand conditions
industrial policies, 307, 312-315, 320, 354-355, 406-408
danger of interventionist approach, 406-407
See also economic opening; economic policy, recommendations for; import substitution; protectionism; trade policies
industrialization, meaning of, 367, 370-371
industry associations and business chambers. *See* business chambers and industry associations infant industry argument. *See* protectionism
inflation, 28-29, 29 table 2.6, 120, 139, 162, 202, 205, 218, 309-311, 316-317, 328, 376-377, 378-379, 383, 409-410
informal economy, 16-17, 199, 200 table 6.3, 209, 360
information resources
business press, 198
Central Office of Statistics and Informatics, 196-197
industry statistics, 197
information disclosure, 197
market research, 197
policy recommendations, 388-389
infrastructure. *See* electricity generating capacity; factor conditions; telecommunications; transportation
infrastructure policies, 324-326
input prices. *See* pricing policies
Interalúmina (Interamericana de Alúmina, C.A.), 16, 152, 154, 184, 264
interest rates, 1, 3, 18, 27, 29, 32, 93, 111, 114, 120, 159, 165, 228-230, 234, 282, 283, 308-311, 379, 382
policy recommendations, 379, 382
investment
efficiency, 313-314
in specific industries. *See* industry name

requirements going forward, 360, 361 table 10.1, 364-366, *See also* chapters 4 and 5.
response to economic opening, 39-40, 40 table 2.11, 186, 310-311, 319, 322-323
See also capital formation, foreign direct investment
Ipostel. *See* postal service

Jatar, Ana Julia, 300, 318
judiciary. *See* legal system and judiciary
JUNAC (Cartagena Agreement Commission), 160-161

labor force
    costs, comparative, 202, 202 table 6.4, 203 fig. 6.3, 204 fig. 6.4
    educational profile, 200-201, 201 fig. 6.2
    low-cost labor, reliance on, 203, 241
    skills shortages, 153, 158, 199, 211, 296
    worker attributes, 200-202, 205-206
labor law and labor policies, 326-331
    collective contracts, legal regime, 218, 328-329
    dismissal and severance, legal regime, 164-165, 203-205, 329-332
    retroactivity provisions, 204-205, 330
    Labor Law of 1936, 327, 329, 425
    labor policy and competitiveness, 331, 391
    mandated wage increases, 219, 219 table 6.7, 328
    mandated worker benefits, 331
    policy recommendations, 393-395, 400-401, 444 table A.3
labor/management relations, 2, 218-222, 444 table A.3
    collective bargaining, 218-220, 328-329
    joint efforts to increase productivity, 220-222
    labor unions, private sector, 218
    labor unions, public sector, 218, 334
    multi-abilities program, Procter & Gamble, 221
    pay-for-learning program, Ford Motor Company, 221
    recommendations for firms, 424-427
Layrisse, Francisco, 154
legal system and judiciary
    Civil Code, need for reform, 403
    Commercial Code, need for reform, 233, 403
    contracts, enforcement of, 348-349
    firm strategies, effect on, 349
    judges, independence of, 348, 404
    judiciary, functioning of, 348-349
    legal environment, for firms, 348-349
    policy recommendations, 390-391, 403-404
Lusinchi, Jaime, 289, 323

Machado Zuloaga Group. *See* Sivensa
Madosa, 252, 285, 288, 421
Makro, 39, 298, 341
Mantex, 164, 165
Maraven, 170, 319
Marte Televisión, 77, 81, 265
Mavesa, 237, 288
MCCA. *See* CACM
Mendoza Group, 16, 345
mineral wealth. *See* natural resources
Miss Venezuela, 53-57, 79
Mitsubishi Venezolana, 39, 182, 292

NAFTA (North American Free Trade Agreement), 51, 61, 315, 415
natural resources
    agriculture. *See* agriculture
    competing on, generally, 240
    electricity generation, 182-183, 182 table 6.2
    falling rates of return, 187-189
    fishing resources, 187, 367, 368 table 10.2
    mineral deposits, 13, 14 table 2.1, 184-185
    natural gas, 106-107, 126, 131-132, 180 table 6.1, 181-182
    oil production and reserves, 13, 147, 148, 180-181, 180 table 6.1
    physical geography and geology, 94, 185
    policies, 320-321
    policy recommendations, 392-393, 443 table A.1
    pricing, 116-118, 316-317, 320-321, 392-393
Nestlé de Venezuela, 214
NICs (Newly industrialized countries), 45, 405

ODC Group (Diego Cisneros Organization), 16, 55, 56, 287, 298
OECD (Organization for Economic Cooperation and Development), 24, 58
oil industry. *See* petroleum industry

oil prices
    during 1970s-1980s, 21, 33, 109, 149
    during 1990s, 149, 314
    impact on economy, 149, 308-310
    projections for, 364
oil producton and reserves. *See* natural resources
oil revenues
    contribution to the economy, 13, 15, 18-21, 23, 27, 33, 308
    foreign exchange earnings, percentage of, 308
    insufficient to support rising standard of living, 7, 363-366
    movements in real oil income, 1970-1993, 21, 22 fig. 2.2
    taxes on oil as percentage of government revenue, 21, 149
OPEC (Organization of Petroleum Exporting Countries), 21, 149, 150, 180, 364
Orimulsion, 148, 224

Palmaven, 157
Papeles Venezolanos, 90
PDVSA (The Venezuelan Oil Company, Inc.), 15-16, 37-38, 107, 109, 112, 115, 116, 117-118, 120, 147-150, 170, 171, 180, 181, 182, 189, 224, 236, 237, 253-254, 255, 259, 262, 264, 289-290, 291, 321, 330, 339, 357, 364, 382, 422, 425
Pequiven, 107, 109, 111, 112, 114, 116-118, 120, 189, 259, 262-263, 321, 365, 416
Pérez, Carlos Andrés
    coup attempts against, 5, 310
    first term, 310
    removal from office in 1993, 5, 354
    second term, 2-4, 231, 310-311, 314-315, 316-317, 318-319, 321, 322-323, 325-326, 328, 339, 342, 344, 345, 351, 354
Pérez Jiménez, Marcos, 99, 312-313
petrochemical industry, 105-121, 108 table 4.6, 110 table 4.7, 113 fig. 4.4, 173 table 5.1, 262-263, 263 table 7.1, 292-293, 361 table 10.1, 365
petroleum industry, 1, 147-150, 151 fig. 5.1, 170, 173 table 5.1, 189, 262-263, 263 table 7.1, 361 table 10.1, 364
pharmaceutical industry, 300-301, 317, 318
Phelps Group, 16, 71, 76-77, 298
Polar Group, 16, 216, 224, 226, 250, 251, 287, 298, 425
Polilago, 115
population, 32, 33 table 2.7, 200, 366
Porter, Michael, 9, 11, 50-53, 57, 59-61, 67, 279

postal service, 196
    Ipostel, 196
    private sector alternatives, 196
price controls. *See* pricing policies
pricing policies
    economic opening, during, 316-317
    import substitution, during, 280-281, 295, 297, 316
    input prices, 85, 93-94, 116-118, 183, 313, 316
    policy recommendations, 378-379, 388
    price controls during import substitution, 186, 281, 388
    price controls, second Caldera administration, 317, 388
    public services, 247
    See also natural resources, transfer prices
privatization
    benefits of, 81-82, 88, 325, 382-385
    CANTV, 3, 15-16, 17, 28, 40, 194, 290, 315, 319, 382
    economic opening, during, 4-5, 325-326
    obstacles to, 315-316, 326, 383
    policy recommendations, 383-385
    specific industries. *See* industry name
Pro-Competition Superintendency, 298, 300-301, 318, 389
    See also competition policy
Procter & Gamble de Venezuela, 39, 70, 221, 226, 250, 257, 293
productivity and productivity growth, 24-26, 26 table 2.5, 370-371, 374, 431-432
prospects for firms and industries, 357-372, 361 table 10.1
    See also individual industries
protectionism
    impact on firm behavior, 261, 280-283, 295, 406
    impact on industries, 134, 88-89, 92-93, 109-110, 122-123, 133-138, 162-163, 186
    infant industries, 48, 133, 405-406
    reasons to avoid, 324, 405-406
    state-led development, 1960s-1980s, 313-314
    See also import substitution; industrial policies
public administration
    and competitiveness, 345
    bureaucratic controls, 345-346, 347-348
    centralization of power, 351
    Congress, functioning of, 291, 346-347
    corruption, 99, 350-351

Index

decentralization efforts, 351-352, 402-403
Executive Branch, functioning of, 346
organization, problems of, 346-34
policy recommendations, 401-409, 450 table A.8
political capture, 349-350
reforms, 352-353
state and municipal governments, 351, 352
technical support for, 346-347
public services, 32, 42, 247, 346
See also education, social policy, telecommunications, transportation
public spending, 27-28, 236, 309, 310, 312, 376
See also debt, public
pulp and paper industry, 83-94, 85 table 4.2, 88 table 4.3, 91 fig. 4.2, 173 table 5.1, 258-259, 270-271, 292, 361 table 10.1, 365-366, 368-370, 369 table 10.2

Química Venoco, 107, 115, 132-133, 254, 282, 421

RCTV (Radio Caracas Televisión), 55, 70, 71, 72, 76-81, 82-83, 252, 265, 268
related and supporting industries
and competitiveness, 51-52, 55, 56, 78-79, 128, 258, 261-262, 422-423, 446 table A.5
barriers to entry, 258
capital goods, suppliers of, 258-259
natural resources, suppliers of, 258-259
role of state-owned companies, 258
supplier-buyer relations, 51-52, 260-261, 274
research and development
centers for, 224-225, 339
distribution of researchers by discipline, 223
expenditures on, 224, 225, 338-340
number of researchers, 223
policy recommendations, 399-400, 401
private sector, role of, 225-226, 281-282, 339
public sector, role of, 223-224, 338-339, 340
universities, role of, 211, 223-224
See also science and technology policies, technological resources
rice industry, 158-162
rivalry. *See* competition and rivalry

science and technology policies

firm capabilities, development of, 339-340
intellectual property protection, weakness of, 168, 340-342
new technology, development of, 340
policy recommendations, 399-400
results of, 339-340
state promotion of science, 338-339
See also research and development, technological resources
Sidor (Orinoco Steel Works, Inc.), 15, 16, 122-128, 129, 130, 131, 133, 199, 222, 255, 265, 291, 297, 358, 365, 417
Siemens, 214, 216-217
Simón Bolívar Airport. *See* transportation
Simón Bolívar University, 193, 211, 212, 339
Sivensa, 16, 122, 124-127, 130, 170, 216, 221, 224, 237, 257, 264, 265, 285-286, 288-289, 294, 297, 416, 425
Smurfit, 90, 292
social policies
and competitiveness, 342-343
Day Care Homes Program, 344
direct subsidy programs, evaluated, 343, 344-345
nongovernmental organizations, involvement of, 345
Program of Attention to Mother and Child, 344
School Network Program, 344-345
social benefit programs, 5, 343-344
software industry, 167-169, 169 fig. 5.6, 173 table 5.1
Sonográfica, 78, 268
Sonorodven, 78, 268
standard of living. *See* competitiveness; economy, Venezuelan
state-owned enterprises. *See* economy, Venezuelan; firm strategy and structure, by type of firm
steel industry, 121-133, 121 table 4.8, 132 fig. 4.5, 264-265, 266 table 7.2, 361 table 10.1, 365
subsidies, 1, 2, 3, 4, 5, 21,27, 33, 45, 46, 48-49, 84, 87, 88, 89, 93, 110, 111, 123, 124, 133, 137, 138, 142-143, 149, 151, 159, 160, 162, 163, 183, 186, 190-191, 197, 233, 236, 240, 249, 256, 264, 280, 281, 283, 290, 303, 309, 310, 312, 313, 317, 320-321, 322-324, 343, 344-345, 350, 353, 354, 372, 376, 379, 382, 392, 404-406, 407-408, 421, 425, 432, 439
agriculture. *See* agriculture, subsidies
elimination during economic opening, 3, 4, 89, 93, 111, 124, 138, 159, 283, 310, 322-323

export, 33, 48-49, 137-138
gasoline, 190-191, 320-321
Sudamtex, 164, 165

taxation
    business assets tax, 377-378
    corporate income tax, 319, 377-378
    debit tax on banking transactions, 312
    oil revenues tax, 149
    personal income tax, 377-378
    policy recommendations, 376, 377-378
    tax base, 28, 377
    value-added tax, 5, 28, 310, 311
    See also economy, Venezuelan
technological resources
    and competitiveness, 58-59, 114-116, 222
    levels of technological learning, 222, 225-226, 339-340, 399-400
    See also research and development; science and technology policy
telecommunications
    CANTV, 3, 15, 40, 80, 194-195, 224, 247, 257, 289, 290, 310, 315-316, 319, 324-325, 326, 330, 358, 370, 382
    CONATEL, 195, 390
    growth of sector, 55, 194-195, 265-266
    new services, 80-81, 194-195
    opening of sector to competition, 79-80
    rates and rate increases, 194, 195-196
    regional comparisons, 195
    teledensity, 194
telenovela industry, 69-83, 82 fig. 4.1, 173 table 5.1, 248, 265-268, 267 figure 7.1
textile industry, 162-166, 166 fig. 5.5, 173 table 5.1, 261
tourism sector, 94-105, 96 table 4.4, 97 table 4.5, 105 fig. 4.3, 173 table 5.1, 370
TQM (total quality management), 285
trade policies, 312-315, 386-387
    antidumping laws, 386
    GATT membership, 314-315
    policy recommendations, 386-387
    reduction in average tariff rates, 314
    regional trade pacts, 315, 386
    specific industries. *See* industry name
trading partners, 37-39, 37 table 2.9
    See also exports and export performance; imports
training, management, 217-218, 400
training, technical
    INCE, 102, 165, 213-214, 215, 216, 264, 331, 337-338, 397-399
    in-house training programs, 102, 216
    non-governmental organizations, role of, 161-162
    policy recommendations, 397-399
    private sector spending, 214-217
    technical education and training policies, 337-338
    technical schools, secondary and tertiary, 213-214
transfer pricing, 392-393, 443 table A.1
    electricity, 183, 392-393
    natural gas, 116-118, 321, 392-393
    petrochemicals, 116-118, 392-393
    policy recommendations, 392-393, 443 table A.1
    See also pricing policies
transportation
    airports, 192-193
    Caracas Metro, 170, 193, 217, 255, 313, 425
    gasoline prices, 190-191, 321
    highway system, 128, 190
    land freight, 191
    ports, maritime, 191-192, 193
    sea freight, 191-192
    subsidies, 190-191
    urban, 193

Univisión, 74

Value-added tax. *See* taxation
Velásquez, Ramón J., 5, 28, 162, 318, 324, 403
Venalum (Venezuelan Aluminum Industry, Inc.), 15, 16, 38, 132-133, 151-154, 255, 264, 290, 297, 416
Venepal, 90, 237, 286
Venevisión, 71, 77-81, 82-83, 252, 265, 268
Venezuela Competitiva, organization, formerly National Center for Competitiveness, 197, 224, 389, 429-431
Venezuela Competitiva, research project, 9-12
Viasa (Venezuelan International Airlines, Inc.), 3, 15, 40, 310, 315, 325-326, 383
Vollmer Group, 16

Warner-Lambert, 39, 293
World Bank, 3, 198, 237

zero-coupon bonds, 230, 235, 312

FLORIDA STATE
UNIVERSITY LIBRARIES

MAR 31 1997

TALLAHASSEE, FLORIDA